Economics

for the IB Diploma

2nd Edition

SEAN MALEY
JASON WELKER

Published by Pearson Education Limited, 80 Strand, London, WC2R 0RL.

www.pearson.com/international-schools

Text © Pearson Education Limited 2022
Development edited by Sarah Wright
Copy edited by Jeremy Toynbee
Proofread by Mike Hamilton and Samantha Lacey
Indexed by Georgina Bowden
Designed by © Pearson Education Limited 2022
Typeset by © SPi Global
Picture research by © SPi Global
Original illustrations © Pearson Education Limited 2022
Cover design © Pearson Education Limited 2022

The rights of Sean Maley and Jason Welker to be identified as the
authors of this work has been asserted by them in accordance with the
Copyright, Designs and Patents Act 1988.

First published 2022

24 23 22 21
10 9 8 7 6 5 4 3 2 1

British Library Cataloguing in Publication Data
A catalogue record for this book is available from the British Library

ISBN 978 1 292 33757 9

Printed in Slovakia by Neografia

Acknowledgements

Inside front cover: [**Shutterstock.com**/Dmitry Lobanov]

Text Acknowledgements:
Adam Smith: Adam Smith, The Wealth of Nations, 1776 10, 27;
African Development Bank: Adapted from the African Development
Bank Group 625; **Arab News:** Data taken from Arab News, Editorial
648; **Bracken Darrell:** Bracken Darrell. CNBC, Logitech CEO says
company boosted webcam supply for back-to-school rush. 85;
Christine Bauer-Ramazani: Major U.S. Federal Regulatory Agencies.
Used with permission from Christine Bauer-Ramazani. 157; **Arthur C.
Pigou:** Quote by Arthur Pigou's 175; **CSIMarket, Inc:** Data from
TYSON FOODS INC SEGMENTS. 207; **Bank of England:** Demand and
Output. Bank of England 263; **CREDIT SUISSE GROUP AG:** Global
wealth report 2019, CREDIT SUISSE GROUP AG 351; **Centre for
Research in Social Policy:** Data taken from Centre for Research in
Social Policy and represented as table. 354; **Christopher Chantrill:** Data
taken from UK Public Revenue, presented by Christopher Chantrill 405;
Christopher Chantrill: UK Public Spending. https://www.
ukpublicspending.co.uk/ 413; **Benjamin Franklin:** Benjamin Franklin,
America's founding father 538; **Asia Society:** Extracts from Amartya
Sen: A More Human Theory of Development. Asia Society 580; **Cato
Institute:** Easterly, William "Why aid doesn't work?" CATO Unbound.
Cato Institute. 643; **Donald Trump:** Statement by President Trump on
the Paris Climate Accord 171; **Garrett Hardin:** Quote by Garrett Hardin
171; **Federal Reserve Bank of St. Louis:** Data taken from Federal
Reserve Bank of St. Louis 240; **Federal Reserve Bank of St. Louis:** U.S.
Bureau of Labor Statistics, Unemployment Rate [UNRATE], retrieved
from FRED, Federal Reserve Bank of St. Louis; https://fred.stlouisfed.org/
series/UNRATE, August 3, 2020. 296; **Federal Reserve Bank of St.
Louis:** FRED Graph. FRED, Federal Reserve Bank of St. Louis 314;
Federal Reserve Bank of St. Louis: Data taken from Federal Reserve
Bank of St. Louis 315; **Eurostat:** Data taken from Eurostat and
represented as graph 409; **Eurostat:** Data taken from Eurostat 409, 410,
411; **Federal Reserve Bank of St. Louis:** FRED Economic data taken
and represented as graph. 597; **Daily Monitor:** Taken from Sunday
Monitor, Andrew M Mwenda, Uganda 12 June 2005 648; **Government
of Canada:** Annual Financial Report of the Government of Canada,
Fiscal Year 2017–2018. Government of Canada 371; **Lippincott
Williams & Wilkins:** Say, Jean Baptiste, and Charles Robert Prinsep. A
Treatise on Political Economy: or, The Production, Distribution, and
Consumption of Wealth. Printed for Longman, Hurst, Rees, Orme, and
Brown, 1821. 28; **Macmillan:** John Maynard Keynes, A Tract on
Monetary Reform, 1923 31; **Milton Friedman:** Quote by Milton
Friedman 38; **Marty Samuelsson:** Quote by Marty Samuelsson 49;
Michael Hallsworth: How to stop touching our faces in the wake of the
Coronavirus 5 March, 2020. The Behavioural Insights Team, https://
www.bi.team/blogs/how-to-stop-touching-our-faces-in-the-wake-of-
thecoronavirus/ 162; **Macmillan:** Arthur C. Pigou, 1920, The Economics
of Welfare 173; **HG.org:** Legal resource, Truth in Advertising and
Marketing and Other FTC Regulations. HG.org. 183; **JK Galbraith:**
Quote by JK Galbraith 216; **Organisation for Economic Co-operation
and Development:** OECD Regional Well-Being - How Is Life in
Southern-Kanto? Being. Used with permission 250; **Organisation for
Economic Co-operation and Development:** Consumer confidence
index (CCI) 2014-2020. Used with permission from OECD. 261;
Organisation for Economic Co-operation and Development:
Business confidence index (BCI).OECD 265; **Organisation for
Economic Co-operation and Development:** Business confidence
index (BCI). Used with permission from OECD 265; **Organisation for
Economic Co-operation and Development:** Data from Organisation
for Economic Co-operation and Development (OECD) 290;
Organisation for Economic Co-operation and Development: Data
from Organisation for Economic Co-operation and Development
(OECD) 291; **IndexMundi:** Inflation Rate (Consumer Prices) by Country
- Thematic Map - World. Used with permission from Index Mundi 309;
Milton Friedman: Quote by Milton Friedman 318; **John Maynard
Keynes:** Quote by John Maynard Keynes 318; **Margaret Thatcher:**
Quote by Margaret Thatcher 318; **New England Chamber of
Commerce:** Extracts from New England Chamber of Commerce, 1960s

334; **Hannah Arendt:** Quote by German-American thinker Hannah Arendt 340; **Our World In Data:** Total Population Living in Extreme Poverty by World Region. Our World in Data 353; **Organisation for Economic Cooperation and Development:** Poverty. OECD Instance. OECD Income Distribution Database, Used with permission. 354; **Our World In Data:** The gender wage gap in selected countries. International Labor Organization, visual: Our World in Data 361; **Karl Marx:** Karl Marx, slogan in 1875 363; **Organisation for Economic Co-operation and Development:** Based on Revenue Statistics 2019, OECD 370; **Organisation for Economic Co-operation and Development:** Data from Personal Income Tax: Top statutory and marginal tax rates for employees, OECD Tax Statistics (database), OECD, 2020 371; **Macmillan Publisher:** John Maynard Keynes, The General Theory of Employment, Interest and Money, 1936 414; **Jules Selmes:** Jules Selmes/Pearson Education Ltd 477; **MarketWatch, Inc.:** US president Donald Trump, May of 2020 513; **International Monetary Fund:** International Monetary Fund – Balance of Payments and International Investments Position Manual – 6th edition, page 109. 532; **Hans Rosling:** Hans Rosling, Factfulness: Ten Reasons We're Wrong About the World—and Why Things Are Better Than You Think 559; **Our World In Data:** Roser, Max. Human Development Index (HDI). Our World in Data, 25 July 2014 560; **Organisation for Economic Co-operation and Development:** Life expectancy at birth, OECD Data 578; **John Donne:** Quote by John Donne. 599; **International Association for Medical Assistance to Travellers:** Malaria, International Association for Medical Assistance to Travellers 604; **Malay Mail:** Adapted from Proton will review export strategy, says Mustapa. Malay Mail 616; **Malay Mail:** Proton will review export strategy, says Mustapa. Malay Mail 616; **Lexico.com:** FOREIGN AID: Definition of FOREIGN AID by Oxford Dictionary on Lexico.com Also Meaning of FOREIGN AID. Lexico Dictionaries 629; **Organisation for Economic Co-operation and Development:** Untying aid: the right to choose by OECD 630; **Organisation for Economic Co-operation and Development:** Compare your country: Aid statistics by donor, recipient, and sector by OECD 632; **Organisation for Economic Co-operation and Development:** Compare your country: Aid statistics by donor, recipient, and sector by OECD 633; **Progress Publishers:** Karl Marx, Critique of the Gotha Program, 1891 29; **Penguin Random House:** Thaler R and Sunstein C R, 2009, Nudge: Improving Decisions About Health, Wealth and Happiness (revised and expanded edition), Penguin Books, Penguin Group, New York 128; **Oxford Poverty & Human Development Initiative (OPHI):** Data taken from Oxford Poverty & Human Development Initiative (OPHI). 357; **Penguin Books Ltd:** Ha-Joon Chang '23 Things They Don't Tell You About Capitalism' (Penguin Books Ltd; 2010) ISBN 978-1-60819-166-6 459; **Peter Singer:** Outline of Peter Singer on Famine, Affluence, and Morality. Peter Singer, Australian philosopher 572; **Russ Roberts**: Quote by American economist Russ Roberts. 599; **The World Bank Group:** Agriculture, Forestry, and Fishing, Value Added (% of GDP). World Bank national accounts data, and OECD National Accounts data files. 69; **Yale School of Management:** Do you need a nudge? by Yale Insights, Yale School of Management. 158; **United Nations Framework Convention on Climate Change:** Paris Climate Agreement 2016 178; **The Associated Press:** Former Bumble Bee CEO Gets Jail In Price Fixing Conspiracy , June 18, 2020 By Associated Press 238; **U.S. Department of Justice:**

Former Bumble Bee CEO Sentenced To Prison For Fixing Prices Of Canned Tuna. The United States Department of Justice, 17 June 2020. 238; **The World Bank Group:** Data taken fromWorld Bank. 245; **Wikimedia Foundation, Inc.:** List of Countries by GDP (Nominal) per Capita. Wikipedia, Wikimedia Foundation, 29 June 2021 246; List of Countries by GDP (PPP) per Capita. Wikipedia, Wikimedia Foundation, 29 June 2021 246; **The World Bank Group:** Data taken from GDP, PPP (constant 2017 international $) - Argentina, Australia. World Bank 253; GDP of selected countries, 2015–2019. World Bank 255; **Trading Economics:** United States GDP Growth Rate. Trading Economics 257; European Union GDP Annual Growth Rate. Trading Economics 257; China GDP Growth Rate. Trading Economics 257; **The International Labour Organization:** Statement from United Nations International Labour Organization 289; **The Brookings Institution:** Aaronson, Stephanie, and Francisca Alba. The Unemployment Impacts of COVID-19: Lessons from the Great Recession. Brookings, Brookings, 15 Apr. 2020 303; **The World Bank Group:** Data from World Bank 335, 344, 346, 347,348, 348; **Wikimedia Foundation, Inc.:** Dennis Wikipedia using World Bank Data 1999-2019 348; GINI index World Bank up to 2018. Wikimedia Foundation, Inc. 350; **United Nations:** Extracts from United Nations Sustainable Development Goals 351; **United Nations:** United Nations Sustainable Development Goals 352; **United Nations Development Programme:** Extracts taken from Human Development Reports 355; Multidimensional Poverty Index, Dimensions and weighting. United Nations Development Programme 356; **The World Bank Group:** Data taken from World Bank. 383, 462; **W. Strahan and T. Cadell, London:** Adam Smith, The Wealth of Nations (Book 1), 1776 442; **Thomas Jefferson:** Quoted by Thomas Jefferson, 1814 447; **World Trade Organization:** WTO in brief by World Trade Organization. 491; **The Slate Group:** Arvind Panagariya, Think again: international trade, Foreign Policy, 1 November 2003 494; **XE.com Inc.:** XE.com, dollar exchange rate in the UK, 2nd October 2020 505; XE.com, swiss francs in euros July-September 2011 508; XE.com, dollars per euro 2014 to 2016 524; US Dollar to Chilean Peso - USD to CLP. Xe 552; **Wikimedia Foundation, Inc.:** Managed Float Regime. Wikiwand 520; **US Census Bureau:** Data taken from US Census Bureau. 553; **The World Bank group:** World Bank via Google public data explorer 555; **United Nations:** United Nations World Commission on Environment and Development, 1987 564; **United Nations:** Communications Materials – United Nations Sustainable Development. United Nations. Used with permission. 566; **United Nations:** Communications Materials – United Nations Sustainable Development. United Nations. 566; **The World Bank group:** Data from THE CHANGING NATURE OF WORK. World bank. 570; **United Nations Conference on Trade and Development:** Commodity Dependence: A Twenty Year Perspective, UNCTAD 570; **United Nations Development Programme:** Human Development Index HDI by United Nations Development Programme 581; **World Bank:** Data taken from UNDP 2019, World Bank. 582; Gender Inequality Index, UNDP 583; Data taken from UNDP GII, 2019. 583; Inequality-adjusted Human Development Index (IHDI), United Nations Development Programme 584; Inequality-adjusted Human Development Index (IHDI), United Nations Development Programme 585.

(Continued after page 702)

Contents

Contents

Introduction

This Economics for the IB Diploma 2nd Edition Student Book offers International Baccalaureate (IB) Economics students an inspiring way to learn and prepare for the IB examinations at both higher level (HL) and standard level (SL). It will help you to prepare for your examinations in a thorough and methodical way as it follows the syllabus outline, explaining and expanding on the material in the subject guide.

This book is based specifically on the new IB Economics curriculum (first examinations in May 2022) and emphasises the use of the nine key concepts that run through the course: scarcity, choice, efficiency, equity, economic well-being, sustainability, change, interdependence, and intervention. The book contains the following useful features:

- Relevant learning outcomes identified at the start of each section to help you identify what you need to know at each step.
- HL and SL content clearly distinguished, with all HL exercises and sections clearly marked (all unmarked content is for both HL and SL students).
- Fully referenced tables and coloured diagrams accompanied by clear explanations in the text.
- Practice examination questions at the end of each chapter reflecting the appropriate form and content of questions that you will find in the new exam papers.
- Links to Theory of Knowledge (TOK) conveniently highlighted throughout to help broaden your knowledge and keep you thinking about the wider applications of your learning.
- Two additional chapters offering specific advice on writing the Internal Assessment and preparing for External Assessments such as Papers 1, 2, and 3, and the Extended Essay.
- A full glossary of IB Economics subject-specific terms included at the back of the book, for easy reference.

In addition, the book includes access to an eBook version which contains:

- Links to around 100 author videos, offering clear explanatory lessons on all the essential diagrams and concepts.
- Links to online databases and sources of information (via the 'Research and inquiry' features), enabling you to apply the course concepts and carry out further research.
- Worksheets and revision quizzes for every chapter, providing additional support.

How to use this book

Throughout the book you will see a number of coloured features interspersed within each chapter, providing different information and stimulus.

Learning outcomes

These appear at the start of each section. They contain the learning outcomes for the section you are about to read and set out which aspects of learning will be covered.

Learning outcomes

At the end of this section you will be able to:

- distinguish between positive and **normative economics**
- explain how economists use models, theories, logic, the *ceteris paribus* assumption, empirical evidence, and **refutation** in their analysis of human behaviour.

Case study

Globally inclusive case studies that reference real-world examples (in the same way that Paper 1 requires real-world examples to be at the centre of your discussion).

Case study – cell service providers and oligopoly

America's cell phone service market has been narrowed down to three major providers after the acquisition of Sprint by T-Mobile in spring of 2020. America's Federal Trade Commission initially denied the request to merge, citing the undue market power exerted by a more concentrated market. They also cited T-Mobile's previously aggressive pricing as a source of competitive behaviour that would diminish after the merger. Together, AT&T, Verizon, and T-Mobile now control 98% of the US cell provider market.

Research and inquiry

Highlights areas for further inquiry and research.

Worked example

Examples that show you (in detail) how to work out necessary calculations.

Worked example 6.3

Consider the market for cotton t-shirts. Assume that when the price of blank cotton t-shirts rises by 10%, the quantity supplied increases by 15%. With these values we can easily calculate PES:

$$PES = \frac{\%\Delta Q}{\%\Delta P}$$

$$= \frac{15}{10}$$

$$= 1.5$$

Research and inquiry

To see real-world examples of increased demand from changes in tastes, conduct a news search using the term 'rise in popularity'.

For discussion and debate:

1 List five found examples of taste and preferences increasing demand for a product.

2 Generate five of your own examples of products that have, for taste reasons, fallen out of favour.

Exercise

In-text exercises to test your knowledge and understanding of that part of the course.

Exercise 7.2

1 Identify a common product you use or consume.
2 What is the **maximum price** you would pay for that good?
3 What is your consumer surplus for that good?
4 Draw an equilibrium diagram of the market for the good, indicating consumer and producer surplus.
5 Identify the consumer, producer, and community surplus for this market.

Theory of Knowledge

These stimulate thought and consideration of TOK issues as they arise and in context.

TOK

Certain individuals depend on particular goods for their very survival, e.g. people with diabetes need insulin to live. If one were to learn that insulin providers were raising their prices ever higher on diabetic patients, would you be obliged to act? This raises a question around the ethics of knowledge: 'How can we know when we should act on what we know?'

Video suggestion

These indicate that a clickable link is available (via your eBook) to one of over 200 author videos. These will help you to review the section of the book you have just read.

Video suggestion:
You have read about it, now you can review what you have just learned by watching a video by the author!
▶ Simply click here in your eBook for a video on the law of demand.

Practice exam questions

At the end of each chapter are some practice questions of the style and weight you can expect to find in the examination papers.

Practice exam questions

Paper 1, part (a) questions

1. Explain how economics addresses scarcity by answering the three basic questions of economics. (10 marks)
2. Distinguish, using a diagram, the difference between a curved PPC and a straight-line PPC. (10 marks)
3. Explain how a production possibilities curve helps demonstrate the concepts of scarcity, choice, and opportunity cost. (10 marks)
4. Explain, using a circular flow diagram, how the consumers and producers are interconnected in a free market economy. (10 marks)

You are now ready to start. Good luck with your studies!

Introduction to economics

What is economics?

1

1.1 What are some of the basic concepts in economics?

Learning outcomes

At the end of this section you will be able to:

- explain the social nature of **economics**
- distinguish between the study of **microeconomics** and **macroeconomics**
- explain the nine key concepts of IB Economics
- analyse the concepts of **scarcity**, choice, and **opportunity cost**
- explain the three basic economic questions that must be answered by any economic system
- distinguish between **market**, planned, and mixed economies.

Look around you. What do you see? Are there tall buildings made of steel? Paved roads and parking lots? Shopping malls? Fields of crops awaiting harvest? Homes built of wood, brick, and glass? Factories producing goods for consumers? Perhaps you see a thick forest or a view of hills stretching to the distance. Or do you see school buildings? Now ask yourself, how did things get to be this way?

There are many ways to attempt to answer these questions. Biologists tell a story of evolution based on natural selection. Physicists answer difficult questions by studying the elemental forces of nature that shaped our universe over billions of years, while mathematicians observe the quantifiable variables of our lives and seek to understand our world through numbers. Every field of science views the world through a lens shaped by its own tools and methodologies. Economics is no different.

Economics is a social science devoted to solving the problems posed by **scarcity**. Our existence on Earth is defined by limited resources and the seemingly unlimited wants, or **demands**, on those resources. For example, a central question in some societies is how much food can be responsibly grown in a given area, when resources like water and fertile soil are diminishing. Scarcity nearly always forces us to make **choices** between competing priorities, such as the perceived choice between **economic growth** and **sustainability**. Economics hopes to inform that choice-making to help societies get the most out of their resources.

Relatedly, a central goal of economics is to seek out **efficiency** wherever possible. Given scarce resources, a growing population and its wants, extracting the highest possible value from those resources is a top priority. However, the pursuit of economic efficiency does not guarantee a relatively equal access to resources. Economists also argue that **equity** should be considered a priority alongside or against pure efficiency. Are resources allocated without bias or prejudice? As the gap between the rich and poor in many countries continues grow, questions of equity are raised.

Economics also tries to widen its focus to broader measures of **economic well-being**, rather than purely monetary success. As such, factors of daily life such as the overall health, safety, and security of a country's population are now taken into account.

How is economics a social science?

A **social science** is a field of academic scholarship that examines the interactions between humans, our institutions, our organisations, and the natural and social environment we inhabit. A distinguishing feature of economics is human interdependence, which focuses on how people interact with each other to improve their economic well-being. Individually and in groups, humans are influenced and enabled by their values and their natural surroundings. This web of motivation poses a challenge to economists seeking a degree of certainty about causal relationships.

As a social science, economic theories are based on logic and empirical data, using models to represent and analyse this complex reality. Physical sciences work somewhat differently, and an understanding of the basic distinction may be useful. Physical sciences seek clear comparisons between an independent variable and its effect on other variables with control group testing. **Social sciences** seek the same controlled environment but this process is complicated by the many possible motivations and causal factors for human behaviour.

Testing the effectiveness of an idea like **universal basic income** (UBI) (the provision of direct cash payments to citizens as a form of poverty relief), for example, is complicated by other factors that may also influence the control group at the same time, such as political, regional, or group-specific issues. Social scientists nevertheless try to approximate control conditions using comparative data sets and statistical analysis. Because individual and collective motivations and behaviours are complex and diverse, understanding them entails the interaction of a variety of disciplines such as philosophy, politics, history, and psychology. Awards for economics have increasingly gone to research that blends economics with one of these other disciplines.

Adding another layer of complexity is the dynamic nature of economics. With physical sciences one can isolate a variable and examine its properties with a reasonable expectation that those properties are stable or may change in predictable ways. However, the events under study in economics are subject to change, possibly in real time. A surge in consumer confidence, for example, may have many causes and can just as quickly drop should events change.

What is the difference between microeconomics and macroeconomics?

Economics is broadly divided into two categories of study, **microeconomics** and **macroeconomics**. Microeconomics is the study of specific markets, such as the market for goods and services, as well as the market for **labour**. It examines the motivations and general rules of behaviour guiding buyers and sellers in these markets, and includes the concepts of **supply**, demand, and **equilibrium** prices. While microeconomics assumes a free market system that uses prices to help allocate resources, it also attempts to account for failure of the free market, where government corrections are required.

Macroeconomics centres on national economies as a whole, with a focus on the overall performance of a national economy. The health of an economy is measured using concepts such as national economic growth, employment levels, and price level stability. Discussions of inflation rates, **unemployment rates**, and **income** distribution are common.

A major focus of this branch of economics is understanding the role governments play in the management of the national economy using the tools of fiscal and **monetary policy**. Macroeconomics, too, seeks to work out useful theories and reliable rules to guide policy making, with the hope of achieving greater national prosperity.

The key concepts of IB Economics

Throughout this book, you will focus on real-world economic issues through the lens of nine key concepts.

Concept	Main idea
Scarcity	Scarcity refers to the limited availability of economic resources relative to society's unlimited demand for goods and services. Economics is the study of how to make the best possible use of scarce or limited resources to satisfy unlimited human needs and wants.
Choice	Since not all needs and wants can be satisfied, economic decision makers continually make choices between competing alternatives. Economics studies the consequences of these choices, one of which is the 'opportunity cost', where certain needs and wants go unsatisfied because resources have been allocated elsewhere.
Efficiency	Efficiency is a quantifiable concept, determined by the ratio of useful output to total input. Allocative efficiency refers to making the best possible use of scarce resources to produce the optimum combinations of goods and services, thus minimising resource waste.
Equity	Equity refers to the idea of fairness. Fairness means different things to different people and might not be the same as equality. In economics, the term 'inequity' may apply to the distribution of income, **wealth**, or human opportunity. It is an issue both within and between societies. How far markets and governments can or should create greater equity or equality in an economy is an area of much debate.
Economic well-being	Economic well-being relates to the prosperity and quality of life enjoyed by members of an economy. It includes: • present and future financial security • the ability to meet basic needs • the ability to make economic choices and so achieve personal satisfaction. Economic well-being varies greatly within and across nations.
Sustainability	Sustainability in economics is about meeting the needs of the present generation without compromising the ability of future generations to meet their needs. The current generation's economic activities can create harmful environmental outcomes, such as resource depletion or degradation, that will negatively affect future generations. This concept is becoming increasingly important in economic analysis.

Change	Economic theory focuses not on the *level* of the variables it investigates, but on their *change* from one situation to another. Empirically, the world that is studied by economists is always subject to continuous and profound change at institutional, structural, technological, economic, and social levels.
Interdependence	Individuals, communities, and nations are not self-sufficient. In a highly interdependent economic world, decisions by consumers, companies, **households**, workers, and governments generate many, often unintended, economic consequences for others. An awareness of this is essential when conducting economic analysis.
Intervention	Intervention in economics usually refers to government involvement in the workings of markets where those markets fail to achieve societal goals such as equity, economic well-being, or sustainability. In the real world, there is often disagreement among economists and policymakers on the need for, and extent of, government intervention.

What is the problem of choice?

As we are about to look at, a lack of resources compels humans at all levels to make decisions about how to allocate resources. Be it time, effort, or **money**, we all make choices about what is important to us. Economics seeks to enhance the economic well-being by clarifying and guiding those choices.

What is scarcity?

Scarcity is defined as the state of having unlimited wants and limited resources. Scarce resources are those things, both natural and manufactured, that are used in the production of the goods and services that humans consume to survive and to enjoy life. The problem with scarcity is that while resources are finite, the wants and needs of humans are infinite. There are simply not enough resources available in the world to satisfy the limitless wants of the world's people. Over time, scarcity is intensified by the natural human desire for more material wealth, safety, and comfort. In doing so, humans use up more and more of the world's limited resources.

How is scarcity related to sustainability?

The problem of sustainability is brought into focus by increasing scarcity. For example, the scarcity of **land** resources for human farming has led more and more territory to be converted from natural use to agricultural use. This increased demand or want for food growing space is in conflict with sustainable production because soil erosion and deforestation contribute to environmental degradation. With the alarm over climate change, there are calls for economics, in its role of clarifying the **choices** around **resource allocation**, to play a part in developing sustainable systems that solve scarcity.

What are the factors of production?

Humans provide for their basic needs by combining what economists call the '**factors of production**' into goods and services. All are required for the production of any good or service that might be exchanged in an economy.

Land

Land resources are those things that are 'gifts of nature'. The soil in which we grow food is scarce because fertile land is in limited supply but there is a huge desire for the food that is grown in such land. Wood is a scarce resource because ultimately all wood comes from trees, which are grown on scarce land. Minerals such as copper and tin, and resources such as oil, coal, gas, and uranium are scarce. These materials are all used to produce energy and other things we desire but they are all in limited supply and the supplies do not renew themselves.

Labour

Labour refers to the human resources used in the production of goods and services. In a world of nearly 8 billion people, it may sound silly to say labour is scarce, but it most certainly is. Labour is the human work, both physical and intellectual, that contributes to the production of goods and services. Some types of labour are more scarce than others. For example, factory workers are desirable in huge numbers in some parts of the world. In China and India, they are not very limited but are greatly desired, therefore they are scarce. Medical doctors are desired in all parts of the world, but they are more limited in number than people able to work in factories. Therefore, doctors are scarce relative to factory workers.

Capital

Capital refers to the tools and technologies that are used to produce the goods and services we desire. The word 'capital' is also sometimes used to refer to the money that individuals and businesses need to acquire the tools and technologies of production. More and better tools enhance the production of all types of goods and services but the amount of capital in the world is limited, so capital is a scarce resource.

Entrepreneurship

Entrepreneurship can be defined as the innovation and creativity applied in the production of goods and services. By combining the other three factors into desirable goods and services, this creativity and innovation have contributed more to improvements in the well-being of the world's people than any other resource. The physical scarcity of land, labour, and capital does not necessarily apply to human ingenuity, which can be renewed and developed through training and education. The basic economic problem of scarcity has led to the development of various economic systems and their methods for allocating the resources of land, labour, and capital, and distributing the output produced.

What is opportunity cost?

Every economic decision involves costs. The opportunity cost is what must be given up in order to undertake any activity or economic exchange, specifically the next best alternative to the use of the money or time. Opportunity costs are not necessarily monetary; rather, when you buy something, the opportunity cost is what you could have done with the money you spent on that thing. Even non-monetary exchanges involve opportunity costs, as you might have chosen to do something different with your time.

For example, think about your decision to sign up for this economics class. You could have studied several other subjects: geography, history, psychology, perhaps business. Your decision to study economics was your choice of how to use the scarce resource of time during your last two years in school. The cost of your decision is the foregone opportunity to study one of the other subjects, and all the skills and knowledge you would have learned had you chosen another subject.

You may be saying to yourself: 'No, the cost of me taking economics is the tuition fees or taxes my parents are paying to support my education at this school.' That is also true. But in economics, we define costs as more than just the monetary expenses involved in an economic transaction. The *opportunity cost is the opportunity lost* when making a decision of how to use our scarce resources, whether it is time, money, labour, land, or capital.

To choose one item in place of another in this way is to make a **trade-off**, a sacrifice of one thing to get another. We face these kinds of trade-offs every day of our lives. On a Friday night, you may face several trade-offs: you can go to a movie with friends at the cost of playing video games with your sister, for example, if that is your next favourite alternative.

The problem of scarcity and the need for choice gives rise to another fundamental reality faced by individuals everywhere: the reality that nothing is free. In answering the basic economic questions, choices must be made and those choices inevitably involve costs, since resources are scarce.

What is a free good versus an economic good?

A **free good** is something that is so abundant that it can easily satisfy our unlimited wants for it. In other words, it has zero, or nearly zero, economic costs. It is difficult to imagine a free good except perhaps on a local or regional basis. For coastal cities, salt water is essentially free. For desert residents, sand is essentially free. However, industrialisation has made resources like clean air and clean water less free and more scarce in the last 150 years. This leads to the conclusion that to produce nearly anything is to incur some cost, specifically an opportunity cost. Finally, there's an old adage that says that 'there is no such thing as a free lunch'. Which is to say that even something that is free to you, like a gift, has incurred a cost to someone else. Nearly all goods are therefore considered **economic goods**, goods which have some cost to society. The lack of free goods again presses the point of scarcity in human existence and the need to make choices about how to use the Earth's resources.

What are the basic economic questions?

The existence of scarcity in our world also gives rise to some basic economic questions that any society must answer with its own economic system. They do so to improve their economic well-being, influenced by their values and enabled by their natural surroundings. Some economic systems rely on customs and traditions to answer these questions, some rely on the commands of a central authority or government, and some rely on free exchanges between individuals in a market system. Regardless of whether it is governed by tradition, planned, or exchanges in the marketplace (see Chapter 2), there are three basic economic questions that any economic system must address.

What should be produced?

This is the decision to prioritise one type of output relative to another, and will reflect a society's choices. Should society's scarce resources (land, labour, and capital) be used to grow food, make clothes, toys, and tools, or should they be used to provide services such as healthcare, entertainment, and haircuts? *What* a particular economy should produce is one of the basic questions an economic system should answer. An economy based on tradition may answer 'produce what has always been produced: food for survival'. A wartime economy may use resources for armaments. A centrally **planned economy** may choose to produce whatever the government decides is most crucial to meeting society's needs, while a market economy leaves the answer up to the interactions between the supply and the demand of self-interested consumers and producers.

How should it be produced?

This is the choice of production methods. Should production be labour intensive or capital intensive? Should robots replace workers whenever possible or should workers be a protected resource? To what extent will technological innovation affect the way things are produced? Economic systems must address the question of how society's output will be produced. Whatever the system, economists see economic efficiency as a primary goal.

For whom should it be produced?

This is answered by the distribution of resources throughout the economy. In other words, who gets what, and how is that determined? Is this decided by prior access to family wealth or is social movement possible? Do social relationships take precedence over education and skill levels? What roles do identity characteristics like gender, ethnicity, race, and religion play in the allocation of resources? Are levels of **consumption** based on social standing? Gender or age? Race or religion? Or should output be allocated fairly across all sections of society? The distribution of a society's income studies the issue of equity in resource allocation in more detail.

The basic economic questions arise from the basic economic problem of scarcity. Once we recognise that scarcity exists, we must confront these questions in order to determine how to deal with the problem of scarcity in our allocation of resources and the goods and services they are used to produce.

What models exist to answer the basic economic questions?

The two types of economic system are the free market and the planned economy. Free markets, in their purest form, exclude any government action, and in fact allow for no functioning government at all. Planned economies, by contrast, use total state control of the factors of production, which can functionally lead to state control in many other aspects of life as well.

Each system has benefits and flaws. Mixed economies try to resolve the drawbacks of each by combining their approaches in a way that suits their priorities. As stated in the conceptual understandings at the start of this chapter, debates exist in economics regarding the potential conflicts between economic growth and equity and between free markets and government intervention. This is because the free market view of the future assumes constant economic growth to satisfy human needs, and ignores growing income inequality and other **market failures**, as well as general resource scarcity. People who think inequality and scarcity threaten the general well-being of all argue that smart intervention is needed for economies to organise for long-term sustainability.

What is a free market economy?

A **free market economy** is a system of resource allocation dependent on the private ownership of the factors of production and on the free exchange of goods and services in a price system. Private buyers and sellers satisfy their wants by paying for each other's products in a free exchange.

What should be produced is determined by the market itself. Sellers seek to satisfy the desires of buyers, and determine what to produce based on what generates the highest prices. The price system guides how goods are produced as well. High prices indicate scarcity and firms will move to produce those goods that bring higher prices. Low prices suggest abundance, and firms will be slow to produce these goods. In a free market system, the private owners of land, labour, and capital, including entrepreneurs, receive the benefits of the system in accordance with their value in the free market.

One of the founders of modern economics, Adam Smith, wrote in the 1770s that the 'market' (a place where buyers and sellers meet to engage in exchanges with one another) was the most efficient means for allocating scarce resources. It therefore led to the greatest amount of benefit for the largest number of people, especially when it was left free of government control.

With regard to markets, Smith advocated a **laissez-faire** approach to the government's management of the nation's economic activity. 'Laissez-faire' is a French term that translates as 'let it be'. A government, said Smith, should let an economy be free, since individual agents in a free market will interact in a manner that results in outcomes beneficial for both the individual and society. Smith believed that freedom and the pursuit of self-gain would not lead to chaos and anarchy, but to a socially beneficial outcome whereby society's wants and needs are satisfied by the 'invisible hand' of the market rather than an iron fist.

▲ Statue of Adam Smith on the Royal Mile in Edinburgh

> 'Whoever offers to another a bargain of any kind, proposes to do this. Give me that which I want, and you shall have this which you want, is the meaning of every such offer; and it is in this manner that we obtain from one another the far greater part of those good offices which we stand in need of. It is not from the benevolence of the butcher, the brewer, or the baker that we expect our dinner, but from their regard to their own self-interest. We address ourselves, not to their humanity but to their self-love, and never talk to them of our own necessities but of their advantages.'

Adam Smith, *The Wealth of Nations*, 1776

The idea that individuals pursuing their self-interest could end up contributing to the well-being of others was rooted in Smith's moral philosophy that humans' personal happiness partly is based on the well-being of those around them, that people are **interdependent** to some degree. Smith believed that in a complex society made up of thousands or millions of individuals whose interests do not always overlap, an economy governed by tradition or command could not possibly achieve a more beneficial outcome for the greatest number of people than a system in which individuals are able to pursue their own self-interest.

Freedom of **choice** was a fundamental basis for Smith's economic and social philosophy, and to this day freedom remains a key characteristic of the economics we study and of the policies that economic theory helps shape in both national and international economies. Most economies combine elements of the free market with some degree of government intervention – these are mixed economies. The degree to which government is involved varies greatly between countries, and is a central point of argument in each country's politics.

Advantages of a free market economy

- People are relatively free within the market system to choose from a variety of jobs or businesses, and to choose how they produce and for whom.
- When the market fosters competition, firms have the incentive to innovate, improve products, and increase efficiency.
- Consumers tend to dominate because consumers vote with their purchases. Markets respond quickly to consumer preferences to gain more profit.
- In an open system that depends on self-interest, the price system sends more accurate information about the scarcity of resources to buyers and sellers.

Disadvantages of a free market economy

- Markets can become dominated by monopoly or **oligopoly** interests that stifle competition and raise prices for all.
- **Public goods** (such as national defence and streetlights) will not be produced because the free market cannot provide them profitably.
- **Demerit goods** (goods that have harmful effects on society such as pollution and tobacco) will be overproduced.
- **Merit goods** (goods that have positive effects on society such as vaccines and education) will be underproduced.
- Extreme gaps between the few rich and many poor develop and have negative social effects.

What is a planned economy?

A planned economy answers the basic questions with the central government making all the decisions. In their extremes, they are sometimes referred to as command economies, suggestive of the control the government exerts over the lives of its citizens. The specific answers as to *what* to produce will vary from country to country, depending on its own priorities, but at the discretion of the government. The government may choose to prioritise capital goods over consumer goods, or military goods over consumption. Likewise, the method, or *how* to produce, will be determined by the authorities. Decisions about the labour market (who gets what jobs), capital market (which firms get machinery, which do not), and land use (which resources will be developed) all happen under central planning. Entrepreneurship, to the extent that it can flourish at all, does so within the limits of state control. It is the state also, who determines *to whom* production is distributed. The state sets **wages** and prices and so completely allocates incomes and wealth.

The most noted planned systems were implemented in Mao's China, Stalin's Soviet Union, the Democratic People's Republic of Korea (North Korea) and Castro's Cuba. In each case, these leaders sought to move the economy of their country from an agricultural base to an industrial and manufacturing base. The mechanism used to pursue this goal involved total control of the nation's resources by the government.

Typically, a planned economy requires state ownership of the factors of production and is guided by the principles of socialism – the notion that society should be organised to the benefit of all its citizens. These principles place the objective of equality above that of efficiency. Socialist economies aim to achieve fairness within society by allocating resources and output based on the common needs of humans rather than the individual pursuit of self-interest that underlies market economies. Private ownership of factors of production is therefore abolished. All agricultural and industrial output is appropriated by the central government and is reallocated among the nation's people in what is intended to be a fair and equitable manner.

Because of the lack of individual **property rights** and the incentive to achieve maximum efficiency in the use of resources (which characterise private ownership), the planned economies of the 20th century eventually became highly and notoriously inefficient. Ultimately, they were unable to provide their nations' people with the basic necessities for a healthy and happy existence. Both Russia (the core of the former Soviet Union) and China eventually abandoned the planned system of economic management. Of the notable Cold War command systems, only Cuba and North Korea have remained fundamentally planned economies.

The failure of planned economies to achieve sustainable and meaningful improvements in the well-being of their people can be tied to the lack of an effective mechanism for determining the most efficient allocation of society's scarce resources. Central planners, it turned out, were too prone to making mistakes in their determination of what was best for society. Massive inefficiencies and high levels of corruption emerged as producers in the economy focused less on producing quality products that society truly demanded, and more on meeting the strict production targets passed down from the central government.

An economic system that does not appropriately harness incentives towards achieving efficiency in production will eventually collapse under the mounting inefficiencies that emerge while attempting to manage the activities of millions of individuals across the nation. This helps explain why the prominently planned economies of the 20th century failed to thrive and why most of them eventually adopted some market-based economic reforms granting individual ownership of property and encouraging the pursuit of self-interest.

Advantages of a planned economy

- Countries that value equity can provide resources to the poor, ensuring basic housing, income, and healthcare.
- Countries that emphasise full equality can minimise income gaps by paying equalised wages across the labour market.
- The state can establish priorities and move the economy in their direction. For example, the priority could be to move from an agricultural economy to an industrialised one, as the Soviet Union did under Stalin in the 1930s.

Disadvantages of a planned economy

- The incentives for innovation and entrepreneurship are greatly reduced because the system rewards individual productivity poorly.
- Organising an economy is complex. Routine decisions about resource allocation in one market, such as how much wood to allocate to paper production, are very difficult to balance across a whole country.
- State control eliminates competition, and so removes the incentive to find efficiency, lower costs, and improve products.
- Citizens have little freedom of choice in their work, housing, or where they live because the government determines all three.

Case study – central planning's worst disaster?

In 1949, the People's Republic of China emerged from the Chinese Civil War, after Mao's Communist Party of China defeated Chang Kai-Shek's Nationalist army in a decades-long conflict. The new state was founded on the principles of Marxist-Leninst socialism, which held wide appeal to a very poor and agrarian population. After consolidating power over the course of the 1950s, Mao declared that China must make the great leap to an industrial economy in 1958. This programme, called the Great Leap Forward was to follow the Stalinist drive to industrialise in the 1930s by collectivising agriculture and using the **surplus** food to power production in heavy industry. Hundreds of thousands of government officials fanned out across the country to direct the plans. Mao tried to mobilise the population in a way similar to the days of the Revolution, and ordered village communes to produce steel in backyard furnaces. Peasants threw every kind of wooden household object to heat the furnace and all kinds of metal equipment into the furnaces, to be melted into steel. The result was massive inefficiency. The metal produced was a pig iron that needed refining by large smelting plants the country did not have. Worse, countryside peasants spent so much time on the furnaces they neglected their crops. The result was one of the worst famines in history, killing between 30 and 50 million people. One lesson among the many tragedies of this period was the wilful ignorance of scarcity and value, something that markets provide and central planners rarely can capture without market signals.

Backyard furnaces in China during the Great Leap Forward era

How would you categorise your own country's economy? Is it closer to a free market economy or is it more planned? Some ways to check: Ask if the country's higher education system is free to students? Is healthcare provided by a single government entity? Are taxes perceived to be relatively high, compared to similar countries? Are the largest companies owned by the government? Another way is to look up the 'government spending as a percentage of GDP'. (GDP being **gross domestic product**, or the size of the overall economy.)

Prepare to discuss your results with those in your class to compare the degree of government intervention in your country's economy.

What is a mixed economy?

A **mixed economy**, as the name suggests, seeks to combine aspects of planned and market economies to suit a country's needs. All countries, unofficially if not officially, have mixed economies in that they combine private and public control of some resources. A mixed economy may have a strong private sector for goods and services, with workers earning varied salaries, firms choosing who their workers are, and allocating resources based on their profitability. That country may also have government provision in other sectors, such as health care, national defence, and education. It may also have a strong social safety net to reduce **poverty** and help the unemployed. These government interventions would be paid for by taxing firms and individuals. Mixed economies rely on cultural and political influence to decide the appropriate place and degree of intervention, and where markets should be free.

Advantages of a mixed economy

- Solutions to market failures can be managed on a case by case basis, not bound to ideology.
- Governments can use tax **revenues** earned through its market system to support underproduced merit goods like education and healthcare.
- Governments can provide popular goods and services but also limit demerit goods.
- A balance of dynamic market forces and government support can increase overall well-being.

Disadvantages of a mixed economy

- There is a potential for social division over the allocation of resources and tax rates.
- There can be political conflict over the role of the government in regulating production and consumption.

1.2 The production possibilities curve model (PPC)

Learning outcomes

At the end of this section you will be able to:

- explain, using a PPC diagram, how the **production possibilities curve** (production possibilities frontier) model may be used to show the concepts of scarcity and choice
- using a PPC diagram, show and explain a situation of unemployed resources and inefficiency
- using a PPC diagram, demonstrate the concept of trade-offs and opportunity cost
- explain how a PPC may demonstrate the idea of increasing and constant opportunity costs.

The existence of scarcity and the reality that every economic decision involves trade-offs and costs can be illustrated in what will be the first of many economics models you will learn about in this course. The production possibilities curve (PPC) is a model economists use to demonstrate the fundamental economic concepts you have been reading about so far (Figure 1.1).

The PPC model makes several assumptions:

- the amount of resources (land, labour, capital, entrepreneurship) is static
- the level of technology is also held constant
- an economy produces only two goods (capital or consumer goods, for example)
- any point on the PPC line represents the full use of all resources and technology, and is therefore economically efficient
- points inside the curve are levels of output that are inefficient, not using all resources available
- points outside the curve are impossible unless conditions change
- to change from one point on the curve to another point on the curve is to reallocate resources, increasing output of one good at the expense, or opportunity cost, of another
- changing preferred outputs along the efficient PPC line are shown by movements along the PPC
- movements along the PPC will demonstrate the trade-offs between production of one good in terms of another, or how much of one good is lost when producing more of the other good
- constant opportunity cost PPCs are shown by straight-line PPC
- increasing opportunity cost PPCs are shown by a curved, bowed-out PPC.

A kind of personal PPC can be used to demonstrate some of these basic concepts. The PPC in Figure 1.1 illustrates the trade-off Sarah faces in deciding how to use her 10 hours of free time each week. She can spend her free time doing one of two things, playing or working.

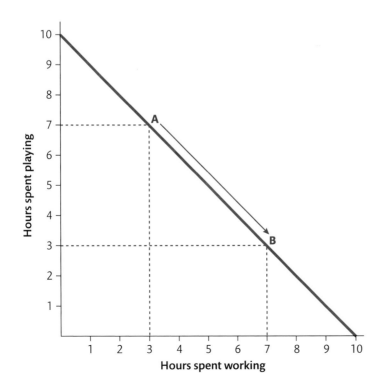

Figure 1.1 Sarah's production possibilities curve

Assume that point A represents Sarah's decision in week 1, when she allocates seven hours to play and three hours to work. Her decision to allocate her limited time in this manner involves an opportunity cost, which is the benefit she would have gained from spending more time working and less time playing.

Assume that point B represents Sarah's decision in week 2, when she has decided to spend seven hours working and only three hours playing. The opportunity cost of working four additional hours is the four fewer hours she gets to spend playing and all the enjoyment she foregoes as a result of her decision.

This simple PPC demonstrates several concepts fundamental to economics.

- **Scarcity**. Because resources are scarce, there is a limit to the amount of production or consumption an individual (or a nation) can undertake. Time is the scarce resource in Figure 1.1. With only ten hours of free time, Sarah must decide how to allocate her time among competing activities.
- **Trade-offs and choices**. The two axes in a PPC represent two trade-offs faced by an individual, firm, government, or society. The axes may represent any economic activity that can be undertaken by an individual, firm, or nation in the employment of its scarce resources. Because we face trade-offs, we must make choices, which involve costs.
- **Opportunity cost.** Nothing is free. More time playing comes at the expense of the benefits from time spent working. Likewise, a nation that chooses to produce a certain good faces costs in the form of the other goods that could have been produced with the same resources.

The law of increasing opportunity cost

More commonly, the PPC is used to illustrate a nation faced with a decision regarding what types of goods to use its scarce resources to produce. The PPC in Figure 1.2 assumes that Country I can produce two goods – pizzas and robots.

The law of increasing opportunity cost explains why the PPC is bowed outwards from the origin. The law says that as the output of a particular product increases, the opportunity cost of producing additional units rises.

Varied resources: Country I's PPC in Figure 1.2 has a convex shape (it bows out from the origin). The reason for this lies in differences in the production of pizzas and robots. Pizzas and robots require very different resources in their production. Pizzas are land intensive (large amounts of land are needed to grow the ingredients). Pizzas also require a particular type of labour and capital: farmers and cooks need not have advanced degrees and extensive expertise in engineering to grow ingredients and make pizzas. The land and labour resources required to make robots are very different than those for pizza. The type of labour needed is highly skilled and educated. Because Country I's land, capital, and labour resources are not equally suitable to making either robots or pizzas, the opportunity cost of increasing production of robots increases in terms of pizzas the more robots are produced.

Increasing opportunity costs to production are shown by the country losing larger amounts of one good as it tries to increase production of another. For example, as this country increases output of robots, it gives up more and more units of pizza each time. Notice, for instance, that when robot production increases from 300 to 400 units, the

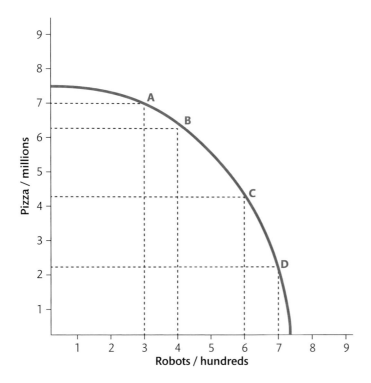

Figure 1.2 The increasing cost PPC bows outwards due to the very different resources involved

cost of the additional 100 robots is just under one million pizzas (since pizza production falls from 7 million to a little over 6 million). But as robot production increases, however, from 600 to 700 units, the additional 100 robots costs Country I around *two* million pizzas (since pizza output falls from around 4 million to 2 million pizzas).

Why did the opportunity costs double for the same increase in output? Why did Country I have to give up twice as many pizzas to increase robot production by 100 units from 600 to 700 than it did to increase production by the same one hundred units two levels before, from 300 to 400? The explanation lies in the fact that as Country I started making robots (between 100 and 400) only the resources best suited for robot design and production were employed. Electrical engineers and highly educated technicians who had been employed in the pizza industry quit making pizzas (which they were never any good at anyway) and started making robots. The land, labour, and capital that was best for making pizzas remained employed in the pizza industry, and at first Country I was able to switch over to the production of robots at a relatively low cost.

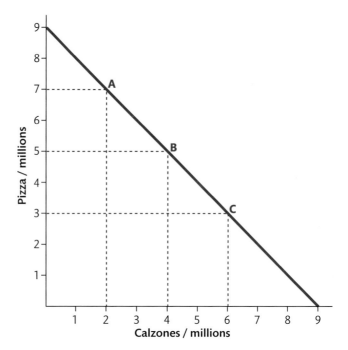

Figure 1.3 The constant-cost PPC derives from the one to one trade-off between pizza and calzones

However, as robot production intensified, resources were increasingly moved out of pizza production, and into the robot industry. This meant switching resources that were well-suited to pizza making and forcing them into robot making. Accordingly, to produce 700 robots, highly skilled pizza makers and land better suited for growing wheat and flour and tomatoes and dairy cows had to be shifted into robot production. The cost of robots in terms of pizzas increases the more robots Country I produces. Because costs increase with each interval of output, the law of increasing opportunity costs is at work.

Constant-cost PPCs

Similar resources: Not all PPCs are bowed outwards. If the two goods represented in a PPC are very similar in their production, requiring similar types of labour, capital, and land resources to produce, then the PPC for the two products is a straight line, such as Country I's PPC for pizzas and calzones (Figure 1.3). A calzone is basically a pizza folded in half. Therefore, the opportunity cost of one calzone is always only one pizza, so the PPC is a constant sloping curve, and the trade-off is always one to one. Real-world examples of similar resources used in the production of two goods include the growing of corn and wheat, or the production of smartphones and tablet computers.

Efficiency, inefficiency, and economic growth

The PPC can also be used to illustrate the economic concepts of efficiency, inefficiency, and economic growth. Look now at Figure 1.4. Points A, B, C, and D are all on the curve; at each of these points Country I is producing some combination of goods and using its existing resources (land, labour, capital, and entrepreneurship) efficiently. This means that nearly every person of working age who wants a job has a job, the land that can be used for production of pizza ingredients and robot components is being used and the nation's existing capital (factory equipment, ovens, and other tools) is operating

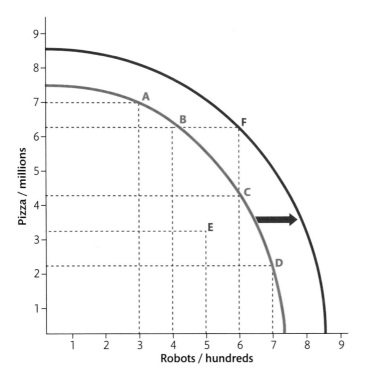

at full capacity – no capital is sitting idle. At these points, an increase in total output is not possible without an increase in inputs first. A nation achieving its production possibilities is producing at its **full employment level of output**. For this reason, the PPC is often given the alternative name of production possibilities frontier (PPF).

A nation not achieving **full employment** of resources is producing at a point inside its PPC. If Country I is producing 500 robots and 3.2 million pizzas (point E), it is under-utilising its land, labour, and capital. A country is said to be inefficient if it is producing at a point inside of its PPC. This means that **unemployment** is likely to be high, land that could be put into cultivation of food or production of minerals is not being used, and existing capital is sitting idle. An economy producing inside its PPC may be in a **recession** – this means that the level of output has fallen below the full employment level achieved when producing on its PPC.

Clearly the PPC can also illustrate the possibility of economic growth. A point outside the PPC is unattainable given the existing quantity and quality of resources, but it is clearly desirable. At point F in Figure 1.4, Country I would produce 600 robots and consume over 6 million pizzas. This is clearly beyond the current production possibilities, but it may be attainable in the future if the economy grows.

Economic growth is defined as an increase in the total output of a nation over time, indicating an increase in economic well-being. Growth is possible if a nation experiences an increase in the quality or the quantity of productive resources (land, labour, capital, and entrepreneurship), or an increase in technology. Economic growth is shown with a PPC in Figure 1.4. In order to achieve a level of production and consumption corresponding with point F, Country I must increase the amount of land, labour, or capital in the country or improve the productivity of these resources. Such a change would create a new PPC boundary line, with a new set of trade-offs between one type of production and another. Most importantly, more of all goods, in this case pizza and robots, can now be produced.

TOK

How realistic are economic models? How can we know what to include or exclude in a model?

Consider the above model, the PPC. To what extent do you think some of the assumptions above (two types of output, resources are static), are very realistic? To what degree do they identify useful ideas? What could be included to make it more realistic? How would that affect the clarity of the model?

Productivity is defined as the output attributable per unit of input. If Country I's workers became better at producing pizzas and robots, either through better training and education or through an increase in the quality of the technologies used to produce these goods, then the national output of Country I would grow and the country would move towards point F. **Investments** in public education by the government or investments in better technology and more capital by the country's businesses could lead to economic growth. Economic growth is an objective that plays a significant role in macroeconomics.

1.3 The circular flow of income model

Learning outcomes

At the end of this section you will be able to:

- describe, using a diagram, the circular flow of income between households and firms in a closed economy with no government
- outline that the income flow is numerically equivalent to the expenditure flow and the value of output flow
- explain how the circular flow demonstrates the interdependence of all sectors of the economy
- describe, using a diagram, the circular flow of income in an open economy with government and financial markets, referring to **leakages**/withdrawals (savings, taxes and **import expenditure**) and **injections** (investment, government expenditure, and **export revenue**)
- explain how the size of the circular flow will change depending on the relative size of injections and leakages.

The idea that the exchanges between individuals are *voluntary* and that anyone engaging in such exchanges benefits from them is fundamental to the market economic system. This implies that when one person voluntarily gives another something that the second person wants, the first person must be getting something he or she wants in return. Thus, both parties are better off following the exchange. In other words, market economics is not a zero-sum game. When one person wins, it does not necessarily mean that someone else loses. Both derive some benefit from the trade, or they would not voluntarily make it.

The circular flow model (Figure 1.5) shows the flow of money through the economy, as money moves from buyers to sellers, and then from sellers to individuals in the form of income. Thus money circulates through the economy. The model assumes that all exchanges in a market economy take place in either the 'product market' or the 'resource market'. In our study of market economies, we will assume that the demand for resources by firms, and for goods and services by households, is met in one of these two markets. Households are the 'owners' of productive resources, which are the inputs firms need in order to produce goods and services. To acquire the inputs for production, firms must pay households for their resources in the resource market. Households earn their income in the resource market and then buy the finished products provided by firms in the product market.

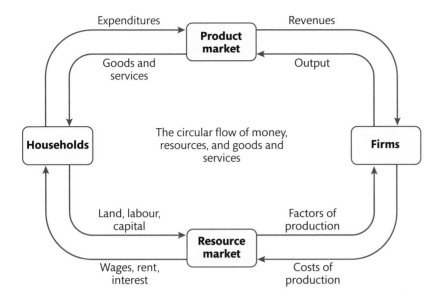

Expenditures   Revenues

Product market

Goods and services   Output

Households

The circular flow of money, resources, and goods and services

Firms

Land, labour, capital   Factors of production

Resource market

Wages, rent, interest   Costs of production

Figure 1.5 Money and resources flow in opposite directions around the **circular flow model**

Thus, in Figure 1.5, money payments flow clockwise in the outer loop while resources, goods, and services flow counter-clockwise in the inner loop. In the resource market, households provide firms with the factors of production (land, labour, and capital) they demand in order to produce their output. But these inputs are not free; firms face costs in acquiring them. These costs translate into money incomes that households receive for the resources they provide; wages for labour, rent for land, and interest for capital.

Once firms have acquired all the inputs necessary to produce their finished products, they sell their products to households in the product market. The money households earn in the resource market goes to pay for the goods and services they demand in the product market. Household expenditures on goods and services translate into revenue for the firms.

Thus, the money earned by households in the resource market is ultimately earned by firms in the product market, and the circular flow is complete. Inputs turn into outputs, income turns into revenue.

Figure 1.5 illustrates at a basic level how market economies function. Buyers and sellers are **interdependent**. A drop in one sector affects the others. Reduced incomes in the resource market will reduce spending in the product market.

The circular flow model with injections and leakages

We can now introduce additional elements into the model to make it more realistic. The previous model was self-contained but the new model will acknowledge that there are other actors in the system and that money exits and enters the system in a variety of ways. Money that exits the system is referred to as 'leakages', while money that enters the system is called 'injections'.

The government sector: taxes and spending

Probably the single largest actor not included in the simple model is the government. The government has a profound impact on even the most avidly free market economies. Governments draw tax money from the population, a leakage of income out of the model. However, that money should eventually re-enter the model as **government spending** on everything from salaries to **infrastructure**. (Even if we assume that some of the money is lost through corruption, it may also eventually re-enter as consumer spending.) This idea, that the flow of money never truly escapes the model, is one that holds true with the other new actors in the model.

The foreign sector: imports and exports

The previous model assumed a closed economy, hardly a realistic notion in a world of increasingly globalised trade. If we assume that some of the money spent in either the factor or product market is spent on imported goods, then that income will leak from the system. However, roughly the same amount of money should enter in the form of **exports** sold to other countries. This tendency towards a balance of import and export flows is explained in more detail in Chapter 26. For now, it is sufficient to acknowledge the leakage and injection that takes place with the addition of the **foreign sector** to the model.

The financial sector: savings and investment

Some consumers save a portion of their money, rather than spend it. Savings would slow down the flow of expenditure and eventually income. However, money that is saved in banks is made available to borrowers. These borrowers then inject the savings back into the economy in the form of investment, whether as capital goods or by the purchase of housing by households. Thus, the leakages of savings re-enter the system through loans made by the financial sector.

Figure 1.6 The circular flow model showing leakages and injections

▼

Figure 1.6 illustrates the new, more complicated circular flow model, one that includes injections and leakages via three sectors: the government, foreign, and banking sectors. Injections are insertions of money into the circular flow and include government

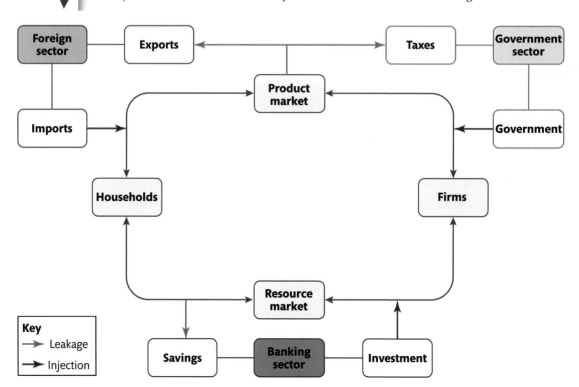

spending, export purchases, and investments. Leakages are the diversions of money outside the circular flow and occur when the government collects taxes, **imports** are purchased, or when people save money. Figure 1.6 shows the government sector taking taxes away from firms and households, then injecting the money into the flow again. It shows imports leaking money out of the economy, while exports inject it back in. It shows savings leaking out of the economy, while investment from the savings injects it back in.

While the new model is still a simplified one, it makes an allowance for some realities. If one sector leaks more than it injects, the flow merely becomes smaller. For example, if imports are greater than exports, the flow may be reduced. If government spending, an injection, is greater than taxes in any given year, the flow will increase. Of course, in that event, most governments will borrow money to do the spending. So, it is likely that, in some future year, taxes will be more than spending to pay off the debt. Although there is a tendency for the leakages and injections to be equal, in the real world it is unlikely that they will be at any particular time.

Practice exam questions – assessment tips (Paper 1 for HL and SL)

Your Paper 1 exam will consist of three pairs of essay questions. You will choose one of them. Each pair may come from any of the four units: Introduction to Economics, Microeconomics, Macroeconomics, the Global Economy. Each pair has part (a) worth 10 marks and part (b) worth 15 marks. You will have 75 minutes to answer this two-part question.

Part (a) will require you to define terms, explain concepts, and, almost always, use a diagram to do so. Most questions, but not all, state the need for diagrams, but even those that do not explicitly say so may still require a diagram for full credit. It is important to connect the diagram to your explanation. Unexplained diagrams do not count for much. The use of real-world examples is desirable, as it helps illustrate the idea.

More information on external assessment is found in Chapter 31. Below are examples of part (a) questions.

Practice exam questions

Paper 1, part (a) questions

1. Explain how economics addresses scarcity by answering the three basic questions of economics. (10 marks)
2. Distinguish, using a diagram, the difference between a curved PPC and a straight-line PPC. (10 marks)
3. Explain how a production possibilities curve helps demonstrate the concepts of scarcity, choice, and opportunity cost. (10 marks)
4. Explain, using a circular flow diagram, how the consumers and producers are interconnected in a free market economy. (10 marks)

How do economists approach the world?

2

2.1 Economic methodology

At the end of this section you will be able to:

- distinguish between positive and **normative economics**
- explain how economists use models, theories, logic, the *ceteris paribus* assumption, empirical evidence, and **refutation** in their analysis of human behaviour.

As you start down this path towards learning economics, you will slowly start to *become an economist*, which means you will start to look at the world a little differently. The *economic way of thinking* is one rooted in logic, reasoning, and both *positive* and *normative* analysis of quantitative and qualitative data drawn from observations of the interactions of various agents in society, often examined using models. By the end of this journey, you will be an *economist*, and you will never look at the world the way you did before studying economics!

The role of positive economics

Economists may not always agree on everything. An economic statement is *positive* or *normative* depending on whether it is purely an expression of factual information or an expression of values or opinions based on facts.

Positive economics deals with what *is*. It focuses on observations and expressions based purely on factual evidence. For example, it is a fact that when the price of doughnuts rises, the number of doughnuts that consumers demand falls. This is not an issue that economists would find it necessary to debate. In fact, the relationship between the price of a good and the **quantity demanded** by consumers is so widely agreed upon that it has become an economic law (the **law of demand**).

Positive economics is rooted in the use of **logic**. An economist undertaking positive analysis will apply a set of tools, often mathematical, always based on formalised principles or economic 'laws', to predict the outcome of a particular event in the world. For example, a positive economic observation might be, 'if the government increases the **minimum wage**, then more people will seek jobs and at the same time employers will need to lay workers off, therefore unemployment will increase'. This statement is based on the basic economic laws of supply and demand and the *ceteris paribus* **assumption**, which economists use to hold 'all else equal' when predicting how a particular change will affect a market or society.

Economists have formalised supply, demand, and many other principles in **models** that can be used to predict and explain how society functions. There is **empirical evidence** to support these models, and therefore it would be difficult to **refute** the above positive economic statements.

The role of normative economics

Not every economic statement is irrefutable, however. Some are more an expression of a particular economist's opinion or values. Consider the statement, 'Doughnuts should be taxed because at their current price they are over-consumed and contribute to obesity.' This may be true in that doughnuts can cause health problems, but the view that they 'should be taxed' is refutable. Therefore, this statement is normative. Normative economics deals with what *should be* rather than what is. Normative economics deals with areas of the subject that are open to personal opinion and belief.

Or consider the statement, 'The government should raise the minimum wage, since many retail workers cannot afford a decent quality of life.' How does this differ from the previous, positive statement about the minimum wage? The previous observation is based on economic theories and real-world evidence, while this statement is based on the subjective viewpoints of the person making it. While it may be true that it is hard for minimum wage workers to afford a decent quality of life, the claim that the solution is a higher minimum wage is refutable by anyone willing to argue that the resulting negative impact on employment outweighs the benefits of the higher wage.

Positive economic analysis examines human interactions through the lens of quantifiable, irrefutable, evidence-based observations. There is no role for values or ethics in the realm of positive economics. Normative economics, in contrast, allows for the expression of the economist's values or personal views based on the quantifiable evidence observed in a particular market or realm of social interaction.

Normative economics places value on certain principles over others, such as the importance of equity over efficiency, or vice versa. Equity in economics refers to *fairness*. This differs from the concept of equality, where resources are distributed evenly across society. Equity is when there is an equal opportunity for individuals in society to achieve economic advantages.

Let us examine two economic statements about education.

A. There is a direct relationship between the level of education attained and one's income later in life.

B. Taxing the incomes of the rich at a higher rate to help pay for publicly-funded schools will benefit society since everyone will have equal access to education regardless of income.

Which of these is a positive statement and which is normative? If you said A is the positive statement then you are correct. B, on the other hand, is a normative statement based on the fact presented in A. While education does, in fact, correlate to higher incomes, whether or not the best way to achieve that outcome is to tax the incomes of the rich is refutable. The statement places a value on *equity* over *efficiency*. Many people would argue that taxing the incomes of the rich creates a negative incentive to work hard and earn higher incomes, and therefore reduces efficiency across the economy. Others may counter that the money taxed at higher levels is less useful to, or needed by, the relatively rich than the money contributed to support the relatively poor.

TOK

What assumptions do economists make when they apply economic theories to the real world?

To what extent does the distinction between positive and normative statements exist in other academic disciplines?

2.2 A history of economic thought

Learning outcomes

At the end of this section you will be able to:

- outline the broad history of economic thought from the 18th century through the early 21st century.

Economics is a social science, and like other sciences the theories and principles on which it is based have changed throughout history. As different practitioners have emerged, each has applied their own unique methodology and perspective to their objective observations of society's economic interactions.

The 18th century – the foundation of classical economics

Economies, the systems by which goods are produced and exchanged in society, have existed since the **specialisation** of human labour arose during the first Agricultural Revolution around 12,000 years ago. The *study* of how economies function is a relatively recent field. Modern economics as a field of study has its roots in the 18th-century English Enlightenment, when the philosopher Adam Smith described how the pursuit of individual self-interest in free markets could result in socially desirable outcomes, as some in society seek to get rich by producing what others demand.

Adam Smith was one of the first theorists of what was later described as *classical economics*, the unifying principle behind which was the idea that the value of any commodity or good is derived from the amount of labour used to produce it. This *labour theory of value* is reflected in the following quote from Adam Smith's *The Wealth of Nations*.

> 'The value of any commodity, therefore, to the person who possesses it, and who means not to use or consume it himself, but to exchange it for other commodities, is equal to the quantity of labour which it enables him to purchase or command. Labour, therefore, is the real measure of the exchangeable value of all commodities. The real price of every thing, what every thing really costs to the man who wants to acquire it, is the toil and trouble of acquiring it.'

Adam Smith, The Wealth of Nations, 1776

A Neolithic rock carving: the first Agricultural Revolution happened during the Neolithic period

The 19th century – free markets for all

Utility theory

The fields we now refer to as microeconomics and macroeconomics were not yet formed when Smith was writing about the pursuit of self-interest guiding commercial interactions as if by an *invisible hand* in the late 18th century. Microeconomics as a field of study emerged only in the 19th century with the development of utility theory, which was used to explain the behaviour of individuals who are able to consistently rank their choices in order of their personal preferences.

As economic agents, individuals make rational decisions about what to buy and consume and how to allocate their limited resources (time, labour, money, etc.) based on their *utility functions* for various choices. **Utility** in economics is the happiness or satisfaction derived from any particular good, service, or activity that an individual could choose to consume or pursue.

Utility theory formed the conceptual foundation of what would later emerge as the market demand and supply models, on which much of microeconomic analysis is still based. The demand for any particular good in a market is derived from the aggregated utility functions of all the consumers in that market. Likewise, a **supply curve** is little more than the aggregated **marginal costs** of all the producers in a market, determined by the diminishing marginal returns experienced as more units of a variable input are added to a fixed factor of production.

Economists talk about individuals' behaviours *on the margin*. These are behaviours based on the value of an additional unit of something. The classical economists of the early 19th century were the first to examine the concept of the margin, and it forms the basis of microeconomic theories to this day.

The laissez-faire approach

Another classical economist of the early 19th century, Jean-Baptiste Say, laid the groundwork for what would be known as the laissez-faire approach to macroeconomics, which says that the best means by which to manage a national economy is to not manage it at all, but to 'let it be'. **Say's Law** observed that *supply creates its own demand*. Say explained that:

> ' … a product is no sooner created than it, from that instant, affords a market for other products to the full extent of its own value'

> Jean-Baptiste Say (Translated by CR Prinsep), *A Treatise on Political Economy*, 1821

The act of paying workers in one factory creates demand for the products from another factory equal to the value of the labour provided in Factory A. Upon this observation the belief emerged that an economy left to its own unregulated and unhindered activities will reach a state of equilibrium where full employment is achieved. Surpluses and **shortages** of goods, services or labour (in other words, unemployment or overemployment) will be eliminated as the market finds a balance between production and consumption. Macroeconomic shocks like recessions, stagnation, and involuntary unemployment, according to Say's Law, are resolved automatically by the free market's rebalancing between the amount produced and consumed.

The 19th century – Marx's critique

Classical economists had faith in the morality of free markets and the socially beneficial outcomes of the pursuit of individual self-interest. That faith was called into question in the mid-19th century by several philosophers, most notably Karl Marx. His critique of the free market theories of the likes of Smith and Say was rooted in the inequality that had emerged under the market system predominant at the time. Marx believed that under the market system, human labour had become a disposable 'commodity' like the slave labour on which the economies of ancient Rome and Greece had been based.

Marx argued that workers were the slaves of capital and capitalists were the slave masters. Marx defined 'capital' as the wealth possessed by individuals that is used to extract profits from the production of commodities and 'capitalists' as the wealthy owners of capital.

Marx believed the capitalist system exploited labour, because the owners of capital paid workers less than the value of the output they produced, thus extracting 'surplus value' from the working class to enrich the capitalist class. This exploitation would create an imbalance over time as the growing classes of exploited labourers would see their wages pushed downward. As the gap between the rich and poor grew, the conditions for revolution would emerge, the capitalist system would be overthrown and workers themselves would take control of the means of production.

The ideal society, according to Marx, was one in which the factors of production were communally owned, and everyone in society would be rewarded equally for his or her labour.

> 'In a higher phase of communist society, … only then can the narrow horizon of bourgeois right be crossed in its entirety and society inscribe on its banners: From each according to his ability, to each according to his needs!'
>
> Karl Marx, *Critique of the Gotha Program*, 1891

▲
Karl Marx in 1875

The 20th century – a battle of ideas

Marxism would form the basis for the communist regimes that emerged in the 20th century in places such as Russia (the Soviet Union), China, North Korea, and Cuba. Some degree of Marxist ideology underlies the socialist states that still exist, reflected in the degree of state ownership of the major industries in modern economies such as Canada, China, Sweden, the UK, and elsewhere. No modern economies demonstrate the continuous cycle of class struggle and ongoing revolution that Marx foresaw, and for the most part experiments with pure communism based on Marxist principles have been abandoned for the mixed market/government-run economies typical of most countries in the 21st century.

We can see that by the end of the 19th century the two poles of the economic spectrum had been firmly established by economic theorists, from Smith and Say at one end to Karl Marx at the other. Finding the balance between them has been the struggle of every economy in the two and a half centuries since Smith established the groundwork for the field of modern economics.

In the 20th century, the tug and pull of free market capitalism at one extreme and state-run communism at the other came to a breaking point as the world's superpowers collided, not only on the battlefields of the First and Second World Wars, but also in the factories, fields, mines, and offices of the global economy. The Great Depression of the 1930s struck a devastating blow to both the capitalist economies of the West and the communist states of the East. With the Second World War that followed, the question of the extent to which government should play a role in the economic lives of a country's people came to the forefront of history. With the communist Soviet Union and the capitalist USA both emerging victorious from the war against Nazism and fascism, a new paradigm for understanding macroeconomics was needed. The man that emerged from the war as the intellectual thought leader of 20th century economics was John Maynard Keynes.

Keynes' voice emerged from a crisis. By 1929, the first great experiment in Marxist-style communism had been underway for seven years in the Soviet Union. The USA was at the tail end of its 'Roaring Twenties', a decade that saw record growth in economic activity and the emergence of the thriving monuments to capitalism that investors still worship today: stock exchanges like those in New York, London, and elsewhere across the capitalist world. In October 1929, a collapse of share prices on the New York Stock Exchange, caused by an unregulated and wildly speculative stock market, triggered a global financial crisis. The ensuing collapse of the banking system ushered in a decline in economic activity that would later be known as the Great Depression.

Unemployed men lining up outside a soup kitchen in Chicago, February 1931

The depression caused problems for the laissez-faire doctrines of the classical economists. The economies of the world failed to self-correct from the slump in output and employment as classical theory suggested they would. Instead, unemployment reached shocking levels across the rich world. In the absence of government safety nets such as unemployment benefits, health insurance, food and housing **subsidies**, and other programmes that are fairly standard in developed economies today, the decline in economic activity resulted in increased poverty and unparalleled human suffering. The free market principles of Adam Smith and Jean-Baptiste Say, it would appear, had failed the people of the USA and Europe. The Great Depression called for a new interpretation of macroeconomic principles, and Keynes stepped in to fill that void.

Keynes's 1936 book *The General Theory of Employment, Interest, and Money* introduced theories that still predominate macroeconomics today. He observed that following economic crises, such as the 1929 stock market crash, economies are unlikely to self-correct, or return to full employment equilibrium, as the classical theory predicted they would, but would instead risk ever-falling spending and shrinking output. This, in his view, was due to several factors, including the propensity for households to save more during economic downturns, businesses' reduced willingness to invest, the inflexibility of wages and prices, and the public's increased preference for 'liquidity' (i.e. the desire to hoard cash during downturns), all factors that cause the overall level of spending to spiral downward, and unemployment to rise during recessions.

Without government intervention, argued Keynes, slumping economies would become stuck in a 'liquidity trap', in which reduced spending leads to rising

unemployment, which reduces business optimism, further reducing spending and employment. Consumers reduce spending, and so firms earn less revenue and fire more workers. This reduces consumer incomes further, hurting sales to firms. The resulting 'deflationary spiral' would see recessions turn to depressions that would last for years if governments did not step in to help restore full employment.

One of Keynes's greatest innovations was to view the economy as working as a complete system. Keynes developed modern macroeconomic theory through his 'general theory', which viewed a nation's economy as a giant machine that could be controlled through various levers. A fall in household consumption could be counteracted by a tax cut and an increase in government spending, which would boost overall demand and help maintain full employment. A decline in business investment could be corrected by increasing the supply of money, which would cause **interest rates** to fall and thereby increase the expected rate of return on new business investment, stimulating demand once more.

Keynes's work recognised that while the self-correction predicted by the theories of his 19th-century predecessors would eventually come true in the long run, it was not enough for economic policymakers to sit idly by during an economic downturn and wait for prices and wages to adjust, while millions of households suffer the hardships that go with unemployment, including poverty, hunger, homelessness, and depression:

> '... this long run is a misleading guide to current affairs. In the long run we are all dead. Economists set themselves too easy, too useless a task if in tempestuous seasons they can only tell us that when the storm is long past the ocean is flat again.'

> John Maynard Keynes, *A Tract on Monetary Reform*, 1923

The *fiscal and monetary policy* tools that governments and **central banks** rely on today to combat recessions and prevent depressions were first envisioned by Keynes. The models we learn in IB Economics, including that of **aggregate demand** and **aggregate supply**, are *Keynesian models*. Keynesian economic theory found a middle ground between the laissez-faire, free market capitalism of Smith and Say and the state-run, centrally planned communism of Marx. For this reason, Keynesian economics has, since the middle of the 20th century and into the 21st, become the target of criticism and revision from thinkers on both ends of the economic spectrum: the free market advocates call Keynesianism quasi-socialist, while those who favour the collectivism of centrally planned economies would say Keynes's approach does not go far enough to regulate and plan the nation's economic activity.

One of Keynes's most vocal critics was the Austrian economist Friedrich von Hayek, who believed that the central decision making at the core of communism and socialism undermined liberty and could only reduce people's standards of living. He believed no central authority could possibly possess the knowledge of human desires to allocate resources efficiently in a way that maximises society's well-being. Any central planning, including the government interventions advocated by Keynes to regulate economic activity and promote full employment during economic slumps, could only lead to authoritarianism. It was a slippery slope, argued Hayek, from a government increasing its deficit spending during a recession to help keep workers employed, and total government control over the lives of the nation's workforce.

Hayek and other followers of the Austrian School of Economics offer a blueprint for an economic system rooted in liberty: free markets, private property, and individuals pursuing their own self-interest, much as theorised by Smith, are the true path to prosperity, and thus government should play only the smallest of roles in the economic lives of their people. The tug of war between free markets and intervention that we see today, as we have shown, has its roots in 19th- and 20th-century debates between the likes of Smith, Say, Marx, Keynes, and Hayek.

TOK

Many economists argue that economics as a social science is in its infancy, and that with time, as empirical testing methods and the quality of data improve, it will become more reliable in making accurate predictions. Do you agree with this statement?

Case study – the battle of ideas in governments' responses to the COVID-19 pandemic

The Keynesian/Austrian debate over the extent to which government should play a role in the economy played out in the decades following the Great Depression and the Second World War, as the governments of Europe, North America, and other rich, developed parts of the world debated the structure of their economies and the role the government should play both in good times and during economic downturns. Given the cyclical nature of booms and busts, economies experience periods of rising prosperity and economic hardship, often swinging between the two every decade or so. Recessions, as periods of declining economic output are called, tend to come along, even in the most developed economies, once every decade or so on average, and can be triggered by a myriad of factors, either on the 'demand side' of the economy or on the 'supply side'.

In 2008 there was a 'demand-side' recession in the USA and Europe, triggered by a collapse in house prices, the effects of which reverberated throughout the world's financial markets. Millions of workers became unemployed around the world, increasing poverty and hardship as governments debated, then struggled to address the downturn with appropriate responses.

The year 2020 marked the next major global economic slump, brought on by the coronavirus pandemic, this one both a 'demand-side' and 'supply-side' recession. Demand for all sorts of goods and services fell as people were forced to stay at home and limit their social interactions for months on end, while supply chains were hobbled as factories and offices adjusted to new requirements to limit the spread of the virus.

The anti-Keynesian argument for responding to COVID-19 emerged in the United States in the summer of 2020, as conservative policymakers in the Republican party of the US government took strong positions opposing future stimulus involving cash payments to individuals and extended unemployment benefits to support people who lost their jobs in the recession. By late 2020, US government support for unemployed workers ended, as some policymakers argued that continued expansion of benefits would create an incentive for people to remain unemployed voluntarily, thus slowing the economic recovery.

Meanwhile, governments around the world once again faced the challenge of addressing the economic consequences of a downturn in the **business cycle**, and just as in the 1930s, the extent to which government should intervene was at the core of the debate. The Keynesians in government, at least during the early months of the pandemic, seemed to win these debates, as rich-country governments mounted massive spending campaigns to prop up demand while households were forced to stay home, and millions lost their jobs. In the USA, the federal government extended unemployment payments of $600 per week to anyone who lost their job due to the pandemic. In many cases, workers' incomes increased under the generous government spending packages relative to what they made while employed.

However, by summer 2020, months into the pandemic, the Keynesian fervour of many governments began to wane and concerns over the cost of continued support for the economy began to win over. By late 2020, the role the government would continue to play in the economic recoveries of pandemic-stricken countries was called into question, as elected officials began to argue that the economy would eventually need to recover 'on its own', much as an Austrian economist of the 20th century might have argued.

In addition to the macroeconomic intervention questions, many economists grappled with specific questions of epidemiology, public safety, and education with regards to school shutdowns. Emily Oster, Professor of Economics at Brown University and pictured at the start of this chapter, created a crowdsourced database to evaluate the degree of COVID-19 spread in schools, and to weigh this against the costs of missed schooling. Her use of cost and benefit analysis helped persuade school districts to open safely more quickly.

The debate between the Keynesians and the Austrians of the 20th century is very much alive and well in the 21st century, as evidenced by government responses to the coronavirus pandemic. In the future, more economic crises will inevitably occur, and the role of government in response to each will once again be debated in the parliaments and congresses of the world's capital cities.

The 21st century – blurred lines
Behavioural economics

From Smith to Keynes and Hayek, economics has evolved from a branch of philosophy in the 18th century to a social science with principles rooted in mathematical logic by the late 20th century. Today the field is undergoing a renaissance once more as innovative economists engage in dialogues with psychologists, ecologists, sociologists, and experts in various other fields. Several recent Nobel prizes in economics have been awarded to economists exploring the field of **behavioural economics**, which studies the effects of psychological, cultural, social, cognitive, and emotional factors on the decisions individuals make in the social and commercial realms. Behavioural economics has broadened our understanding of economic interactions beyond the view of humans as the purely rational, utility-maximising agents that we were understood to be by the classical economists.

Ecological and environmental economics

As growing populations and rising incomes have put an increasing strain on the world's natural resources and the environment, fields of economics that focus on the relationship between economic systems and the environment have become increasingly popular. *Ecological economics* is an interdisciplinary field that views the economy as a subsystem of the Earth's larger ecosystem. It focuses on the threat to the ecosystem of continued development of technology and the substituting of physical capital for natural capital. *Environmental economics*, on the other hand, shares more of the traditional beliefs of the classical and Keynesian schools of economic thought, but broadens its cost–benefit analysis to incorporate external, environmental impacts of the behaviours of producers and consumers. Both these fields are increasingly emerging as leading fields of study in the 21st century as societies have begun to

TOK

Economics, like any science, is evolving as students of the subject become leading thinkers themselves and formulate new ideas that catch on and become mainstream paradigms. As a social science, it might be the case that there are fewer 'hard truths' in economics than in the physical sciences. The social aspect of the field leads some to call into question its validity, as humans can be fickle creatures who tend not to abide by strict rules of behaviour, as atoms and molecules do in the physical world.

Discussion questions:

1 To what extent have individual thinkers shifted the paradigms of economics through their contributions to the field over the last 300 years?

2 How likely is it that the economics we study today is the same economics that future students will study?

3 Does the fact that the paradigms of economics are always changing make the field any less relevant to the world we live in today?

face the increasing scarcity of natural resources and the environmental impacts of unchecked economic growth and development.

A common critique among ecological and environmental economists of the classical economic model (that based on the works of Smith, Say, and other 18th- and 19th-century thinkers) is that its focus on the mathematical modelling of human behaviour fails to take into account the contexts within which economic interactions take place, including human psychology, society, culture, and the natural environment. The classical economists can perhaps be forgiven for under-emphasising the natural environment in their analysis, given that the human population at the turn of the 19th century was only around 1 billion people. However, as population and incomes have grown, the need to re-examine economic philosophy through the lens of *sustainability* has become increasingly urgent.

A recent model of **sustainable development** is that of the *doughnut economy*, developed in 2012 by University of Oxford economist Kate Raworth. The doughnut economy, according to Raworth, is one in which the 'safe and just space for humanity' exists where we have achieved a 'social foundation' but do not live beyond the Earth's 'ecological ceilings'.

In order for the whole of the world's population to live within the 'safe and just space', significant economic growth is still needed in developing countries, where the social foundation has not been achieved for roughly 1 billion people. Wherever there is a shortfall within any of the 12 social foundations (visible on the inside of the doughnut), economic growth and development are required. However, if all 12 are achieved, further economic growth threatens to 'overshoot' one or more of the nine ecological ceilings, resulting in environmental degradation, and ultimately reductions in living standards as human systems become unsustainable.

All this is to say that *economics* is an ever changing and evolving field of study. The theories you study in this course are only a sample of the myriad branches of social science that have emerged in its short history. Where the field goes in the future is up largely to young learners like yourself, and what you choose to focus your studies on as you progress through the field in the years to come.

Practice exam questions

Paper 1, part (a) questions

1. Using examples, distinguish between positive and normative economic analysis. (10 marks)
2. Explain how the 20th century 'battle of ideas' between John Maynard Keynes and his Austrian critics, including Friedrich von Hayek, reflected the earlier ideological debates between the free market theories of Adam Smith and the communist theories of Karl Marx. (10 marks)
3. How do behavioural economics and ecological economics demonstrate the evolution of economic thought as the field incorporates the work of other social and physical scientists? (10 marks)

Microeconomics

How do consumers and producers make choices in trying to meet their economic objectives?

- Interaction between consumers and producers in a market is the main mechanism through which resources are directed to meet the needs and wants in an economy.
- Consumer and producer **choices** are the outcome of complex decision making.
- Welfare is maximised if allocative **efficiency** is achieved.
- Constant **change** produces dynamic markets.

Demand

3

3.1 Demand

At the end of this section you will be able to:

- define a market
- state the law of demand
- explain the negative relationship between price and quantity demanded
- **HL** explain the income and substitution effects
- **HL** explain the law of diminishing **marginal utility**
- analyse the relationship between an individual consumer's demand and **market demand**
- draw a **demand curve** and explain that it represents the relationship between the price and the quantity demanded of a product, *ceteris paribus*.

What is a market?

A market is any place, physical or virtual, where the buyers and sellers of goods and services meet. In most languages, the term 'market' has connotations of a direct and tangible experience, like buying fruit from a local grocery, or meat from a nearby butcher. These are markets in the traditional sense, but in the modern world a market can be defined more broadly as any instance where buyers and sellers come together for the exchange of goods and services.

These interactions can happen at any time or place. Direct buying and selling usually happens in a specific place, such as when trading your cash for a farmer's fresh eggs. But markets can also operate indirectly, when buyers and sellers communicate remotely. In commodity markets, buyers can purchase massive amounts of basic goods like coffee or wheat at international meetings with representatives of the farmers, never meeting the actual producers. This indirect buying and selling may also happen online – for example, when a share trader buys a stock that you have offered up for sale. In this case, the buyer and seller have no contact at all.

Product versus resource markets

Another way to think of markets is to distinguish between product markets and resource markets. Economists view product markets as wherever consumers purchase goods or services directly from producers. In the resource market, businesses make payments to the owners of resources such as land, labour, capital, and entrepreneurship. In a market economy, the recipients of these payments are private individuals or households.

Examples of markets, by type and definition, include the following.

- *Retail*: corner shops selling directly to customers who are the end-users of the product or service.
- *Wholesale*: businesses buying in large quantities to re-sell or transform into final products.

- *Geographic*: markets can be defined as local, regional, national, or international.
- *Online*: while the majority of goods are still sold directly, greater amounts are sold online every year.
- *Foreign exchange*: buyers and sellers exchange one currency for another.
- *Financial markets*: a market exists for company shares (stocks) and government or corporate bonds.
- *Labour markets*: firms are the buyers and workers are the sellers in the market for labour.

What is demand?

As stated above, every market transaction involves a buyer and a seller. The economic concept of demand takes the consumer perspective, examining what motivates and limits buyers in any given market. More specifically, consumers can be private households in the market for end-user consumer goods and services in the product market. Businesses also act as consumers in the product and resource market.

Demand is defined as the quantity of a good or service that a consumer or group of consumers are willing and able to purchase at a given price, during a particular time period. Note that the quantity of demand is limited to those who are both willing and *able* to buy the good.

What is the law of demand?

The law of demand states that as the price of a good increases, the quantity demanded of the good decreases. The opposite is also expected to hold as true: as the price of a good decreases, the quantity demanded of that good increases.

The law of demand implies a negative or indirect relationship between the two variables of price and quantity demanded. As a result, most demand curves have a downward-sloping shape. This concept rises to the level of a 'law' in economics because it conforms closely to everyday reality. As individuals, we are less likely to buy any good as the price rises (exempting, for the moment, speculative goods like gold or company stocks, which may be bought with the expectation that they could be re-sold at a higher price). As the price goes up, our common sense (and budgets) generally tell us to economise and buy less. And the reverse tends to be true as well. When the price of something declines, we grow less concerned about the price and may buy a little more of it as a result, and perhaps others will start to switch to it also, increasing the amount demanded.

As an example, we can determine a city's demand for chocolate bars in a given week. A demand schedule is a list of prices and quantities that show the amount demanded at each price for a given time period. Table 3.1 shows the city's chocolate bar demand schedule for one week. For example, at a price of $2.50, 5000 bars would be purchased. Demonstrating the law of demand, as the price falls to $2, the quantity demanded rises to 10,000 bars.

The information on a demand schedule can also be plotted as a graph to give us a demand curve. Figure 3.1 plots the price and the quantity demanded to derive the demand for chocolate bars.

Table 3.1 Demand schedule for chocolate bars

Price of chocolate bars (P) $	Quantity of chocolate bars demanded per week (Q) (thousands)
2.50	5
2.00	10
1.50	15
1.00	20
0.50	25

Chocolate bars on sale in Canada

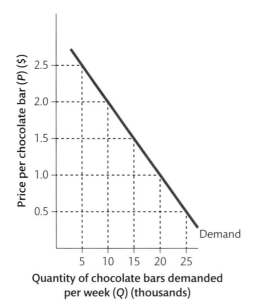

Figure 3.1 The demand curve for chocolate bars shows demand increases as the price decreases

Demand

3

In Figure 3.1, the vertical axis shows the price of the good (the independent variable), while the horizontal axis shows the quantity demanded of chocolate bars (the dependent variable) per week. The curve is downward sloping, reflecting the negative slope and negative relationship between the two variables. It is also said that price and quantity demanded have an inverse relationship, because as one rises the other falls. In the diagram, as price rises from $.50 to $1.00, the quantity demanded falls by five thousand bars per week.

What is *ceteris paribus*?

The term *ceteris paribus* is a Latin term meaning that we are holding all other variables constant or frozen, while we examine how different prices change the amount demanded. Many other things can influence any decision to buy goods. Holding those factors constant permits us to isolate one variable (price) and quantify the effect a change in price has on another variable (the quantity demanded).

HL Why do economists assume the law of demand is essentially correct?

The following are some of the factors that underlie the law of demand.

- The **income effect**: A decrease in the price of a good or service that is being consumed means that consumers experience an increase in real income, usually allowing them to purchase more of the product. Real income refers to income that is adjusted for price changes, and implies the actual buying power of a consumer. As the price of a good decreases, the quantity demanded increases because consumers now have more real income to spend. With more buying power, people sometimes choose to buy more of the same product. So, in our example, as the price of bars falls from $2.00 to $1.50, part of the 5,000-bar increase in quantity demanded will be accounted for by some chocolate consumers buying even more chocolate bars, because they can afford to at the lower price. Their real income has risen, and they choose to buy more bars with that extra buying power.

- The **substitution effect**: When the price of a product falls, relative to other products, there is an incentive to purchase more of the product, since the marginal utility/price ratio has improved. As the price of a good decreases, consumers switch from other substitute goods because its price is comparatively lower. A substitute good is a good that is easily switched for another. In our example, as the price falls from $2.00 to $1.50, some portion of the 5000-bar increase in demand is from buyers of cookies, another sweet snack food, who see a drop in the price of chocolate bars and switch, or substitute, chocolate bars for their beloved cookies. More specifically, at lower prices, each consumer gets more utility per dollar of spending now that the price is lower.

- The **law of diminishing marginal utility**: This law states that as we consume additional units of something, the satisfaction (utility) we derive for each additional unit (marginal unit) gets smaller (diminishes). The law of diminishing marginal utility does not state that extra consumption causes a decline in total satisfaction. It merely states that, in this instance, a second or third bar of chocolate will be less satisfying than the first bar. It may still be delicious and add to one's total level of benefit, but the rate at which it satisfies has dropped with each successive bar consumed.

Economics asserts that some principles are relatively certain, such as the law of demand. Are some types of knowledge less open to interpretation than others?

TOK

Video suggestion:
You have read about it, now you can review what you have just learned by watching a video by the author!

Simply click here in your eBook for a video on the law of demand.

Economists use the term 'util' for a hypothetical standard unit of satisfaction. If, using the example below, satisfaction was measured in units of utility, one might say for a typical consumer that the first bar is worth 10 utils, but the second bar only 8 utils. Still satisfying, but not as much so as the first bar. The third bar consumed would provide the consumer with a smaller number of utils, and so on. In an extreme case, it is possible that a consumer eating repeated bars would find that some future bar would produce negative satisfaction, making them ill, and actually decreasing their overall enjoyment of eating chocolate bars.

This concept helps explain the law of demand because it is logical that a consumer would only buy a second or third unit of a good when the price was lower, reflecting their lower utility for extra units of the good. In our example, as price falls from $2.00 to $1.50, some portion of the increase of 5000 bars consumed is accounted for by consumers buying more bars at a cheaper price, reflecting their lower utility per bar. Therefore, because utility is lower for additional units, it is only at lower prices that more will be demanded.

Figure 3.2 reduces demand to the individual demand for chocolate bars each month. The diagram shows how a graph can reflect the law of diminishing marginal utility, and how the relationship mirrors that shown in the demand curve in Figure 3.1. The theory of marginal benefit says that the price we are willing to pay for a good is a reasonable approximate measure of our satisfaction from the good – that is, our benefit. If we are willing to buy ten bars at a price of $2, then we are **signalling** to the world that our benefit is at least $2 from the tenth bar.

Because a demand curve reflects what we are willing to pay for a good, it is an approximate reflection of the marginal benefit (MB), the extra benefit from each additional unit, that we receive from consuming additional units of a good. If our consumer were to consume an 11th bar, we would have to assume that his or her satisfaction from it would be less than $2-worth, and that the only way he or she would buy more than ten bars is if the price were lowered to something below $2. Thus, we see the concept of diminishing marginal utility at work in the everyday demand curve.

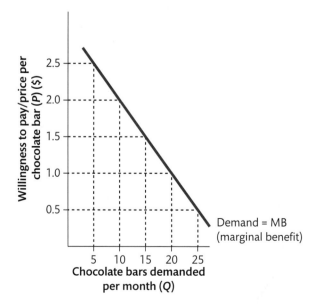

Demand = MB (marginal benefit)

TOK Is the assumption of **rational consumer choice** realistic?

In recent years, a group of economists and psychologists have questioned the assumption of rational consumer choice suggested by utilitarian theory. The school of *behavioural economics* has developed in part by examining the notion that consumers both (a) have **perfect information** at their disposal to make decisions and (b) make choices based on entirely objective information when they do. This topic will be covered more extensively in Chapter 8.

As an introduction, try making two lists.

- First, write down items you buy or decisions you make that are highly researched, where you think carefully over the choice. Label that list 'tough choices'.

- Next, write down purchases or decisions that are made quickly without much thinking. Label this list 'easy calls'.

- Identify two or three ways you gathered information to make each type of decision.

Figure 3.2 A graph of individual demand for chocolate bars illustrates how the decrease in **marginal benefit** is similar to the decrease in overall demand

Video suggestion:
You have read about it, now you can review what you have just learned by watching a video by the author!

 Simply click here in your eBook for a video on the income and substitution effects.

John Stuart Mill, 1806–97 ▶

Case study – John Stuart Mill's theory of utilitarianism

Among the more direct attempts to apply economic principles to moral thinking was that of John Stuart Mill, who in the 19th century formalised a philosophy of human interaction rooted in the very economic concept of the pursuit of utility. Working as a philosopher and social theorist, Mill developed a moral viewpoint called utilitarianism.

Mill wrote that a fundamental method of evaluating moral questions was based on the greatest happiness principle. In other words, the course of action that is most morally justified is that which creates the greatest happiness for the most people.

While the utilitarian philosophy has been eclipsed by many others since Mill's time, the pursuit of utility (happiness) has become embedded in modern economic theories which hold that individuals in a market economy (whether consumers or producers) will engage in activities that help them achieve the greatest level of utility (profit).

Mill was influenced by thinkers like Jeremy Bentham, an English philosopher and political radical, and his own father, the Scottish philosopher and economist James Mill. His moral philosophy was applied controversially. On questions of women's rights and slavery, for instance, Mill's thinking was viewed by many as radically progressive and even dangerous to the prevailing ideas of the time.

Discussion questions:

1   Utilitarianism holds that the individual pursuit of utility is itself morally good. How is this similar to and different from the economic view of utility and profit maximisation?
2   Does modern economic theory attach moral values to the behaviours of individual consumers and producers in a market economy?
3   To what extent does the pursuit of individual happiness contribute to or interfere with the achievement of social harmony?

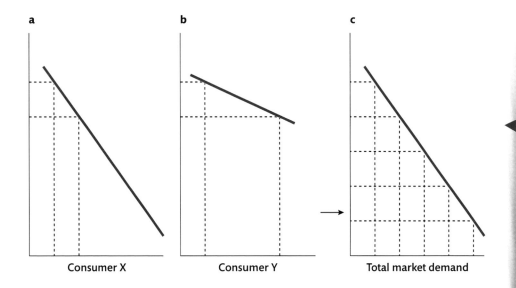

a

Consumer X

b

Consumer Y

c

Total market demand

Figure 3.3 Total market demand is the sum of all individual consumers' demands

How is the individual demand of consumers related to total market demand?

To get the total market demand for a good, we take the sum of all the individual demand curves for the same good. Therefore, if we started with the demand for Consumer X, and added it to the demand for an additional consumer, Consumer Y, we would have the market demand for chocolate bars between those two people (Figure 3.3). If Consumer X were to buy one bar at $2.50 as shown on Figure 3.3a, and Consumer Y were to buy one bar at $2.50 as shown on Figure 3.3b, then the market demand together may only be two bars at a price of $2.50. At a price of $2.00, Consumer X would buy two, Consumer Y would buy four, and the market demand would be six.

This summation continues at every price until the market demand for chocolate bars is complete (Figure 3.3c). The final market demand for the city adds all the individual demand curves, with the quantities at each price. Note that the demand curve for Consumer Y is flatter than that for Consumer X. This is because each has a different **elasticity**, a concept covered in Chapter 4. However, the slope is still downwards, reflecting the law of demand.

3.2 What are the non-price determinants of demand?

Learning outcomes

At the end of this section you will be able to:

- explain the effects of various non-price determinants of demand
- distinguish between movements along the demand curve and shifts of the demand curve
- draw diagrams to show the difference between movements along the demand curve and shifts of the demand curve.

Until now, we have held constant (*ceteris paribus*) all of the other factors that could influence the demand for goods so that we could exclusively examine the effect of price changes on the amount of demand. All of those other factors can be referred to as the non-price determinants of demand: the variables that will cause overall demand for a good to increase or decrease.

The non-price determinants of demand fall into five main categories:

- income
- tastes and preferences
- future **price expectations**
- price of related goods (in the case of **substitutes** and **complements**)
- number of consumers.

Income

People tend to increase their spending when their income improves. But whether an increase in income actually increases demand for any particular good depends on whose income rises, and on their relationship to that good.

Normal goods

These are goods for which demand increases as income rises and falls as income falls. Examples of **normal goods** would be cars, cinema tickets and restaurant meals. This principle is dependent on the income for a particular population. The relatively poor, given an increase in incomes, may view bicycles as a normal good, while richer populations would not. The demand for restaurant meals is shown in Figure 3.4. Notice that the change in the determinant moves the entire demand curve to the right. At all prices, consumers want more of the good. In this case, an increase in income for normal goods shifts the demand curve to the right. This increases the demand for restaurant meals at every price.

Inferior goods

These are goods for which demand decreases as income rises and increases as income falls. **Inferior goods** are generally considered to be a cheaper alternative to higher quality goods. Examples of inferior goods could be, for middle-income and richer populations, bicycles and bus tickets. Other typical examples include raw food

Figure 3.4 Restaurant meals are an example of a normal good: an increase in income shifts the entire curve to the right

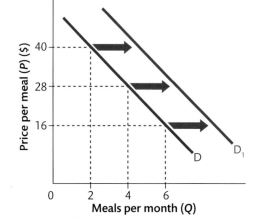

ingredients like baking flour and millet, since richer consumers are more likely to buy the finished product. Previously used goods like used cars and clothing are also good examples. In these cases, an increase in income would result in a shift of the demand curve backwards or to the left.

Taste and preferences

Demand changes with consumer tastes and preferences. Goods become more or less popular because of fashion, current events, and word-of-mouth recommendations between friends or co-workers.

Future price expectations

Consumers think and act according to the information they receive about the world. Sometimes consumers believe that the price of a good will change in the near future. This can influence their decisions about buying particular goods at that moment. If consumers believe that the price of a good is likely to climb rather quickly, they will be inclined to purchase more immediately. This means that an expectation of higher future prices will cause consumers to buy more now (an increase in demand now, a shift to the right). An expectation that prices will decline soon is likely to cause consumers to defer their purchases until the product becomes cheaper (a decrease in demand now, a shift to the left).

Price of related goods

Goods may be substitutes for each other, complementary to each other, or not related at all.

Substitute goods

These are goods that one might easily use in place of another. A substitute good (demand) is one for which demand will increase when the price of another good increases. Demand for a substitute good will decrease when the price of its substitute decreases. Because they are so similar, an increase in the price of one may lead consumers to switch consumption to the substitute. Therefore, the price of one good and the demand for a substitute have a positive relationship. As the price of one increases, demand for the other increases.

There are many examples among branded goods such as fizzy drinks, or fast food outlets. Other examples include margarine and butter, buses and train travel, and chicken and beef.

Figure 3.5 shows how an increase in the price of fizzy drink C causes an increase in the demand for its substitute, fizzy drink P. The demand curve for the latter moves to the right, increasing the amount demanded at every price.

Complementary goods

These are goods that are typically used in combination with each other. Therefore, they are also purchased and consumed together, and the demand for one is decreased by the price increase of the other. Therefore, an increase in the price of a complementary good will appear to the consumer as an increase in the price of enjoying the combined

Research and inquiry

To see real-world examples of increased demand from changes in tastes, conduct a news search using the term 'rise in popularity'.

For discussion and debate:

1 List five found examples of taste and preferences increasing demand for a product.

2 Generate five of your own examples of products that have, for taste reasons, fallen out of favour.

Research and inquiry

For discussion and debate:

Generate a list of three pairs of complementary goods.

1 Look up the prices of each.

2 Speculate how high the price of one would have to go to affect the demand for the other.

3 How would demand for the complementary good change?

Generate your own list of three pairs of substitute goods.

1 Look up the prices of each.

2 Speculate how high the price of one would have to go to affect the demand for the other.

3 How would demand for the substitute good change?

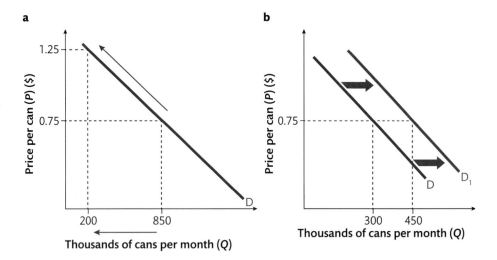

Figure 3.5 An example of a substitute good: an increase in the price of one drink (a) results in a rightward shift in demand for another (b)

experience of both goods. As a result, the demand for complementary good will decrease. Examples include goods such as phones and phone cases, computers and printers, cameras, and memory cards.

In Figure 3.6, a decrease in the price of digital cameras, shown as a movement along the curve (Figure 3.6a), causes an increase in the demand for memory cards (Figure 3.6b). The demand curve for memory cards shifts forwards, or to the right, reflecting an increase in the amount of demand for memory cards at every price.

Number of consumers

All businesses hope to market their goods to the widest audience possible. Two ways that the number of eligible buyers can change are through new markets and demographic change. New markets opened by political change or trade agreements will increase potential demand. In the last few decades, many companies have relocated major operations to China and India partly because they hope to sell their product in the world's largest newly opened market. All of these companies are attempting to increase the number of potential buyers.

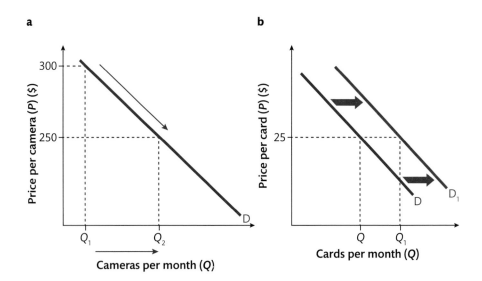

Figure 3.6 An example of a complementary good: a fall in the price of digital cameras (a) results in a rightward shift in demand for memory cards (b)

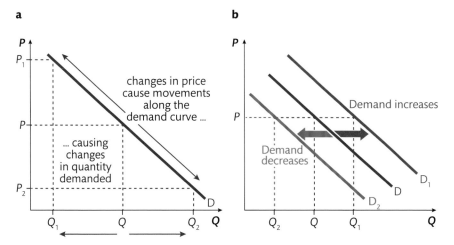

Correspondingly, a decrease in the potential number of buyers shrinks demand. For example, if a trade restriction were to prevent the importing of Japanese electronics into China, demand for Japanese electronics would drop. Demographic change refers to shifts in the type of consumers within a market. Changes in the proportional ages of a population can cause major change in demand. As populations age, demand for health services are likely to increase. If a population grows younger, demand for education-related services will be higher.

Shift in demand and movement along a demand curve

One significant difference between changes in price and changes in the non-price determinants of demand is that a change in price will cause only a movement along the demand curve. Something other than price must change to shift the entire curve.

Figure 3.7 shows the distinction between a change in price and a change in the actual non-price determinants of demand. A change in price causes a movement up and down along the demand curve, changing only the quantity demanded. In Figure 3.7a, as price rises from P to P_1, the quantity demanded decreases from Q to Q_1. In Figure 3.7b, changes in the non-price determinants of demand shift demand at all prices to the right or left. An increase in demand, from D to D_1, increases the amount of demand at P from Q to Q_1. But it is true that the quantity demanded will be higher at all prices with the new D_1 demand curve. Conversely, as demand decreases from D to D_2, the quantity demanded at all prices decreases.

Using our example, in Figure 3.8a, a change in the market price from $1.50 to $2.50 causes a movement along the demand curve and a decrease in the quantity demanded from 15,000 to 5000. However, when the non-price determinants of demand change, there is a shift of the entire demand curve. The quantity demanded will change at each price.

In Figure 3.8b, the initial demand is indicated by curve D. If one of the determinants of demand were to change and cause an increase in demand, the new demand curve would be D_1, a shift outwards or to the right. More is being demanded at every price. For example, at $1.50, where once only 15,000 were demanded, now a quantity of 20,000 are demanded. The same is true at all prices, all because of a

Figure 3.7 Price changes cause movements along the demand curve (a), while changes in non-price determinants shift the whole curve (b)

Research and inquiry

A series of age-based demographic statistics can show how populations may be growing younger or older, and so predict the demand for certain types of age-related goods and services. Generally, a *dependency ratio* measures the combined number of younger (school age) people and older people (over 65 years) as a proportion of working age people. Higher dependency ratios suggest more pressure on public services for both groups, and a squeeze on the earnings of the working age population. For our purposes, it is possible to separate the measure into the *youth dependency ratio* and the *elderly dependency ratio*.

Conduct an internet search to identify the three countries with the highest and lowest values in each category.

For discussion and debate:

1 How do you think the demand for particular goods and services is affected by these extremes?

2 Using an example product for each, explain your reasoning.

Video suggestions:
You have read about it, now you can review what you have just learned by watching some videos by the author! Simply click here in your eBook for videos on the determinants of demand and changes in demand versus changes in quantity demanded.

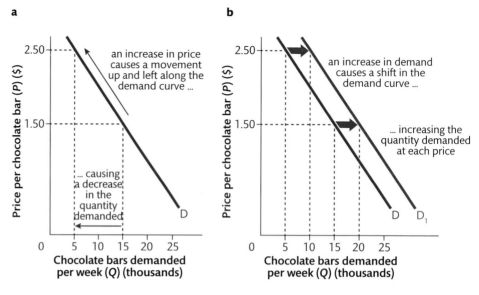

Figure 3.8 Price of chocolate bars goes up (a) and general demand for chocolate goes up (b)

change in the *ceteris paribus* variables for chocolate bar demand. The same process works in reverse as well. If demand were to decrease, then there would be smaller quantities demanded at each price and a shift of the demand curve backwards or left would occur.

Exercise 3.1

Consider headlines 1 to 7, and for each:

- state whether there is a shift or a movement along the demand curve
- state the kind of shift
- create a diagram to demonstrate the shift
- identify the determinant that caused the shift.

1. A summer heatwave affects the market for electric fans.
2. The price of toy airplanes increases.
3. A formerly communist country is now eligible to buy cars from the rest of the world.
4. Consumers are expecting the price of beef to rise significantly in the coming weeks.
5. Diamond sellers are worried about the impact of the recession.
6. The price of toothpaste drops unexpectedly.
7. As the population grows older, the market for bicycles is changing.

Practice exam questions

Paper 1, part (a) questions

1. Distinguish between a shift of the demand curve and a movement along a demand curve. (10 marks)
2. Explain the relationship between individual demand and the total market demand for a good. (10 marks)
3. Using three determinants of demand, explain why demand for petrol-powered cars may decrease. (10 marks)

Practice exam questions – assessment tips (Paper 2 data response questions)

Your second assessment paper will provide a set of text and/or data, to which seven questions are matched, *a* through *g*. Practice with Paper 2 questions will make you familiar with the way the questions are asked.

Part (a) asks for a definition, usually one from the list of terms in the IB Guide.

Part (b) may require a calculation or diagram directly from the text or data.

Parts (c) through (f) will ask for a diagram and explanation that is related to the text.

Part (g) is typically worth more points and requires a longer answer that includes the same types of synthesis and evaluation demonstrated in part (b) of Paper 1.

You are given 1 hour, 45 minutes for Paper 2.

Practice exam questions

Paper 2 questions

Below are questions that align with part (a) and (c) question prompts.

High Demand for Bicycles Causes Shortage

The stay-at-home orders imposed by governments battling the pandemic around the world have provoked a sharp increase in the demand for bicycles, as people seek to enjoy the outdoors safely.

'We sold four times as many bikes as usual last week,' said Marty Samuelsson, owner of Big Swede Bikes in Sussex. 'All of our basic and mid-range models are sold out.' Samuelsson said that most buyers are workers stuck at home and in front of screens all day. 'They are anxious to get out and move.'

'If you want a weekend bike now, you should go online to re-sale or used bike sites. We are having trouble even finding parts for them.'

The increased demand for bike parts comes as consumers are looking to repair and upgrade their current bikes. 'It's very frustrating,' said Samuelsson, 'there are sales and repairs we can't make because of the shortage.'

---

1. Define demand.
2. Using a diagram, explain the change in the market for bicycles.

Elasticities of demand

4

4.1 What is price elasticity of demand?

Learning outcomes

At the end of this section you will be able to:

- define the concept of PED
- calculate PED using an equation
- explain, using diagrams and PED values, the various degrees of price elasticity.

In Chapter 3 you learned about the fundamental relationships between the price of a particular good and the quantities that consumers demand. The law of demand holds true in almost every market. At higher prices, consumers buy lower quantities, and at lower prices, consumers buy more. To extend our analysis of demand, it is useful to introduce an additional component into our analysis of the relationships between price, demand, and supply.

This concept of **elasticity** examines the responsiveness of consumers or producers to a change in a variable in the marketplace. Elasticity measures how much one factor changes in response to a change in a different factor. While the law of demand tells us that when the price of a good increases, the quantity demanded will decrease, the **price elasticity of demand (PED)** tells us *by how much* the quantity demanded of a good will decrease when price increases. PED is a measure of the responsiveness of consumers to a change in price.

In theory, if a small increase in price leads to a proportionally large decrease in quantity demanded, consumers are said to be very price sensitive, and demand is therefore *price elastic*. In contrast, if a large increase in price has little effect on the quantity of a good demanded, consumers are not very price sensitive, and demand is said to be *price inelastic*.

How is PED measured?

To measure the sensitivity of consumers to changes in price, we must compare the change in quantity demanded of a particular good with the particular price change of the good that led to the change in demand. To accommodate the different levels of output and price, we measure changes in percentages, not raw values. The formula for determining the PED coefficient is:

$$PED = \frac{\text{percentage change in quantity demanded}}{\text{percentage change in price}}$$

or
$$PED = \frac{\%\Delta Q_D}{\%\Delta P}$$

where $\%\Delta Q_D$ is the percentage change in quantity demanded (Δ, delta, signifies change), and $\%\Delta P$ is the percentage change in price. Thus, to calculate PED we divide the percentage change in quantity demanded of a good resulting from a particular percentage change in price by that percentage change in price.

Worked example 4.1

If the price of rice rises by 15% and the quantity demanded decreases by 10%, the PED for rice is:

$$\text{PED} = \frac{\text{percentage change in quantity demanded}}{\text{percentage change in price}}$$

$$= \frac{-10}{15} = -0.66$$

If the price of a smartwatch falls by 20% and the quantity demanded increases by 40%, the PED is:

$$\text{PED} = \frac{\text{percentage change in quantity demanded}}{\text{percentage change in price}}$$

$$= \frac{40}{-20} = -2$$

Note that in each case the final PED is expressed as a negative integer. Why? Because the law of demand says that P and Q_D always have an inverse relationship, the value of PED will always be negative. What is important is the size of the number, denoting the strength of the response, so economists generally show PED as an absolute value for simplicity, i.e. we omit the minus sign. (Absolute value is the size of a real number regardless of its sign.)

However, we may not know the percentage changes in quantity and price, and would therefore be required to calculate them. The formula for calculating PED between two prices when percentage changes are not known is:

$$\text{PED} = \frac{(Q_{D2} - Q_{D1}) \div Q_{D1}}{(P_2 - P_1) \div P_1}$$

where Q_{D2} is the quantity demanded following the price change, Q_{D1} is the original quantity demanded, P_2 is the new price, and P_1 is the original price. Using this formula, we can determine the PED between two prices knowing only the values of quantity demanded and price.

Worked example 4.2

Let us assume that a telecommunications firm offers a typical monthly mobile data package for RM80 (RM is the symbol for the Malaysian ringgit, the currency of Malaysia) and sells 100,000 contracts per month. After increasing the price to RM100, the quantity demanded falls to 80,000 contracts. Assuming no other variables changed, how responsive are consumers to the change in price of the product? To determine the PED for the contracts, we can apply the price and quantity information to the equation above.

$$PED = \frac{\text{percentage change in quantity demanded}}{\text{percentage change in price}}$$

or $\quad PED = \dfrac{(Q_{D2} - Q_{D1}) \div Q_{D1}}{(P_2 - P_1) \div P_1}$

Percentage change in quantity demanded, the top part of the equation, is:

$(Q_{D2} - Q_{D1}) \div Q_{D1}$

$= (80{,}000 - 100{,}000) \div 100{,}000$

$= -0.2$

Next, we multiply the result by 100 to get the value expressed as a percentage.

$0.2 \times 100 = 20\%$

Percentage change in price, the bottom part of the equation, is:

$(P_2 - P_1) \div P_1$

$= (100 - 80) \div 80$

$= 0.25$

Next, we multiply the result by 100 to get the value expressed as a percentage:

$0.25 \times 100 = 25\%$

So, for the mobile data contracts:

$$\frac{\text{percentage change in quantity demanded}}{\text{percentage change in price}} = \frac{20}{25} = 0.8$$

The PED for these contracts as the price increased from RM80 to RM100 per month is 0.8. A price increase of 25% led to a decrease in quantity demanded of only 20%. This suggests that consumers did not reduce their quantity demanded quite as much as the price rose, suggesting **inelastic demand**.

What is the theoretical range of elasticity values?

The possible PED values can range from, in theory, 0 to infinity. In reality, most PED values will fall between those two extremes. Depending on the degree to which quantity demanded changes when price changes, demand can be price elastic, price inelastic, or unitary elastic. For simplicity, we will here examine the absolute value of the PED coefficient, which enables us to analyse positive numbers when comparing the elasticities of different goods.

PED = 0 → perfectly inelastic demand

For the elasticity value to equal 0, any change in price is met with no change in quantity demanded. The price of the good could rise ever higher, with consumers

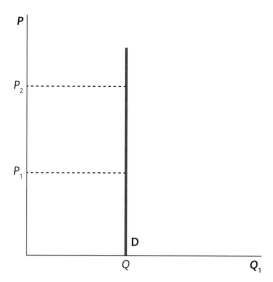

Figure 4.1 The curve for perfectly inelastic demand is vertical ▶

buying exactly the same amount. The existence of goods for which demand is perfectly inelastic is highly unlikely, but theoretically possible. To grasp how this might appear on a demand curve, see Figure 4.1.

In Figure 4.1, the product price rises from P_1 to P_2, and the quantity demanded remains at Q. Thus, **perfectly inelastic demand** is shown as a vertical demand curve. In terms of the PED equation, the price rise from P_1 to P_2 could be any amount, but the percentage change in quantity would remain zero. To divide zero by any number results in zero, the PED value for perfectly inelastic demand is zero. Consumers in this case are completely unresponsive to price changes.

PED = infinity → perfectly elastic demand

For the elasticity of demand to equal infinity, any price increase at all causes the demand to disappear completely. The implication of a PED coefficient of infinity is that any change in price leads to an infinite change in quantity demanded. If the price of such a product increases even by 1% the quantity demanded falls to zero. Figure 4.2 shows an example of this theoretical scenario.

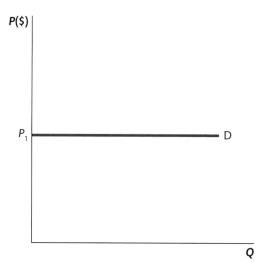

Figure 4.2 The curve for **perfectly elastic demand** is horizontal ▶

The demand curve is a straight line, suggesting infinite demand at the price of P_1. Any increase in price above P_1, however, and none of the product will be bought. Quantity demanded falls to zero, an infinite decrease in quantity. Recalling the PED equation, the quantity demanded change will always be infinity. Anything divided into infinity is equal to infinity. Therefore, the PED value of perfectly elastic demand is infinity, and it is shown as a straight line. Most goods, as stated before, have values between zero and infinity. In real life, most goods will be considered *relatively* inelastic, *relatively* elastic, or perhaps occasionally *unitary elastic*.

PED $< 1 \rightarrow$ relatively inelastic demand

PED values that fall between 0 and 1 are considered price inelastic because the responsiveness of consumers to price changes is less than proportionate to the price change. Recall the data contract in Worked example 4.1 on page 52, prices rose by 25%, but the quantity of contracts sold dropped by only 20%. The PED was equal to only 0.8 (PED < 1). A proportionate response would have been for contracts sold to fall by exactly 25% (PED $= 1$).

Worked example 4.3

When the corner shop's price for cigarettes, a notoriously addictive substance, decreased from Bs21 (Bs is the symbol for the Boliviano, the currency of Bolivia) to Bs14, the quantity demanded rose from 530 to 560 packs per week.

% change in quantity demanded $= (560 - 530)/530 = 0.056$

Next, we multiply the result by 100 to get the value expressed as a percentage:

$0.056 \times 100 = 5.6\%$

% change in price $= \left(\dfrac{14 - 21}{21} \right) = -0.33$

Next, we multiply the result by 100 to get the value expressed as a percentage:

$0.33 \times 100 = 33\%$

PED for corner shop cigarettes $= 0.17$

The PED of 0.17 is far below 1, suggesting that consumers barely responded at all to the price decrease. Thus, demand for cigarettes is relatively inelastic, as consumers only slightly increased their consumption of the good relative to the price decrease.

This change can be seen in Figure 4.3. Notice the demand curve is steeply sloped, but not perfectly vertical like perfectly inelastic demand. The price decreases significantly, the quantity demanded increases very little.

Another way to test the elasticity of demand when a price change occurs is to observe the changes to the total sales value also called the **total revenue**. As price decreases, the total revenue of the firm could increase, decrease, or stay the same.

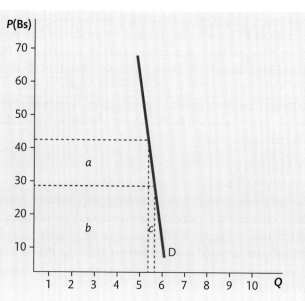

Figure 4.3 Demand for cigarettes is relatively inelastic due to their addictive nature; note the steep demand curve

For price inelastic goods, as price falls total revenues fall. And as price rises, total revenue rises.

Total revenue can be calculated as price (P) × quantity demanded (Q). And it can be shown in the diagrams as boxes measured by the height (P) × length (Q). In Figure 4.3, notice that at a price of Bs42, the areas of total revenue is equal to the combined areas of boxes $a + b$. As the price drops to Bs28, the total revenue area is equal to the smaller combined boxes of $b + c$. By lowering the price, the corner shop has lowered its cigarette revenues because consumers were relatively unresponsive to the change.

PED > 1 → relatively elastic demand

PED values that are greater than 1 are considered price elastic because the responsiveness of consumers to price changes is greater than proportionate to the price change.

Recall the data contract (Worked example 4.2). Prices rose by 25%, so for consumers to be price elastic, consumers that are more responsive would have to reduce purchases by some percent greater than 25% (PED > 1), say 50%, and thus PED = 50% ÷ 25% = 2. Consumers, in that case, responded to the price increase by reducing purchases at two times the rate of the increase, a very responsive reaction.

Worked example 4.4

Assume that the price of movie tickets for a particular movie decreased from $9 to $6, and the quantity sold rose from 250 to 1000 tickets per day. Using the PED formula:

$$\% \ change \ in \ quantity \ demanded = \frac{1000 - 250}{250} = 3$$

Next, we multiply the result by 100 to get the value expressed as a percentage:

$3 \times 100 = 300\%$

$\% \text{ change in price} = \dfrac{6-9}{9} = -0.33$

Next, we multiply the result by 100 to get the value expressed as a percentage:

$0.33 \times 100 = 33\%$

$PED \text{ for movie tickets} = \dfrac{300}{33} = 9.09$

The PED of 9.09 is far above 1, suggesting that consumers were significantly more responsive to the price decrease. Thus, demand for movie tickets is relatively elastic, as consumers increased their consumption by many times the decrease in prices.

This change can be seen in Figure 4.4. Notice the demand curve is relatively, but not perfectly, flat and has a shallow slope. The price decrease causes an apparently significantly larger increase in quantity demanded.

For price elastic goods, as price falls total revenues rise and as price rises, total revenue falls.

In Figure 4.4, notice that at a price of $9, the areas of total revenue is equal to the combined areas of boxes $a + b$. As the price drops to $6, the total revenue area is equal to the much larger area of the combined boxes of $b + c$. By lowering the price, the movie theatre has massively raised its ticket revenues because consumers were extremely responsive to the change in price.

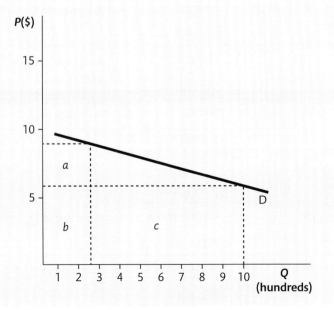

Figure 4.4 The shallow slope of the demand curve for cinema tickets indicates relatively elastic demand

PED = 1 → unitary elastic demand

If a particular percentage change in price results in an identical percentage change in quantity demanded, then demand is said to be unitary elastic. If the price of a good rises by a certain percentage, the quantity demanded falls by the same percentage. From the data contract example, the rise in contract prices of 25% would be matched by a decrease in quantity demanded by exactly 25%.

In terms of total revenue, when the PED is unitary elastic, a rise in price will be offset by the decrease in demand, and there will be no change in total revenue. The same is true for any price decrease: total revenue will not change.

Table 4.1 provides a summary of the relationship between changes in price, changes in firms' total revenues, and the PED value

Price	Total revenue	PED value	Closer look
Price ↑	TR ↑	Inelastic $0 > PED < 1$	% change in Q_D < % change in P
Price ↑	TR ↓	Elastic $1 < PED \rightarrow$	% change in Q_D > % change in P
Price ↓	TR ↑	Elastic $1 < PED \rightarrow$	% change in Q_D > % change in P
Price ↓	TR ↓	Inelastic $0 > PED < 1$	% change in Q_D < % change in P
Price ↑	TR ↑	Unitary elastic $PED = 1$	% change in Q_D = % change in P
Price ↓	TR ↓	Unitary elastic $PED = 1$	% change in Q_D = % change in P

4.2 What are the determinants of PED?

Learning outcomes

At the end of this section you will be able to:

- analyse the determinants of PED:
  - number
  - closeness of substitutes
  - degree of **necessity**
  - time
  - proportion of income spent on the good.

Video suggestions:
You have read about it, now you can review what you have just learned by watching a few videos by the author!

Simply click here in your eBook for videos on PED:

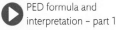 PED formula and interpretation – part 1

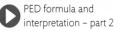 PED formula and interpretation – part 2

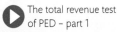 The total revenue test of PED – part 1

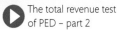 The total revenue test of PED – part 2

When determining whether demand for a good is likely to be relatively elastic or relatively inelastic, perfectly elastic or perfectly inelastic, or unitary elastic, we must consider the various factors that influence how responsive consumers are likely to be to price changes. The degree to which consumers respond to price changes depends on several factors, which can be summarised using the following acronym: PANTS.

P = Proportion of income
A = Addictiveness
N = Necessity or luxury
T = Time
S = Substitutes, number of

Proportion of income

The proportion of the consumer's income that the price of a good represents is a determinant of PED. Demand for goods that make up a large proportion of a consumer's income tends to be more elastic since a particular percentage change in price will appear much larger to a consumer than the same percentage change in price of a good that makes up a very small proportion of income.

Take two examples: household refrigerators and toothpicks. A 50% drop in the price of a refrigerator may mean a saving of up to €500 or more to a family of four who is considering replacing theirs. The saving of €500 is a significant amount of money and will surely be noticeable and therefore have a considerable impact on the number of families considering a new refrigerator.

On the other hand, a 50% fall in the price of toothpicks may represent only a few cents savings on a box of a thousand toothpicks. Toothpicks are already so cheap and make up such a minute proportion of the typical consumer's budget that a fall in their price will have little or no effect on the overall quantity demanded.

Addictiveness

Whether a good is addictive or not affects the PED. Addictive goods such as alcohol, tobacco, drugs, and fatty or salty foods, tend to have relatively inelastic demand. The reason is obvious: consumers with a physical dependence on a good will be unwilling or unable to respond greatly to price increases. This helps explain why certain illicit drugs sell for extremely high prices on the streets of many cities; once a user is addicted, he or she is willing to pay almost anything for a drug like heroin or cocaine. If tobacco were not addictive, the chances are that far more people would quit smoking in response to the high taxes levied on cigarettes by most governments.

Necessity or luxury

The degree of necessity affects its PED. Goods that are necessary to consumers will have less elastic demand than the luxuries we can do without if the price rises. Consumers will likely be less responsive to a 20% increase in the price of natural gas than they will to a 20% increase in the price of Italian leather handbags. We depend on natural gas to heat our homes and to cook our meals, yet we do not need fine leather handbags, therefore can afford to do without them when their prices rise.

Time

The amount of time consumers have to respond to a price change determines the PED. Immediately following a change in price, it is unlikely consumers will adjust their consumption by much. With a sudden price increase, it is difficult to identify suitable substitutes for a good that has increased in price in the **short run**, but in the **long run** new options can be identified and consumers can further reduce their consumption of the more expensive good. If the price of a particular good falls, it will take time for consumers to notice the price change, but once they do it is likely that in the long run market demand will be more responsive to changes in price.

For example, were there a massive increase in petrol prices, say 100%, the drop in car use would be low at first. Consumers cannot switch to alternatives quickly. But over time consumers would find ways to drive less or drive alternative-fuel vehicles.

Substitutes

The number of substitutes a good has is one of the primary determinants of how elastic demand will be. Consumers will be more responsive to changes in the price of a good

Video suggestion:
You have read about it, now you can review what you have just learned by watching a video by the author!

▶ Simply click here in your eBook for a video on the determinants of PED.

with a large number of substitutes than for a good with very few or no substitutes. For most coffee consumers, the drink is a good with almost no perfect substitutes. Coffee consumers are therefore relatively unresponsive to changes in the price of coffee.

Products like patented life-saving medicines are another example of a good that is highly inelastic because of its few substitutes. Insulin is a popular example, because people with type 2 diabetes require insulin to survive. Naturally, demand among people with diabetes is very unresponsive to price changes. This type of market can be subject to market failure, as discussed in Chapter 10, when companies manage to preserve their **market power** over drugs like insulin and raise prices to vulnerable consumers.

TOK Certain individuals depend on particular goods for their very survival, e.g. people with diabetes need insulin to live. If one were to learn that insulin providers were raising their prices ever higher on diabetic patients, would you be obliged to act? This raises a question around the ethics of knowledge: 'How can we know when we should act on what we know?'

4.3 Why does PED matter to businesses and governments?

Learning outcomes

At the end of this section you will be able to:

- discuss the role of PED for firms regarding price changes and their effect on total revenue
- examine the significance of PED for government in relation to **indirect taxes**
- **HL** explain why PED changes along a straight-line demand curve and is not represented by the slope of the demand curve
- **HL** draw a diagram showing the changes in PED along a straight-line demand curve
- **HL** explain why the PED for many **primary commodities** is relatively low and the PED for **manufactured products** is relatively high.

How might businesses make decisions based on PED?

The degree to which consumers respond to changes in the price of a firm's products has major implications on a firm when it is considering raising or lowering its prices. Producers of some goods must be aware of the effect that changes in the prices of other goods will have on market demand for their products. A perfect example is the decision by manufacturers, such as Toyota and Honda, to expand their production of hybrid automobiles in the last decade as petrol prices have risen steadily around the world.

How might governments make decisions based on PED?

Governments must consider elasticities when deciding which goods to place taxes on and whether or not to raise or lower income tax. Levying taxes on goods for which consumers are highly sensitive to price changes will create little tax revenue yet lead to a large decrease in the quantity sold in such markets.

Raising or lowering income tax with the goal of stimulating or reducing overall household spending on goods and services may be futile if consumers' demand is unresponsive to changes in disposable incomes.

Why does PED change along a straight-line demand curve?

Until now, products have been categorised as broadly elastic or inelastic. In reality, elasticity values will change over the course of a particular product's demand curve. It is more correct to state that a found elasticity value is true over a specific range of prices than for the product generally. However, it can be said that in general, products tend to be elastic at higher price ranges, inelastic in the lower price ranges and unitary elastic somewhere in the middle. In fact, the elasticity value should start high, at the top left of the curve, and steadily decline as one moves along the curve.

Figure 4.5 shows that the PED for a particular good is not constant across all prices. The higher the price of a good, the more responsive consumers are to a change in price; the lower the price, the less sensitive consumers are to price changes.

The demand curve shows the quantity demanded for this good at a series of prices between ¥10 and ¥0 (¥ is the symbol for the yuan, the currency of China). At the high price of ¥10, the total market demand is 0 units, so the total revenues for producers is ¥10 × 0 = ¥0. But ten units can be sold for ¥8 each, generating a total revenue of ¥80.

Figure 4.5(b) plots the total revenue in the industry at each price and quantity combination. At a price of ¥6, 20 units are sold for a total revenue of ¥120. It can be assumed that at a price somewhere between ¥6 and ¥4, and a quantity between 20 and 30 units, the revenues earned by producers will be maximised.

We can use the total revenue test described above to help understand the change in elasticity. Generally speaking, at higher prices, demand tends to be relatively elastic for most goods. But as the price falls and the quantity demanded increases, the percentage changes in price become larger and the percentage changes in quantity become smaller, causing the PED to decrease at lower prices and higher quantities.

The observation that a product's PED is high for high prices and low for low prices tends to hold true because of the following.

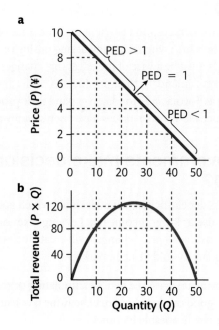

Figure 4.5 The varying degrees of price elasticity along a linear demand curve (a) are reflected in the shape of the total revenue curve (b)

- At higher prices, consumers tend to feel a higher proportion of their income being affected by the same percentage change in price.
- Mathematically, at the upper left range of the demand curve the PED values reflect higher incremental percentage price changes and lower incremental percentage quantity changes.
- Similarly, in the lower right range of the demand curve, prices are changing at higher incremental percentages, while quantity demanded is changing at lower incremental percentage levels.

To confirm the concept, we can calculate the PED coefficient between two sets of prices.

Worked example 4.5

Using the example in Figure 4.5, the price first falls from ¥8 to ¥6, and then from ¥4 to ¥2. If the total revenue test holds true, we should find that PED is greater than one at the high prices and less than one at the low prices.

Between ¥8 and ¥6, the PED coefficient is 4, so demand is elastic, supporting our observation that an increase in total revenue following a decrease in price proves that consumers are relatively responsive to the lower price.

Between ¥4 and ¥2 the percentage decrease in price is larger than it was between ¥8 and ¥6, since the starting price is now lower. Additionally, although quantity demanded increases by the same number of units as it did after the earlier ¥2 price drop, the percentage increase in QD is smaller since the starting quantity is now larger.

When price falls from ¥4 to ¥2, the total revenue in the industry declines from ¥120 to ¥80. This is evidence that consumers are no longer very responsive to lower prices, and that the percentage increase in quantity demanded must be smaller than the percentage decrease in price.

The PED coefficient of the above example at the higher price range is 4, but at the lower price range is only 0.66, proving that a fall in price resulting in a decrease in total revenue is evidence of the inelasticity of demand between two points on a demand curve. At lower prices, consumers are no longer as responsive to price decreases as they were at higher prices. If the industry or firm were to decrease output and raise its price from ¥2 to ¥4, firms would experience an increase in total revenue because the inelastic nature of demand at low prices means that consumers are relatively unresponsive to the higher price, thus despite the lower quantity sold, the industry's revenues would rise.

HL Why is the PED for primary commodities lower than the PED for manufactured products?

Primary commodities are typically Earth-based products that come from the categories of mining, forestry, and agricultural goods. Iron, timber, cocoa, and tea are all examples of primary commodities. Demand for these goods tends to be inelastic because there are few close substitutes, and therefore firms and consumers have little choice but to pay the market price.

Industries that use iron to produce steel and other metals have a difficult time replacing iron, and are therefore not responsive to higher iron prices. Makers of chocolate, of which cocoa is the essential ingredient, are price inelastic when it comes to cocoa prices.

In contrast, manufactured goods usually have many more substitutes, and are therefore more price elastic by comparison. Consumer electronics are produced by hundreds of different makers, with just as many brand marks. If the price of one maker's electric toothbrush rises, for example, there are many more available at a more affordable price. In turn, producers are aware of the different price sensitivities among consumers, and will offer a range of slightly differentiated products, with more or fewer features, and prices to match consumers' willingness to spend.

Exercise 4.1

Answer the questions using the product information in the table below.

Product	New price $	Old price $	New quantity demanded	Old quantity demanded
1. Paper clips, per box	2.00	1.00	400	380
2. Petrol, per litre	1.00	1.30	5000	4500
3. Brand X bottled water	5.00	4.00	120,000	240,000
4. Fancy watch	3000	3300	600	900
5. Electricity, per kilowatt hour	0.40	0.30	100	110

a. Calculate the PED value.

b. State whether the good is price elastic, inelastic, or unit elastic.

c. Calculate the change in total revenue.

d. Does the change in total revenue confirm your finding for the PED value? Explain.

e. Identify the most likely determinant of price elasticity of demand.

4.4 What is income elasticity of demand?

Learning outcomes

At the end of this section you will be able to:

- define YED
- explain how the different signs (+/−) reflect different types of income elasticity
- using diagrams, show income elastic, income inelastic, and inferior goods
- calculate changes in YED from provided data
- **HL** explain the importance of YED for firms, and for explaining sectoral changes in the economy.

Income elasticity of demand (YED) measures the responsiveness of consumers' demand for a particular good to a change in income. As a determinant of demand introduced in Chapter 3, changes in income have different effects on the demand for different goods depending on the nature of the good in question, on whether the good is a 'normal' or an 'inferior' good.

If a good is a normal good, then rising income leads to greater demand. Normal goods tend to be service-related or more expensive versions of everyday goods. Examples of normal goods include restaurant meals, taxi rides, clothes, air travel, streaming packages, or anything else consumers tend to buy more of as their incomes rise.

If a rise in income leads to a decrease in consumption of a particular good, that good is said to be inferior. Inferior goods tend to be necessities, and may include items such as fast food, generic brand groceries, public transport, second-hand clothes or any other product consumers tend to consume less of as incomes rise. Because consumers' demand for certain goods responds differently to changes in income, the YED coefficient can be either negative or positive.

YED is found by dividing the percentage change in quantity demanded for a good by the percentage change in the consumer's income.

$$YED = \frac{\%\Delta Q_D}{\%\Delta Y}$$

$\%\Delta Q_D$ is the percentage change in quantity demanded, and $\%\Delta Y$ is the percentage change in income. If the percentage changes in quantity and price are not known but the values are known, then the simple YED formula can be used to determine the coefficient:

$$YED = \frac{(Q_{D2} - Q_{D1}) \div Q_{D1}}{(Y_2 - Y_1) \div Y_1}$$

where Q_{D2} is the quantity demanded following the income change, Q_{D1} is the original quantity demanded, Y_2 is the new income, and Y_1 is the original income.

If there is a direct relationship between income and demand, then the YED coefficient will be positive, indicating that the good in question is a normal good. If, on the other hand, the relationship between income and demand is indirect, in which case a rise in income would lead to a smaller quantity and a fall in income to an increase in the quantity, then the YED coefficient will be negative, indicating the good in question is inferior.

YED is $+ \rightarrow$ normal good
YED is $- \rightarrow$ inferior good

YED can be applied to measure the change in an individual's consumption of particular goods following a change in the individual's income, or it can be applied to analyse the effects of changes in national income on the demand for particular goods and services in a nation as a whole.

For instance, it is fairly typical for recessions (a general decrease in income when the country's gross domestic product (GDP) shrinks) that the demand for expensive durable goods and discretionary leisure tends to fall. Automobiles and expensive vacation travel decrease. A recession would likely cause inferior good demand to rise, including that of fast food, discounted home goods, and camping supplies.

Interpreting the YED coefficient

As with the other types of elasticity covered in this chapter, YED can be elastic, inelastic, or unitary elastic. The value of YED gives us information about the extent to which the good is responsive to changes in income.

If YED is less than 0, or negative, the goods are considered inferior goods.

$$YED \text{ for public transport} = \frac{-3\%}{5\%} = -0.6$$

For example, if a 5% rise in income leads to a 3% fall in the demand for public transport, the YED for public transport is $-3 \div 5$ or -0.6. The negative sign indicates that public transportation is an inferior good, and the fact that the absolute value of the YED coefficient is less than one is evidence that demand is income inelastic. Public transport consumers are negatively responsive to changes in their income.

As stated above, positive YED values are considered normal goods. Within that category, products can be divided into necessities and luxuries.

If YED is between 0 and 1, demand is said to be income inelastic. These goods are assumed to be necessities. For example, if a 50% rise in income leads to only a 10% increase in the demand for noodles (pick your favourite), then the good is considered a necessity.

$$YED \text{ for dried noodles} = \frac{10\%}{50\%} = 0.2$$

Consumers do buy more as their incomes rise, but not by the same rate as the rate of increase in income.

If YED is greater than 1, demand is said to be income elastic, and these goods are broadly considered **luxury goods**. As an example, as incomes rise, consumers may quickly switch from an inferior good like cheap athletic shoes to more expensive shoes.

If a good is highly and positively income elastic, then a particular percentage change in income will lead to a larger percentage change in the quantity demanded for the good. For example, if a rise in consumer income of 5% results in a 12% increase in the quantity demanded of hybrid cars, the YED for hybrid cars is $12 \div 5 = 2.4$.

$$YED \text{ for hybrid cars} = \frac{12\%}{5\%} = 2.4$$

Demand for hybrids is said to be income elastic, and a luxury good.

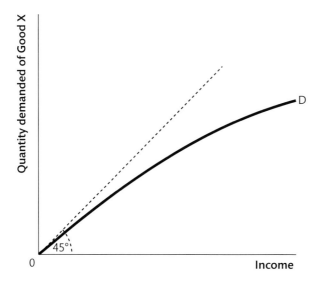

Figure 4.6 Demand (D) for necessity goods grows at a slower rate than disposable income

What is an Engel curve?

The **Engel curve** is named after the German statistician Ernst Engel, who was among the first to examine the relationship between income and demand for particular goods and services. The change in disposable income is shown on the horizontal axis, while the volume of demand for Good X is shown on the vertical axis.

Figure 4.6 shows an essential or necessity good. Were the rate of consumption equal to the rate of increased income, the line would follow the 45-degree line. For this necessity good, observe how consumption grows slower than the rise in disposable income.

Figure 4.7 shows a superior or luxury good. Its consumption grows faster than the rise in disposable income. Note the positive relationship between the two variables, but the diminishing rate of increased consumption.

Figure 4.8 shows an inferior good. Consumption decreases as disposable income rises. Note the negative correlation between the two variables, with consumption falling as income rises.

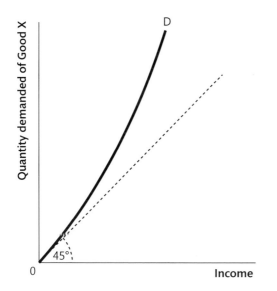

Figure 4.7 Demand for luxury goods rises faster than disposable income

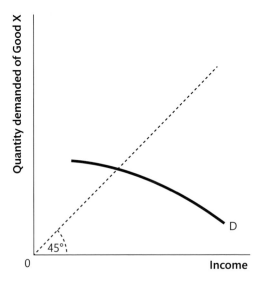

HL Why is it important to understand the YED?

Income elasticity can help inform the decision making of firms, who are trying to maximise profits, and governments, who are trying to improve the overall economic well-being.

Income elasticity and firms

Understanding YED allows businesses and governments to analyse the effects of changing incomes among consumers and taxpayers on the level of demand for particular goods in an economy. A firm that must decide on production numbers for its product may wish to determine whether the incomes of its consumers are likely to rise or fall in the future.

If a firm produces a good that is considered inferior, then a recession could be good for business and it will increase its output in order to meet the rising demand among consumers whose incomes are harmed by the recession. Producers of normal goods, on the other hand, may scale back production as incomes decline. Understanding the responsiveness of consumers of their products to changes in income better enables firms to produce at a more efficient level of output over time.

Income elasticity sectoral change in the economy

Governments, in steering their economy towards prosperity, must face the basic economic question of 'what' to produce. Governments try to forecast which goods will rise in demand, and then shift production away from lower demand goods. Income elasticity provides a clue to greater demand because global income is generally expected to rise year by year. Assuming that incomes rise, demand for superior and luxury goods are likely to grow in demand much faster than necessity goods.

The theory of sectoral change in economies identifies three sectors to any economy.

- **Primary sector**: 'gifts of the Earth', such as agriculture, mining, fishing, and forestry products, are considered primary commodities.
- Secondary sector: manufactured goods take the raw materials of the primary sector and turn them into finished goods. These products range from simply produced tools, furniture, clothing, and consumer goods, to sophisticated machinery and technology.

- Tertiary sector: this consists of services offered to the public, including healthcare, food service, financial services, bureaucratic, educational, and computing services.

Income elasticity helps explain why most countries seek to diversify their production away from exclusively primary production and into manufacturing and services. Generally primary production tends to be more income elastic overall, being mostly necessity goods. As incomes rise globally, demand will instead increase for manufactured goods, which tend to be more income elastic, superior goods, and luxury goods. Services, too, tend to be highly income elastic.

To take advantage of this understanding, countries seek to leave farming and mining behind, and to industrialise in order to capture the expected profits from rising global demand in manufactured goods and services. This follows the model set initially by the UK in the Industrial Revolution of the 1800s, and followed by most rich nations since then.

Knowing this is more complicated than enacting it. In today's global trading environment, a country keen to diversify its output (say, start producing steel), will face highly developed competition from all over the world. Even with some allowances from the **World Trade Organization (WTO)** to protect newly formed industries, these industries face challenging odds.

Case study – India's structural transformation

The trend in countries away from primary production towards secondary and tertiary production is evident in the case of India. This chart measures the value added to GDP by sector over the last several decades. In 1969, India's primary sector added the most value to GDP. Thirty years later, it is the smallest contributor and is still declining. Manufacturing rose slightly but stopped increasing, while services have steadily increased. Those in charge of India's economy now should question whether further sectoral change is possible, with over 15% of the economy still devoted to agriculture. Should India seek to increase manufacturing again? Should it aim to shift away from agriculture? Knowing what you do about income elasticity, what information would you use to make this decision?

TOK What practical problems does economic theory attempt to solve? Discuss, using examples from the concepts in this chapter.

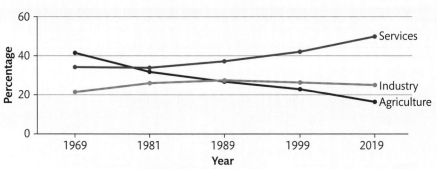

- → Agriculture forestry and fishing value added (% of GDP)
- → Industry (including construcion) value added (% of GDP)
- → Services value added (% of GDP)

Practice exam questions

Paper 1, part (a)

1. Using three determinants of price elasticity of demand, provide real-world examples and explain how they demonstrate a high or low level of elasticity. (10 marks)
2. Using the expected values of price elasticity of demand, explain the concepts of perfectly elastic and perfectly inelastic PED. (10 marks)
3. Using the expected values of PED, explain the concepts of relatively elastic, relatively inelastic, and unitary elastic PED. (10 marks)
4. Explain how businesses might use price elasticity of demand to know how to raise or lower total revenue. (10 marks)
5. **HL** Explain why PED values may change over the course of a single straight-line demand curve. (10 marks)
6. Explain, using expected values, how income elasticity of demand demonstrates how consumers buy more or less of a product based on changes to their income. (10 marks)
7. Using diagrams, explain how products may qualify as income elastic, income inelastic, and inferior goods. (10 marks)

Paper 2, parts (a) and (c) and (g)

Country P Seeks to Enter High-value Industries

For decades, Country P has struggled to raise export revenues from their main agricultural base of products like sugar, corn, and soy. Barely considered a middle-income country, Country P's leaders see the future in more sophisticated processing of their crops, hoping to capture more of the value, and in manufacturing, where they believe more profits are waiting.

'The market sets the prices,' said one government minister. 'If the price of raw sugar is 13 US cents a pound, we can't charge a higher price. Even though our sugar is better!' Knowing their product is price elastic has made sugar producers want to move into sugar processing, where they can get a higher price.

'Sugar processing is where the money is,' said a leading industry expert. 'By manufacturing sugar into many forms, we capture the profits rather than sending them to the US or Europe.

'Some government ministers want to move away from agricultural-based products almost entirely. 'We need to be making our own clothes, furniture, and technology,' said a member of the Finance Office. 'As the world gets richer, we need to sell higher value products, not just basic goods. We need fewer farmers every year, and those people come to the cities looking for jobs. We have the labour, but now we need to have industries to hire them.'

1. Define price elastic. (2 marks)
2. Explain why sugar producers in Country P cannot raise their prices above the world market level. (4 marks)
3. Explain what would happen to Country P's sugar revenues if they lowered their prices below world prices. (4 marks)
4. **HL** With respect to Country P, discuss the validity of the following statement: 'As the world gets richer, we need to sell higher value products.' (10 marks)

Supply

5

5.1 What is supply?

Learning outcomes

At the end of this section you will be able to:

- state the **law of supply**
- explain the positive causal relationship between price and **quantity supplied**
- `HL` explain the assumptions underlying the law of supply:
  - `HL` the **law of diminishing marginal returns**
  - `HL` increasing marginal costs
- describe the relationship between an individual producer's supply and **market supply**
- explain that a supply curve represents the relationship between the price and the quantity supplied of a product, *ceteris paribus*
- draw a supply curve.

Any market transaction requires two parties, buyers and sellers. Demand explores the buyers' side of things, while supply takes the perspective of the sellers. Supply is defined as the quantity of a good that producers are willing and able to produce at a given price over a particular time period, *ceteris paribus*. A supply curve shows us the relationship between the price of a particular good and how much of that good producers will send to market at that price.

Figure 5.1 shows the weekly supply of chocolate bars in a major city. On the vertical axis is price per chocolate bar, and on the horizontal axis is quantity of chocolate bars supplied.

Again, all other variables are held constant (*ceteris paribus*) so that we may clearly see that relationship between price and quantity supplied. As the supply curve shows, this is a direct relationship: at higher prices sellers wish to provide more chocolate bars to the market, while at lower prices less chocolate is supplied.

Figure 5.1 Higher prices lead to a greater quantity supplied

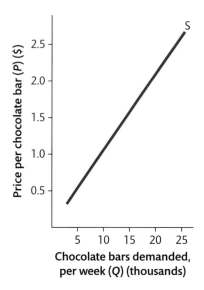

Table 5.1 Supply schedule for chocolate bars

Price of chocolate bars (P) $	Quantity of chocolate bars supplied per week (Q) (thousands)
0	0
0.50	5
1.00	10
1.50	15
2.00	20
2.50	25

Like demand, the relationship between price and quantity supplied can be shown with a table or supply schedule, as well as with a supply curve. Table 5.1, a supply schedule for chocolate, shows that as price increases from $0.50 to $2.50, the quantity supplied increases as well. The supply schedule in Table 5.1 reflects the same relationship between price and quantity as the supply curve in Figure 5.1.

What is the law of supply?

The relationship between a good's price and the quantity producers will be willing and able to supply to the market is, like the relationship between price and quantity demanded, so widely established and agreed upon that it has risen to the level of an *economic law*. The **law of supply** states that, *ceteris paribus*, there is a direct relationship between a good's price and the quantity supplied. As price increases, more of a good is supplied by firms. As price decreases, less is supplied.

The law of supply is reflected in the upward-sloping supply curve, as in Figure 5.1. As price increases from $0.50 to $2.50, there is a movement upwards along the supply curve. Thus, there is a positive relationship between price and quantity supplied. Why do economists hold this relationship to be so true as to be considered an *economic law*? There are two assumptions underlying the law of supply, the first of which leads to the second.

Video suggestion:
You have read about it, now you can review what you have just learned by watching a video by the author!
▶ Simply click here in your eBook for a video on the law of supply and the determinants of supply (watch up to 6:10).

HL The law of diminishing marginal returns

The first assumption that explains the law of supply is that as more resources are allocated towards a good's production in the short run, the productivity of additional resources decreases. In other words, the output attributable to additional units of a **variable resource** added to **fixed resources** decreases the more of the variable resource is employed.

Okay, that was a mouthful. Let us break that down with an example. Assume a bakery makes only croissants, and in order to do so it requires four resources:

1 bakers (labour)
2 raw materials (ingredients)
3 ovens (capital)
4 a space to work (land).

The **short run** is defined as the fixed capital and land period. In the short run our bakery owner cannot acquire more ovens or space to work, but she can employ more or less labour and use more or less raw materials. In our example the labour and ingredients are the **variable resources** and the ovens and bakery space are the **fixed resources**.

Now, let us go through a scenario in which our bakery owner wishes to change her level of output in the short run. She can increase or decrease the number of croissants she bakes daily by employing more or less labour and raw materials. Let us assume she has only two ovens in her workspace. Table 5.2 shows a possible production schedule for our bakery, given its fixed amount of capital and workspace, but with different numbers of bakers employed.

Table 5.2   Bakery production schedule

Number of bakers employed	Number of croissants produced each hour (total product = TP)	Number of croissants attributable to the last worker hired (marginal product = MP)
0	0	—
1	25	25
2	55	30
3	80	25
4	98	18
5	108	10
6	110	2
7	105	−5

Let us put the values from our production schedule into a graph showing the total product and the marginal product of labour. Figure 5.2 shows the *productivity curves* (total product and marginal product) for our bakery.

Figure 5.2 shows us that the rate at which the bakery can increase its output of croissants in the short run is not constant; rather, it diminishes as output increases.

Figure 5.2   It is important to distinguish between total product and marginal product

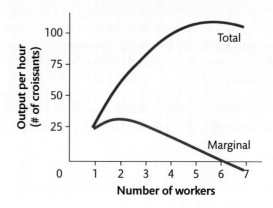

The first baker can make 25 croissants, while the addition of a second worker increases output to 55. The second worker's marginal product, in other words, was 30 croissants. The **marginal product of labour** is the amount of output attributable to the last worker hired, or the change in total product experienced when one more worker is employed.

What happens to the marginal product of labour in the short run as more workers are hired? We can see in Figure 5.2 that beyond the second worker, marginal product decreases; in other words, as more workers are hired and put to work using the bakery's two ovens, the number of croissants each additional worker is able to produce decreases. While total product increases, it does so at a decreasing rate, and eventually, with the addition of the seventh worker, the bakery's output of croissants actually decreases. The marginal product of the seventh worker is negative; he or she actually gets in the way of the other six workers and makes the bakery less productive than it would have been with fewer workers.

The law of diminishing marginal returns describes the predictable outcome of adding more and more of a variable resource (usually labour) to fixed resources (land and capital). Because the ratio of capital to labour decreases as more labour is added to a fixed amount of capital, the productivity of labour diminishes in the short run as output increases.

What does this have to do with the shape of the supply curve, you ask? That brings us to our second explanation for the law of supply.

HL Increasing marginal costs

We just defined *marginal product* as the output attributable to additional units of a variable resource added to fixed resources towards a good's production. Let us isolate the marginal product curve from our bakery example in its own graph, seen in Figure 5.3.

After the second worker, additional workers become less and less productive due to the lack of additional capital (ovens) needed to keep them more productive. **Firms** must consider the productivity of labour when deciding the optimal amount of labour to employ: the baker in the example would be irrational to hire a sixth or seventh worker, for example, due to the fact that these two workers contribute

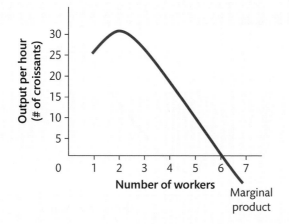

TOK

Do businesses need to know and understand the law of supply?

We learn economic laws and are taught that they are immutable, meaning they are *always true*. An increase in a good's price will lead to an increase in the quantity supplied, assuming all else is held constant. While economists might observe this relationship in real-world markets, does that mean that individual business owners really need to understand it to operate?

An object in motion stays in motion until acted upon by an outside force. This is Newton's first law of motion, learned in any physics class. Laws in economics might be like laws in the physical science: a ball needs to *know* or *understand* Newton's first law just as much as an individual business owner needs to know or understand the law of supply. Whether there is knowledge of the laws or not is irrelevant; a ball will remain in motion regardless of its level of understanding, just as a market will respond to price changes regardless of the understanding of the agents participating in that market of the underlying laws that describe its operation.

Do you agree or disagree with the thoughts above? Discuss!

Figure 5.3 A more detailed look at the bakery's marginal product curve

almost nothing (only two croissants per hour for the sixth worker) or actually decrease overall production (by five croissants each hour for the seventh worker!).

How do firms determine just how many workers to employ, then? What businesses care about, just like any rational economic agent, is *marginal costs* and *marginal benefits*. **Marginal cost** is defined as the cost of producing an additional unit of output, and it is a function of the marginal product of labour.

Employ a fourth baker? ▶

Because the productivity of labour decreases as labour is added to a fixed amount of capital and land in the short run, the firm needs more and more workers to produce less and less additional output, meaning that additional output becomes more and more costly to firms in the short run. Marginal cost (the cost of additional output), therefore, is inversely related to the marginal product of labour. When additional workers are *more* productive than those hired before them (as was the case with the second worker in our bakery example), the cost of the output attributable to the worker is lower than that produced by previous workers. However, when additional workers are *less productive* (as with Workers 3 through 7 in our bakery), the output they produce increases in cost to the business owner.

Figure 5.4 shows the short-run marginal cost for a typical producer. Notice that marginal cost decreases as output increases at first (reflecting the fact that additional workers are *more productive* when added to fixed capital at first), but then marginal cost increases as output increases (as marginal product decreases, increasing the cost of additional output).

Figure 5.4 In contrast to marginal product, marginal cost tends to go up as output increases ▶

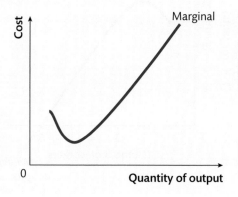

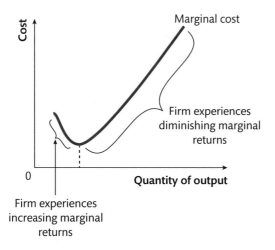

Figure 5.5 Marginal cost is related to the marginal product of labour

A **firm's** marginal cost curve is downward sloping over the range of output during which the marginal product of labour increases (known as *increasing marginal returns*), but marginal cost increases when the marginal product of labour decreases (known as *diminishing marginal returns*). Figure 5.5 identifies the ranges of output over which the firm experiences increasing and diminishing marginal returns of labour.

What are the implications for a producer facing an upward-sloping short-run marginal cost curve for their willingness to supply more of a good to the market? Well, this brings us back to the law of supply, which describes the direct relationship between a good's price and the quantity supplied. The law of diminishing marginal product results in the cost of additional units of output increasing as a firm produces more of its product in the short run. For this reason, the only way a firm is willing and able to bring more of its product to the market is if the product's price increases, as described by the law of supply.

HL Marginal cost as an individual firm's supply curve

Strictly speaking, a supply curve describes the total quantity that all producers in a market are willing and able to produce at any given price; it is a *market supply curve*. There is no such thing as an individual firm's supply curve. However, a firm's marginal cost curve basically represents what that firm is willing and able to produce at any given price. Consider Figure 5.6, which puts price and cost on the vertical axis and quantity of output on the horizontal axis.

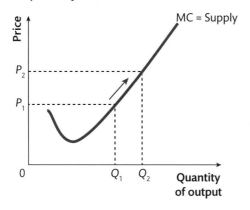

Figure 5.6 The marginal cost curve equates to an individual firm's supply curve

77

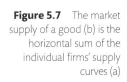

The price has increased from P_1 to P_2, and with it the firm has increased its output from Q_1 to Q_2. The higher price allows the firm to cover the higher marginal cost of the Q_2 level of output relative to the lower cost Q_1 level of output. As such, the marginal cost curve is an individual firm's supply curve: it shows how much output a firm is willing and able to produce for the market at a given price.

Relationship between an individual producer's supply and market supply

If we were to aggregate all the individual supply curves of the producers in a market, we would end up with the market supply curve. For example, if our baker from the example earlier in this chapter were to settle on an output of 50 croissants per hour at a price of $2, and there were 20 bakeries of similar size facing similar costs in the same city, then the city's market supply would be 1000 croissants at the market price of $2. Figure 5.7 illustrates such a scenario.

The market supply of a good is the *horizontal sum* of the individual firms' supply curves in that market. The law of supply dictates that any change in the market price will lead individual firms to change their level of output based on the cost of producing the good, thereby causing the market quantity supplied to increase or decrease depending on how the price changed. Figure 5.8 shows what happens when the price of croissants decreases from $2 to $1.50.

A decrease in price has caused a movement along the individual bakery's supply curve and a movement along the market supply curve. The next question is, what can cause a shift in market supply, or, in other words, an increase or decrease in supply?

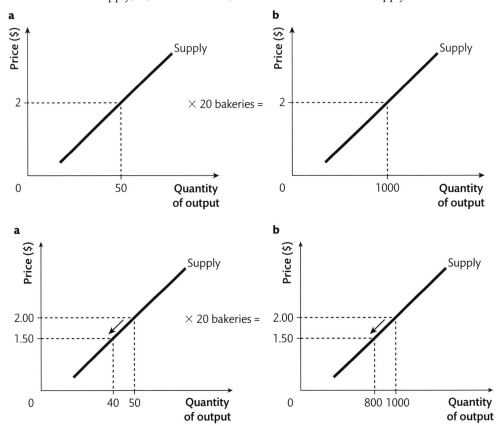

Figure 5.7 The market supply of a good (b) is the horizontal sum of the individual firms' supply curves (a)

Figure 5.8 A movement along an individual firm's supply curve (a) is reflected in the market (b)

5.2 What are the non-price determinants of supply?

Learning outcomes

At the end of this section you will be able to:

- analyse the non-price determinants of supply:
  - changes in costs of factors of production
  - prices of related goods
  - indirect taxes and subsidies
  - future price expectations
  - changes in technology
  - number of firms.

Aside from price changes, a variety of non-price factors can also affect supply. These non-price factors are called determinants, as in demand theory. They will cause the supply curve to shift outwards or inwards to reflect a change in the market at every price.

As shown in Figure 5.8, a change in a good's price causes a movement along its supply curve. However, when non-price determinants of supply actually change, there is a shift of the entire supply curve. When supply shifts, the quantity supplied changes at *every price*. Consider the market supply for chocolate bars in Figure 5.9.

Chocolate bar supply has shifted from S_1 to S_2. At every price a greater quantity of chocolate bars is now brought to the market (10,000 bars at $0.50 instead of 5000 and 20,000 bars at $1.50 instead of 15,000, and so on). The process also works in reverse. If supply were to decrease, then there would be smaller quantities supplied at each price and an inward shift of the supply curve would occur.

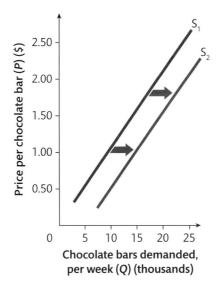

Figure 5.9 An increase in supply will shift the supply curve to the right

There are several determinants of supply, a change in any of which would cause a market supply curve to shift:

- changes in costs of factors of production
- prices of related goods
- indirect taxes and subsidies
- future price expectations
- changes in technology
- number of firms.

Let us look at each of these in turn, using the chocolate industry, guest lodging, and the market for ethanol as examples.

Changes in costs of factors of production

The ability of a firm to produce is intimately related to the costs of production. Higher costs obviously make it more difficult to earn profits, all other things being equal. If firms are selling chocolate bars for $2 per bar and costs rise from $1.50 to $1.75, profits per bar will fall by $0.25. This reduction in profits may provoke some producers to quit production, or to simply produce less chocolate and shift resources to the production of something else that is more profitable.

What causes the costs of production to change? Most generally, the price and availability of the factors of production will influence costs. As discussed in Chapter 1, the broad categories of the factors of production are land or natural resources, labour, financial and productive capital, as well as entrepreneurship or management. For example, if there is a disruption to the supply chain for cocoa beans, the price of cocoa beans will increase and the cost of producing a bar of chocolate will rise. This increased resource cost will shift the market supply curve to the left, as shown in Figure 5.10.

Furthermore, if the factors of production for chocolate were to become cheaper, costs would decrease and the supply curve would shift to the right. For example, if chocolate factory workers' wages or machine rental fees were to fall, the profitability of chocolate production would increase and the supply of chocolate bars would increase accordingly. This would mark an increase in the quantity supplied at every price. At all prices, firms would produce more bars of chocolate.

Figure 5.10 Higher costs will result in a decrease in supply overall

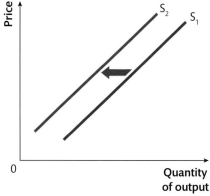

Prices of related goods

From the producer perspective, firms have a choice as to what to produce. Firms can substitute the supply of goods from those earning lower prices to those getting better ones. This is most clearly demonstrated by goods that offer **joint supply**. Joint supply occurs when two or more goods are derived from the same product. Animal products are an example. The various parts of an animal can be sold for different purposes, such as skin for leather and meat for consumption. When the demand for leather products increases, more resources will be allocated towards raising animals for leather, increasing the supply of meat in turn.

Another example of joint supply is corn. Corn can be used to produce a variety of goods, including corn syrup and ethanol (alcohol) for fuel. Should the price of ethanol increase, corn producers may choose to sell more corn on the ethanol market and reduce the amount supplied for corn syrup.

Figure 5.11(a) shows an increase in the price of ethanol, perhaps in response to concerns about fuel supplies. The quantity supplied increases in accordance with the law of supply. This is shown as a movement along the supply curve for ethanol from 10 million litres to 20 million litres. To farmers, ethanol is relatively more profitable than before, and they switch their supply from other corn-based products to ethanol. As a result, in Figure 5.11(b), the supply of corn syrup shifts to the left as producers substitute corn from the corn syrup market to the market for ethanol.

As we can see in Figure 5.11, one determinant of supply for corn syrup is the price of a related good with which it is in joint supply, ethanol.

To return to our chocolate example, let us consider how a change in the price of hot cocoa powder, a good that is in joint supply with chocolate bars, might affect the market for chocolate. If cocoa powder is becoming less popular among consumers, the price might fall, causing the quantity supplied of cocoa powder to decrease. Producers will view chocolate bars as a more profitable alternative to cocoa powder, and thus will allocate more resources towards the production of chocolate bars. A decrease in the price of cocoa powder, a good in joint supply with chocolate, would cause the supply of chocolate to increase.

Figure 5.11 Where goods are in joint supply, an increase in the supply of one leads to a decrease in supply of another

▼

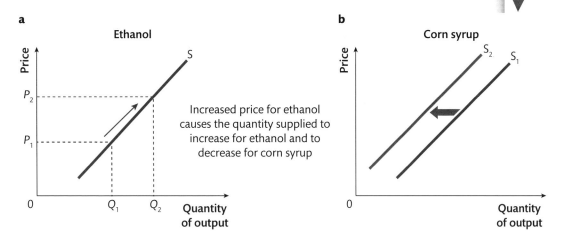

Indirect taxes and subsidies

Taxes and subsidies can also strongly influence supply decisions. Businesses view an indirect tax (defined as a tax on *consumption*, rather than on *income*) on their product as an increase in the cost of production. Indirect taxes are taxes on goods or services that are collected at the point of sale, and then transferred by the seller to the government, therefore an indirect tax is essentially another cost of production born by firms. A tax increases the marginal cost of producing a good because a tax is now added to the other costs of producing each unit. Thus the market supply decreases when taxes are increased or a new tax is imposed, shifting the supply curve to the left and reducing the amount produced at every price.

Historic Florence

Consider the example of a tax placed on short-term rentals (think Airbnb). Assume the city government of Florence, Italy, has decided that due to the huge numbers of summer vacationers, there is a need to increase government revenue in order to maintain the city's ancient infrastructure. The city decides to impose a 50% tax on all short-term rentals. The cost to property owners of operating a short-term rental thus increases by 50% at every price. This means that a €100 per night apartment will incur an additional €50 to the owner (on top of all other costs of maintaining the apartment, such as rent or mortgage payments, utilities, cleaning fees, and so on).

The increased cost created by the new tax will make using apartments for short-term rentals less profitable, thus decreasing the supply of short-term rentals at every price. Figure 5.12 shows the effect of a 50% tax on short-term rentals on the supply of such units in Florence, Italy.

An apartment costing €100 per night now costs owners €150, which includes a €50 tax paid to the city government. As a result of the increased cost of renting out apartments, the supply decreases from S_1 to S_2. Now, at €100 fewer apartments are put up for short-term rental, reducing the quantity available from Q_1 to Q_2.

Subsidies, on the other hand, have the opposite effect. A **subsidy** is when the government pays a producer to make more of the good. While there are different ways to subsidise production, we will focus on per-unit subsidy. This type of subsidy pays the firm for each unit produced. This has the effect of reducing production costs. Therefore, an increase in subsidies will have the effect of shifting supply to the right, successfully encouraging more supply of the product at every price.

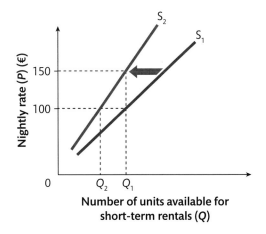

Figure 5.12 A new tax would cause a shift in the supply curve for short-term rentals

Consider a government plan to increase the affordability and thus the use of rooftop solar panels. The German government decides to subsidise each 100-watt solar panel by €50. Producers now receive a €50 'bonus' from the German government for each 100-watt panel that comes off their production lines, essentially offsetting the other costs that go into solar panel production, reducing their marginal costs and increasing the market supply.

Future price expectations

We know how a change in a good's *current price* affects supply: producers will bring more to market when the price rises and less when the price falls. But what about the *expected future price*? Even when there is no actual change in a good's price, but producers expect its price to change in the future, the supply can be affected.

Consider the market for an agricultural commodity, such as avocados. Let us assume there is a new administration in the USA that ran its campaign on the promise to 'get tough' with America's trading partners, and producers in all markets expect increased taxes on imported products. Farmers in California, who can grow any variety of fruits and vegetables, and who know that 80% of avocados consumed in the USA are imported from Mexico, now assume that the price of imported avocados is about to increase thanks to the expected import duties. The very expectation of future price increases will lead American farmers to allocate more of their resources towards avocado production today, increasing the supply being produced.

On the flip side, if a good's price is expected to fall in the future, rational producers would allocate fewer resources towards the good's production today (due to the expectation of decreased future profits), shifting the supply inward.

Higher expected future prices should cause a good's supply to increase today, while the expectation of a price decrease should cause supply to decrease today.

Changes in technology

New production technologies will positively impact a good's supply due to the impact new tech has on firms' productivity. Productivity is the amount of output per unit of input. If a new technology allows a firm to use fewer factor resources in the production process (less labour, less energy, less waste in its application of raw materials, etc.), it will spend less on production. If it can get more out of its resources while still getting the same prices, then it will earn more profit on each unit, thus supply will increase.

Research and inquiry

What are some real-world examples of goods or services that are taxed and subsidised in your community/country? Conduct a local news search for terms like 'excise tax' or 'subsidies', then answer the following questions.

For discussion and debate:

1 What is one good on which a specific tax is placed in your country?

2 What is one good or service that your country's government subsidises?

3 What are the government's intended effects of the taxes and subsidies you identified for questions 1 and 2?

4 In your opinion, are the government interventions in the above markets successful? Why or why not?

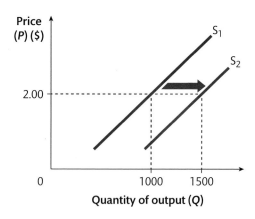

Figure 5.13 The entry of more firms into a market will shift the supply curve to the right

Productivity can be enhanced in different ways. Managerial insight can lead to better methods of production. This can also happen via the creation of better incentives for workers, changing production schedules, or adding new and specialised jobs to increase efficiency. Generally, though, productivity is enhanced through better technology. For example, robotic systems can replace expensive labour. Data management can reduce accounting costs and find new ways of marketing products. Both methods and machines play an important role in reducing costs and improving efficiency.

Using our initial example, if chocolate producers adopted a software program that improved workflow and minimised inefficiencies in staffing at their factories, the cost of producing chocolate would decrease and chocolate supply would increase, meaning more chocolate bars would be produced at every price.

Number of firms

The final non-price determinant of supply is perhaps the easiest to understand: the number of firms in a market. Let us revisit our bakery example from earlier in this chapter. We assumed that there were 20 bakeries producing 50 croissants each hour at a price of $2 per croissant. What happens to market supply if more bakeries open up in the city? Obviously, there will be more croissants produced at every price, or in other words, supply increases. Figure 5.13 shows the effect of increased competition in the bakery market.

Without any change in the costs of the individual bakeries, market supply has increased due to the influx of more competition in the market. Of course, if firms drop out of a market or allocate their resources towards a different market, then the supply decreases and a smaller quantity is produced at every price.

Video suggestion:
You have read about it, now you can review what you have just learned by watching a video by the author!
Simply click here in your eBook for a video on the law of supply and the determinants of supply (watch from 6:10 until the end of the video).

Case study – market supply of webcams

As the summer of 2020 unfolded, schools the world over weighed the costs and benefits of reopening for face-to-face instruction as the COVID-19 pandemic continued with varying degrees of intensity around the world. One thing was certain; more schools than ever would be conducting remote learning of some sort, meaning there would be record demand for the technologies required to allow students to interact with their teachers and classmates from home.

In a July 2020 interview with American financial news broadcaster CNBC, the CEO of a company that manufactures USB webcams for personal computers said 'We're working like crazy to make sure we have enough [products], especially for colleges and for education of all levels ... We've really expanded our capacity of webcams to make sure ...'

For discussion and debate:

1 Is the change described here an example of the law of supply at work, or does it describe a change in the supply of webcams?
2 Which determinant or determinants of supply are driving the changes described by the CEO? Explain?
3 **HL** What is likely to happen to the cost of producing additional webcams in the short run as the industry ramps up production?

5.3 Movements along and shifts of the supply curve

Learning outcomes

At the end of this section you will be able to:

- distinguish between movements along and shifts of the supply curve
- show these using diagrams.

To wrap up our examination of supply, we'll revisit the two main concepts introduced in this chapter, and examine how each relates to the *law of supply*. In any market, two things can disrupt the current level of output produced by firms: a change in the good's price or a change in a non-price determinant of supply.

When price changes, *ceteris paribus*, there is a movement along the supply curve from a smaller quantity to a larger quantity or vice versa. When chocolate prices fall, firms have a harder time covering the costs of production, making chocolate production less profitable, leading them to allocate some of their limited resources out of chocolate production. A decrease in price thus causes a *movement along the supply curve*.

However, when any factor affecting supply other than price changes, the entire supply curve shifts. A change in costs of factors of production, in the prices of related goods, indirect taxes or subsidies, future price expectations, changes in technology, or the number of firms will cause supply to *shift*, increasing or decreasing the quantity brought to market at every price.

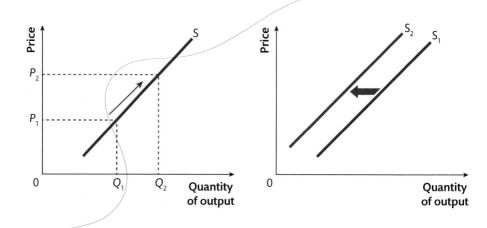

Figure 5.14 It is important to distinguish between the effect of change in price and a change in a non-price determinant of supply

Can laws in economics, such as the law of demand and the law of supply, have the same status as laws in the natural sciences?

TOK

To review, we'll look at the difference between these two outcomes one more time. Figure 5.14 shows the difference between the effect of a price change and a change in a non-price determinant of supply.

Understanding the law of supply, the determinants of supply, and the differences between changes in supply and changes in the quantity supplied provide us with one more tool to analyse the outcomes of real-world market interactions between buyers and sellers. In the next chapter we'll dive deeper into supply, looking at the *responsiveness* of producers to price changes, building on the knowledge of elasticity that was introduced in Chapter 4.

Practice exam questions

Paper 1, part (a) questions

1. Explain the difference between a movement along the supply curve and a shift in the supply curve. (10 marks)
2. Using an appropriate diagram and your knowledge of the determinants of supply, explain why the supply for solar power might increase. (10 marks)

Elasticity of supply

6

6.1 What is price elasticity of supply?

In the last chapter we introduced the concept of supply, defined the *law of supply*, and learned the various factors that can cause a change in a good's supply. We now know that there is a direct relationship between price and quantity supplied: a price increase allows producers to cover the additional cost of producing more of their output and therefore leads them to bring more to market, and the opposite happens when price falls. In the same way as Chapter 4 looked more closely at demand, this chapter will move beyond the basic relationship between price and quantity supplied, and ask *how much* the quantity supplied will change in response to a particular price change.

Price elasticity of supply (PES) measures the responsiveness of producers of a particular good to a change in the price of that good. PES is a quantitative indicator of producer sensitivity to price changes. Depending on how quickly producers are able to ramp up production following a price increase, or scale back production when prices fall, our PES value, and thus the *elasticity of supply* will be either high or low. This has implications for markets, including those for primary commodities like minerals, those for high tech manufactured goods like smart phones and electric cars, digital goods markets, labour markets and service industries. PES values can vary based on numerous factors, which we will explore in this chapter.

How is PES calculated?

The PES coefficient, like that for the different elasticities of demand introduced in Chapter 4, is determined by calculating the percentage change in quantity observed following a particular percentage change in price, and dividing it by the percentage change in price.

Worked example 6.1

We can use the supply schedule for chocolate from Chapter 5 to calculate the PES for chocolate between various prices.

Price of chocolate bars (P) $	Quantity of chocolate bars supplied per week (Q) (thousands)
0	0
0.50	5
1.00	10
1.50	15
2.00	20
2.50	25

First, the formula:

$$PES = (\%\Delta \text{ in } Q_S)/(\%\Delta \text{ in } P)$$

If the percentage changes in quantity and price are not known, they can easily be calculated, giving us the following formula for PES:

$$PES = ((Q_2 - Q_1) \div Q_1)/((P_2 - P_1) \div P_1)$$

where Q_2 is the quantity following the price change and Q_1 is the original quantity while P_2 is the new price and P_1 is the original price.

First we'll measure elasticity when price increases from $0.50 to $1.00.

$P_1 = \$0.50$

$P_2 = \$1$

$Q_1 = 5$

$Q_2 = 10$

$$PES = \frac{(10 - 5) \div 5}{(1 - 0.5) \div 0.5}$$

$$= \frac{5 \div 5}{0.5 \div 0.5}$$

$$= 1$$

The elasticity coefficient between $0.50 and $1.00 is equal to 1. For this supply schedule, any combination of prices and quantities we choose will yield the same PES value. For example, let us see what happens when the price increases from $2.00 to $2.50.

$P_1 = \$2.00$

$P_2 = \$2.50$

$Q_1 = 20$

$Q_2 = 25$

$$PES = \frac{(2.50 - 2) \div 2}{(25 - 20) \div 20}$$

$$= \frac{0.25}{0.25}$$

$$= 1$$

Again, we see that there is a constant PES value of 1 on this supply schedule. Any change in price will be met by a proportional change in quantity. When price increases by 50%, quantity increases by 50%.

The term for a supply curve along which price and quantity always change by the same percentage is *unitary elastic* (meaning an elasticity value of 1).

Let us look next at a supply curve that is not unitary elastic, but along which the elasticity coefficient is less than one.

Worked example 6.2

Consider the market for housing in a densely populated city. Figure 6.1 shows a supply curve for the annual supply of new homes in Rio de Janeiro.

From the supply curve we can draw values upon which we can calculate PES. Let us first determine the responsiveness of home builders between the prices of R$200 per square foot and R$400 (R$ is the symbol for 'real' (plural: reais), the Brazilian currency).

$P_1 = R\$200$

$P_2 = R\$600$

$Q_1 = 100$

$Q_2 = 130$

Figure 6.1 Supply curve for new homes in Rio de Janeiro, Brazil

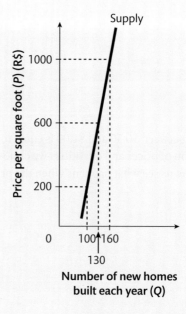

$$PES = \frac{(130 - 100) \div 100}{(600 - 200) \div 200}$$

$$= \frac{0.3}{2}$$

$$= 0.15$$

And using R\$600 as a starting price we can calculate the PES when the price rises to R\$1,000 per square foot.

$P_1 = R\$600$

$P_2 = R\$1,000$

$Q_1 = 130$

$Q_2 = 160$

$$PES = \frac{(160 - 130) \div 130}{(1,000 - 600) \div 600}$$

$$= \frac{0.23}{0.67}$$

$$= 0.35$$

Both of our elasticity coefficients are smaller than that which we calculated for chocolate. The builders of new homes in Rio de Janeiro are relatively *unresponsive* to price changes compared to the producers of chocolate. Any increase in price is met with a proportionally *smaller* increase in quantity supplied.

Rio de Janeiro, Brazil

Recall from Chapter 4 that elasticity coefficients of less than one put the good's elasticity in the *inelastic range*, meaning that the percentage change in quantity is less than the percentage change in the good's price.

Finally, we can look at a good for which the supply is relatively elastic.

Worked example 6.3

Consider the market for cotton t-shirts. Assume that when the price of blank cotton t-shirts rises by 10%, the quantity supplied increases by 15%. With these values we can easily calculate PES:

$$PES = \frac{\%\Delta Q}{\%\Delta P}$$

$$= \frac{15}{10}$$

$$= 1.5$$

With an elasticity coefficient of 1.5, producers of cotton t-shirts are the most responsive to price changes from among our three examples. A particular change in price will be met with a proportionally larger change in quantity supplied – supply is *elastic*.

What are the possible ranges of PES?

A good's supply can be inelastic, unitary elastic, or elastic, and the PES coefficient can range from zero to infinity. On the extremes, a good could theoretically have a *perfectly inelastic supply* or a *perfectly elastic supply*.

Perfectly inelastic means that no matter how much the price increases or decreases the quantity supplied remains fixed and unchanged. Consider the market for tickets to a hugely popular show in London's West End. There is one performance per day in a theatre that contains 1000 seats. The daily supply of tickets for this show is shown in Figure 6.2.

Figure 6.2 The supply of tickets for popular theatre shows is inelastic due to limited theatre capacity

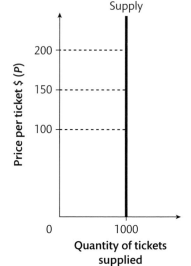

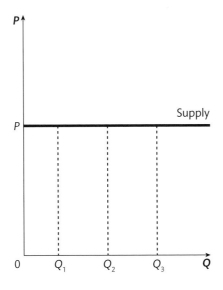

Figure 6.3 The perfectly elastic supply curve is horizontal

Supply for tickets is perfectly inelastic. The PES coefficient is equal to zero – no matter what people are willing to pay, the quantity is fixed at 1000.

At the other extreme is a good with *perfectly elastic supply*. Any change in price will lead to an *infinite* change in the quantity supplied. While examples of this from the real world are rare if impossible to find, the idea behind perfectly elastic supply is useful in understanding the ranges over which the elasticity coefficient can vary.

Supply can be close to perfectly elastic for a good if large inventories exist for that good or if the good has a marginal cost of zero (meaning there is no cost to produce and bring to market an additional unit of the good). Inventories are the amount of a good held in stock by a firm. If a good's price rises and large inventories exist, producers can respond to the increase in price instantly by releasing their inventories onto the market to meet the increase in consumer demand. Even in the short run, supply can be perfectly elastic in markets in which firms have substantial quantities of inventory.

Digital goods (think songs and movies on streaming services, computer software, smartphone apps, weapon packs in online video games, digital study guides, or downloadable files like pdfs), incur no marginal cost to their producers. In other words, to sell *one more* song, *one more* pdf study guide, or *one more* weapons pack in World of Warcraft costs nothing to the companies that sell these digital goods online. Therefore, once a price is set, as much or as little of such goods can be sold without the price having to increase or decrease.

For example, a publisher might sell downloadable pdf study guides through its website. The supply of these digital study tools is perfectly elastic. In a particular month he may sell five study guides or 150 study guides, but no price increase is necessary for the publisher to be willing to make more of them available. Likewise, if students were suddenly willing to pay less, the publisher would not 'decrease' the quantity supplied. Instead, fewer would be sold at the same price.

To summarise, a good's elasticity of supply can range from perfectly inelastic (PES = 0), to inelastic (PES > 0 and < 1), unitary elastic (PES = 1), elastic (PES > 1) and perfectly elastic (PES = ∞). In the next section we'll examine the factors that determine the PES.

In 2019, ticket prices for the hit Broadway musical *Hamilton* rose higher than $850 at the box office, and some sold for much more on the secondary market. The show was the costliest musical ever to show on Broadway, but some commentators observed that even at $850, the show might have been underpriced, due to the difficulty people still faced in getting tickets.

For discussion and debate:

1 What is the price elasticity of supply of tickets to a show like *Hamilton*?

2 Why doesn't the high price lead to more tickets being made available by the show's producers?

3 What could change in the long run that could increase the responsiveness of the producers of *Hamilton* to the high ticket price?

Exercise 6.1

Calculate the PES for the following goods using the values provided. For each, indicate whether supply is inelastic, unit elastic, or elastic.

1 The price of commercial air travel falls by 20% and the number of seats offered on commercial flights decreases by 5%.
2 The price of corn increases from $25 per bushel to $30 per bushel and the amount of corn brought to market increases by 40%.
3 The average price of cellular data plans increases from $50 to $75 and the number of plans supplied by cellular providers increases from 100 million to 150 million.
4 When the price of milk doubles, the amount supplied increases by half.

Answers:

1 PES of commercial air travel $= -5\% \div -20\% = 0.25$. Air travel supply is inelastic.
2 PES of corn $= 40\% \div [(30-25) \div 25] = 40\% \div 20\% = 2$. Corn supply is elastic.
3 PES of cellular data plans $= [(150-100) \div 100] \div [(75-50) \div 50] = 50\% \div 50\% = 1$. Supply of cellular data plans is unit elastic.
4 A doubling of the price of milk is a 100% increase. An increase by half is a 50% increase. The PES of milk $= 50\% \div 100\% = 0.5$. Milk supply is inelastic.

6.2 What are the determinants of PES?

Learning outcomes

At the end of this section you will be able to:

- explain the determinants of PES, including:
  - time
  - mobility of factors of production
  - unused capacity
  - ability to store stocks
- **HL** explain why the PES for primary commodities is relatively low and the PES for manufactured products is relatively high.

A good's PES depends on time, the mobility of factors of production, the degree of unused capacity, the ability to store inventories, and the rate at which costs increase.

Time following a change in price

An important determinant of how responsive producers are to price changes is the amount of time following a change in price over which producers are able to adjust their output. Figure 6.4 shows three possible supply curves for the same product, corn.

Assume the price of a bushel of corn increases from $5 to $6. The three supply curves in Figure 6.4 represent the supply of corn in the *market period*, the *short run*, and in the *long run*.

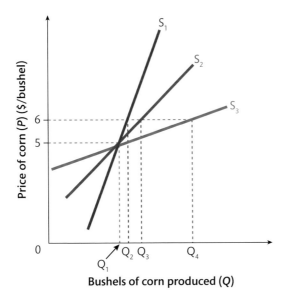

◀ **Figure 6.4** PES increases over time as producers adapt

S_1 – the market period

The period immediately following a change in price is known as the market period, and during this time supply is highly inelastic. In the market period, producers do not have the time to adjust their output to changes in price. Corn producers can release the little inventory they have and can perhaps harvest their crop earlier than planned, but the amount of land, labour and capital allocated to growing corn is fixed in the market period. Quantity can increase minimally, from Q_1 to Q_2, due to the fixed factors of production and limited inventory on hand.

S_2 – the short run

Within a few months of the increase in price, corn growers will be able to increase the intensity with which they use their fixed capital and land resources for growing corn. More labour and better or more fertiliser and pesticides can be applied to the existing crop in an attempt to increase the yield in order to meet the rising price. The short run is the period of time over which land and capital are fixed, but labour is variable and therefore the intensity with which land and capital are used can increase, resulting in more elastic supply than was possible in the market period. In the short run, output increases from Q_1 to Q_3 bushels of corn; supply is more elastic than it is in the market period due to producers' ability to mobilise variable resources such as labour and other easily added inputs towards corn production.

S_3 – the long run

In the long run, supply is highly elastic. The long run is defined as the period of time over which all factors of production are variable. In the case of corn, the long run may be one or two years, a period of time over which farmers can switch land that was being used for other crops to corn production and bring idle land into production of corn as well. In addition, farmers can allocate more capital and labour towards growing corn, allowing them to be much more responsive to the increase in price. In the long run, output can be increased from Q_1 bushels to Q_4 bushels, reflecting a much more responsive supply than that observed in the market period and the short run.

Over time, producers are much more responsive to changes in the price of a good. In the period immediately following a change in price, all factors of production are fixed and therefore firms are unable to change their output much. In the short run, capital and land are fixed but firms can hire more workers to respond to a price increase or lay workers off to adapt to falling prices, thereby using existing land and capital more or less intensively. In the long run, all factors of production are variable, so firms can be highly responsive to changes in market price.

Mobility of the factors of production

The more mobile the factors of production (the labour, land and capital resources needed for the production of a good), the more responsive a firm can be to changes in price. Whether a good is land intensive in its production or labour and capital intensive makes a significant difference to producers' ability to quickly shift resources into or out of production following a change in price.

Low-tech manufactured goods (e.g. clothes, toys, and simple electronics) and low-skilled services (e.g. haircuts, laundry services, and housekeeping) tend to have relatively elastic supply. Producers can easily hire more workers and acquire more raw materials and capital resources to meet increases in demand for such goods, thus they are highly responsive to increases in the price. When price falls, producers of these goods find it quick and easy to lay off workers, take capital out of production, and cancel orders for raw materials, thus they can respond quickly to decreases in demand as well.

HL   Heavy industry and primary commodities

The easy mobility of resources for manufactured goods and low-skilled services allows for supply of these items to be relatively responsive to changes in price.

The harder it is to shift factors of production into or out of the production of a good, the more inelastic the good's supply will be. The markets for heavy industrial goods such as airplanes, residential and commercial construction, and automobiles, high tech goods, and highly skilled services (e.g. doctors, financial experts, or university professors) tend to exhibit highly inelastic supply. Additionally, primary commodities that are land intensive in production, such as coffee, rice, corn, wheat, coal, oil, gas, and minerals also exhibit immobility of the factors of production, even in the long run, relative to less capital-intensive goods or lower skilled services.

It is extremely time consuming and costly to bring into production new plants for heavy industrial goods and primary commodities to meet rising demand, or to take them out of production in response to falling prices. Thus, the supply of such goods tends to be relatively inelastic.

Primary commodities likewise require substantial amounts of land and capital to produce. These are fixed resources that cannot be quickly put into production or taken out of production once a substantial investment has been made towards the extraction of a particular commodity. For instance, if diamond prices are rising, the quantity of diamonds brought to market will increase only minimally (assuming there are not large inventories of diamonds on hand). Why is this? It is because locating new potential sites for diamond mines is extremely difficult and expensive. Also, once a site is located, installing the machinery and training the workers to extract the diamonds is very time consuming and requires a substantial capital investment. When diamond prices fall, the firms that extract diamonds are unlikely to walk away from their mines, given the large investment they have made in getting them operational.

Diamonds are just one example of a primary commodity of which supply is highly inelastic, even in the long run, due to the substantial amount of fixed land and capital that goes into their production. Manufactured goods, on the other hand, tend to have relatively elastic supply curves due to the ability to quickly mobilise factors of production into and out of the manufacturing process. The lower tech and more simple a good's production process, the more elastic supply tends to be, while higher tech, more capital-intensive goods typically display a more inelastic supply.

The degree of unused capacity

Excess capacity refers to the amount a firm is able to produce in the short run without having to expand its plant size and the amount of capital and land employed in production. If an industry is operating at a level of output at which it has large amounts of unused capacity, then producers are able to quickly and easily respond to changes in the good's price. If, however, an industry is operating at or near full capacity, supply will be highly inelastic in the short run, as in order to meet any increase in demand, firms must first acquire new capital equipment and open new factories to meet the rising demand for their output. Such expansion takes time and means that supply will be relatively inelastic following a change in price.

The ability to store inventories

If large inventories of a good can easily be stored in warehouses or kept on hand by producers, then supply of the good can be highly responsive to changes in the price. Items such as video games, software, low-tech manufactured goods, and certain non-perishable commodities can be produced in large quantities that are not necessarily sold but added to inventories to be stored and used to meet future demand. If, in the future, prices for such goods rise, producers can quickly and easily release stored inventory onto the market to meet the increase in price. Likewise, when the price for non-perishable commodities falls, producers can respond by putting supply into inventory and quickly reducing the quantity available in the market.

However, not all goods can be easily stored. When the prices of perishable goods such as milk, fruit, some grains, and large-scale industrial goods such as airplanes

Stockpiled goods

97

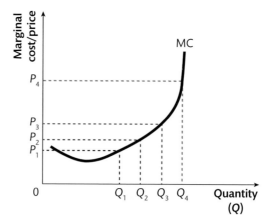

Figure 6.5 The marginal
cost curve becomes steeper
due to capacity constraints ▶

and ships rises, producers have a very limited stock to dip into. Likewise, some goods'
inventories cannot be added to when price falls. The producers are not very responsive
and must accept a lower price to sell the current output that would otherwise go bad or
be very costly for the firm to store.

The rate at which costs increase

Recall from Chapter 5 that an individual firm's 'supply curve' for a good is actually the
firm's marginal cost curve. One of the explanations for the direct relationship between
price and quantity supplied was the fact that marginal cost (the cost of an additional
unit of a good's output) increases as output increases for most goods, due to the
diminishing marginal returns experienced as more labour is added to a fixed amount
of capital and land to increase production. The rate at which costs increase is therefore
a determinant of a good's PES.

Consider the market for cotton candy, which requires three inputs to produce: labour
(the person operating the cotton candy machine), land (the physical space the machine
is located and the raw ingredient, which in this case is sugar, an agricultural product),
and capital (the cotton candy machine). Figure 6.5 shows the marginal cost curve for a
single cotton candy producer.

At lower quantities the cotton candy producer is able to increase her output (Q_1 to Q_2)
with only a minimal increase in price (P_1 to P_2), due to the fact that her marginal costs
increase only slightly. However, at higher quantities (Q_3 to Q_4) the same increase
in output requires a much larger increase in price (P_3 to P_4) due to the increasingly
constrained capacity of the cotton candy machine. The intensity with which the
labourer can work the machine is limited when output is at Q_4, and supply becomes
increasingly inelastic as the rate at which costs increase becomes greater in the short
run. To increase responsiveness to price changes, a second cotton candy machine is
needed, which would once again lower the marginal cost as excess capacity is restored.

6.3 Why does PES matter?

This chapter extended your understanding of the economic principles behind market
supply by focusing on the responsiveness of producers to changes in price. The
formula for elasticity of supply measures the percentage change in quantity supplied
over the percentage change in price. We learned that goods can have perfectly

inelastic supply (think theatre tickets) or perfectly elastic supply (digital downloads). Understanding how firms respond to price changes helps all businesses to be prepared for changes in variables such as price, government policy, and market demand. These can affect business decisions on how much to produce now and how to prepare for the future.

In later chapters we'll examine how government interventions in markets, such as indirect taxes, subsidies, **price ceilings**, and **price floors**, will have dramatically different impacts on buyers and sellers depending on the relative elasticities of demand and supply. For now, it is time to put our knowledge of both demand theory (Chapters 3 and 4) and supply theory (Chapters 5 and 6) together to explore the concept of **market equilibrium**, which will be introduced in Chapter 7.

Video suggestion:
You have read about it, now you can review what you have just learned by watching a video by the author!
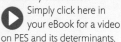 Simply click here in your eBook for a video on PES and its determinants.

Practice exam questions

1a. Explain the factors which influence price elasticity of supply. Illustrate your answer with reference to the market for a commodity or raw material. (10 marks)

  b. Discuss the importance of price elasticity of supply for producers of primary commodities in less developed countries. (15 marks)

2. Using examples, explain why supply of primary commodities tends to be more inelastic than that of secondary commodities. (10 marks)

Competitive market equilibrium

7

At the end of this section you will be able to:

- explain, using diagrams, how demand and supply interact to produce market equilibrium
- analyse, using diagrams and with reference to **excess demand** or **excess supply**, how changes in the determinants of demand and/or supply result in a new market equilibrium.

This chapter will draw together many important concepts from everything you have learned so far. As described in Chapters 1 and 2, free market systems depend on interaction between consumers and producers as the main mechanism through which resources are directed to meet the needs and wants in an economy. This is the relationship from which these societies answer the questions of *what* to produce *how* to produce and *for whom* to produce. Having examined demand and supply separately, we now combine them to analyse markets more completely.

Market equilibrium

When demand and supply are combined, there is a tendency for the market to reach a market equilibrium. Equilibrium is defined as a state of rest, self-perpetuating in the absence of any outside disturbance. This suggests balance or stability. Market equilibrium is defined as the point where the quantity of a product demanded is equal to the quantity of a product supplied. This creates the market-clearing price and quantity where there is no excess demand or excess supply. The price at which the quantity supplied and demanded are equal is called the equilibrium price. At this price, the amount purchased is exactly equal to the amount sold. There is no surplus product available on the market, nor are there shortages of supply at that price. For this reason, the equilibrium price is also called the market-clearing price. Everything put on the market, at that price, is sold.

Returning to the example of chocolate bars we used in Chapter 3, the total market schedule shows the equilibrium price is $1.50 per bar (Table 7.1). At that price, the amount supplied and demanded is 15,000 bars per week. All the bars offered on the

Table 7.1 Demand and supply schedule: chocolate bars

Price of chocolate bars (P) $	Quantity of chocolate bars demanded per week (Q_D) (thousands)	Quantity of chocolate bars supplied per week (Q_S) (thousands)
2.50	5	25
2.00	10	20
1.50	15	15
1.00	20	10
0.50	25	5

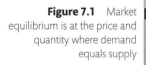

Figure 7.1 Market equilibrium is at the price and quantity where demand equals supply ▶

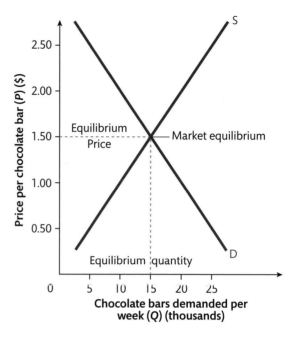

market are purchased by consumers. Prices set above or below the market price will result in market disequilibrium, because there will be excess supply or demand.

On a diagram, the equilibrium price is found at the intersection of supply and demand. In Figure 7.1, the supply and demand intersect at $1.50. At that price, as noted previously in the table, the quantity supplied is 15,000 bars, and all those bars are purchased as quantity demanded is also 15,000. The market 'clears' because there are no extra bars available, nor any shortage at that price.

Market disequilibrium

A market disequilibrium occurs at any price at which the demand and supply quantities are not equal. Let us look at specific examples of market disequilibrium, and analyse the results of attempting to set prices anywhere other than the equilibrium price.

Excess supply

Excess supply occurs where the price of a good is higher than the equilibrium price, such that the quantity supplied is greater than the quantity demanded. Table 7.2

Table 7.2   Demand and supply schedule: chocolate bars

Price of chocolate bars (P) $	Quantity of chocolate bars supplied per week (Q_S) (thousands)	Quantity of chocolate bars demanded per week (Q_D) (thousands)	Specific consumer surplus (demand price – market price) $
2.50	25	5	1.00
2.00	20	10	0.50
1.50	15	15	0.00
1.00	10	20	—
0.50	5	25	—

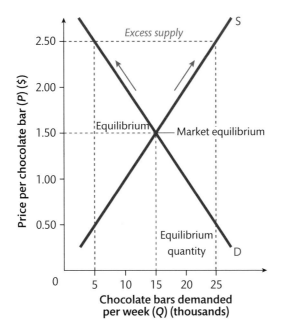

Figure 7.2 A price higher than the equilibrium price results in excess supply

and Figure 7.2 show the market price to be $1.50. If the producers of these chocolate bars had an exaggerated sense of their value, they might set the price too high. Let us say, for example, that they greedily set the price at $2.50 per bar. At that price, the quantity demanded is much smaller than at the equilibrium price. Quantity demanded drops from 15,000 to 5000 bars per month. This is equivalent to a movement along the demand curve, as shown in Figure 7.2, to a price of $2.50 and quantity of 5000 bars.

As price increases, the quantity demanded decreases or moves upwards and left along the demand curve. At the same time, setting the price higher induces producers to increase production as they expect higher profits at higher prices. Quantity supplied thus moves in the opposite direction, moving upwards along the curve to a quantity of 25,000.

Thus, we can say at $2.50, an excess supply for bars exists, with more quantity supplied than demanded. What happens to this surplus? Producers can only sell the extra goods if they lower the price. As they do so, more quantity is demanded, and producers reduce production. This narrows the gap continuously until the surplus is reduced to zero at the market-clearing, equilibrium price.

Excess demand

Excess demand occurs where the price of a good is lower than the equilibrium price, such that the quantity demanded is greater than the quantity supplied. Let us take up the opposite case and assume that firms are not aware of the market value of their bars, and they under-price them at $0.50, as shown in Figure 7.3. At this price, the quantity demanded is much higher, now 25,000 bars, while the lower price is not well received by producers. They scale back production to only 5000 bars. This gap between relatively higher quantity demanded and lower quantity supplied is called excess demand.

When excess demand exists, market forces take over. With relatively scarce amounts of the good on the market at $0.50 (an excess demand of 20,000 bars) some consumers

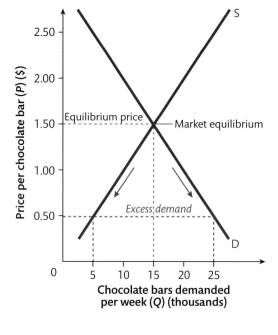

Figure 7.3 A price lower than the equilibrium price results in excess demand

start to bid the price higher in an attempt to get more of the good. As bars quickly fly off the shelves, producers also realise they can charge a higher price. So, at the higher price of $1.00, producers make more (10,000 bars) and some consumers drop out of the market, reducing the quantity demanded to 20,000. Now the shortage is smaller (10,000 bars) but there is still a shortage. This prompts producers to raise the price again, with some consumers dropping out again, a process that continues until all of the extra demand is satisfied at the market-clearing price of $1.50.

Therefore, at any price other than the market-clearing price, either excess supply or demand will exist. Furthermore, unless firms are compelled by law to keep their prices at some disequilibrium level (too high or too low), market forces will urge producers and consumers towards a market-clearing price where everything offered is purchased.

What causes changes to market equilibrium?

The tendency of a market towards equilibrium is strong. When prices are too high or too low, the market tends to clear eventually. And when markets are in balance, it requires some external force or event to alter that balance. Recall that for all equilibriums, like the one above, *ceteris paribus* is in effect. All other factors are being held constant. However, in reality, market forces are dynamic, and market equilibriums are changing often. Shifts in either market supply or demand will change the market equilibrium, changing the market-clearing price, and quantity as well.

Shifts of demand

Ceteris paribus, an increase in demand will increase the scarcity of the good, and cause a temporary shortage. That shortage will cause the price to be bid higher and higher, to a point where quantity demanded and supplied meet. At that new market equilibrium, the result is an increase in the equilibrium price and quantity.

For example, suppose consumer demand for mango juice significantly increased following reports that it contained very high levels of antioxidants. As a result, demand

Video suggestion:
You have read about it, now you can review what you have just learned by watching a video by the author!
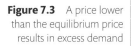 Simply click here in your eBook for a video on market equilibrium, disequilibrium, and allocative efficiency.

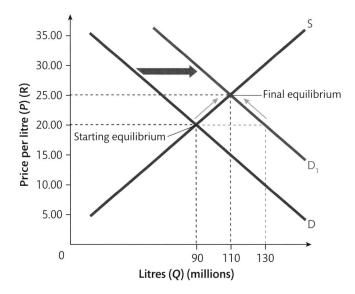

Figure 7.4 Following a rise in demand, the equilibrium price will settle further up the supply curve

for all products using mango increased, shifting demand for mangos to the right. As shown in Figure 7.4, demand for mangos shifted to the right, causing a temporary shortage at the old equilibrium price of R20.00 (R is the symbol for the rand, the currency of South Africa). The quantity demanded (Q_D) is thus far greater than the quantity supplied (Q_S). In this case, the excess demand is 40 million litres. As producers realise they can raise the price, they produce more, a movement upwards along the supply curve. And as consumers see the higher prices, they decrease the quantity demanded, a movement up and left along the new demand curve. The quantities of supply and demand settle at the new equilibrium price of R25.00 and equilibrium quantity of 110 million litres. As a result of the increased demand, prices are higher and quantities greater than before.

Figure 7.5 Following a fall in demand, the equilibrium price will settle further down the supply curve

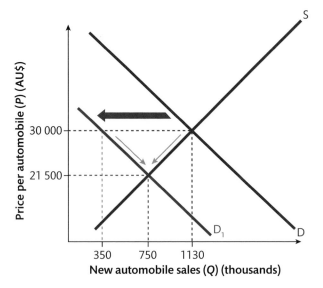

Conversely, a decrease in demand will decrease the scarcity of the good, and cause a temporary surplus. That surplus will cause the price to drop lower and lower, to a point where quantity demanded and supplied meet. At that new market equilibrium, the result is an increase in the equilibrium price and quantity. For example, a decrease in a country's income might decrease the demand for all normal goods. Automobile sales, in particular, tend to be immediately affected by decreases in income, and a recession causes a decrease in demand for automobiles.

In Figure 7.5, a decrease in demand of this type results in a temporary surplus of 800,000 automobiles at the equilibrium price of AU$30,000 (AU$ is the symbol for Australian dollar, the currency of Australia) (fewer new automobiles being sold); producers cut prices to entice buyers (increasing quantity demanded, moving down along the new demand curve). Eventually, the market settles at a new, lower market price and quantity (AU$21,500 and 750,000 automobiles): fewer automobiles are being sold at lower prices.

Shifts of supply

Supply shifts can also have important effects on price and quantity. When supply increases, a good becomes less scarce and a temporary surplus occurs. This causes the price to drop until settling at the price where quantity supplied and demanded are equal.

In Figure 7.6, the market for rubber ducks shows the effect of synthetic rubber production. Synthetic rubber is much cheaper than rubber collected from rubber trees, so it becomes much less costly to produce rubber items, including rubber ducks. As a result, the supply of rubber ducks shifts to the right. A temporary surplus of 7 million ducks exists at the old equilibrium price of S$3.75 (S$ is the symbol for Singapore dollar, the currency of Singapore). This surplus is eliminated by cutting prices and selling off the excess supply. Consumers do their part by buying up the residual amounts at successively lower prices, an increase in quantity demanded at each lower price. The increase in supply therefore results in a lower equilibrium price for rubber ducks at S$2.25, and a higher equilibrium quantity of 12 million sold.

A decrease in supply will have the opposite effect. When supply decreases, a good becomes more scarce and a temporary shortage occurs. This causes the price to rise until settling at the price where quantity supplied and demanded are equal.

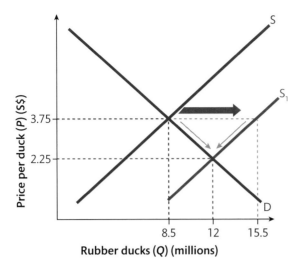

Figure 7.6 Following an increase in supply, the equilibrium price will settle further to the right along the demand curve

Figure 7.7 shows a decrease in supply, in this case the effect of a deep winter freeze across the Mediterranean which damaged orange crops in Cyprus, Greece, Italy, and Spain. As a result, the number of oranges available for juice products decreased dramatically. Oranges are an input cost for orange juice, so the supply of orange juice decreases, shifting supply to the left. The reduced supply causes a temporary shortage of 700 million litres at the old equilibrium price of €1.50 per litre. Producers therefore begin to increase their prices, and consumers respond by decreasing the quantity demanded. The final price and quantity settle at €2.10 per litre and 550 million litres consumed. Thus, the decrease in supply has caused a decrease in quantity available and increased prices.

Video suggestions:
You have read about it, now you can review what you have just learned by watching some videos by the author! ▶ Simply click here in your eBook for videos on the effect on market equilibrium of changes in demand and/or supply.

Case study – the 1973 oil crisis

Perhaps the greatest single supply shock in the modern era occurred with the 1973 oil crisis. The Organization of the Petroleum Exporting Countries (OPEC) launched an embargo of oil in response to US support of Israel during the Yom Kippur War. The price of oil quadrupled to a then-record $12 per barrel. This resulted in long queues at petrol stations, **price controls**, and **rationing** in the USA, Europe, and Japan. It also stoked inflationary tendencies at work during this period, and is credited with starting the era of stagflation (higher price levels and low economic growth).

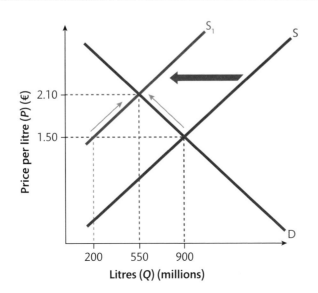

Figure 7.7 Following a decrease in supply, the equilibrium price will settle further to the left along the demand curve

For each of the following headlines (1) create a fully labelled diagram of the product, (2) show the shift and the changes to equilibrium price and quantity, and (3) identify and label the determinant of demand or supply that caused the shift for each.

a. Heavy rainfall affects the market for rubber boots.
b. Diplomatic agreements open the market for Chinese airplanes to several new countries.
c. Consumers learn that cars will be much more heavily taxed starting with next year's models.
d. House-building companies are gloomy about new business during the recession.
e. A baby boom 15 years ago influences the market for popular music and cosmetics today.
f. The government places more regulations on food preparation after several poisoning scares.
g. A maker of t-shirts moves production to a country with significantly lower labour costs.
h. A severe winter frost decimates the crop of grapes from which French champagne is made.
i. Country X joins the EU and its wheat farmers reap massive subsidies.

7.2 What role do prices play in allocating resources?

Learning outcomes

At the end of this section you will be able to:

- explain why scarcity necessitates choices that answer the 'What to produce?' question
- explain why choice results in an opportunity cost
- explain, using diagrams, that price has a signalling function: rising prices signal scarcity and falling prices signal abundance
- explain, using diagrams, that price has an incentive function, which results in a reallocation of resources when prices change
- discuss how a price system helps perform the rationing of resources in a free market economy.

The concept of scarcity was introduced in Chapter 1. Because human wants are unlimited in a world of limited resources, choices must be made about what to produce and what to consume. Such choices will always incur an opportunity cost, which is the value of the next best alternative use of the resource. To act efficiently, and to improve one's overall economic well-being, one needs reliable information about the relative scarcity of the resources being used.

How does a functioning price system signal scarcity?

Resource allocation is the manner by which society selects which resources are used for what purposes. These decisions about the allocation of precious resources derive important information from a functioning price system. When markets operate freely, the price system is the organising principle around which all resources are allocated. The interaction of supply and demand tells us those goods which are most scarce (lowest supply relative to demand) because they have the highest prices, and least scarce (lowest demand relative to supply) because they have the lowest prices.

In **competitive markets**, we have seen that buyers and sellers come to a settlement or agreement on the appropriate market price. This is not done through any central command or by the guidance of some overseeing body of government. Instead, the establishment of a market price happens when countless buyers and sellers, each making rational choices about their scarce resources, make the best decision for themselves. Buyers are conscious of their time and income levels, while suppliers watch closely their costs and the selling potential for their goods. This decentralised, seemingly random process produces one of the most important benefits of competitive markets: an efficient rationing of resources through the price system. Free markets serve an important signalling function, where signalling is understood to be the sending of a signal revealing relevant information to a participant in a transaction.

Rising prices signal scarcity

In Figure 7.8, if the demand for a good were to increase, a temporary shortage would exist at the current price. All of the extra demand would bid the price upward from P_1 to P_2 to reflect that there is more demand for the good relative to the same amount available. A decrease in supply would likewise indicate more scarcity, and prices would rise.

Falling prices signal more abundance

If demand for a good decreases, it is wanted less, and the price drops accordingly. Were supply to increase, there would be more abundance and less scarcity, dropping prices as well.

Without price information, it is very difficult to make informed, efficient decisions about production. Centralised economies make mistakes for this reason. In these situations, planners fight over resources, like rubber, steel, and textiles, to be used

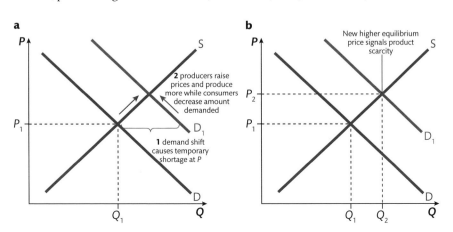

Figure 7.8 Rising prices signal scarcity following a rise in demand (a) with a new higher equilibrium price (b)

in production of other goods. What are these resources worth? They do not know, and may overuse steel, for example, in the building of automobiles, when it is more desperately needed in building construction, or railway repair. Without prices, making a rational decision, based on costs and benefits, is nearly impossible.

How does the price system influence incentives in a free market economy?

When prices rise and fall, producer and consumer incentives are changed. Incentives refer to events that cause behaviour to change, in this case the behaviour of consumer and producers. When a resource or product rises in price, buyers try to use it less frequently, and producers try to make more of it to increase their profits. If, in Figure 7.8, the price increase occurred in the market for high-quality beef steaks, cattle ranchers would have a greater incentive to sell more, and would respond by trying to offer more of their animals up for sale. If a supply decrease caused the price rise, steak buyers have a new incentive to reduce their consumption and find substitutes.

It works the other way as well. When the price of a resource drops, buyers will find reason to use it more since it is cheaper. Firms will be discouraged from production because the low prices offer less reward for their time.

What is the rationing function of the price system?

Rationing is a term used to describe an artificial process by which goods, services, or resources in general are distributed. In a price system, resources are rationed because prices indicate scarcity, and the resources are available to anyone willing and able to buy them. This may seem obvious, but compare that with other rationing systems to see the difference. One might allocate resources, as in a planned system, by groups of government officials deciding what is important to produce, and what is not. Because of the lack of signalling and incentive functions described above, this leads to inefficient outcomes. Surpluses and shortages of critical goods are a common feature of planned systems.

The value of a price system is that nearly all the relevant information about the market is revealed naturally, without outside intervention. Figure 7.8 shows how a competitive market uses supply and demand to ration resources in this way. As demand for a good increases, a temporary shortage occurs (Figure 7.8a). Firms see the shortage and begin to raise the price of the good. This acts as incentive to produce more, helping to relieve the shortage. At the same time, consumers reduce the quantity they demand, and there is a movement up and to the left along the demand curve. Eventually, the price settles at a new equilibrium (Figure 7.8b). The rise in prices has told consumers to ration their consumption and producers to make more.

To take an example from the resource market, Figure 7.9 shows a market for capital equipment (i.e. any kind of machinery or service that is used in production). Here, an increase in the supply of this resource sends critical information to the producer, who buys the capital equipment as an input for the products. The information about lower prices says that this resource is more available and will cost less. A wise producer may look for ways to use this resource more frequently, and for ways to use other, relatively more expensive resources, less frequently. A rational reaction to this information would be for producers to look for ways to hire more capital equipment (which now costs less) and less labour.

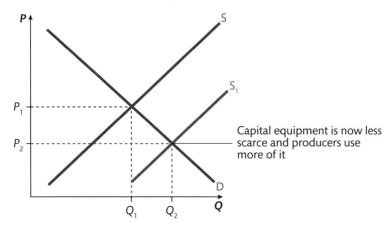

Figure 7.9 Lower prices would signal to producers a greater availability of capital equipment

Thus, the forces of supply and demand work towards an efficient allocation of resources. This is what Adam Smith referred to when he coined the term the 'invisible hand of the market'. Market forces, Smith argued, consistently and accurately guide us to produce and consume to get the best outcomes. Buyers and sellers are rationing resources, based on prices, to get the most from what they have. In the process, consumer wants are satisfied with the least possible cost to society.

PPE prices soared in the first half of 2020

Research and inquiry

Command economies, because they do a poor job of placing a value on goods, are famous for producing shortages. A noteworthy shortage occurred in 1980 when, in parts of the Soviet Union, milk was in such short supply that it was rationed by medical prescription. Little or poor-quality food often led to work stoppages. A chronic lack of medical supplies and basic necessities had a long-term debilitating effect on the population. Even nurses were scarce because the job was difficult and did not pay.

For discussion and debate:

1 Conduct an internet search for 'soviet food shortages' and observe cases across several decades. Were the shortages a result of crop failure or failures of the planning system?

Case study – demand for PPE

Market shocks can raise serious ethical dilemmas about the ways a free market system will ration resources. As the COVID-19 pandemic began in 2020, demand for certain types of medical equipment rose rapidly. Hospitals, governments, and individuals were suddenly hunting down surgical masks, ventilators, coronavirus tests, and personal protective equipment (PPE). The PPE prices soared because of the scarcity, perceived scarcity, and people taking advantage of the panic. For example, stories emerged about celebrities and powerful government officials getting tested regularly, when in most countries getting a test was very difficult. Billionaires were believed to be buying up ventilators to personally keep in reserve, even if they were healthy.

Discuss the following question: To what degree will a free market system solve or exacerbate a shortage of resources during a health crisis?

7.3 How do competitive markets achieve efficiency?

At the end of this section you will be able to:

- explain the concepts of **consumer surplus** and **producer surplus**
- identify consumer surplus and producer surplus on a demand and supply diagram
- explain the concept of social or community surplus and identify it on a demand and supply diagram
- explain that allocative efficiency is achieved where MB = MC and that this is at equilibrium price
- explain that allocative efficiency is where community surplus is maximised
- explain that at any price other than the equilibrium price there will be reduced community surplus and a welfare loss
- HL calculate consumer surplus, producer surplus, and deadweight loss from a diagram.

Competitive markets can also yield benefits beyond the signalling, incentive, and rationing functions explained above. Your study of free market equilibrium encompasses the key concept of efficiency. Recall from Chapter 1 that 'efficiency is a quantifiable concept, determined by the ratio of useful output to total input'. In this section, we will employ a specific measure of efficiency to analyse the qualities of a market equilibrium. Allocative efficiency refers to making the best possible use of scarce resources to produce the combinations of goods and services that are optimum for society, thus minimising resource waste. To understand allocative efficiency in the context of market equilibrium, it is useful to examine the concepts of *consumer surplus, producer surplus,* and *community surplus.*

Consumer surplus

Consumer surplus is the benefit consumers receive when they pay a price below what they are willing to pay. The difference between the two is considered a buyer's consumer surplus for that product. Let us return to our example of chocolate bar demand in a major city. A partial demand schedule is shown in Table 7.3 on page 114.

The equilibrium or market price for chocolate bars is, as with all other markets, the intersection of supply and demand. In Table 7.2 (page 102), it is evident that the equilibrium price is $1.50, where 15,000 bars are sold. However, a closer look at the demand schedule tells us right away that there are chocolate fans who are willing to pay considerably more than the market price. Here it is $1.50, where 15,000 bars are expected to be sold. For each buyer willing to buy at a price of $2.50, and who only pays $1.50, the consumer surplus is $1.00. For only that group of consumers the consumer surplus is found this way:

Price willing to pay ($2.50) − Equilibrium price ($1.50) × Quantity (5000) = Total consumer surplus at that price = $5,000

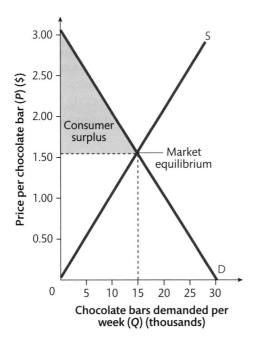

Thus, the demand schedule reveals that this consumer surplus can be calculated as the difference between what consumers are willing to pay and the market price they ultimately pay (Table 7.2).

The total market consumer surplus can also be shown on a diagram, as the area between the demand curve and the market price (Figure 7.10).

The demand curve reflects the demand schedule. Each point shows the highest price consumers are willing to pay for the product. The difference between what a consumer is willing to pay and any market price below that is considered consumer surplus. Thus, the area of the triangle below the demand curve extending down to the market price is the total area of consumer surplus. It can be inferred (from the schedule or the diagram) that any decrease in price will have the effect of increasing consumer surplus, *ceteris paribus*. Any increase in the market price will shrink that difference, causing a decrease in consumer surplus.

HL Calculating consumer surplus from a diagram

To calculate the area of consumer surplus, use the formula for calculating the area of a triangle:

$$area = \frac{(base \times height)}{2}$$

In the example above:

$$consumer\ surplus = \frac{15,000\ bars \times \$1.50}{2} = \$11,250$$

Note the consumer surplus is expressed in money terms, and should reflect the units and amounts of the market being studied.

Table 7.3 Demand and supply schedule: chocolate bars

Price of chocolate bars (P) $	Quantity of chocolate bars supplied per week (Q_S) (thousands)	Quantity of chocolate bars demanded per week (Q_D) (thousands)	Specific producer surplus (market price – supply price) $
2.50	25	5	—
2.00	20	10	—
1.50	15	15	0.00
1.00	10	20	0.50
0.50	5	25	1.00

Producer surplus

It is also possible to see the same type of benefit accruing to producers. Producer surplus is the benefit producers receive when they receive a price above the one at which they were willing to supply the good. A close look at the supply schedule in Table 7.2 should reveal this phenomenon. Even at the lowest price listed, some producers are willing to produce. Perhaps they are very efficient. They would produce 5000 bars at a price of just $0.50. However, because the prevailing market price is $1.50, $1.50 is what they receive for every unit sold. Therefore, they enjoy a producer surplus of $1 per unit. Table 7.3 shows the producer surplus at each price.

The total market producer surplus can also be shown on a diagram as the area between the supply curve and the market price (Figure 7.11). Each point on the supply curve shows the lowest price at which producers are willing to sell the product. Any market price above that is considered producer surplus. Thus, the

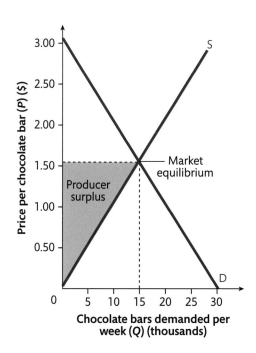

Figure 7.11 Producer surplus is the difference between the market price and the lowest price at which producers are willing to sell

area of the triangle above the supply curve extending up to the market price is the total area of producer surplus. It can be inferred (from the schedule or the diagram) that any increase in price will have the effect of increasing producer surplus, *ceteris paribus*. Any decrease in the market price will shrink that difference, causing a decrease in producer surplus.

> **HL** **Calculating producer surplus from a diagram**
>
> To calculate the area of producer surplus, use the formula for calculating the area of a triangle:
>
> $$area = \frac{(base \times height)}{2}$$
>
> In the example above:
>
> $$producer\ surplus = \frac{15,000\ bars \times \$1.50}{2} = \$11,250$$
>
> Note the producer surplus is expressed in money terms, and should reflect the units and amounts of the market being studied. Also, note that in this case, the amount of consumer and producer surplus is equal. Were the general elasticities of demand and supply different, the size of each surplus would also be different.

Community or social surplus

Taken together, consumer and producer surplus are equal to **community surplus**, also called **social surplus**. We will use the concept of community surplus to analyse the concept of allocative efficiency in the section that follows.

Allocative efficiency and competitive markets

Allocative efficiency is generally considered to be in effect if society is getting the goods and services it wants most in the right amount. More specifically, allocative efficiency is achieved if society produces enough of a good so that marginal benefit (MB) is equal to marginal cost (MC). This most directly relates to the 'what' should be produced question of economics. Through the price system, free and competitive markets should bring consumers what they desire. But a look back at marginal cost and benefit theory makes the case clearer.

You will recall from Chapter 3 that the MB derived from any good tends to drop as more is consumed. In other words, satisfaction tends to decline with extra consumption, and the demand curve's downward slope reflects this principle. Also, recall from Chapter 4 that the additional cost of producing more and more units tends to increase. In other words, the MC tends to rise as more is made. This explains why MB (demand) tends to slope downwards, and MC (supply) tends to slope upwards.

Video suggestion:
You have read about it, now you can review what you have just learned by watching a video by the author!
▶ Simply click here in your eBook for a video on consumer surplus and producer surplus.

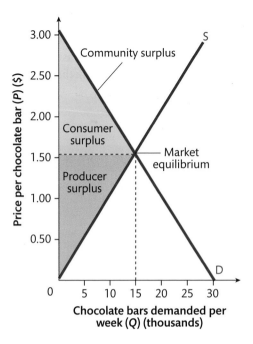

Figure 7.12 Community surplus is also known as social surplus

Figure 7.12 Community surplus is also known as social surplus

Figure 7.12 shows a market producing at equilibrium, with consumer surplus represented by the area above equilibrium price and below the demand curve, and producer surplus by the area below equilibrium price and above the supply curve. Allocative efficiency asks whether a market produces what consumers want, and part of the answer comes from the demand/marginal benefit curve. Figure 7.13 reproduces the demand curve showing that what consumers are willing to pay for a good is our best guess at the value (or benefit) society places on it. It also shows a supply curve indicating the rising cost to producers with each rise in output, reflected in the **minimum price** at which sellers will offer up each new level of chocolate bars.

 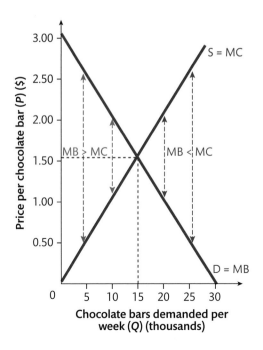

Figure 7.13 Allocative efficiency is achieved where marginal benefit is equal to marginal cost

Allocative efficiency is achieved when, in a free market, supply (MC) is equal to demand (MB). This is true in Figure 7.13: at $1.50, MC = MB. At any other price or quantity, the market does not achieve equilibrium, nor allocative efficiency. At a price of $2.50, the MB is much higher ($2.50) than MC to society ($0.50). This result suggests the market is producing too little, and that more of the good should be produced and consumed. Why? There is still consumer and producer benefit to be captured by increasing quantity, at least until the point where MB = MC. However, any quantity and price combination beyond 15,000 units will see marginal costs to society rise above the benefits of those units (MC > MB). This suggests that the market is producing too much of the good, and output should be scaled back.

If allocative efficiency is achieved, welfare is maximised. We can also demonstrate the fact of **allocative efficiency** in free markets another way. Allocative efficiency is also achieved when community surplus is at its maximum. In other words, when supply (MC) equals demand (MB), community or social surplus will have its largest possible value, and largest area on the diagram. In Figure 7.14a, compare the allocatively efficient result with one where the price is set artificially high. This could be legally required, as with a price floor (of which there is more discussion in Chapter 9), or it could also be a mistake by sellers eager to get a higher price.

In Figure 7.14b, the price is raised to P_1. At that price, MB is greater than MC. A movement along the demand curve occurs, as consumers reduce their quantity demanded in response to the higher price at P_1. The area of consumer surplus is significantly smaller. The area of producer surplus will likely rise because producers receive a higher price. Most importantly, whole areas that were once community surplus (in orange), a combination of consumer and producer surplus, disappear. That loss of surplus is designated as a welfare loss, or deadweight loss (DWL). DWL is a situation where the market loses producer or consumer surplus.

Figure 7.14 Allocative efficiency maximises welfare (a), but **allocative inefficiency** results in deadweight loss and reduced welfare (b)

▼

a

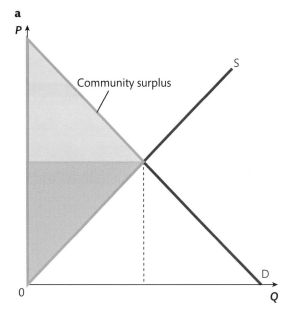

b

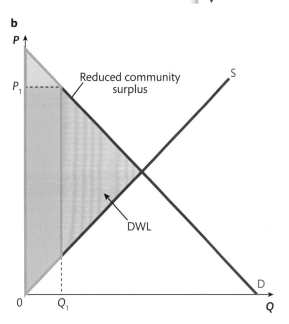

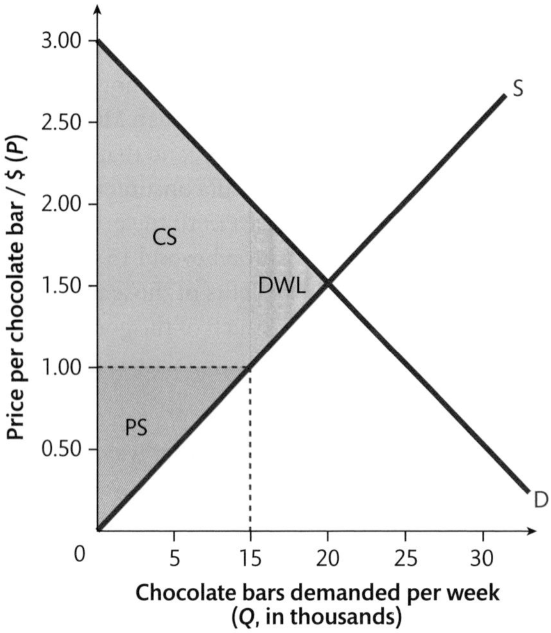

Figure 7.15 Calculating deadweight loss

TOK

As a subject, economics is sometimes reduced to being all about 'supply and demand', or rather the **competitive market equilibrium** you have studied in this chapter. Why is this area of knowledge so important?

Figure 7.15 reinforces the notion that it is only at the free market equilibrium price and quantity that allocative efficiency will be achieved, and community surplus will be maximised. You will study examples of government intervention in Chapter 9 where the equilibrium is not allowed to be in place, and a similar loss in welfare will be the result.

HL Calculating DWL from a diagram

To calculate the area of DWL, use the formula for calculating the area of a triangle:

$$area = \frac{(base \times height)}{2}$$

In the example above:

$$deadweight\ loss = \frac{5{,}000\ bars \times \$1}{2} = \$2{,}500$$

Note the DWL is expressed in money terms, and should reflect the units and amounts of the market being studied.

Exercise 7.2

1 Identify a common product you use or consume.
2 What is the **maximum price** you would pay for that good?
3 What is your consumer surplus for that good?
4 Draw an equilibrium diagram of the market for the good, indicating consumer and producer surplus.
5 Identify the consumer, producer, and community surplus for this market.

Practice exam questions – assessment tips (Paper 1, part (b))

In Chapters 1 and 2, you were introduced to the part (a) sections of Paper 1 assessment. Part (b) requires students to evaluate and sythesise information, as well as using the economics skills you have employed in part (a). Expect to see command terms such as: *compare and contrast, discuss, evaluate, examine,* and *justify.*

Part (b) asks students to see many perspectives on the question and to develop a balanced argument. Competing ideas should be explored and weighed by the writer to show serious judgement.

Part (b) answers are best illustrated with real-world examples that you have collected over the course of your study in each topic. Your instructor may provide some, and your research and inquiry may also.

And, as with part (a) questions, be aware that diagrams are typically useful, if not required, to gain full marks. Below you will find several part (a) questions and a full Paper 1 question.

Practice exam questions

Paper 1, part (a) questions:

1. Using a diagram, explain how an increase in demand for a good will change the market equilibrium.
2. Using a diagram, explain the concepts of consumer surplus, producer surplus, and community surplus.
3. Explain that allocative efficiency is achieved where community surplus is maximised.

Paper 1, full question

a. Using a diagram, explain the effect of a wheat shortage on the price of bread. (10 marks)
b. Discuss the ways a functioning price system uses the signalling and incentive functions to ration resources in a free market economy. (15 marks)

HL Critique of the maximising behaviour of consumers and producers

8

8.1 What classical ideas are being challenged by behavioural economics?

Learning outcomes

At the end of this section you will be able to:

- discuss how classical theory views consumer behaviour
- evaluate the concepts of consumer rationality, utility maximisation, and of perfect information, providing real-world examples.

As is described in Chapter 2, the assumptions and theory presented in this book so far rest largely on a foundation of classical economic theory, a collection of ideas formulated by various economists in the late 1700s to the mid-1800s, primarily in Britain. Adam Smith, Jean-Baptiste Say, and David Ricardo were among the more prominent writers who asserted that humans should be assumed to be rational beings, who weigh the costs and benefits of any decision and act to make their own lives better.

This view may sound obvious and commonplace to modern readers. However, at the time of their writing, this notion was part of a broader movement of liberalism which asserted that 'man' had intrinsic liberty to act freely and independently of traditional bases of authority. Emerging as a distinct branch of Enlightenment thinking, liberalism challenged the prevailing notions of hereditary privilege, state religion, absolute monarchy, and the divine right of kings. Liberalism promoted the concept of natural rights for all people, the rule of law rather than by fiat, and general democracy rather than traditional authoritarianism.

Within economics, Smith and the other classical economists challenged the view of colonial wealth-building by advocating for **free trade** rather than the mercantilist approach that appeared to serve Britain so well at the peak of its empire. Ricardo advanced the concept of **comparative advantage**, about which you can read in Chapter 22, which asserted the virtue of free trade for all actors, regardless of power or efficiency. On the microeconomic level, classical economists presented humans as *homo economicus*, or 'economic man'.

Homo economicus is the idea that human beings are pursuing their own self-interest, acting in a consistently rational manner, while making themselves as 'happy' as possible, on their own terms.

Rational consumer choice

The idea that people are constantly weighing the costs and benefits of any decision and acting in their own interests falls under an area of economic thought known as *rational consumer choice*. This has application in areas outside consumer choice, for example when deciding how much time is reasonable to work and how much time to spend on leisure. However, within consumer theory, rational choice applies mainly to our view of goods and services. We buy, according to classical economists, whatever we like best, taking into account our preferences. Rational choice theory centres on individual preferences and assumes that what is beneficial or not is decided on a personal level.

The perceived value of any good or service matters only to the individual buyer. It is not possible to assign universal value. However, these collective preferences determine the market demand for a good.

Utility maximisation

Recall from Chapter 3 how the concept of utility helped explain the law of demand. Economists broadly define utility as 'satisfaction' or 'contentedness'. Classical economic thought assumed that each of us are utility maximisers, in that all humans seek as much satisfaction or contentment as possible. This view allows for perceived acts of selflessness or charity as ones that generate psychic happiness, if not material success, and still can be considered rational acts for the individual. As applied to consumer theory, utility maximisation assumes that we buy what we buy to maximise our total utility, one purchase at a time. In other words, we buy the most 'important' things, those with the highest utility relative to what we can afford, first, and then move down the line to less essential or less satisfying goods.

Perfect information

Classical free market theory also asserts that buyers hold all the necessary information to make a buying decision. To buy an electric fan, for example, one would know all the product models available, their features, levels of quality, and reliability. And buyers would weigh these variables against their own preferences and budget, and shop accordingly. This theory holds that this is true for all consumers at all times, and for all products. Therefore, whether evaluating supermarket purchases or healthcare procedures, plastic toys or financial instruments, consumers know and understand all their options fluently.

Collectively, the classical economists asserted that homo economicus will always maximise his or her own utility, making rational choices, and using perfect information. It is this view that behavioural economics began to challenge in the middle of the 20th century.

8.2 What does behavioural economics say about the assumptions of rational decision making?

Learning outcomes

At the end of this section you will be able to:

- compare and contrast behavioural economics and classical economics
- examine how cognitive **biases** like rule of thumb, **anchoring**, **framing**, availability, and **imperfect information** conflict with the notion of rational choice.

Behavioural economics is a branch of economic research that adds elements of psychology to traditional models in an attempt to better understand decision making by economic actors. It challenges the assumption that actors will always make rational choices with the aim of maximising utility.

While the classical view of economies as self-regulating mechanisms on the national level was challenged contemporaneously by socialist thinkers like Karl Marx and Friedrich Engels in the 1800s, disputations of the notion of homo economicus only developed a century later, in the mid-1900s. Prominent work in the field has only been recognised by the Nobel Committee in recent years, starting with the awarding of prizes related to behavioural economics in 2002, then 2013, and 2017. Since then, many governments around the world have established behavioural economics groups to inform policy and to create more positive social outcomes by guiding the actions and choices of their citizens.

What is cognitive bias?

Cognitive biases are systematic deviations from rational judgement. The study of cognitive bias has influenced behavioural economics to question the basis of rational decision making as a valid assumption about human behaviour. Cognitive biases are attempts to solve the problem posed by *imperfect information*, which is the idea that consumers are unlikely to be able to absorb and process all correct information to make decisions in a way that rational choice theory would assume. In the absence of the time, energy, and concentration needed to make rational choices, we rely on these biases instead.

Rules of thumb

Also known as heuristics, these are mental short-cuts for decision making to help people make a quick, satisfactory, but often not perfect, decision about a complex choice. 'I only shop when there are sales' is an example. Or 'I always buy my airplane tickets early, because that is when prices are lowest.' These short-cuts will shape choices, even when more research and a fuller understanding of all options would produce a different outcome.

Anchoring

Anchors are mental reference points, relating to ideas or values, which are used to make decisions. One way to look at anchors is that by using them you are giving too much 'weight' to the first piece of information you learn. Anchors can establish a value, imprinting it on our mind. There it serves a reference point for decisions. Retail shops use anchoring by displaying a manufacturer's recommended retail price (MRRP) far above their expected price, and listing a 'sale' much closer to their desired market price. Buyers, influenced by this anchoring effect, may assume they are getting a good deal.

As an illustration, imagine a shopper excited to buy a simple white t-shirt that has been marked down by 75%, from ₹1,600 (₹ is the symbol for the rupee, the currency of India) to ₹400, and thinking he is getting a 'good deal'. In reality, the t-shirt's equilibrium price is closer to ₹400 than to ₹1,600, but the 75% 'sale' creates the perception that it is a great deal.

Framing

Framing is the way that choices are described and presented. Changing the framing of a choice may affect tastes and preferences. Both options have the same outcome, but framing influences the choice.

For example, if given the opportunity to 'save 90 out of 100 lives' or 'risk losing 10 out of 100 lives' many would choose the 'save' option.

Below are some common choices that all have the same outcome. Which would you choose?

* Meat that is advertised as '75% fat free' or '25% fat'.
* A $1,000,000 lottery ticket that says '1 in 10,000 are winners' or '9,999 in 10,000 are losers'.
* Birth control that is '99% effective' or that has a '1% failure rate'.
* Signalling cheap prices by listing a toaster for $19.99, or signalling luxury or taste by round number prices, like a designer bag for $700.

Like other cognitive biases, framing undermines the idea that consumers absorb all the relevant information around every choice, weigh the options completely, and take the more beneficial choice. If consumers behave consistently in a rational way, framing would have little effect.

Availability

Availability bias makes us believe that something is more likely because we have heard of it or that comes to mind first. No deliberate calculation of risk or rewards is involved. Examples could include the following.

* A popular movie depicting shark attacks makes beachgoers reluctant to swim.
* Local news watchers see crime stories every night and vastly overestimate the actual amount of violent crime.
* A spate of colder than usual weather might condition some to ignore data on the incremental process of climate change because their current experience says otherwise.
* Pharmaceutical advertising may underestimate the effectiveness of therapies that do not involve taking medicine and overestimate those that do.

▲

Framing can influence consumer choices. Why would '1% fat', which is the same idea, have a less positive response than '99% fat free'?

Research and inquiry

Find your own examples of cognitive biases shown here. Conduct an internet search for such examples and share them with your class. Do these examples apply to you?

8.3 How does behavioural economics explain consumer decision making?

Learning outcomes

At the end of this section you will be able to:

* discuss how a dual system model of decision making differs from the classical view of rational choice
* examine the concepts of **bounded rationality**, **bounded self-control**, and bounded selfishness, identifying real-world examples.

Behavioural economists Daniel Kahneman and Amos Tversky developed a model that allowed for both views of decision making (that described by the classical economists and those explored by 20th-century behaviouralists) to co-exist.

The dual system model

Kahneman and Tversky's dual system model describes System 1 as the impulsive, irrational, and cognitively biased approach to decisions. System 1 allows for quick decisions based on short-cuts, limited available information, and is susceptible to framing and anchoring effects. System 2 thinking, in contrast, refers to deliberative, reflective, and careful thinking that would more closely resemble the rational analysis implied by homo economicus.

System 1 is used whenever solving problems or making decisions 'without thinking'. It is intuitive, emotional, fast, and prone to error. You would use System 1 when:

- quickly adding 50 + 50
- having a casual chat with your friend
- reading the text on the cover of a magazine
- buying a sweet or dessert after a meal.

System 2 thinking is employed when doing more complex tasks, and involves slow, thoughtful, logical processing. You would use System 2 when:

- multiplying 265×19
- finding the cause of a mysterious ache or pain
- deciding how to invest your money
- buying a house or property.

Of course, humans toggle between these two approaches, depending on their time, interest, and the cost of a particular decision (monetary or intrinsic), among many possible variables. Because we make thousands of decisions every day, System 1 allows us to reserve our time and focus for decisions that we believe require System 2.

Behavioural economics, therefore, builds a case that the notion of humans as cold, rapid cost–benefit calculation machines should be expanded to include a more realistic concept of rationality.

What is bounded rationality?

Bounded rationality suggests that most consumers and businesses do not have enough information to make fully informed choices and so opt to satisfice, rather than maximise their utility. **Satisficing** is a combination of the words 'satisfaction' and 'suffice', meaning that to arrive at this kind of a choice is to find an acceptable, or 'good enough', choice in that context.

Influenced by our cognitive biases, and pressed for time to make thousands of choices every day, humans rely on bounded rationality to make choices. We may not have the brain power to calculate sophisticated decisions, and therefore resort to System 1 thinking and make decisions based on short-cuts, framing, and emotion.

Choosing ice cream in a large supermarket can be a daunting task, with many brands, flavours, and choices on offer. To optimise your choice and select the 'best' may require consultation with your friends or family, checking online reviews, even the sourcing of the milk used (if that is important to you). It is far more likely that one will rely on **rules of thumb** and anchoring, among other cognitive biases, to decide. You may avoid

Research and inquiry

Decoy pricing is a strategy that uses behavioural economic theory to increase revenue by presenting limited choices appealing to cognitive biases. For example, by presenting three differently priced product options, it might point the customer to a medium-priced option by encouraging them to perceive a cheaper version as inferior and a higher-priced version as too expensive for them.

For discussion and debate:

1 Conduct an internet search for examples of decoy pricing.

2 Summarise one example and share it with your class.

ice cream priced too high based on rules of thumb. Furthermore, among the more typically priced brands, you may buy what is on sale if you perceive it to be discounted based on your perceived 'right price'.

Some of behavioural economics research casts doubt on the rigidity of foundational economic concepts, such as the law of demand. In one prominent study, researchers surveyed wine consumers and asked for their perceptions of the quality of wine at different prices. In response, drinkers reported higher levels of satisfaction from wine they were told cost more, even when they were served cheap wine. This suggests that pricing itself can influence the perceived benefits of a good, rather than exclusively a factor on the cost side. Moreover, it also suggests that some businesses might actually be able to sell more of some goods at higher prices than if they were priced lower: a contradiction of the law of demand.

Herd behaviour

The existence of market bubbles also challenges the notion of cold rationality. In markets for financial assets, for instance, if buyers truly behaved in fully rational ways, investors would quickly notice the overvaluation of assets, such as stocks or mortgage bonds, and would sell them off before prices escalated significantly. But often they do not, and prolonged overvaluations (bubbles) take hold, indicating that instead of being rational decision makers, investors are subject to a 'herd mentality'.

Risk and loss aversion

Another facet of bounded rationality is in the area of risk. Generally, research indicates that people tend to feel losses more painfully than the pleasure received from an equal reward.

One way to know if you are risk averse is to ask how you would answer this dilemma: Given two envelopes, one with zł500 (zł is the symbol for the złoty, the currency of Poland) cash and one with zł0, you are asked to either choose from the two envelopes or accept a cash amount instead.

- If offered zł250 cash and you accept, you are 'risk neutral' because you accepted a payoff equal to the probability of your expected payoff from the choice between envelopes.
- If offered zł355 and you decide to try the envelopes, you are generally 'risk tolerant' because you rejected a cash payment that is higher than the expected return of zł250 from the envelopes in the hope of getting lucky and getting the zł500.
- If offered zł245 and you accept, you would be 'risk averse' because you would accept less than the expected payoff from choosing envelopes, since you would prefer the guarantee of zł245 over the 50% chance you get the envelope with nothing in it.

Loss aversion is observable in the use of 'free trials' to consumers. If offered a free trial for a streaming service or grocery delivery service, consumers are less likely to quit after the trial and 'lose' the product. In the same manner, shoppers are not influenced by a 5-cent reward for bringing their own bags, but will do so more often if charged 5 cents.

Economists use the ultimatum game to demonstrate how humans behave irrationally depending on the situation. In the game, one player is given $100 and will offer a split with the other player. If offered less than $50, what would you do? Players rejected such offers much more frequently than offers of $50 or more. This defies rationality, because the players stood to receive no money at all before the game. Why not accept any offer, $1 or higher? $1 is better than $0. But the player's decisions were complicated by notions of what is ethical or fair.

Bounded self-control

Another way of explaining seemingly irrational behaviour is the concept of bounded self-control. In reality, consumers are often not rational in their self-control and do not stop consuming, even when it is sensible to stop. They consume even though the price of the good or service is greater than the marginal utility they gain from consumption.

To understand how consumers could so directly contravene their own rational assessments, the idea of hyperbolic discounting is useful. This is the idea that people can discount future costs in favour of current consumption. Should one buy and eat a second slice of chocolate cake? Consumers can easily devalue the costs of such consumption, which in a small way will contribute to health problems later, and make the less beneficial choice. Tied to this idea of bounded self-control is the idea that people sometimes have difficulty in delaying gratification, and would rather indulge in short-term rewards.

Bounded selfishness

Also known as bounded self-interest, bounded selfishness allows for the fact that people act on behalf of the well-being of others, not only themselves. Why race into a burning building to save a stranger? Why donate money to charity? Acting in accordance with rational cost–benefit analysis, you may not. Bounded selfishness recognises that people sometimes act on perceived moral grounds, or with regard to the social norms of others even when that comes at some risk of a net loss in satisfaction.

Is behavioural economics really new?

To what degree does behavioural economics really challenge the rational behaviour world view? Behavioural economists tend to assert that the less-than-rational individual is a new paradigm, one that should be added alongside the classical view. Critics of this view argue that a definition of humans as rational largely incorporates all the poor decisions described above, that even if a calculation about costs and benefits discounts future costs (see cake example above), this choice still qualifies as a rational choice on its own.

In this view, time and effort used to evaluate all the alternatives is also a cost, and cognitive biases that are described negatively actually help us reduce those costs and make decisions quickly. Furthermore, if rational thinking were only defined as System 2 thinking, nobody on Earth would be considered rational because everyone uses short-cuts. Rational choice has always, it is argued, been subjective, and that the model allows for cognitive bias.

Research and inquiry

Do the wealthy give more to charity than the less wealthy? Explore the notion of bounded selfishness by researching the connection between income level and charity. Look for giving rates expressed as a percentage of income to find a more accurate comparison.

What behavioural economics has contributed, some say, is a more realistic depiction of rational thinking, one that is very good at describing situational behaviour that may appear at-odds with obvious cost–benefit analysis. Nonetheless, if the place of behavioural economics within classical theory is not completely settled, its role in shaping decision making in business and government is more popular than ever.

8.4 Can behavioural economics help governments improve social welfare?

Learning outcomes

At the end of this section you will be able to:

- examine the general approach taken by **nudge theory** towards business decisions and government policy
- discuss how **choice architecture** works to alter choice among consumers and citizens
- compare and contrast default, mandated, and **restricted choices**
- evaluate the extent to which nudge theory can support social welfare.

Governments have begun to take notice of behavioural economics, and in some cases have even launched agencies that put its theories to use in improving social welfare, including through education, legislation, and enforcement. 'Nudging', another application of behavioural economics, uses choice architecture to preserve an aspect of free will while structuring the options to subtly guide behaviour.

What is nudge theory?

Nudge theory rose to prominence with the publication of Richard Thaler and Cass Sunstein's 2008 book *Nudge: Improving Decisions About Health, Wealth, and Happiness*. In it, the authors draw on elements of psychology and economics to develop techniques targeted at specific populations to alter their choices. It has been employed in the private sector and by governments, most notably those of the USA, Singapore, China, and the UK. A nudge, according to Thaler and Sunstein, should not forbid any options or significantly change their incentives. Nudges must be 'cheap and easy to avoid. Nudges are not mandates. Putting fruit at eye level counts as a nudge. Banning junk food does not.'

Therefore, nudge theory is a form of subtle government intervention, but one that does not change the basic cost–benefit analysis. Taxes, subsidies, and price controls all change the fundamental cost–benefit ratio, while nudge policy presents the choice in a different way, to encourage the socially beneficial choice.

Some prominent examples of successful nudge experiments include the following.

- Putting healthy food at the cash desk of train station kiosks in Dutch train stations.
- Making organ donation the **default choice** in Spain, where citizens must opt-out of the programme if they do not wish to donate.
- On energy bills, the display of average use by neighbours and conservation tips to reduce energy consumption in the UK.

What is choice architecture?

Choice architecture is a collection of tactics designed to shape decision making that use the layout, sequencing, and range of choices that are available. Firms and governments use choice architecture to generate more of the results they desire.

Nearly all retail environments employ choice architecture to maximise profits. Luxury goods with high prices are prominently displayed. To find necessities, one must hunt to the further reaches of the store. When entering a large department store, the sales of fragrances, makeup, and beauty products are staged on the main floor, while shirts and shoes will be further away. Supermarkets put sweets at the cash desk, knowing that after an hour of shopping, few customers can resist the temptation.

What are defaults?

Defaults are choice frameworks where one option is pre-selected and the decision maker must take active steps to opt-out of the scheme. Organ donation, as noted above, as well as the enrolment of college students into health insurance plans, and enrolment into savings plans, all have used default options to encourage the desired behaviour.

Defaults are believed to be successful in part because the decision maker views the default choice as an endorsement of the selection by a more informed party. Default selection may be influenced by status quo bias: the notion that behavioural inertia reduces people's appetite for change, as well as the extra effort required to opt-out of a choice. Defaults tend to work well in situations where the 'presumed consent' fits the target population. However, this can lead to strong objections where such a presumption is out of line with popular sentiment. When installing software, consumers generally prefer having a recommended setting rather than choosing from many alternatives. With organ donation, the presumption can be taken negatively.

What are mandated choices?

Mandated choices are when consumers are required to state whether or not they wish to take part in an action. Also known as a choice requirement, one that typically forces a choice before continuing along a process. Compared to defaults, required choice presents the options as relatively equal, and any choice as more explicitly voluntary. In the organ donation example, mandated choice is sometimes more popular than default mechanisms. For example, in the US state of Illinois, people are asked if they would like to choose organ donation as they are receiving their drivers licences. This has increased the positive response rate significantly.

What are restricted choices?

Restricted choice is when the choice of a consumer is restricted, but still exists. The placement of healthy food at eye level is an example. With little effort, junk food lovers can still buy what they want, but consumers who are acting quickly will buy a healthy option with that subtle change in placement. Restaurants use restricted choice and anchoring to encourage spending by having a menu item that is much more expensive than all the others. They do not expect many to order the item, but to instead order the next most expensive. Having been anchored by the higher price, consumers feel permission to order the next lower option. Credit card companies have managed to lower the payback rate, and therefore earn more on interest, by stating a 'minimum amount due' on all bills.

Research and inquiry

Using your school's library research engines and your own search tactics, investigate how choice architecture influences decision making in different contexts (for example, its role in a supermarket, or how it may influence the rate of organ donation in different countries).

A social credit system is a means of generating a unified reputation score on one's behaviour in a prescribed set of community interactions. Using nudge theory rather than laws to affect behaviour, the system has positive behaviours add to one's score, and negative ones reduce it. Examples of negative behaviour that can be cited are playing loud music, failure to sort personal waste, and generally dishonest behaviour. Positive acts, like giving money to charity or volunteering, can add to the score. Based on such 'trustworthiness' scores, a citizen may be approved or denied choices of housing, travel, and use of public services.

For discussion and debate:

1 Conduct an internet search into the different examples of social credit systems in various countries.

2 Using multiple perspectives of the possible stakeholders affected by such a policy, discuss the ways in which social credit systems may have positive and negative effects.

Nudge theory can be viewed as an attempt to apply the behavioural critique of classical economics to improve social outcomes. If consumers do not behave rationally, in the strictest classical sense, because of time constraints, complexity, or emotion, nudge-based policymaking can fill the information gap, save time, and improve results. Firms, too, can use this approach to raise profits (though not always to improve social outcomes).

At the same time, critics are debating whether nudges amount to 'liberal paternalism' that denies true freedom of choice and the extent to which nudges become 'shoves' and the state's behaviour becomes coercive. Preliminary studies of the acceptance of policies based on nudge theory suggests that countries with high trust in government regard it most positively, and those with low trust in government regard it with the most suspicion.

What about the maximising behaviour of producers?

Producers and consumers have rather oppositional aims when each is 'maximising' on their own behalf. As we have seen, the theory suggests that consumers are generally trying to maximise their *utility*. Producers, we assume, are trying to maximise *profits*. Throughout this chapter, we have called into question whether rational consumers really maximise utility all the time, and it is fair to question whether producers always maximise profits. In fact, in Chapter 11, we will explore business strategies that specifically avoid pure profit maximisation, such as satisficing and increasing **market share**.

Case study – behavioural economics used to fight a pandemic

The coronavirus pandemic and consequent spread of COVID-19 disease starting in 2020 was viewed as a complicated scientific, health, economic, and behaviour problem. Early on, it became evident that part of the solution to the spread of the virus was changing behaviour. 'Bending the curve' meant reducing rates of infection to avoid overwhelming health systems and to buy time to develop treatments and vaccines. In particular, the need for everyone to behave differently made spread prevention a collective action problem. In these problems, everyone would be better off if everyone cooperated but may not do so because of competing interests that make it difficult to work together.

Remember the assumption of perfect information? In the best of times, and under clear scientific consensus, techniques like vaccinations against common disease have become areas of controversy. In a pandemic where little is known, information changes daily, and initial opinions are revised, many people found it difficult to process and understand the complex sets of information shared every day. 'Is there enough testing? How many cases is too many? How big a risk am I taking going to the gym?' Information is decidedly imperfect.

Behavioural economics and psychology also described other reactions to the pandemic. Besides status quo bias, one area of cognitive bias at work in the crisis was loss aversion as people rushed to stores and stocked up on food, cleaning products, and toilet paper. Was this rational? Game theorists point out that if everyone believes the stores will be sold out, it makes sense to ensure your own supply. Another was optimism bias, the idea that one's odds of suffering the disease were lower than they actually were, going to clubs, religious gatherings, and densely populated events.

Because the virus required collective action, governments were challenged to encourage self-sacrifice, trust, and cooperation. As the causes of COVID-19 became more clear, nudge theory was employed to educate the population to the risks, and to aggressively attack the status quo bias against preventative actions. To change behaviour without draconian legal tactics, authorities, schools, and businesses resorted to several different nudge techniques.

- Posting clear signs encouraging social distancing of between 1 and 3 metres.
- Multi-media advertising of the need to wash hands.
- Community leaders modelling mask-wearing to encourage compliance.
- Marking floors with socially distanced places to stand while waiting in line at the cash desk as an example of choice architecture.
- Social media campaigns to wash hands thoroughly, while singing 'happy birthday'.
- Government press conferences in the UK with messages written on the front of the podium, in camera view, saying 'Stay Home. Protect the NHS. Save Lives'.
- The free distribution of masks to the poor or anyone who wanted them.

Social distancing and mask wearing in public

Some measures like quarantine orders, mask requirements in public spaces, and work-from-home rules were also reinforced by fines and threats of imprisonment. However, in most instances, authorities relied on the more direct and indirect persuasive tactics. Here, as in the examples of nudge tactics above, social trust as well as trust in one's government, played a key role in predicting compliance with the new rules.

Discussion questions:

1 What kind of rules did your school or local government put into place to encourage safe behaviour?
2 What kinds of biases did these tactics attempt to diminish?
3 Was compliance widespread or fragmented? Why do you think this was true?
4 Would you change some of the tactics employed, or when they were employed?
5 Why might guidelines based on nudge theory be preferable to legal enforcement?

Practice exam questions

Paper 1, part (a)

1. Distinguish between the classical view and behavioural view of rational decision making. (10 marks)

Paper 1, full question

a. Using three cognitive biases, explain how consumers can be guided when making buying decisions. (10 marks)
b. Evaluate, using real-world examples, the degree to which nudge theory may be used to create more socially efficient outcomes. (15 marks)

Real-world issue 2

When are markets unable to satisfy important economic objectives — and does government intervention help?

- The **market mechanism** may result in socially undesirable outcomes that do not achieve **efficiency**, environmental **sustainability**, and/or **equity**.
- Market failure, resulting in allocative inefficiency and welfare loss.
- Resource overuse, resulting in challenges to environmental **sustainability**.
- Inequity, resulting in inequalities.
- Governments have policy tools that can affect market outcomes, and government **intervention** is effective, to varying degrees, in different real-world markets.

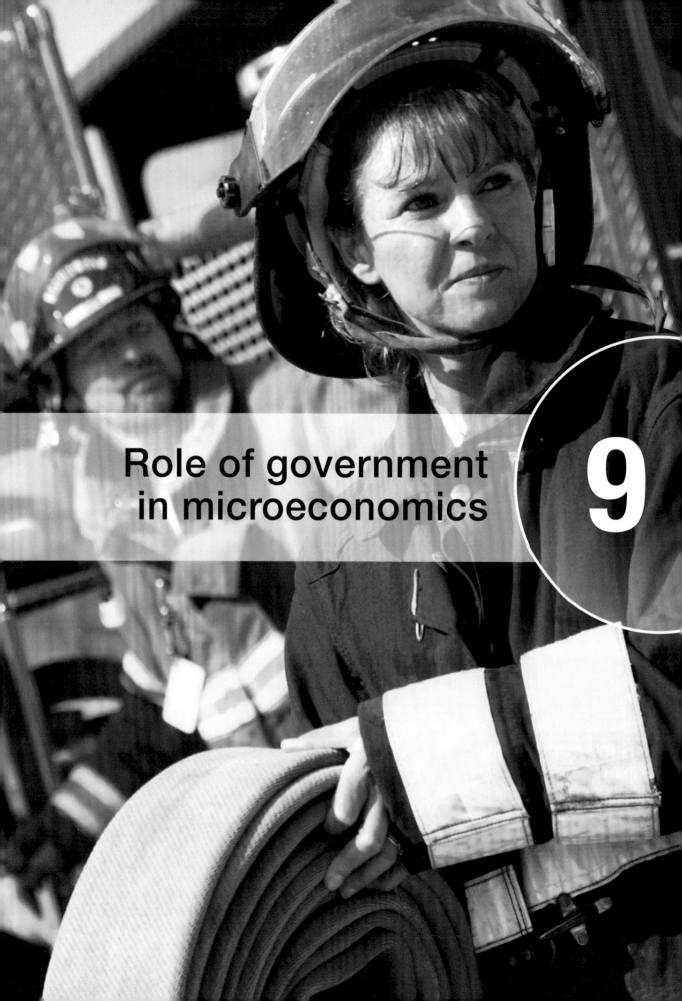

Role of government in microeconomics

9

9.1 Reasons for government intervention in markets

Learning outcomes

At the end of this section you will be able to:

- comment on the reasons for government **intervention** in markets.

In Chapter 1 we introduced a different range of economic systems, with completely free market economies and centrally planned economies at the two extremes and the most common systems, mixed economies, found in the middle of the spectrum between free market and centrally planned economies. Every national economy in the 21st century (except perhaps that of North Korea) falls somewhere in between the two extremes of the spectrum of economic freedom; in other words, almost all economies exhibit some characteristics of free markets and some of planned economies. Government intervenes in the economy in various ways to promote economic objectives that are unmet by the free market system.

When are markets unable to satisfy important economic objectives?

Markets are great at providing society with most of the goods and services people desire. When there is a large enough group of willing buyers for a product, their demand signals potential producers that there is a willingness to pay for the good or service. In response, entrepreneurs form businesses to gather the resources needed to produce the good and to supply it to the buyers. Like magic, a market is formed to satisfy society's wants.

However, the market mechanism may result in undesirable outcomes that do not achieve **efficiency**, **environmental sustainability**, and/or **equity**. When markets fall short of these desired outcomes, there may be a need for government intervention.

When markets fail

Additionally, **market failures** may result, in which particular goods are either overproduced or underproduced due to the existence of negative or positive effects imposed on third parties arising from their production or consumption. Sometimes markets fail to achieve **allocative efficiency**, as it is described in Chapter 7, and in these cases government intervention might help promote a more desirable level of production that increases overall social welfare.

When sustainability is threatened

Markets also sometimes result in resource **overuse**, which threatens the overall sustainability of the economic system as a whole. A system is sustainable when it is able to endure in its current form indefinitely for generation after generation. The market often under-values or under-prices non-renewable resources, resulting in their exploitation in the present at a rate that depletes them faster than they can be replenished. When resources are overused today, they will be unavailable for future generations, thus the system under which they are exploited becomes unsustainable.

To fund government

The very existence of a government requires a funding mechanism to allow the government to operate. It may seem odd to state this, but the government itself is a good that is not provided under a free market system. To finance the functions of government, some degree of intervention in the market is necessary. Taxes on income, production, or consumption, for instance, help generate the revenues necessary for the government system to function; thus, intervention in markets is a necessary condition for the very existence of government.

To promote equity

Governments may also intervene in the market to support firms or households through subsidies or transfers (when income is reallocated through taxes from one group in society to another). Government intervention can influence both the level of production and of consumption in a market to correct market failures or to promote equity.

Does government intervention help?

Governments have policy tools that can affect market outcomes, and government intervention is effective, to varying degrees, in different real-world markets. However, government intervention does not always improve market outcomes, and one of the roles economists play as social scientists seeking to understand markets is to evaluate the extent to which government intervention is necessary, and when it exists how well it achieves its stated intention, be that to raise revenues for government, to help producers or consumers, to incentivise more or less production of a good, to provide a good that might not be provided by the free market, or to regulate a good's production or consumption to promote sustainability, equity, efficiency, or any other welfare-increasing outcome that might not have been possible under free market conditions.

9.2 Price controls

Learning outcomes

At the end of this section you will be able to:

- explain why governments impose price controls, giving examples
- **HL** analyse the impacts, using diagrams, of price ceilings and price floors on market outcomes
- comment on the possible consequences of price controls for markets
- discuss the consequences for **stakeholders** of imposing price controls.

While free markets have many virtues, there are situations where the outcomes are not optimal for all the participants. In some of these situations, the government enacts maximum prices or minimum prices in order to benefit either consumers or producers.

Price ceilings

A price ceiling is a maximum price imposed by the government below the equilibrium price in a market. In this market situation, the government determines that there is a

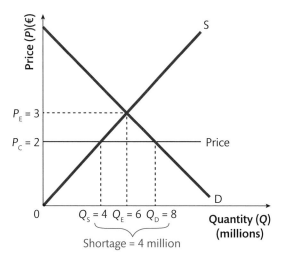

Figure 9.1 The imposition of a price ceiling leads to shortage

potential for higher than desired prices, and makes a goal of keeping prices low. Often governments take this step to make basic goods and services more affordable for lower income households. Thus, by preventing an increase, the government places a 'ceiling' on the price of a good.

Assume the French government wishes to keep baguettes (a small loaf of bread) affordable for people of all income levels; therefore, the government sets a maximum price of €2 per baguette in the market. Without the price ceiling, let us assume the equilibrium price of baguettes would be €3. Figure 9.1 shows the daily baguette market with the price ceiling in place.

Under free market conditions, the price of a baguette would be €3 (P_E) and the equilibrium quantity would be 6 million baguettes per day (Q_E). The French government has imposed a ceiling price of €2 (P_C), however, which has led to a greater quantity demanded (8 million) and a smaller quantity supplied (4 million). The lower price imposed by the government has sent signals to French consumers to demand

137

more baguettes and to French bakers to bake fewer baguettes. The laws of demand and supply drive a wedge between the quantities demanded and the quantity supplied, resulting in a daily shortage of baguettes.

What are the effects of price ceilings?

As we can see from Figure 9.1, a price ceiling has several effects on the market, including the following.

Shortages

With a binding price ceiling (i.e. one that is actually below the equilibrium price) producers will reduce output while consumers demand more, creating a shortage in which there is excess demand for the product.

Rationing

Without price to guide the rationing of the good, consumers and producers will use other means to determine who receives the product. Some methods of rationing include government-created ration cards or vouchers, which may have their own system by which consumers receive the product (perhaps 'family size' if the product is a staple food). Waiting in line for a scarce good is common. Additionally, special barter deals may be arranged with the seller, which effectively increase the price of the good.

Decreased market size

With the reduced quantity supplied, less of the good is produced, reducing employment opportunities in the affected industry and the actual level of consumption among buyers.

Increased consumer surplus

The intent of a price ceiling like that on baguettes in the example is to make a staple good more affordable to consumers. To that end it succeeds, but the trade-off is fewer overall consumers. While some people are able to buy the price-controlled good at a discount compared to the equilibrium price, fewer people overall will have access to the good. In the case of our baguettes, this may mean that bakeries are sold out of fresh baguettes by 11 a.m. every day, and people who cannot make it to the bakery by that time are unable to have a fresh loaf of bread. At a higher price, bakers might be willing to bake enough bread to keep their shelves stocked all day long.

Elimination of allocative efficiency

Allocative efficiency is achieved when marginal benefits (MB, represented by the demand curve) equal marginal costs (MC, represented by the supply curve). The price ceiling eliminates this efficiency. Now, the price is set by the government, not where MB = MC. Society is not producing enough of the good with the price ceiling in place. Figure 9.2 shows the deadweight loss (DWL) that results from a binding price ceiling.

- The lower price has increased consumer surplus relative to what it would have been at equilibrium.
- Producer surplus is reduced, since less of the good is sold at a lower price.

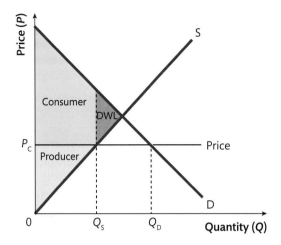

- The red area represents the DWL, or the loss of overall efficiency and welfare created by price ceiling. The increase in consumer surplus is less than the decrease in producer surplus, so overall the market is made worse off.

Emergence of black markets

The disequilibrium created by a price ceiling puts pressure on sellers to withhold their output from the formal market and instead sell it on the informal or black market. Whenever there is an imbalance between the quantity demanded of a good and the quantity supplied, sellers will turn to the black market to meet the excess demand by selling their product at a higher price than the government's ceiling price. This undermines the validity of the price control's intended outcome; instead of buying baguettes at the more affordable €2 each, buyers may be forced to turn to the black market where they can be purchased at €4, a price higher than what the market would have provided them for without any government intervention.

What are some examples of price ceilings?

Besides staple foods, governments have implemented price controls on all sorts of goods and services in an effort to aid consumers. Some **common markets** in which the government places maximum prices include health insurance, taxi fares, diapers and baby food, certain prescription drugs, and, notably, the market for low-income housing.

Rent controls, as price ceilings in the housing market are called, have been employed by countless cities around the world to control increases in rental rates for housing within their jurisdictions in order to make housing more affordable for middle and lower income residents. The city of Oakland, California, for instance, has a rent control law that prohibits the rate of increase in rents from exceeding the rate of inflation. For instance, if inflation for 2020 turned out to be 1%, then no landlord in the city of Oakland would be allowed to increase rent by more than 1% between 2020 and 2021, no matter what the conditions in the market for housing are.

Figure 9.3 shows the impact rent controls might have had on the market for two-bedroom apartments in the city of Oakland assuming that housing demand increased at a steady rate between 2020 and 2021.

The actual demand for two-bedroom apartments has increased from *D* in 2020 to *D* in 2021. With higher demand landlords are motivated to charge higher rents; the

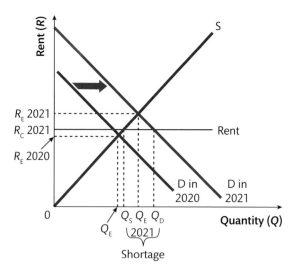

Figure 9.3 Rent controls limit the rate of increase in rents but also lead to shortage

equilibrium rent increases from R_E 2020 to R_E 2021. However, due to the city's new law limiting rent increases to the rate of inflation, the allowable increase in rent is only to R_C 2021. At this lower than equilibrium rental rate, the quantity supplied of apartments only increases incrementally, from Q_E 2020 to Q_S, while the quantity demanded increases more dramatically (to Q_D), resulting in a shortage of affordable housing of $Q_D - Q_S$.

As with all price ceilings, the intended beneficiaries of the rent control are both helped and harmed. The lucky renters who are able to find apartments at R_C 2021 are better off than they would have been had rent been allowed to increase to R_E 2021. However, there is now excess demand for affordable housing. Some families that wish to rent an apartment are unable to find an available unit. Landlords who might have been willing to put their units onto the rental market at R_E 2021 are unwilling to do so at R_C 2021, due to the reduced potential for profits at the government's allowable rental rate.

Price ceilings create winners (the lucky consumers who get the good at the controlled price) and losers (consumers who are cut out of the market and producers). When binding, they reduce market size, require a system of rationing, and reduce allocative efficiency, creating more harm than good for the market overall.

However, when implemented carefully, which might mean combining them with other forms of government intervention such as subsidies (outlined later in this chapter), price controls can improve access to essential items like food, sanitation products, and affordable housing, to those who otherwise might be unable to afford these goods. In this way, price ceilings can increase equity and equality in society, levelling the playing field for those who otherwise might be left behind by the free market system.

Price floors

Whereas a price ceiling is set by the government below equilibrium to help consumers, a price floor is the opposite: a minimum price set above the equilibrium price in a market aimed at helping producers of the good.

Price floors are often established to help producers of essential commodities like food crops earn an income that allows them to continue in the market even when equilibrium prices fall to a level at which they might otherwise choose to leave the

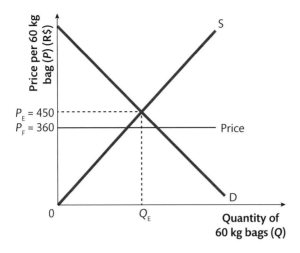

Figure 9.4 A price floor set below the market equilibrium price has no effect

market. Another popular price floor used in many countries is the minimum wage, which is used to guarantee 'working class' individuals a living wage and to prevent the blatant exploitation of lower income labourers by employers that have the power to control the wage rate they pay their workers.

Consider the market for coffee, shown in Figure 9.4. Coffee is one of Brazil's key agricultural products and a source of income for thousands of Brazilian farmers. In an effort to protect the incomes of coffee farmers, and assure they can cover the costs of keeping their plantations operational year after year, Brazil's government sets a price floor for coffee of R\$360 (R\$ is the symbol for the real (plural: reais), the Brazilian currency) per 60 kg of coffee. As long as the market equilibrium price is higher than R\$360, this floor price remains non-binding. But if market conditions drive the price below R\$360 reais, the government steps in to enforce its floor price.

At the current equilibrium price (P_E) of R\$450 the government's price floor is non-binding. In other words, it has no effect on the market. However, if market conditions were to change in a way that the equilibrium price were to decrease, the price floor would become binding and the government would step in to enforce the minimum price. Figure 9.5 shows a situation in which the supply of coffee increased (perhaps due to coffee imports from Ecuador), driving the market price down to R\$300 per 60 kg bag.

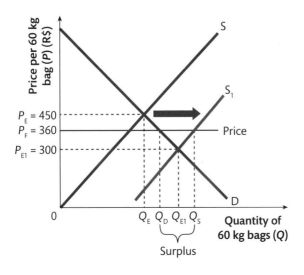

Figure 9.5 A price floor comes into effect where an increase in supply drives the market equilibrium price down

Supply has increased, driving equilibrium price down to R\$300 at P_{E1}. The price floor of R\$360 is now binding; sellers are not allowed to sell coffee below this price. Therefore, the quantity demanded increases only slightly, from Q_E to Q_D, while the quantity supplied increases more than it otherwise might have from Q_E to Q_S. There is now a surplus of coffee in the Brazilian market, also known as excess supply.

In order to enforce its price floor and avoid the emergence of black markets in which coffee growers unload their excess supply at illegally low prices, Brazil's government must intervene further and purchase the extra beans from farmers. This, in essence, props up market demand and keeps the price steady at R\$360. We will examine the effect of government payments to sellers later in this chapter when we look at subsidies.

What are the effects of price floors?

As with price ceilings, binding floor prices will have several effects on a market, including the following.

Surplus output

The laws of demand and supply dictate that a price set above equilibrium will necessarily result in reduced quantity demanded and increased quantity supplied. The excess supply this creates is known as a surplus (not to be confused with consumer surplus and producer surplus, which represent welfare and should be maximised, a 'surplus' represents wasted resources and should be avoided).

Reduced market size

Whereas price ceilings reduce the market size because less is produced, a price floor reduces the market size because less is demanded.

Allocative inefficiency

When quantity supplied exceeds quantity demanded, the MC (represented by supply) producers face is higher than the MB (represented by demand) that consumers derive from the last unit of the good produced. In other words, resources are overallocated towards the price-controlled good since the cost of producing the last unit exceeds the value consumers place on it.

Figure 9.6 The increase in producer surplus under a binding price floor is less than the loss of consumer surplus, creating deadweight loss

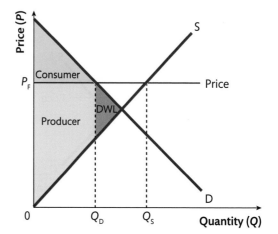

- The higher price has increased producer surplus relative to what it would have been at equilibrium.
- Consumer surplus is reduced, since less of the good is demanded at a higher price.
- The red area in Figure 9.6 represents the DWL, or the loss of overall efficiency and welfare created by price ceiling. The increase in producer surplus is less than the decrease in consumer surplus, so overall the market is made worse off.

Informal markets

Output that remains unsold due to a price floor might be bought by the government (in the case of coffee in Brazil), but in the absence of a government scheme to purchase surplus output it might also be disposed of (every year dairy farmers dump tonnes of milk down the drain thanks to excess output resulting from price control schemes) or, in some cases, sold on the black market. Unlike in the case of price ceilings, in which case shortages are relieved by goods being sold on the black market at prices higher than the government's maximum price, when price floors are in place excess output might end up being sold at prices below the floor price on the black market. Such undercutting of the government's price floor undermines the intended effect of the price control, but also prevents the excess output from going to waste.

What are some examples of price floors?

Perhaps the most commonly used price floor is the minimum wage. Most countries have them, and in many cases individual states, provinces, or municipalities will impose a minimum wage that is higher than the national wage floor. Minimum wages are very controversial, and for good reason. Helping workers at the lowest rung of the income ladder seems like an easy way to increase equality in society and reduce the gap between rich and poor that inevitably arises under the market economic system.

Figure 9.7 shows the effect of a $15 minimum wage imposed by the American city of Seattle on the market for fast food restaurant workers. The previous minimum wage of $10 per hour was non-binding, meaning that no fast food restaurants were actually paying a wage that low. Instead, the equilibrium wage rate had been $12, deemed too low by the city's governing council for a worker to be able to afford to live in Seattle.

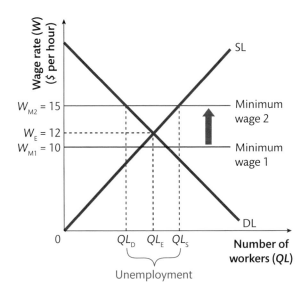

Figure 9.7 A minimum wage creates unemployment

Research and inquiry

Starting in 2014, the US city of Seattle began phasing in a minimum wage increase from the state of Washington's minimum of $9.47 per hour to $11, then a year later to $13 per hour, and finally, in January 2017, to $15 per hour. In a 2017 study, the University of Washington, located in Seattle, released a study of the impact of the city's minimum wage policy.

Perform a web search using the terms 'Seattle minimum wage study' to find articles about the study's finding or even the study itself. Investigate the study's key findings, then discuss the questions below with your class or answer them yourself.

For discussion and debate:

1   Did the Seattle minimum wage study support or refute the conclusions of our analysis of minimum wages on the level of employment as demonstrated in Figure 9.7?

2   We concluded in our analysis that 'workers who are unable to find a job at the higher minimum wage are worse off'. What evidence is there in the Seattle minimum wage study to support or refute this conclusion?

3   What were the limitations of the Seattle minimum wage study? What did the researchers conclude they could do in future studies to provide a clearer picture of the effects of increasing the minimum wage?

SL represents the supply of labour in the fast food industry, or how many workers are willing to work in fast food restaurants at a range of wage rates. *DL* represents the demand for workers, or how many workers fast food restaurants are willing to employ at a range of wage rates. W_{M1} is the previous minimum wage; it was below the actual market wage rate of $12 ($W_E$), therefore it was non-binding. When city council votes to raise the minimum wage to $15, the price floor becomes binding; at the higher wage rate more people wish to take jobs in fast food restaurants (up from QL_E to QL_S) while restaurants wish to employ fewer people (down from QL_E to QL_D).

The increase in the quantity supplied of labour in the face of layoffs by fast food restaurants creates a situation in which unemployment results. More job applications are being submitted to restaurants that are actually looking to replace workers with technology or simply make their existing employees do more work with reduced staffing. As with other price controls, minimum wages have their winners and losers.

Winners of minimum wages

Workers who are able to find jobs at the binding minimum wage are better off than they would have been with no minimum wage; they will have more disposable income and will enjoy a higher quality of life.

Some argue that overall demand is increased by a minimum wage. Because the higher wage earners spend their additional money into the circular flow (often on goods like food, rent, and consumer goods), overall demand increases. This increased demand offsets the increased wage job losses or may even create more employment opportunities in those industries.

Losers of minimum wages

Workers who are unable to find jobs at the higher wage rate are worse off. They may remain unemployed until an opening comes up at a fast food restaurant or may seek work in another industry. However, with most minimum wages applying across all industries the outcome may just be higher unemployment across the economy.

Producers (fast food restaurants in this example) are worse off. Wages are the resource cost of labour; higher resource costs are a determinant of supply, so the market supply curve of industries affected by minimum wages should decrease, resulting in higher prices, less output, and reduced profits.

Consumers in the affected industry are worse off. As stated above, reduced supply drives prices up in the industries in which minimum wages have increased producers' costs. Higher prices lead to reduced quantity demanded and less consumer surplus among the consumers of the finished product. Fast food consumers should expect higher menu prices when a binding minimum wage is imposed in the market for fast food workers.

As with price ceilings, price floors are complicated in that there are not clear winners and losers. Some producers are made better off by price controls, but not all. Government should think carefully before imposing price floors on a market, and consider important questions like whether surpluses will be created, and if so, what is the least inefficient way to dispose of the excess supply and whether unemployment will increase, and if so, who will support affected workers when they can no longer find a job due to an increase in the minimum wage.

HL Calculating the effects of price controls

With some simple maths is it possible to calculate the effects of price controls on a market.

Worked example 9.1

Consider the maximum price imposed by the city of London on taxi fares of £8 per kilometre. At peak commuting hours, the fare the market is willing to pay is much higher than the maximum, at £12 per kilometre. Therefore, the price ceiling is binding during peak hours. With only 10,000 kilometres of taxi transport provided and 15,000 kilometres demanded, there is a shortage of taxis during peak hours.

With the price ceiling in effect, we can calculate the impact on consumers (or commuters, in this case), producers (taxi drivers), and the market as a whole.

Consumer surplus has increased. Before the price ceiling consumer surplus was represented by the green triangle above P_E and below the demand curve (dotted green in Figure 9.8). With the maximum fare in place, there is a new area representing consumer surplus, shown as dotted green in Figure 9.9. The change in consumer surplus can be determined by adding the new dotted green rectangle below £12 and above £8 and subtracting the top portion of the DWL triangle.

$$Increase\ in\ CS = (12-8) \times 10,000) - \frac{(15-12) \times 2000}{2}$$

$$= 40,000 - 3000 = 37,000$$

The maximum fare causes consumer surplus to increase by £37,000.

$$Loss\ in\ PS = (12-8) \times 10,000 + \frac{(12-8) \times 2000}{2} = 40,000 + 4000$$

$$= 44,000$$

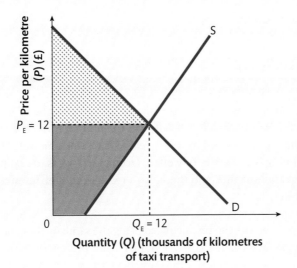

Video suggestion:
Price controls can be described as the bluntest of instruments at a government's disposal for influencing market outcomes. For this reason, they are often heavily criticised by economists.

▶ Simply click here in your eBook for a video in which economist Milton Friedman answers a student's question about the wisdom of the government's use of wage and price controls.

Questions for discussion:

1 How might governments justify the use of price controls as a 'cure for inflation'?

2 In his analogy of a kettle on a stove, is the kettle's lid used as an example of a price floor or a price ceiling?

3 If Friedman opposes price ceilings as a way of preventing prices from rising, what does he think is a better way to maintain low and stable inflation in an economy? (Hint: this one requires some knowledge of macroeconomic policy, which of course you have not studied yet, but give it your best shot!)

Figure 9.8 Total surplus in the market for taxi transport without any price controls is maximised, even at peak hours

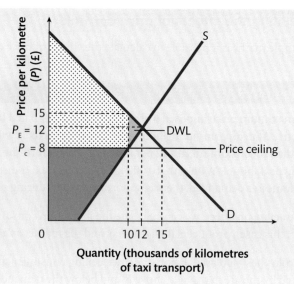

Figure 9.9 With a maximum price for taxi journeys imposed there is a loss of community surplus at peak hours

Taxi drivers are worse off. We can see that a portion of their surplus from before the price ceiling has been transferred to consumers. In addition, the lower portion of the DWL triangle in Figure 9.9 is also lost to producers. The sum of these two areas represents the loss in producer surplus.

Producer surplus is reduced by £44,000. This represents the lost income and welfare of taxi drivers who are willing to drive fewer kilometres and allowed to charge a lower fare than they would if the market were allowed to set its own equilibrium price.

Finally, we can calculate the amount of DWL resulting from the price control, which represents the lost surplus across the entire market resulting from the government intervention. There are two ways to calculate DWL. It can be found by subtracting the loss in producer surplus from the increase in consumer surplus, or by calculating the area of the red DWL triangle in Figure 9.9.

$$DWL = 37,000 - 44,000 = -7000$$

or

$$DWL = \frac{(15-8) \times 2,000}{2} = 7000$$

The first method gave us a negative result. This is because the £7,000 of DWL does in fact represent a *loss of welfare* in the market for taxi transport. Calculating the area of the red triangle yielded the same amount. The end result of the price ceiling is a transfer of welfare from taxi drivers to taxi passengers, but a loss of overall surplus (and therefore a reduction in **efficiency**) in the taxi transport market.

The effects of price floors can be calculated using the same method: finding the areas of rectangles and triangles on our graphs that represent the changes in producer and consumer surplus or the DWL from the government's intervention in the market.

9.3 Indirect taxes and subsidies

At the end of this section you will be able to:

- explain why governments impose indirect taxes
- distinguish between specific and ad valorem taxes
- **HL** draw diagrams to show specific and ad valorem taxes and analyse their impacts on market outcomes
- discuss the consequences for market stakeholders of imposing an indirect tax.

How do indirect taxes affect a market?

Indirect taxes are those taxes placed on goods and services. They are described as indirect because the government collects the revenues from the supplier after the supplier has collected them from the purchaser. Therefore, the government collects the money from the consumer indirectly. A sales tax is collected by the seller and delivered to the government: it is an indirect tax.

Indirect taxes can take either of two forms:

- a specific tax – the amount of the tax is a fixed value per unit of output, such as $2 per pack of cigarettes
- an ad valorem tax – the amount of tax is a percentage of the sale, such as a value added tax (VAT) of 19% on the sales of most goods is an ad valorem tax.

The term 'excise tax' is used to refer to the taxing of one type of good, like cigarettes, alcohol, or hotel accommodation. Excise taxes can be either specific or ad valorem.

In contrast, income taxes are collected by the government directly from the individual or household, and are therefore called **direct taxes**. Firms generally view taxes as an increase in their operating costs because the tax is likely to erode the profitability of their product. For this reason, economists show the effect of the tax as a decrease in supply: a shift left of supply at all prices. This shift is shown differently, however, depending on whether the tax is specific tax or ad valorem tax.

What is a specific tax?

Specific taxes charge a fixed amount to be paid for every unit of a good sold. Figure 9.10 shows the initial effect of a specific, per-unit tax of ₦6,000 (₦ is the symbol for the naira, the currency of Nigeria) on tyres. The supply curve shifts upward the amount of the tax, from S to S_1. This is a parallel shift because the amount of the per-unit tax is the same no matter the price or quantity of units. Whether a tyre sells for ₦60,000 or ₦150,000, the tax the seller must pay to the government will be the same at ₦6,000 per tyre.

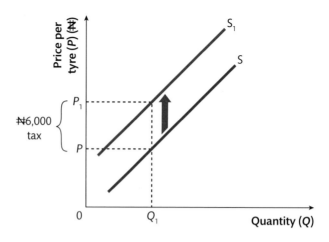

Figure 9.10 A specific, per-unit tax will shift the supply curve upwards ▶

What is an ad valorem tax?

In contrast to direct taxes, ad valorem taxes base the tax on a percentage of the purchase price. Therefore, the higher the price of the good, the greater the amount of tax paid by producers to the government. Consider the effect of an ad valorem tax of 50% on tyres. The seller will pay the government ₦50,000 for a tyre that sells for ₦100,000 but will have to pay ₦25,000 on a tyre that sells for ₦50,000. Figure 9.11 shows the effect of an ad valorem tax. Supply still shifts upward by the amount of the tax, but the distance between S and S_1 grows as the price increases. This reflects the increased amount of tax charged as the price increases.

While the value of the tax increases at higher prices, the percentage of the tax relative to the price is the same. $P_1 - P$ is half the distance between P_1 and 0. $P_3 - P_2$ is half of $P_3 - 0$, but larger than $P_1 - P$. As price has increased, the amount of tax the seller has to pay the government increases with it.

Video suggestion:
You have read about it, now you can review what you have just learned by watching a video by the author!

▶ Simply click here in your eBook for a video on the effects of a tax on supply.

Who shares in the burden of a tax?

Let us look at the effect of a specific per-unit tax imposed on a market with a downward-sloping demand curve and an upward-sloping supply curve. Figure 9.12 shows decrease in supply resulting from a specific, per-unit tax of $P_1 - P_E$.

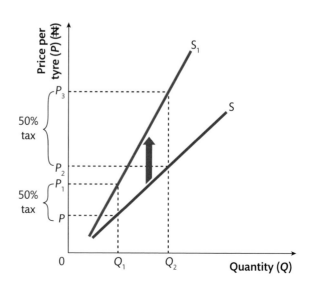

Figure 9.11 An ad valorem tax will cause the new supply curve to diverge from the original one ▶

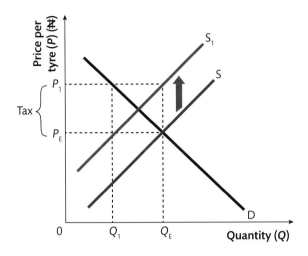

Figure 9.12 Adding the full amount of a specific tax to the price creates a surplus

The tax has shifted the supply curve vertically. As a result, sellers have raised the price from P_E to P_1 (the full amount of the tax). Let us examine the effects of their attempt to pass the entire tax onto consumers by raising the price by the full amount of the tax: the quantity demanded has decreased from Q_E to Q_1, while sellers continue to produce Q_E units of the good. In other words, there is a surplus in the market. Q_E is no longer an equilibrium price, and consumers are not willing to pay the new price of P_1 to buy the output sellers are producing.

Figure 9.12 shows what happens when sellers attempt to make buyers pay the full amount of an indirect tax. Figure 9.13, on the other hand, shows the more likely outcome when the government imposes an indirect tax on a good, but when buyers and sellers *share the burden* of the tax.

Figure 9.13 shows the same tax 'wedge' between supply and demand, but now the price has increased not by the full amount of the tax but only a portion of the tax amount, from P_E to P_{E1}. Consumers pay more for the product, but the quantity demanded has not fallen by as much as it did when they were asked to pay the full tax. Now, producers share a portion of the tax's burden by keeping a lower price of P_2 after they have paid the government. The market is in a new equilibrium at P_{E1} and Q_{E1}, unlike when the full tax was passed onto consumers, which resulted in a disequilibrium in the market. The consumers' tax burden is represented by the dotted green area, producer burden by the red shaded area. The two areas together represent the total tax revenue.

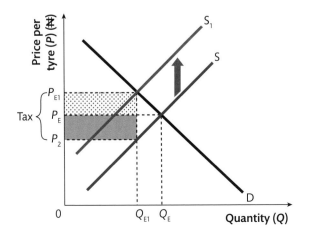

Figure 9.13 A new market equilibrium is found when consumers and producers share the tax burden

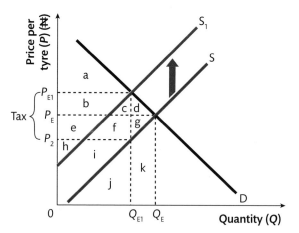

Figure 9.14 The graph can be used to analyse the effects of indirect taxes

In nearly every case, a tax imposed on a particular good or service, or even ad valorem taxes like the *value added tax* (VAT) or *sales tax* (a tax on nearly all goods and services that is a common source of government revenue in nearly every country), the burden is shared by consumers and producers. Consumers pay more when taxes are imposed on consumption, but producers also end up making less than they would if there were no consumption taxes.

What other effects does a tax have on a market?

We can analyse the effect of indirect taxes on various stakeholders, including consumers, producers, the government, and the market as a whole, by taking a closer look at the impact the tax has on our market supply and demand diagram.

Figure 9.14 places labels in the different areas of the graph representing consumer and producer surplus.

Without a tax, consumer surplus in the market would be represented by the triangle above P_E and below the demand curve, or area 'abcd'. The tax has resulted in an increase in price to P_{E1} and a decrease in consumer surplus to area 'a', meaning consumers have lost an area of surplus equal to 'bcd'.

Producers are also worse off after the tax, with producer surplus falling from 'efghi' to only 'hi', a decrease represented by the area 'efg'.

The tax has harmed both producers and consumers; so who benefits? Taxes are paid to the government, which uses tax revenues for all sorts of activities, which in theory should provide benefits to the public. Therefore, not all of the surplus lost to consumers and producers is lost to society; there is an area of tax revenue on our graph represented by 'bcef' that goes back to the government for the provision of other goods and services.

Consumers are worse off, producers are worse off, the government collects revenues, and society as a whole, it turns out, experiences a DWL (a decrease in overall community surplus) represented by the triangle 'dg'.

We can also look at the impact on sellers' revenues. Before the tax sellers in this market earned revenues determined by multiplying the number of units sold (Q_E) by the equilibrium price (P_E), or the large rectangle 'efghijk' in Figure 9.14. With the tax, producer revenues have fallen; less output is sold, and after paying the tax, sellers get to keep less money per unit. Total revenues after the tax are represented by area 'hij'.

Why do governments impose indirect taxes?

Indirect taxes can be imposed by governments to discourage the production or consumption of a good deemed harmful by the government. When a tax is imposed to correct the market failure of *over-consumption* or *over-production* it is called a *Pigouvian tax*, after economist Arther Pigou, whose work first explored the use of taxes to incentivise more socially optimal market outcomes. Beyond correcting market failures, indirect taxes can provide significant government revenue to finance regular government operations including the provision of important public goods such as healthcare, infrastructure, and education.

One argument against the use of consumption taxes for revenue generation, however, is that they are **regressive**, which means a tax on consumption places a larger burden on lower income households than it does on higher income households. Regressivity refers to the proportion of a consumer's income that is spent on a particular tax. Any consumption tax, because it is calculated as a specific amount, or as a percentage of the taxed good's price, is the same regardless of which consumer buys the good. A lower income consumer earning, say, ₦1.2 million per year, would therefore pay the same amount of tax on any particular good as a richer consumer, earning say ₦24 million per year. However, for the richer consumer, any tax paid represents a smaller proportion of her income than it does for the lower income individual. Therefore, it places a smaller burden on the rich than it does the poor.

Indirect consumption taxes, while effective at generating revenue, can exacerbate **inequality** in society, as the incomes of the poor are strained more than the incomes of the rich. In comparison, direct, graduated taxes on income, which will be explored in the macro section of this textbook, are *progressive*, which means the burden increases as a percentage of incomes as incomes rise.

Video suggestions:
You have read about it, now you can review what you have just learned by watching some videos by the author!
▶ Simply click here in your eBook for videos on the effects of a per-unit tax in the cases of inelastic demand and elastic demand.

9.4 How do subsidies affect a market?

Learning outcomes

At the end of this section you will be able to:

- explain why governments provide subsidies, and describe examples of subsidies
- draw a diagram to show a subsidy, and analyse the impacts of a subsidy on market outcomes
- discuss the consequences of providing a subsidy on the stakeholders in a market, including consumers, producers, and the government
- plot demand and supply curves for a product from linear functions and then illustrate and/or calculate the effects of the provision of a subsidy on the market (on price, quantity, consumer expenditure, producer revenue, government expenditure, consumer surplus, and producer surplus).

A subsidy is a payment made by the government to a firm for the purpose of increasing the production of a good. Governments may have several different motivations to subsidise.

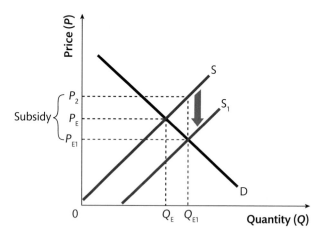

Figure 9.15 The benefit of a per-unit subsidy is shared between consumers and producers

- To increase the consumption of some goods by lowering the price. This might address a positive externality such as the underconsumption of some healthcare services.
- To support a particular industry by helping with production costs. The industry might be considered critical for economic security – e.g. steel – or might be one of political influence.
- To address a **balance of payments** deficit by increasing export revenue. Subsidies may lower costs enough to make a particular good more competitive on the world market.

Subsidising a product will cause the supply curve to shift downwards by the amount of the subsidy. Firms find that their costs of production are lower at every price, making production at every price more profitable. Therefore, supply expands and more is produced at every price. Figure 9.15 shows the supply shift for a per-unit subsidy.

The supply curve has shifted 'downward' by the amount of the subsidy, increasing the equilibrium quantity and decreasing the good's price. The price, however, does not fall by the full amount of the subsidy. Recall from our examination of indirect taxes that a taxed good's price does not rise by the full amount of the tax. The same principle applies here. A subsidy benefits both producers and consumers. While the price consumers pay decreases, it does not fall by the full amount of the subsidy. Instead, producers end up receiving some of the subsidy and collect money from the government for each unit they produce. The per-unit subsidy essentially drives a wedge between supply and demand, increasing both quantity demanded and quantity supplied.

How do subsidies affect consumers and producers?

Let us examine the welfare effects of the subsidy by adding labels to the different areas on our graph and looking at how consumers, producers, the government, and the market as a whole are affected. Figure 9.16 adds area labels to our subsidy graph.

Before the subsidy, consumer surplus in the market was represented by area 'ab'. The subsidy has caused the price to fall to P_{E1} and the quantity demanded to increase to Q_{E1}. As a result, consumer surplus increases by the area 'efg'. Consumers are better off.

Producer surplus before the subsidy was area 'eh' (below P_E and above S). The subsidy acts like a 'top off' to the price consumers pay. While consumers enjoy a lower price

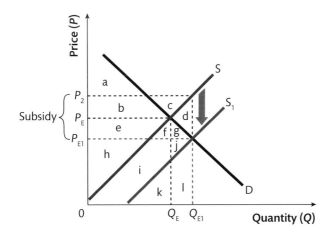

Figure 9.16 The effects of a subsidy can be analysed by looking at the areas in the graph

of P_{E1}, after the government has paid producers for each unit sold (Q_{E1} units), producers take home a higher price of P_2. Therefore, producer surplus increases, since both the quantity and the price collected for each unit sold have increased. Producer surplus thus increases by area 'bc', and is now the whole area below P_2 and above S. In the end, the areas of consumer and producer surplus overlap, as seen in Figure 9.17.

Consumers pay a lower price than producers receive. Both consumer and producer surplus are higher than they were before the subsidy.

It would appear on the surface that a subsidy is a win–win proposition. If both stakeholders are made better off, then who is made worse off? What we are missing from this conclusion, of course, is the government, whose limited funds have been allocated away from other purposes to subsidise the production and consumption of a certain good. The third element of our analysis is to look at the subsidy's cost to taxpayers.

This can be found by looking back at Figure 9.16 and identifying the area representing the total cost of the subsidy, which is the per-unit subsidy multiplied by the number of units sold, or $(P_2 - P_{E1}) \times Q_{E1}$, an area represented by 'bcdefg'.

Finally, we can compare the combined increases in consumer and producer surplus to the cost imposed on the government. Consumer surplus increased by 'efg' and producer surplus by 'bc', for a combined increase in surplus of 'bcefg'. The cost to taxpayers, again, was 'bcdefg'. Comparing the two, we can see that the cost to

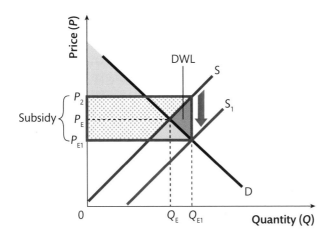

Figure 9.17 Like other forms of intervention, subsidies create a deadweight loss

Video suggestion:
You have read about it, now you can review what you have just learned by watching a video by the author!

▶ Simply click here in your eBook for a video on the effects of a per-unit subsidy.

taxpayers exceeded the benefit to producers and consumers, specifically by an amount represented by area 'd'.

Not surprisingly, subsidies, just like the other forms of intervention in markets we have studied in this chapter, create a DWL. In this case, the subsidy's cost to taxpayers outweighs the benefits it creates for consumers and producers. On our graph, the DWL can be seen as the triangle wedged between supply and demand between the free market equilibrium quantity and the subsidised quantity, as in Figure 9.17.

In Figure 9.17 the dotted yellow area represents producer surplus, the green area consumer surplus, and the red area the DWL. The rectangle outlined in red, meanwhile, is the cost the subsidy imposed on taxpayers. This is money that could have been spent on something else, or simply left in taxpayers' pockets to spend on whatever they like in the marketplace.

So once again we are left with a question: if subsidies impose more costs on society than the benefits they create, then why do governments use them? Well, as with taxes and price controls, there are situations in which subsidies are justified to improve overall economic well-being. Sometimes the free market under-allocates resources towards the production of certain goods, such as renewable energy, healthcare, affordable housing, nutritional foods, public transportation, and so on. Subsidies are a way for the government to prioritise socially beneficial goods or goods that are deemed strategic assets, without which the economy would struggle to function efficiently.

Another example is military and aerospace technology. There simply would not be much of a market for high tech aerospace equipment if it were not for the government's support of such industries over the decades. Subsidies make it appealing for producers to enter new markets and remain in them, even in the face of extraordinarily high start-up and operating costs.

Without subsidies, there are entire industries that would not exist in our economy today. That is not to say that all subsidies are justified. Frequently firms survive market slumps or changing tastes and preferences among consumers only because of government support, and there are many economists who argue that when private demand is not enough to keep an industry alive, it should not be the job of government to do so.

Nonetheless the close ties between large industries and the governments of the world is a fact of life and despite economists' best arguments against government support of certain industries, it has persisted and will continue to do so. Only when the affected good would be under-provided by the free market is subsidising its production justifiable, according to most economists. We will explore examples of market failure, including positive **externalities** and public goods, under which economists argue that subsidising output can increase total welfare in society, in a later chapter.

HL Calculating the effects of indirect taxes and subsidies

As we demonstrated in the section on price controls, calculating the effects of a government's intervention in the free market can be as simple as finding the areas of different shapes in our diagrams.

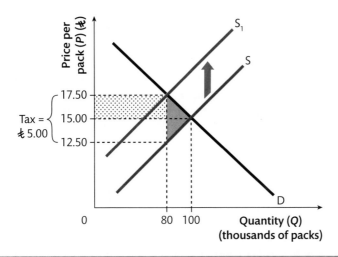

Figure 9.18   This graph can be used to calculate the impact of a specific tax on cigarettes

Worked example 9.2

Consider the effect of the ₺5 (₺ is the symbol for the Turkish lira, the currency of Turkey) per pack tax on cigarettes shown in Figure 9.18.

From this graph we can easily calculate the tax's impact on consumer surplus, producer surplus, government tax revenues, and total welfare.

First let us calculate the lost consumer surplus, represented by the dotted green rectangle and the top half of the red DWL triangle.

Decrease in consumer surplus

$$= ((₺17.5 - ₺15) \times 80,000 \ packs)$$

$$+ \frac{(₺17.5 - ₺15) \times 20,000 \ packs}{2}$$

$$= ₺200,000 + ₺25,000$$

$$= ₺225,000$$

Consumer surplus is reduced by ₺225,000. The loss in producer surplus can also be calculated.

Decrease in producer surplus

$$= ((₺15 - ₺12.5) \times 80,000 \ packs)$$

$$+ \frac{(₺15 - ₺12.5) \times 20,000 \ packs}{2}$$

$$= ₺225,000$$

Both consumer and producer surplus have decreased by ₺225,000 as a result of the ₺5 cigarette tax. Next we can calculate the amount of tax revenue generated, which is represented by the green and dotted yellow areas in Figure 9.17.

$$Tax\ revenue = (₺17.5 - ₺12.5) \times 80,000\ packs$$

$$= ₺400,000$$

Not surprisingly, a ₺5 tax applied to 80,000 packs of cigarettes generates ₺400,000 in tax revenue. Finally, we can calculate the DWL resulting from the tax, or the red area on the graph. There are two ways to do this: (1) we can simply subtract the tax revenue from the total loss of consumer and producer surplus; or (2) we can find the area of the red triangle. Either way will yield the same result, so let us do the latter:

$$Deadweight\ loss = \frac{(₺17.5 - ₺12.5) \times 20,000\ packs}{2} = ₺50,000$$

The DWL is ₺50,000, representing the net loss of community surplus in the market resulting from the ₺5 tax.

As mentioned earlier in this chapter, taxes like those on cigarettes may be justified despite the resulting DWL in the market if it is determined that the good's production or consumption are socially harmful, as is almost certainly the case with cigarettes, which are considered a *demerit good*, or one that creates harmful effects for those who consume it and for third parties, such as non-smokers who suffer the effects of second-hand smoke.

Using the same methods, the effects of subsidies can be calculated, allowing us to weigh the monetary benefits and costs of government intervention in the markets for particular goods.

9.5 Other forms of government intervention in markets

Learning outcomes

At the end of this section you will be able to:

- explain the need for direct provision of services by government, giving examples
- analyse the effects of regulation and legislation
- comment on government use of 'nudges' to influence markets, including the default option and social reinforcement.

Direct provision of services

Government intervention in the markets for particular goods can take the form of price controls, taxes, or subsidies, but in each of these cases there must first be an actual market for the good. In some cases, the free market itself fails to provide certain goods or services, and government provision is required. In Chapter 10, we will examine the market failure known as *public goods*, or goods that the free market will not provide due to certain characteristics they exhibit.

Vaccines are an especially good example. Vaccines for polio, smallpox, and hepatitis are estimated to have saved millions of lives in the past. As a reference, immunologists estimate that 80% of the population must receive a vaccine if herd immunity is to be achieved. Left to the free market, it is likely that fewer than 80% of people would be willing and/or able to purchase and receive the coronavirus vaccine. Therefore, the government must intervene to provide the vaccine at little or no cost to consumers. Through government provision, the vaccine can be provided for 'free' and nearly everyone will receive it, thereby achieving herd immunity.

Government provision takes the concept behind subsidies to its logical extreme. Rather than simply supporting the provision of a good by paying producers a specific amount for each unit they sell, the government pays for the entire production and may even handle the good or service's distribution. Beyond healthcare goods such as vaccines, other examples of services governments provide include education, police and fire services, road construction and maintenance, and even health insurance in many rich countries. Governments have determined that without public intervention, the markets for these and other public goods would fail to provide them at anywhere near an adequate level to allow for an efficiently functioning economy and a healthy, well-educated society.

Command and control – regulation and legislation

Another way the government can intervene in the markets for particular goods is through regulation and legislation. Governments make the rules by which certain industries have to play, and by tweaking these rules certain behaviours can be incentivised or required by producers and consumers. Environmental and health regulations, workplace safety regulations, **anti-monopoly regulations**, and a host of other rules by which markets must comply allow the government to act as referees in the free market economy.

Below is a list of regulatory agencies in the USA, along with a brief description of the role they play in the markets for different goods and services.

- Consumer Product Safety Commission (CPSC) enforces federal safety standards.
- Environmental Protection Agency (EPA) establishes and enforces pollution standards.
- Equal Employment Opportunity Commission (EEOC) administers and enforces Title VIII or the Civil Rights Act of 1964 (fair employment).
- Federal Aviation Administration (FAA) regulates and promotes air transportation safety, including airports, and pilot licensing.
- Federal Communications Commission (FCC) regulates interstate and foreign communication by radio, telephone, telegraph, and television.
- Federal Deposit Insurance Corporation (FDIC) insures bank deposits, approves mergers, and audits banking practices.
- Food and Drug Administration (FDA) administers federal food purity laws, drug testing and safety.
- Federal Reserve System (the FED) regulates banking; manages the **money supply**.
- Federal Trade Commission (FTC) ensures free and fair competition and protects consumers from unfair or deceptive practices.

TOK

Given the demonstration of the distinct types of government intervention shown in this chapter, it begs the question of which policies are best in which situations. How does one decide that? More specifically, what knowledge criteria should government policymakers use to make choices between alternative policies?

Each of these agencies intervenes in a different market with various ends in mind, the result being that the 'free market' is less free, but perhaps more equitable, safer, and more likely to act in the greater interest of society as a whole and not just in the interests of the producers and/or consumers within the market itself. In adhering to the regulations laid out by government agencies, industries face higher costs, possibly reducing the supply of their goods as a result, reducing some of the negative effects their consumption or production might have on society.

HL Consumer nudges

A more recent form of government intervention, introduced in Chapter 8, is the government's use of **consumer nudges**. Nudges can tweak the incentive structure ever so slightly, without relying on government regulations, rules, mandates, or laws; thereby nudges offer fans of free markets and free societies a means of promoting socially desirable outcomes without taking away people's freedoms.

Two examples of nudges at work are the cases of the 'default option' and 'social reinforcement'.

Case study – pension enrolment default option

In a 2009 Q&A article for the publication *Yale Insights,* Richard Thaler provides an example of how changing the 'default option' can lead to better outcomes for both individuals and society.

> 'A default option is simply what happens if you do nothing. Normally, nothing happens, but sometimes even when you do nothing, something happens.'

> 'A good example is in the area of pension policy. In many company sponsored, optional retirement plans, the default option is not to join. If you are going to join, you have to fill out some paperwork. Some companies have tried the opposite default, which is that you are enrolled unless you fill out some paperwork. We know that speeds enrollment greatly and doesn't really cost anything … No one is forced to join it. People sign up of their own free will, but in the first company where we did this we more than tripled savings rates.'

Almost everyone understands that saving a part of their income is important, both for the individual who needs to plan for their future retirement but also for the economy as a whole, which depends on household savings to provide funds for private and public sector investment. Without savings, the circular flow of the economy is slowed and less economic growth can take place. The nudge Thaler describes above is a simple way to increase the amount of savings in the economy, without *requiring* anyone to save more. Simply by making the default option to *be enrolled* in a pension plan, rather than to *not be enrolled*, the amount of savings tripled.

Case study – social reinforcement during a pandemic

Nudge theory has also been applied in the current fight against the COVID-19 pandemic. Early on in the pandemic, the UK's Behavioural Insights Team, a public–private partnership that 'exists to improve people's lives and communities … often using simple changes to tackle major policy problems' (in other words, the British government's 'nudge unit') tackled the challenge of nudging people to touch their

▲ An image of a fly applied in the centre of a men's urinal is a classic example of a nudge aimed at improving users' aims

faces less in response to scientists' claim that coronavirus transmission was likely to take place when people touched contaminated surfaces and then transferred the virus to themselves by touching their eyes, nose, or mouth.

The BIT's suggestions to help change people's face-touching behaviours included people asking their friends and family to use verbal reminders whenever they saw one another touching their faces, such as shouting 'FACE!' whenever one attempted to do so. Another suggestion was for people to enforce self-conscious behaviours to replace subconscious face-touching, such as folding their arms in front of them or putting their hands in their pockets. Over time these conscious behaviours could become subconscious (like face touching is for many people) and replace the more dangerous behaviour. According to the BIT, 'These may seem to be absurdly small and unimportant things to be discussed. In fact, they are crucial. Creating substitute behaviours and new barrier-forming habits are the most effective way of curbing face touching.'

As the infection rate rose across the UK, and even the country's prime minister, Boris Johnson, fell ill with the virus, the efficacy of nudge theory came into question and ultimately, as many countries, regions, and locales did, mask mandates were passed and the public was asked to cover their faces. Thus, social reinforcement aimed at limiting face touching became a moot point, as with a mask on, people are far less likely to touch their face as well as transmit the virus to those whom they might be standing near.

Despite its status as a relatively new branch of economics, within the umbrella category of *behavioural economics* (discussed in Chapter 8), nudge theory is being employed not just by private businesses, but by governments to create the conditions under which individuals make decisions that are in both their own self-interest and society's self-interest, when they might otherwise have acted in an irrational way that harms social and even personal well-being.

Practice exam questions

1. Explain, using a diagram, the effect of a specific tax on various stakeholders. (10 marks)

2. Explain, using a diagram, the effects of a per-unit subsidy on various stakeholders. (10 marks)

3a. Explain the concepts of maximum and minimum price controls. (10 marks)

  b. Evaluate the idea that government intervention in the form of price ceilings and price floors is well intentioned, but often leads to undesirable side effects. (15 marks)

4a. Using an appropriate diagram, explain the likely effects of a decrease in the maximum price set for petrol (gasoline), which is already set below the market price. (10 marks)

  b. Evaluate the effects of this kind of government intervention into the market for petrol. (15 marks)

5a. Using a diagram explain the effect on various stakeholders of a high specific tax on alcohol. (10 marks)

  b. Evaluate the effectiveness of a policy that would impose substantially higher levels of taxation on the sale of alcohol. (15 marks)

Market failure: externalities, public goods, and the market's inability to achieve equity

10

At the end of this section you will be able to:

- define the concept of market failure as a failure of the market to achieve allocative efficiency
- distinguish the concepts of marginal private benefits (MPB), **marginal social benefits (MSB)**, marginal private costs (MPC) and **marginal social costs (MSC)**
- analyse the failure of the market to achieve a social optimum where MSB = MSC
- explain, using diagrams, the meaning of **positive and negative externalities of production and consumption**, giving examples of merit and demerit goods
- comment on the problems of unsustainable use of **common pool resources**.

Socially optimal output

We have so far looked at how effective markets can be in bringing society what it wants with efficiency. However, the strict conditions that apply for free markets to achieve socially optimal outcomes are not always in effect. Market failure is any situation where the allocation of resources by a free market is not efficient. These situations, from society's viewpoint, could be improved on if resources were allocated differently. Market failure is most often associated with the existence of externalities, common pool resources, public goods, **asymmetric information**, and market power.

First, it is important to remember that many markets function quite well if left free and competitive. Consumers enjoy allocative efficiency, and large amounts of producer and consumer surplus are produced. You will recall that the demand and supply curves introduced in Chapters 3 and 5 also represent the marginal benefit (MB = D) and marginal cost (MC = S) curves. Furthermore, allocative efficiency is achieved where MB equal MC. Normally, this is where supply meets demand.

We can now expand the idea of marginal analysis to include society's benefits and costs, and so MB becomes MSB (marginal social benefit) and MC becomes MSC (marginal social cost). The difference between MB and MSB is that MSB includes any external benefits that may arise from a good's consumption. Likewise, MSC includes the marginal *private* cost of producing a good plus any external costs to the rest of society. External benefits and costs are called *externalities* by economists, and include any spillover effects arising from a good's production or consumption imposed on a third party that was not directly involved in the market.

When a good's production and consumption do not create any externalities, the marginal *private* cost (MPC) (in other words, supply), and the marginal *private* benefit MPB (demand) are equal to the MSC and the MSB. In such a case the market equilibrium output is the socially optimal, allocatively efficient level of output.

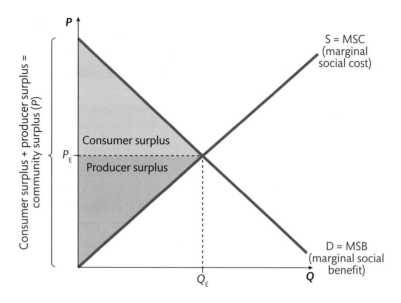

Figure 10.1 Community surplus is maximised at market equilibrium

Figure 10.1 shows the supply (MSC) and demand (MSB) curves at market equilibrium.

At P_E and Q_E, to produce any greater quantity would cause costs to exceed benefits. Any less output, a quantity to the left of Q_E, and some portion of consumer/producer surplus is left unenjoyed. Therefore, at equilibrium community surplus is maximised, where community surplus is the combination of producer and consumer surplus. The market illustrated in Figure 10.1 is allocatively efficient, thus there is no market failure taking place.

At competitive market equilibrium, economists argue that there exists a state of Pareto optimality. 'Pareto optimal' refers to a market situation where no one can be made better off without making someone else worse off. Look again at Figure 10.1. There are no other possible combinations of price and quantity that can improve one group's situation without hurting the other. If the price were higher than P_E, consumers would be worse off. If price were below P_E, producers would be worse off. If the quantity produced were greater than Q_E, society's costs (MSC) would be greater than its benefits (MSB), so everyone would be worse off. If the quantity were less than Q_E, some amount of community surplus would be lost. Thus, maximisation of community surplus, achieved where MSB = MSC, is synonymous with Pareto optimality.

Competitive markets provide Pareto optimality by maximising community surplus. These markets also tend to be allocatively efficient, delivering the goods society wants by matching MSB and MSC. However, markets often do not meet the conditions of free competition, and we admit that markets can fail. When resources are not allocated in an optimal or socially efficient manner, this is called market failure. When this occurs, it is left to governments to address the problem to help society get the most from its resources. This chapter considers various forms of market failure and evaluates the solutions most often proposed to deal with them.

What are externalities?

There are many instances where someone outside of a transaction, a third party, may suffer the costs or enjoy the benefits of someone else's transactions. When this occurs,

Video suggestion:
You have read about it, now you can review what you have just learned by watching a video by the author!
▶ Simply click here in your eBook for an introductory video on market failure.

it is called an externality. Someone outside the original transaction is being affected by it, either positively (enjoying benefits) or negatively (suffering costs).

When the side effects are good, it is called a positive externality. When the side effects are bad, it is called a negative externality. Another term for externality is 'spillover', which suggests that costs or benefits have gone beyond the initial actors in the transaction. Thus, someone suffering the effects of a negative externality may be bearing some of the spillover costs. Someone feeling the effects of a positive externality is enjoying spillover benefits.

When an externality occurs, there is a difference between society's experience and that of the individual firm or consumer. No longer can we assume that the private benefit is equal to society's benefit or that social cost is equal to private cost.

Positive externalities of consumption

A positive externality occurs when a good's production or consumption creates spillover benefits on the rest of society that exceed the benefits enjoyed by the individual consumers of the good itself. In other words, the MSB derived from the good's consumption exceeds the MPBs. In the case of a positive production externality, the good's cost to society is lower than its cost to the firms producing the good itself. In both cases (consumption and production externalities) the result is a situation in which the market equilibrium quantity of the good is less than the socially optimal quantity.

Consider the market for healthcare in Figure 10.2.

Healthcare is a service that provides health benefits to individuals who have access to it, but also to society as a whole. When my neighbour has good health, I am more likely to remain healthy. When an employee in a company I work for is healthy, my company is more productive and all employees and the business's owners are better off as a result. Healthcare is a service that creates social benefits that exceed the private benefits, thus MSB is greater than MPB.

The problem is, if left alone the market will provide only a Q_E level of healthcare. At Q_E the MSB (point 'a' on the graph) is higher than the marginal social cost (point 'b').

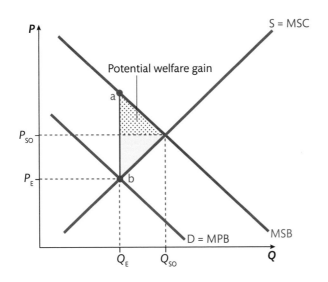

Figure 10.2 Positive consumption externality

The optimal amount of healthcare, however, is at Q_{SO} (socially optimal quantity), where MSB = MSC. Thus, the free market will not produce enough healthcare by itself. And, if society's true value for healthcare were included, if demand were reflected in the MSB curve, the demand would be higher than it is. Society would gain considerably by consuming more healthcare. The amount of the potential gain in welfare is shown by the dotted blue triangle. The potential welfare gain is congruent with deadweight loss (DWL); it is the welfare that the market is losing out on by not producing at the optimal quantity.

Merit goods

Healthcare is an example of a good whose consumption creates positive externalities. These are known as *merit goods*: goods that are under-consumed because the benefits they create are not purely private, therefore private individuals will only consume as much as they demand for themselves, neglecting to take into account the social benefits they create. As a result, if left entirely to the free market the level of consumption will be less than the socially optimal level.

Other examples of merit goods include the following.

- **Education**. Like healthcare, getting an education makes the individual who receives it better off, but also society, as an educated workforce is more productive, pays more in taxes, and results in a more prosperous society as a whole.
- **Open spaces (such as parks)**. There are private parks, like Disneyland, that allow paying customers to come and enjoy beautiful spaces and entertaining rides. However, open spaces provide social benefits beyond the enjoyment of those who actually use them, such as contributing to public health, cleaner air, habitat for flora and fauna, and so on. Because the benefits of public spaces are not purely private, they tend to be under-provided by the free market.
- **Security**. Public safety is another good that would be under-provided by the free market because its provision is expensive and the benefits of providing it are not purely private. The richest in society may be able to afford private security; but we cannot all have bodyguards. This does not mean that we do not all need security. Because its benefits are not purely private, but mostly social, public safety is, in most countries, left up to public security forces, e.g. police and sheriff departments.
- **Renewable energy**. The consumption of renewable energies, like wind and solar power, benefit not just the individuals who choose to install solar panels on their roofs, but also others in society, who will see their own electricity bills get cheaper as a result of the reduced demand for non-renewable energy. Additionally, as most renewables are non-polluting, their consumption results in cleaner air quality, reduced health effects of energy consumption, and a more sustainable economy, all which benefit society as a whole, not just the individual business or household who chooses renewables over non-renewables.
- **Public transportation**. Taking the train or bus to work reduces traffic and therefore benefits drivers who drive themselves in cars. While the bus passenger benefits by having a relatively cheap and stress-free option for commuting, drivers of private automobiles enjoy spillover benefits in the form of less traffic and a more speedy commute. Thus, the benefits of public transportation are not purely private but social as well.

Positive externalities of production

While most of the goods described above can be understood as goods whose externalities result from their consumption, other goods create positive externalities through their production. When it is the process of manufacturing a good that creates spillover benefits, rather than the consumption of the good, we can analyse the market from the supply side, rather than from the demand side. Consider the market for honey. In order for bees to make honey, their keepers must constantly provide them access to pollinating plants. Farmers whose crops require pollination by bees are a third party, not directly involved in the honey market, who benefit from the production of honey.

The costs of making honey can be very high. But because the benefits of honey production are enjoyed by farmers who do not make or sell honey, but whose crops get pollinated by honeybees, the social cost of honey production is actually *lower than* the private cost. Figure 10.3 shows the market for honey, a good with a positive production externality.

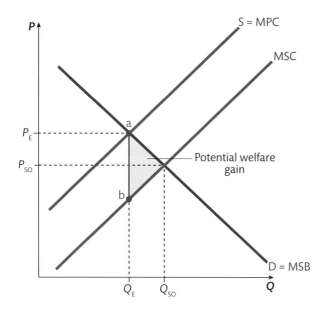

Figure 10.3 Positive externality of production

The private costs of honey production are greater than the social costs, since its production creates spillover benefits for farmers growing crops that depend on the activities of pollinators like honeybees. If beekeepers act only in their own self-interest, they will produce less honey (Q_E) and it will sell for a higher price (P_E) than what is socially optimal (Q_{SO} and P_{SO}). At Q_E the MSB of honey (point 'a') is higher than the MSC (point 'b'). Honey production benefits society more than it costs. Therefore, not enough honey is produced.

The existence of positive externalities of consumption and production results in market failures. In both cases the good creating externalities will be underproduced by the free market. Later in this chapter we will examine ways the government can intervene in response to merit goods and goods that create positive externalities through their production to promote a more socially optimal level of production and consumption.

Video suggestions:
You have read about it, now you can review what you have just learned by watching some videos by the author!

▶ Simply click here in your eBook for videos on positive externalities of consumption and positive externalities of production.

Negative externalities of production

Sometimes, the most innocuous products cause problems for other people, but not for the consumer who enjoys using it nor for the producer who is paid for it. Third parties, who had no part in the transaction, suffer costs ranging from the small to the very large, from lost money to poor health. These production costs are called negative production externalities. Beyond private costs, the external costs suffered by others increase the overall social costs.

There are many examples of negative production externalities.

- Coal is produced with significant air pollution as a by-product, along with the deaths of hundreds of miners working in dangerous conditions every year.
- Oil production appears to be growing more and more costly, as spills and refinery pollution cause significant external losses worldwide, not to mention the depletion of reserves.
- Textile manufacturers in developing countries have faced accusations of exploiting child labour, allowing dangerous work spaces, or paying workers a lower than living wage, externalising some of the costs of the production of their goods onto the communities from which their factory workers come.
- Chemical-intensive industries such as industrial agriculture have long abused the environment by discharging harmful by-products from their activities into the water, air, and soil.

The list could go on and on. If one were to dig deep enough, the production of almost any industrially manufactured good could be said to create spillover costs on the environment, the communities employed in their production, on human health, or on other third parties not directly involved in the goods' production.

Using MB and MC analysis, it is possible to represent negative production externalities using a typical market diagram. Figure 10.4 illustrates the market for a good that creates environmental pollution in its production processes.

Note that the supply curve has been split. MPC is another name for the supply curve representing the costs paid by the firm to produce. At the market equilibrium price of P_E, quantity Q_E is produced. At that quantity, the external costs to society are quite

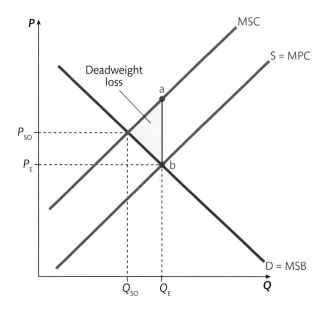

Figure 10.4 Negative production externality

high, represented by the distance between points 'a' and 'b'. This implies that if the good were priced to cover all of the relevant costs, the price would be much higher. At the market equilibrium quantity of Q_E, however, the cost the good imposes on society (point 'a') is higher than the benefit society derives from the good's production (point 'b'). *Too much* of the good is produced by the free market.

In fact, the entire MSC curve lies above the MPC curve, showing that the private costs of production are less than the costs to all of society at every price. This is not a shift to the left of the supply curve, merely a more accurate representation of the full costs of production. You could refer to the MSC curve as the 'true' supply curve because it shows all the costs to society.

Moreover, if the marginal social costs are the accurate costs to society, the intersection of MSC with the MSB curve should provide the optimal equilibrium point, the best allocation of resources, at the point where MSC = MSB. The socially efficient price and output would be P_{SO} and Q_{SO}. When all the costs are added into the process, it appears that the optimal amount of production is Q_{SO}, significantly less than Q_E. We can also conclude that the equilibrium price would be higher, at P_{SO}, than the current free market price of P_E.

The above implies that goods whose production creates a negative externality are overproduced, and are sold at prices that are too low, or below what the market would show if all costs were added in. Furthermore, because production is not where MSCs are equal to MSBs, resources are being misallocated. The distance between MSC and MPC at Q_E represents the negative externality at that point. If the optimal output and price are Q_{SO} and P_{SO}, then the production beyond that amount produces the negative externality, shown by the area of the shaded triangle, which again, is the DWL.

Negative externalities of consumption

Spillover costs can occur on the consumption side as well. They are the negative effects that are suffered by a third party when a good or service is consumed. In these cases, a person's use of a product affects others adversely. A surprising number of products create obvious third party costs.

- Cigarettes create second-hand smoke when consumed that can make non-smokers ill.
- Alcohol consumption increases the chance of automobile accidents and domestic abuse, meaning even non-drinkers can suffer the effects of alcohol abuse.
- Gambling is considered to be addictive, and the gambling industry has ruined the lives of many families whose loved one has fallen victim to it.
- Private automobiles are responsible for tens of thousands of premature deaths each year, are responsible for a significant percentage of the planet's carbon emissions, and cause clogged streets and reduced productivity due to traffic congestion in many of the world's cities.

Recently, some have argued that the consumption of high-fat diets, which contribute to heart disease, constitutes the same kind of consumer spillover cost. In the case of a negative externality of consumption, the costs are seen on the MB curve.

While this may seem counter-intuitive, remember that this is a consumption externality and, therefore, it is the demand (or consumption) side where the costs occur. For negative externalities of consumption, the MSBs are less than the benefits enjoyed by the private consumer. In other words, the benefit of a fast food meal enjoyed by a consumer is greater than society's benefit. This is because the consumer is a part of society, so their enjoyment is part of the total. But others will eventually pay some of the costs of eating fatty foods (by paying higher insurance premiums or taxes for government health programmes). This cost to others actually reduces the overall benefit to society. Figure 10.5 shows the negative externality of fast food consumption where MSB falls below the MPB.

The amount of fast food that is actually consumed (Q_E) corresponds with a social cost (point 'a') that exceeds the social benefit (point 'b'). More fast food is consumed than what is socially optimal (Q_{SO}), and therefore there is a DWL imposed on society. In the case of fast food, the DWL triangle represents the additional healthcare costs borne by members of society for whom fast food is not a regular part of their diet, but who face higher healthcare costs nonetheless.

Figure 10.5 Negative consumption externality

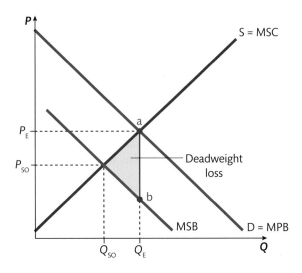

Demerit goods

Goods that create negative externalities through their production are known as demerit goods. The word 'demerit' literally means 'to take away good', or 'negative good'. In contrast to a 'merit' good, which could be understood as a 'good good'. Demerit goods are ones whose consumption harms society, but for whom the individual consumer does not suffer some of the good's negative effects. Tobacco, cars, prostitution, and alcohol are all demerit goods. The free market will provide more of these goods than what is socially optimal, thus they represent a market failure.

Common pool resources

Another form of market failure is the existence of what are called common pool, or common access, resources. American ecologist Garrett Hardin warned of what he called the '**tragedy of the commons**' in a 1968 essay. Hardin explained that when there exist common resources, for which there is no private owner, the incentive among rational users of the resources is to exploit it to the fullest potential in order to maximise their own self-gain before the resource is depleted. The tragedy of the commons, therefore, is that common resources will inevitably be depleted due to humans' rational, self-interested behaviours, leaving us with shortages in key resources essential to human survival.

The classic example is that of a herd of stock animals using a common pasture. Each animal's owner has a strong private incentive to place his animals in the pasture for feeding. The cumulative effect of this, however, is the long-term destruction of a once lush resource, as overgrazing renders the pasture unusable. The lack of private ownership of the pasture has allowed individuals to graze their animals to the fullest extent possible while the grazing was good, ultimately depleting the pasture and rendering it useless to all. Economists and environmental scientists have also applied the idea to the world's common fishing waters, citing the dwindling of fish stocks everywhere.

The critical problem is that common access resources like open grassland and the world's oceans are essentially 'free' to the user, but use of them depletes the availability of the resource to everyone else. Economists and scientists call these subtractable resources. Because users do not pay a market price for use of the good, they have little incentive to ration it wisely. Economists call this behaviour the **free-rider problem**: those who benefit and draw from a resource but do not have to pay for it. Examples are abundant.

- Water sources in nearly every country are receivers of toxic waste, thus diminishing ecosystems.
- Forests on public lands (which are owned by the 'public' and not any private individual) are slashed for wood and to make way for farming, which reduces oxygen production and erodes the soil.
- The atmosphere is infused with pollutants generated from industry, cars, and the methane output of animals that are kept for meat production.

Case study – public health as a common pool resource

An imminent example of the tragedy of the commons is the threat to public health arising from people who may choose not to vaccinate themselves and their families against COVID-19. Given the 95% effectiveness rate of vaccines currently

Video suggestions:
You have read about it, now you can review what you have just learned by watching a few videos by the author! ▶ Simply click here in your eBook for videos on negative externalities of production and consumption.

available, epidemiologists estimate that up to two-thirds of the population will need to receive a vaccine in order to achieve 'herd immunity' – the state in which the virus is no longer able to spread within the community due to a lack of viable vectors.

Common pool resources are **non-excludable**, but **rivalrous**. This means that no individual can be excluded from consuming a common resource, but when one person consumes it the benefit enjoyed by all other consumers is diminished. Consider the example of fish in the ocean. Anyone with the right boat and equipment can go into the ocean and catch as many tuna as they want, since ocean fish are non-excludable. But a fish caught by one person can obviously not be caught by another person, so fish are rivalrous.

Now let us consider our vaccine example. Unless there is a law passed requiring that everyone get vaccinated, individuals will have the freedom to choose whether or not to receive the vaccine. In other words, no one can be excluded from making the decision not to get it (it is non-excludable). However, if more than one-third of any given population does not receive the vaccine, then the virus can be expected to persist within that community and continue to spread. Therefore, the decision not to get the vaccine is rivalrous; it diminishes the benefit the vaccine provides the rest of society through the increased likelihood that the pandemic will continue spreading within the community, albeit in a diminished capacity.

The vaccine question is a classic example of the free-rider problem: individuals who choose not to receive a vaccine will still benefit from everyone else in their community getting vaccinated, but they personally do not have any input into achieving the disease's eradication. A common pool resource is one for which there is no cost for anyone to use (it is non-excludable). Not having a vaccine is essentially a no-cost decision in many places. Therefore, when people are free to choose not to receive a vaccine, the efficacy of the vaccine at eradicating COVID-19 (or any other disease) is undermined, for if more than a small minority make this decision, the disease is likely to persist within the community.

Governments have put systems in place to incentivise vaccination, including, in the USA, the passing of the 1986 National Childhood Vaccine Injury Act, a law which recognises potential injuries, disabilities, and conditions that might result from a long list of different vaccines and provides victims a means of receiving compensation for vaccine-related injury or death. By offering compensation to victims of vaccine injuries, the government relieves the pharmaceutical companies that manufacture them from the potential legal exposure that might result from patients who feel they are owed compensation following an adverse reaction to a vaccine suing the companies themselves. The Vaccine Injury Act increases the MPB of receiving a vaccine (in other words, demand for vaccines is greater, since parents can expect compensation following a potential injury), while stabilising the supply (since manufacturers are more willing to supply vaccines when the government is there to cover injury claims). Thus, government intervention is employed to correct the market failure of too few people receiving vaccines.

Ultimately, the tragedy of the commons arises from a tendency among humans to act in their own rational self-interest while undervaluing the collective consequences of their individual actions. A fisher who ignores catch limits on ocean fish, a factory owner who refuses to invest in air-pollution reducing technologies, a chemical plant or farmer who knowingly allows runoff into freshwater sources, a neighbour who drills a well and pumps more than 'a fair share' out of a common aquifer – these are just some examples of the tragedy of the commons and how it impacts our world today.

In his 1968 essay Garrett Hardin said:

> 'Ruin is the destination towards which all men rush, each pursuing his own best interest in a society that believes in the freedom of the commons. Freedom in a commons brings ruin to all.'

Wherever common pool resources exist (which is everywhere) sustainability is threatened, and negative externalities of consumption and production will persist. The goal of sustainable development is to avoid resource depletion and encourage environmentally benign forms of economic progress. Recognising the obstacles to sustainability posed by the tragedy of the commons allows us to better assess the ability of society to grow and develop in a sustainable manner.

Video suggestions:
You have read about it, now you can review what you have just learned by watching some videos by the author! Simply click here in your eBook for videos on the tragedy of the commons.

10.2 Government intervention in response to externalities and common pool resources

Learning outcomes

At the end of this section you will be able to:

- explain, using diagrams, the use of policy responses, including market-based policies (taxation and **tradable permits**), and government regulations, to the problem of negative externalities of production and consumption
- evaluate, using diagrams, the use of government responses, including subsidies, legislation, advertising to influence behaviour, and direct provision of goods and services
- evaluate, using diagrams, possible government responses to threats to sustainability, including legislation, **carbon taxes**, cap and trade schemes, and funding for clean technologies
- explain, using examples, that government responses to threats to sustainability are limited by the global nature of the problems and the lack of ownership of common resources.

When the free market fails to achieve a socially optimal outcome, the government may choose to intervene to either increase or decrease the amount of production and consumption or to regulate the market in a way that promotes sustainability.

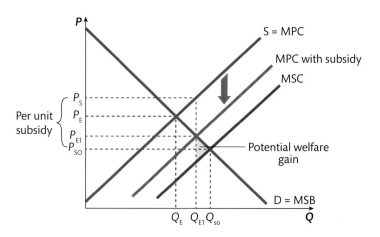

Figure 10.6 In the case of a merit good, a per-unit subsidy moves price and quantity supplied closer to socially optimised levels

Subsidies

When a market under-produces a good, as in the case of merit goods or goods whose production creates positive externalities, measures that increase the good's production are required. The government can actively encourage more production through the payment of subsidies. This may occur in the form of a lump-sum payment to the industry, or more commonly as a per-unit subsidy. The goal would be to reduce the MPC of production so that private producers have an incentive to produce more of the good.

Figure 10.6 shows the effect of a subsidy for a merit good, affordable housing, provided by the government to developers who choose to build middle- to low-income housing in an urban area.

The private cost of building additional low-income housing decreases due to a per-unit subsidy of $P_S - P_{E1}$. As a result, the supply of affordable housing increases, the equilibrium price falls to P_{E1} and the quantity demanded increases to Q_{E1}. There is still a positive externality from affordable housing, therefore a potential welfare gain still exists; however, the market is more efficient following the subsidy than without it because Q_{E1} is closer to the socially optimal level of housing (Q_{SO}) than the amount constructed without the subsidy (Q_E). Government intervention has made the market for affordable housing more efficient by reducing the private cost so that it is closer to the social cost, thus increasing equilibrium output.

The subsidy, however, is paid for by tax revenues, and is drawn from other areas of the government budget. So again, the opportunity cost of using these resources must be considered. Furthermore, the granting of such subsidies can create a political problem. Other industries may see an opportunity to be subsidised, which may lead to a barrage of appeals to the government for subsidies on the basis of the external benefits their products create.

Taxes

When demerit goods impose spillover costs on third parties, or when a good's production harms the environment or human health, government intervention to reduce the quantity of the good produced may be in order. Whereas subsidies can increase market output, indirect taxes, as we know, will lead to a decrease in output. A tax on a good meant to reduce its output to a more socially optimal level is known as

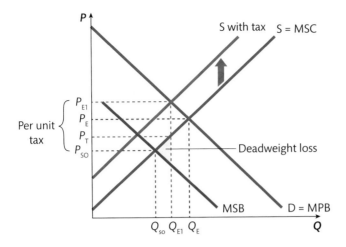

Figure 10.7 The imposition of a Pigouvian tax on a demerit good moves price and quantity supplied closer to socially optimised levels

a Pigouvian tax, after economist Arthur Pigou, who in his 1920 work *The Economics of Welfare*, first distinguished between 'marginal private net product' and 'marginal social net product', or what we refer to as equilibrium quantity and socially optimal quantity. Pigou argued:

> 'It is … possible for the state, if it so chooses, to remove the divergence [between social and private costs] in any field by 'extraordinary encouragements' or 'extraordinary restraints' upon investments in that field. The most obvious forms which these encouragements and restraints may assume are, of course, those of [subsidies] and taxes.'

A Pigouvian tax, in other words, is one that 'restrains' the investments in an industry to 'remove the divergence' between MPCs and MSCs. The classic example of a Pigouvian tax is that on cigarettes, although many other examples exist, including taxes on sugary beverages, fatty foods, petrol (gasoline), non-renewable energies, alcohol, marijuana (in countries where it is legal), and carbon emissions. Figure 10.7 shows the effect of a tax on alcohol, charged to the sellers, but shared by both producers and consumers.

A per-unit tax of $P_{E1} - P_T$ has been imposed on alcoholic beverages, increasing the cost to sellers and thus reducing supply from $S = MSC$ to S with tax. Equilibrium price has increased to P_{E1} and quantity demanded has decreased to Q_{E1}. The tax burden is shared by sellers (who receive only P_T for each unit of alcohol sold) and buyers (who pay more for each unit bought).

Pigouvian taxes are 'corrective' taxes in that they help to correct the market failure. The amount of alcohol bought after the tax (Q_{E1}) is closer to the socially optimal quantity (Q_{SO}). The DWL from alcohol consumption (domestic abuse, drunk driving, reduced productivity, and poorer health) is smaller thanks to a government intervention that required alcohol sellers and consumers to share in the burden that alcohol places on society, thereby 'internalising' the externality.

Carbon taxes

Of course, taxes on alcohol and cigarettes are so common that they are expected in nearly every country. Few people question their effectiveness at both reducing consumption from what it might be without taxes but also at raising revenues for city, state, provincial, or federal governments (depending on which tax authority collects the tax revenues). More controversial is the use of Pigouvian taxes to limit the consumption of goods that are less avoidable than cigarettes, alcohol, or marijuana: taxes on goods that nearly everyone has to buy just to get through the week.

Carbon taxes, for example, have been proposed in many countries as a means of shifting consumers away from carbon-intensive fuel sources such as gas, coal, diesel, and petrol, and towards renewable energy and transportation fuels such as wind and solar energy and more fuel efficient or even zero emissions cars like hybrids and electric vehicles.

Industrial emissions, Antwerp, Belgium

A carbon tax would be levied on manufacturers of different products based on the amount of carbon dioxide emitted through the good's production. For instance, let us assume the US government places a tax of $30 per metric tonne of carbon emitted anywhere in the USA. Every producer in every industry would be required to track their carbon emissions, report their figures to the government, and pay $30 per tonne emitted in tax. The result would be an increase in the MPC of producing any good that emits carbon through its production process. Not all goods, of course, are responsible for carbon emissions, but even intermediate goods like minerals, plastics, chemicals, and other inputs used in the production of goods that are thought of as relatively 'clean' will be taxed. Thus, the tax will be passed on through the chain of production, increasing the costs of most manufactured goods throughout the economy.

The higher cost would reduce the supply of affected goods, driving the price up and reducing the quantity demanded. Opponents of carbon taxes point to the assumed macroeconomic impacts of reduced overall output, higher prices, and lower standards of living among households whose incomes are stretched due to higher prices. Whereas, supporters argue that revenues from carbon taxes can be used to pay for income tax cuts for households, and with increased disposable incomes consumers will be free to buy goods that are less carbon intensive, which will become more attractive due to their lower prices. Over time the carbon tax will generate much needed government revenue, but more importantly will incentivise producers and consumers to shift their production and consumption patterns away from carbon-intensive goods and towards a more sustainable pattern of economic behaviour.

Legislation and regulation

Corrective subsidies and taxes provide governments with means of 'encouragement' or 'restraint', in the language of Pigou, to narrow the divergence between private costs and social costs in markets where externalities exist. A potentially more blunt instrument of government intervention is the use of legislation and regulation. In Chapter 9 we gave examples of government agencies in the USA that are tasked with overseeing and regulating the activities of various industries, from the aviation industry to the transportation sector to the markets for energy and education. When governments pass laws or make rules that *require* certain behaviours of producers and consumers, they are intervening in markets to try and produce more socially optimal outcomes than what might be achieved otherwise.

Some examples of government regulations and legislation to correct market failures include things as common and familiar as speed limits on public roads, minimum ages to drink and smoke, laws against child labour, the regulation of toxic substances, the illegality of hard drugs, workplace safety laws, and requirements that children attend school until a certain age. In each of these cases the government has determined that without rules and regulations, private individuals and producers might make decisions that they deem to be in their own self-interest ('I am late to work, therefore I will drive 150 kilometres per hour on this state highway'!) but which are clearly not in the interest of society as a whole.

Case study – the ethics of individual liberty versus social good

Rules, regulations, and laws are the glue that hold society together in the face of the sometimes-fierce libertarian instincts of many people within a community. A case in point is the conflict in the USA over the wearing of cloth face coverings in public during the COVID-19 pandemic. Millions of Americans refused to wear masks voluntarily, thus when those who were knowingly or unknowingly infected with the coronavirus ventured into public places, they were highly likely to spread the virus through seemingly innocuous activities like breathing, sneezing, coughing, or simply carrying on a conversation with others.

Because simple appeals from public health officials were not enough to get the majority of the population to wear masks, governments at different levels, from the city to county to state, passed 'mask mandates', which were essentially temporary laws requiring that citizens wear masks in public. Violators could be cited with a fine or arrested depending on the provisions of the mandate.

In this case, government intervention is required to reduce the MPB of 'not wearing a mask' to essentially zero, since the socially optimal number of people who should NOT be wearing masks in public during a pandemic is zero. Another way to look at it is there are external benefits of wearing a mask right now; therefore by fining or arresting people who do not wear masks, it increases the MPB of wearing a mask so that it is closer to the MSB, thereby reducing the potential welfare gain of masking up.

Discuss the trade-off society faces between individuals' freedom to make decisions about their own health and the conflict with successfully achieving public health. Do you think mask mandates were the right approach for governments to take during the COVID-19 pandemic?

Research and inquiry

Carbon taxes are still rare, but very popular among economists who would like to see Arthur Pigou's vision of 'removing the divergence' between social and private costs applied on a larger scale than the targeted taxes on individual goods like alcohol and cigarettes.

To further explore the potential effects of a carbon tax on the US economy, do a web search for the 'RFF E3 Carbon Pricing Calculator'. Once you have located the calculator, play around with it by trying different carbon tax rates and tax growth rates, examining the different effects on annual emissions and on tax revenues.

For discussion and debate:

1 How much less carbon would the USA emit in the year 2030 with a $30 per tonne CO_2 tax, increasing at 1% above inflation each year, compared to the amount it would emit without a carbon tax?

2 What percentage of 2005 levels of CO_2 would the US emit in 2030 with a $30 per tonne carbon tax increasing at 1% above inflation each year?

3 How would your answers to (1) and (2) change if the tax were increased to $50 per tonne?

4 Explain the slope of the annual gross revenue curve. What happens when you increase the rate at which the carbon tax increases annually? Why do revenues from the carbon tax decrease over time?

5 What are the opportunity costs of imposing a tax on all carbon emissions? What are the benefits? In your opinion, are the benefits worth the costs?

Education – awareness creation

Whereas regulations, mandates, rules, and laws are examples of government intervention in markets to *require* behaviour that is more socially optimal (staying in school until the age of 16, driving at a reasonable speed, drinking only when you are of an appropriate age, or wearing a mask during a public health crisis), educating the public on good behaviour presents another, perhaps less direct, means of promoting socially desirable market outcomes.

Examples of education for reducing market failures are health education in general, which may aim to educate young people about the importance of a healthy diet and avoiding tobacco and drugs, and even driver's education, which makes sure that only people who have been instructed on safe vehicle operation are allowed on the roads, thereby reducing instances of traffic accidents and deaths.

Public and private organisations that promote safer behaviours are essentially aiming to increase the MPB of those behaviours, thereby reducing the potential welfare gain from healthy and safe practices.

Tradable permits

When the goal of an intervention is to reduce the amount of a good that is produced or consumed, taxes, regulations, or education can be employed, but another method is to simply require a permit for each unit of the good a user wishes to consume. Consider the example of carbon dioxide once more. Earlier in this chapter we discussed carbon taxes as a means of internalising the external costs of producing goods that emit carbon in their production. A carbon tax generates revenue for the government and creates a disincentive for firms to use carbon-rich production methods. A tax acts as a 'punishment' for polluting, but offers no 'reward' for firms that clean up their act. In colloquial terms, a tax is 'all stick, but no carrot'.

Now consider a tradable pollution permit. The government could issue permits to every manufacturer in the country that would allow them to emit a certain amount of carbon dioxide based on the industry and historical levels of pollution. Some firms may already be using 'green' production methods and may not need the permits they are issued. Other firms, meanwhile, may be using older, less efficient means of production and might require more permits than they are issued. The beauty of a tradable pollution permit is that rather than paying the government for each tonne of carbon dioxide a firm emits (which a carbon tax requires), a heavy polluter instead must pay another firm for additional permits. The total amount of pollution can thus be capped at a 'safe' level by the government, and rather than paying the government to pollute at whatever level they desire, firms must acquire a permit from among the limited number available from other firms that are polluting less and therefore do not require the permits they possess.

Tradable pollution permits act as both a carrot and a stick, since they reward good behaviour and punish bad behaviour. In contrast, a carbon tax only punishes bad behaviour. Firms that adopt greener production methods are rewarded by being able to sell unneeded permits. Additionally, the government can control the total level of pollution by limiting the number of permits available. Supply of permits is perfectly inelastic, in other words; increased demand for carbon dioxide emitting technologies does not lead to increased emissions, only a higher cost to pollute. In the long run,

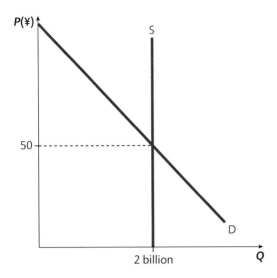

Figure 10.8 The supply of tradable pollution permits is fixed according to the number issued by government

demand for polluting technologies should decrease, since permits are in essence a complementary good that must be purchased in order to produce goods that emit carbon dioxide. If the government wants to reduce pollution, it simply issues fewer permits, which increases the cost to pollute and further rewards firms that reduce their emissions.

Figure 10.8 shows the market for tradable permits for the emission of carbon dioxide by producers. Each permit allows a firm to emit one tonne of carbon dioxide. A firm that emits 50,000 tonnes each year, in other words, would be required to hold 50,000 permits.

The government has issued 2 billion permits that allow for 1 metric tonne of carbon dioxide pollution each. Supply is set by the government, while demand is downward sloping. The cheaper it is to pollute, the more polluting firms will wish to do. However, the amount of pollution permitted is fixed; so, what happens if demand for polluting technologies or products increase? Let us assume that economic growth increases the demand for all kinds of carbon dioxide-related production, from energy to industrial use. Figure 10.9 shows what happens when there is more demand for pollution permits.

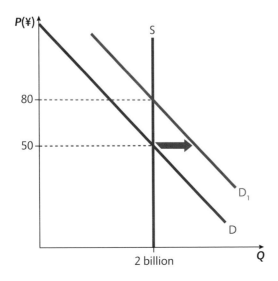

Figure 10.9 As demand for pollution permits rises, higher prices reward and incentivise 'greener' firms

Producers now demand more pollution permits, but the quantity supplied has stayed fixed at 2 billion. The cost to pollute, however, increases to ¥80 (¥ is the symbol for the yuan, the currency of China) per tonne. As overall demand for pollution has increased, firms that have reduced their emissions are able to sell their permits to those that wish to pollute more, increasing the greener firms' profits and making pollution less profitable. Total emissions, meanwhile, remain unchanged.

International agreements

Many of the market failures we have discussed in this chapter are global in nature, not local. Global carbon dioxide emissions contribute to climate change, a market failure arising from the common access resource that is our atmosphere, which is non-excludable but rivalrous. International agreements provide a means of holding countries accountable towards taking steps that help prevent the tragedy of the commons.

In an effort to overcome the global challenge of climate change, world leaders have come together several times in recent decades in an effort to work out agreements over steps all countries will take to share the burden of reducing greenhouse gas emissions. The 2016 Paris Climate Agreement is one example.

The Paris Agreement central aim is to strengthen the global response to the threat of climate change by keeping a global temperature rise this century well below 2°C above pre-industrial levels and to pursue efforts to limit the temperature increase even further to 1.5°C. Additionally, the agreement aims to strengthen the ability of countries to deal with the impacts of climate change. To reach these ambitious goals, appropriate financial flows, a new technology framework and an enhanced capacity building framework will be put in place, thus supporting action by developing countries and the most vulnerable countries, in line with their own national objectives.

TOK

Other examples of international agreements aimed at reducing the harmful impacts arising from negative externalities of the unsustainable exploitation of resources associated with common access resources include:

- Basel Convention on the Control of Transboundary Movements of Hazardous Wastes and their Disposal (1989)
- Convention on Biodiversity (1993)
- Convention on International Trade in Endangered Species (1973)
- Montreal Protocol on Substances that Deplete the Ozone Layer (1987)
- Stockholm Convention on Persistent Organic Pollutants (2001)
- United Nations Environment Programme (UNEP) (founded 1972)

In each of these agreements, a global common pool resource is being protected. When international cooperation is required to achieve sustainability, international agreements are the best way to get countries to work together.

Several challenges arise that may limit the effectiveness of international agreements at protecting common pool resources: monitoring the extent to which participating countries adhere to their pledged reductions in harmful activities, for one. There is no 'world government' that can track or enforce limits on air pollution by participating countries. In most cases, one country cannot 'punish' another country for failing to meet emissions targets or to take necessary steps to protect a particular resource or endangered species.

Without agreements, the free-rider problem arises once more. Why should Vietnam require its industries to reduce greenhouse gas emissions by 30% if Bangladesh continues to allow its producers to pollute at ever increasing levels? The costs of mitigating climate change would be unfairly borne by certain countries, while others free ride on their actions and enjoy the climate benefits without making any sacrifices.

Where in your own life do you see the free-rider problem at play? Are there free-riders in your school or your community who do not take the best action for society as a whole in pursuit of their own self-interest? Give some examples.

International agreements present a version of what economists call the 'prisoner's dilemma'. Assume, for example, that 100 of the most developed countries agree to reduce greenhouse gas emissions by 5% per year starting in 2020. The climate benefits of countries undertaking such reductions would be enjoyed by all, but by some countries more than others (those with expansive, low-lying, heavily populated coastal zones, for example, which would benefit from a reduction in sea level rises).

However, if every country assumes that all other countries are taking the difficult steps to reduce their emissions, then it becomes less important for any individual country to reduce its own emissions. One country, in other words, could free ride on the good behaviour of all the other countries. The problem is, when more than one country (say, a dozen, or 25, or 50!) of the hundred in the agreement make the same rational decision that it is no big deal if they do not reduce their emissions since they will enjoy the climate benefits of everyone else reducing theirs, then we end up in a situation where the international climate agreement fails altogether.

The 'prisoner's dilemma', a thought experiment used by game theorists to predict the outcome of situations like this, predicts that when multiple agents must cooperate to achieve an outcome that is good for all, but not the best possible outcome for each individual agent, the agents tend to 'cheat' and pursue the outcome that benefits each agent the most; thus the effort to achieve the socially optimal outcome fails. Often **game theory** is used to analyse the behaviour of oligopolistic firms in imperfectly competitive markets (Chapter 12), but it applies rather well to understand why international environmental agreements are often unsuccessful at achieving their stated environmental aims. Once again, the selfish behaviours that give rise to the free-rider problem described earlier in this chapter contribute to market failures even at the international level.

10.3 Public goods

Learning outcomes

At the end of this section you will be able to:

- using the concepts of rivalry and excludability, and providing examples, distinguish between public goods (**non-rivalrous** and non-excludable) and private goods (rivalrous and **excludable**)
- explain, with reference to the free-rider problem, how the lack of public goods indicates market failure
- discuss the implications of the direct provision of public goods by the government.

What are public goods?

Earlier in this chapter we defined common pool (or common access) resources as ones that are *non-excludable* but *rivalrous*. No individual can be excluded from consuming or participating in the use of a common pool resource, but their use or consumption is rivalrous, meaning one person's use diminishes the benefit the good provides to the rest of society. As a result, common resources tend to be *over-consumed*, leading to an unsustainable depletion of such resources.

A similarly defined, but very different, type of good is one that is non-excludable, but also non-rivalrous. A public good, such as national defence, is one that every person is able to benefit from but that one person's benefit or use of does not diminish the benefit or use enjoyed by the rest of society. National defence, by which we mean the existence of armed forces that protect all people within a country's borders from aggression by foreign forces, benefits everyone within the country's borders. No individuals within the country are excluded from the protection the defence force provides.

However, when one more person, or a hundred, or a million more people, enter the country, their presence does not subtract from the value the defence force provides the people who were already there. This is in contrast to a common pool resource like fresh drinking water. A million people who move into a watershed will put increasing strain on the supply of fresh drinking water, while contributing to sources of water pollution, diminishing water supply and quality for everyone else. Fresh drinking water, in contrast to defence, is non-excludable, but rivalrous. Defence, meanwhile, is both non-excludable *and* non-rivalrous.

The market failure that arises due to the existence of public goods is that due to the inability to exclude certain people from benefiting from the good and the fact that the benefits are universal (for everyone), there is no incentive for private firms to provide the good. Without government, pure public goods would not be available. This explains why armies, navies, air forces, and other defence forces are always 'national'. Private militias or paramilitary groups, in contrast, provide defence to the private parties that hire or finance them, or to the small communities from which their ranks are drawn. The services of private defence forces are excludable; if you are not part of the community paying for protection, you cannot expect to receive protection.

Other examples of pure public goods include things like roads and sidewalks, streetlights, lighthouses, fire departments, police and sheriff departments, the legal system, and the criminal justice system. Consider streetlights. Once a street is lit, no individual walking, driving, or cycling along that street at night can be excluded from using the light to see where they are going. Nor does having a second or third or fourth person within the arc of a particular streetlight diminish the benefit the light provides all other users. Streetlights are non-rivalrous and non-excludable. So, who installs and pays for the operation of streetlights? Well, usually that is the municipal government of the area in question. Why not a private business? Because, of course, it would be impossible to charge each individual who benefits from the light for its use.

Direct government provision of public goods is most common, but in some cases private sector firms might be contracted to provide goods at public expense. Motorways like Germany's autobahn, Italy's autostrada, or the interstate highway system in the USA, while financed at taxpayer expense, are rarely constructed by government employees themselves; rather, private contractors will bid for the jobs, and enter into a contract *with* the government, earning a profit in the process. In contrast, most militaries are fully public; servicemembers in national armies are directly employed by the state. The same could be said for publicly-funded school teachers and doctors and nurses working at public hospitals. In most developed countries today, however, the provision of public goods is made possible by partnerships between the government and the private sector.

The market failure of public goods is perhaps the ultimate market failure. Whereas other goods that we have studied in this chapter are either *over-* or *under-provided* (demerit and merit goods) or *over-consumed* (common pool resources) in the free market, there simply is no market for pure public goods. Owing to their non-excludability, the free-rider problem explained earlier in the chapter exists for public goods as well: individuals who benefit from the good may do so without doing anything to help pay for the good. This is why the provision of public goods is left to the government and paid for not by the willing expenditures of the users of the good at the point of consumption, but through the obligatory collection of direct or indirect taxes, collected by the state, and used to provide the goods that otherwise would not be provided. Government provision is the only solution to the market failure of pure public goods.

Video suggestions:
You have read about it, now you can review what you have just learned by watching some videos by the author!
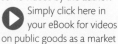 Simply click here in your eBook for videos on public goods as a market failure.

HL 10.4 Asymmetric information

How does information asymmetry lead to market failure?

Learning outcomes

At the end of this section you will be able to:

- explain, using examples, that market failure may occur when one party in an economic transaction (either the buyer or the seller) possesses more information than the other party
- HL evaluate possible government responses, including legislation, regulation, and provision of information.

Market theory presupposes that all actors are in possession of the same perfect levels of information regarding market transactions. All consumers, for instance, will know the variety of prices and quality levels available for a particular good. Of course, this is highly unlikely, as consumers are constrained by time and access to such information. Even in the digital information age, when far more information on any product is widely available, consumers make a decision about the opportunity cost of absorbing all the alternatives, and rarely possess anything close to perfect information.

What is adverse selection?

With this reality in mind, it is more than likely for consumers to make 'mistakes' regarding purchases, in pure market theory terms. Today, consumers are also more likely to be subjected to sophisticated marketing techniques that aim to limit information and choice. One variety of asymmetric information has one party in a transaction holding more information than the other party. For example, the seller of a plot of land might know that neighbouring land will, in the near future, be used for a chemical plant, while the buyer is ignorant of this information. The buyer will pay too much for the land – an example of market failure.

Adverse selection refers to a situation where the seller has more information about the characteristics or the quality of a good than the buyer, or vice versa. A used car dealer may withhold information about the service history of a vehicle that a customer is considering buying in order to make the car more attractive to the buyer, thus earning a higher selling price. Without correct information, the buyer will pay too much, and across several transactions the seller will extract consumer surplus from their customers who are ill-informed about the true nature of the cars they are buying; more used cars will be sold at higher prices than what is optimal for the market as a whole.

Entire industries can experience adverse selection if producers withhold information they know to be true from their customers. Cigarette producers in the tobacco industry were aware of studies linking smoking to cancer for decades, but withheld or denied knowledge of the adverse health effects of their product, assuring consumers that there was nothing to fear by consuming a 'healthy' volume of cigarettes each day. The result of withholding scientific facts from their customers was higher than optimal cigarette usage and a public health crisis that was only brought under control once the government began regulating and taxing tobacco firms to reduce supply of and demand for their products to a more socially optimal level.

Adverse selection can also occur when the product is relatively complex for the average person to understand. The 2008 financial crisis was partly caused by the sale of complicated mortgage loans to borrowers, as well as the repackaging of those loans to potential investors. Health and life insurance policies are notoriously complex. Finally, consider the 'terms and conditions' statements that app and websites require for our use. Do we ever read them?

What is moral hazard?

Another market failure arising from asymmetric information occurs when a party provides misleading information and changes behaviour after a transaction has taken place.

An example is a life insurance company that takes on a customer who, in his or her application, claims that he or she does not participate in any extreme sports or work in a job that is particularly hazardous, but then takes up sky diving and takes work as a coal miner. Sky diving and working in mines are both extremely dangerous activities; if the insurance company had known their client was going to be participating in these activities, they would have thought twice about taking them on as a customer, or at the very least charged much higher premiums to cover the increased risk the individual's lifestyle poses.

Moral hazard describes the tendency for individuals to engage in activities that they might not otherwise participate in because of a previously agreed upon arrangement that mitigates the risk to the individual's financial well-being. Another example of moral hazard is when someone rents a car and takes out the full insurance coverage; once he or she leaves the lot he or she is not financially responsible for any damage to the vehicle, including damage they may cause. Therefore, the renter is likely to drive the car far more recklessly than she would if it were their own property on which he or she would share in the cost of any repairs to damage done.

What are appropriate responses to asymmetric information?

The result of market failures arising from information asymmetry is that too much of some goods are consumed at too high of a price (in the case of adverse selection), or too low of a price (in the case of moral hazard: think of how the insurance company or the car rental agency would have adjusted their premiums or rental rates if they had known the truth about how their clients would act once the contract had been signed). The solutions to these market failures lie in improving access to information, and there are both private and public examples of appropriate responses.

Government responses to asymmetric information include consumer protection legislation, regulation, and direct provision of information. These include laws that make it illegal for producers to supply false information about their products (such as truth in advertising laws, which require that advertisements on the television, radio, or the internet, are 'truthful, not misleading, and, when appropriate, backed by scientific evidence'), and the existence of regulatory agencies (some of which were mentioned in Chapter 9) whose responsibility is to monitor and require certain disclosures of firms in various industries; both aim to improve access to information among consumers.

Beginning on 2 January, 2020, the US Department of Agriculture's Bioengineered Food Disclosure Law, for example, began requiring all US food manufacturers to disclose on their packaging when a food includes ingredients that are or may be bioengineered. Doing so allows consumers who may have concerns about bioengineered foods to make informed decisions at the point of purchase, and avoid such products should they wish to do so.

Private responses to asymmetric information are myriad. There are publications that can be purchased, such as *Consumer Reports* (a subscription-based magazine), that are dedicated to offering potential buyers detailed product reviews of different categories of goods so they can make informed decisions before buying. Amazon, the world's largest online retailer, includes a robust customer review feature that allows shoppers to read reviews for individual products, such as a set of Bluetooth earbuds, before buying; these private solutions make it increasingly difficult for sellers to withhold information about their products with the aim of exploiting unwitting consumers.

Video suggestions:
You have read about it, now you can review what you have just learned by watching some videos by the author! Simply click here in your eBook for videos on asymmetric information as a market failure.

10.5 The market's inability to achieve equity

Learning outcomes

At the end of this section you will be able to:

* **HL** discuss how the workings of a free market economy may result in an unequal distribution of income and wealth.

Why do markets sometimes fail to achieve equity?

Throughout this chapter, and indeed the first ten chapters of this book, we have examined the strengths and weaknesses of the free market system at providing society with the goods and services it wants and needs. When private property rights are clearly established, when perfect information is shared among buyers and sellers, when markets are competitive and the private costs and benefits are equal to one another, and when the goods produced are both excludable and rivalrous, we generally accept the market system as being the best system for producing a good or service.

The signalling mechanism of prices allows buyers to communicate to potential sellers the value they place on the good and sellers to signal to buyers the relative scarcity of different resources and goods. Thus, free markets tend to achieve allocative efficiency and to maximise societal welfare.

However, markets fail in many ways, too, many of which have been explained in detail in this chapter. The results of market failures range from the over-provision of some goods to the **under-provision** of others, to the lack of a market altogether for yet others. When markets fail, the effects can be felt on the environmental, health, and societal levels among others. One of the social consequences of market failure is the inability of the market to achieve equity, or *fairness*, which leads to an unequal playing field in which certain groups in society enjoy higher incomes and a greater level of wealth than others.

Inequities (or unfairness) that are intrinsic to the market system lead to inequality: a situation in which a relatively large percentage of the world's wealth is shared by a tiny proportion of the population. Some of the most unequal countries are, perhaps not surprisingly, those in which government plays the smallest role in the economy. The under-provision of merit and public goods like education, healthcare, security, and infrastructure means that those with wealth can afford to access such goods on the free market, while those without wealth must get by without them (or only have access to poorer quality services). The inequitable distribution of income and goods by the free market leads to generational inequality, where people who are born poor are likely to remain poor while those lucky to be born in rich families are given opportunities in life that almost guarantee they end up rich.

To promote greater equity, governments intervene in the free market to:

- provide or support the provision of merit and public goods
- break up monopolies that tend to result in wealth concentration among the owners of capital
- regulate or tax industries whose externalities disproportionately harm the poor
- redistribute income through **progressive taxation** systems
- provide social safety nets in a way that helps elevate the living standards of those who the market system might otherwise leave behind.

Inequity is, it could be argued, the ultimate result of market failure, and government intervention, when done well, helps to make markets *moral*, while protecting the system of incentives and rewards that make the market system so effective at delivering the goods and services we all need and want.

Practice exam questions

1a. Using an appropriate diagram, explain how negative
     externalities are a type of market failure. (10 marks)

  b. Evaluate the measures that a government might adopt
     to correct market failure arising from negative externalities. (15 marks)

2a. What are positive externalities and how do they arise?
     Illustrate your answer with examples. (10 marks)

  b. To what extent should governments attempt to influence
     markets where positive externalities exist? (15 marks)

3a. 'National policies and international agreements must be
     implemented in order to reduce global environmental
     problems'. Using the concept of market failure, explain the
     statement above from an economist's point of view. (10 marks)

  b. With reference to both national policies and international
     agreements, discuss three solutions that could be
     recommended by economists. (15 marks)

4. How does the under-provision of merit goods by the free
   market give rise to inequality in society? (10 marks)

HL Market power:
perfect competition
versus monopoly

11

11.1 Introduction to market structures

Learning outcomes

At the end of this section you will be able to:

- describe, using examples, the assumed characteristics of **perfect competition**:
  - a large number of firms
  - a **homogeneous product**
  - freedom of entry and exit
  - perfect information
  - perfect resource mobility
- describe, using examples, the assumed characteristics of a monopoly:
  - a single or dominant firm in the market
  - no close substitutes
  - significant **barriers to entry**
- describe, using examples, barriers to entry, including:
  - **economies of scale**
  - branding
  - legal barriers.

In Chapter 10 we examined many ways that markets fail to achieve socially optimal outcomes. Whenever the market equilibrium quantity of a good is greater than or less than the socially optimal quantity, a market failure exists. While externalities, common pool resources, public goods, and information asymmetry all give rise to market failures of their own, perhaps the most common situation in which markets fail to achieve efficiency is when there exists **imperfect competition**. The degree of competition in a market tells us, before we even consider the characteristics of the good or services in question, whether the market is even capable of achieving a socially optimal, allocatively efficient, level of production.

Let us back up. A market's *structure* refers to the degree of competition among producers or suppliers in general (since this could apply to labour markets as well). Any particular market's structure falls along a spectrum of competition, from *perfect competition* on one end to *pure monopoly* on the other. Figure 11.1 provides a conceptual image of such a spectrum.

The two ends of our spectrum are where we will begin our examination of market structures, beginning with perfect competition.

What is a perfectly competitive market?

A *perfectly competitive market* is one in which individual firms produce such a small proportion of the overall supply of the product that altering their own output has no

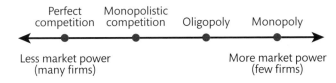

Figure 11.1 The less competition a firm faces, the more power it has in the market

187

influence over the market price of the product. In this regard, firms in such an industry are **price-takers**; this means that they find it impossible to charge a price higher than that charged by their competitors, nor can they successfully offer their output at a lower price since competition forces the price down to the producers' lowest average cost.

In addition to perfectly competitive markets consisting of a large number of identical, price-taking firms, the model also assumes that the firms:

- produce completely identical products (the goods are not differentiated and act as perfect substitutes for each other)
- can enter or exit the market very easily (with effectively no barriers to entry or exit)
- will produce where marginal social benefit equals marginal social cost, achieving allocative efficiency (this is assuming there are not externalities arising from the good's production or consumption).

While perfectly competitive industries are rare in the real world, examples of markets with some of these characteristics do exist in certain industries, including some agricultural commodities, such as coffee or cocoa, low-tech manufactured goods, certain types of low-skilled labour, markets in which there are many firms producing nearly identical products or millions of households supplying an identical resource (such as labour). Despite being rare, perfectly competitive markets are worth studying for what they teach us about resource allocation and the efficiency resulting from high levels of competition between firms.

Assuming there are no spillover benefits or costs (externalities) in the production or consumption of the product, perfectly competitive markets result in the most socially optimal level of output and price of any of the four market structures, and are therefore considered allocatively efficient. Shortages and surpluses are non-existent in perfectly competitive markets, wherein the high level of competition ensures that the marginal social benefit of a particular product will align with the marginal social cost and neither too much nor too little will be produced. The perfectly competitive model can be held up as an example of perfect efficiency when compared to less competitive market models in which the price-making market power of individual firms results in a level of output that is lower than and a price that is higher than that achieved under perfect competition. This provides evidence that efficiency decreases as markets become less competitive.

What is a monopoly?

Let us move now to the other end of our market structure spectrum, to monopoly. A monopoly is a market where one firm dominates the market for a good that has no substitutes and where significant barriers to entry exist. To most people, monopoly might seem akin to autocracy, where one company makes the rules, sets the prices, and controls its destiny. As you will see, monopolies can occur in different types of markets and take many forms.

The Dutch East India Company offers a historical example of a monopolistic firm. Throughout the 17th and 18th centuries the company exerted nearly total control over the spice trade between Europe and Asia, giving it monopoly power in the European spice market. Its power was derived from its control of access to spices, and thus its dominant market share. Trade with Asia took place almost entirely along sea routes controlled by the company, so the limited volume of spices that made it to the continent over land accounted for such a tiny share of total sales that the Dutch East India Company enjoyed a high degree of monopoly power.

More recently, Mark Zuckerberg's Facebook has emerged as a dominant player in the social media industry, where Facebook-owned apps controlled 56% of the market (based on site visits in May of 2020). As the dominant firm in the social media market Facebook has great power over the fate of its customers: not only the users whose private information the company stores and sells access to, but just as importantly the thousands of businesses that pay for online ads on Facebook's platforms. Its market power gives Facebook great influence over prices for online ads and earns the company substantial profits.

Another well-known modern-day monopolist is Jeff Bezos, former CEO and now executive chairman of the board of Amazon, the world's largest online retailer, which controls 49% of America's online retail market (and an increasing share of the markets in the rest of the world, where the company is rapidly expanding its operations). Amazon's dominance has not necessarily harmed consumers, who benefit from the firm's economies of scale and wide selection of goods that can be delivered right to their doors, but traditional brick and mortar retail businesses have suffered as Amazon has increasingly taken over the markets for countless goods that used to be purchased locally in physical outlets.

None of the three examples above describe a pure monopoly, or a market with only a single seller. That is because such markets are extremely rare. Examples include nationalised industries like railways and airlines (in some countries) or natural monopolies (defined later in this chapter) for local utilities such as the electric company, the garbage collection company, or the wastewater treatment company. In markets for consumer goods monopolies are rare, and the two forms of imperfect competition in the middle of our spectrum are the dominant market structure: **monopolistic competition** and oligopoly. These will be explored in detail in Chapter 12.

For now, let us examine the characteristics of a monopolistic market.

Single seller

When a firm controls the market entirely and is the only producer of the good, it is called a pure monopoly. The term 'monopoly' is derived from the Greek *mono* (single) and *polein* (to sell). However, the case where a single firm controls a dominant share of the market is much more common than a pure single seller.

No close substitutes

Being the single seller of a good would hold little value if that good were easily replaceable with something else. Therefore, for true monopoly power, a firm must be selling something that has no substitutes.

Price-maker

As the single seller of a good without substitutes, the firm will have some power to set the price of the good. The extent of that power is limited by the overall demand for the good, but this power can be considerable. In contrast to the perfect competitor, which must accept whatever price is set in the larger market, the monopolist has significant price-making power.

Barriers to entry

A monopolist keeps the dominant position because there are significant barriers to other firms' entry into the market. In the absence of competition, the firm can maintain its price-making power, and will continue to make **abnormal profits**. Entry barriers may include:

- legal barriers (permits or licences required by government but held by a single or a few firms)
- economies of scale (prohibitively high fixed costs to enter a market), patents, or copyrights
- control or ownership of key resources, and other factors that prevent competition from entering a market.

Where an industry sits along our spectrum of competition determines several factors, such as the level of efficiency and the degree to which the firm achieves socially optimal levels of output, the price level of the goods being produced, the amount of consumer surplus relative to producer surplus, the profitability of the firms in the market, and the amount of deadweight loss (DWL) resulting from production.

The more firms there are competing in a market, the closer the market will come to achieving allocative and productive efficiency. The less competitive a market, the more likely firms are to earn profits, but at the expense of consumer surplus and allocative efficiency. These and other concepts will be explored further in this chapter and the next.

11.2 Profit maximisation

Learning outcomes

At the end of this section you will be able to:

- explain the meaning of economic costs
- distinguish between explicit costs and implicit costs
- analyse the difference between total revenue, **average revenue**, and **marginal revenue**
- illustrate, using diagrams, the relationship between total revenue, average revenue, and marginal revenue
- calculate total revenue, average revenue, and marginal revenue from a set of data and/or diagrams
- distinguish between economic profit and normal profit
- analyse why a firm will continue to operate even when it earns zero economic profit
- explain the meaning of loss.

Businesses, like individuals, respond to incentives in the pursuit of their economic objectives. The goal of individual consumers in a market economy is to maximise their utility or happiness which, in the economic realm, is achieved through increased consumption of goods and services made possible through increased income. Individuals, therefore, seek to maximise their incomes by selling their productive resources (land, labour, and capital) to those firms that demand them in the resource market.

The objective of most firms, conversely, is to maximise their profits through the production and sale of their various goods and services in the product market. The interaction of firms and individuals in the resource and product markets is the defining activity of the market economic system. In the pursuit of their goal of profit maximisation, firms must accomplish two distinct objectives: reducing costs and increasing revenues until the difference between the two (the profit) is maximised.

Costs in economics are those things that must be given up in order to have something else. Costs can be explicit or implicit. Explicit costs are the monetary payments that firms make to the owners of land, labour, and capital in the resource market (i.e. rent, wages, and interest, respectively). Implicit costs include the opportunity costs of entrepreneurs who decide to allocate their time and energy to one enterprise over other possible economic activities (in economics, the implicit cost of an entrepreneur is called normal profit, a concept that will be defined later in this chapter).

Revenue is the income earned from a firm's sale of its goods or services to consumers in the product market. A firm's profit is the difference between its total revenue (TR) earned in product market and its total cost (TC) in the resource market, as shown in the following equation:

$$Economic\ profit = TR - TC$$

Table 11.1 shows the costs and revenues (in euros) faced by a bakery that correspond with different daily output levels of its most popular product, croissants. Assume the bakery sells its croissants in a competitive market at a price of €3 per croissant. At this price the bakery can sell as many croissants as it wishes. Therefore, its total revenues at each level of production equal the number of croissants produced times the price ($TR = P \times Q$).

Table 11.1   Short-run costs of production

Number of croissants produced (Q)	Total cost (€)	Marginal cost (€)	Average cost (€)	Total revenue (€)	Marginal revenue (€)	Average revenue (€)
0	100	—	—	0	3	3
20	120	1	6	60	3	3
40	130	0.5	3.25	120	3	3
60	150	1	2.5	180	3	3
80	180	1.5	2.25	240	3	3
100	220	2	2.20	300	3	3
120	270	2.5	2.25	360	3	3
140	330	3	2.36	420	3	3
160	400	3.5	2.5	480	3	3
180	480	4	2.67	540	3	3
200	570	4.5	2.85	600	3	3

From Table 11.1 we can analyse some of the key cost and revenue figures a business must consider in deciding on how to maximise its profits.

Total cost

The firm's TC includes its fixed costs, which are the costs of its capital and land resources (which do not change with the level of production) and its variable costs, which are the costs of labour and raw materials (and do change with the level of production). For our bakery, the fixed costs equal €100 per day, evidenced by the fact that even when the bakery is producing zero croissants it still faces a TC of €100. This may include the rent it pays on its bakery space and the utilities it pays (water, sewerage, electricity, gas, etc.), none of which vary much with the level of output.

Also included in the bakery's TC are its variable costs, or the costs of the resources that must be added to its fixed resources in order to actually produce croissants. As discussed in Chapter 5, a firm's variable costs include the labour and raw materials that must be employed as more output is produced.

Total costs therefore equal the sum of a firm's fixed and variable costs. Not surprisingly, TC increases as output increases, since more variable resources must be employed to produce more croissants.

Marginal cost

A business, like an individual, tends to make decisions based less on total costs and revenues, but on marginal costs and revenues. A firm's marginal cost shows how much the *last unit of output* cost to produce. Since more resources are needed to produce more output, the cost of additional units of output tends to increase. Recall from Chapter 5 that, according to the law of diminishing returns, as more variable resources are added to fixed resources to increase output, the productivity of additional variable resources decreases due to the decreasing ratio of labour to capital. Therefore, the cost of additional units of output tends to increase in the short run.

In our bakery's marginal cost column, we can see that the cost of additional croissants eventually increases. At first, when the bakery goes from 0 to 60 croissants, the marginal cost decreases; this is due to the fact that the first workers and raw materials employed were more productive than those employed before them due to the abundance of capital (baking implements, ovens, etc.) available to them. However, beyond the 60th croissant the marginal cost (the cost of additional croissants) increases. The 60th croissant costs the bakery €1 to produce, the 100th costs €2, the 140th €3, and so on, until the 200th croissant, which costs the bakery €4.50 to produce. The reason additional croissants cost more to produce, recall, is the *diminishing marginal returns* (Chapter 5) experienced as the bakery employs more workers and adds more raw materials to its fixed capital.

Average cost

Marginal cost, we will see, helps a producer decide the optimal level of output to produce, since at a certain point the cost of an additional unit will exceed what the unit can be sold for and it will therefore stop making sense to increase production. However, once the optimal level of output is decided, the question of whether a profit or a loss is being earned requires a business to know its average cost (which can be compared to its average revenue, or the price of the output).

Average cost is simply the *per-unit cost of production*. It is found by dividing the firm's TC by its total output, or the quantity produced.

Total revenue

A firm's revenue is the amount it earns from the sale of its product, and can be found by multiplying the firm's output by the price it is sold for. Revenue should not be confused with profit, which is the firm's revenue minus its costs.

Marginal revenue

The change in a firm's total revenues experienced when output is increased by one unit is the firm's marginal revenue. Again, firms make decisions based as much on *marginal analysis* as anything else. As we will soon see, by comparing the marginal revenue and the marginal cost from an additional unit of output, a producer will be able to determine whether an increase in output will increase or decrease its overall profits.

In a perfectly competitive market like that in which our bakery produces croissants, a firm's marginal revenue is always equal to its price, since additional units of output can be sold at whatever the market price happens to be. Later in this chapter we will see that in imperfectly competitive markets, like monopolies, marginal revenue is always *less than price*, since in order to sell additional units of output an imperfect competitor (as a **price-maker**) must lower its price. For our bakery, however, marginal revenue (MR) = P.

Average revenue

We have defined total costs and **average costs**, TR and marginal revenue, and now define *average revenue*. This one's really simple. In any industry, the average revenue is the price the output sells for. It is the TR divided by the quantity. Recall that TR equals quantity multiplied by the price. Therefore, by the transitive property, price equals average revenue. When we compare a firm's average revenue at a particular level of output to its average cost, we will be able to calculate the firm's *per-unit profit*.

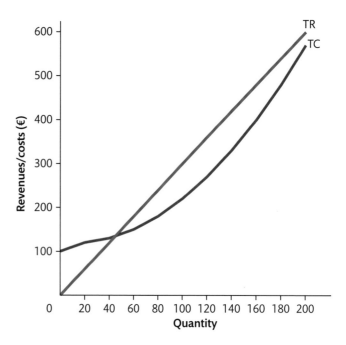

Figure 11.2 Comparing TR and TC reveals the bakery is in profit at outputs above 40 croissants

What is the profit-maximising rule?

We have already defined a firm's economic profit as its total revenues minus its total costs. As an agent interested in maximising its profits, a firm's goal is to find the optimal level of output at which the difference between its TR and its TC is maximised.

Let us first look at a graph of our bakery's total revenues and costs over its possible levels of output. Figure 11.2 shows these values, with TR in green and TC in red.

Any level of output at which total revenues are greater than total costs represent a profit-earning situation for the bakery. Beyond about 40 croissants, in other words, our bakery *can* earn a profit. Below 40, the cost of producing each croissant exceeds revenues; it is not worth the bakery considering a very low level of output, in other words.

To find the *profit-maximising* level of output, however, we must consider the per-unit and marginal costs and revenues. Figure 11.3 shows the bakery's marginal costs (MC), average costs (AC), MR, and average revenue (AR) over its range of possible output.

The first thing to notice is that the firm's MR and AR curves are the same. That is evidence that this bakery sells its product in a perfectly competitive market, in which it is a *price-taker*. The bakery has no control over the market price of croissants, therefore it can sell as few (0) or as many (200) as it likes at the equilibrium price of €3. Demand for the individual seller's output is perfectly elastic in a competitive market.

The question the seller faces, therefore, is not what *price* to charge, rather what *quantity* to produce in order to maximise profits. Figure 11.4 shows the bakery producing at its profit-maximising level of output, where MR = MC.

At 140 croissants the cost of the last croissant equals the price the bakery could sell it for (MC = 3 and MR = 3). The bakery breaks even on the 140th croissant *but earns a profit on every croissant it produced up to that point.*

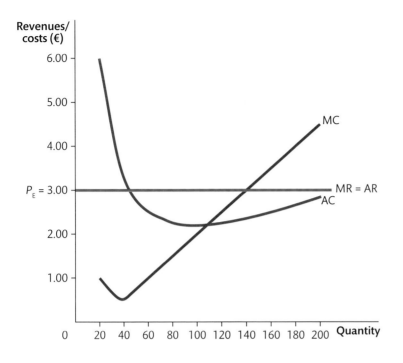

Figure 11.3 Firms look at marginal costs and revenues in order to set output at the **profit-maximising** level

Using the data from our table we can calculate the bakery's profits at its profit-maximising level of output of 140, shown in Table 11.2.

The firm's profit equals €420 − €330, or €90 per day, when it produces 140 croissants at a cost of €2.36 per croissant.

The per-unit profit can also be calculated. With a price of €3, and a cost of €2.36, the bakery earns a profit of €3.00 − €2.36 = €0.64 per croissant.

You may have noticed that the profit-maximising quantity is not, in fact, the quantity at which the bakery's average cost is lowest, which is where the marginal cost curve

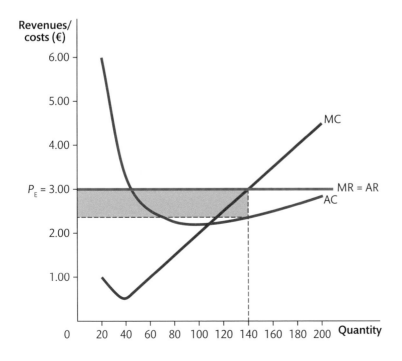

Figure 11.4 The profit-maximising level of output is where MR = MC

Table 11.2 Profits at profit-maximising level of output (140)

Number of croissants produced (Q)	Total cost	Marginal cost	Average cost	Total revenue	Marginal revenue	Average revenue
140	330	3	2.36	420	3	3

crosses the average cost curve somewhere between an output of 100 and 120. This is the *cost-minimising* level of output, where the per-unit cost of croissants is lowest. However, producing at the *cheapest* quantity does not necessarily maximise the bakery's profits. Figure 11.5, which shows the amount of profit the bakery would earn at the cost-minimising level of output, illustrates why.

In Figure 11.5 our baker is producing around 105 croissants, the quantity at which its average cost is lowest. The red dotted rectangle represents the firm's economic profit at the cost-minimising level of output. Profit, recall, is the firm's TR minus its TC. Our graph shows per-unit, not total, revenues and costs, therefore, the dotted red area represents (AR − AC) × Q, or the per-unit profit multiplied by the number of units.

How do we know that the cost-minimising level of output is not necessarily the profit-maximising level of output? Because the blue triangle represents possible additional profits the firm could earn by producing more croissants. For each croissant between 105 and 120, where the marginal cost equals the marginal revenue, the next croissant will sell for more than it costs to produce (MR > MC).

To summarise, a firm that faces an upward-sloping marginal cost curve in the short run, explained by the law of diminishing marginal returns (Chapter 5), can maximise its total profits by choosing to produce at the level of output where the cost of the last unit produced (MC) equals the revenue the firm earns from its sale (MR).

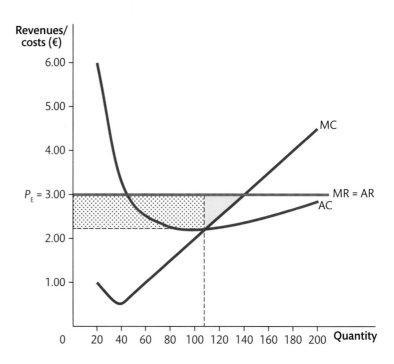

Figure 11.5 The cost-minimising level of output is where average cost is lowest

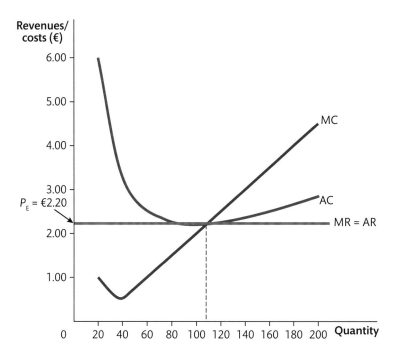

Figure 11.6 At a lower price the firm is breaking even (only earning **normal profits**)

What is the difference between normal profit and abnormal profit?

Our bakery, when producing 140 croissants at a cost of €2.36 and selling them at a price of €3 apiece, is enjoying what economists refer to as abnormal profit. Abnormal profit is earned when a firm covers all of its explicit and implicit costs of production, and then some. Let us look at a situation in which only a normal profit is being earned. Figure 11.6 shows what happens if the market price of croissants falls and our bakery is only able to sell them at a price equal to its minimum average cost of €2.20.

The market price has fallen, and with the lower price the firm's profit-maximising quantity has decreased to 105 croissants. At that quantity, the average cost is equal to the price of €2.20; the bakery is 'breaking even'. This may make it sound like the firm is earning no profits, but economists distinguish between the experience of a firm that is covering all its costs and earning a *normal level of profit* and a firm that is earning an *abnormal profit*, as our bakery was at a price of €3.

A normal profit is earned by a firm that is covering all its explicit costs and implicit costs. Let us distinguish between the two.

Explicit costs

Explicit costs are the monetary payments a firm makes to the owners of the resources it employs in the production of its output. Wages for workers, raw material costs, energy and transport costs, rent payments for factory or retail space, and interest payments to banks are all explicit costs a firm may face.

Implicit costs

Implicit costs refer to the opportunity costs faced by the entrepreneur who undertakes a business venture and who could otherwise have earned money by hiring his self-owned resources out to another employer. The founders of all business enterprises face implicit costs that represent the foregone wages of the entrepreneur who chose to start a business as opposed to earning a wage working for someone else. Also considered an implicit cost is the normal profit an entrepreneur expects to earn above and beyond all his or her explicit costs.

Normal profit is the entrepreneur's implied value of his or her own talent; it is the cost to do business, and if a firm's revenues do not cover the normal profit, the firm owner may choose to shut down and direct his or her efforts towards another industry or area of employment.

To demonstrate the difference between explicit and implicit costs, imagine a chemist who chooses to leave her job paying €100,000 at a pharmaceutical company to start her own research firm. Her explicit costs as a new business owner are the wages she must pay herself and her five researchers, the rent she pays for her lab space, and the interest she pays the bank for the loans she took out to acquire equipment for her laboratory.

The chemist's implicit cost is her perceived value of her entrepreneurial talent, represented by the profit she expects to earn above and beyond her old salary to compensate her for the risk she took when starting her own business. Assume the chemist expects to earn the €100,000 she sacrificed when she left her old job, plus an additional €50,000 to compensate her for the risk she took by starting her own lab. The €50,000 is her normal profit, which she must earn in order for her to consider the venture worth her while.

Back to our bakery example. When our baker is selling her croissants for €2.20 apiece she is covering her explicit costs (paying her employees and her rent and utilities, buying raw materials, etc.) but she is also earning a normal profit. In other words, she is making just enough above and beyond her explicit costs to make it worth her while to remain in the market. Any less than €2.20 per croissant and the bakery owner would decide it was not worth her keeping the bakery open, even though she would still be able to pay her workers and her rent and could still afford all the ingredients to keep operating.

What are 'economic losses'?

When the market price at which an individual firm can sell its product is equal to the firm's minimum average TC, the firm is able to earn a normal profit, but not an abnormal profit. When the price is below the firm's minimum AC, even a normal profit is not possible, and the firm is facing a situation where it is minimising its **economic losses**. Let us consider what happens to our bakery when the price of croissants in the market falls below its minimum AC of $2.20. Figure 11.7 shows such a situation.

In Figure 11.7 the price has fallen to €1.50. According to the profit maximisation rule, the bakery should produce where MC = MR, which is at a quantity of 80 croissants. Not surprisingly, the lower price leads the bakery to reduce its output (as predicted by the law of supply). The problem is, at the lower price the firm is not able to cover all its costs of production: the average cost is now higher (around €2.25) than average revenue. The baker is losing about €0.75 for each croissant she sells. She is no longer covering all the explicit and implicit costs, thus she is not earning the normal profit she requires to remain in the market.

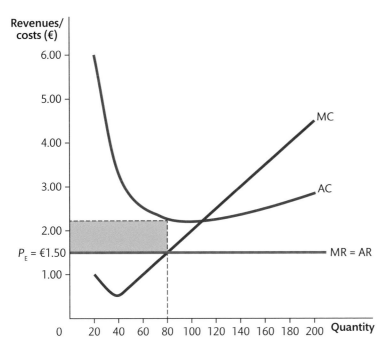

When a firm experiences economic losses, it is only a matter of time before it will shut down and leave the market. When a firm's losses exceed its total fixed costs, or the costs of paying rent and utilities, the firm will have to shut down. In the short run, losses may be endured as the business owner waits for prices to rise again or attempts to take steps to reduce her explicit costs. Alternatively, a business owner's expected level of normal profit may decrease, which would lower the AC and perhaps allow a firm to remain in the market even when losses are being earned.

Alternative business objectives

So far we have assumed that all firms are interested first and foremost in maximising their profits, which requires them to always produce where their marginal cost equals their marginal revenue. There may be alternative objectives driving firm behaviour, including satisficing, **corporate social responsibility (CSR)**, or increasing market share. We'll examine each of these in turn.

Satisficing behaviour

When a firm aims to earn a profit but not necessarily maximise its profit due to its promotion of alternative objectives, the term used is 'satisficing behaviour'. While there is no single 'satisficing rule', a firm intentionally earning, but not maximising profits, could be said to be satisficing.

A firm that is satisficing might produce at an output level that is not maximising its profits but is earning enough profit for the business to do well while also pursuing other objectives. Satisficing behaviour might allow a firm to pursue one of the other alternative business objectives described here.

Corporate social responsibility

When a business voluntarily engages in activities that aim not to increase its profits, but to better the community in some way unrelated to its business model, it might

Research and inquiry

Global corporations nearly all have a CSR mission, and they often love to talk about their work in CSR in the media and through their websites. Projecting an image of themselves as responsible global citizens is a key objective of most corporations that engage in CSR.

CSR reports are sometimes issued annually by corporations to inform their shareholders and the public about their efforts to promote sustainability, health, education, or other outcomes not directly related to the companies' bottom lines. Take a few minutes to skim the CSR reports from three global corporations, then discuss the questions that follow. Below are links to three such reports, but you can feel free to do a web search for a corporation of your choosing.

- Nestle (food industry): https://www.nestle.com/csv
- Glencore (mining): https://www.glencore.com/sustainability
- Microsoft (computer software): https://www.microsoft.com/en-us/corporate-responsibility

For discussion and debate:

1 For each of the three companies you investigated, identify three issues not directly related to their industries on which their CSR report focused.

2 What motivations do you think drive corporations whose key focus could be on maximising profits for their shareholders to undertake CSR? Are there any clues on the CSR reports for the three companies you chose to investigate?

3 Is there a trade-off between being responsible corporate citizens and maximising profits? Why or why not?

be engaging in CSR. CSR could aim at promoting objectives such as environmental sustainability, public health, education, **economic development**, or human rights. Firms that engage in CSR may be satisficing, meaning they are pursuing profits but sacrificing some profitability to promote other ends.

Examples of CSR firms might engage in include voluntarily investing in renewable energies to reduce their carbon emissions, donating to charities, participating in fair trade (which may increase the costs of their inputs but promotes higher wages among those engaged in their production), requiring employees to volunteer in their communities, or making socially or environmentally beneficial investments when they are not necessary to achieve maximum profits.

Increasing market share

A third objective that may require firms to sacrifice profits in the short term is the pursuit of growth in order to increase its market share. As we will see later in this chapter firms in competitive markets are unlikely to earn substantial profits over the long run. Competition forces prices downward and with them profits. Therefore, increasing market share is a sure way to increase profitability, and to that end firms might be willing to sacrifice profits in the short run (or even operate at a loss) in order to attract consumers away from their competition and gain market share over time, allowing them to be more profitable in the future.

An example of this is the ride-sharing market, which includes large firms like Uber and Lift. Neither of these firms has been profitable in their first decade of operation; they charge fares that are competitive but not profitable, with the goal of becoming the dominant ride-sharing operation in any given market. Should their strategy work, Uber or Lift expect that someday, once they have emerged the winner in the **price war** in which they are engaged, their market power might allow them to charge higher fares and earn abnormal profits sometime down the road.

The pursuit of objectives other than profit maximisation is common among firms in imperfectly competitive markets, due to the ability to focus on things like social and environmental welfare and increasing their market share. Firms in perfectly competitive markets, we will see soon, are forced to minimise costs at all times in order to avoid the losses that would ultimately force them to shut down in the face of high levels of competition.

Business growth

Finally, an objective similar to increasing market share is a business's goal of increasing its scale of production. Rather than targeting a larger market share, firms may aim to increase the size of their operations in terms of growing their quantity of output, which typically allows production to occur at a lower average cost due to increased economies of scale. While economies of scale and lower costs often correspond with greater profits, the two objectives are different and may require a firm to target not their profit-maximising quantity, rather a level of output beyond what may be the most profitable in the short run.

A classic example of business growth as an economic objective is the American online retailer Amazon, which for most of its first two decades operated at a loss in order to increase its scale, allowing it to achieve lower and lower average costs over time. In the process of growing its operations, Amazon also happened to chip away at the market share of brick and mortar retail businesses, and it became the dominant online retailer in America and in many other countries.

11.3 The perfect competition market model

Learning outcomes

At the end of this section you will be able to:

- compare and contrast, using a diagram, the shapes of the perfectly competitive firm's average revenue and marginal revenue curves
- analyse how the assumptions of perfect competition imply that each firm is a price-taker
- explain, using a diagram, that the perfectly competitive firm's average revenue and marginal revenue curves are derived from market equilibrium for the industry
- explain, using diagrams, that it is possible for a perfectly competitive firm to make economic profit (supernormal profit), normal profit, or negative economic profit in the short run
- explain, using a diagram, why, in the long run, a perfectly competitive firm will make normal profit
- explain, using a diagram, how a perfectly competitive market will move from short-run equilibrium to long-run equilibrium
- compare and contrast allocative efficiency and productive efficiency.

The defining characteristic of a perfectly competitive market is that there are *many sellers*. So many, in fact, that no single seller has any control over the market price; each firm therefore is a price-taker. Figure 11.9 shows the situation in the market for croissants, of which our individual bakery is one single firm.

At the current level of demand and supply the equilibrium price is €3 and around 10,000 croissants are produced and sold. The market is made up of many small bakeries that are each producing a tiny fraction of the total market output. Let us assume that there are 70 bakeries, each making 140 croissants each day, which accounts for the market output of 10,000 croissants.

When we combine our market model with our model for the individual firm used earlier in the chapter, we can see how the demand for each individual bakery's croissants is determined. Figure 11.10 puts the individual firm and market models side by side, to show that the price, demand, MR, and AR seen by an individual firm in a competitive market is derived from the market equilibrium price.

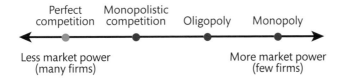

Figure 11.8 Firms in a perfectly competitive market are at the least-powerful end of the competition spectrum

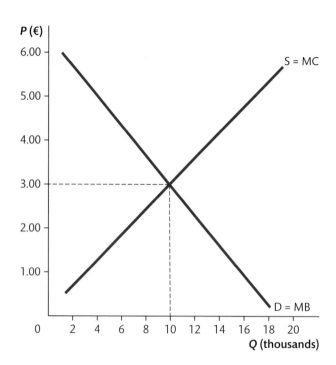

Figure 11.9 A perfectly competitive market for croissants ▶

Video suggestion:
You have read about it, now you can review what you have just learned by watching a video by the author!

▶ Simply click here in your eBook for a video on demand, MR, and profit maximisation for a perfect competitor.

Demand for the individual bakery's croissants, you will notice, is horizontal, meaning demand is *perfectly elastic*. The bakery has no price-making power; any attempt to raise its price and it will not sell any croissants, since there are 69 other bakeries willing to sell at €3.

Short-run versus long-run equilibrium in perfectly competitive markets

The market and firm shown in Figure 11.10 is in a short-run equilibrium, since supply equals demand, but not a long-run equilibrium. The existence of abnormal

Figure 11.10 Within a perfectly competitive market (a) any single firm (b) is a 'price-taker', charging the market equilibrium price ▼

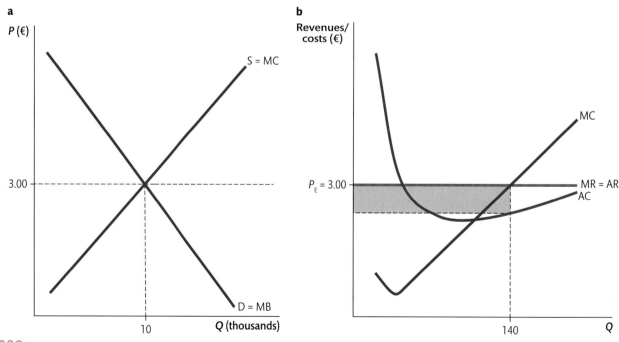

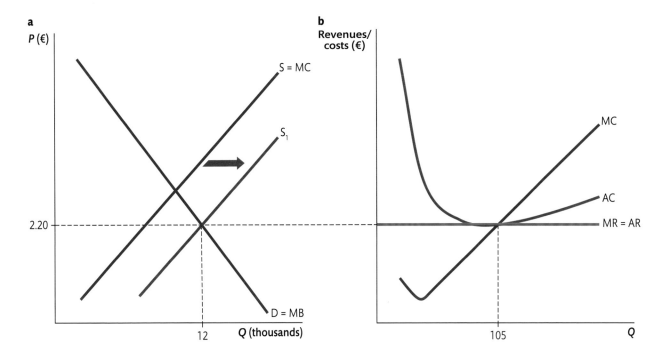

a

P (€)

S = MC

S₁

2.20

D = MB

12   Q (thousands)

b

Revenues/
costs (€)

MC

AC

MR = AR

105   Q

Figure 11.11   In the long run, abnormal profits are eliminated by the entry into the market of other producers, driving the price down

profits (red rectangle) will attract new firms to the market, as the low barriers to entry characteristic of perfectly competitive markets make it easy for new bakeries to enter or for existing bakeries to increase their output of croissants in order to capitalise on the profits available.

As bakeries increase the highly profitable product, the market supply will increase in the long run and the equilibrium price will be driven down until **abnormal profits** are eliminated. Figure 11.11 shows this process unfold: supply of croissants increases, equilibrium price decreases, and abnormal profits are eliminated.

Abnormal profits attracted more competition to the market for croissants, increasing market supply to S_1 and driving the price down to €2.20. Each individual baker now has a smaller market share; while individual output falls to 105, total output increases to over 12,000 croissants due to the influx of new competitors.

A perfectly competitive market is in a long-run equilibrium when only normal profits are being earned by individual sellers. The existence of abnormal profits or of losses will lead to either an inflow or outflow of sellers until the market reaches equilibrium at each individual seller's minimum average cost, where only normal profits can be earned. Let us consider how the market for croissants would be affected by a fall in demand that drove the market price down to €1.50. Figure 11.12 shows the result of a fall in market demand on the individual producer.

Demand has fallen to D_1 in the market, leading to a lower price and economic losses for the individual bakeries as MR falls with the price. The market is no longer in a long-run equilibrium as individual firms will begin leaving the market due to losses. As they do so market supply will decrease driving the price back to the long-run equilibrium of €2.20. Figure 11.13 shows how the market will adjust in the long run following the decrease in demand shown in Figure 11.12.

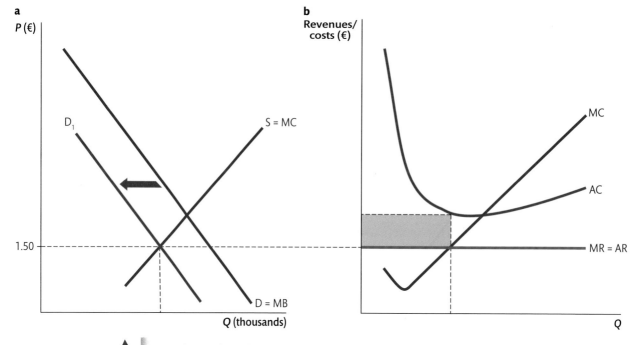

Figure 11.12 If the price drops due to lower demand, individual firms will suffer economic loss and leave the market

Figure 11.13 The long-run market equilibrium is where only normal profits are earned by individual firms

The market is back in equilibrium at €2.20, which equals the individual bakeries' minimum average cost. At this price, only normal profits are earned, so there is no incentive for new sellers to enter the market nor for existing sellers to leave. The market, in other words, is in equilibrium.

Allocative and productive efficiency

A competitive market in long-run equilibrium achieves what economists refer to as perfect efficiency. The socially optimal quantity is produced (where MSB = MSC) and individual producers are using their resources in the least cost, most efficient manner possible.

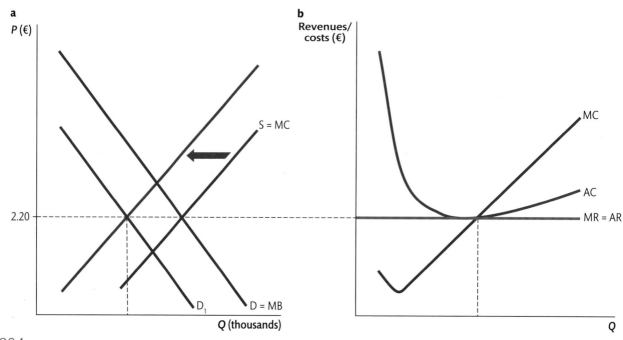

Allocative efficiency, as we have learned, occurs when market output occurs where marginal social benefit equals marginal social cost. Competition assures that output will take place at the allocatively efficient level. Imperfectly competitive markets, as we will see in the next section, produce at a level of output that is less than socially optimal. Their ability to control prices allows imperfect competitors to charge a higher price by restricting output. As a result, imperfectly competitive markets under-allocate resources to their goods, transferring surplus from consumers (who pay a higher price) to producers (who earn more profits).

When we look closely at Figures 11.10 and 11.12, in which the firm is earning abnormal profits and losses, respectively, we can see that in both cases the firm's average cost is higher than their minimum AC of €2.20. Profits allow a firm to produce more than it would under long-run equilibrium and charge a price that is higher. Losses require a firm to reduce its output to a level where the AC is higher than the minimum. In both cases, the firm is productively *inefficient*. When the market adjusts in the long run, however (firms enter to eliminate profits or leave to eliminate losses), the remaining firms are forced once again to produce at the quantity where their AC are lowest, resulting in productive efficiency in the long run.

We began this chapter by explaining that perfectly competitive markets, while rare in the real world, are worth studying because they form a basis on which to compare the relative efficiency of more realistic market models. As we have shown here, perfect competition, a model in which many firms that have identical costs and produce identical goods, which are able to enter or exit the market easily in response to profits or losses, result in a socially desirable outcome in which resources are allocated efficiently and used to produce output in the most efficient manner possible.

11.4 The monopoly market model

Learning outcomes

At the end of this section you will be able to:

- explain that the average revenue curve for a monopolist is the downward-sloping market demand curve
- explain, using a diagram, the relationship between demand, average revenue, and marginal revenue in a monopoly
- explain, using a diagram, the short- and long-run equilibrium output and pricing decision of a profit-maximising (loss-minimising) monopolist
- explain the role of barriers to entry in permitting the firm to earn economic profit
- explain, using diagrams, why the profit-maximising choices of a monopoly firm lead to allocative inefficiency (**welfare loss**) and productive inefficiency
- explain the meaning of the term '**natural monopoly**' and draw a diagram to illustrate.

When a single firm controls a dominant share of total market sales, it has monopoly power over the market. Recall from earlier in this chapter that *pure monopolies*, in which there is only a single seller, are rare; but industries in which a large firm accounts

Video suggestion:
You have read about it, now you can review what you have just learned by watching a video by the author!

▶ Simply click here in your eBook for a video on short run and long-run equilibrium in perfect competition.

Video suggestion:
You have read about it, now you can review what you have just learned by watching a video by the author!

▶ Simply click here in your eBook for a video on efficiency in perfectly competitive markets.

Figure 11.14 Monopoly power allows large firms to influence price ▶

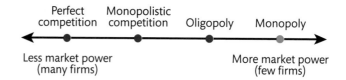

The following table shows hypothetical figures reflecting the market demand for beef in the USA, of which a single firm, Tyson, accounts for over 40% of market sales, giving it significant monopoly power in the industry. Demand for beef is inversely related to the price. Table 11.3 shows the demand for beef as seen by Tyson, as well as the total and marginal revenues Tyson would experience at a range of prices.

When a firm has a dominant share of the market, it is a *price-maker*. This means simply that in order to sell more output, it must lower the price of its goods. Similarly, price increases lead to less quantity demanded. In other words, monopolists face a downward-sloping demand curve. Contrast this with the perfectly competitive seller, for whom demand is perfectly elastic and horizontal, determined by the price set by the market as a whole. Since a monopolist is the market's main supplier, the market demand curve *is* the firm's demand curve.

The following table shows hypothetical figures reflecting the market demand for beef in the USA, of which a single firm, Tyson, accounts for over 40% of market sales, giving it significant monopoly power in the industry. Demand for beef is inversely related to the price. Table 11.3 shows the demand for beef as seen by Tyson, as well as the total and marginal revenues Tyson would experience at a range of prices.

Next let us plot Tyson's demand and MR curves on a graph. Figure 11.15 plots beef demand and MR as seen by Tyson Foods.

The price-making firm faces a downward-sloping demand curve and an MR curve that slopes twice as steep as demand. Because the price for all its output must be lowered to sell additional units, the monopolist sees its MR decrease faster than the price, and so MR will drop at two times the rate of decrease in the price.

Table 11.3   Demand for beef

Price ($ per kg)	Quantity demanded (millions of kg per week)	Total revenue (millions of $)	Marginal revenue $MR = \dfrac{\Delta TR}{\Delta Q}$
14	0	0	—
12	2	24	12
10	4	40	8
8	6	48	4
6	8	48	0
4	10	40	−4
2	12	24	−8

Source: https://csimarket.com/stocks/segments.php?code=TSN

The profit-maximising monopolist

To determine the profit-maximising level of output a monopolist must consider the same variables as a competitive firm: its MR (shown in Figure 11.15) and its MC. The MC and average cost curves for a monopolist, assuming it employs variable resources like labour and raw materials in combination with fixed resources like capital and land, will look similar to any other firm's: MC will slope down then up, reflecting the law of diminishing marginal returns, and AC will slope down until MC crosses it, then increase as additional units of output cost more than the average, pulling the average up.

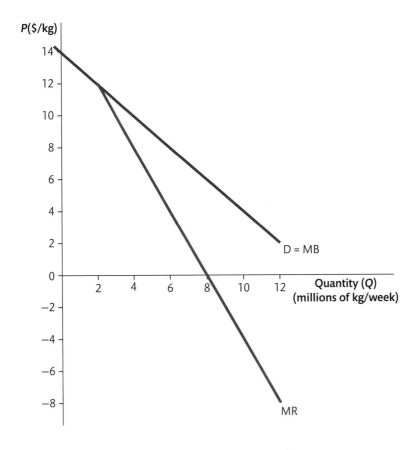

Figure 11.15
The monopolist must drop prices to sell additional units

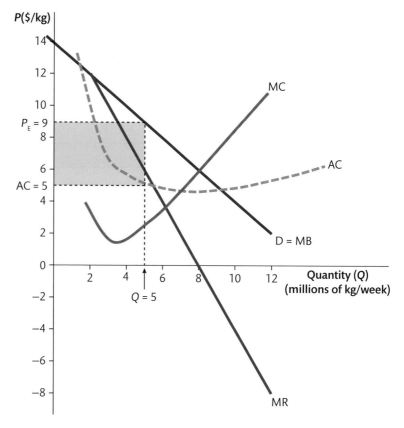

Figure 11.16 adds the MC and AC curves to our graph showing Tyson's demand and MR in the beef market.

The price-maker has chosen to produce at its profit-maximising quantity and price, determined where the MC (the increase in total costs attributable to the last kilogram of beef produced) equalled the MR (the increase in TR attributable to the last kilogram of beef produced). The firm will produce 5 million kg of beef and charge a price of $9 per kg. With an average cost of $5 per kg, Tyson Foods can expect to earn a profit of $4 per kg, or $20 million in total ($4 × 5 million = $20 million).

When firms in competitive markets earn abnormal profits like those shown in Figure 11.16 they can only be expected to last until new competition is attracted to the market; ultimately the inflow of new businesses and increased market supply will drive the price down and eliminate the profits. However, due to the nature of monopolies, high barriers to entry prevent competitors from entering, allowing the monopoly to maintain its abnormal profits in the long run. In the case of beef production, large economies of scale allow firms like Tyson to produce beef with great efficiency using expensive, high tech processing machinery, making it difficult for smaller firms to join the market, even when significant profits can be expected.

Let us do a thought experiment and imagine how the price and quantity in the market might look if it were perfectly competitive. We know that in a competitive market, entry eliminates profits, and that in the long run the equilibrium price and quantity will occur where demand equals supply, or where marginal benefit equals MC. We can determine where the competitive market equilibrium would occur by looking at the monopolist's MC curve, which instead of representing the MC of a single firm, would represent the market supply in a competitive market, because at each price there is a different

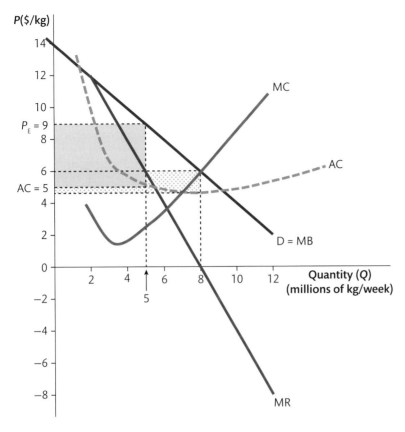

Figure 11.17 At the competitive market equilibrium, profits are approximately half those at the monopolist's equilibrium

quantity supplied. The demand curve, rather than representing demand for one company's beef, would represent total market demand from all companies. Figure 11.17 compares the likely competitive market equilibrium with the monopolist's equilibrium.

A competitive market would produce where MC = MB, at a quantity of 8 million kg and a price of $6 per kg. Compared to a market under monopoly, a competitive market would, not surprisingly, produce more output at a lower price. Notice, however, that the profit rectangle would be smaller (yellow dotted area) if Tyson were to sell more beef at the lower price. Abnormal profit at the competitive price and quantity would be in the range of $10 million (around $1.25 per kg × 8 million kg), just one-half of what the firm earns at its monopoly price and quantity.

Video suggestion:
You have read about it, now you can review what you have just learned by watching a video by the author!
Simply click here in your eBook for a video introducing pure monopoly.

Allocative inefficiency and welfare loss

It is important to observe that because of the tendency of monopolies to restrict their output below the level that would be produced in a competitive market and charge a higher price, there are several consequences for consumers, producers, and overall efficiency in the market.

First, because less output is produced, the monopolist fails to achieve allocative efficiency, which occurs when equilibrium is where marginal benefit equals marginal cost. Monopolies are allocatively inefficient. Figure 11.18 illustrates the reason monopolies are allocatively inefficient because at the monopolist's equilibrium quantity, the MB > MC.

By restricting its output to maximise profits the monopolist under-allocates resources towards its good. Society would be better off by producing at the perfectly competitive

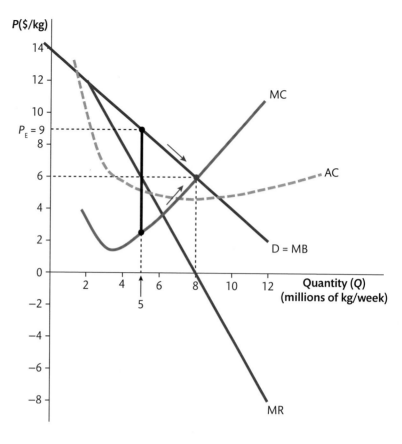

Figure 11.18 At the monopolist's equilibrium, marginal benefit is greater than marginal cost

level of output where MB = MC, since the last unit produced would create as much value for society as it cost to produce it.

Second, because consumers pay a higher price and get less of the good under monopoly than they would under perfect competition, there is less consumer surplus and a loss of total welfare in the market. Figure 11.19 shows the DWL arising from a single seller dominating the US beef market.

The red shaded area in Figure 11.19 represents the DWL, or loss of social welfare, resulting from a single firm dominating the market for beef. The top half, above the competitive price of $6, represents lost consumer surplus, while the bottom half represents the producer surplus that would exist if more producers were able to compete in the market. Overall, the market is worse off because fewer firms are producing beef and consumers are paying a higher price for less beef than they would get under a more competitive market.

Do monopolies always earn profits?

We have assumed that due to its market power, its ability to set prices, the lack of competition, and the high barriers to entry, a monopoly is likely to earn abnormal profits, unlike less fortunate (and less powerful) companies struggling to survive in perfectly competitive markets. Just because it is the sole seller does not guarantee that a monopoly will earn abnormal profits, however. Monopolists, just like firms in competitive markets, are subject to the changing tastes and preferences of consumers, changes in incomes, change in the prices of complementary goods, changes in expectations, and other determinants of demand. Likewise, input prices, regulations,

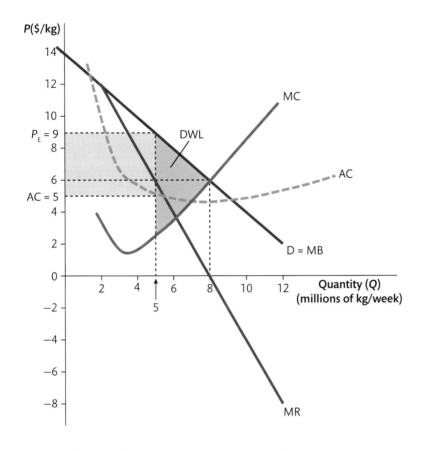

Figure 11.19
The monopoly results in deadweight loss

taxes, and subsidies can all change, causing a monopolist's costs to increase and reducing or eliminating its abnormal profits.

Figure 11.20 shows a situation in which demand for a monopolist's product decreased. For instance, assume that Americans' demand for beef drops dramatically, due to changing dietary preferences or a health scare such as mad cow disease/BSE outbreak that hit the UK in the 1980s.

A decrease in demand for beef has forced the firm to lower its price in order to maintain sales. The firm still produced where MC=MR, but this now corresponds with a much lower price, at which P_E =AC. The firm is now breaking even; it is earning only a normal profit.

Another scenario could see an increase in marginal and average cost, leading to economic losses. Figure 11.21 shows the result from an increase in government regulation or taxation of the beef industry, driving Tyson's costs up, eliminating its profits and even causing economic losses.

A combination of reduced demand and higher costs has driven our once profitable beef producer into loss minimisation mode. If it is to return to profitability the firm will have to find a way to increase demand for its product (through marketing, differentiation, or improvements in quality), or reduce its costs (increase efficiency, lobby for lower taxes or reduced regulation).

As we can see, monopoly power does not guarantee abnormal profits will always be earned. What it does promise is that profits will not be eliminated through the increase in competition that results in more competitive markets only breaking even in the long run.

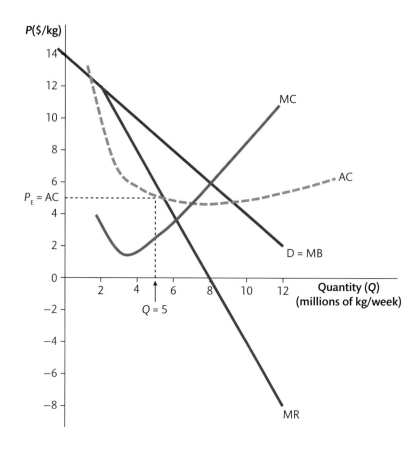

Figure 11.20 A reduction in demand would lower the monopolist's profits

Figure 11.20 A reduction in demand would lower the monopolist's profits

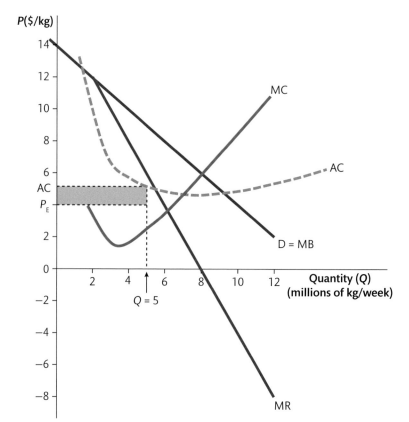

Figure 11.21 Increased costs further lead to economic losses

What is a natural monopoly?

From our analysis above we can conclude that in the case of typical consumer goods monopoly is a less socially desirable market structure than perfect competition. Higher prices and lower output mean less consumer surplus and a loss of total welfare. Monopoly power is a market failure, since resources are under-allocated towards the monopolised market's output. The quantity produced is less than the socially optimal quantity, since the marginal benefit of the last unit produced is greater than the marginal cost.

Not all industries that are monopolies necessarily need to be monopolies; sometimes firms have monopoly power for legal or technical reasons.

- When a firm has an exclusive permit from the government to provide a particular good
- When a firm has 'cornered the market' for a particular resource needed to produce the good.
- When a firm has priced competitors out of the market using predatory pricing strategies.

Any of these sources of monopoly power could be considered economically inefficient and therefore undesirable to some extent.

However, there is a type of monopolistic industry in which the dominance of a single firm is economically justifiable and actually beneficial for society; such a market is known as a natural monopoly. A natural monopoly is an industry in which a single firm produces all the output because of its large economies of scale, and in which demand for the good is low relative to the very high fixed costs. In the graph below we see a natural monopoly, recognised because demand intersects AC while it is still downward sloping.

Figure 11.22 shows a naturally monopolistic electricity company's AC and MC and the monthly demand for electricity.

If the firm is left to produce at its profit-maximising price and quantity, it will limit its production to 30 million kwh (where MC = MR) and charge a price of Mex$6.00 (Mex$ is the symbol for the Mexican peso, the currency of Mexico) per kWh. The socially optimal quantity of electricity (where MB = MC) is 60 million kWh and the socially optimal price is Mex$1.00 per kWh.

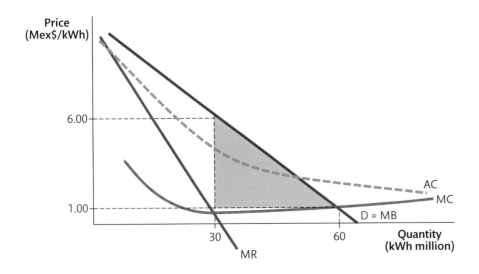

Figure 11.22 A natural monopoly such as a utilities company underprovides important goods without government intervention

213

Figure 11.23 At the socially optimal price the company makes losses and would leave the market in the long run

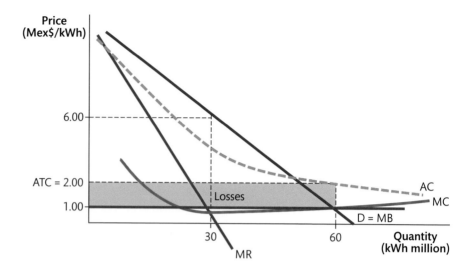

Figure 11.23 At the socially optimal price the company makes losses and would leave the market in the long run

Clearly, the utility company, if left to pursue its profit-maximising agenda, will overcharge for and underproduce electricity. There is a loss of consumer surplus represented by the red triangle as a result of the monopoly abusing its power.

To ensure that a naturally monopolistic industry produces at a level closer to the allocatively efficient or socially optimal price and quantity (where MB = MC), either subsidies or price controls should be imposed by the government. Figure 11.23 shows the effect of a price ceiling set by the government at the socially optimal price of Mex$1.00 per kWh of electricity. As a result, the electricity company has increased its output to the socially optimal level (60 million kWh in this case). There is one problem with a price ceiling set at the socially optimal price in a natural monopoly, however. It will always be at a price lower than the firm's AC, meaning the firm will experience economic losses. The red area on the graph above represents this utility company's losses when it is forced to charge the socially optimal price of Mex$1.00. At this price, the company will choose to shut down in the long run.

The solution, therefore, is for the government to provide the firm with a lump-sum subsidy to cover the losses it experiences when producing at the socially optimal level. In the case of our utility company, the subsidy would have to equal at least the level of losses the firm experiences at Mex$1.00 per kWh. We can calculate the losses the firm will experience at a price of Mex$1.00 and a quantity of 60 million kWh. The firm's average cost is Mex$2.00 and its AR (the price) is Mex$1.00. With these values we can calculate the firm's losses.

$$\text{Economic losses} = (\text{AC} - \text{AR}) \times \text{Q}$$

$$= (\text{Mex}\$2.00 - \text{Mex}\$1.00) \times 60 \text{ million}$$

$$= \text{Mex}\$1.00 \times 60 \text{ million}$$

$$= \text{Mex}\$60 \text{ million}$$

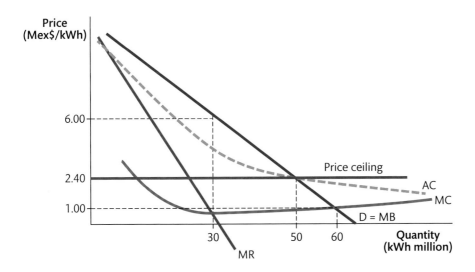

A Mex$60 million lump-sum subsidy (payment) from the government to the utility company will assure it is able to stay in operation even while charging the socially optimal price of Mex$1.00 per kWh and producing the socially optimal quantity of 60 million kWh.

Another option for regulating natural monopolies that would not involve providing lump-sum subsidies is to establish what is called a 'fair return' price ceiling. This is a price ceiling set at the price where demand crosses the firm's AC, as seen in the Figure 11.24, in which the government has set a price ceiling equal to the firm's AC.

A price ceiling of Mex$2.40, which is equal to the firm's AC, will increase quantity demanded to 50 million kWh and make electricity more affordable, promoting a more socially optimal level of production and price. Since the firm breaks even, no government subsidy is necessary. This is called a 'fair return' price because the firm charges a price that earns it a normal profit. No abnormal profit is earned at the expense of consumers who would be unable to afford electricity.

Subsidies and price controls are two commonly used interventions in naturally monopolistic utility industries such as electricity, water, gas, public transportation, waste management, and recycling. Capping the price that monopolistic producers are allowed to charge at or closer to the socially optimal price (where MB = MC) and using subsidies to cover any resulting losses will assure that essential services are provided at a relatively low cost and at a relatively high level to society.

In our final chapter in the Microeconomics unit we will do a deep dive into the two remaining market structures, both of which lie in the middle of our spectrum of competition: monopolistic competition and oligopoly. While the lessons taught by our study of the perfect competition and monopoly market models will help us better evaluate the consequences for consumers and producers of the other two market structures, they are quite rare in the real world. In contrast, the vast majority of markets for the consumer goods that we buy on a daily basis are produced by monopolistic competitors or oligopolistic firms.

Video suggestion:
You have read about it, now you can review what you have just learned by watching a video by the author!
▶ Simply click here in your eBook for a video on natural monopoly and the need for government regulation.

Practice exam questions

1a. Using a suitable diagram, explain the difference between short-run equilibrium and long-run equilibrium in perfect competition. (10 marks)

b. To what extent is the perfectly competitive market likely to exist in the real world? (15 marks)

2a. Using a diagram, explain how allocative and productive efficiency will be achieved in long-run equilibrium in perfect competition. (10 marks)

b. Evaluate the view that consumers, not producers, are the main beneficiaries of perfectly competitive market structures. (15 marks)

3a. A firm in perfect competition is producing at the profit-maximising output, but making a loss. Using diagrammatic analysis, explain how this is possible. (10 marks)

b. Discuss the claim that all costs are identical among different firms in a perfectly competitive market. If this claim is correct, then why do some firms shut down before others when earning economic losses? (15 marks)

4a. Explain, using an appropriate diagram, how the monopolist determines the profit-maximising level of output and price. (10 marks)

b. Discuss the view that competitive markets are always more efficient than monopolies. (15 marks)

5a. Explain, using examples and an appropriate diagram, the concept of a natural monopoly. (10 marks)

b. To what extent do natural monopolies act against the best interest of society? (15 marks)

6a. Explain how a monopolist may earn economic profits in the long run. (10 marks)

b. Evaluate the view that, compared to competitive markets, monopolies will always harm the consumer. (15 marks)

7. 'Monopoly price is higher and output smaller than is socially ideal. The public is the victim'. (JK Galbraith, 1974)

a. Explain the economic reasoning behind the statement that 'monopoly price is higher and output smaller than is socially ideal'. (10 marks)

b. Do you agree that the public is always the 'victim' of monopoly? Justify your answer. (15 marks)

HL Market power: monopolistic competition and oligopoly

12

Learning outcomes

At the end of this section you will be able to:

- describe, using examples, the assumed characteristics of monopolistic competition:
  - a large number of firms
  - differentiated products
  - absence of barriers to entry and exit
- explain that **product differentiation** leads to a small degree of monopoly power and therefore to a negatively sloping demand curve for the product
- examine, using a diagram, the short-run equilibrium output and pricing decisions of a profit-maximising (loss-minimising) firm in monopolistic competition, identifying the firm's abnormal profit (or loss)
- explain, using diagrams, why in the long run a firm in monopolistic competition will make normal profit
- discuss, using a diagram, why neither allocative efficiency nor productive efficiency are achieved by monopolistically competitive firms
- compare and contrast, using diagrams, monopolistic competition with perfect competition, and monopolistic competition with monopoly.

What are the characteristics of monopolistic competition?

We have so far looked at two extremes in the market: monopoly and perfect competition. Monopoly sits at one end of the spectrum of competition, with the most market power. In this chapter, you are going to examine two models that are more commonly found in the real world: monopolistic competition and oligopoly. Our guiding principle of distinction, relative market power, is still in effect here. With that in mind, monopolistic competition can be seen as a step up from perfect competition in terms of market power whereas oligopoly is a step closer to the ultimate market power of a monopoly firm.

Monopolistic competition is a market structure where there are many buyers and sellers, producing differentiated products, with no barriers to entry or exit, and it is based on the following assumptions.

Many firms, most of them small in size

This trait is shared with perfect competition, without being quite as extreme. The number of firms is high enough that it is unlikely, but not impossible, for one firm to influence the market. Cooperation between firms is not possible as there are too many firms for this to take place.

Figure 12.1 In monopolistic competition, many small firms use product differentiation to influence price

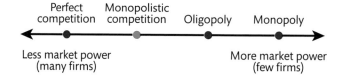

Perfect competition — Monopolistic competition — Oligopoly — Monopoly

Less market power (many firms) ← → More market power (few firms)

Relatively free entry and exit

Like perfect competition, there are few barriers to entry and exit. It is rather easy to get into or out of the business.

Product differentiation

Product differentiation is a form of **non-price competition**, where a firm competes in areas other than price to win customers. Differentiation marks the most significant departure from perfect competition, where products are completely identical. Monopolistic competitors strive to differentiate their products in the hopes of deriving some market power (price-setting ability). Product differentiation occurs when consumers perceive a product as being different in some way from other substitute products. Firms differentiate products in a number of ways.

- **Appearance.** Shape, colouring, materials, 'look and feel', as well as packaging can influence perceptions of a product.
- **Service.** Firms can be faster with assistance and sales, or offer additional help with home delivery, product guarantees, and more.
- **Design.** Products having the same function can be designed for more ease of use or with more fashionable styling.
- **Quality.** Variations in quality can bring higher or lower market power, depending on the good.
- **Expertise/skill.** The perceived level of skill can significantly differentiate one firm from another, especially in service industries.
- **Location.** Some firms will benefit from location, such as the last petrol station for 100 kilometres, or exchange bureaus and convenience stores in airports.
- **Brand reputation/image.** Many firms spend advertising money persuading and reminding customers how their products are superior or priced well (creating a brand image can also differentiate one firm from another).
- **Distribution.** Selling online rather than through traditional retail outlets is a means of differentiating.

Examples of monopolistically competitive industries include restaurants, bars, nail salons, jewellers, car mechanics, plumbers, book publishing, clothing, shoes, restaurants, consumer services, and specialist retailers of all kinds.

How is monopolistic competition distinguished from perfect competition and monopoly?

Monopolistic competition shares attributes with both monopoly and perfect competition. However, the single distinguishing feature of monopolistic competition, when compared with perfect competition, is product differentiation. The degree to which a firm can 'create' demand for its goods is the degree to which it can create market power, or price-setting ability.

Figure 12.2a shows a perfectly competitive firm with no such power. It is a small firm in a massive market, and the price and demand curve for the firm is set in the overall market. Its demand curve is, therefore, perfectly elastic. Because goods in perfect competition are exact substitutes, any attempt to get a higher price will fail; none of the higher price goods will sell.

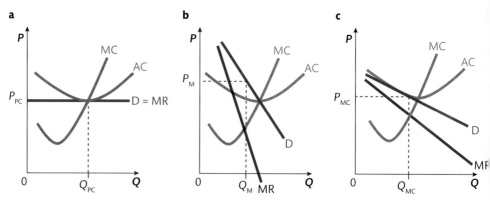

Figure 12.2 Elasticity of demand in monopolistic competition (c) falls somewhere between that for a perfectly competitive market (a) and a monopoly (b)

In contrast, firms in the monopoly market face a downward-sloping demand curve (Figure 12.2b). This curve is relatively steep, suggesting a generally inelastic demand for the good. This comes from the fact that the monopolist is the only provider of the good, so no substitutes are available. Thus, demand is relatively more inelastic or rigid.

The firm showing monopolistic competition (Figure 12.2c) is viewed as a hybrid of the previous two. It is relatively elastic; consumers are price sensitive because there are similar goods available from many producers. However, the firm that successfully differentiates its product may have inspired a belief that its goods are not exactly the same as other goods, and may be somewhat better.

This gives us insight into the behaviour of the monopolistic competitor. A more steeply sloping demand curve, where demand is more inelastic, means more market power. It means more power to set higher prices and earn higher profits. A more inelastic demand for your good, it is logical to conclude, is highly desirable for your bottom line.

Firms often advertise to persuade consumers of the uniqueness of a particular brand. By differentiation and advertising, a firm can make its product appear essential or necessary to more buyers, and thus inspire brand loyalty and inelasticity of demand. Thus, firms can increase the demand for their product, moving it outwards, and also make demand steeper at the same time.

What are the short- and long-run profit possibilities for the monopolistic competitor?

The monopolistically competitive firm operates under the same demand, revenue, and costs situation as the monopolist, except for its much more elastic demand curve.

Short-run profits

In the short run, a monopolistic competitor can earn abnormal profits. Figure 12.3 shows the monopolistic competitor producing quantity Q_E where marginal cost (MC) and marginal revenue (MR) are equal. Like the monopolist, the monopolistic competitor sets the price at that quantity by charging as much as the demand at that quantity will allow, P_E. At Q_E, average costs (AC) are below the price P_E, therefore abnormal profits are being earned. The area of the shaded box gives the total abnormal profit. In a numerical example, this could be calculated using the formula: *total abnormal profit* $= (AR - AC) \times Q_E$.

Short-run profits to long-run normal profits

As it is relatively easy to enter and exit the industry, the profit-making industry will get attention and new entrants rather quickly. When this occurs, the demand experienced

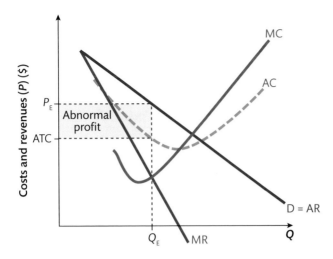

Figure 12.3 Monopolistic competition allows abnormal profits in the short run

by each individual firm will decrease, shifting demand to the left. This will cause MR to intersect MC at a smaller quantity, reducing output and profitability for the firms in the industry.

If abnormal profits are still present, this process of new entrants to the market will continue until all the abnormal profits have been eliminated. The long-run result is normal profits, as shown in Figure 12.4. Here, demand ($D = AR_1$) and marginal revenue (MR_1) for the individual firms has shifted to the left so that it is only touching a portion of the AC curve. Thus, only normal profits are earned.

Short-run losses

The monopolistic competitor may also experience losses in the short run. Figure 12.5 shows the firm producing at the profit-maximising/loss-minimising point where MR = MC, and so producing Q_E output. The firm sets the price as high as demand will allow at P_E, but this still falls below the AC experienced by the firm at this level of output. As a result, the firm is clearly making losses, shown by the area of the shaded rectangle.

Short-run losses to long-run normal profits

Where firms are losing money, some will be forced to shut down. As firms shut down, the remaining demand is divided between fewer firms; thus the demand curve faced by

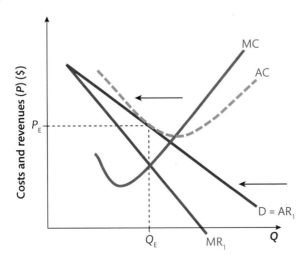

Figure 12.4 In the long run, abnormal profits will be eliminated as they attract new entrants to the market, reducing the individual firms' demand

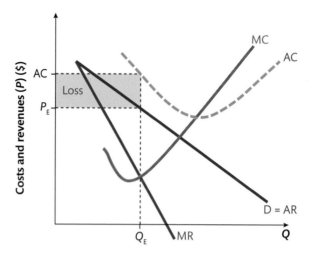

Figure 12.5 The monopolistic competitor may experience short-run losses

each firm shifts to the right. This increases output because the new MR = MC quantity will occur at a point to the right of the previous equilibrium. Also, because demand shifts upwards and outwards, the firms remaining in the market will experience a decrease in losses. This process will continue, with particularly weak firms shutting down, and demand increasing for the remaining firms, until normal profits are attained.

In Figure 12.6, demand has shifted right to $D = AR_1$, reflecting the increased demand and market share enjoyed by this firm as a result of some of its competitors leaving the market. And it shows demand equal to the AC at the profit-maximising quantity of Q_e. Firms will no longer leave the industry if they are making normal profits. Therefore, after the long-run adjustment to short-run losses, only normal profits are attained.

Exceptional cases of long-run profits in monopolistic competition

Since the long run is basically a series of short runs and monopolistic competitors can earn profits in the short run by differentiating their products, continual differentiation may enable firms to earn abnormal profits, even in the long run. In particular, when monopolistic competitors grow large enough and enjoy some economies of scale, they can also lower their costs to maintain profits. For example, restaurants generally are subject to long-run normal profits as many are small family-run businesses, but some large restaurant chains may sustain their profits for long periods of time by taking advantage of differentiation, advertising, and economies of scale.

Figure 12.6 Short-run losses adjust to long-run normal profits as some firms leave the market

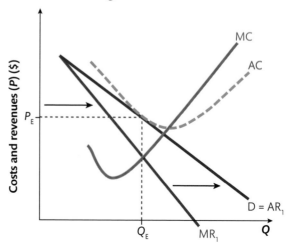

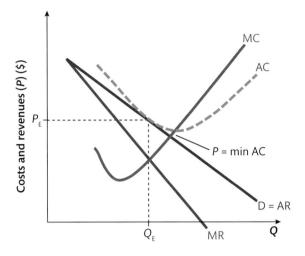

Figure 12.7 Productive efficiency, where MC = AC, is not achieved in monopolistic competition

Do monopolistic competitors achieve efficiency?

As with monopoly and perfect competition, we assess the efficiency of monopolistic competition based on whether the firm achieves allocative and productive efficiency. As detailed previously, allocative efficiency is achieved where P or (AR) = MC, and productive efficiency is achieved where P = minimum AC. When viewed in terms of the long-run equilibrium, it seems clear that neither form of efficiency is achieved in monopolistic competition.

Productive efficiency

Figure 12.7 shows long-run equilibrium for the monopolistic competitor. In Figure 12.7, the firm's productively efficient quantity is noted. The monopolistic competitor produces too little and at too high a price to qualify.

Allocative efficiency

In Figure 12.8, the firm's allocatively efficient point is indicated by the point where D = MC. Clearly the monopolistic competitor produces at a price above and quantity below that. Thus, allocative efficiency is not achieved and a welfare loss, shown as the grey triangle, occurs. Recall that whenever firms produce at a level where the price, as a proxy for marginal benefit, is higher than the MC, a welfare loss occurs. The shaded

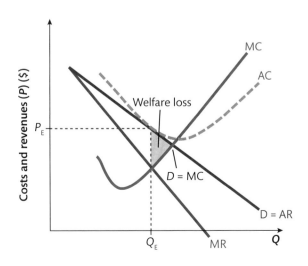

Figure 12.8 Allocative efficiency, where D = MC, is not achieved in monopolistic competition, leading to welfare loss

Research and inquiry

Small firms hit hard by the pandemic

The COVID-19 pandemic that started in 2020 hit service industries especially hard because these firms offer in-person contact. Car services, beauty salons, bars, restaurants, and dentists were at times forbidden to see customers, and after restrictions ended customers only returned slowly.

For discussion and debate:

1 Conduct a brief search for examples in one of the above industries, or any monopolistically competitive industry of your interest.

2 Select a country and investigate the effect of the pandemic on the number of firms remaining.

3 Has the number of firms recovered?

4 How would the loss of competitors be shown on a short-run to long-run diagram?

area represents the loss of consumer and producer surplus that takes place when firms do not produce the allocatively efficient level of output.

Because the monopolistic competitor has a downward-sloping demand curve and MR curve, it will not achieve either type of efficiency, both of which would require the firm to produce more output at a lower price; but as a profit maximiser it will not do so. As a result, monopolistically competitive firms are often said to have excess capacity.

How does monopolistic competition compare to perfect competition?

Perfect competition is the closest market structure to monopolistic competition, especially in the number of firms and the ease of entry. How do they compare overall?

Profitability

In the long run, both industries achieve only normal profits. Because it is easy to enter and exit, profits are consistently 'competed away' while attrition reduces losses over the long run.

Efficiency

Perfect competition is more efficient. While the perfect competitor achieves both types of efficiency, the monopolistic competitor achieves neither.

Product variety

Choice and variety are greater among monopolistic competitors. Product differentiation provides consumers with a wider range of choices than perfectly competitive firms. This expanded choice is consistent with the free market idea of allowing consumers and producers to act based on price information and the profit incentive.

How does monopolistic competition compare to monopoly?

While they share a name, monopolistic competition and monopoly share some characteristics, while also having several key distinctions from one another as market structures.

Profitability

Monopolists can earn long-run profits because they have barriers to entry. The monopolistic competitor will see profits eroded by new entrants.

Efficiency

Neither industry is efficient. Their downward-sloping demand curves restrict output and price goods higher than in perfect competition, lowering efficiency on both allocative and productive grounds.

Product differentiation

The monopolist faces no real competition, thus its product is unique. Monopolistic competitors do face competition, and so have an incentive to differentiate their products from those of other firms.

Service industries have been hit hard by COVID-19 restrictions

Economies of scale

Cost savings of economies of scale are far more likely under monopoly, whereas the monopolistic competitor is unlikely to grow large enough to see these benefits.

12.2 What is an oligopoly?

Learning outcomes

At the end of this section you will be able to:

- describe, using examples, the assumed characteristics of an oligopoly:
  - the dominance of the industry by a small number of firms
  - the importance of interdependence
  - differentiated or homogeneous products
  - high barriers to entry
- examine why interdependence is responsible for the dilemma faced by oligopolistic firms – whether to compete or to collude
- discuss how a concentration ratio may be used to identify an oligopoly
- define the terms 'collusion' and 'cartel', give examples, and state that they are usually (in most countries) illegal
- discuss the incentive of cartel members to cheat
- analyse the conditions that make cartel structures difficult to maintain
- discuss the behaviour of oligopolies including reference to 'tacit collusion', price leadership by a dominant firm, strategic non-collusive decision making, non-price competition, and the risk of price wars.

One step further up in the realm of market power lies oligopoly. From the Greek for 'few authorities', the oligopoly model represents a significant concentration of market power within a few firms.

Oligopoly is defined as a market structure where a few sellers dominate the market. There may be more than a few in the entire market, but a small group exert significant market power. Examples of oligopoly markets include smartphone operating systems, computer operating systems, passenger airlines, cellular phone service in most countries, and the US beer industry.

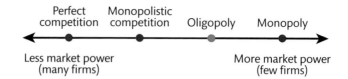

Oligopoly and monopolistic competition are grouped together in this chapter because it is sometimes difficult to discern a clear difference between the two in the real world. As more areas of local and national economies expand to a global scale, the frequency of oligopoly has increased.

Assumptions of the model

Oligopolies can be very different from each other. What follows is an attempt to summarise some key points of similarity and comparison.

A few large firms

Concentration ratios can mislead one into thinking that all the firms share their concentration equally. This may be the case. However, it is also possible that one firm is significantly larger than the other three or four. What can be said is that the market is dominated by a small group of firms that are relatively large compared to the others.

High barriers to entry

Oligopolies are characterised by high barriers to entry. These barriers may be the same types as those enjoyed by monopoly firms: high initial fixed costs, access to resources, economies of scale, legal barriers such as licences and patents, and the employment of aggressive anti-competitive tactics.

Differentiated or non-differentiated (homogeneous) goods

Oligopolies may produce differentiated goods, like the monopolistic competitor. Oligopoly industries like soaps, soft drinks and sodas, breakfast cereals, and automobiles all strive mightily to differentiate their products in hopes of drawing customers away from their competitors. Other oligopolies, typically in the provision of raw materials like timber (wood), oil, and aluminium, produce essentially the same good.

Interdependence

A distinct feature of oligopolies is that with relatively few firms in the industry there is a tendency towards interdependent relationships between firms. In other words, a firm's actions in the market are watched by its competitors, which may react with actions of their own. Recall that in more competitive markets, the actions of one firm had no effect on the overall market. With an oligopoly, the single firm is large enough, relative to the market, to affect the market by its actions.

Strategic thinking

One result of interdependence is that firms are inclined to think strategically, considering the possible reactions of other firms to any particular initiative. As they do so, the firms have relatively few other firms to monitor, and this leads to a choice between following the strategies employed by most of the other firms, or to compete with them.

With oligopoly, firms are regularly tempted to cut prices to win customers away from competitors. This type of **price competition** can reduce profits throughout the industry, especially if it leads to a protracted 'price war'. An alternative approach would be to keep prices high, either passively or in active coordination with other firms. This is only possible because the collective firms have enormous market power. The strategy can yield extra profits as a result. Thus, the oligopoly must choose between opposite strategies, to compete or to collude. This is explored in the remaining sections of this chapter.

How does a concentration ratio help us identify an oligopoly?

Oligopolies markets may have just a few firms, or they may have several more. A common method of determining whether or not an industry operates under oligopoly conditions is called the concentration ratio. A concentration ratio attempts to quantify the density of market power held by a certain number of firms. It is expressed as CR_X, where X is the number of firms controlling a certain percentage of the market. A value for CR_{10} would tell us how much of the market is controlled by the top ten firms. The higher the percentage, the greater the market power. Typically, the CR_4 is the guideline measure for determining the type of industry. Figure 12.10 shows the CR_4 percentage criteria for classifying a firm as a particular type of industry.

Concentration ratios are calculated by taking into account the total sales revenues of the top firms and dividing them by the industry's total revenues. What a concentration ratio does not show is the relative size of each firm, which is also important for market leadership. For example, a CR_4 of 90% would indicate a near monopoly situation even if the four firms were approximately equal in sales. However, if one firm held 70% and the other three held the remaining 20%, concerns about the large firm's dominance would be greater. It is likely that the 70% firm would lead the market for many strategic decisions, including price setting.

For example, in the USA, the domestic airline industry is concentrated among Delta (22%), American (21%), United (18%) and Southwest (15%) for 76% of the market, which places the industry in the zone of oligopoly, and with roughly equal market share. In the market for organ dialysis, two firms dominate with Fresenius (49%) and DaVita (43%) in an apparent duopoly. In e-commerce, Amazon has half the market (49%), with eBay (7%) and many smaller firms. In social networking, Facebook has an 85% market share, followed by LinkedIn (10%), and Twitter (5%).

Economists will point out that concentration alone should not be a basis for assessing market power. Other questions should be asked: Are prices higher than expected? Is output lower? Are there other harmful market effects? Nevertheless, concentration ratios provide a clear starting point for evaluating an industry's level of competition.

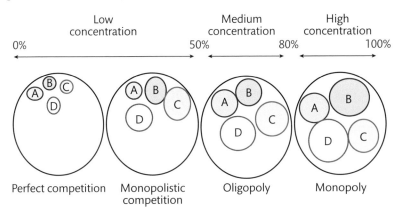

Figure 12.10 The higher the concentration ratio, the greater the market power

What is the difference between collusive and non-collusive oligopolies?

This section explores in further detail the distinction between firms that actively cooperate to fix prices and restrict output (i.e. collusive oligopolies) with firms that do not (i.e. **non-collusive oligopolies**). Collusion need not be explicit, it can be tacit and happen without specific coordination. But it can also be formal and explicit, with agreed strategies that seek to maximise profits for the entire industry.

Formal versus informal collusion

Informal or tacit collusion occurs when a single dominant firm establishes price leadership. The leading firm sets general price levels, and smaller firms follow with comparable prices. While no specific agreement exists, the informal understanding can endure because the smaller firms resist the urge to cut prices as the dominant firm would be able to survive any price wars. This does not prevent all forms of competition. Firms may still compete on service or brand power, or on another basis of non-price competition. Industries that have seen instances of price leadership include rental cars and breakfast cereals.

Informal collusion, while perhaps more common than the formal kind, is still somewhat difficult to achieve. Cost and demand differences among firms cause each firm to have their own incentives. Firms are still tempted to cheat. And this kind of price-fixing may also be illegal.

What is a cartel?

When oligopolists agree to take specific market action in a coordinated and sustained effort to enhance profits, a cartel is at work. A cartel is a group of competitors that successfully limit competition and keep prices above a competitive norm. Cartels differ from occasional acts of market coordination by being continuous business arrangements. Firms can coordinate a variety of market behaviours together. They can restrict output to drive up prices. They can fix prices within a specified range. They can decide to restrict innovation and avoid extra costs of research and development. They can agree not to advertise or in any way compete with each other.

When the firms agree to fix the market price and output level, they are essentially acting as one industry. Figure 12.11 shows the **collusive oligopoly** in action. It functions just

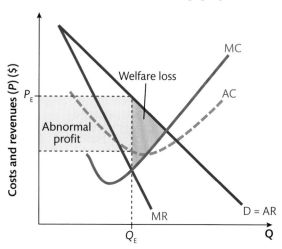

Figure 12.11 A collusive oligopoly functions like a monopoly, leading to welfare loss

as a monopoly would, with firms producing at the profit maximisation output where $MR=MC$, setting price at the demand curve at P_E, and enjoying whatever profits are produced, shown by the shaded area of the diagram.

Recall that monopolies keep prices high, and output low, and that this results in a net loss of welfare, a loss of consumer and producer surplus compared to competitive markets, shown in the shaded grey area. This would be true of collusive oligopolies, who imitate monopoly in their pricing and output decisions.

While overt collusion across whole industries is rarely achieved, most price-fixing takes place covertly on the specific market level, for particular products like illness-specific drugs, or airline routes between cities. However, public attention to the market power of concentrated industries is growing. In recent years, governments have investigated Apple for fixing the price of ebooks, the top five German car makers for car prices, Google for internet search advertising, and Swiss airlines for shipping rates.

The most famous and public cartel is the Organization of Petroleum Exporting Countries (OPEC), a group of 12 oil-producing countries founded in 1965. OPEC regularly meets to set production **quotas** in the hope of establishing the 'right price' for oil in world markets. OPEC countries possess nearly 80% of latent oil reserves, and currently produce 30% of all oil. Thus, they have considerable influence on world oil markets. In fact, OPEC is a useful example to keep in mind when observing the dual tendencies to collude or compete. After agreeing to production quotas with a target oil price in mind, countries are tempted to produce and sell secretly. This, of course, would lower world prices and reduce profits for all.

The paucity of outright collusive cartels provides a clue to the difficulties oligopolists face when attempting to work together in a sophisticated fashion. Price and production fixing is specifically illegal in the EU, the UK and the USA, which drives the practice underground, if it is practised at all, in those areas. Aside from illegality, the incentive to cheat other firms makes collusive cartels less common. Firms, it should also be noted, are not all alike in their demand and costs situations. Some firms could compete on cost, which would make them more likely to compete rather than collude, on prices. Their opponent might need higher prices to survive, and so they each face different incentives regarding collusion. Furthermore, even if firms successfully coordinate and earn very high abnormal profits, this could encourage entry into the market by potential competitors, reducing the market power of the remaining firms.

Non-collusive oligopoly

Non-collusive oligopoly occurs when firms do not cooperate and, therefore, exist in a strategic environment where one must consider the actions and reactions of other firms at all times. Even when firms actively collude, the tension between the strategies to compete and to collude is still in force. Firms may agree to collude but still have strong incentives to cheat on this arrangement.

Non-collusive oligopoly players are constantly weighing the possible decisions taken by their opponents, requiring *strategic behaviour* to a much larger degree than the other firm types. As the prisoner's dilemma and the example below will also show, firms in an oligopoly are interdependent on each other's actions. One's behaviour relies on the actions of another, also a feature that is unique among the four types of firms.

Game theory offers an opportunity to demonstrate the strategic thinking and interdependence involved in non-collusive oligopolies. Game theory uses applied mathematics to understand how individuals act strategically, where their success depends on the choices made by others in the so-called 'game'. The simplest form of game theory can illustrate the quandary posed to the oligopolist. Called the prisoner's dilemma, this form of a game has two players, in effect a duopoly.

In the original game, two prisoners are held for questioning regarding a robbery. They are held separately, and face the dilemma of colluding to stay silent and receiving a modest sentence on a lesser charge, or 'cheating' on their agreement and confessing, thereby securing the lowest possible sentence for themselves and the highest for their opponent. In the end, both have the same incentive to cheat/confess and are rather likely to do so. What is important is that the prisoners face divergent incentives, to collude or compete, and are influenced by what the other player may do.

The above dilemma can be applied to market duopoly, where firms are deciding on whether to maintain their price or lower it, a common dilemma for oligopolistic firms. In Figure 12.12, two cola companies, Company C and Company P, are assessing their incentives. If the firms split the market 50% each, and both maintain their price, then their profits will be $5 billion each.

However, if Company C lowers the price and Company P does not, it will win over vast numbers of new customers and earn $7 billion, mostly at the expense of Company P, who will earn only $1 billion. (This might be enough profit to allow Company C to buy Company P and become a monopoly.) Of course, the reverse is true, as Company P will dramatically out-earn Company C if it lowers price and Company C does not. Thus, both firms have a strong incentive to compete (lower price) rather than to collude. At the same time, if they both compete and lower price they both wind up with $4 billion profits, and have lost $1 billion in profits. The dilemma each faces, to compete or collude, reflects the interdependence of these firms.

Game theory would help firms make strategic decisions when they can know the payoffs of all players and the number of players is relatively small. If the model incorporates additional players or more strategic choices, such as whether to advertise, the calculations become very complex and less reliable. However, where true the duopoly game theory model suggests that firms may not compete on price if they can

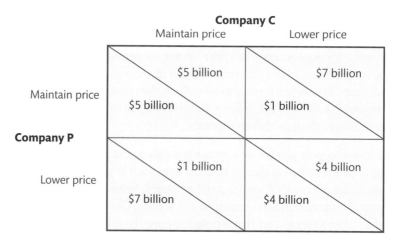

Figure 12.12 This duopoly **payoff matrix** illustrates a common dilemma for oligopolies. Should they collude or compete?

avoid it and will collude if they can do so. That leaves firms to compete in areas other than price to win market share. The above highlights one of the risks oligopolies face in relation to each other. Competitive behaviour on pricing can lead to ever lower prices. The risk of a price war acts as an implicit floor on the desire of firms to compete on price, knowing that it will directly reduce profitability and perhaps hurt the image of the product in the market.

What is non-price competition?

Oligopoly firms often seek ways other than price to maximise profits. Service, design and appearance, quality, and brand power are among the most typical forms of non-price competition. Evidence of non-price competition among oligopolists occurred in the early decades of commercial flight, when most airlines were heavily regulated on the prices they could charge customers. As a result, airlines competed in every other way possible, including offering lavish meals with beverages. Only after **deregulation** did 'budget' airlines offer an alternative, with no meals and reduced services, to attract price-conscious customers.

Furthermore, as with monopolistic competition, actual differences in product are only important insofar as they are perceived to be different by consumers. This is where advertising plays a pivotal role in oligopoly as well as monopolistic competition. Firms spend lavishly with the purpose of convincing the public of sometimes rather small differences in products. Recall that they do so in the hope of yielding abnormal profit (at least temporarily, until the competitor copies or counters the innovation), or of preventing a loss of market share (the fate of firms that choose not to compete).

Furthermore, strategic brand differentiation can mask the ownership concentration in a market. Supermarkets may appear to offer thousands of choices, but many brands are owned by a few food, beverage, and consumer product firms, creating an illusion of choice and more power to set prices than the consumer might imagine.

12.3 When should governments intervene to reduce market power and what do they do?

Learning outcomes

At the end of this section you will be able to:

- identify the risks and advantages of excess market power
- explain the market conditions that may provoke government intervention
- examine the ways governments seek to limit market power and discourage anti-competitive practices
- discuss the effectiveness of government measures to restrain market power.

What are the advantages and risks with oligopoly and excess market power?

While oligopoly tends to have the most complicated type of firm, it is possible to establish some areas of criticism and possible benefit.

Economic risks

Disadvantages to oligopoly are the apparent lack of allocative and productive efficiency. Like monopoly and monopolistic competition, the downward-sloping demand curve of the collusive oligopoly has the same effect. Figure 12.11 shows the oligopolist raises price above MC ($P > $ MC), and so allocative efficiency is not achieved and a welfare loss occurs. Oligopoly also brings the profit-maximising level of output to the left of where AC is at its minimum. Thus, productive efficiency is also not achieved.

The other major problems with oligopoly involve the tremendous incentives to coordinate and collude. These incentives seek merely to take advantage of the firm's market size and to discourage the competition that could yield innovation and efficiency. Excess market power such as this is likely to result in higher prices and less output for the market, reducing consumer welfare. It also acts as a transfer of income from buyers to sellers that is less likely to happen in a competitive market.

Economic advantages

Oligopolies, like a monopoly, may earn continuous abnormal profits as a result of the barriers to entry. Thus, firms do have the economic resources to conduct research and development. When profits invested into R&D result in better products, more choice, and lower prices, overall consumer welfare may rise.

Natural monopolies are a good example of beneficial monopoly power. As you read in Chapter 11, these monopolies are granted by governments to reap the benefits of economies of scale for public utilities and transport. Prices are in fact lower and output higher with natural monopolies, rather than with multiple producers. While they need regulation and subsidies to achieve near-allocative efficiency, the single producer model is the basis for greater social welfare.

How do governments discourage and restrain excess market power?

To enjoy the benefits of competitive markets, governments must protect the market from practices aimed at dominating or rigging it in a few firms' interests. Where governments perceive a market failure, they can intervene in the market to correct it. Each government sets its own level of tolerance of market power, and attention to market power can vary from election to election. Government intervention may include the following.

Legislation and regulation

Anti-trust laws form a body of anti-monopoly law that seeks to keep markets competitive. Anti-trust law seeks to protect consumers and producers from **unfair competition**. Such laws typically forbid or restrict:

- price-fixing
- bid-rigging
- mergers, horizontal and vertical
- anti-competitive bundling of products
- predatory pricing.

Furthermore, governments often create 'watchdog' agencies whose role is to enforce antitrust laws and ensure fully competitive markets. The EU Competition Commission, the UK Competition and Markets Authority, and the US Federal Trade Commission are all examples of such agencies. Their powers and responsibilities include:

- setting quality conditions
- establishing market rules and prices
- investigating claims
- issuing fines
- making criminal indictments of offending executives
- recommending a break-up of offending companies.

Government ownership

Industries can also be taken over by the government, or nationalised, if there are sufficient welfare gains or positive externalities to be captured by public provision. Natural monopolies, because they provide necessities like water, gas, or electricity, are often under complete government control.

Fines

The power to levy major fines can discourage anti-competitive behaviour. By issuing fines, government authorities affect the cost–benefit ratio that firms weigh when deciding to seek market power advantages. Such fines are nearly always appealed in court and negotiated after the fact. The effectiveness of fines depends on the degree to which they match the social costs of the offence, and discourage the market power-seeking behaviour. Fines that are too light, for example, simply reduce the profitability of the practices without discouraging the behaviour by making them unprofitable or loss making, or holding managers accountable.

Case study – cell service providers and oligopoly

America's cell phone service market has been narrowed down to three major providers after the acquisition of Sprint by T-Mobile in spring of 2020. America's Federal Trade Commission initially denied the request to merge, citing the undue market power exerted by a more concentrated market. They also cited T-Mobile's previously aggressive pricing as a source of competitive behaviour that would diminish after the merger. Together, AT&T, Verizon, and T-Mobile now control 98% of the US cell provider market.

Research and inquiry

To find recent examples of market power being challenged by government action, conduct an internet search using the following terms: 'EU Competition Commission' or 'Federal Trade Commission', paired with 'price-fixing', 'fines', or 'market power'.

For discussion and debate:

1 List the agency and industry.

2 Identify the main allegations against the firms involved.

3 List the possible government interventions in response.

4 Discuss how the interventions may help address the market power violations in the case.

Case study – internet advertising and oligopoly

Internet advertising is a growing business that tends to be dominated by a few small firms. In 2019 in the USA, Google (37%), Facebook (22%), Amazon (8%), and Microsoft (8%) collectively made up 75% of the market. Based purely on CR_4 standards, the industry could qualify as a highly concentrated oligopoly.

Discussion questions:

1 Aren't the above companies' services 'free' to users? Who is being charged by whom in this situation?

2 Why might the concentration of market power in this industry be a problem for consumers or the public?

3 What evidence would help you decide if this level of concentration is a problem?

4 How could the government intervene to protect social welfare and restore competition?

Practice exam questions

Paper 1, part (a)

1. Explain, using examples, how monopolistically competitive firms use differentiation to increase market power.   (10 marks)

2. Explain, using a diagram, the degree to which monopolistically competitive firms achieve allocative and productive efficiency.   (10 marks)

3. Explain, using a diagram, what happens to a monopolistically competitive firm that experiences short-run abnormal profits.   (10 marks)

4. Explain, using a kinked demand curve, the existence of price rigidities in an oligopoly market.   (10 marks)

Paper 1, part (b) questions

1. Evaluate the view that market power negatively affects consumer welfare.   (15 marks)

2. Using real-world examples, evaluate the view that governments should strictly enforce anti-market power laws and regulations.   (15 marks)

3. Using real-world examples, discuss the forms of government intervention used to address extreme market power.   (15 marks)

4. Using real-world examples, discuss the position that collusive oligopolies should be investigated and forcefully controlled.   (15 marks)

Paper 2

Former Bumble Bee CEO Sentenced to Prison for Fixing Prices of Canned Tuna

Christopher Lischewski, former Chief Executive Officer and President of Bumble Bee Foods LLC, was sentenced to serve 40 months in jail and pay a $100,000 criminal fine for his leadership role in a three-year antitrust conspiracy to fix prices of canned tuna, the Department of Justice announced.

Lischewski was charged on May 16, 2018, in an indictment returned by a federal grand jury in San Francisco. After a four-week trial in late 2019, he was convicted on the single count of participating in a conspiracy to fix prices of canned tuna. In imposing Lischewski's 40-month prison sentence, the Court found that Lischewski was a leader or organiser of the conspiracy and that it affected over $600 million dollars of canned tuna sales.

'The sentence imposed today will serve as a significant deterrent in the C-suite and the boardroom,' said Assistant Attorney General Makan Delrahim of the Justice Department's Antitrust Division. 'Executives who cheat American consumers out of the benefits of competition will be brought to justice, particularly when their antitrust crimes affect the most basic necessity, food. Today's sentence reflects the serious harm that resulted from the multi-year conspiracy to fix prices of canned tuna.'

'This sentence is the result of our commitment to holding corporations and senior leadership accountable for their actions, whether they operate in the food supply industry or elsewhere,' said FBI San Francisco Division Special Agent in Charge, John F. Bennett. 'This brings us closer to our goal; allowing our citizens to be able to purchase food in an unbiased market within an efficient and fair economy, free of corporate greed.'

Bumble Bee pleaded guilty and was sentenced to pay a $25 million criminal fine. In September, StarKist Co. was sentenced to pay a statutory maximum $100 million criminal fine. In addition to Bumble Bee and StarKist, four executives, including Lischewski, were charged in the investigation. The other three executives pleaded guilty and testified in Lischewski's trial.

The sentence announced today is a result of the Department's ongoing investigation into price fixing in the packaged-seafood industry, which is being conducted by the Antitrust Division's San Francisco Office and the FBI's San Francisco Field Office. Anyone with information on price fixing, bid rigging, or other anticompetitive conduct related to the packaged-seafood industry should contact the Antitrust Division's San Francisco Office.

a. Define *price-fixing*. (2 marks)
b. Explain how the firm's behaviour is an example of formal collusion. (4 marks)
c. Explain, using a diagram, how this collusive oligopoly earns large abnormal profits. (4 marks)
d. Explain, using examples, how tuna firms might engage in two kinds of non-price competition. (4 marks)
e. Evaluate the effectiveness of government intervention to restrain market power. (8 marks)

Macroeconomics

Why does economic activity vary over time and why does this matter?

- **Change** in the conditions of the demand and supply sides of the economy cause economic activity to vary over time.
- Fluctuations in economic activity impact the **economic well-being** of individuals and societies.
- Different schools of macroeconomic thought identify different causes and offer different solutions for macroeconomic problems.

Measuring economic activity and illustrating its variations

13

13.1 How is the overall level of economic activity measured?

This chapter begins the study of macroeconomics, the study of national economic activity. With it, the scope of the subject changes from the individual markets of microeconomics to the broader measures of total well-being. In seeking to improve the general livelihood of their citizens, governments tend to prioritise four macroeconomic concerns or objectives:

- **full employment**, as measured by a *low unemployment rate*
- **economic growth**, as measured by *increasing national income*
- **price stability**, as measured by a *low inflation rate*
- **income distribution**, as measured by a more *equitable distribution of income*.

This chapter will explain how each objective is measured, starting with gross domestic product, or GDP, as a measure of national income. This measure of economic activity is determined in three different ways, and to grasp those different approaches it is useful to revisit the circular flow model of the economy from Chapter 1.

How is national income measured?

When economists set out to add up the value of a country's economic output, they have an enormous task. The equivalence of expenditure to income guides them as they seek to check the validity of their conclusions. With this in mind, economists have three main methods of counting national income:

- the spending (**expenditure**) **approach**
- the **income approach**
- the **output approach**.

In Chapter 1, you looked at the circular flow model of the economy showing the movement of resources and money through the economy. That model included leakages and injections for the trade, banking, and government sectors.

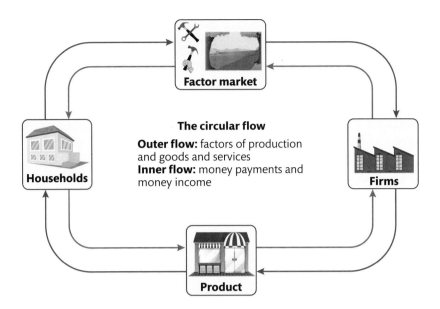

Figure 13.1 shows a simplified model, showing the economy roughly divided into two types of market, with two types of economic agents interacting (households and firms). In the goods and services market, households bought goods and services, and in exchange paid money to the firms. In the market for factors of production, firms buy land, labour, capital, and entrepreneurship from households. Households, in a free market economy, own these factors, and thus earn income in the form of rent, wages, interest and profits, respectively. Money flows in one direction while goods, services and factors of production flow in the other.

The circular flow model illustrates that each of the three methods should derive essentially the same national income result. All of the goods and services produced will be measured with the output method. All of that output is eventually bought, and those expenditures are recorded with the expenditure methods. Furthermore, each and every transaction involves money spent on the buyer side that will be income on the selling side.

The identity of output as equivalent to the value of income may at first seem odd, or an overly tidy result. However, when viewed at the level of an individual transaction, the identity becomes clearer. Consider the purchase of an apple from your local market for NZ$1 (NZ$ is the symbol for New Zealand dollar, the currency of New Zealand). This price represents the value of the output to you, the consumer. To the seller, it represents income. Some portion of that NZ$1 goes to the grower, transporter, wholesaler, and final market. This income may go to pay wages, to profits, even to rent. Thus, we can say that spending on output must, at the same time, represent income to the factors of production.

The expenditure approach

The expenditure (spending) method counts the total spending on final new goods and services in a given year. Final goods are ready for consumption; this category does not include goods that will be input goods or are raw materials for other production.

Apples bought at the grocery store count as final goods, apples sold to a baker for apple pie are not counted until they are sold in their final form. This approach places such spending into four broad categories.

- **Consumption (C)**. Consumption includes the durable and non-durable goods and services purchased by private individuals and households.
- **Investment (I)**. Investment refers to spending by firms on new capital equipment and by households on new housing.
- **Government spending (G)**. Government spending is all spending on government purchases, which includes salaries for workers as well as capital goods spending and transfers.
- **Net exports (X – M)**. Net exports deducts the outflow of import purchases (M) from the inflow derived from export revenue (X).

The expenditure approach can be expressed as:

$$GDP = C + I + G + (X - M)$$

GDP is gross domestic product, which is commonly defined as measuring the final value of all goods and services produced in a country in a given period, usually a year.

An example of the expenditure method is shown in Table 13.1. This shows the spending totals for each sector in the US economy for 2019. In the USA, a free market economy, the largest spending sector is consumption. This is typical of free market economies. Next is government spending, then private investment, and net exports. Net exports is expressed as a negative number (US$–659 billion), which means that the USA imported that much more than it exported in that year.

The income approach

The income approach to **national income accounting** attempts to count GDP through the market view of the circular flow of income. The income approach roughly approximates to the returns for factors of production described in Figure 13.1. Wages, interest, rent, and profits are the factor payments made for labour, capital, land, and entrepreneurship. These forms of income are used to buy goods and services in the product market, and should be roughly equivalent to those expenditures.

Again, it is assumed that for every transaction there is a buyer and a seller. A buyer's spending is recorded by the expenditure approach, and that same spending is recorded as revenue income on the income approach. Thus, we economists assume the identity as:

$$W + I + R + P = C + I + G + (X - M)$$

$$(GDP\,from\,income) = (GDP\,from\,spending)$$

Table 13.1 Expenditure approach to GDP: USA, 2019 (US$ billion)

(C) personal consumption expenditure	14,188
(I) gross private domestic investment	3,766
(G) government expenditures	3,569
(X – M) net exports goods and services	−659

Research and inquiry

How is your country's GDP composed? Which of the four spending categories would you think is the largest? The smallest? To find out, conduct an internet search using the term 'GDP by composition by end use'. Now check a country you expect to be very different from your own. Compare the results. Was one sector considerably larger than another's sector? What factors do you think influenced this difference?

The output approach

The output approach takes a completely different view when adding the overall level of economic activity. Like the other approaches, the output approach seeks to ascertain the total value of all final goods and services produced in a year. When adding production, however, it would be easy to double count by counting goods that are intermediate goods and then counting the final product. To avoid this, economists attempt to identify the value added at each stage of the production process. An automobile's raw materials, then parts, then the whole are calculated separately to measure each interval of production. The total is then added to the national income number.

As you study macroeconomics, it is useful to keep in mind that the overall economic activity of a country can go by any of these categorisations:

$$GDP = national\ output = national\ income = national\ spending$$

Exercise 13.1

The table below shows sample figures for the GDP of Nigeria, calculated using the expenditure approach.

	US$ million
Household consumption	969,600
Government expenditure	60,600
Investment, gross private	179,376
Exports	144,228
Imports	159,984
Total	1,193,820

1 Which sector of GDP is Nigeria's largest? Is this result a surprise?
2 Calculate the percentage of spending by each sector.
3 Why is it necessary to subtract imports from exports?
4 How does this compare to the size of the sectors in the country you researched in our research and inquiry?

Video suggestion:
You have read about it, now you can review what you have just learned by watching a video by the author!
▶ Simply click here in your eBook for a video on measuring GDP using the income approach and the expenditure approach.

How significant is household spending in the Nigerian economy?

13.2 What is GNI and how is it distinguished from GDP?

GDP defines its measurement of income *geographically*. All output that is domestically produced, regardless of who owns the factor of production, is measured in a country's GDP. For example, the sales of many UK-owned firms that have factories or outlets in Ireland will count towards Ireland's GDP. And similarly, Irish firms operating in the UK will add their sales to the UK's GDP. **Gross national income (GNI)** instead measures income by *nationality of ownership* of the factors of production wherever they are. GNI is specifically defined as the total money value of all final goods and services produced in an economy in one year, plus net property income from abroad.

GNI statistics track income flows by subtracting from GDP any income to foreign factors of production. At the same time, it adds any factor income from domestically owned factors of production located in other countries. In our Irish example, Irish production in the UK would be subtracted from UK GDP and added to Irish GDP to help arrive at Irish GNI. Meanwhile, the UK-owned firms' production in Ireland would be subtracted from Ireland's GDP and added to the UK's to arrive at each country's GNIs. The term for this is 'net property income' from abroad, which takes the sum of income from domestically owned assets abroad, minus the income from foreign-owned assets within the country. It is possible to summarise the method of accounting for GNI as:

$$GNI = GDP + \text{ net property income from abroad}$$

What accounts for the differences between GNI and GDP depends on the country. Countries that have a much higher GNI than GDP are likely to have workers or firms overseas who send income back to home country accounts. Correspondingly, the presence of foreign workers and firms, and the profits and income they repatriate, is lower by comparison. Countries with higher GDP than GNI may have significant foreign presence, in either workers or companies. Therefore, they suffer a net income loss when GDP is compared to their GNI. Net income is reduced by the outflow of foreign-earned income on the country's soil.

What is the difference between nominal and real GDP, and between nominal and real GNI?

Nominal GDP measures output in current values, while real GDP will adjust the measure for inflation levels. Economists hope to determine the actual level of output produced every year and to avoid accidentally counting changes to price levels instead. Because GDP is counted by tabulating the transaction prices charged at the time, price changes can distort attempts to measure actual output. Economists seek to distinguish between the nominal value of output as it is shown in current prices and the real value. Nominal values may be higher (inflated) or lower (deflated) than they were in the previous period. Real GDP seeks to adjust for that and show the value of output at constant prices.

For example, consider a car manufactured and sold for ₩15 million (₩ is the symbol for the won, the currency of South Korea) in a given year. One year later, exactly the same car was manufactured and sold for ₩18 million. Simple mathematics tells us that the price has increased by 20%, but nothing about the car is actually 20% greater than in the previous year. So, a nominal measure of GDP for the second year would count every car sold at a 20% increase in price as a contribution to national output, when really it is only an increase in the price of the good. This is how price increases from inflation could cause GDP to be overestimated, causing us to think the economy is doing better than it is in reality.

When taking account of goods and services at their current prices, economists use the term 'nominal'. Nominal GDP is simply the value of goods and services produced in a country in a given year, expressed in the value of the prices charged for that year. In the example above, the new car would have added ₩3 million to nominal GDP, providing an artificially high estimate of how much output actually grew.

- Price level rises (inflation): nominal GDP exaggerates value of output compared to real output.
- Price level falls (deflation): nominal GDP underestimates value of real output compared to actual output.

The same distinction between real and nominal values applies to GNI.

$$Real\ GNI = Nominal\ GNI\ adjusted\ for\ inflation$$

Similarly, rising prices in a measured year can result in an overestimate in real output due to inflated GNI numbers, while falling prices may underestimate the real level of output by showing deflated GNI numbers.

Exercise 13.2

Calculating real GDP and real GNI using a price deflator

To adjust for inflation, economists use a price deflator, which is defined as a coefficient that removes the impact of inflation when measuring economic statistics. The GDP deflator is a price index that expresses price level changes relative to a base year value of 100. If the base year is 2010 and the value of the GDP deflator is 155 in 2020, prices have increased 55% from 2010 (deflator = 100) to 2020 (deflator = 155).

To adjust nominal GDP to real GDP use the following equation:

$$Real\ GDP = \frac{Nominal\ GDP}{Price\ deflator} \times 100$$

For example, if Country X has $1.6 billion in nominal GDP and a 125 deflator:

$$Real\ GDP = \frac{\$1,600,000,000}{125} \times 100$$

$$= \$1,280,000,000$$

Nominal GDP has been 'deflated' from $1.6 billion to $1.28 billion.

Using the figures below, calculate the expected values in each blank.

Nominal GDP (US$ million)	GDP deflator	Real GDP
726,000	219	
2,356,002		2,012,442
1,843,994	142	
	110	459,432
396,421	95	

What is real GDP/GNI per capita?

While real GDP adjusts for price changes, economists use another measure to adjust for population size. After all, we would expect countries with large populations to have large economies: their supply of labour resources and **human capital** can be a tremendous advantage. At the same time, it is important for a country to be growing enough economically to keep pace with the growth of its population. A simple mathematical adjustment provides a more accurate picture. By dividing GDP by the population size, we arrive at a per capita (per head) income for the country. Per capita GDP is the amount of national income divided by the population size. It gives us a better sense of the approximate standard of living in a country than total GDP does.

Table 13.2 shows the difference between sheer size of a country's economy and the value compared to population size. Viewed this way, our top five countries are completely different.

In total terms, all of the above are large diverse economies in countries with hundreds of millions of people. On a per capita basis, only the USA ranks in the top 10 of both size and average GDP. China ranks 68th, Japan 27th, Germany 18th, and India 142nd. Clearly, a better measure of average economic well-being is per capita GDP.

Table 13.2 The top five countries by total nominal GDP are very different to the top five by nominal GDP per capita

Country (GDP rank)	Total GDP (US$ trillion) [per capita rank]	Country per capita rank	Per capita GDP (US$)
United States	21,374,418.88 [10]	Monaco	185,741
China	14,342,902.84 [68]	Liechtenstein	173,356
Japan	5,081,769.54 [27]	Luxembourg	114,705
Germany	3,845,630.03 [18]	Switzerland	81,994
India	2,875,142.31 [142]	Ireland	78,661

Exercise 13.3

Calculate real GDP/GNI per capita

Using the figures below, calculate the expected values in each blank.

Nominal GDP (US$)	Population	Per capita GDP (US$)
3,600,000,000	80,000,000	
7,364,000,000	300,000,000	
	9,000,000	75,000

What is real GDP per capita using PPP?

Look closely and you will notice that Table 13.2 uses nominal measures of GDP. This may explain why all of the top five per capita GDP countries are places where the cost of living is relatively high. Without adjusting for cost of living, the higher overall price levels in those countries are inflating their nominal GDP numbers relative to the rest of the world.

Adjusting for domestic inflation, using real GDP numbers, would only help us measure the value of output relative to previous years within that country. Economists have developed a method to adjust for cost-of-living differences between countries. Called **purchasing power parity (PPP)**, this adjustment is based on the theory that **exchange rates** between currencies are in equilibrium when their purchasing power is the same in each of the two countries.

Why do this? The spending power of a Norwegian kroner may be very different from that of the Thai baht. Resources, goods, and services may be more expensive in Norway than in Thailand, which means that more income may be needed to enjoy the same standard of living as in Thailand.

PPP is based on the law of one price, which states that an identical good in one country should cost the same in another country, and that the exchange rate should reflect that price. For our purposes here, PPP is a tool to assess more accurately the standard of living available for a given amount of income in a country.

For example, the Norwegian krone equivalent of $100 (Nk588) may buy a certain amount of food, perhaps three pizzas. The Thai baht equivalent of $100 (THB2994)

Table 13.3 High-income countries may move down the ranking for per capita GDP once the cost of living is taken into account …

GDP selected high-income countries: per capita GDP adjusted with PPP accounting			
Country by GDP per capita (rank)	**GDP per capita/ thousands (US$)**	**GDP per capita PPP/thousands (US$)**	**GDP/capita PPP rank**
Luxembourg (3)	114,705	109,100	4
Switzerland (4)	81,994	61,400	11
Ireland (5)	78,661	72,600	7

may buy six pizzas, because staple goods are cheaper in Thailand. This means that every $100 of income earned in Norway will buy less in goods and services than the same amount in Thailand. Therefore, Norway's high GDP per capita may overrate the standard of living there.

When the purchasing power is factored into national income measures, it produces a refined view of the GDP data. Table 13.3 shows how the per capita GDP leaders in Table 13.2 are adjusted for purchasing power in their countries. In each case, PPP adjustments reduced the per capita GDP. All of these are West European countries, where the cost of living tends to be higher.

In the case of middle- and low-income countries shown in Table 13.4, these result as having GDP per capita PPP greater than their nominal GDP values. This suggests that when ranked against other countries nominally, their potential standard of living is underestimated. What these countries also share is some level of regional underdevelopment within the country. Economists pay attention to PPP-adjusted GDP levels to better understand the attainable quality of life, and to compare one country with another in this regard.

How can national income statistics be used to measure economic well-being?

The compilation of good economic data is not easy. It requires enormous administrative work, as well as persistent and rigorous mathematical analysis. It can also be quite expensive. The US government's primary agency for national income accounting, the Bureau of Economic Analysis, spends nearly $100 million dollars a year to do this job. A logical question is whether this kind of information is worth that

Table 13.4 … while middle- and low-income countries may move up the ranking

GDP selected middle- and low-income countries: per capita GDP adjusted with PPP accounting			
Country by GDP per capita (rank)	**GDP per capita/ thousands (US$)**	**GDP per capita PPP/ thousands (US$)**	**GDP/capita PPP rank**
Egypt (141)	2,000	15,000	93
Thailand (93)	6,595	17,800	86
Mongolia (120)	3,620	12,820	101

kind of money or, as an economist would say, is the opportunity cost too high? This is a dimension of positive (rather than normative) economics that everyone agrees on – the need for accurate data. Furthermore, when agencies openly publish the methods used to obtain the data, it allows experts to determine the full value of the information. Economists would justify the pursuit of correct information on the grounds that it can be useful for comparisons between countries and for the evaluation of economic performance over time.

Comparing country by country

As our previous tables have shown, national income can help us compare the relative standard of living across countries, especially on a per capita basis. This leads to further evaluation of a country's economic progress and prospects for further growth.

Evaluation of economic performance over time

Policymakers and economists of all kinds can use the data to evaluate the overall performance of the economy. Making good policy to affect the economy depends on good information as the basis for those decisions. Questions such as 'Has our expansionary fiscal policy been effective?' or 'Did reducing the money supply help reduce inflation?' can be intelligibly answered with good data.

- These results can inform further changes to government policies.
- Voters can use these results to assess the effectiveness of the current governing approach, and therefore confirm or evict current office holders.
- Businesses can use this information to forecast changes in markets and predict demand.

What are the limitations of national income statistics?

Does wealth make one happy? This age-old question arises quite appropriately when the question of GDP and well-being is raised. In other words, to what degree does a higher GDP per capita mean a better quality of life? Economists use the term 'welfare' to describe a way of speaking about the quality of life. We would assume that, *ceteris paribus*, more income is better than less income. And so, we could easily conclude that countries ranked according to per capita income levels could be ranked in the same order for welfare.

However, it is possible to argue that GDP only partly represents our view of a country's true welfare. Some have contended that GDP has little relevance for the everyday person. Economists have noted that national income accounting sometimes exaggerates well-being, and sometimes underestimates it. And sometimes, it misleads in unpredictable ways.

How do national income statistics underestimate economic well-being?

Increasing life spans

The fact that people are living longer is not included. Longer life expectancy is a universal goal among all countries. Most countries have seen their life expectancies climb. GDP does not tell this story.

Black market and parallel market activity is not included

For some countries, the estimated value of black market or parallel market activity is quite high. The income generated in these markets is not counted in final GDP numbers. Just as importantly, this income is not taxed by the government and therefore reduces the government's ability to produce public and merit goods like education, healthcare, and infrastructure.

Unpaid output is not counted

In other words, GDP only counts paid work. Volunteer efforts, which can be considerable in some countries, are not counted. Housework and childcare done by parents at home, while clearly desirable socially, are not counted. Furthermore, the work of poor farmers in subsistence economies is not counted, since these families will eat the product of their labour, rather than sell it. GDP figures show countries with subsistence economies to be less developed than perhaps they really are.

Rising quality, falling prices

Technological and managerial techniques are expected to improve the choice, quality, and safety of most of our material goods and services. These improvements are unseen by GDP figures, which merely report the type of output and the purchase price value of the product. For example, consider the calculators that many students use in their maths classes. To replicate the collective computing power of these small, inexpensive machines in a single computer would once have required a machine the size of a room, costing thousands of dollars. However, the falling price of these instruments would be recorded as reduced income for the vendors, and a fall in GDP.

How do national income statistics overestimate economic well-being?

Negative externalities

GDP numbers will include clearly negative social behaviours and transactions as net positives for national output, despite their ill effects. These include the environmental damage from many kinds of production. Furthermore, the money spent to jail criminals, fight wars, and consume unhealthy products all add to GDP figures, without contributing much to overall welfare.

Under-reporting the loss of natural resources

The degradation of rainforests is more likely to count as increased production than the despoiling of potentially valuable resource bases and watersheds. Strip mining of metals, the destruction of endangered species, and other environmentally harmful endeavours count as adding to GDP, though their long-term consequences may be devastating.

What other information about economic well-being do national income statistics fail to give us?

Composition of output

Does the economy produce large amounts of demerit goods, such as weapons or cigarettes, or spend money controlling the damage of natural disasters and criminal activity? Or instead does the economy have more hospitals and doctors than average, with greater access to education? Raw GDP numbers do not communicate the types of production, or their value to society.

Quality of life

Community activity that includes participation in groups beyond the family (e.g. social clubs, volunteer participation, church groups, sports, or outdoor activities) have been linked to greater life satisfaction. Faith in government, trust in the law and the courts, a sense of mutual responsibility among citizens, all these are desirable qualities for any country, but are unreported by national income data.

Distribution of income

In other words, national income cannot tell us who gets what. Income distribution can be very divergent, with a large gap between rich and poor. Furthermore, there is no guarantee that those at low-income levels are experiencing growth along with growth in GDP. While GDP may grow, individuals at the lowest levels of income may experience decreased standards of living.

13.3 Alternative measures of overall economic well-being

Learning outcomes

At the end of this section you will be able to:

- explain and comment on alternative measures of overall economic well-being:
  - **Better Life Index**
  - **Happiness Index**
  - **Happy Planet Index**.

In response to the criticism that macroeconomic measures like GDP and GNI offer a very limited view of economic well-being, economists in different realms have offered alternative approaches to measuring overall quality of life.

What is the OECD Better Life Index?

The Organisation for Economic Co-operation and Development (OECD) is an intergovernmental economic organisation with 37 member countries. It was founded in the early 1960s to share information, identify common policy issues, identify good policy and coordinate policies that may require collective action. OECD members are typically high-income countries that describe themselves as committed to democracy and a market economy. The OECD developed the Better Life Index (BLI) first published in 2011. The BLI is a composite measure that adds 11 dimensions of well-being into one summary score. The BLI includes (continued on the following page):

- housing
- jobs

The BLI emphasises user interactivity by allowing users to prioritise some dimensions over others and 'create your own' BLI. You can choose to emphasise income and health, for example, and see how the rankings change.

For discussion and debate:

1 Find the Create Your Better Life Index on the OECD website.

2 Toggle the indicators to reflect the aspects of life you value most highly.

3 Create your own index.

4 Screenshot and share your rankings.

5 Discuss with your classmates.

   a. Which countries dropped in your rankings, which rose?

   b. What accounts for the changes?

- education
- civic engagement
- life satisfaction
- work–life balance
- income
- community
- environment
- health
- safety
- Happiness Index
- Happy Planet Index.

The BLI continues to broaden its measure of well-being by adding an examination of gender disparities across the OECD. In other words, it shows how different are the levels of satisfaction that men and women enjoy on the various indicators within each country. One interesting feature of the BLI is a regional comparison tool. An example is shown below. Taking, for example, the Seoul region of South Korea as a starting point, the BLI will display regions with similar levels of well-being in the same categories.

Figure 13.2 shows Southern-Kanto, an area that includes Tokyo. It has similar rankings in the same dimensions in what could be very different types of regions such as Sardinia and Central Portugal.

What is the Happiness Index?

The United Nations publishes the World Happiness Report every year, a product of the United Nations Sustainable Development Solutions Network. One portion of this report includes rankings of national happiness based on self-reported surveys of individuals in over 150 countries. Inspired by the Government of Bhutan's Gross National Happiness index, the survey asks respondents to rank their life from 0 to 10, with 0 being the worst possible life and 10 being the best. High rankings on the Happiness Index tend to correlate with six key variables that support well-being: income, healthy life expectancy, social support, freedom, trust, and generosity.

Figure 13.2   The OECD Better Life Index shows which regions in other countries have a similar well-being profile

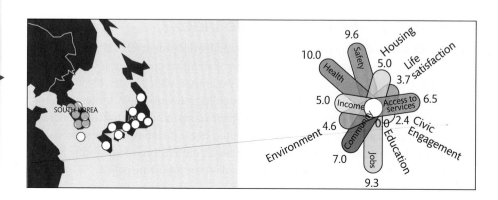

What is the Happy Planet Index?

The Happy Planet Index (HPI) is an index of well-being that incorporates environmental impact. By weighting a country's ecological footprint in the index, the HPI combines self-reporting happiness surveys with life expectancy, as well as equality of outcomes within a country on happiness and life expectancy. Perhaps the most significant feature of the HPI is trying to adjust for the level of sustainable resource use. Because GDP may include ecologically 'expensive' activities in terms of external costs, the HPI will revalue sustainable use. The environmental impact is estimated by quantifying the amount of natural resources used on a per capita basis.

As you might guess, HPI rankings can be very different from GDP, BLI, or happiness scores. The top five HPI countries in the most recent ranking were middle-income countries like Costa Rica, Mexico, Colombia, Vanuatu, and Vietnam. Moreover, some countries that are typically top scoring in the other measures drop considerably on the HPI. Australia, with cities often ranked as the best quality of life in the world, dropped to 105 on the HPI, and the USA to 109.

Research and inquiry

Find your country's ranking in GDP per capita, the BLI, Happiness Index, and Happy Planet Index.

For discussion and debate:

1 What accounts for the differences in rankings?
2 Do the results surprise you in any way?
3 Speculate as to what policies might help your country move up or down a particular index.

Video suggestion:
You have read about it, now you can review what you have just learned by watching a video by the author!
▶ Simply click here in your eBook for a video on the limitations of GDP.

13.4 What is the business cycle?

Learning outcomes

At the end of this section you will be able to:

- explain, using a business cycle diagram, that economies tend to go through a cyclical pattern characterised by the phases of the business cycle
- explain the **long-term growth trend** in the business cycle diagram as the **potential output** of the economy
- distinguish between a decrease in GDP and a decrease in GDP growth.

The business cycle is a term used to describe the fluctuations of national income from expansion to contraction to recovery. It can also be associated with changes in price levels. Economies tend to rise and fall, sometimes with warning and at other times rather suddenly. The fluctuations of GDP, and the important changes in employment that go with it, are often called the business cycle because there sometimes appears to be a pattern of increase and decrease, followed by another increase and then decrease. However, as Figure 13.3 shows, a more appropriate term might be the business roller-coaster.

Economic growth, as you now know, is an increase in the GDP from one year to the next. But sometimes, the economy shrinks. A recession is defined as two consecutive quarters of declining national output. In other words, if real GDP contracts over a six-month period, it is classified as a recession.

The lowest point of a recession is called the recessionary trough, seen here at the bottom of the GDP line. Nobody really knows exactly when this point is reached until output has begun to recover and growth has resumed. Hopefully, the economy

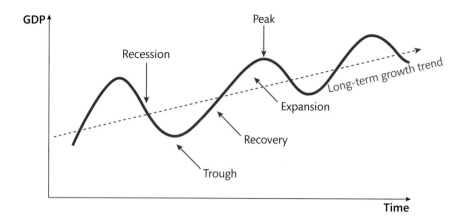

Figure 13.3 In the business
cycle there are peaks and
troughs along the road to
long-term growth

will quickly enter a recovery period. Recovery, shown as the GDP line rises from the trough, is defined as an increase in GDP from a recessionary level to match the level of output produced before the recession. The economy is getting back to where it was before the contraction. Should the economy grow beyond its previous level of output, it is called expansion. For most countries, expansion happens in short bursts, rather than a steady level of growth. When these bursts hit an apex (just before a recession) it is called the peak. Again, a peak is only observed after a recession begins.

The specific ways an economy can go from recession to recovery, and from recovery to expansion to recession again, are covered in detail in the chapters that follow. What is important to note here is that short-term fluctuations, the highs and lows of the roller coaster, can be quite dramatic. In the early years of industrial capitalism, when severe recessions were common, Karl Marx identified this tendency for swelling and collapse in his Crisis Theory, and predicted that these convulsions would inspire class struggle between labour and capital interests. These predictions appeared to come true with the rapid rise in the popularity of socialist movements after the Second World War until and into the Great Depression era of the 1930s. At that time, John Maynard Keynes labelled the phenomena a 'boom and bust' cycle that required massive government intervention, but not socialist revolution, to control. Today, it is widely accepted that the job of government policymakers is to 'smooth out' the peaks and troughs, to allow for more economic stability whenever this is possible. The economic crises of the 20th and 21st centuries have inspired calls for more government intervention to avoid major recessions and to have steady, reliable growth instead.

Also important is that the roller coaster moves generally upwards. While wide swings between peaks and troughs can cause significant pain and political instability, an upward average trend should be present in nearly all economies. Look again at Figure 13.3 and note the trend line that runs through the peaks and troughs. The trend line suggests that, over the long term, the economy is growing. This may mean an improvement in the standard of living, if the growth matches population growth and is distributed widely. While economists agree that GDP is not the only measure of national well-being, most agree that a growing economy is an essential ingredient for rising living standards.

TOK
Most economists agree that a growing economy is an essential ingredient for rising living standards. In the absence of statistics and news information about the economy, how might people judge whether the economy is doing well?

Paper 1, part (a)

1. Using a circular flow diagram, explain how two methods
   of measuring GDP will produce similar results.   (10 marks)

Paper 2, parts (a) and (b) and (g)

Australia and Argentina: divergent stories

In terms of overall size, the economies of Argentina and Australia started at similar
points in the early 2000s. Their stories diverge, however, in the experience of each
over the last decade. For Australia, the growth of *real GDP* has been steady, reliable,
nearly constant. For Argentina, economic performance has been much more
volatile, with several recessions in that short span.

a. Define *real GDP*.   (2 marks)
   Define *recession*.   (2 marks)
b. Using a diagram, explain the business cycle experience of
   Argentina from 2006 to 2011.   (4 marks)
g. Discuss the view that GDP can provide conclusive evidence
   of a country's overall economic well-being.   (15 marks)

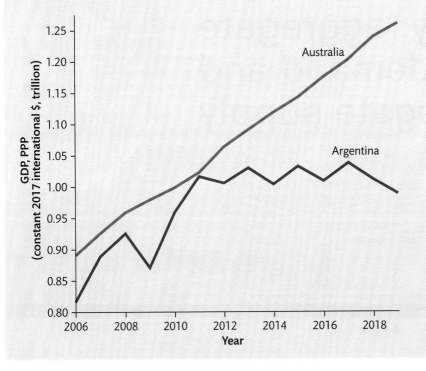

Figure 1 GDP, Australia and Argentina

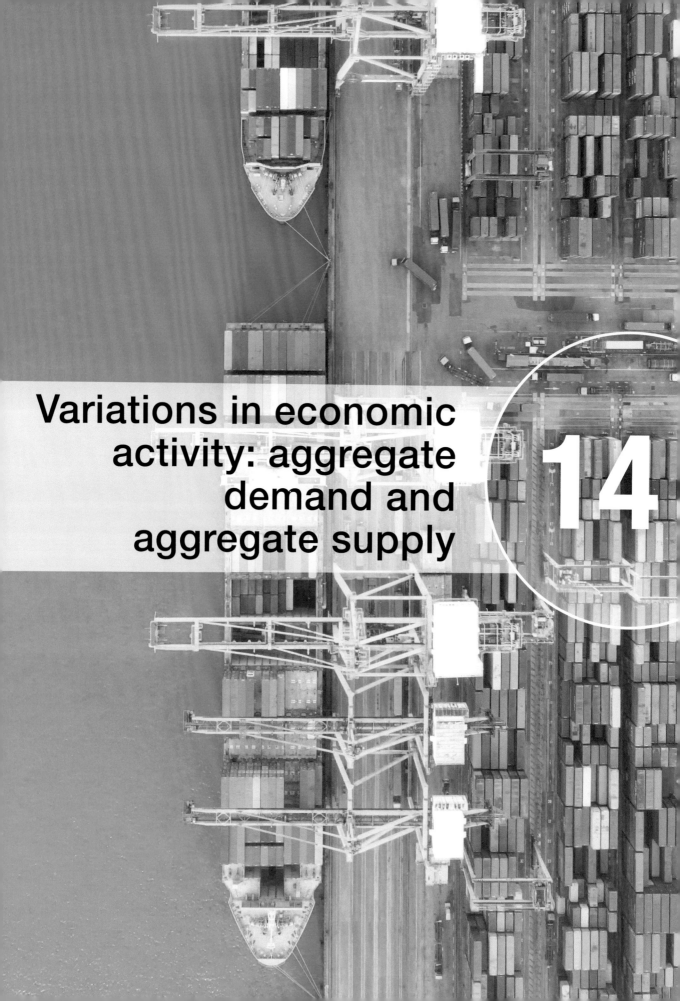

Variations in economic activity: aggregate demand and aggregate supply

14

14.1 What is aggregate demand?

Learning outcomes

At the end of this section you will be able to:

- distinguish between the microeconomic concept of demand for a product and the macroeconomic concept of AD
- construct an AD curve
- explain why the AD curve has a negative slope
- describe consumption, investment, government spending, and net exports as the components of AD
- for each of the various factors, explain how changes in the components of AD can lead to a shift in the AD curve.

It was December 2019 and on the eve of a new decade the economies of the world were operating under conditions that most would describe as 'business as usual'. The decade began, however, with a slow and unsteady recovery from what was later coined the Great Recession, the biggest global collapse since the 1930s. In the run-up to 2019, most of the world had been experiencing stable and steady economic growth for the second half of the 2010s.

Figure 14.1 shows the GDPs of the USA, the EU, and China from 2015 through to the end of 2019.

Almost no one on New Year's day of 2020 could have predicted that within a couple of months, nearly every country in the world would be in the midst of a record-setting decline in economic activity. Unemployment rates reached all-time highs, businesses

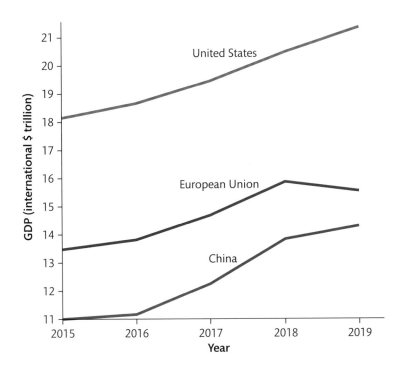

Figure 14.1 GDP of selected economies, 2015–19

large and small faced bankruptcy and closure, and governments scrambled to devise emergency measures to prop up their economies and protect the livelihoods of billions of their citizens.

Figures 14.2a-c tell a bit of the story of what unfolded in the world's three largest economies in the first half of 2020.

What happened in the early months of 2020? Well, we all know about the global pandemic that swept across nearly every country in the world. However, in addition to the public health crisis, the world's economies found themselves in an *aggregate demand and aggregate supply crisis* due to the unprecedented response required to slow the spread of COVID-19. The stay-at-home orders and forced shut downs of all but 'essential businesses' constrained both aggregate demand (AD) and aggregate supply (AS) in a manner and with a speed never experienced in modern history. While the Great Depression of the 1930s unfolded over months and years, the shocks that struck the countries of the world between February and April of 2020 occurred over just days and weeks.

To understand the causes and consequences of the economic collapse that occurred during the first half of 2020 (and in some places continuing well through the summer and fall), we must apply a new economic model that builds on the basic concepts introduced in our study of microeconomics. The concepts of *demand and supply*, which apply to the markets for individual goods and services, will be adapted to apply to entire nations' economies. The *aggregate demand and aggregate supply model* (AD/AS) is the subject of this chapter.

We begin by looking at AD, defined as the total spending in an economy consisting of consumption, investment, government expenditure, and net exports.

If we think of AD relative to its microeconomics counterpart, demand, the differences are clear: Demand represents the amount of a *particular good* that consumers are willing to buy at a range of prices in a period of time. AD, meanwhile, is the amount of *total output*, or all goods and services produced by an entire country, that households, businesses, the government, and foreigners are willing to buy in a period of time at a range of price levels. It is broken down into its four components, each representing a category of spending undertaken by a different stakeholder in a country's economy.

What are the components of AD?

Demand for a nation's output comes from households, from firms, from the government, and from foreign consumers of domestically produced goods, services, and resources. The four components (with the abbreviation for each) that make up a country's aggregate demand are as follows.

- **Consumption (C):** Consumption measures all spending by domestic households on goods and services during a particular period of time.
- **Investment (I):** Investment is short for gross domestic private investment, and measures the total spending by firms on capital equipment.
- **Government spending (G):** Government spending is short for gross government investment and spending and measures a country's government's expenditures on goods and services.
- **Net exports (X – M, or Xn):** Net exports measures the total income earned from the sale of exports (X) to foreigners minus the total amount spent by a nation's

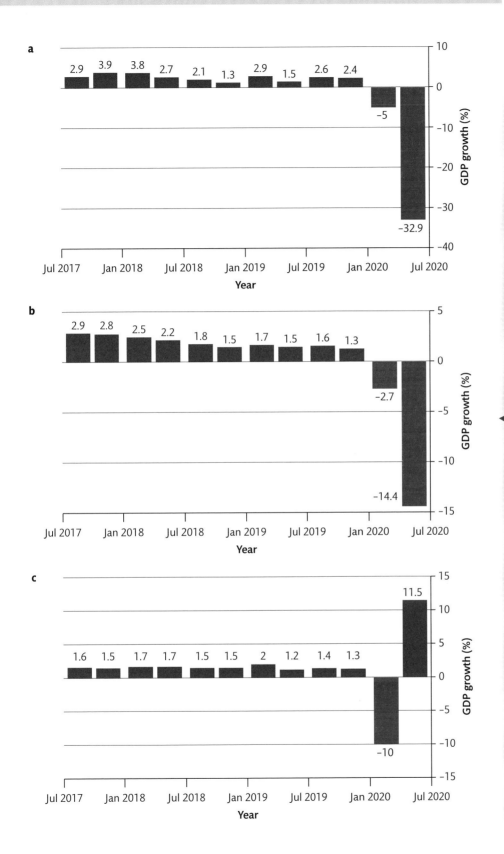

Figure 14.2 GDP growth rates July 2017 to July 2020 (a) USA (b) EU (c) China

households, firms and government on goods and services imported (M) from other countries. Net exports can be negative or positive, depending on whether a nation spends more on imports than it earns from the sale of its exports.

AD can therefore be expressed using the following formula:

$$AD = C + I + G + (X - M)$$

The AD curve

The AD curve describes the relationship between the price level and the quantity of goods and services demanded in a country. Consider Figure 14.3, showing the AD for a hypothetical economy.

Recall from Chapter 13 that the GDP deflator price index measures the average price level of all the goods and services in a country. The vertical axis in our AD model depicts the average price level as measured by the deflator. Along the horizontal axis we see the amount of national output (in billions of dollars) demanded by households, firms, the government, and foreigners at every possible price level.

In later graphs, we will use the label 'rGDP' for 'real GDP' along the horizontal axis, and 'PL' for 'price level' along the vertical axis. When identifying levels of national output, we will use Y, which is short for 'national income' and PL on the vertical axis.

The negative slope of the AD curve reflects the fact that at lower price levels, more of a nation's output is demanded, while at higher price levels less output is demanded, assuming all else is held constant. Households, firms, the government, and foreigners will demand more of a country's goods and services as their average prices fall, and less as their prices rise. In this regard, AD is a reflection of the microeconomic concept of demand, which observed that at lower prices, more of a particular good is demanded, and vice versa. The same logic applies to total output. When a nation's goods become

Figure 14.3 The **aggregate demand curve** shows the relationship between average price levels and total demand for goods and services in a nation's economy

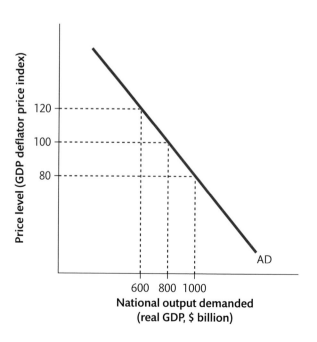

cheaper, *ceteris paribus*, households, the government, businesses, and foreigners wish to buy more of them, while at a higher price level a smaller amount of output is demanded.

A change in the price level, therefore, causes a movement along the AD curve, while a change in one of the components of AD causes the whole curve to shift, meaning more or less output will be demanded at every price level. In the following section we will break down each of the components of AD and describe what factors can cause changes in C, I, G, or Xn.

What are the factors that can cause a shift in AD?

Any change in the components of AD (consumption, investment, government spending, or net exports) that is not due to changes in the price level leads to a shift of the AD curve. When a determinant of one or more of the components of AD changes, the entire AD curve will shift in or out, and the quantity of output demanded at every price level will change.

Assume, for example, consumption increases. The result is an increase in AD and an outward shift of the AD curve. Figure 14.4 demonstrates how this would be illustrated in our AD model.

Owing to an increase in consumption, households are now willing to buy more output at every price level (at AD_1) compared to before (at AD).

Any change in the level of business investment, government spending, or net exports will likewise cause the AD curve to shift. Consider the impact of a decrease in exports to other countries, which would cause the net exports component of AD to decline. Figure 14.5 shows the effect of a decrease in one of the components of AD.

Owing to a decrease in demand for its exports, Snowlandia has seen its AD shift inwards, meaning less of the country's output is demanded at every price level.

Video suggestion:
You have read about it, now you can review what you have just learned by watching a video by the author!
Simply click here in your eBook for an introductory video on aggregate demand.

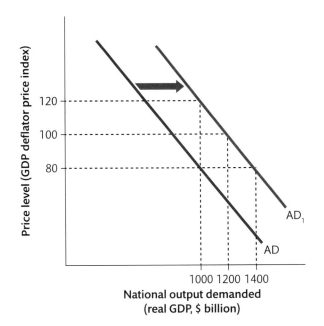

Figure 14.4 An increase in any one determinant of AD results in a rightward shift of the AD curve

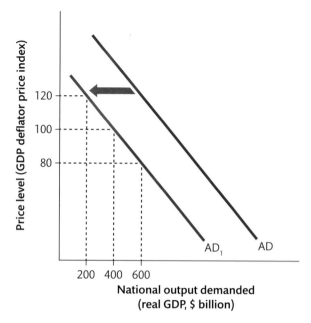

Figure 14.5 A decrease in, say, exports would shift the AD curve to the left

Let us look more closely at the factors that determine the level of each of the components of AD, beginning with consumption, for most countries the largest single component of aggregate demand.

What are the determinants of consumption?

The level of household consumption may increase or decrease at every price level, thereby causing a shift in aggregate demand, due to the following factors:

- consumer confidence
- interest rates
- wealth
- income taxes
- level of **household indebtedness**
- expectations of future price levels.

Consumer confidence

The 20th-century economist John Maynard Keynes used the term 'animal spirits' to describe the confidence (or lack of confidence) among households and firms in an economy. Consumer confidence is an economic indicator that measures the degree of optimism that consumers feel about the overall state of the economy, and is therefore an important determinant of overall household consumption.

During periods of economic growth with low unemployment and stable prices, confidence tends to be high and consumer spending strong. In periods of macroeconomic uncertainty, when overall output is falling, unemployment is rising and prices are declining, consumer confidence can collapse and households will reduce their consumption and increase savings in the expectation of future economic hardships.

Figure 14.6 shows the Organisation for Economic Co-operation and Development's (OECD) consumer confidence index, as measured between 2014 and the summer of 2020.

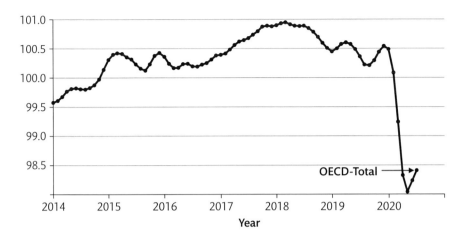

Figure 14.6 The OECD's **consumer confidence** index, 2014–20

Not surprisingly, with the onset of the 2020 pandemic, the index took a steep dive, part of the explanation for the fall in output described at the beginning of this chapter.

Interest rates

When most people think of interest rates they are likely to think of the return they can get by placing their money in a savings account or perhaps the additional amount they have to pay a bank or a credit card company when repaying money they borrowed. Both of these are correct understandings of what an interest rate is. However, from a purely economic perspective, the interest rate is simply the *opportunity cost of spending money*.

For example, assume an individual has €100 cash in his pocket. He can decide whether to spend that money today on a new outfit or to place that money in the bank and spend it sometime in the future. If the interest rate is 2%, then the opportunity cost of spending his €100 today is only €2 over the next year, as this is his expected rate of return by saving the money. However, assume instead the interest rate is 10%. Now he stands to earn €10 in interest income over the next year. The opportunity cost of spending his cash today is now five times greater than it was with the lower interest rate.

Splashing out on a new suit

We can begin to see how interest rates might affect consumption. At higher interest rates, there is a greater opportunity cost to spending money today, while at lower interest rates the opportunity cost of current spending is lower since less future income is foregone by spending money now.

Another way to think about it is from the perspective of a borrower. Much household spending in the economy is financed through borrowing. This is particularly true for expensive items (sometimes called durable goods by economists), such as cars, boats, new household appliances, or other items that people may not have cash available for. Car dealers make loans to buyers to allow them to take home a new car. Appliance retailers might do the same to allow a shopper to equip their kitchen with shiny new appliances. These loans come with an interest rate attached, and any amount borrowed must be repaid with interest. When interest rates are low, households are inclined to borrow more to finance the purchase of durable goods. At higher interest rates, the cost of borrowing is higher, so consumption will be lower.

All else equal, a decrease in the interest rate should cause household consumption to increase and AD to shift out, while higher interest rates should cause a decrease in consumption and a contraction in AD.

Wealth

Household wealth is another important determinant of the level of household consumption. Wealth is not to be confused with income. Income is the money households *earn* during a particular period of time. Wealth is the value of all of a household's assets minus the size of its liabilities. In other words, wealth is what someone *has* minus what they *owe*. Later in the chapter we will look at the 'what they owe' side of this equation when we consider the level of indebtedness as a determinant of consumption, but here let us look at 'what someone has'.

In many countries, the primary source of household wealth is, not surprisingly, the house itself. While houses are not the only source of wealth, they are the most significant for the typical middle-class citizen in most developed countries. In the USA, for example, 52% of households own stocks, but 50% of all the stocks owned are in the hands of the top 1% of households. Meanwhile, 65% of American households own their own home, meaning a significant proportion of the wealth encapsulated in the US housing market is in the hands of a majority of the US population.

Houses are an asset the price of which fluctuates with supply and demand, just like the prices of all assets. When house prices are rising, household consumption tends to rise, because households feel wealthier. The psychology of this relationship is straightforward. If Mia, a UK businessperson, earns £60,000 per year and lives in a house that is valued at £250,000, she will base her consumption in a given year on both her actual income and her perceived wealth, which includes the equity she has in her house. If, however, her home is valued the following year at £350,000, Mia's wealth has increased by 40%. Without any change in her income, Mia's perception of her own wealth has increased. Mia is now inclined to increase consumption, perhaps by taking on new debts to buy big ticket items like a new car or boat, since the value of her biggest asset has increased substantially.

This hypothetical situation can be observed in real-world data. Figure 14.7 shows the actual relationship between changes in house prices in the UK and UK household consumption.

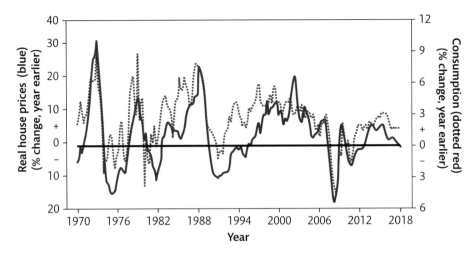

Figure 14.7 UK household consumption changes in line with real house prices

There is almost a perfect correlation between the two variables. When house prices rise, UK households consume more (1994–2006). But when house prices fall, consumption falls lockstep (2006–09).

Consumption, which measures the amount households spend on finished goods and services, rises and falls with household wealth, and in many countries, the main source of wealth is the house itself. A recent example of the power of house prices on consumer spending is the Great Recession of 2008–10 (which can be seen in the dip during these years in Figure 14.7). A collapse in house prices in the USA, the UK, and across the EU, triggered a financial crisis and a collapse in consumer spending that sent the world's largest economies into a deep recession, with unemployment rising to levels not seen since the 1930s in many countries. Eventually, the housing markets stabilised and with the recovery in house prices came a recovery in consumer spending, as households across the developed world saw their wealth recover from the shocks of the late 2000s.

Income taxes

The level of income taxes in a country is one factor influencing household consumption over which the government has direct control. When income taxes are reduced, households are left with more disposable income, increasing demand for all goods and services at every price level. Higher income taxes reduce disposable incomes and cause consumption to decrease.

Changes in the level of taxation aimed at stimulating or contracting aggregate demand are a tool of a government's fiscal policy, which will be explored in more detail in Chapter 20.

Level of household indebtedness

As mentioned earlier in the section on wealth, another factor influencing consumption is the level of indebtedness among a nation's households (or 'what they owe'). Sources of debt can include the money owed for all kinds of spending, but in most countries household debt is largely made up of *mortgage debt*, or money owed to banks for the purchase of a home.

In the short term, taking on debt allows a household to *increase* its consumption, since the money borrowed can be spent on cars, boats, or education fees. But when a household's debt burden grows too large, banks and other lenders (like car dealerships or credit card companies) will think twice before making additional loans, as the risk of lending increases

Adam Smith, the father of modern economics, laid out his foundational theories in his 1776 book *The Wealth of Nations*. Smith called into question the prevailing 18th-century *mercantilist* definition of wealth, under which wealth consisted of the nation's accumulated reserves of gold and silver. The way to increase wealth was by boosting exports and restricting imports in order to build up reserves of gold and silver.

Smith disputed this. To learn more, read about the broad themes of *The Wealth of Nations* on the Adam Smith Institute website (https://www.adamsmith.org/the-wealth-of-nations).

For discussion and debate:

1 If not gold and silver, what did Adam Smith consider to be the true wealth of a nation?

2 What were two ways Smith believed national wealth could be increased?

3 What are some of the threats to wealth accumulation Smith observed and warned us about?

4 How did Smith's definition of wealth differ from that introduced in this chapter? What is the modern term used to describe what Smith considered 'the wealth of a nation'?

as a consumer's debt load grows larger. Additionally, servicing past debts (making interest payments on past debts) increasingly dips into consumers' disposable income, leaving them with less money at the end of each month to buy other things. Just paying back past debts reduces the amount of disposable income available for new consumption.

So, debt is a double edged sword. At first, increasing household debt equates with increasing consumption; but over time, high debt levels force consumers to tighten their belts and pay down past debts before taking on new ones, and the interest payments themselves act similarly to taxes, reducing disposable incomes today and forcing households to consume less, reducing AD across an economy.

Expectations of future price levels

A final determinant of household consumption is the expected inflation rate. There is a micro equivalent here: recall from Chapter 3, Demand, that 'future price expectations' is one of the determinants of demand for particular goods. Similarly, if a nation's consumers expect the average price level of all goods to increase in the future (in other words, they expect higher inflation), then the demand for output today increases. It is perfectly rational to spend money now while it is worth more rather than wait until the future when the value of your money has decreased. Inflation essentially decreases the value of money, since more dollars or euros or yen are needed to buy the same amount of goods when inflation increases.

Similarly, expected deflation will constrain current spending. If households expect the average price level to fall in the future, the rational thing to do is reduce spending today and wait for lower prices tomorrow, which increase the value of money in the future.

There are implications for policymakers of the power of expectations over consumer spending. In Chapter 19, Demand management: monetary policy, we will study the role of central bankers in targeting a low and stable level of inflation through their control of the economy's money supply. By doing so, policymakers can manage future price expectations and help prevent unexpected shocks to consumption and aggregate demand that threaten to plunge the business cycle into unwanted peaks and troughs.

What are the determinants of investment?

Investment is defined as the addition of capital stock to the economy, or more simply, expenditure by firms on capital equipment and technology. Nearly all investment in an economy is undertaken by business firms; the one exception is when households purchase houses or real estate. A house purchase is distinct from consumption, since the home is not a *consumable good*; rather, a house is an asset that can be used to make money in the short term (a homeowner may choose to rent it out) or, in the longer term, be resold at a higher price (assuming house prices rise over time, which they tend to do).

Many of the determinants of investment will sound similar to those for consumption, so we will not go into quite the detail we did in the last section. The factors affecting investment are:

- interest rates
- business confidence
- technology
- **business taxes**
- level of **corporate indebtedness**.

Interest rates

As with household consumption, business spending is *interest sensitive*. The same principles apply: at higher interest rates the opportunity cost of borrowing money or spending cash a business already has increases, since more future income is given up by not saving. At lower interest rates borrowing costs are lower, making more potential investments attractive to a business owner.

For instance, if the expected rate of return on the purchase of a 3D printer for a toy manufacturer is 7% (meaning the purchase of the printer would increase revenues by 7%) but the increase in costs due to the added interest payments is 5%, then the investment stands to increase profits by 2%. However, if interest rates are higher, the cost of borrowing to buy the 3D printer increases, and the investment may not prove profitable.

Higher interest rates will constrain investment spending and AD, while lower interest rates will stimulate investment and AD. Central banks have a role in controlling monetary policy and setting interest rates. In Chapter 19, we will look more closely at the role of central banks in managing levels of investment and consumption in an economy.

Business confidence

Again, just as household spending is influenced by consumer confidence, investment spending is subject to changes in the level of business confidence. The OECD tracks a business confidence index, which 'provides information on future developments, based upon opinion surveys on developments in production, orders and stocks of finished goods in the industry sector. It can be used to monitor output growth and to anticipate turning points in economic activity. Numbers above 100 suggest an increased confidence in near future business performance, and numbers below 100 indicate pessimism towards future performance.'

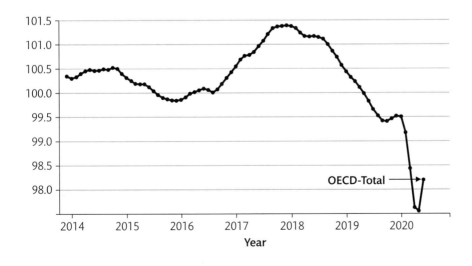

Figure 14.8   Business confidence index for OECD member countries, 2014–20

Not surprisingly, business confidence and consumer confidence track very closely with one another. When households are feeling good about the current and future economic outlook, they are likely to spend more, which leads businesses to invest in order to be able to meet the expected increases in future demand from their customers.

When business confidence falls, however, spending on new capital equipment and technology is likely to slow down as well, contributing to a decrease in AD. The decline in confidence in early 2020 is a result of the stay-at-home orders and forced shutdowns that contributed to the recessions across the world during the COVID-19 pandemic.

Technology

The availability of new technologies are assumed to be followed by bouts of increased investment. There are countless historical examples to choose from, such as the invention of early industrial technologies like the cotton gin, the steam engine, and later the railroads, to later innovations in automobiles, air travel, and high-speed trains. More recently, the internet has given rise to perhaps the longest and largest boom in business investment, as e-commerce, gaming, communications, entertainment, and other industries have increasingly moved online.

The year 2020 saw an explosion in investments in video-conferencing and remote-working technologies as hundreds of millions of workers were forced to work from home due to the closures of shared work spaces. People expected that this might be a turning point in how workers in the high-skilled sectors interact with one another. New technologies will continue to develop, leading to increased investments from businesses as they look to capitalise on the enthusiasm for, and reap the benefits of, innovations in various sectors.

Business taxes

Once again we return to a determinant of AD that government can directly affect. You will recall from Chapter 5, Supply, that taxes and subsidies are determinants of supply. A cut in business taxes will increase business profits and incentivise new spending on capital goods. The expected return on any potential investment increases when the government promises to take a smaller share of profits that investment earns. Similarly, higher taxes make new investments less profitable and will lead firms to retain more of their earnings in order to pay their taxes.

Level of corporate indebtedness

Just as with households, increases in corporate indebtedness promise to stimulate spending in the short term, but reduce it in the long term. Managing debt payments requires firms to find a balance between spending their revenues on new capital and servicing the debts accrued from the purchase of existing capital. If a firm takes on too high a debt level to expand its operations today and then its revenues grow too slowly to allow it to easily service past debts, then the firm's debt burden will prevent it from taking on new investments in the future.

So, as with households, debt is a double edged sword. Too much debt will slow investment, but not enough will slow it as well. The *right amount* of debt will allow firms to pay interest on past loans while growing their operations and earning revenues that cover costs, allowing for a sustainable level of expansion over time.

What determines the level of government expenditures?

Government spending includes a broad range of expenditure: publicly-funded schools and universities, national defence, highways and roads, parks and hospitals. Governments may spend directly on the provision of goods and services or they may subsidise provision of certain goods by the private sector.

The proportion of total AD made up of government spending varies hugely across nations. Government spending makes up the largest proportion of the economies of northern and western European nations such as Denmark, Sweden, the Netherlands, France, and Germany. In these countries, the government provides services such as healthcare and education to all citizens, paid for almost entirely by taxpayers.

In countries with large government sectors, taxes on households and firms tend to be much higher than in those where government spending makes up a smaller proportion of AD. This makes sense since ultimately all government spending on goods and services must be financed by the nation's taxpayers.

The level of government spending in a nation in a particular year depends on the government's fiscal policy, which refers to the government's use of taxes and spending to stimulate or contract the overall level of AD in an economy. **Fiscal policy** is explained in detail in Chapter 20, but what you need to know here is that its use can raise or lower the level of government spending in a given period to help meet macroeconomic objectives.

What are the determinants of net exports?

In a global economy, nearly every nation depends to some degree on foreign demand for its output as a component of its AD. Net exports measures the spending by foreigners on a nation's goods and services minus the amount spent by domestic households and firms on imports from other countries. Net exports is, therefore, the only component of AD that can be negative. This occurs when a nation spends more on imports than it earns from the sale of its exports.

Case study – net exports for the USA and Germany

In 2019, the USA's net exports were about −$500 billion. Yes, that is *negative* $500 billion. Germany, on the other hand, experienced net exports of around $274 billion (yes, greater than zero). How can we understand the discrepancies between these two large economies' net exports? While the USA sold a lot of stuff to the rest of the world (exports), they imported a half a trillion dollars *more* than they exported. Meanwhile, Germans love imports as much as Americans do, but the German economy specialises in the production of goods that the rest of the world also craves, and as a result Germany exported goods whose value exceeded imports by over a quarter of a trillion dollars.

The determinants of a country's net exports are:

- income of trading partners
- exchange rates
- trade policies.

Income of trading partners

The macroeconomic health and household incomes of a nation's trading partners determine demand for the nation's exports. For example, Canada's largest trading partner is the USA (75% of Canada's trade takes place with the USA).

Case study – Canada

As incomes in the USA fell during the recession of 2008–09, Canada's exports fell from $460 billion in 2008 to $323 billion in 2009, a decline of 30%.

However, during the same period, Canada's imports from the rest of the world also declined, from $415 billion to $327 billion, a decline of 21%. Canada's net exports in 2008 were $44 billion but in 2009 fell to –$4 billion, a decline of $48 billion in one year. Falling incomes in the USA are the most likely explanation for this massive decline in Canada's net exports, supporting the fact that household income in trading nations is a major determinant of a nation's net exports.

Exchange rates

An exchange rate is the value of one currency expressed in terms of another. For example, if US$1 = €0.8, then $1,000 will buy €800 worth of German goods. However, if the dollar *appreciates*, say to $1= €1, then suddenly Americans' ability to buy German goods improves, as US$1,000 will now purchase €1,000 worth of Germany's output.

A stronger currency will cause demand for *imports* in a country to increase, and demand for that country's *exports* to fall. A weaker currency, on the other hand, will lead to an increase in exports and decrease in exports (assuming all else is held constant, of course). The relationship here is a bit counterintuitive: while a 'strong currency' sounds like it should be good for an economy, from an AD perspective it is actually contractionary, since a stronger currency causes net exports to fall. On the other hand, when currency **depreciation** (decrease in the exchange rate) occurs, net exports increase as a country's goods get cheaper abroad and imports get more expensive.

Trade policies

In Chapters 22 and 23 we will study the advantages and disadvantages of *free trade* and *protectionism*, which can be defined as government policies that limit the flow of imports or promote exports in order to boost domestic AD and employment. The extent to which a government intervenes in the international flow of goods and services will directly influence its net exports.

Export promotion policies like subsidies to domestic producers that make their output cheaper to foreigners will increase the export component of *Xn*. **Import substitution** policies such as **tariffs** (taxes on imports) or quotas (physical limits on the quantity of imports allowed) will shift domestic consumers away from foreign-produced goods and increase demand for domestic output, increasing net exports in the process.

We have looked closely at the demand side of the macroeconomy. We now know that changes in a country's price level, *ceteris paribus*, will cause a movement along the AD curve, leading households, the government, businesses, and foreigners to demand more or less output. We also now know that, autonomous of the price level, there are determinants of AD that can cause aggregate spending to expand or contract,

Video suggestion:
You have read about it, now you can review what you have just learned by watching a video by the author!

▶ Simply click here in your eBook for a video on movements along the AD curve versus shifts in AD.

increasing or decreasing the amount of national output demanded at every price level. But to truly understand the causes behind macroeconomic shocks like the Great Depression (1930s), the Great Recession (2008–10) and the 2020 COVID-19 recessions, we must incorporate another element into our macroeconomic model, and that, of course, is aggregate supply.

14.2 What is short-run aggregate supply?

Learning outcomes

At the end of this section you will be able to:

- define the term aggregate supply
- explain, using a diagram, why the SRAS curve is upward sloping
- explain, using a diagram, how the AS curve in the short run (SRAS) can shift due to factors including:
  - changes in resource prices
  - changes in business taxes and subsidies
  - supply shocks.

With our definition and graphical analysis of AD complete, it is time to consider the 'supply side' of the economy. Aggregate supply (AS) is the quantity of goods and services that a country's producers are willing and able to produce at a range of price levels in a period of time. The **short-run aggregate supply (SRAS)** curve describes the relationship between the price level and the quantity of goods and services supplied in an economy in the period of time during which wages (the price of labour) and other input prices are fixed, or inflexible.

In the **short run**, a nation's output will vary with the level of AD; when AD increases, the level of output will increase and when AD decreases the level of output will decrease. Later in this chapter we will examine **long-run aggregate supply (LRAS)**, which is dependent not on the level of demand, but on the availability of resources in the economy.

The SRAS curve

The term 'short run' in macroeconomics is defined as the 'fixed-wage period'. At the core of this concept is the debate over how long it takes prices and wages to adjust to changes in demand. The fixed-wage period describes the period of time following a change in AD or the price level over which the wage rate paid to workers in an economy is fixed. Wages will remain fixed (or at least, relatively inflexible) in the short run due to several factors, including labour contracts, minimum wage laws, the ability for workers to collect unemployment benefits for a period of time after losing their jobs, and the power of **labour unions**.

Owing to these and other factors, firms are unable to raise and lower wages quickly in response to a macroeconomic shock such as an increase or decrease in AD, and therefore workers are more likely to be hired and fired in the period following such a shock rather than their wages simply adjusting to the level of demand in the economy.

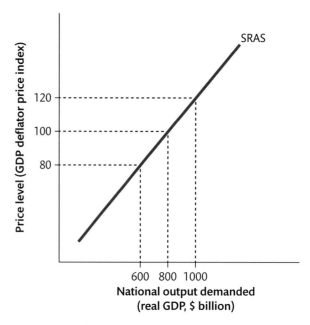

Figure 14.9 Aggregate supply has a direct relationship with price levels in the short run

When the prices for which producers can sell their output rise, while the wages they must pay their workers and the prices of other inputs remain fixed, producers will wish to supply a greater quantity of goods and services due to the opportunity for higher profits resulting from an increase in the price level. At lower prices levels, producers will reduce the quantity of output they supply and reduce the amount of labour they employ as the prospect of losses force suppliers to reduce output and employment.

This direct relationship is reflected in an upward-sloping SRAS curve, as seen in Figure 14.9.

There is a positive relationship between price levels and real GDP. At higher price levels, producers will supply a greater quantity of output. The corresponding increase in employment causes the unemployment rate to decrease in the economy. However, low unemployment is achieved in the short run only by accepting a higher price level, therefore more inflation. The upward-sloping SRAS curve has implications for policymakers that we will examine in more detail in later chapters: in order to achieve a lower unemployment rate, policymakers may have to accept a higher inflation rate, a trade-off that could result in negative consequences for certain stakeholders in an economy.

Sticky versus flexible wages and prices

The SRAS curve is upward sloping because of sticky wages and prices. To better understand the implications of sticky wages for a nation's producers, look at the SUV case study, which focuses on how a single producer would be likely to respond to a sudden decrease in demand for its output.

Case study – sticky wages

Assume that demand for luxury sport utility vehicles (SUVs) suddenly decreases. 'Tekla', a manufacturer of a popular model of SUV, the 'Unibog', is faced with a collapse in demand.

Tekla's CEO must cut costs or face bankruptcy. In a world in which wages were perfectly flexible, the CEO could simply reduce every worker on the Unibog assembly line's wage by, say, 30%, in order to 'weather the storm' of falling demand for Unibogs. However, Tekla's workers are unionised, and the union has threatened a strike should the firm try to reduce wages. Additionally, there is a state-wide minimum wage that prevents Tekla from cutting wages by 30%. Finally, the government provides generous unemployment benefits, so many of Tekla's workers may choose to leave their jobs should their pay fall by 30% and simply collect unemployment benefits while they search for a new job.

Tekla's ability to cut workers' wages is limited by labour union power and government regulations. Therefore, our CEO, facing 'sticky wages', must reduce employment instead. Rather than lowering everyone's pay by 30%, the boss must lay off 30% of the firm's workers and reduce production numbers in order to cut costs in the face of falling demand.

Now consider how sticky wages affect the national economy. In a country in which all employers face the same constraints as the case study example, Tekla, falling output prices will be met by falling employment and reduced output. In other words, in the short run, when wages are sticky, there is a direct relationship between the price level and the level of output and employment. Falling prices lead to less output and less employment, while rising prices lead to more output and more employment.

What causes shifts of the SRAS curve?

A change in the average price level causes a movement along the SRAS curve. Any factor that causes production costs to change will cause the SRAS curve to shift. When any of the following changes, AS will either decrease and shift inwards or increase and shift outwards.

- **Wage rates:** Higher wages cause SRAS to decrease, lower wages cause SRAS to increase.
- **Resource costs:** When rents for land, interest rates, or raw materials prices increase, SRAS will decrease. Lower resources costs cause SRAS to increase.
- **Energy and transportation costs:** Higher oil or energy prices will cause SRAS to decrease. Cheaper energy and transportation cause SRAS to increase. Changes in energy and transport costs are referred to as *supply shocks*.
- **Government regulation:** Regulations impose costs on firms that can cause SRAS to decrease. Reduced regulation makes it cheaper to produce output, increasing SRAS.
- **Business taxes/subsidies:** Taxes are a monetary cost imposed on firms by the government, so higher taxes will cause SRAS to decrease. A tax cut or increased subsidies to producers reduce firms' costs and cause SRAS to increase.
- **Exchange rates:** If producers use imported raw materials, then a weaker currency will cause these to become more expensive, reducing SRAS. A stronger currency makes imported raw materials cheaper and increases SRAS.

A shift in SRAS results in a larger or smaller amount of output being produced at every price level. Assume, for example, the government has reduced environmental

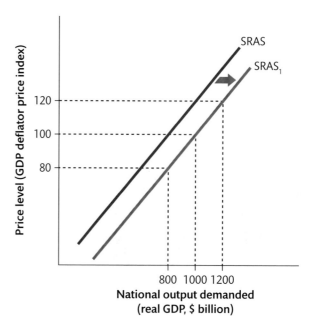

Figure 14.10 Reduced regulation would result in an outward shift of the SRAS curve

regulations, making it cheaper for firms to produce their output as they are not required to pay for costly waste-reduction and air purification technologies. As a result of reduced regulation, the country's producers are willing to produce a greater quantity of output at every price level. The impact is an outward shift of the SRAS curve, as seen in Figure 14.10.

The shift from SRAS to SRAS$_1$ reflects an increase in aggregate supply resulting from reduced government regulation. Falling wages, lower energy prices, reduced business tax rates, and a stronger currency would cause a similar increase in SRAS. Higher wages, rising energy prices, increased regulation or taxation, or a weaker currency would cause SRAS to decrease, as in Figure 14.11.

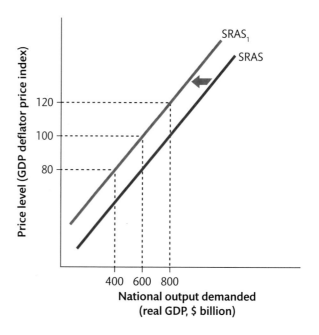

Figure 14.11 Reduced regulation would lead to a decrease in SRAS

Owing to a depreciation of the currency, causing imported raw materials to become costlier, SRAS has shifted inwards, resulting in a smaller quantity of national output produced at each price level.

Our analysis above assumes that the wage rate (the cost of labour) is fixed, and therefore firms will respond to varying price levels by changing their output and levels of employment. But what if wages were perfectly flexible, rising or falling depending on what happens to aggregate demand and the price level in the economy? According to classical economic theory, wages and prices are fully flexible in the **long run**, and therefore there is no trade-off between inflation and unemployment. In the next section we will examine the classical view of AS and a 20th-century interpretation of the model known as the Keynesian view.

14.3 What are some alternative views of AS?

Learning outcomes

At the end of this section you will be able to:

* explain, using a diagram, why the **monetarist/new classical model** of the LRAS is vertical at the level of potential output (full employment output)
* explain, using a diagram, how the Keynesian model of the AS curve has three sections corresponding to different levels of spare capacity in the economy
* suggest what could cause shifts in supply according to these models.

It might seem odd that in the 21st century, almost three hundred years after the start of the first Industrial Revolution, in an era of globalisation, high-speed internet, instantaneous communication and connectivity between countries, and rising incomes the world over, there is still debate about whether an economy's output is dependent or independent of the price level and the amount of demand in the economy. Yet, alternative views of AS still persist, the result being that our model of AD/AS is actually a hybrid model, in which there is not one, but two, AS curves.

What is the monetarist/classical view of LRAS?

The SRAS curve described above represents how producers will respond to changes in demand and the price level in the fixed-wage period. However, over time, economists observe that wages that were fixed in the short run are likely to become *flexible* in the long run. In other words, even as things like unemployment insurance, minimum wage laws, labour unions, and contracts contribute to sticky wages, over time, following a change in AD, wages will become flexible, and either fall (if demand is weak and the price level is low) or rise (if demand is strong and prices are high).

The LRAS curve shows the level of output achieved in an economy when wages and prices are fully flexible and adjust to the economy's price level. In a world of flexible wages, a firm like Tekla would be able to maintain its level of output and employment even as demand for Unibogs falls. In such a scenario falling prices would simply be offset by a decrease in wages and other input prices. Sellers would maintain their 'full employment' level of production and consumers would simply pay lower prices for

Video suggestion:
You have read about it, now you can review what you have just learned by watching a video by the author!

▶ Simply click here in your eBook for a video on SRAS.

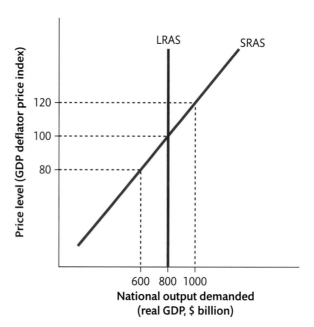

Figure 14.12 In contrast to the upward-sloping SRAS curve, the LRAS curve is vertical

their output. Workers would earn lower nominal wages, but since prices fall across the economy as a whole, real wages and real output would not be affected.

In the case of a rising price level, firms would face higher wages and thus would not be willing or able to increase their output as the price level rose. And while workers' nominal wages would increase, their real wages and the level of real output would remain constant as all prices increased across the economy.

In the long run, all prices and wages are fully flexible, while in the short run some input prices (namely wages) are fixed. A consequence of flexible long-run prices and wages is the lack of a long-run trade-off between inflation and unemployment. The LRAS curve is vertical at a country's full employment level of output, or the real GDP that would be produced when all resources are fully utilised and wages have fully adjusted to the price level in the economy. Figure 14.12 shows a hybrid view of aggregate supply, including both the upward-sloping SRAS curve and the vertical LRAS curve.

In Figure 14.12, the LRAS curve is vertical at an output of $800 billion, meaning that once wages and price have fully adjusted and resources are fully employed, the country should produce this much output, which is considered the *full employment level of output* at which unemployment will settle at a *natural rate*. In the short run, when wages are fixed, output will increase or decrease for the reasons outlined in our Tekla example.

What is the Keynesian view of AS?

A third version of the AS curve is attributed to the depression-era economist John Maynard Keynes, who recognised the downwardly inflexible nature of wages in the short run, but understood that as an economy approached its full employment level, the limited degree of spare capacity for increased production would drive wages and other resources upwards, limiting potential output at a certain level.

Figure 14.13 shows the three-segmented Keynesian view of AS, on which there is a horizontal segment (at levels of output well below full employment, where there

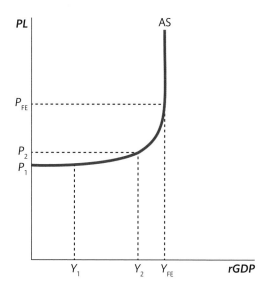

Figure 14.13 The Keynesian AS curve has three segments determined by capacity

is ample spare capacity in the economy), an upward-sloping segment (as output approaches full employment, when spare capacity begins to decrease), and a vertical segment (beyond full employment, where there is no further spare capacity).

Each level of output in Figure 14.13 corresponds with a different level of spare capacity in the economy. Y_{FE} represents the economy's *full employment* output level. There is no spare capacity, meaning nearly all workers are employed and capital is being used at maximum productivity. Any attempt to increase output beyond Y_{FE} will only cause inflation, but no actual increase in output. In other words, beyond Y_{FE} AS is *perfectly inelastic*. Any increase in prices will be met by no change in output due to the lack of available resources needed to actually expand output.

Y_2 represents a level of output below full employment, at which there is some degree of spare capacity available for increased output. However, the fact that resources are close to being fully employed means that an increase from Y_2 to Y_{FE} will be accompanied by a greater proportional increase in the price level. In other words, between Y_2 and Y_{FE} AS is relatively inelastic. An increase in the price level will be met with a proportionally smaller increase in output, due to the limited availability of resources to expand output.

At Y_1 the economy is producing well below its full employment level. There is considerable spare capacity in the economy, meaning that AS is nearly perfectly elastic. Any increase in prices will be met with a proportionally large increase in output as firms will scramble to hire the abundance of available workers and put idle capital back into production to profit from the rising price level. At Y_1 the economy has a large negative output gap, or a gap between what it is actually producing and what it could produce if resources were fully employed.

The Keynesian view of AS acknowledges that wages are downwardly inflexible, which explains the horizontal range of AS below full employment. However, at or beyond full employment wages are highly flexible and will rise to prevent an economy from producing beyond its full employment level, due to the fact that increases in demand for resources will be checked by the increasing scarcity and rising costs of resources, limiting the nation's potential output.

Video suggestion:
You have read about it, now you can review what you have just learned by watching a video by the author!
Simply click here in your eBook for a video on long-run aggregate supply and the Keynesian AS model.

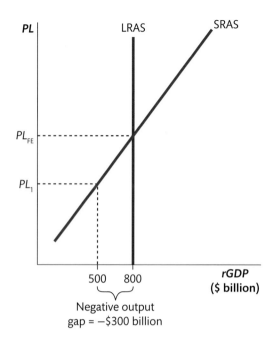

Figure 14.14   Output below or beyond full employment is known as an output gap

What are output gaps?

In both the hybrid SRAS/LRAS and in the Keynesian AS models, output can be shown to take place either *at full employment*, *below full employment*, or, in the case of the SRAS/LRAS model, *beyond full employment*.

The existence of *output gaps* results from a situation in which an economy is producing at a level of output below or beyond full employment. Assume, for example, that the economy is producing at an output of $500 billion in Figure 14.14.

With the economy producing just $500 billion when it could be producing $800 billion, an output gap of –$300 billion exists. The economy is producing a level of output that is $300 billion below what it would be if all resources were fully employed. The lower price level of PL_1 explains why the output gap exists; at PL_1 firms cannot afford to pay workers the expected wage rate they earned at the higher output and price levels of $800 billion and PL_{FE}. We can assume that this economy is experiencing sticky wages, and that once wages adjust, output should return to the full employment level.

In the Keynesian AS model, a negative output gap can also arise because of sticky wages. Figure 14.15 shows such a situation.

Owing to sticky wages, firms have reduced output and employment as the price level has fallen to P_1. The economy is producing below full employment and has spare capacity in the form of idle workers and capital.

Positive output gaps are possible in the short run in the SRAS/LRAS model. Figure 14.16 shows such a situation.

At $1 trillion the economy has a $200 positive output gap. How is it possible that an economy can produce an output level that is beyond its full employment level? According to the SRAS model, even at full employment an economy still has *some* spare capacity, meaning some workers and capital will be available to hire and put towards production. Given the stickiness of wages in the SRAS model, an increase in

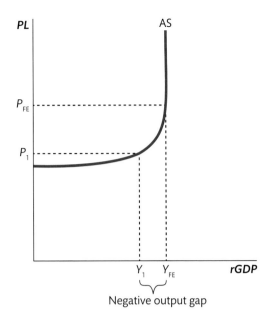

Figure 14.15 A negative output gap is also possible in the Keynesian AS model

the average price level (to PL_1 in Figure 14.16) will lead producers to wish to increase output and employment, which they are able to do to a limited extent.

In contrast, the Keynesian model predicts that an economy producing at full employment is unable to increase output due to scarcity of resources. In Figure 14.17 we can see what will happen at price levels beyond that prevailing at the full employment level in the Keynesian model.

The price level has risen, but output remains at Y_{FE}. Because resources are fully employed, higher prices lead only to higher costs and no increase in output.

The competing views of AS offer economists and policymakers various models on which to base their predictions of how an economy might respond to macroeconomic shocks like changes in the level of AD, changes in resource costs, exchange rate

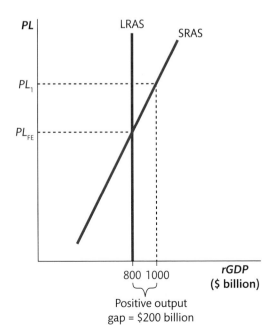

Figure 14.16 Positive output gaps are possible in the SRAS/LRAS model

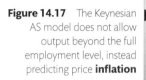

14 Variations in economic activity

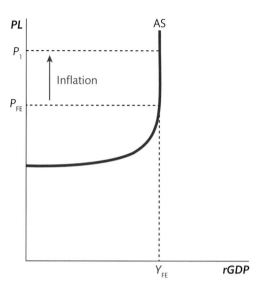

Figure 14.17 The Keynesian AS model does not allow output beyond the full employment level, instead predicting price **inflation**

variability, taxation, or subsidies, changes in interest rates, **inflation rates**, or other variables. At the core of the debate between advocates of the SRAS model, the LRAS model, and the Keynesian AS model is the extent to which wages and other costs of production respond to changes in the price level.

To understand what might cause a change in the equilibrium price level and the level of national output, we must combine our models of AD and AS to determine macroeconomic equilibrium, which we will do later in this chapter. First, we'll look at factors that can cause shifts in LRAS and the Keynesian AS curves.

What can cause shifts of the LRAS and the Keynesian AS curves?

The LRAS curve corresponds to the production possibilities curve (PPC) because they both represent maximum sustainable capacity, or full employment output. An increase in a country's maximum sustainable output will shift both the PPC and the LRAS curves outwards.

Full employment output increases when there is an increase in either the quality or the quantity of a country's factors of production.

- **Labour:** An improvement in the productivity of labour or in the size of a country's workforce will increase a country's maximum sustainable capacity, shifting the PPC and LRAS curves outwards.
- **Land:** An improvement in the efficiency with which land resources are used through improved technology (better farming, mining, fishing, or logging techniques) will increase the potential output produced on a fixed amount of land. An increase in the amount of land available to a country (through territorial expansion or land reclamation) will increase maximum sustainable capacity and shift the PPC and LRAS curves outwards.
- **Capital:** Technological improvements increase productivity in the manufacturing, service, and primary (agriculture, mining, etc.) sectors of the economy and increase the maximum sustainable capacity, shifting the PPC and LRAS curves outwards.

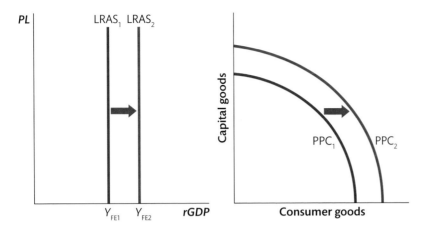

Figure 14.18 Shifts of LRAS curve correspond to those of the PPC

- **Entrepreneurship:** Entrepreneurship refers to the willingness of individuals to pursue creative and risky ventures aimed at providing new and unique products to the marketplace. An increase in entrepreneurship or an influx of entrepreneurial talent in a country will increase the economy's maximum potential capacity and shift the PPC and LRAS curves outwards.

An outward shift of LRAS and the PPC illustrate *economic growth*, or an increase in the actual and potential output of goods and services in a country over time. In Figure 14.18 we can see the effect of economic growth in an AS model and in a PPC model.

In Figure 14.18 the country has experienced an increase in its potential output due to an increase in the factors of production. In the LRAS model output increases from Y_{FE1} to Y_{FE2} (Y_{FE} = full employment national output), and in the PPC the curve has shifted outwards, indicating a higher level of maximum sustainable output.

In the Keynesian model, a shift in AS can be seen as an increase in the potential output achieved at the vertical range of aggregate supply, as seen in Figure 14.19.

A change in the quantity or quality of factors of production, improvements in technology, or increases in efficiency could explain the shift in AS shown in Figure 14.19. At every price level up to full employment the economy can now produce more output.

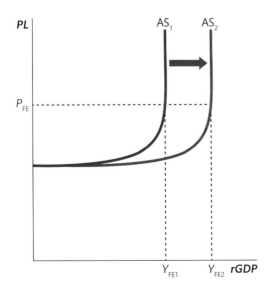

Figure 14.19 An outward shift of the Keynesian AS curve results in an increase in output at the vertical range of AS

Beyond full employment future increases in output are impossible due to limited resources, and only inflation will occur if producers attempt to further expand output.

Let us now combine our models of AD and AS to examine what determines *macroeconomic equilibrium*.

14.4 What is meant by macroeconomic equilibrium?

Learning outcomes

At the end of this section you will be able to:

- explain, using a diagram, the determination of short-run equilibrium, using the SRAS curve
- explain, using a diagram, that if the economy is in equilibrium at a level of real output below the full employment level of output, then there is a **deflationary (recessionary) gap**
- discuss why, in contrast to the monetarist/new classical model, the economy can remain stuck in a deflationary (recessionary) gap in the Keynesian model
- explain, using a diagram, that if AD increases in the vertical section of the Keynesian AS curve, then there is an inflationary gap
- explain why, in the monetarist/new classical approach, the economy will always return to the full employment level of output in the long run
- examine, using diagrams, the impacts of changes in the long-run equilibrium.

A country's full employment level of output is its maximum sustainable output assuming all resources are efficiently employed. The macroeconomic equilibrium real output and price level, on the other hand, is what a country's economy achieves at a particular period of time given the level of aggregate demand and AS in the economy. Macroeconomic equilibrium can occur below, at, or even beyond full employment.

What is short-run equilibrium in the AD and SRAS/LRAS model?

Short-run equilibrium occurs when the aggregate quantity of output demanded and the aggregate quantity of output supplied are equal, at the intersection of the AD and SRAS curves. In Figure 14.20 the economy is in a macroeconomic equilibrium at an output of $800 billion and a price level of 100.

Notice that at its current equilibrium, the country is also producing its full employment level of output. The AD curve intersects the SRAS curve and the LRAS curve in the same place. Resources are fully utilised and unemployment is low.

The short-run equilibrium output can be at the full employment level of output, above it, or below it, depending on whether the economy is experiencing a negative or positive output gap. A positive shock in AD (resulting from an increase in either

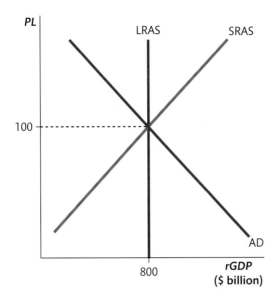

Figure 14.20 Equilibrium is at full employment output, where AD = SRAS = LRAS

consumption, investment, government spending, or net exports) causes output, employment, and the price level to rise in the short run. Assume, for example, that there is a depreciation of the currency, causing net exports to increase as foreigners demand more of the country's goods. The economy will move from an equilibrium at full employment to a situation in which both the price level and output increase in the short run, as in Figure 14.21.

Owing to a positive demand shock, the economy is temporarily producing at a short-run equilibrium level of output that is beyond its full employment output. Notice that the GDP deflator price index (used to measure the price level) has increased from 100 to 115, equating to a 15% inflation rate. The output gap between equilibrium output and full employment level of output is also called an *inflationary gap*. The economy is essentially overheating – the unemployment rate is lower than it would be at full employment and inflation is higher than it should be.

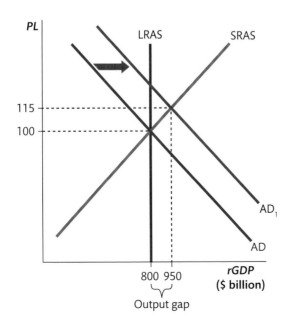

Figure 14.21 Short-run equilibrium can be beyond full employment in the case of a positive output gap.

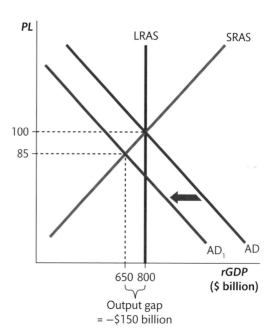

Figure 14.22 A negative output gap, resulting in output below full employment level, is also called a recessionary gap

Next let us assume there is a negative demand shock due to an increase in income taxes and reduced government expenditures. A fall in private and public spending will cause AD to decrease. Figure 14.22 shows the effect of a negative demand shock on macroeconomic equilibrium.

Owing to sticky wages, firms are forced to lay off workers and reduce their output as the price level falls from 100 to 85. Costs must be cut in the face of falling prices, and the only way to reduce costs is to reduce output and employment since wages cannot be lowered in the short run. The fall in output causes a negative output gap (also called a *recessionary gap*) of $150 billion, representing the amount by which equilibrium output is below the country's full employment output.

Inflationary and recessionary gaps are short-run phenomena arising because wages are sticky. In the case of AD increasing to create an equilibrium beyond full employment, firms must compete for the limited number of available workers in order to increase output in response to increased demand and rising prices. While wages remain fixed, firms demand more labour and increase their output in the short run.

What is long-run equilibrium in the AD and SRAS/LRAS model?

In the long run, nominal wages will begin to rise following a positive demand shock or fall following a negative demand shock. In the case of a positive output gap, workers will have more bargaining power as the labour market tightens and they will begin to demand pay hikes to keep up with the rising prices. As the nominal wage rate rises, firms will find it less and less attractive to continue employing more workers and some firms will be forced to cut back on output and employment. Notably, as the nominal wage rate is a determinant of SRAS, it will decrease in the long run, pushing prices up further and causing output to fall back to its full employment level. Figure 14.23 shows how the economy will adjust in the long run following an inflationary gap.

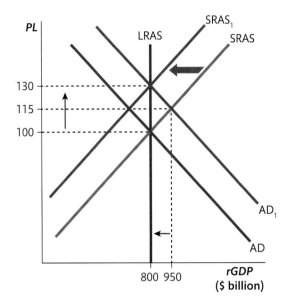

Figure 14.23 The long-run adjustment following a positive demand shock ends with limited output and a rise in prices

The initial increase in output to $950 billion proved unsustainable as tight labour markets led to rising wages and a reduction in output and employment back to the full employment level of $800 billion. The price level is driven up initially by rising AD, and then by decreased SRAS caused by rising nominal wages. In the long run, output is limited by the available stocks of land, labour, and capital. The short-run boost in output caused by stronger export demand proves temporary as the economy is unable to sustain its higher output due to limited resources.

The process of self-adjustment following the positive demand shock described above is the result of the flexibility of wages in the long run. An economy will return to its full employment level of output following any shocks to AD or AS once wages and other input costs have adjusted to the price level. A similar story unfolds following a negative demand shock and a recessionary gap.

A recessionary gap will likewise be resolved in the long run once wages have adjusted to the lower price level. Going back to our negative demand shock resulting from a tax hike and decreased government spending, we can assume that in the long run the excess supply of labour resulting from the fall in equilibrium output and employment will eventually lead to a fall in the nominal wage rate. As government benefits for unemployed workers expire and labour unions lose their bargaining power, new contracts offering lower wages will eventually be accepted and firms will once again begin hiring workers and increasing output due to the falling costs of production. Figure 14.24 shows how an economy will self-adjust from a recessionary gap.

The recession caused by the fall in AD eventually comes to an end as wages decrease in the long run, causing SRAS to increase. Firms rehire workers who are now willing to accept lower wages, restoring output to its full employment level. While the nominal wage rate falls, real income and output return to full employment as lower wages are offset by lower prices across the economy.

A country's equilibrium level of output can be above or below its full employment output in the short run, creating inflationary or recessionary gaps. However, in the long run, when wages and other input costs have fully adjusted to the price level, national output will return to its full employment level. This process of self-adjustment

Video suggestions:
You have read about it, now you can review what you have just learned by watching a few videos by the author!
Simply click here in your eBook for videos on short-run equilibrium in the AD–AS model, demand and supply shocks in the AD–AS model, and long-run equilibrium in the AD–AS model.

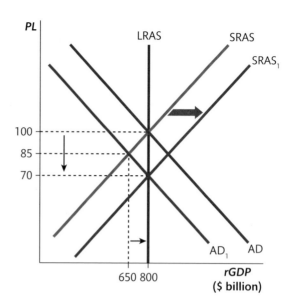

Figure 14.24 The long-run adjustment following a negative demand shock restores full employment, with lower wages offset by the lower price level

is the foundation of the classical theory of LRAS, which as we have shown is vertical at full employment output. In the long run there is no trade-off between unemployment and inflation. The unemployment rate will always settle at a 'natural rate' (a concept to be explored in Chapter 15), even as inflation rises and falls with changes in the level of aggregate demand.

What is equilibrium in the Keynesian model?

The Keynesian model offers a slightly different prediction of what will happen to an economy that experiences an output gap. First of all, we must remember positive output gaps are not possible in the Keynesian model. An economy at full employment that experiences a positive demand shock will see inflation, but no increase in output, due to the upward flexibility of wages in an economy where resources are already fully employed. Figure 14.25 illustrates the outcome of such a scenario.

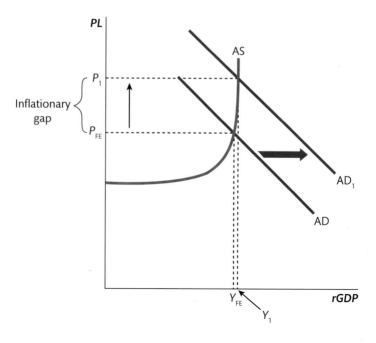

Figure 14.25 Any positive demand shock results in an **inflationary gap** according to the Keynesian model

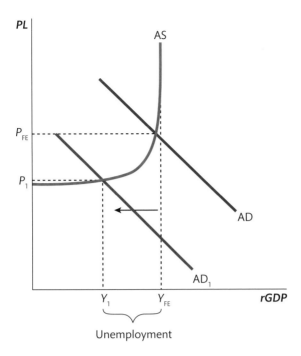

Figure 14.26   In the case of a negative demand shock, the Keynesian model predicts persistent recession

Greater demand has caused a negligible increase in output (which remains around Y_{FE}) but a substantial rise in inflation.

Wages are flexible upwards, but sticky downwards, which means following a negative demand shock, the economy is likely to end up 'stuck' in a recession, as seen in Figure 14.26.

When AD falls, the economy experiences a decrease in output and a rise in unemployment. Unlike the classical LRAS model, the Keynesian model assumes wages will remain sticky, even in the long run, preventing the economy from self-adjusting. For this reason, Keynes predicted economies in recession could remain stuck in a deflationary/recessionary cycle where falling employment leads to falling incomes, reducing consumer confidence and household incomes, causing demand to fall further. Uncertainty and pessimism prevail across the economy, leading businesses to reduce investment, further exacerbating the economic slump.

14.5 What are the assumptions and implications of the models?

Learning outcomes

At the end of this section you will be able to:

- explain that the Keynesian approach to macroeconomics is one of 'demand-management' to promote macroeconomic objectives such as full employment
- explain that the monetarist/new classical model of the economy implies that a 'laissez-faire' approach to the economy is best.

The persistence of recessions and inability of economies to self-correct is the defining distinction of the Keynesian model from the monetarist/new classical, LRAS model. Some context to Keynes's theories might help understand this profound difference. Keynes's model was based on his observations of the economies of Europe and North America during the 1930s, when the Great Depression saw unemployment rates of up to 25% persist for years across the developed world. Despite the predictions of the classical theorists like Say and Smith, wage flexibility never prevailed, and the world's economies remained trapped in the vicious cycle of deflation and unemployment for years on end.

One implication of the Keynesian model, as we will see, is that an economy left to its own devices, reliant on the 'free market mechanism' of prices to send signals to producers and consumers, may *not* be enough to manage fluctuations in the business cycle over the long term. Keynesian economics, to this day, approaches macroeconomic policy with an *activist* mindset. Under this approach governments must do more than just create an environment where markets can thrive. They must look for instances where the market fails to achieve the efficiency and flexibility necessary for full employment to prevail, and in such instances governments must intervene to *manage* the level of aggregate demand, stimulating it or contracting it in order to avoid the two evils apparent in the Keynesian model: persistent unemployment, recession, and deflation on one hand, and uncontrolled inflation on the other.

Keynesian economics is sometimes referred to today as 'demand-side' economic theory, since in the Keynesian view an economy's ability to achieve and maintain full employment is dependent upon managing the level of demand in the economy, since sticky wages will prevent AS from rising or falling to meet the level of demand at the full employment equilibrium.

The monetarist/new classical models of SRAS and LRAS, on the other hand, predict that, at least in the long run, flexible wages and prices will allow an economy to self-correct from any macroeconomic shocks it may experience. Therefore, the best approach policymakers can take to 'managing' the economy may just be to not try and manage it at all. The supply-side, 'laissez-faire' (let it be) school of economic thought is one embraced by small government, conservative-minded government officials and policymakers the world over.

TOK

Macroeconomists in the 21st century tend to align themselves with either the Keynesian, demand-side school of macroeconomic thought or the new classical, supply-side school of thought. To what extent do political beliefs and ideologies, such as the debate over whether government can solve problems or whether government is the problem, influence a person's preference for one school of macroeconomic thought over another? Discuss.

Case study – the global recessions of 2020

The global recessions of 2020 were crises of both AD and AS. As governments shut down their economies and issued stay-at-home orders during the first wave of the pandemic, both AD and AS experienced unprecedented shocks.

1 Using an AD/AS diagram, illustrate the effect on equilibrium output of government orders that forced all but 'essential' businesses to close during the months of April and May.
2 On the same diagram as above, illustrate the effect of the stay-at-home orders which limited consumers' ability to engage in normal patterns of consumption.

One of the first responses of governments in Europe and North America during the economic shutdowns was the expansion of unemployment insurance programmes aimed at providing workers in non-essential businesses with incomes during the shutdown.

3   How did the extension of unemployment benefits contribute to the stickiness of wages during the pandemic?
4   Using a Keynesian AD/AS model, show the impact that the extension of unemployment benefits would have likely had on equilibrium output and employment in the months following the shutdowns of spring 2020.

As summer 2020 unfolded and the world's economies began returning to some semblance of 'normal' the debate among government policymakers turned to the extent to which additional government support was required to help struggling households and firms during what was expected to be an unsteady economic recovery. Two schools of thought emerge: One (let us call it side A) argued that continued support of struggling workers and businesses was essential to prevent the economy from becoming trapped in a longer than necessary recession. The other (side B) argued that rolling back government support was essential to speeding the economic recovery.

5   Which of the sides of the debate over the best policy response represents a Keynesian view of the economy, A or B? Which represents the monetarist/new classical 'supply-side' view? Explain.
6   Using two different AD and SRAS/LRAS models, explain and illustrate the desired long-run economic outcomes as envisioned by those arguing:
    a.   Side A
    b.   Side B.

Practice exam questions

1a. Using the Keynesian AD/AS diagram, explain why an economy may be in equilibrium at any level of real output.   (10 marks)
  b. Evaluate the view that an economy will always self-correct following a negative output gap.   (15 marks)
2.   Explain how an increase in the level of taxation can influence the level of aggregate demand in an economy.   (10 marks)
3.   Using an AD/AS diagram, explain one reason why deflation may lead to a higher level of unemployment.   (4 marks)
4.   Assume an economy is currently producing at its full employment level of national output. Using an AD/AS diagram, explain the effect of a decrease in real interest rates on equilibrium national output in the short run and in the long run.   (10 marks)
5.   Evaluate the view that an increase in aggregate demand will always correspond with an increase in national output.   (15 marks)
6.   Explain how a rise in consumer confidence and business confidence might affect equilibrium national output.   (10 marks)

Macroeconomic objective: low unemployment

15

Concepts

The level of employment is a critical indicator of an economy's overall health. Therefore, low unemployment is a primary macroeconomic objective of policy makers the world over. Employment is viewed as a measure of overall **economic well-being** because wages from work are most households' primary source of income, and national income is a measure of living standards.

Changes in unemployment can be rapid, and can cause major social disruption as a result. While some forms of unemployment may be accepted as normal, rising unemployment levels can threaten the **interdependence** of the economy's circular flow. As fewer people have jobs, spending on goods and services falls, thereby reducing revenues for firms. Such events inspire governments to stage forms of **intervention** to reduce the causes and effects of unemployment.

15.1 The meaning of unemployment

Learning outcomes

At the end of this section you will be able to:

- explain what is meant by unemployment
- define the unemployment rate
- explain how the unemployment rate is calculated
- calculate the unemployment rate from a set of data
- explain the difficulties in measuring unemployment, including hidden unemployment and unemployment rate disparities by subgroups.

What is the unemployment rate and how is it calculated?

From an economic perspective, to be unemployed means that you are actively seeking but unable to find work. A person who is not working is not necessarily unemployed. According to the United Nations International Labour Organization (ILO), to be considered unemployed in an economic sense a person must 'be out of work and willing to accept a suitable job or start an enterprise if the opportunity arises, and actively looking for ways to obtain a job or start an enterprise'.

Governments monitor the level of unemployment by calculating the unemployment rate, which is found by dividing the number of unemployed people by the labour force then multiplying by 100 to establish a percentage.

$$\text{Unemployment rate (\%)} = \frac{\text{number of unemployed}}{\text{labour force}} \times 100$$

According to the **World Bank**, a country's labour force is the sum of employed and unemployed persons aged 15–64 (although the exact age range may vary from nation to nation). Persons who are neither employed nor seeking employment are not in the labour force; this includes retired persons, full-time students, those taking care of children or other family members, and others who are neither working nor seeking work.

Examples of people who are part of the labour force include the following.

- A part-time retail sales clerk, who is also going to college, is part of the labour force because she is employed.
- A full-time nurse is part of the labour force because he is employed.
- A factory worker whose plant closed and who is applying for jobs at other firms is part of the labour force because she is unemployed.
- A recent college graduate interviewing at different companies for his first job is part of the labour force because he is unemployed.

Examples of people who are not part of the labour force include the following.

- A stay-at-home parent is not part of the labour force because he or she is not employed nor seeking employment.
- A college graduate who volunteers in a community centre is not part of the labour force because, although she is working, she is not formally employed nor is she seeking employment.
- A discouraged worker who has been looking for a job for 18 months but has given up the job search is not part of the labour force because he is no longer seeking employment.
- An engineer who goes back to school to earn a teaching degree is not part of the labour force because she is not currently seeking employment.

Figure 15.1 Average unemployment rates for 17 selected developed and developing countries, 2018–20

▼

Figure 15.1 shows average unemployment rates over the years 2018–20 for 17 developed and developing countries. National governments employ their own means of collecting unemployment data, but the Organisation for Economic Co-operation and Development (OECD) uses the method devised by the ILO. Therefore, the data in

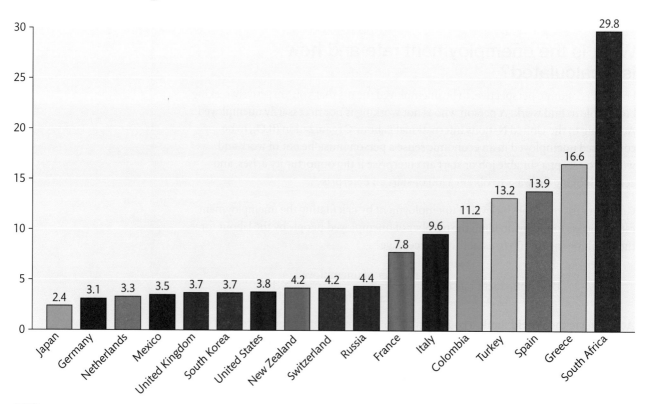

Figure 15.1 can be compared with confidence despite the fact that the figures reported by each individual nation may vary due to different methods of collection.

Unemployment rates vary across countries depending on the current macroeconomic conditions and institutional factors in each, such as the existence of social safety nets, the education levels of the workforce and the evolving structures of the economy, among others.

What are the difficulties in measuring unemployment?

Methods of data collection

The source and method of calculating the unemployment rate can vary significantly, affecting the degree of comparability between countries. One method is to report unemployment claims. Another is to rely on survey data of thousands of people. Counting unemployment benefit claims may undercount the actual rate of unemployment, especially during prolonged recessions, which may last longer than the period of time government provides benefits to unemployed workers. Survey methods are often considered more reliable but may also miss marginal populations (immigrants, undocumented workers) that are unlikely to be captured by household surveys.

Disparities by group

Subgroups within the broad population may have higher or lower unemployment rates than the overall national figure.

- **Regional disparities:** Larger countries tend to have greater variance than smaller ones. Turkey is among the countries with the largest variance, with a 20-point difference between regions with the lowest and highest rate.
- **Ethnic/racial disparities:** Unemployment rates are typically higher among ethnic minorities, especially those that have experienced formal and informal discrimination. Countries that identify indigenous populations typically also report higher unemployment rates among those populations.

- **Gender variance:** The ILO reports that globally approximately 75% of men participate in the labour force, compared to only 50% of women. Many women, therefore, may not have work but are not counted in the official unemployment figures (see below). Officially, the unemployment rate for women is 6.1% while for men it is only 5.1% (ILO). However, this varies tremendously by country. Algeria reports that unemployment for women is twice as high as for men, while Saudi Arabia reports four times the level of unemployment for women as for men.

(Source: OECD. https://www.oecd-ilibrary.org/)

What is 'hidden unemployment'?

The true level of joblessness can be masked by the specific rules guiding the calculation of the unemployment rate: what is left uncounted is considered hidden unemployment.

Workers leave the labour force

Any unemployed worker who leaves the labour force may still be without a job, but will not be counted as unemployed. At times, this leads to the unemployment rate significantly undercounting the actual number of jobless. People leave the labour force for many reasons, including:

- Forced retirement: Workers above the age of 50 may find it difficult to find employment and retire 'early'.
- Return to school: Some choose to go back to school for more training rather than compete in a bad labour market.
- Family childcare: In countries without subsidised childcare, workers may decide their low wages are not sufficient to cover child care costs and so decide to stay at home.

Discouraged workers

Especially during recessions, when the number of cyclically unemployed people grows dramatically, workers may find it difficult to find new jobs. Whatever their motivations, when discouraged workers stop looking for a job, they leave the labour force, and are therefore no longer considered unemployed. These people, when added to the official figures, can raise the 'true' level of unemployment by several percentage points.

Part-time workers still technically employed

A worker paid for one hour of work per week is still considered employed, even if that worker is seeking a full-time job. The official unemployment rate will not show the degree to which workers seeking full-time employment can only find part-time work.

The quality of employment is unknown

Unemployment figures do not reflect the level of wages or the working conditions of a country's labour force. Developing countries with few social services may have low unemployment rates, yet their workers may experience a high level of poverty relative to workers in richer economies, simply because the alternative is **absolute poverty**, or the state of being unable to afford even the basic necessities of life.

Underemployment

The unemployment rate does not reflect the degree to which qualifications match actual jobs. Highly skilled workers working low-skills jobs (engineers working as housekeepers) are examples of such *underemployment*. Countries with a poor match often have workers shifting to informal and temporary work to earn money.

Exercise 15.1

Calculate the missing values in this table of labour market data.

Country	Labour force (millions)	Number of unemployed (millions)	Unemployment rate (%)
Germany	43.5	1.3	
Tunisia		0.64	16
South Korea	28.3		4.1
Mexico	57.1	1.94	

15.2 What are the causes of unemployment?

Learning outcomes

At the end of this section you will be able to:

- explain, using a diagram, how the labour market sets the equilibrium wage and quantity of labour
- describe, using examples, the meaning of frictional, structural, seasonal, and **cyclical (demand-deficient) unemployment**
- distinguish between the causes of frictional, structural, seasonal, and cyclical (demand-deficient) unemployment
- explain, using a diagram, how a deflationary gap causes cyclical unemployment
- explain, using a diagram, that **structural unemployment** is caused by changes in the demand for particular labour skills or changes in the geographical location of industries
- explain, using a diagram, how labour market rigidities, such as a minimum wage, contribute to structural unemployment
- explain that the **natural rate of unemployment (NRU)** is composed of structural and **frictional unemployment**
- evaluate government policies to reduce the different types of unemployment.

What is the labour market?

A labour market is where households and firms meet to buy and sell labour. In the real world, labour markets are not tangible places, rather they exist for different industries where there are employers looking to hire workers and households looking for jobs.

Video suggestions:
You've read about it, now you can review what you've just learned by watching a few videos by the author!

 Simply click here in your eBook for videos on the limitations of the unemployment rate.

Research and inquiry

You can research the gender unemployment gap in your country by using the online tool provided by the ILO.

For discussion and debate:

1 Is it higher or lower than the world's average gap?

2 If higher, what legal and cultural factors may have contributed to this result?

3 If lower, what legal and cultural factors may influence this result?

An example of a labour market is that for international school teachers: around the world there are thousands of international schools that employ tens of thousands of teachers across all subject areas.

In the market for any particular type of labour, it is households that provide workers to an industry and firms that demand workers. In Chapter 7 we studied product markets, in which households are the demanders and firms are the supplier. In labour markets, which are an example of a factor market, the roles are reversed. The supply curve therefore reflects the willingness of households to provide workers to a particular market at a range of wage rates (the price of labour) and the demand curve represents the willingness of firms to hire workers at a range of wages.

Consider our example, one with which you might relate, of the market for international school teachers. In the international teacher marketplace the buyers, representing the demand for labour, are international schools and the sellers, representing the supply of labour, are households whose family members are willing and able to teach in international schools. Much like in a product market, there is a 'price' for labour, which is called the *wage rate*, and there is a quantity of labour, which can be interpreted as the number of workers currently employed or the total number of hours worked, depending on how you look at it.

The equilibrium wage rate and quantity of labour employed in any particular market is determined by the demand for and supply of labour at any given time. In Figure 15.2 the demand for labour (DL) represents how many teachers all the international schools are willing and able to employ at a range of wage rates. At higher wage rates, the number of teachers demanded is lower, as schools will choose to have larger class sizes or offer more online classes due to the high cost of employing teachers. However, at lower wage rates the number of teachers demanded is much greater, and schools will have much smaller class sizes and opt for more face-to-face classes due to the comparatively low cost of employing teachers. In other words, there is an inverse relationship between the wage rate and the quantity of labour demanded.

Labour supply (SL), representing all households who might be willing to enter the international teaching field, is up-sloping, reflecting the direct relationship between the wage rate and the quantity of labour supplied. At higher wages more people are willing to become international teachers, due to the comparatively high income relative to

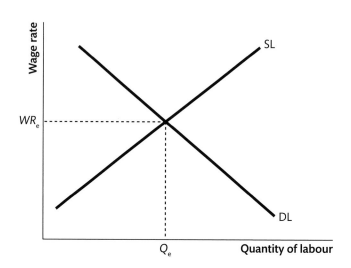

Figure 15.2 Market for international school teachers

other professional fields. At lower wage rates, fewer people are willing to teach in international schools, since other careers will appear more attractive due to the low wage offered to teachers.

As in all markets, the equilibrium level of employment (Q_e) and wage rate (WR_e) are where the demand and supply meet. Later in this chapter we will learn that unemployment arises due to a disequilibrium in the labour market, or when the wage rate does adjust efficiently to the level of demand for and supply of a particular type of labour, resulting in structural unemployment. But first we will look at a type of unemployment that can occur in a nation as a whole, not just in a particular labour market. For this we use the AD/AS diagram, and then we will use the labour market diagram to demonstrate changes in a particular labour market.

What happens when demand for all types of labour decreases?

Cyclical (demand-deficient) unemployment

Without question, the type of unemployment that poses the greatest problems and, therefore, the one which policymakers attempt to avoid at all costs is cyclical unemployment. Cyclical unemployment affects all types of labour, not just workers in a particular labour market. Workers whose skills are in demand given the structure of the nation's economy but who lose their jobs because of a fall in total demand for the nation's goods and services are **cyclically unemployed.**

Cyclical unemployment arises due to fluctuations in the nation's business cycle. It is also referred to as demand-deficient unemployment (simply meaning workers lose their jobs because of weak demand). Cyclical unemployment occurs when a contraction in private or public spending (consumption, investment, government spending or net exports) reduces aggregate demand and leads to a fall in national output. Reduced output requires fewer workers, and so firms lay off workers.

The most dramatic example of cyclical unemployment in the modern era is almost certainly the increase in joblessness that resulted from the decline in economic activity accompanying the spread of the novel coronavirus, SARS-CoV-2, and the resulting COVID-19 pandemic of 2020. Most of the decade preceding the onset of the global pandemic had been characterised by growing economic output and record low unemployment rates the world over; but within the span of a couple of months, across countries both rich and poor, the unemployment situation rapidly deteriorated as economies were shut down and consumers forced to stay at home.

In the two months between February 2020 and April 2020, unemployment in the United States went from a near historic low of 3.5% to the highest level the country had seen since unemployment statistics began being measured in the 1950s, at 14.7% (Figure 15.3). Nearly 20 million Americans lost their jobs in the first two months of the COVID-19 pandemic: the result not of any shift in the structure of the American economy nor by the decision of millions of people to quit their jobs in search of another job, rather because of a massive fall in the total demand for goods and services brought on by the mandatory stay-at-home orders imposed on the citizens of all 50 states.

A public health crisis aside, cyclical unemployment is normally the result of more regular fluctuations in an economy's business cycle. For example, the last global

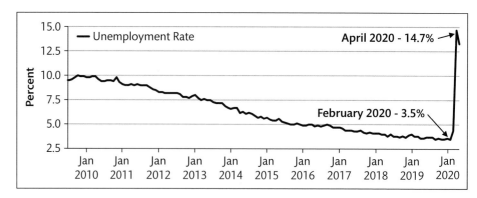

Figure 15.3 US unemployment rate, 2010–20

recession of 2008–9 saw unemployment rise around the world as household wealth declined amid a collapse in housing prices, triggering a decrease in aggregate consumption across Europe and the United States. Between 2009 and 2013 the Greek economy saw unemployment climb from 8% to 27%, largely as a result of a debt crisis that required the Greek government to massively reduce its public sector spending. In other cases, cyclical unemployment can result from declines in private sector investment or in response to falling exports.

In other words, cyclical unemployment arises whenever workers lose their jobs not because of a lack of skills, a change in the composition of the economy's output or any other structural shifts in the economy, rather because of a decline in either household consumption (as was the case in 2009 and 2020), government spending (Greece between 2009 and 2013), private sector investment, net exports or any combination of these.

Cyclical unemployment arises because of the short-run 'stickiness' of wages illustrated by the upward sloping short-run **aggregate supply curve**. When aggregate demand falls, firms are forced to reduce the level of employment rather than simply reducing wages to offset the decline in revenues resulting from falling sales. Recall that wage 'stickiness' simply refers to the fact that wages are not perfectly responsive to changes in demand for labour due to things like labour contracts, minimum wage laws, the ability for workers to collect unemployment benefits from the government, and the influence of labour unions in wage negotiations. The result of wage rigidity is that even as demand for labour falls during a recession, firms are unable to slash wages and must lay workers off instead. The result is cyclical unemployment.

Cyclical unemployment is shown in an aggregate demand (AD)/aggregate supply (AS) model as the gap between equilibrium national output and full employment national output when a deflationary gap exists following a decrease in AD.

In Figure 15.4 aggregate demand has fallen from AD to AD1 due to a contraction in either consumption, investment, government expenditures or net exports. Falling demand leads to a decrease in the price level from PL_e to PL_1 and a decrease in equilibrium output from Y_{fe} (full employment national income) to Y_e (equilibrium national income, which in this case is below full employment).

The notion that wages tend to hold steady during a recession originated with the Keynesian explanation of the Great Depression of the 1930s, and has several rationales.

1 Firms choose to fire some workers and retain the rest at full wages to avoid the morale reducing effect of lower wages.

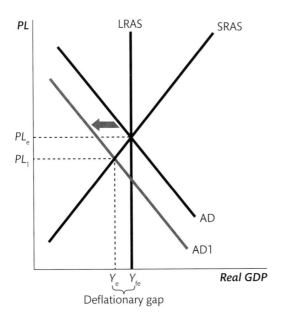

◀ **Figure 15.4** Keynesian model: a deflationary gap causes cyclical unemployment

2   Unemployment benefits may reduce the need for workers to automatically take any lower-paying job after being laid off.

3   Unions can negotiate wages that are higher than average, and may also lock firms into those wages for several years at a time, regardless of a sudden recession.

Because of this wage stickiness, the equilibrium wage holds for some time, creating a surplus of workers in the economy, otherwise known as cyclical unemployment.

If wages were perfectly flexible, the economy would be able to maintain output at the full employment level even as aggregate demand decreased. Recall that the monetarist/new classical view of aggregate supply assumes that wages are perfectly flexible and thus the economy is always at its full employment level of output. Figure 15.5 shows that in a world of perfectly flexible wages and prices, a fall in aggregate demand would result in no change in output and employment, but a much larger decrease in

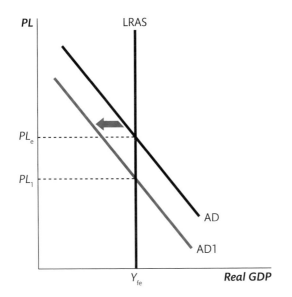

◀ **Figure 15.5** Neo-classical model: flexible wages and prices allow the economy to remain at full employment when AD falls

297

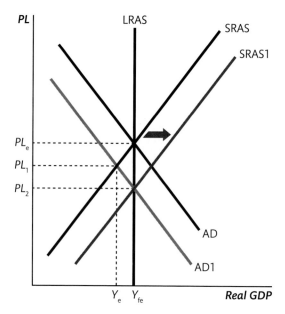

Figure 15.6   Cyclical unemployment is eliminated in the long run when wages fall and the economy self-corrects

the aggregate price level, as workers' nominal wages are slashed in response to weak demand, while employment and output remain at the full employment level.

However, in the real world wages are sticky in the short run, therefore a disequilibrium results in the nation's economy when aggregate demand decreases: as demand for output and workers decrease, wages remain stubbornly high, therefore firms must lay workers off to reduce their costs in the short run. In the long run, cyclical unemployment may be reduced as wages adjust to the decreased demand across the economy.

Only over time, whatever period it takes for wages to fall, will cyclical unemployment begin to decrease and the economy settle at a new, lower wage rate, while employment recovers. Recall from Chapter 14 that in the long run an economy self-adjusts following a negative demand shock; high cyclical unemployment puts downward pressure on wages, and as wages fall the quantity of labour demanded increases, causing employment and output to slowly increase back towards the full employment level.

Figure 15.6 shows the self-adjustment that takes place to reduce cyclical unemployment in the long run following a demand-deficient recession. In later chapters, we will explore government interventions that could help either avoid cyclical unemployment altogether or help reduce it without having to wait for wages to decrease in the long run, an outcome based more in classical/monetarist economic theories than in observations of real world economic outcomes.

What happens when demand for a particular type of labour decreases?

Structural unemployment

We have just learned about the most harmful type of unemployment: that which results from a demand-deficient recession. Workers can also find themselves unemployed for reasons other than a decrease in aggregate demand. When a worker loses her job due to the changing composition of the nation's economy, the individual becomes structurally unemployed. Structural unemployment is a form of involuntary unemployment among workers whose skills are no longer in demand. Automation may replace workers with technology. Firms may move operations 'off-shore', outsourcing production to lower-cost countries. Shifts in technology may make some jobs, and the skills for producing them, irrelevant.

Structural unemployment arises when demand for a *certain type* of labour decreases, as opposed to demand for *all labour* decreasing (as in the case of cyclical unemployment). As with cyclical unemployment, however, the stickiness of wages is at the core a cause of structural unemployment, as we will see below.

An example of structural employment occurs when a developing country moves from an agricultural base to a manufacturing base. New farming techniques are less labour intensive and more capital intensive. Farmers whose skills were passed down through generations find themselves unemployed as their old techniques for tilling the land are replaced by new technology. Likewise, as a more developed nation transitions from a manufacturing base to a larger service sector, factory workers' skills may no longer be in demand, while the demand for highly educated and highly skilled 'knowledge workers' increases.

In both of these examples, the nation as a whole is getting richer as productivity grows and the country shifts from the primary to the secondary and tertiary sectors. However, structurally unemployed workers typically face a longer path back to gainful employment, and government intervention sometimes is desirable.

Structural unemployment is shown using a labour market diagram, as in Figure 15.7. Initially, textile production in South Korea pays US$10 per hour and Q_e is the equilibrium quantity of labour. The demand for textile workers in Korea decreases from DL1 to DL2; this is caused by structural factors such as the relocation of textile factories to lower-cost production in China or Morocco or the increased use of automation in textile manufacturing. The decreased demand for labour puts downward pressure on wages, but due to institutional factors outlined earlier in this chapter the wage rate remains stuck at US$10, resulting in a disequilibrium in the labour market as the number of workers demanded falls to Q_d while the number of workers wishing to work remains at Q_e.

Figure 15.7 Market for textile workers: structural unemployment arises when demand for labour falls

Because textile wages in South Korea cannot fall to the level required to 'clear the market' (that is, firms decide it is once again worth hiring back unemployed workers, who are now more competitive compared to overseas workers or compared to technology), textile jobs will leave the country and relocate to lower-wage economies. Previously employed textile workers in South Korea have become structurally unemployed. If they wish to work again they must either accept a wage rate competitive with what workers in China or Morocco earn or learn skills that will allow them to gain employment in an industry in which labour is still in demand at the wage rates expected of workers in South Korea.

Structural unemployment can be resolved by the free market when one of two things happen: either the equilibrium wage rate in the affected industry must fall to a level that 'clears the market', or the supply of labour in the industry must decrease until the quantity of labour supplied once again equals the quantity demanded at a wage rate that workers are willing to accept. For supply to decrease, structurally unemployed workers in the affected industry must leave that industry and either exit the labour force or seek employment in another sector.

The emergence of structural unemployment in an economy may at first seem incredibly undesirable, as those who have been 'made redundant' are the unfortunate victims of economic change. However, structural unemployment is considered a 'natural' form of joblessness as it is expected that as a nation grows, its production will become more capital intensive and it will incorporate into the global economy, causing both a change in the makeup of its output and the types of skills demanded of its workers. Generally, however, the existence of structural unemployment accompanies economic growth and an increasingly diverse and globalised national economy, thus it is both natural and desired.

Economists view unemployment derived from an effective minimum wage as part of structural unemployment as well. Recall from Chapter 9 that putting a price floor on labour can cause unemployment. Figure 15.8 shows a labour market diagram in the

Figure 15.8 Market for retail employees with a minimum wage ▶

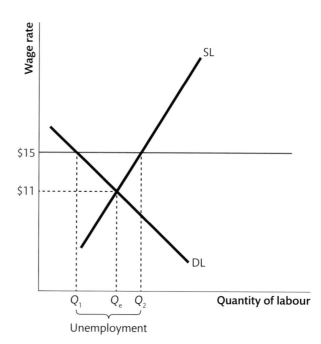

market for retail shop workers who before government intervention were earning an equilibrium wage rate of US$11 per hour. The government has established a minimum wage at US$15.

The imposition of $15 minimum wage has caused a movement up and to the left along the demand for labour curve from Q_e to Q_1, as the quantity demanded for retail workers has fallen. At the same time, more workers are drawn into the labour market by the higher wage, shown by a movement upward along the supply of labour curve, from Q_e to Q_2. With retail businesses demanding fewer workers while more people desire to work in retail, there emerges a disequilibrium in the labour market, resulting in unemployment of $Q_2 - Q_1$.

Unlike with cyclical unemployment and most kinds of structural unemployment, a minimum wage causes unemployment to increase not because of a fall in demand for labour, but because of a government intervention that is intended to help workers. While some workers are indeed made better off (those who are still employed at Q_1 in the market above), some are inevitably harmed (those who are left without a job at the higher wage).

Strategies for reducing structural unemployment include increased worker training and improved education and protectionism.

- Governments could offer assistance to workers relocating from job-poor areas to ones that are job-rich.
- Protectionist policies, such as tariffs and subsidies, can be used as a short-term method of slowing the trend away from some industries. However, this is more likely to prolong the decline of the industries, and works against the concept of economic efficiency outlined by comparative advantage theory. Tariff revenues could be spent on transitioning to more promising forms of production and employment.
- To reduce structural unemployment over the long term, a nation must invest heavily in public education and training for adult workers in the skills that will be needed for the future economy, as well as developing systems of matching education to the skills currently in demand by industries.

What are frictional and seasonal unemployment?

Workers who are in between jobs or just entering the labour force for the first time are referred to as frictionally unemployed. A person may be relocating to a new area and seeking a new job. Someone may be leaving a job in an attempt to find a better one. Students finishing university and graduate school with fresh training may spend time looking for a job. One example is a worker who quits his job in retail with the training and expectation of taking up a job as a nurse. During the period of time between the old job and the new job, which he is fairly certain he will be able to acquire rather quickly, he is frictionally unemployed.

Frictional unemployment is generally short term (three months or less) and is often voluntary, meaning the unemployed person has chosen to seek employment in a different location or industry. The key characteristic of the frictionally unemployed is that they possess skills that are demanded by the nation's employers, thus their prospects for employment are generally positive. Another characteristic of frictional unemployment is that it tends to decrease during recessions, when workers are fearful of losing their current jobs, and tends to rise during economic expansions when job prospects are better.

Workers who do seasonal labour (for example, golf course employees, migrant farmers, ski-lift operators or summer-camp instructors) may be unemployed between seasons. **Seasonal unemployment** is also considered a type of voluntary unemployment as many such workers choose their jobs for the freedom and other benefits such employment offers.

Government policies that affect incentives among the labour force may increase or decrease the level of frictional and seasonal unemployment. The longer unemployment benefits can be collected, the less the incentive to rush the job search process and take the first decent job offered. Additionally, if information about employment opportunities around the country is readily available and systems exist to quickly match frictionally unemployed workers with employers through job centres or online employment services, then the duration of frictional unemployment and its prevalence in the economy may be reduced.

Case study – cyclical, structural, or frictional unemployment: you decide!

When the novel coronavirus struck in late 2019 and early 2020, the effects on unemployment around the world were immediate and severe as economies saw jobless rates double or even triple in the span of a few weeks. But even within countries themselves there were extreme variations in the virus's impact on employment between regions, provinces, or states.

Figure 15.9 shows the unemployment rates in ten US states in early April, 2020, just one month after the US president declared the COVID-19 pandemic a 'national emergency'.

Considering what you have learned about unemployment in this chapter, answer the following questions:

1   What is likely to account for the large variation in unemployment between the states with the highest rates and the states with the lowest rates in the early months of the COVID-19 pandemic?
2   Why might a state like Hawaii, where tourism makes up 21% of the economy, have experienced the greatest unemployment effects of the coronavirus?
3   Is the high unemployment resulting from the COVID-19 pandemic structural, frictional, seasonal, or cyclical? Explain your answer.
4   This data is from just one month into the coronavirus outbreak in the United States. What do you think most likely happened to the unemployment rates in the states hardest hit at this stage versus those least affected in the months that followed?

What is the natural rate of unemployment?

An economy producing at full employment still experiences frictional, seasonal, and structural unemployment. These combined are known as the natural rate of unemployment (NRU). This can be a confusing concept because the term 'full

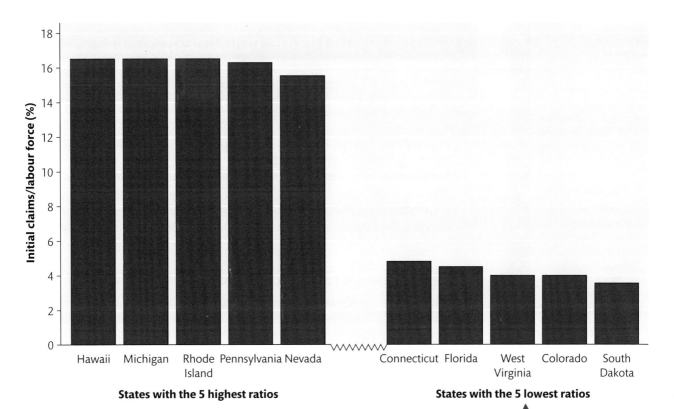

States with the 5 highest ratios   **States with the 5 lowest ratios**

Figure 15.9 Unemployment rates in ten US states, 9 April 2020

employment' makes it sound as if everyone has a job. Nonetheless, economists believe that a dynamic economy requires people to change jobs for structural or frictional reasons, and that some level of unemployment is natural, even desirable.

$$\text{structural unemployment} + \text{frictional unemployment} = \text{natural rate of unemployment (NRU)}$$

The NRU varies widely from country to country. Its variance depends on several factors, including factors that influence the levels of both structural and frictional unemployment:

- low information about job vacancies and available talent
- labour immobility, the instance of qualified workers unable to relocate to available positions
- mismatch of workers' training/education and skills needed by employers
- hysteresis, or the fact that unemployed workers become less employable the longer they are out of work
- labour laws that protect jobs that are no longer needed
- the level of unemployment benefits provided.

As countries try to manage their overall economies, the NRU is used as an important guideline for the calibration of fiscal and monetary policy. *Ceteris paribus*, if a country's unemployment rate exceeds the NRU, some cyclical unemployment is occurring and will require an expansionary response. Conversely, when unemployment drops below the NRU, the labour market may be considered 'tight'. In this case, the heated job market may indicate rising wages and future inflation. Policymakers may then choose contractionary policies to 'cool off' the potential inflation.

TOK

Using the concepts of 'natural rate' of unemployment and 'full employment', how might the language we use to describe economic circumstances affect our perception of individuals in society who are affected by those circumstances?

Further thoughts

While structural and frictional unemployment are considered 'natural' forms of unemployment that exist in an economy that is producing at its 'full employment' level, the reality for those experiencing unemployment in a healthy economy may be no less unpleasant than that experienced by someone who has lost their job due to a recession. However, when economists consider some types of unemployment 'natural', it risks diminishing the hardships of those experiencing unemployment.

1 How could economists employ language to assign terms that better reflect the experiences of unemployed workers, many of whom are struggling to support their families while they search for work?

2 How do different languages translate the concept of unemployment? Does it have different connotations in those languages than it does in English?

15.3 The costs of unemployment

Learning outcomes

At the end of this section you will be able to:

- discuss possible personal and social consequences of unemployment, including increased crime rates, increased stress levels, increased indebtedness, homelessness, and family breakdown
- discuss possible economic consequences of unemployment, including a loss of GDP, loss of tax revenue, increased cost of unemployment benefits, loss of income for individuals, and greater disparities in the distribution of income.

What are the personal costs of unemployment?

Unemployment can be a personally traumatic experience. More broadly, the social and economic consequences of unemployment can be severe and long-lasting as well, which explains why maintaining a low level of unemployment is an important macroeconomic objective.

Decreased household income and purchasing power

An obvious consequence of the unemployment of one or more members of a household is a decline in a household's income and consequently its standard of living. The decline in personal income could result in foreclosure or repossession of a mortgaged or rented home, or worse, an inability to feed the household.

Increased levels of psychological and physical illness

A significant personal consequence of unemployment is the psychological and even physical toll it imposes on the unemployed. Some studies have shown that higher unemployment rates are correlated with higher rates of depression, cardiovascular disease, suicides, and psychiatric hospital admittances.

What are the social consequences of unemployment?

Increased poverty

Regions or cities in which unemployment occurs may become depressed and therefore less attractive to new investment by businesses. The low income levels of the largely unemployed population can therefore deter businesses from starting or expanding businesses, further contributing to the unemployment and poverty problem in that area.

Transformation of traditional societies

Unemployment in particular regions or sectors of the economy can lead to social upheaval. Where farming and hunting offer economic self-sufficiency on a familial or small village level, the social web flows from these relationships. Economic development, especially the move from labour-intensive home production to capital-intensive organised production, can separate a labourer's work from these relationships, and sever them from their traditional social web. China's shift, over the last 40 years, to massive industrialisation, is an example of this on a grand scale.

What are the economic consequences of unemployment?

Downward pressure on wages for the employed

High unemployment means the supply of available labour has increased in the nation. Since wages are determined by supply and demand, an increase in the labour supply can lower the equilibrium wage rate for those who still have jobs, forcing them to accept pay cuts and reducing the real incomes of all workers.

Lower level of aggregate demand

Closely related to wage losses is the level of consumption. A major component of aggregate demand, consumption is primarily determined by disposable incomes. Unemployment lowers households' disposable income and consumption, reducing the level of demand and output in the nation as a whole. This leads to more unemployment and can pull an economy into a recession.

Under-utilisation of the nation's resources

Unemployment means a nation is not fully utilising its productive resources, therefore a nation with high unemployment is producing within its PPC at a level below that which is most beneficial to an economy trying to improve the economic well-being of its people.

Brain-drain

Skilled workers may choose to leave a country with high unemployment if job opportunities are more abundant elsewhere. This further leads to a fall in the production possibilities of the nation with high unemployment.

A turn towards protectionism and isolationist policies

Rising unemployment is often blamed by politicians and policymakers on competition from cheap foreign producers. This can lead to the rise of protective tariffs and quotas or increased government spending on subsidies for domestic producers. Such policies lead to a misallocation of society's scarce resources and in the long run will make the nation less competitive in global markets.

Increased budget deficits

Unemployed workers do not pay income taxes, but instead receive monthly payments from the government to assist them until they find work. High unemployment reduces the total tax revenues received by a government while simultaneously increasing public expenditures on financial support for the unemployed, pushing national budgets towards deficit. It therefore necessitates either a decrease in government spending on public goods, such as infrastructure, education, defence and healthcare or an increase in government borrowing to finance its budget deficit. As you will see in Chapter 22, large government budget deficits bring their own set of problems to a nation's economy.

The individual, social, and economic consequences of unemployment are not limited to those outlined above, but it should be clear that the costs of unemployment are wide-ranging, thus making low unemployment a worthy and important goal for macroeconomic policymakers.

Video suggestions:
You've read about it, now you can review what you've just learned by watching a few videos by the author!
 Simply click here in your eBook for videos on 'Types of Unemployment, the Business Cycle, and the Natural Rate of Unemployment (NRU)'.

Video suggestions:
You've read about it, now you can review what you've just learned by watching a few videos by the author!
 Simply click here in your eBook for videos on 'Factors that can cause the Natural Rate of Unemployment to change'.

Research and Inquiry

For discussion and debate:

1. Conduct a search to determine the NRU for your country. This is sometimes referred to as the long-term unemployment rate.

2. Next seek out the NRU for two other countries. What, based on what you know of each country, might account for the differences?

3. Investigate the NRU over several decades (try 1990, 2000, and 2010) for one of the countries you selected. Has it changed much? Can you make a guess as to why this may have happened?

Practice exam questions

Paper 1 questions

1a. Distinguish, using examples, between the causes of structural, seasonal and demand deficient unemployment. (10 marks)

2a. Explain the difficulties in measuring unemployment. (10 marks)

3a. Explain, using a diagram, how labour market rigidities such as the minimum wage contribute to structural unemployment. (10 marks)

Paper 2 questions

Germany Unemployment Rises, Budget Deficit Set to Increase
July 2020

Germany's unemployment rate rose in June from 6.2%, up from 6.1% in May, and a percentage point higher than in March, when it scored 5.1%. Jobless claims are more than 600,000 higher than the same time last year.

Germany's labour force is currently 43.5 million people. This number may drop if the crisis continues and workers drop out of the labour force as discouraged workers. By 2021, some economists project 3 million people will be unemployed.

Unemployment has risen more slowly and less severely in Germany due to 'short-work' programmes that subsidise wages to firms up to 60% of previous levels, encouraging firms to retain employees through the crisis. Also known as 'furloughs', these programmes pay firms to pay workers, even if there is little work or demand for the firm's output.

One result of the extra spending on firms and workers is that Germany also announced recently that it expects to borrow a record 218 billion Euro in 2020, the country's largest deficit spending ever. Its debt to GDP ratio will rise from below 60% to above 75% for the current year.

---

a.   i. Define *unemployment*. (2 marks)

     ii. Define *budget deficit*. (2 marks)

b.   i. Assuming the labour force is stable, calculate the expected unemployment rate for Germany in the next year. (2 marks)

     ii. Using the formula for calculating the unemployment rate, explain the effect of an increase in the number of discouraged workers. (3 marks)

c. Explain, using a diagram, that demand deficient unemployment is caused by a fall in aggregate demand. (4 marks)

d. Explain, using a diagram, how Germany's wage subsidy programme acts as an automatic stabiliser for aggregate demand. (4 marks)

e. Explain two reasons unemployment is difficult to measure accurately. (4 marks)

f. Using examples, explain two types of unemployment. (4 marks)

g. Using information from the text and your own knowledge of economics, discuss the economic, social, and personal consequences of unemployment. (15 marks)

Macroeconomic objective: low and stable inflation

16

16.1 What is inflation and how is it measured?

Learning outcomes

At the end of this section you will be able to:

- distinguish between inflation, disinflation, and deflation
- explain how a CPI measures changes in prices
- **HL** construct a **weighted price index**, using a set of data provided
- calculate the inflation rate from a set of data
- analyse the limitations of the CPI in measuring inflation and the alternative measures used by economists
- draw a diagram to show how demand-pull inflation is caused by an increase in AD
- use a diagram to explain cost-push inflation.

In addition to maintaining a low level of unemployment, governments and central banks also focus their policies on maintaining a stable rate of increase in the average price level of goods and services in a nation; in other words, *low and stable inflation*. Maintaining price level stability is considered a fundamental objective of macroeconomic policy, since price level instability can have negative effects on a nation's economic health.

Inflation is defined as an increase in the average price level of goods and services in an economy over time. Deflation, on the other hand, occurs when the average price level of goods and services decreases over time. The key word in these definitions is 'average' since inflation does not measure changes in the relative prices of particular goods. For instance, certain types of technology (e.g. smartphones, electric cars, and solar panels) have come down in price considerably in the last decade due to expansion of their markets and productivity gains in their manufacturing. The fall in prices of these particular goods does not mean that nations have experienced deflation, since only certain types of goods have become cheaper. Even as certain goods have fallen in price, the overall price levels of most countries have risen over the last decade.

Figure 16.1 provides a snapshot of the levels of inflation across every country in the world. The further left the colour is in the key, the lower the inflation rate, with the lowest rates recorded in 2019 being at around 1% (Saudi Arabia). The further to the right-hand side of the key, the higher the inflation rate, with the highest rate in 2019 being around 90% (Venezuela). The meaning of these values will be made clearer in the next section of this chapter.

So why does inflation matter to economists? Another way of understanding inflation is that it causes the value of money to decrease over time. An increase in the price level essentially makes money less valuable and reduces its purchasing power. In an environment of inflation, a particular amount of money will buy less in the future than it does in the present. Therefore, inflation encourages households and firms to spend now rather than postponing spending until the future when prices are higher. The anticipation of future inflation can trigger a positive feedback loop in which households increase their spending now, thereby causing inflation and encouraging further increases in spending. The increased spending worsens scarcity across the

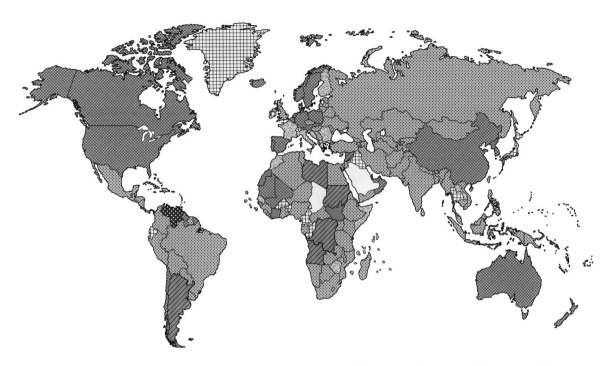

| -1.00 – -0.15 | -0.15 – -0.70 | 0.7 – 1.6 | 1.6 – 2.4 | 2 – 25 | 25 – 47 | 47 – 70 | 70 – 92 |

▲

Figure 16.1 Worldwide inflation variations, 2019

economy, fuelling more inflation and eroding people's real incomes and wealth over time. If left unchecked, inflation can destroy economic value.

So high inflation is bad. Does that mean that its opposite, deflation, is good? Deflation occurs when the average price level decreases over time. A fall in prices results in an increase in the value of money, since its purchasing power increases. A particular amount of money will buy more in the future than it does in the present when deflation occurs. Deflation incentivises savings over consumption and investment, since households and firms will wish to postpone purchases until the future when prices are expected to decline. Much as anticipated inflation can trigger an inflationary spiral, anticipated deflation can create a deflationary spiral in which spending falls, driving prices down, encouraging even less consumption and investment. As we learned in Chapter 14, falling demand will lead to rising unemployment in the short run, as firms faced with sticky wages are forced to reduce the size of their workforce. Deflation, therefore, can lead an economy into a period of rising unemployment and prolonged recession.

Okay, so high inflation is bad, deflation is bad, what are policymakers to do, then? A final term requiring a definition is disinflation. Disinflation refers to a decrease in the rate of inflation from a higher level to a lower level. Generally speaking, disinflation is a desirable outcome in a country that is experiencing high inflation. However, if inflation is already very low, disinflation may be undesirable because it could push the economy into deflation.

Have you heard the story of Goldilocks and the three bears? If not, here is the gist of it. A little girl wanders into the woods and finds a cabin with the door left open. Inside are three bowls of porridge left on the dining table. Goldilocks is hungry, so she takes a spoonful from the first bowl: too hot. She tries the second bowl: too cold. So she tries the third bowl: *just right*. She eats up all the porridge. Goldilocks then spots three rocking chairs. Chair one is too hard, chair two too soft, but chair three is *just right*. Finally, she wanders upstairs to the bedrooms, as she is tired after her walk and her snack. There are three beds. The first bed is too hard, the second bed is too soft, but the third bed is *just right*.

Too hot, too cold, just right ▶

Much like Goldilocks, economic policymakers must target a rate of inflation that is neither *too high*, nor *too low*, rather one that is *just right*. The target inflation rate may vary depending on the underlying macroeconomic conditions of a particular economy, but in the more developed countries of Western Europe, East Asia, and North America, the *just right* level of inflation is believed to be between 2% and 3%. And these are the inflation 'targets' for policymakers in those countries. In Chapters 19, 20, and 21 we will explore the role of policymakers at targeting a low and stable rate of inflation in more detail. For now, we will move onto inflation measurement, the limitations of measuring inflation, and the causes and costs of inflation and deflation.

How do price indexes help economists measure inflation?

Changes in price levels are monitored on a monthly or quarterly basis by most governments. The method for collecting inflation data is similar across countries, and employs a tool known as a price index. The **consumer price index**, or CPI, measures the change in income a consumer would need in order to maintain the same standard of living over time under a new set of prices as under the original set of prices.

HL Calculating a weighted price index

Calculating a price index involves the government conducting a regular survey of the prices of hundreds or even thousands of different consumer and producer goods. The basket of goods measured for the CPI may include items such as clothing, food, fuel, electricity, rents, airline tickets, bus fares, laptop computers, and so on. It also includes services, and its composition may be updated annually or biannually as new types of products become fashionable among consumers.

A price index is found by dividing the price of a basket of goods in one period by the price of the identical basket of goods in a base period and multiplying by 100.

To determine the price index, first a base period index must be established. For instance, imagine a country where the typical consumer only buys three goods: pizza, haircuts, and coffee. Table 16.1 shows the prices and quantities purchased of the three goods by a typical consumer over three years, along with the amount spent.

Table 16.1 Prices of three consumer goods over three years, 2019, 2020, and 2021.

Good or service	Quantities purchased	Price in 2019	Amount spent in 2019 $(Q \times P)$	Price in 2020	Amount spent in 2020 $(Q \times P)$	Price in 2021	Amount spent in 2021 $(Q \times P)$
Pizza	20	$10	$200	$10.50	$210	$12	$240
Haircuts	10	$20	$200	$19	$190	$22	$220
Coffee	40	$8	$320	$10	$400	$9	$360
Total basket price		In 2019	$720	In 2020	$800	In 2021	$820

The 'quantities purchased' assigns a *weight* to each of the goods in the CPI basket. The more a consumer purchases of a good, the more weight that good has in the overall CPI measurement.

Assume 2019 is the base year, and we want to calculate the CPIs for 2019, 2020, and 2021:

$$\text{CPI for 2019} = \frac{\text{Price of the basket of goods in 2019}}{\text{Price of the basket in base year}} \times 100 = \frac{720}{720} \times 100$$
$$= 100$$

$$\text{CPI for 2020} = \frac{\text{Price of the basket of goods in 2020}}{\text{Price of the basket in base year}} = \frac{800}{720} \times 100$$
$$= 111.1$$

$$\text{CPI for 2020} = \frac{\text{Price of the basket of goods in 2021}}{\text{Price of the basket in base year}} = \frac{820}{720} \times 100$$
$$= 113.9$$

The CPI for 2019 is 100, which makes sense since 2019 is our base year. The price of the same basket of goods in 2020 increased from $720 to $800, giving us a CPI of 111.1. In 2021 prices continued to rise, with the same basket of goods going up to $820, giving us a CPI of 113.9.

In Worked example 16.1 the CPI increased in each of the three years. Notice also that not all three goods are weighted equally in the basket. While coffee is the cheapest of the goods, it carries more weight since coffee is consumed at twice the rate of pizza and four times the rate of haircuts. A change in the price of coffee, therefore, will have a greater proportional effect on the CPI than a change in the price of a good that is consumed less than coffee.

Video suggestion:
You have read about it, now you can review what you have just learned by watching a video by the author!

▶ Simply click here in your eBook for a video on calculating a CPI.

What does the CPI tell us, then? It tells us whether the *average weighted price level* of the goods consumed by the typical consumer have increased or decreased over time. To determine the inflation rate, however, we must calculate the rate of change in the CPI between two periods of time.

Calculating the inflation rate from a price index

The inflation rate is measured as the rate of change in the CPI between two periods of time. While inflation can be measured quarterly or even monthly, it is standard to report inflation annually. To do so, we must divide the change in the CPI between two years (year 1 and 2) by the original CPI (year 1) and multiply the result by 100.

Worked example 16.2

Using our CPI data from the previous worked example we can calculate inflation between 2019 and 2020 and between 2020 and 2021:

$$\text{Inflation between 2019 and 2020} = \frac{111.1 - 100}{100} \times 100 = 11.1\%$$

$$\text{Inflation between 2020 and 2021} = \frac{113.9 - 111.1}{111.1} \times 100 = 2.5\%$$

This country experienced inflation between all three years, of 11.1% between 2019 and 2020 and then 2.5% between 2020 and 2021. Average prices rose between 2019 and 2021. Another way to say this is that a typical consumer would need to experience a 13.9% increase in their nominal income in order to maintain the same standard of living in 2021 as she enjoyed in 2019.

Video suggestion:
You have read about it, now you can review what you have just learned by watching a video by the author!

▶ Simply click here in your eBook for a video on calculating inflation using a CPI.

What are the limitations of the CPI in measuring inflation?

The official inflation rate, like other macroeconomic measurements, is an aggregate measure, in this case of the average price level of what the typical household consumes. However, not all households' consumption patterns will be accurately reflected by the CPI.

Different effect on consumers of different income levels

For example, a lower income household may be more affected by inflation in their everyday consumption decisions than a wealthier household. Poorer consumers tend to spend a greater percentage of their income on goods and services, whereas richer consumers tend to save more. Therefore, an increase in the CPI could have a disproportionate effect on lower income consumers than on the rich.

Additionally, the composition of the basket of goods consumed by different households will be very different. Higher income households may be able to substitute imported goods for domestically produced goods when domestic inflation accelerates, sheltering them from rising prices at home.

Changing consumption patterns

The inability of the CPI to reflect the consumption patterns of all households is one obvious shortcoming of its usefulness as a measurement of economic well-being. Another is that the consumption patterns in a nation may change faster than the composition of the collection of goods whose prices are included in the CPI measure, which may only be updated once a decade or so, even as the goods purchased by actual consumers change every year. If the goods in a CPI are not updated frequently, the usefulness of the inflation rate will diminish as consumers switch to newer, different products.

Improvements in product quality not captured

Additionally, the CPI might overstate inflation as prices rise even as the quality of the goods consumers are buying increases exponentially. For example, a £25,000 car purchased in 2010 might have increased to £30,000 by 2020, a 20% increase in price (an average of 2% per year over ten years). However, the quality of the car purchased in 2020 may have increased exponentially. Improvements in safety, comfort, entertainment, and navigation systems, self-driving or 'autopilot' capabilities, and other factors affecting the consumer's experience of the 2020 model are not reflected in that average 2% increase in its price over ten years. When technology and product quality increase disproportionately compared to goods' prices, the inflation rate will overstate the burden of higher prices on consumers.

Volatility of energy and food prices

Another limitation of the CPI is that it could be skewed by the price volatility of particular 'core' goods, namely energy and food prices. Because of the inelastic nature of demand and supply for energy and food (see Chapters 4 and 6), small shifts in demand or supply can cause large changes in prices of these goods.

For example, in 2020 the price of a barrel of crude oil dropped from $61 on 1 January (before the COVID-19 pandemic began) to $11 on 21 April (when most economies were on shut down during the first wave of the pandemic). In the USA, where oil and other fossil fuels are important sources of energy production, *energy* is given a considerable weight in the overall CPI (7%). Motor fuel, of which oil is the key input, is weighted at 3% of the overall CPI. Together energy and motor fuel account for 10% of value of the consumer price index. The price of oil, an input into both of these, fell by 82% between January and April. Given the considerable weight of goods that use oil, this drop would have impacted the CPI in a noticeable way, despite the fact that lower oil prices say little about how prices across all other industries changed during the shutdown.

In order to provide a picture for how *most* goods and services are changing in price, not including those energy and food commodities whose prices tend to fluctuate more wildly, economists measure what is known as the core CPI to determine *core inflation*. Core inflation measures the price of a basket of goods consumed by the typical household, excluding energy and food. It gives a clearer picture of the long-run trends in living costs, ignoring short-run fluctuations in certain commodity prices.

Figure 16.2 compares the USA's CPI for all items (known as the 'headline' inflation rate, in blue) to the core CPI (in dotted red) between January and July 2020. The area shaded in grey indicates the period during which the US economy was officially in a recession.

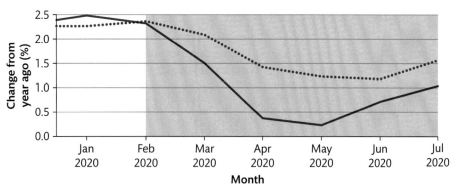

Figure 16.2 Core inflation was less volatile than headline inflation in the USA, January–July 2020

As we can see, the core inflation rate was much more stable during the first half of 2020, while headline inflation fell from 2.5% in early January to 0.2% by May, a significant amount of disinflation. Core inflation, which excludes the change in food and energy prices, meanwhile, remained more stable, falling from 2.26% in January to 1.2% in May. All other goods beside food and energy, in other words, experienced a much less precipitous slowdown in inflation compared to what was experienced when including food and energy.

CPI is not useful to producers

Another limitation of the CPI is that it is useful only for communicating the effect of price changes on consumers, but lacks relevance to a whole other group of stakeholders in an economy, producers. For this reason, many governments also use a second price index, known as the producer price index (PPI), to communicate the impact of changing prices on firms. The PPI includes more primary commodities, such as those produced by the mining, manufacturing, agriculture, fishing, and forestry sectors, as well as natural gas, electricity, construction, and other goods that are more likely to be purchased by a country's business firms, rather than the finished goods and services purchased by households.

Figure 16.3 shows that while the CPI and PPI generally rise together over time, the PPI (blue) appears to be far more volatile than the CPI (dotted red). This fits with what we know about primary commodities. Supply and demand both are relatively inelastic compared to manufactured goods, resulting in greater fluctuations in price when relatively small changes in their demand or supply occur.

Also notice that during recessions (shaded grey in the chart), the PPI tends to experience steep declines, while the CPI typically experiences slower growth (disinflation) or a relatively small drop (mild deflation). This is explained by the fact that demand for primary commodities is also relatively *income elastic*, and that primary commodities are a *normal good*. Normal goods see demand decrease when incomes fall (as they do during recessions).

Additionally, given the relatively steep decrease in commodity prices during recessions relative to consumer prices (which include more manufactured goods), we can assume that producers of primary commodities face more income elastic demand than producers of finished goods and services. This may have to do with the ability to

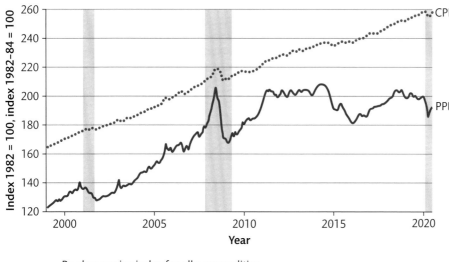

Figure 16.3 A comparison between the CPI and PPI of the USA between 2000 and 2020 shows how the PPI is relatively volatile

— Producer price index for all commodities
•••• Consumer price index for all urban consumers: All items in US city average

store inventories of primary commodities. When a recession begins, firms may cancel orders for newly extracted or produced inputs (causing prices to tumble) and instead dip into existing inventories while they reduce output and wait to see how aggregate demand evolves as the recession unfolds.

The CPI as it is reported by governments offers a measure of inflation as it affects an 'average' consumer. It is just that though – a single metric that has some advantages but also many shortcomings as an indicator of economic welfare. To accommodate for its disadvantages, several alternative measures of inflation are employed, including the 'core' inflation rate and the PPI. Next we'll look a little deeper into the causes of inflation.

What are the causes of inflation?

Inflation can be caused by one of two ways, either as a result of an increase in aggregate demand (AD) or as a result of a decrease in aggregate supply (AS).

What is demand-pull inflation?

Demand-pull inflation occurs when there is an increase in total demand for a nation's output, either from domestic households, foreign consumers, the government, or firms (*C, Xn, G,* or *I*). When AD increases without a corresponding increase in AS, the nation's producers cannot keep up with the rising demand, and prices are driven up as goods become scarcer.

Demand-pull inflation can be illustrated in the AD-AS model, as in Figure 16.4.

In the Keynesian model, demand-pull inflation is likely only if AD increases in an economy that is already producing at or close to full employment. An economy in a recession, with lots of spare capacity, is unlikely to experience demand-pull inflation. Figure 16.5 shows an economy with a recessionary gap experiencing an increase in AD, but no increase in inflation.

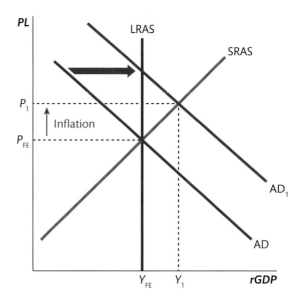

Figure 16.4 Rising demand creates **demand-pull inflation** in the AD-AS model

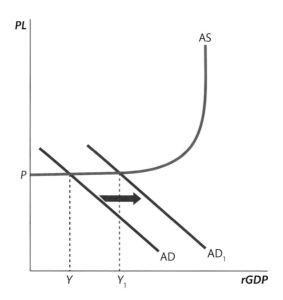

Figure 16.5 The Keynesian model predicts no demand-pull inflation in an economy in a deep recession due to the existence of spare capacity

What is cost-push inflation?

Cost-push inflation, shown in Figure 16.6, occurs as the result of a negative supply shock. This arises from a sudden, often unanticipated, increase in the costs of production for the nation's producers. Cost-push inflation could result from a change in any of the determinants of short-run aggregate supply (SRAS) that causes SRAS to decrease, including an increase in the wage rate, in resources costs, in energy or transportation costs, in business taxes, or a decrease in the exchange rate (causing imported raw materials to become more expensive). A stricter regulatory framework imposed by the government can also cause cost-push inflation if enough of the nation's producers are forced to implement costly new production methods.

Notice one big difference between demand-pull and cost-push inflation: when AD increases and pulls prices up with it, it is also accompanied by a short-run increase in aggregate output (real GDP). Meanwhile, cost-push inflation is accompanied by a fall in

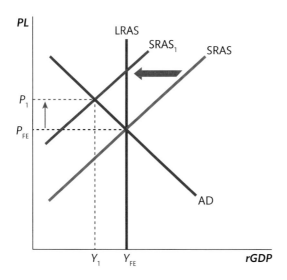

Figure 16.6   A shift in SRAS can result in **cost-push inflation** in the AD-AS model

output, or at the very least a decrease in the rate of economic growth. For this reason, cost-push inflation is sometimes referred to as *stagflation*, which combines the words 'stagnation' and 'inflation'. When SRAS decreases, the economy tends to stagnate, or stop growing. While stagflation does not always equate to a recession, it always means slower growth, since higher costs of production make it less profitable for an economy's producers to increase their output.

Considering demand-pull inflation once again, it might be tempting to argue that it is desirable, since it is also accompanied by an increase in real GDP. However, the short-run increase in output should not be confused with *economic growth* (which will be explored in more detail in Chapter 17). Rather, an economy that produces beyond its full employment level of output is not producing sustainably. Recall from Chapter 14 that when AD increases to an equilibrium beyond full employment, it is only a matter of time before wages and other costs become 'flexible' and begin to rise to adjust to the higher price level in the economy. Workers, who are given bargaining power in a tight labour market, will demand wage hikes that will eventually result in firms reducing their output and laying some of their workers off. The economy will self-adjust in the long run, with SRAS shifting left as wages increase, restoring the full employment level of output at a yet even higher price level.

For this reason, demand-pull inflation is just as undesirable as cost-push inflation and stagflation, since an increase in AD beyond full employment, if left unchecked by the government or the central bank, will lead to a decrease in SRAS and cost-push inflation in the long run.

In later chapters (19, 20, and 21), we will explore government and central bank policies to deal with both demand-pull and cost-push inflation. Here, we will next look at the costs of a high inflation rate to the economy.

What are the economic and social costs of a high inflation rate?

While we have hinted throughout the chapter at the reasons inflation is undesirable, we have yet to break down the costs it imposes on various stakeholders in society. Inflation does more than reduce the purchasing power of money.

Video suggestion:
You have read about it, now you can review what you have just learned by watching a video by the author!

▶ Simply click here in your eBook for a video on demand-pull and cost-push inflation.

Here are a few quotes from famous figures in history that point to some of the costs inflation can impose on society:

Milton Friedman: 'Inflation is the one form of taxation that can be imposed without legislation.'

John Maynard Keynes: 'By a continuing process of inflation, government can confiscate, secretly and unobserved, an important part of the wealth of their citizens.'

Margaret Thatcher: 'Inflation is the parent of unemployment and the unseen robber of those who have saved.'

Uncertainty

High inflation creates an environment of uncertainty among consumers and producers over future conditions. Expectations of higher prices in the future can drive demand for current inputs and outputs, creating shortages as producers struggle to keep up with rising demand. The inflationary spiral described earlier in this chapter is an almost inevitable result from unchecked inflation today. Rising demand leads to shortages, causing input and output prices to rise, causing cost-push inflation and even more demand for current output as buyers expect prices to rise even more.

Low and stable inflation, on the other hand, creates an environment of certainty and stability, as the expectation of moderate price increases prevents panic buying and the resulting inflationary spirals.

Redistributive effects

Another effect inflation has on society is the redistribution of wealth from one group to another. Businesses typically like some inflation, particularly of consumer prices, as it means the prices of the goods they sell increase over time, allowing them to enjoy higher profits. Consumers, on the other hand, find their wallets squeezed in an inflationary environment and must face tough choices about what to cut back on in order to make their money last.

Another redistributive effect of inflation is the transfer of wealth from lenders to borrowers. An individual or a country with lots of debt benefits from inflation, especially when the interest rate owed on that debt is fixed or rises more slowly than the inflation rate. Rising prices mean the value of money decreases, including the value of the money a debtor owes his or her lenders. Money borrowed is worth more than money repaid.

Effects on saving

The Thatcher quote above points to the negative effect inflation has on savers. When the inflation rate increases while interest rates remain the same, the *real rate of interest* savers earn decreases, and may even become negative. For example, assuming you have COL$4 million (COL$ is the symbol for the Colombian peso, the currency of Colombia) in a savings account earning 3% interest annually, as long as inflation remains below 3% the *real value* of your savings increases each year, since your nominal return will outpace the increase in the price level. However, if inflation rises to 4%, 5%, or even higher, every percentage by which inflation exceeds your **nominal interest rates** represents a 1% decrease in the real value of your savings each year.

Remember, one definition of inflation is a 'decrease in the value of money over time'. Money saved decreases in value in an inflationary environment, which also explains why inflation encouraged consumption over savings.

Damage to export competitiveness

On an international level, inflation erodes a country's competitiveness with other economies as domestic prices rise and make the exports less attractive to foreign consumers. Higher domestic inflation will also make imports more attractive to domestic consumers, as prices abroad may be rising less than prices at home. As exports decrease and imports increase the net exports component of AD falls, but more importantly, domestic firms will find demand for their goods at home and abroad to be less than in an environment of low and stable inflation.

Impact on economic growth

Inflation is an expected companion of economic growth. Rising prices send the signal to a nation's producers that demand for output is growing, which leads firms to allocate more resources towards production and increase their output to meet growing demand. The increase in AD and AS that results is what is meant by economic growth: over time the real output of nations grows as prices increase steadily, driving more growth.

Too much inflation, however, creates scarcity and stymies growth. Once again we return to the story of the inflationary spiral. Demand-pull inflation leads to cost-push inflation as wages and other resource costs increase due to the inability of supply to keep up with demand. Low and stable inflation, on the other hand, promotes sustainable economic growth characterised by increasing AS and AD.

Inefficient resource allocation

The shortages inflation creates are a microeconomic phenomenon that can be associated with allocative inefficiency. When prices rise due to shortages, we have a situation in which the quantities supplied and demanded do not match. The marginal benefit of consumers is greater than the marginal cost to producers; in other words, consumers are willing to pay more for scarce goods, so the only way to reduce scarcity is for the price to rise, which reduces the quantity demanded and, over time, increases quantity supplied.

Allocative inefficiency arises in an inflationary environment, as markets fail to achieve equilibrium due to shortages of key inputs and scarcity of finished goods.

Video suggestion:
You have read about it, now you can review what you have just learned by watching a video by the author!
▶ Simply click here in your eBook for a video on the consequences of and solutions to high inflation.

16.2 What is deflation?

Learning outcomes

At the end of this section you will be able to:

- identify the causes of deflation—changes in AD or SRAS
- distinguish between disinflation and deflation
- examine the costs of deflation—uncertainty, redistributive effects, deferred consumption, association with high levels of cyclical unemployment and bankruptcies, increase in the real value of debt, inefficient resource allocation, policy ineffectiveness.

Inflation is one side of the CPI coin. When the price index increases, the cost of living of the typical household goes up and the real value of money goes down. When the CPI falls, the cost of living goes down and the value of money increases. Deflation is a sustained decrease in the average price of a nation's output over time. Deflation exists when the inflation rate is *negative*.

What are the causes of deflation?

Deflation has two causes: a decrease in AD or an increase in SRAS.

Changes in AD

A substantial and sustained decrease in AD can push a nation with low and stable inflation into a deflationary state. Assume, for example, an economy is experiencing 1% inflation. While this is a bit lower than the target inflation rate in most countries (2%–3%), it is still a low rate that should be consistent with economic growth. However, due to an unexpected collapse in the stock market, household wealth is negatively impacted and there is a fall in household consumption. The effect will be a negative demand shock, which will push the economy from economic growth into recession.

Figure 16.7 shows the effect of the negative demand shock on equilibrium national output, employment, and the average price level.

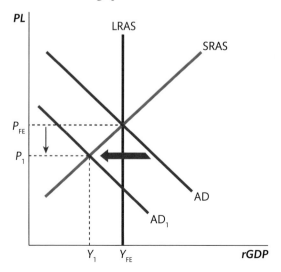

Figure 16.7 A sudden reduction in aggregate demand leads to lower national output, employment, and prices

The collapse in consumption has pushed the economy from price level stability into deflation. The CPI decreases due to a fall in demand for aggregate output and the inability of producers to adjust wages quickly enough to maintain full employment output. Prices decrease, forcing firms to lay workers off. The deflation is accompanied by rising unemployment and a recessionary gap (from Y_1 to Y_{FE}).

Changes in SRAS

Another cause of inflation is a *positive supply shock*. If the deflation caused by a fall in AD is unequivocally bad, then deflation caused by an increase in SRAS is, well, perhaps a good thing. A positive supply shock occurs when SRAS increases due to a decrease in resource costs, wage rates, business taxes, business regulations, or an increase in the value of the currency (causing imported raw materials to become cheaper), or any other factor that causes SRAS to increase.

Figure 16.8 shows the effect of a positive supply shock on equilibrium output, the average price level, and employment.

The supply shock has caused equilibrium output to increase from Y_{FE} to Y_1, while the average price level has decreased to P_1. Employment increases as costs of production fall, leading businesses to increase their output and therefore their demand for labour.

Deflation caused by a positive supply shock could be considered desirable since the fall in output and employment that accompanies deflation from a fall in AD do not occur. The question to consider is, however, whether the positive supply shock is a short-term phenomenon and will be offset by rising wages due to tight labour markets or whether it is permanent, and will eventually lead to an increase in long-run aggregate supply (LRAS) as well.

Only an increase in LRAS, as we will see in Chapter 17, can be considered economic growth. The increase in real GDP resulting from the positive supply shock may be short term, as the economy is producing beyond its full employment level. The resulting deflation and corresponding increase in the real value of people's incomes is unlikely to be maintained if the lower price level is only temporary.

Video suggestion:
You have read about it, now you can review what you have just learned by watching a video by the author!
► Simply click here in your eBook for a video on what causes deflation.

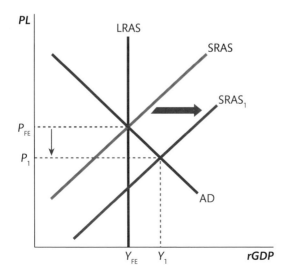

Figure 16.8 A sudden increase in aggregate supply leads to higher national output and employment but lower prices

Disinflation versus deflation

In reality, a decrease in AD or an increase in SRAS are unlikely to immediately cause deflation. Referring back to Figure 16.1 at the beginning of this chapter, only a few countries in the entire world experienced deflation in 2019. That is because the *typical* inflation rate a country producing at or close to full employment experiences is positive – as we have said most countries aim to maintain inflation of between 2% and 3%. However, in developing economies, inflation rates that are much higher are not uncommon. Across the 54 countries in sub-Saharan Africa, for instance, inflation averaged 8.38% in 2019 and 9.32% in 2020. A decrease in AD in one of these countries, therefore, is unlikely to immediately result in deflation, since the inflation rate is already so far in the positive.

The more likely result from a negative demand shock or a positive supply shock, therefore, is *disinflation*, or a decrease in the inflation rate. Typically, disinflation is considered a *good thing*, since bringing inflation down to the 'low and stable' level of 2–3% promotes macroeconomic stability and economic growth. The exception is when an economy is already within its desired range; in such a case disinflation is the first step towards deflation.

What are the costs of deflation?

Many of the costs of deflation will sound similar to those of inflation, only for the opposite reasons. Therefore, we'll summarise them briefly where possible.

Uncertainty

Inflation creates uncertainty about higher prices in the future, deflation about lower prices. When prices are expected to fall businesses will reduce output now and lay off workers in expectation of reduced revenues and profits tomorrow. The resulting uncertainty permeates throughout the economy, depressing both consumer and producer confidence and throwing the economy into a deflationary spiral of falling demand, deflation, high unemployment, and recession.

Redistributive effects

Whereas inflation redistributes wealth from lenders to borrowers, deflation does the opposite. The real burden of a debt increases when prices fall, as the value of the money that has to be repaid is greater than the value of the money that was borrowed. Additionally, while inflation reduces the **real interest rates** on loans, deflation increases the real cost of borrowing. For example, with a nominal interest rate of 3%, and an inflation rate of 2%, the real cost to the borrower of a loan is only 1% (since inflation reduces the value of the money that is repaid). However, with deflation of 2%, the real interest rate is 3% − (−2%), or 3% + 2%, which is 5%. Lenders are better off when there is deflation, while those who borrowed money in the past are worse off. Wealth is redistributed from those who *owe money* to those who are *owed money*.

Deferred consumption

Deflation shifts consumers' expectations towards lower prices in the future, thus affecting the psychology of consumers today. The rational thing to do when prices are expected to fall is to *defer consumption*, or delay purchases until the future when your money will go further. The result is a decrease in current consumption and a fall in AD, along with all the negative consequences a negative demand shock has on employment and output.

Association with high levels of cyclical unemployment and bankruptcies

When prices fall, businesses find it hard to both continue paying their workers and servicing their debts. Businesses have debts for all sorts of reasons, from the mortgages on office or factory space to money borrowed for the purchase of capital equipment. When revenues decrease in a deflationary environment, servicing their debts becomes more difficult for firms, and bankruptcies might result. When firms across the economy go bankrupt, the owners of their debt likewise experience a decrease in the value of their assets, reducing wealth and consumption across the economy.

Cyclical unemployment is that which results from a decrease in AD (Chapter 15). In a deflationary environment, the unemployment rate will increase above the natural rate, indicating cyclical unemployment. When workers whose skills would normally be in demand in a 'healthy' economy lose their jobs, the economy as a whole underperforms, indicating inefficiency and an underutilisation of resources.

Inefficient resource allocation, policy ineffectiveness

Inflation, recall, results from shortages in key inputs and outputs. Deflation, on the other hand, is evidence of surplus goods in the economy. A surplus arises when the quantity supplied exceeds the quantity demanded in the market for a particular good, leading to the good's price to fall over time. Deflation is evidence of this on a macro scale: the amount of output supplied exceeds the amount demanded, meaning prices must fall to clear the markets. Allocative inefficiency results; individual markets are producing at a level of output where the marginal costs of producers exceed the marginal benefits of consumers.

Microeconomic disequilibria correspond with a macroeconomic disequilibrium; the economy is producing below full employment and will only adjust once wages have fallen or aggregate demand increases to a level where it meets aggregate supply at an equilibrium price level and real GDP.

Video suggestion:
You have read about it, now you can review what you have just learned by watching a video by the author!
Simply click here in your eBook for a video on the consequences of and solutions to deflation.

16.3 HL Potential conflict between macroeconomic objectives – low unemployment and low inflation

Learning outcomes

At the end of this section you will be able to:

- draw SRPC and LRPC diagrams showing the relationship between unemployment and inflation
- discuss the view that there is a possible trade-off between the unemployment rate and the inflation rate in the short run
- examine stagflation with reference to an outward shift in the SRPC due to a decrease in SRAS
- evaluate the view that the LRPC is vertical at the natural rate of unemployment.

In the pursuit of certain objectives economic policymakers often find themselves running into conflicts between those objectives. In the pursuit of a more efficient free market, for instance, greater inequality might emerge as tax rates are cut on

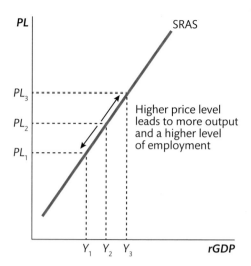

high-income earners and corporations. In the pursuit of economic growth society might face a higher level of environmental degradation. One such potential conflict that might result from the pursuit of the two macro objectives we have examined in Chapters 15 and 16 is that between low unemployment and low inflation.

As we learned when studying short-run aggregate supply in Chapter 14, when the average price level increases, output increases in the short run. At higher levels of output, firms employ more workers; therefore, unemployment decreases as the price level increases. When the average price level decreases, output decreases in the short run. At lower levels of output, firms employ fewer workers; therefore, unemployment increases as the price level decreases.

Figure 16.9 illustrates the relationship between the average price level and employment in the short run, using an SRAS curve.

Owing to the stickiness of wages and other input costs, there tends to be a short-run trade-off between inflation and unemployment. As the price level increases, unemployment decreases and as the price level decreases, unemployment increases. In the long run, as we will see, this relationship does not hold, and there is no trade-off between inflation and unemployment.

The short-run Phillips curve

The short-run trade-off between inflation and unemployment is so fundamental to macroeconomics that economists have developed a model just to illustrate this relationship, the **short-run Phillips curve (SRPC)**. The **Phillips curve** model shows the rate of inflation on the vertical axis and the unemployment rate on the horizontal axis. The curve itself is downward sloping, showing the inverse relationship between the two indicators in the short run.

Assume that in the country represented by the Phillips curve in Figure 16.10 the natural rate of unemployment is 5% and the target inflation rate is between 2% and 3%.

Points along a country's SRPC correspond with different combinations of inflation and unemployment that the economy might experience in the short run.

- At point A the inflation rate is 5% and unemployment is at less than 1%. The economy is producing beyond full employment with a positive output gap.

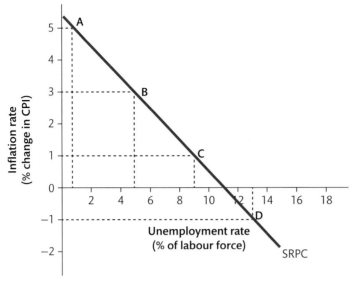

Figure 16.10 The short-run Phillips curve illustrates the fundamental relationship between the rate of inflation and the unemployment rate

- At point B inflation is within the target range of 2–3% and unemployment is 5%, close to the natural rate of unemployment.
- At point C the economy has lower than desired inflation of 1% and unemployment that is greater than the natural rate at 9%. The economy has a recessionary gap.
- At point D the economy has inflation of −1% (deflation) and unemployment of 13%. The economy is experiencing a deep recession.

The long-run Phillips curve

The long-run relationship between inflation and unemployment can be illustrated by the **long-run Phillips curve (LRPC)**, which is vertical at the natural rate of unemployment. Recall from our study of the AD-AS model that the LRAS curve is vertical at the full employment level of output, explained by the fact that wages and other input costs are fully flexible in the long run. Since output always returns to the full employment level in the long run, the unemployment rate will always return to the natural rate of unemployment (NRU).

Figure 16.11 shows both the SRPC and the LRPC, which is vertical at the country's NRU of 5%.

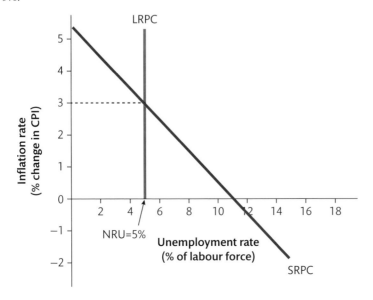

Figure 16.11 The long-run Phillips curve is vertical at the natural rate of unemployment

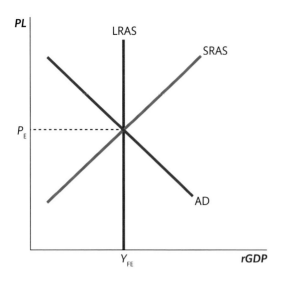

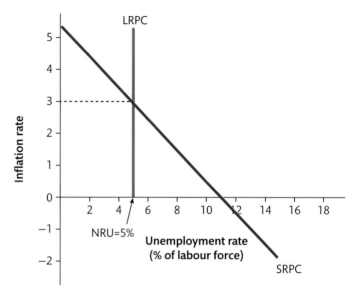

Figure 16.12 AD-AS and the Phillips curve models in long-run equilibrium

Long-run equilibrium corresponds to the intersection of the SRPC and the LRPC. In the short run, when wages and other input prices are fixed, an economy can produce anywhere along its SRPC. However, in the long run, when all prices are flexible, a country will return to its NRU.

Demand shocks in the Phillips curve model

Changes to aggregate demand cause a movement along a country's SRPC. Assume a country is currently producing at its full employment level and is in its long-run equilibrium in both the AD-AS model and the Phillips curve model, as in Figure 16.12.

Let us examine how shocks to AD and SRAS will affect the short-run and long-run Phillips curves.

Positive demand shocks

Figure 16.13 Positive demand shock in the AD-AS and Phillips curve models

A positive demand shock will cause an increase in output, employment, and the price level in the AD-AS model, and a movement up and to the left along the SRPC in the Phillips curve model, as seen in Figure 16.13.

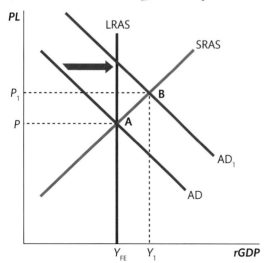

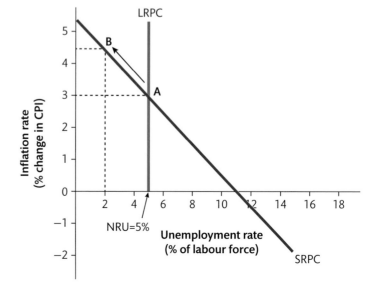

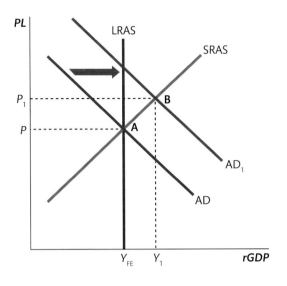

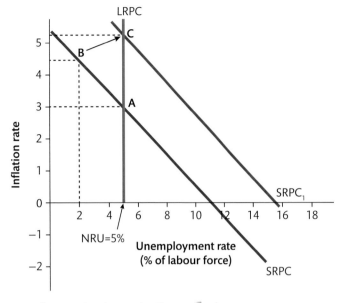

A move from point A to B in the AD-AS model causes a move from point A to point B in the Phillips curve model.

In the long run, an economy producing at point B (beyond full employment) will experience rising wages and input costs, causing the SRAS to decrease and output to return to the full employment level. As this happens, inflation will increase and unemployment will return to the NRU in the Phillips curve model, as seen in Figure 16.14.

Rising wages and other input prices causes the SRAS to shift in, restoring full employment in the AD-AS model at a higher price level. The inward shift of the SRAS causes an outward shift of the SRPC, restoring the NRU in the Phillips curve model at a higher inflation rate.

Negative demand shocks

A negative demand shock will cause a decrease in output, employment, and the price level in the AD-AS model, and a movement down and to the right along the SRPC in the Phillips curve model, as seen in Figure 16.15.

▲
Figure 16.14   Long-run self-adjustment in the AD-AS and Phillips curve models following a positive demand shock

Figure 16.15   Negative demand shock in the AD-AS and Phillips curve models
▼

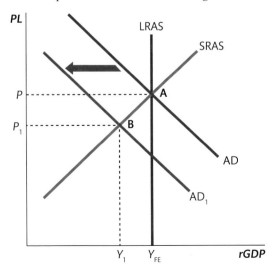

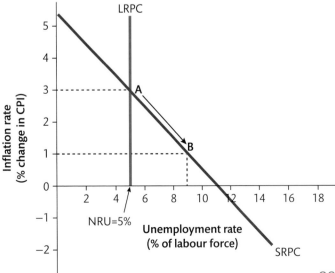

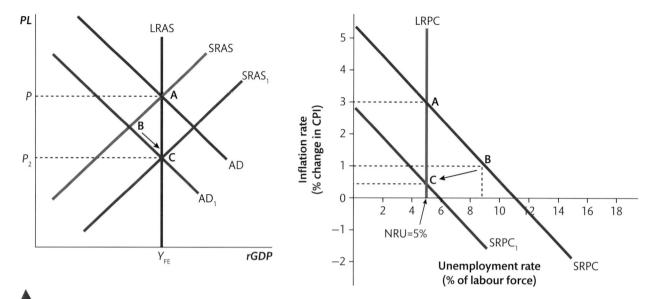

▲

Figure 16.16 Long-run self-adjustment following a negative demand shock in the AD-AS and Phillips curve models

A move from point A to B in the AD-AS model causes a move from point A to point B in the Phillips curve model.

In the long run, an economy producing at point B (below full employment) will experience falling wages and input costs, causing the SRAS to increase and output to return to the full employment level. As this happens, inflation will decrease and unemployment will return to the NRU in the Phillips curve model, as in Figure 16.16.

Falling wages and other input prices caused the SRAS to shift out, restoring full employment in the AD-AS model at a lower price level. The outward shift of the SRAS causes an inward shift of the SRPC, restoring the NRU in the Phillips curve model at a lower inflation rate.

Supply shocks in the Phillips curve model

Whenever a factor leads to a shift in the SRAS curve, the SRPC shifts in the opposite direction.

A negative supply shock causes both higher inflation and higher unemployment. For example, assume there is an unexpected increase in energy prices. SRAS will shift in as the cost of producing output increases. Firms reduce both employment and output, while raising prices to consumers.

A negative supply shock causes higher inflation and higher unemployment. A country experiences stagflation when SRAS shifts in and the SRPC shifts out.

A positive supply shock leads to more output and employment and lower prices. The SRPC shifts inward, allowing a country to enjoy both lower inflation and lower unemployment.

A positive supply shock causes output to increase and the price level to fall. More output means lower unemployment and a lower price level means lower inflation, as shown in Figure 16.18.

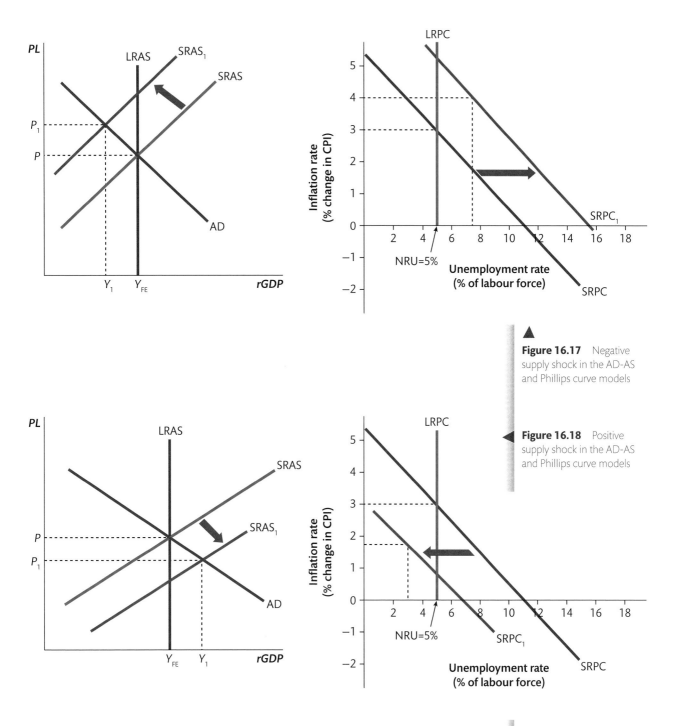

Figure 16.17 Negative supply shock in the AD-AS and Phillips curve models

Figure 16.18 Positive supply shock in the AD-AS and Phillips curve models

Shifts of the LRPC

Factors that cause the NRU to change will cause a shift of the LRPC. Recall that the NRU consists of two types of unemployment.

- Structural unemployment that arises due to changing technology or other factors that result in a mismatch between the skills of a nation's workforce and the needs of employers.
- Frictional unemployment that arises from workers who are between jobs and cannot quickly and easily be matched up with firms that demand labour.

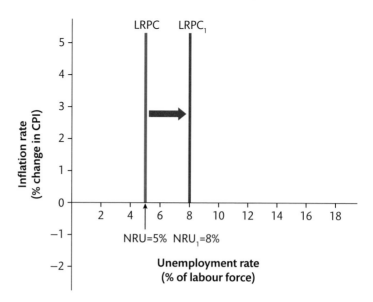

Figure 16.19 An outward shift of the long-run Phillips curve ▶

Video suggestions:
You have read about it, now you can review what you have just learned by watching some videos by the author! ▶ Simply click here in your eBook for videos on the SRPC and the LRPC.

TOK

As our discussion of the Phillips curve demonstrates, there are often conflicts between important macroeconomic objectives. So, which is more important, low inflation or low unemployment? What kind of knowledge criteria should policymakers use to make decisions in favour of pursuing one objective over another?

An increase in structural or frictional unemployment causes an outward shift of the LRPC and a higher NRU, as shown in Figure 16.19.

A decrease in structural or frictional unemployment causes an inward shift of the LRPC and a lower NRU.

Is the Phillips curve model still applicable?

In the decade since the Great Recession of 2008–10 the applicability of the Phillips curve model has been called into question, as the rich economies of Western Europe, East Asia, and North America saw unemployment rates decline from historically high levels during the recession back to, or even below, their natural rates of unemployment by late 2019 (before the onset of the COVID-19 recessions). As employment and output recovered throughout the 2010s, the Phillips curve model would have predicted rising inflation. What happened instead, however, was an apparent 'flattening' of

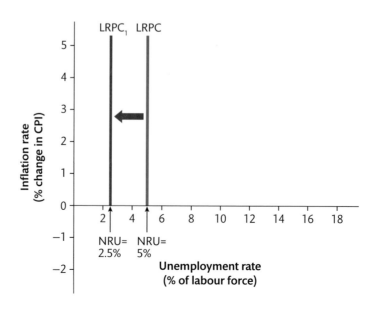

Figure 16.20 An inward shift of the long-run Phillips curve ▶

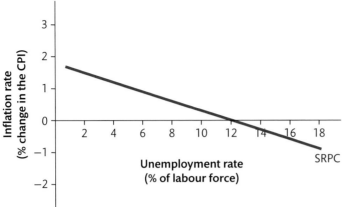

Figure 16.21 There has been a 'flattening' of the Phillips curve since 2010

the SRPC. While unemployment rates fell, inflation rates remained at or only slightly above their recession levels, with many countries struggling to meet even the lower range of their target inflation rates.

The result is a Phillips curve that has flattened out, meaning that the inflation rate has become less responsive to changes in the unemployment rate, as in Figure 16.21.

According to Phillips theory, economic recoveries following a recession should be characterised by falling unemployment and rising inflation, until the NRU is restored. Continued decreases in unemployment below the NRU should cause wages to climb and inflation to accelerate, keeping the rate of expansion in check and forcing output to be restrained by rising costs. However, in the decade since the Great Recession ended, unemployment rates have mostly continued to decrease while inflation has remained below the target rate.

Possible explanations for this breakdown in the inflation/unemployment trade-off are that the unemployment rate might misstate the amount of spare capacity or 'slack' in the economy. As unemployment fell in the USA, Europe, and Japan throughout the 2010s, people who had not been participating in the labour force (women, older folks, students, etc.), who had not been counted as unemployed, were tempted back into work, allowing for expansion without inflation.

Another possible disinflationary influence in the rich world could be the increased globalisation of supply chains, allowing for an increasing number of goods that might have been produced domestically, and thus subject to rising prices as labour markets tightened, to be imported from lower cost countries like China. Although given the relatively small share of rich countries' CPIs made up of imported goods, this theory has its limitations.

The final explanation might just be that prices take time to adjust, and tightening labour markets have not translated into higher inflation due to the stickiness of wages and other costs. Had the world's economies not slipped into another recession in 2020, it is possible that the inflation predicted to result from low unemployment by the Phillips curve could have set in. The COVID-19 induced recessions of 2020, however, have thrown the model into question once more, as unemployment rates climbed throughout 2020, yet inflation rates remained relatively unresponsive. Time will tell whether the Phillips curve model still has a place in economic textbooks as the world crawls its way back towards full employment in the years to come.

Research and inquiry

How have inflation and unemployment changed in the years since the Great Recession and since the COVID-19 recessions of 2020? Follow the link here, https://bit.ly/32al26d, to the GapMinder tool, which allows you to track economic variables for different countries over time. A few developed economies have already been selected for you, but you may choose your own country or any others that you like, to answer the questions that follow.

You can control the years for which data is displayed by using the slider tool at the bottom of the chart. Change the year and watch how the two indicators have changed over time in the countries you selected.

For discussion and debate:

Consider the following questions after observing changes in unemployment and inflation over time.

1 Is there a decade in the last 60 years during which the relationship between inflation and unemployment predicted by the Phillips curve model was most apparent?

2 Describe the relationship between inflation and unemployment in your selected countries over the years since 2008. Does it match what is predicted by the Phillips curve?

Research and inquiry cont.

3 Select three countries: Mexico, the USA, and Germany. Scroll through time over the last 50 years. Is there an 'average' long-run unemployment rate around which the three countries tend to hover? If so, what are they? Why might some countries' natural rates of unemployment be higher or lower than others?

4 Select three countries: Japan, Turkey, and Hungary. Is there an 'average' inflation rate around which the three countries tend to hover? If so, what are they? Why might some countries' average inflation rates be higher or lower than other countries?

Practice exam questions

1. Use the data in the table below to answer the questions that follow.

Year	CPI	Inflation rate (from previous year)
2020	105.3	2.2
2021	106.4	1.0
2022	105.8	—
2023	—	3.2

a. Calculate the missing inflation rate between 2021 and 2022. (2 marks)
b. Calculate the missing CPI for 2023. (2 marks)
c. Explain why governments weight categories in the measurement of a nation's CPI. (2 marks)
2a. Explain the difference between cost-push and demand-pull inflation. (10 marks)

b. Discuss the view that inflation of any amount is undesirable. (15 marks)
3. Outline three limitations to the Consumer Price Index as a means of measuring inflation. (6 marks)
4. Distinguish between deflation and disinflation. (4 marks)
5. What are two factors that can cause a movement along a country's short-run Phillips curve? (4 marks)
6. Outline the consequences of deflation for different stakeholders in an economy. (10 marks)

Macroeconomic objective: economic growth

17

Learning outcomes

At the end of this section you will be able to:

- define economic growth as an increase in real GDP
- calculate the rate of economic growth from a set of data.

'A rising tide lifts all boats.'

– New England Chamber of Commerce, 1960s

The essential truth in this old aphorism suggests that a growing economy will offer prosperity for all. Economic growth is defined as the growth of the real value of output in an economy over time, usually measured as growth in real gross domestic product (GDP). Growth, to put it plainly, is good. This, at least, is the established consensus among macroeconomic policymakers. As a nation's output increases over time, the quantity and quality of goods and services available to the people of the nation increases. One expects that such growth can be used well, and a country can raise its standard of living year by year.

In Chapter 15, you learned about the ways an economy's size can be measured. Generally, GDP or gross national income (GNI) are the primary statistics used for comparisons between countries and within countries over time. Also, one should expect to measure GDP using 'real' or 'purchasing power parity' GDP calculations to adjust for inflation or deflation. In this chapter, we will add to your understanding of economic growth by using new calculations, reviewing our diagramming of economic growth, and discussing the ways growth can go right and wrong.

What is the economic growth rate?

The standard statistic used for measuring economic growth is called the economic growth rate (GR). It is the percentage increase or decrease in real GDP over the previous year. Economists measure the rate of economic growth in a nation by comparing the total value of the output of one year to the output of the previous year. The GR in real GDP is found by the formula:

$$GR = \frac{GDP_2 - GDP_1}{GDP_1} \times 100$$

Economic GRs vary from country to country for year after year based on the macroeconomic conditions within each country. A positive GR indicates the total output of goods and services has increased from one year to the next. Negative growth is evidence of a recession, caused by either a decrease in aggregate demand (AD) or a decrease in aggregate supply (AS). However, a fall in the rate of growth does not necessarily mean an economy is experiencing a recession, rather that the level of output is increasing at a slower rate.

Calculating economic growth

Consider these GDP figures for Egypt:

Year	Real GDP (constant prices, US$)
2014	965,888,437
2015	1,008,117,312
2016	1,051,396,500
2017	1,095,920,375

To calculate the real GDP GR we use the formula:

$$GR = \frac{(GDP_2 - GDP_1)}{GDP_1} \times 100$$

So, in 2015 the GR is:

$$\frac{(1,008,117,312 - 967,888,437)}{967,888,437} \times 100$$

$$= \frac{40,228,875}{967,888,437} \times 100$$

$$= 4.15\%$$

For 2016 the calculation is:

$$\frac{(1,051,396,500 - 1,008,117,312)}{1,008,117,312} \times 100$$

$$= \frac{43,279,188}{1,008,117,312} \times 100$$

$$= 4.29\%$$

And in 2017 it is:

$$\frac{(1,095,920,375 - 1,051,396,500)}{1,051,396,500} \times 100$$

$$= 4.23\%$$

Exercise 17.1

Calculate the value of the GDP GR for 2013 and 2014.

Year	Real GDP (US$, 2017 prices)
2012	37,089,000,000
2013	38,136,000,000
2014	40,658,000,000

Learning outcomes

At the end of this section you will be able to:

- use a PPC curve to illustrate two types of economic growth
- explain, using a diagram, the manner in which a change in AD causes economic growth
- explain, using an LRAS diagram, how sustained economic growth is caused by increases in the productivity, technology, or an increase in the quantity or quality of the factors of production.

PPCs and economic growth

Recall that a production possibility curve (PPC) model is designed to show several economic concepts, among them scarcity, opportunity cost, and trade-offs, but also economic growth. Figure 17.1 shows a country whose two goods are consumer and capital goods. Figure 17.1 illustrates growth in two ways.

Movement from within the PPC to a point on the PPC line

Point X is inside the nation's PPC, indicating that the economy's resources are underemployed or not being used to their greatest efficiency. If the nation were to move from point X to points A or B (both on the PPC), then the nation would experience an overall increase in the total output of goods and services, achieving economic growth. This would correspond with a movement from below full employment in the AD/AS model to a level of output at which the AD curve intersects the long-run aggregate supply (LRAS) curve at the full employment level of output.

Figure 17.1 The PPC model can show two types of economic growth

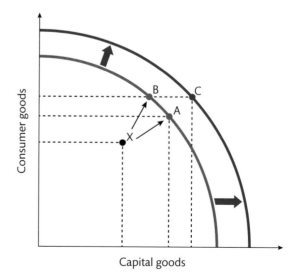

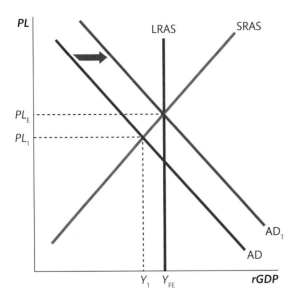

Figure 17.2 An increase in AD leads to an increase in real GDP and economic growth

Economic growth shown as an increase in potential output

An outward shift of a nation's PPC shows that the nation is able to produce and consume more of everything. A movement from point A to point C in Figure 17.1 is only possible through an increase in the quality or quantity of the nation's productive resources, or improved productivity. Increases in these areas could lead to economic growth shown by an outward shift of a nation's PPC. This shift is equivalent to an increase in a country's LRAS, shown in Figure 17.3.

AD/AS and economic growth

Short-run growth

The most useful and detailed model for illustrating economic growth in both the long run and the short run is the AD/AS diagram (Figure 17.2). Economic growth occurs any time a nation's GDP increases. An increase in GDP occurs any time AD increases when an economy is below its full employment level of output. An economy in a recession that begins to recover is, therefore, technically growing as output returns to its full employment level. On a PPC, this is similar to a movement from X to C in Figure 17.1 above.

Long-run growth

As we know from Chapter 14 when we studied AD/AS theory in the long-run, movements of AD by themselves only produce short run changes in growth. In Figure 17.2, during a recession, a rise in AD may fill a recessionary gap. If the economy were starting from Y_{FE}, full employment, a rise in AD would provide a burst of extra activity, as well as higher price levels, but eventually short run aggregate supply (SRAS) would shift left and the economy would land back at Y_{FE} with extra inflation. In short, only shifts of LRAS can increase long-run growth.

Figure 17.3 shows an economy experiencing long-run economic growth. Whatever changes in AD and SRAS occur, sufficient and sustained changes to productivity or in the factors of production produce a shift of LRAS, one which corresponds to an outward movement of the PPC. The increase in LRAS is what allows this economy

Video suggestions:
You have read about it, now you can review what you have just learned by watching a few videos by the author!
▶ Simply click here in your eBook for videos on economic growth in the short run and long run, in the AD/AS model and in the PPC – the capital versus consumer goods trade-off.

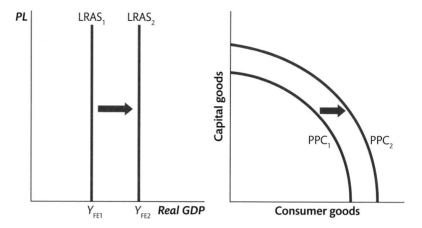

Figure 17.3 Long-run growth involves a shift of LRAS corresponding to an outward shift of the PPC

to achieve a greater level of output in the long run. Without increases in LRAS, this economy's ability to grow is restrained to the full employment level by its limited supply of land, labour, and capital.

17.3 What are the potential consequences of economic growth?

Learning outcomes

At the end of this section you will be able to:

- analyse the impact of growth on living standards
- discuss the possible conflicts between growth and aims of low inflation, environmental protection and sustainability, and income distribution.

While the notion that growth is positive for society may seem obvious, it is worthwhile to identify how growth can affect specific macroeconomic goals and concerns.

Economic growth's impact on living standards

An expanding economy by definition helps people reduce the constraints of scarcity. More of our unlimited wants are likely to be satisfied in a growing economy. Some of those gains will come from better buying power. More income may allow families to buy more nutritious food, or consume greater levels of healthcare than before, leading to greater life satisfaction. Expansion may raise incomes enough to allow people to work less and increase their leisure time or time with friends and family. Moreover, higher income may relieve the strain that money can place on families and improve the stability of marriages and child-rearing.

On a more mundane level, rising GDP will increase tax revenues, allowing the government to buy merit and public goods, increasing living standards. Also, if one assumes that the general quality of consumer goods and services rises over time, one's enjoyment of better cars, appliances, furniture, and entertainment technology can make life more enjoyable.

Sources of potential success and conflict between macroeconomic objectives

Growth can broadly support and also diminish achievements in macroeconomic progress, depending on the composition of increased output.

Economic growth and low inflation

As demonstrated by the short-run Phillips curve (SRPC), the relationship between full employment and inflation is often a negative one. Increases of AD, in particular, are likely to increase growth (corresponding to lower unemployment), while raising prices and thus increasing inflation. Calibrating monetary and fiscal policy to create just the right level of growth, a level that will not push spending too far (beyond a country's ability to match that spending with more goods and services), is a difficult and sophisticated task.

Economic growth's impact on the environment and sustainability

Here the effects of growth depend almost entirely on the composition of output and the manner in which it was made. Clearly, some types of production generate significant environmental spillover costs. As noted in Chapter 10, fossil fuels power or supplement quite a lot of raw economic growth. That growth creates significant and growing risk of climate change, and all the potentially massive planetary consequences that come with it. A region or country that chooses growth in land development, carbon-based power production like coal-electric power, or the relaxing of environmental rules to lure companies to their economy, is choosing immediate growth over sustainable development. However, large investments in green infrastructure would be reflected as positive in environmental terms as well as higher growth numbers.

Emissions from a coal power station

Economic growth's impact on income distribution

Growth does not necessarily lead to rising standards of living. As noted previously, growth may not be distributed evenly, and the gains from growth may be rather tightly concentrated among the wealthy. It is not uncommon for rapidly growing countries to experience large disparities between the relatively rich and poor. In rich countries, these widening gaps are highly correlated with increased social problems. That said, growth provides the resources to correct inequality and redistribute income. Growth may raise tax revenues, especially if the tax system is progressive, and increase spending on merit goods like healthcare and education. A progressive tax rate can also simply reduce inequality by reducing after-tax incomes among the rich and reducing the tax burden on the poor.

Practice exam questions

Paper 1, part (a) question

1. Explain, using a diagram, the difference between short-run economic growth and long-run economic growth. (10 marks)

Paper 2, part (b) question

2. Using real-world examples, discuss the positive and negative effects of economic growth. (15 marks)

Paper 2: 4-mark questions

3. Explain, using a PPC diagram, two ways to show economic growth. (4 marks)
4. Using an AD/AS diagram, explain how an increase in population could lead to economic growth. (4 marks)

Economics of inequality and poverty

18

Learning outcomes

At the end of this section you will be able to:

- analyse the tension between the goals of economic efficiency and economic equality
- distinguish between equality and equity
- explain the difference between distributions of income and of wealth.

What is the tension between efficiency and equality?

Market economies are considered proficient at several things:

- allocating resources efficiently, with the notable exception of externalities of market failure
- encouraging innovation and creativity when property rights exist to protect the inventions brought to market by entrepreneurs
- achieving increases in total output and average standards of living through the pursuit of self-interest and profits in labour, capital, and product markets.

For these reasons, market economies score well in areas of *efficiency*, or, in other words, getting the most out of the scarce resources that are available.

Planned economies, in which society's scarce resources are allocated not by the forces of supply and demand, rather by the very visible hand of the state, failed throughout the 20th century to achieve long-run growth and improvements in the overall living standards of people of the nations in which such economic systems were implemented. What command economies did manage to achieve to some extent, however, was relative equality in the distribution of the nation's income and output across the nation's people. However, critics of the socialist system pointed out that while such economies may have strived to achieve equality, by the time everyone was equal, they were equally poor.

Free market advantages in efficiency, however, are often accompanied by a reduction in equality. A major source of conflict in economics is that between efficiency and equality. There is nothing inherent in a market economy that promotes equality in the distribution of income and output. Freed from the organising principles of state control, most of the new free market 'transition economies' of the formerly communist sphere reported larger and larger gaps between rich and poor. Meanwhile, in the rest of the world, average incomes in most emerging market economies have risen, but the distribution of income has become increasingly unequal. Rich countries have observed the same pattern.

As inequality has grown sharply, more economists are wondering if the trade-off has swung too far in the direction of market efficiency and too far away from equity, especially in the area of income and wealth distribution. If economies are to be judged on overall economic well-being, they think, the social ills generated by inequality may themselves qualify as a form of market failure.

What is the distinction between equality and equity?

First, a distinction is helpful for this discussion. When referring to equity, a notion of fairness is paramount. More specifically, a society that is highly equitable is one where opportunities are accessible to all. This may mean that different people are treated differently to ensure the availability of opportunities. In contrast, equality can be interpreted to mean a standardised result for all. One could view measures to achieve equity as being in service to greater equality across the population, but not necessarily guaranteeing it.

Whereas the market system may fail to promote equity or equality due to the very system of incentives aimed at encouraging efficiency, these are not unachievable goals for economic policymakers. What is fair is not necessarily equal. For instance, a taxation system rooted in the idea that those who can afford to pay the highest tax rates should pay the highest tax rates, while those whose incomes are lowest should pay lower rates is not equal treatment (some are treated differently that others), but it is widely considered to be more equitable.

A market system can be equitable even if it cannot create total equality. To a certain extent, a free market economy is in fact more equitable than a command system, in that every individual is free to improve him- or herself through education and professional growth, and then make his or her labour available to the market. In the pursuit of self-interest, however, there are sometimes those who are left behind. In this regard, it is the responsibility of government to promote equity through policies that give every citizen in society a fair shot at achieving economic success in the free market.

What is the difference between income and wealth distribution?

The term *income* refers to the money earned in all forms over a period of time, typically one year. Wealth refers to the accumulation of income or assets up to that time. For example, a person might earn Ft3.6 million (Ft is the symbol for the forint, the currency of Hungary) in a year from various sources: a primary job, short-term employment projects, and perhaps rental income from a property. The same person may have much more (or less) in net wealth, say from the accumulated value of her savings, rental property, and the equity in her home that equals perhaps Ft17 million. The analysis that follows will largely explore differences in income, which is more flexibly adjusted by government policy, but will also consider inequities in wealth distribution, which tend to be more acute and enduring.

18.2 What is the distribution of income and how is it measured?

Learning outcomes

At the end of this section you will be able to:

- define income distribution and distinguish between relatively equal and unequal distribution of income
- analyse data on relative income shares of given percentages of the population to show differences in income distribution
- draw a **Lorenz curve** and explain its significance
- explain how the Gini index and coefficient is derived and interpreted
- HL build a Lorenz curve from income quintile data.

Economic inequality refers to the degree of distributions of both income and wealth. To what degree are they equal or unequal?

What is the distribution of income?

In order to determine the equality or inequality of income distribution across a nation's population, economists first use income shares, or rather how much of a nation's total income is earned by the richest and the poorest groups of households. Table 18.1 divides five nations' households into five quintiles representing the richest 20% of households down to the poorest 20% and then indicates what percentage of total income is earned by each quintile.

From Table 18.1 you can see that the highest concentration of income among the top 20% of households exists in South Africa, where the richest fifth of the population earns 68.9% of the income. The poorest fifth of South African households, on the other hand, earn only 2.5% of the nation's income. Algeria, another developing country with a population about one-third smaller than

Table 18.1   Income Distribution for Selected Countries (latest data sourced from 2014–2018)

Country	Percentage of total income earned by:					
	First quintile (lowest 20%)	**Second quintile (next to last 20%)**	**Third quintile (middle 20%)**	**Fourth quintile (next to top 20%)**	**Fifth quintile (top 20%)**	**Gini index**
(Perfect equality)	20	20	20	20	20	0
Czech Republic	10.2	14.7	17.7	22	35.4	24.9
Nigeria	7.1	16.2	17.48	22.7	42.4	35.1
Netherlands	8.8	13.8	17.5	22.3	37.6	28.5
Indonesia	6.9	10.9	15.2	22.1	44.9	37.8
Honduras	3.0	7.4	12.7	20.8	56.1	52.1
South Africa	2.4	4.8	8	16.5	68.2	63

South Africa's, displays a more even distribution of income; its richest 20% of households account for 37.6% of the income while the poorest earn 9.39%. Both South Africa and Algeria have large numbers of poor people, but the poorest 20% of people in South Africa are much poorer relative to the poorest 20% in Algeria. South Africa's poor have a much smaller 'slice of the gross domestic product (GDP) pie' than do Algeria's poor. And South Africa's richest are relatively much richer than the top income group in Algeria. Put simply, income is distributed less equally in South Africa than in Algeria.

What is the Lorenz curve?

The Lorenz curve is a graphical representation of a country's income distribution. It plots the cumulative percentage of the nation's income across the cumulative percentage of the population (Figure 18.1). As a general rule, the further away a country's Lorenz curve is from the 45-degree line of equality, the more un-equal the distribution of income.

The line of equality is the 45-degree line, representing a country in which each quintile (20%) of the population earns exactly the same income as each other quintile. No country has perfectly equal income distribution, therefore the line of equality is only used for comparison. The Lorenz curve in Figure 18.1 represents the data shown above for the Netherlands and Honduras. Starting at the origin, for Honduras, the bottom 20% of the population earns 3% of the income. Moving on to the next quintile, the bottom 40% of the population earn 10.4% of the income (3% + 8.4% = 11.4%). This process repeats until the last quintile, where the top 20% of income earners in Honduras account for around 56.1% of the national income.

For the Netherlands, the cumulative income is larger at each quintile, showing that each 20% of the population earns more relative income than in Honduras, keeping

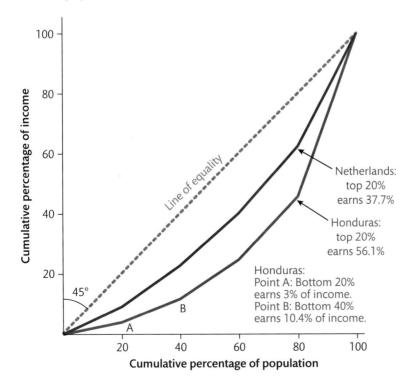

Figure 18.1 The Lorenz curve for the Netherlands and Honduras shows how far they are from a perfectly equal distribution of income

Video suggestion:
You have read about it, now you can review what you have just learned by watching a video by the author!

▶ Simply click here in your eBook for a video on the Lorenz curve and income distribution.

the Lorenz curve for the Netherlands closer to the 45-degree line of equality. As noted above, the top 20% of earners in the Netherlands earn significantly less proportion of total income, 37.7%, compared to 56.1% taken in by the top earners in Honduras. This demonstrates that more unequal distribution of income, the more bowed out (further away) a country's Lorenz curve and more equally distributed income countries will be closer.

What is the Gini coefficient?

Rather than draw Lorenz curves for every country to illustrate the level of income inequality, economists use a tool called the Gini coefficient to quantify the degree of income inequality in a nation. The Gini coefficient is the ratio of the area above a country's Lorenz curve and below the line of equality to the total area below the line of equality. In Figure 18.2, the Gini coefficient is the ratio of area A to the area A + B. The further away the Lorenz curve is from the line of equality, the greater the proportion of area A to the total area below the 45-degree line. Therefore, the higher the value of A ÷ (A + B), the greater the Gini coefficient and the more inequality exists in income distribution in the nation.

On Honduras' Lorenz curve, the ratio of area A to area A + B is 0.52, indicating that the area between the line of equality and the Lorenz curve makes up 52% of the total area below the line of equality. Honduras' Gini coefficient is 0.52.

What is the Gini index?

Economists more commonly refer to the Gini index. This is the Gini coefficient multiplied by 100. A Gini index of 100 would indicate perfect inequality of income distribution in the nation. The top 1% of the population earns 100% of the income. This represents an extreme example and is not technically possible, since even in a

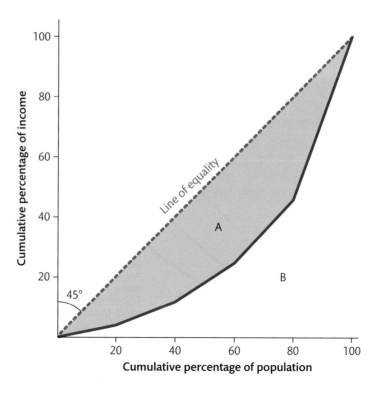

Figure 18.2 The **Gini coefficient** for Honduras is the ratio of area A to the whole of the area below the line of equality

Table 18.2   Gini index for selected countries

Country	Gini index (latest year available between 2015 and 2018)
Norway	27
Switzerland	32.7
Ethiopia	35
China	38.5
Indonesia	39
USA	41.4
Turkey	41.9
Ecuador	45.4
Brazil	53.9
Namibia	59.1

nation in which poverty is extremely widespread the large number of poor require some income just to survive.

On the other extreme, a Gini index of zero would indicate perfect equality of income distribution. The Lorenz curve would lie along the line of equality, meaning every household in the nation would enjoy an identical share of the national income. There would be neither rich nor poor citizens since everyone's income would be the same. Just as a Gini index of 100 is impossible, so is an index of zero. Even in the world's nominally egalitarian countries, such as the communist countries of the Soviet bloc, there existed a rich elite whose share of the national income was larger than others. This was because of their control of essential resources or political connections or corruption.

A Lorenz curve and the Gini index can provide useful comparisons in the income distribution between countries. See above in Table 18.2 showing countries with a range of Gini index values. While these measures of relative equality provide some indicator of relative position in each country, it is not a perfect predictor of levels of economic development. Countries with high development scores like the USA may have rather high Gini coefficients (41.4), while some relatively equal countries may do poorly in overall development terms, like Ethiopia (35). The Lorenz curve and Gini values are only a part of the overall picture in a given economy.

At the same time, these measures of inequality can be useful for comparing a single country's change in income distribution over time. As countries grow more unequal, they may reconsider policies to address it (covered below). If equality is desirable and rising, they can ask what policies are contributing to that and if it is worth any perceived trade-off with economic efficiency.

While it is important to avoid drawing firm conclusions about the link between inequality and development levels, one should consider the geographical evidence for income distribution as well. Figure 18.3 shows distribution of income across the world, based on data points over 20 years. This suggests some clusters of inequality in South America and Southern Africa, as well as patches of more equal distribution

Video suggestion:
You have read about it, now you can review what you have just learned by watching a video by the author!

▶ Simply click here in your eBook for a video on the Gini coefficient.

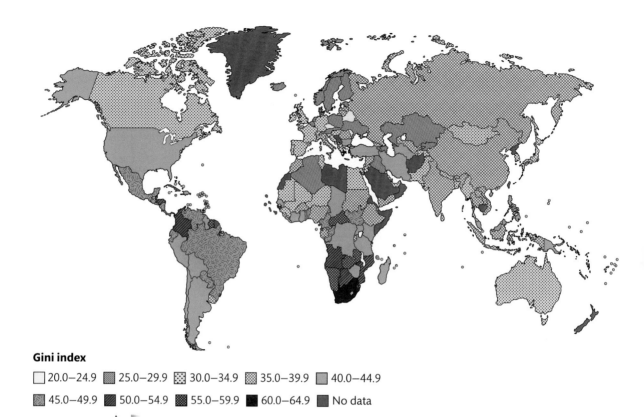

Gini index

| 20.0–24.9 | 25.0–29.9 | 30.0–34.9 | 35.0–39.9 | 40.0–44.9 |
| 45.0–49.9 | 50.0–54.9 | 55.0–59.9 | 60.0–64.9 | No data |

Figure 18.3 The areas towards the end of the key have more income inequality according to this world map, based on Gini index data, 1999–2019

HL How is a Lorenz curve constructed?

To build a Lorenz curve, one needs data on the income shares by quintile (20% shares) or decile (10% shares). With these numbers one can plot each point on the Lorenz curve to show cumulative income at each level.

Each point on the Lorenz curve represents the cumulative income of the poorest quintiles to that point. Thus, each point does not represent only the share of income earned by that quintile, but by all preceding quintiles. For example, in Japan the middle 20% of earners earn 17.30% of income. On the Lorenz curve, however, one

Table 18.3 Income shares and cumulative income shares by quintile for Japan

Quintile	Share of income (%)	Cumulative share of income (%)	Point on Figure 18.4
Lowest 20%	7.40	7.40	Bottom 20% = A
Second Lowest 20%	12.90	7.40 + 12.90 = 20.30	Bottom 40% = B
Middle 20%	17.30	7.40 + 12.90 + 17.30 = 37.6	Bottom 60% = C
Second Highest 20%	22.70	7.40 + 12.90 + 17.30 + 22.70 = 60.3	Bottom 80% = D
Highest 20%	39.70	7.40 + 12.90 + 17.30 + 22.70 + 60.3 = 100	Total 100% = E

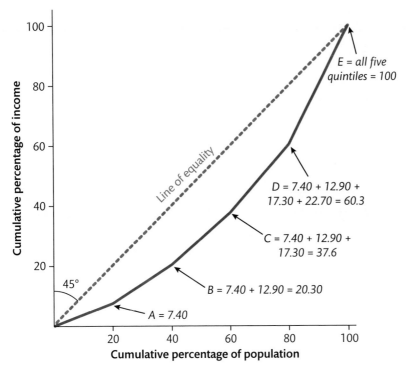

Figure 18.4 Each point on the Lorenz curve for Japan is the total of the income shares for the quintiles preceding it

adds that income to the second lowest (12.90%) and lowest quintile (7.40%) to get the cumulative income earned by the bottom 60% of earners, which is only 37.6% of income (7.40 + 12.90 + 17.30 = 37.6%). We can see this in Figure 18.4.

in Europe, Canada, and Australia. The patterns and differences in income distribution lead to more questions about the sources of inequality. In other words, why do some countries have more equality than others? This is discussed in section 18.3.

What is the distinction between income inequality and wealth inequality?

Income distribution takes into account the yearly earnings of households, without considering the total wealth accumulation. By examining wealth distribution, one can observe the historical summation of yearly income distribution. Some argue this is a better measure of rich and poor since wealth distribution accounts for what households currently own in terms of assets, rather than just what is been earned in a given year.

By this measure, global inequality is more extreme than mere income distribution would lead one to believe. Wealth measurement is more complicated than income measurement, especially when considering debt levels and determining the correct value of assets. Nevertheless, economists recognise that income distribution only tells part of the story, and are increasingly concerned about the concentration of wealth into fewer hands.

In Figure 18.5, notice the difference between countries shown previously with income distribution and compare their wealth distribution.

Sweden, for example, ranks highly in equal distribution of income, but appears to have wealth concentrated narrowly. Likewise, the USA, Russia, Brazil, India, and Saudi Arabia appear to be countries who have the greatest wealth concentrations.

Income inequality ▶

Why does wealth concentration matter? Two reasons stand out. First, if the market system is to work, in accordance with the 'invisible hand' of incentives that inspire competition, effort, and innovation, then rewards must be possible. Where wealth is concentrated without mobility, these incentives are blunted. In other words, if such wealth is transferred from generation to generation and it is difficult to rise up through one's own ingenuity or hard work, then the talents of the clever and hard working are unrewarded.

Figure 18.5 Compare this map of Gini coefficients of wealth inequality by country with the one at Figure 18.3 representing income inequality ▼

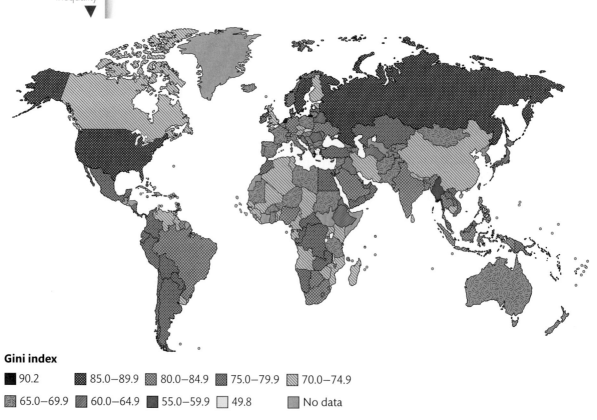

Gini index

- 90.2
- 85.0–89.9
- 80.0–84.9
- 75.0–79.9
- 70.0–74.9
- 65.0–69.9
- 60.0–64.9
- 55.0–59.9
- 49.8
- No data

Second, the concentration of wealth is likely to result in political power and dominance by an elite class. The greater the concentration of wealth, the more important a wealthy individual or family becomes as sources of influence, fundraising, and informal types of support for those seeking office or representation. While authoritarian regimes may simply reflect the merging of state and wealthy interests, such as with the Saudi royal family or Chinese Communist Party, democratic systems of government are also vulnerable to influence by the rise of a billionaire class that is perceived to pursue its own economic interests.

Case study – distribution of wealth

The Swiss bank Credit Suisse publishes a Wealth X Report and in 2019 it stated that 'the bottom half of adults account for less than 1% of total global wealth in mid-2019, while the richest decile (top 10% of adults) possesses 82% of global wealth and the top percentile alone owns nearly half (45%) of all household assets'.

Discussion questions:

1 What characteristics of the free market explain how such a disproportionate amount of global wealth could be held by such a small minority of global population?
2 What are the social and economic consequences of half the world's population holding only 1% of global wealth?
3 What role should the government play in redistributing wealth?
4 Can you think of two policies governments could employ to reduce the large gap in global wealth distribution?

18.3 How is poverty measured and how is it related to inequality?

Learning outcomes

At the end of this section you will be able to:

- distinguish between absolute and **relative poverty**
- explain how international **poverty lines** measure absolute poverty
- explain how standards of minimum income measure poverty levels
- analyse a country's performance using **composite indicators** of poverty
- discuss the difficulties in measuring poverty
- identify and explain the different major causes of inequality and poverty
- discuss the various impacts of income and wealth inequality.

What does it mean to be poor?

Despite the popular belief that there are rich countries and developing countries, in reality there is poverty in every country in the world. There are also incredibly rich people even in the world's least developed countries. So, it is an oversimplification to say that one country is rich while another is poor. Poverty exists everywhere; but in higher income countries, poverty is typically relative, while in the least developed countries, we are looking at absolute poverty. Notably, one of the goals of the **United Nations Sustainable Development Goals** is to 'end poverty in all its forms by 2030'.

Research and inquiry

The 20:20 ratio for income inequality

Economists have been developing new ways to quantify inequality. One that is growing in recognition is called both the 20:20 ratio, and also the 80:20 ratio. Both measure the same way by comparing the median income in the top 20% to the median income of the bottom 20%. That ratio expresses how much more the top earners make compared to the bottom. For example, the OECD ratio from 2015–19 shows that among OECD countries, the Slovak Republic has a 20:20 ratio of 3.2, meaning that on average the top 20% earn only 3.2 times that of the lowest 20%. Selected countries include the Netherlands (4.2), Japan (6.2), and the USA (8.4).

For discussion and debate:

1 Why might the 20:20 ratio be a more useful metric for understanding and communicating inequality than the other measures?

2 Search for the OECD 20:20 or 80:20 ratio and look at the span of countries and their values. Does this match your impression of the relative inequality for them?

3 Speculate as to what a country with a high ratio might do to reduce it, and what the countries at the low end might be doing to achieve this level.

Video suggestion:
You have read about it, now you can review what you have just learned by watching a video by the author! Simply click here in your eBook for a video on the 20:20 ratio as a tool for quantifying income inequality.

How does one distinguish between absolute and relative poverty?

For our purposes, we will define poverty as the scarcity or the lack of a certain amount of material possessions or money. Absolute poverty is measured in terms of the basic need for survival. It is the amount of income a person needs to have in order to stay alive. Relative poverty is a comparative measure of poverty. A person is said to be relatively poor if they do not reach some specified level of income, for example, 50% of average earnings for the country. Both measures convey different and useful measures of poverty.

How can absolute poverty measurements inform our understanding of poverty?

Measures of absolute poverty seek to quantify the number of people without the basic needs for survival including food, shelter, clothing, and basic levels of healthcare and education. International poverty lines are used to make meaningful comparisons between countries. The World Bank's international poverty line in 2020 was valued at $1.90 per day in international dollars in terms of 2011 purchasing power parity, which equalises its purchasing power across all countries and currencies.

The metric used by the World Bank is called the poverty headcount ratio, and by using purchasing power parity it translates the money income earned into wages needed to obtain basic needs. For higher cost of living countries, the poverty line would be higher in nominal terms, reflecting the higher price levels for goods and services. And in some very low-cost countries, it is possible to reduce the poverty line to a level below the $1.90 per day amount.

As one might expect, absolute poverty is more of a problem in developing countries. There has been significant progress in the reduction of absolute poverty (also known as extreme poverty) in the last 20 years. In its Sustainable Development Goals, the United Nations reports that 'Globally, the number of people living in extreme poverty declined from 36 per cent in 1990 to 10 per cent in 2015.' This is an enormous achievement worth marking. At the same time, nearly 700 million people, about 10% of the world's population, still languishes in abject poverty. More alarming is that the World Bank warns the gains of recent years may be entirely wiped out by the COVID-19 pandemic and oil price drop of the early 2020s.

Figure 18.6 shows the dramatic reduction in absolute poverty on a global scale, broken down by regional totals. In several regions extreme poverty has decreased, such as Latin America, East Asia, and South Asia. In some it has decreased only slightly, but from very low levels to start with, including the Middle East/North Africa, and Europe/Central Asia. Only in sub-Saharan Africa have such poverty levels continued to rise. While there will be more discussion of poverty in relation to economic development in the section of the course on the global economy, it is important to understand different measures of relative poverty.

If the average income of a nation rises and the income distribution remains the same, the level of relative poverty will stay the same, while the number of people in absolute poverty will decrease. It is important to keep this distinction in mind as we examine the efforts of policymakers to eradicate poverty. While absolute poverty may be reduced through international economic development strategies (Chapters 27–30),

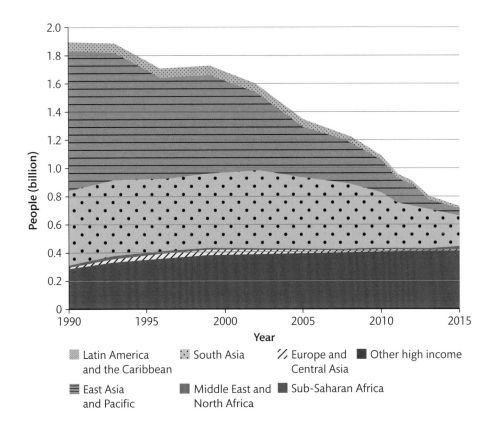

Figure 18.6 There was a marked reduction in the number of people in the world living in absolute poverty, 1990–2015

Legend:

- Latin America and the Caribbean
- South Asia
- Europe and Central Asia
- Other high income
- East Asia and Pacific
- Middle East and North Africa
- Sub-Saharan Africa

relative poverty persists and could lead to macroeconomic instability unless policies aimed at redistributing the nation's income is enacted on a national level. In other words, a country's economic growth may assuage absolute poverty, but may leave relative poverty, and the problems that go with it, in place.

How is relative poverty measured?

Relative poverty is measured in many ways, often according to a national approach that suits the government's macroeconomic goals.

Median income benchmarks

The OECD defines relative poverty as the percentage of people living with less than 50% of median equivalised disposable income. So, if the median income is approximately €22,000 per year in France, someone living on half of that, just €11,000, is at the relative poverty line.

Countries can define their relative poverty line in their own way. Some consider disposable income to be all income after housing payments, others include taxes. Some countries use a measure of 60% below median disposable income rather than 50%. However, the OECD has tried to standardise its estimate using the 50% benchmark. Figure 18.7 shows the relative poverty scores across OECD countries.

The measure shown in Figure 18.7 also shows disparities by gender. In nearly all countries women experience more relative poverty than men. Furthermore, those most likely to experience poverty in all countries are children, youth, the elderly, and women.

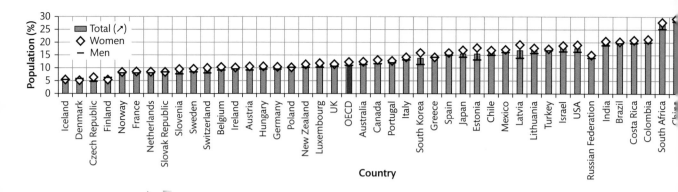

Figure 18.7 Percentage of persons living with less than 50% of median equivalised disposable income, by gender, in 2016 (or nearest year)

Minimum income standards

Another measure of relative poverty has been the creation and use of **minimum income standards (MIS)**. Also sometimes referred to as a 'living wage', the standard is the amount of income one needs to fully participate in society, not to merely get by on a subsistence level. MIS differs from statistical income benchmarks in its approach to identifying those needs. In the UK, MIS researchers ask focus groups of particular socioeconomic cohorts to identify the required goods and services to be included as essential. Different household types, because they have different needs, generate different lists. Older people, single adults, and different family sizes each have different lists and levels.

The 2020 UK estimate for a two person household, one adult and one small child, is shown in Table 18.4.

Table 18.4 UK Minimum Income Standard: the estimate for one adult and small child in 2020.

Weekly outgoings £656.34		Weekly income £656.34	
Food	£58.15	Pre-tax earnings	£789.81
Alcohol	£5.36	Income tax	£110.02
Clothing	£22.48	National insurance	£72.82
Water rates	£10.20	After tax earnings	£606.97
Council tax	£20.98	Working tax credits	£0.00
Household insurances	£1.36	Child benefit	£21.05
Gas, electricity, etc.	£15.55	Child tax credit	£28.32
Other housing costs	£1.92	Childcare tax credit	£0.00
Household goods	£20.71	Housing benefit	£0.00
Household services	£13.50	Council tax support	£0.00
Childcare	£251.76	Income support/Jobseeker's allowance	£0.00
Personal goods and services	£30.58		
Travel costs and motoring	£66.66		
Social and cultural activities	£51.60		
Rent	£85.53		
Mortgage	£0.00		

Note that a living wage is not the same as a minimum wage, which you learned about in Chapter 9. A minimum wage is the legal wage floor while the living wage may be well above this standard. For many researchers and living wage advocates, the point of identifying a living wage is to show the difference between the wages currently available and the level of wages actually needed by families.

What is the multidimensional poverty index?

The standards shown above are single indicators that are limited to showing a single perspective on poverty. A useful contribution to poverty studies is the use of composite indicators that put several characteristics of the problem into one measure: the **Multidimensional Poverty Index (MPI)**, developed by the UN Development Programme (UNDP) and the Oxford Poverty and Human Development Initiative, claims that 'new data demonstrate more clearly than ever that labelling countries – or even households – as rich and poor is an oversimplification'.

As an example of differences within a country, 55% of Uganda's population experience multidimensional poverty, in line with the rest of sub-Saharan African countries. However, in the capital city of Kampala, the rate is only 6%. But in the rural region of Karamoja, the MPI is 96%. On a more specific level, households themselves may experience poverty differently. The report cites that 25% of South Asian children live in a household where one child is malnourished, but another child in the same household is not.

Among those who fall into the category of multidimensionally poor, children are hit hardest, more likely to feel all of the effects of poverty from ill health to poor sanitation. Children are affected far more frequently than adults. The MPI finds that one in three children worldwide are multidimensionally poor, which is only true of one in six adults.

The MPI is calculated by identifying the different aspects of poverty, measuring their frequency and assigning each factor a relative weight based on the likely impact each dimension will have on the experience of poverty. Among the most heavily weighted values involve health and education: nutrition, child mortality, years of schooling and school attendance. Table 18.5 shows the full range of measured dimensions and their weighting.

According to the MPI, households must be deprived in one of the following ways in order to be considered multidimensionally poor:

- at least six standard of living indicators
- three standard of living indicators and one health or education indicator
- two health or education indicators.

So, a family experiencing insufficient levels of electricity, water, housing, fuel, sanitation, and without basic assets will qualify. Or a family without perhaps poor water, sanitation, and electricity with either little schooling or poor nutrition would qualify. In the last case, a family with acceptable levels in standard of living but with poor health or poor education also qualifies.

What does the MPI tell us about poverty?

By this measure, the MPI estimates that 1.3 billion people are multidimensionally poor, nearly double the measure found in extreme poverty by the international poverty

Table 18.5   Multidimensional Poverty Index, dimensions, and weighting

Dimensions of poverty	Indicator	Deprived if living in the household where . . .	Weight
Health	Nutrition	An adult under 70 years of age or a child is undernourished.	1/6
	Child mortality	Any child under the age of 18 years has died in the five years preceding the survey.	1/6
Education	Years of schooling	No household member aged 10 years or older has completed six years of schooling.	1/6
	School attendance	Any school-aged child is not attending school up to the age at which he/she would complete class 8.	1/6
Standard of living	Cooking fuel	The household cooks with dung, wood, charcoal, or coal.	1/18
	Sanitation	The household's sanitation facility is not improved (according to SDG guidelines) or it is improved but shared with other households.	1/18
	Drinking water	The household does not have access to improved drinking water (according to SDG guidelines) or safe drinking water is at least a 30-minute walk from home, round trip.	1/18
	Electricity	The household has no electricity.	1/18
	Housing	Housing materials for at least one of roof, walls, and floor are inadequate: the floor is of natural materials and/or the roof and/or walls are of natural or rudimentary materials.	1/18
	Assets	The household does not own more than one of these assets: radio, TV, telephone, computer, animal cart, bicycle, motorbike, or refrigerator, and does not own a car or truck.	1/18

line measure. Perhaps surprisingly, two-thirds of the multidimensionally poor live in middle-income countries. Half of the multidimensionally poor are children. Between some countries in South Asia, there are massive differences in poverty and education deprivation for girls. The study also analysed ten countries for change over time, and found that the biggest gains came among the poorest groups in each country. This finding roughly corresponds to the reduction in extreme poverty worldwide according to international poverty line measurements.

A distinguishing value of the MPI is that it provides information about the specific nature of poverty in a country, giving policymakers an idea of how to prioritise their poverty reduction goals.

Figure 18.8 shows Laos and Zimbabwe, who each scored the same overall on the MPI. However, they differed in the aspects of life where deprivation hit hardest. For Laos, a much bigger contributor to poverty was fewer years of schooling and attendance, where for Zimbabwe, poverty was more directly related to a lack of necessities for standard of living: not enough fuel, water, electricity, or sanitation. Government officials and **non-governmental organisations (NGOs)** aiming to reduce poverty in each country should therefore target their solutions to the most pressing issues. Measures like the MPI help inform more precise policymaking.

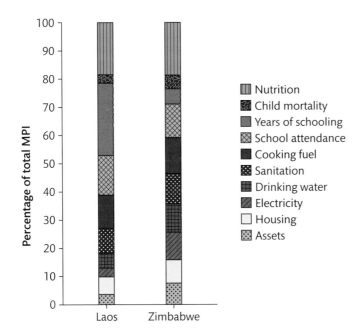

Figure 18.8 While Laos and Zimbabwe score the same overall on the MPI, they differ in the aspects contributing most to poverty

What are the difficulties in measuring poverty?

Despite the apparent progress in the quality and quantity of poverty measures, getting a precise and reliable view of poverty is challenging for a variety of reasons.

- Household survey data is a major source of poverty information. Such surveys are subject to sampling and weighting issues that may distort the true picture of poverty.
- Definitions of poverty vary from country to country. Countries may prioritise the gathering of some kinds of poverty data over others, which makes standardising the data across countries difficult.
- Non-income aspects of poverty, many of which are covered by the MPI, can be even more difficult to measure than income data. Many data points, like nutrition levels, are context specific and so require more resources to collect.
- Country data can be skewed to reflect the priorities of a national government, who may have the incentive to adjust poverty lines to falsely report better outcomes than actually exist.
- Data from conflict zones is notoriously difficult to collect as the disruption to everyday life and communication systems render all kinds of statistical data gathering difficult to perform.

What are some of the major causes of poverty?

Poverty arises from a variety of factors, some of which are related to each other and which also reinforce each other.

Inequality of opportunity

Free market schools of economic thought, from classical to new classical, have emphasised the role of incentives to self-interest to economic growth and self-improvement. One can get rich with effort and cleverness, it is argued, because the system rewards these qualities. However, what if access points to self-improvement are not available?

Those born into households where there is poor nutrition, little healthcare available, and no schooling are starting well behind everyone else. More specifically, a child who is poorly nourished may be more likely to be out sick from school, if such a school is available. One alternative is to work to earn money for one's family, which helps in the short term but limits educational attainment, and caps lifetime earnings. In general quality of life terms, this is a family which spends most of their waking hours working and has little time for anything that brings joy or connection in life. They are consumed by the need to meet basic needs, and few resources to move past this point.

In contrast, those born into a different household may be enrolled into steady schooling, where they can develop their skills and work towards employment in jobs that offer a living wage. They can have access to bank loans to buy property or a business and build their family wealth. Such children have a chance, though not a guarantee, at a future equal to or better than that of their parents.

Both examples above, though simple, illustrate a sort of circular dynamic. However, in the first case, the poor child may be locked into a **poverty trap** that prevents them from improving their standard of living. In the second case, the child raised with certain basic levels of education, health, and income can maintain their level or perhaps even move higher.

How does one measure equality of opportunity?

In one sense, the poverty measures above give a vivid picture of likely opportunity from country to country. The gaps between life chances in a rich and a developing country can be profound. For life spans, the average person in the richest country can live 60% longer, or 30 years, longer than the average citizen of a poor one. Children go to school nearly 10 times longer in rich compared to developing countries, and incomes can be an astonishing 172 times higher, even after adjusting for price levels. When it comes to opportunities from birth, life, as the saying goes, is not remotely fair.

One factor that could mitigate such inequity is if it were still possible to rise from such deprivation. In other words, is it possible to move up the ladder in your country, or are positions fixed? Economists try to measure this by calculating intergenerational income mobility. This refers to the relationship between the socioeconomic status of parents and the status their children will attain as adults. It attempts to measure the likelihood that one's wealth is largely determined by one's inherited advantages.

The idea is that while poverty is undesirable, it may be excusable in societies where upward mobility is possible. If the poor are able to move up, then poverty itself is not as significant a problem as when the poor are trapped in their circumstances.

However, the World Bank estimates suggest that income inequality is highly correlated with upward mobility. In other words, where incomes are most unequally distributed, there is less opportunity.

Worryingly, the narrowing of opportunities for the poor is most pronounced in developing countries. While there is considerable variance from country to country, the World Bank found that in many countries mobility rose in the decades leading up to 1980, but that since then the path to life improvement has become less accessible.

In many poor parts of the world, or poor parts within developing countries, far too many children's standard of living is defined by the level attained by their parents.

Different levels of resource ownership

Relatedly, there are significant differences in the ownership of resources, in particular that of capital. The ownership of capital, in either money or the form of a business, puts one in a position to generate more income from that resource. A relatively small portion of the world's population holds ownership of meaningful physical or financial capital. Over the last several decades the growth in incomes has been far greater as a return on capital than to rises in worker wages or other income sources.

Different levels of human capital

Labour markets tend to reward labour that is highly skilled, and rewards to higher-skilled labour have grown faster than those for lower skilled workers, for a variety of reasons, including greater mobility in physical capital (outsourcing). This increases the value of greater educational attainment, which is an expensive merit good that individuals and countries struggle to afford.

Globalisation and technological change

Globalisation has vastly increased the size of markets for capital owners, it has made the relocation of factories and firms easier. This has made it possible for firms to hop from country to country seeking the lowest labour costs. Globally, wages for manufacturing jobs have been suppressed. Even for low-income countries that draw such investment, the rewards in terms of improved capital and rising wages may be transitory. At the same time, demand for managers and mid-level positions within such companies have been much higher, compounding inequality.

Market-based supply-side policies

As described in Chapter 2, the consensus around free markets and government intervention shifted significantly from the post-Second World War period to the 1970s (Keynesian), to the 1980s into the present (new classical). It was in the 1980s in the UK and the USA that major shifts towards supply-side economic policies took place. While much more will be said of supply-side approaches in Chapter 21, the market-based approach of the 1980s required the rolling back of many layers of government intervention, including many that protected workers and the poor.

Specifically, under UK Prime Minister Margaret Thatcher and US President Ronald Reagan, respectively, both countries reduced social welfare programmes for the poor, believing that they reduced the incentive to work. They lowered **marginal tax rates** as well, believing that lower rates encouraged work and innovation. Both engaged in active efforts to reduce the power of labour unions, which have traditionally served to fortify wages in typically low-wage jobs. These and other market-oriented policies of that era made greater numbers of workers and the unemployed at risk of poverty.

One product of the sweeping anti-regulatory approach of the 1980s was to encourage the deregulation of financial markets. As a result, banking grew quickly, relative to the overall size of the economy, and also as the leading profit maker in the economy. However, it also led to the financial crisis of 2008, which plunged millions into bankruptcy and caused a global recession. Since that time, most of the gains in GDP in rich countries have gone not to the poor or middle class but to the top 20% of earners.

Discrimination (gender, race, and others)

A blind spot in pure classical economic theory is the insistence that racial and gender discrimination should not occur, because it violates the notion that competition seeks out efficiency and quality, regardless of irrelevant factors. More specifically that it is in the best interest of firms, for example, to hire the most talented people regardless of race, gender, religion, or other charateristics. This ignores years of anecdotal, historical, and increasingly data-based evidence that discrimination plays a major role in creating inequality between groups.

The USA demonstrates glaring gaps by race in nearly every standard of living category. The average white family in America holds nearly nine times more wealth ($171,000) than the average Black one ($17,150) , and the yearly income disparity is similar. Of course, the roots of this disparity go back hundreds of years. Nearly all of the African Americans in the USA, a group that made up 16% of the country's population at the peak of slavery, were property themselves from the 1600s to the 1860s. From the 1860s to the 1960s, most American blacks suffered under segregation laws that restricted property ownership, denied black children an education, denied the right to vote, and allowed comprehensive forms of discrimination, especially in employment.

The USA is distinguished, but not alone, in permitting racial discrimination in the basis of its economic system. Ethnic minorities in many countries suffer from racially based discrimination in many areas of economic life.

Gender disparities are another notable source of income inequality. This too varies greatly country by country. Figure 18.9 shows one example of wage inequality by gender, within selected countries. Where the gaps are greatest, policymakers might be left to wonder if norms and policies that discriminate in this way destroy the incentives for self-advancement that are assumed to be open to all. If so, many people may reduce their ambitions because of systematic inequalities of opportunity, and greatly reduce a country's human capital.

Unequal status and power

As a broad source of inequality, unequal status and power refers to the interconnected characteristics of many of the above categories, and include others that may not specifically be mentioned here. A country can have its own combination of inherited wealth, forms of discrimination, lack of opportunity, and lack of enfranchisement that combine with other contextual factors to produce versions of a social underclass. Members of such an underclass are hardly ever united in any common struggle for better treatment and conditions. They typically lead isolated lives, work in soulless employment, and have little opportunity to address their grievances.

Government tax and benefits policies

Despite the classical economic vision of an economically neutral government, most governments have policies in place that reward different groups in different ways. This can help to promote or, as we will observe later in the chapter, to reduce income

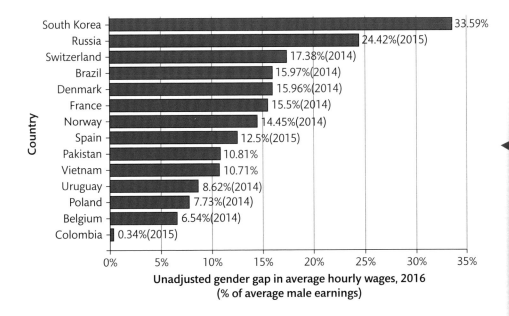

◄ **Figure 18.9** The gender wage gap in selected countries

inequality. As mentioned above, free market **supply-side policies** have accentuated the gap between rich and poor in many ways over the years. For example, differences in tax rates can imply favouritism to classes of work. Where corporate or capital gain taxes are lower than income taxes, it appears that the relatively rich, those who own capital and have shares in companies, pay less than their share to the government relative to wage earners. This effect is compounded when governments insist on reducing pension, health, or other benefits in order to pay down **government debts**.

What are the consequences of inequality and poverty?

Less economic growth

Research into the link between inequality and growth has shown mixed results, with some showing inequality reduces growth and some showing the opposite correlation. The debate has two sides. One may argue that in unequal societies, the increased profits and savings of the rich contribute to higher levels of funding for investment and innovation. Conversely, if inequality reduces the incomes of the poor and squeezes out a middle class, the lack of their spending on goods and services reduces the circular flow and reduces potential GDP. Furthermore, if paired with reduced economic opportunity, inequality has the effect of reducing levels of educational attainment and the development of human capital that would otherwise contribute to potential growth.

Less social stability and social cohesion

Inequality and poverty affect social trust and participation. Unequal societies have lower rates of civic participation, lower voter turnout, and appear to have fewer acts of altruism. The poor, who may not believe the system works for them, are far less likely to join clubs and social groups, and vote less frequently. This only contributes to the comparative political power of the relatively wealthier groups. Moreover, research finds that physical and psychological health levels are much lower in unequal societies. Higher levels of obesity, mental illness, depression, infant mortality are found in unequal societies. This is especially true of inequality in rich countries.

Individual and family struggles

For workers and families, the grinding demands of living without enough resources can have significant damaging effects on emotional and cognitive well-being. Research on poverty, specifically the effects on poor children show a bleak picture. Adults who were poor as children tend to have memory deficits. Brain research indicated that low-income children are more likely to suffer from irregular brain development, and have deficits and verbal and spacial memory. Research on adults has found that the stresses induced by poverty reduce the ability to make evidently beneficial decisions about many types of family economic problems.

18.4 How do tax systems and government intervention affect inequality?

Learning outcomes

At the end of this section you will be able to:

- distinguish between direct and indirect taxes, providing examples of each
- examine the potential role of direct taxes in redistributing income
- compare and contrast progressive, regressive, and proportional taxation, providing examples of each
- **HL** calculate the amount of indirect tax paid from information given
- **HL** calculate total tax and **average tax rates** from a set of data
- discuss the arguments for and against progressive taxation as a method for reducing income inequality.

Governments at many levels hold the power to tax: at the national level, the regional or state level, and the city or town level. They levy taxes in a variety of ways and for many purposes. Generally, governments may tax demerit goods, ones which generate negative externalities, in the hope of reducing consumption of them. These taxes, as well as others, may also fund important government goods and services. Finally, authorities may use tax rates to redistribute income to reduce the gap between high- and low-income groups.

Indirect taxation, such as the specific taxes on demerit goods you studied in Chapter 10, or the value added taxes to goods more generally are one way of collecting taxes. Another method is direct taxes, where the payee pays the government directly via cash, ebanking, or with credit cards. Direct taxes can be in the form of income taxes, property taxes, corporate profit taxes, and wealth taxes. A personal income tax takes a percentage of your salaried income from each year. Corporate profit taxes are similar to a personal income tax in that a particular tax rate is applied to yearly company profits. A wealth tax levies a rate based on the accumulated assets of an individual or family. Property taxes are a particular form of wealth tax, based on real estate holdings.

The rates on all of these taxes can vary, and these differences are where political discussions around equity arise. In some countries, the value added tax (on all goods) and the income tax rate paid by most families, is actually higher than any form of property tax, corporate tax, or wealth tax. This discrepancy famously prompted the multibillionaire investor Warren Buffet to claim that he paid a lower tax rate than his secretary, whose income was hundreds of times lower.

Corporations and the wealthy who can afford it take advantage of loopholes and legally written advantages for investment income. In the case of corporations, rules can be relaxed to lower the rates paid by influential firms. Using publicly available corporate reporting information, the Institute on Taxation and Economic Policy found that 60 US corporations paid $0 in US taxes in 2018. Among them were: Amazon, Chevron (oil), Netflix, General Motors, Eli Lily (pharmaceuticals). The practice of tax avoidance, by wealthy individuals and corporations together, is estimated to cost countries up to $600 billion per year in lost income. Of that figure, $200 billion would be payable to low-income countries, for whom it is much more needed and could otherwise be directed to public works. It is also more than the amount of **foreign aid** sent to low-income countries ($150 billion) each year.

What are the historical perspectives on taxation?

The Marxist view

On the far 'left' of the economic spectrum is Marxist/socialist ideology, which believes that households' money incomes should be made obsolete and each household's level of consumption should instead be based on the labour-value of the output which it produces. In a purely Marxist/socialist economy, money incomes do not matter since the output of the nation will be shared equally among all those who contribute to its production. Private ownership of resources and the output those resources produce are wholly abolished in a socialist economy.

With regards to taxation, the slogan 'from each according to his ability, to each according to his need', made popular by Karl Marx, summarised his idea that a household's consumption should be based on its level of need, rather than the amount of capital it owns and the income it can earn from that capital. The logical conclusion of this idea is that all households in a nation have essentially the same basic needs, therefore household incomes and consumption should be equal across the nation. With that approach in mind, that Marx disapproved of wealth and inequality to begin with, the Marxist view of taxes would be harsh on the highest earners and lower incomes workers would be net receivers of subsidies.

The laissez-faire view

On the other extreme of the economic spectrum is the classical, free market model which argues that the only role the government should play in the market economy is in the protection of private property rights, ensuring that the private owners of resources are able to pursue their own self-interest in an unregulated marketplace where their money incomes are determined by the exchange-value of the resources they own, including capital, land, and labour.

In a market economy, the level of income and consumption of households vary greatly across society because the exchange-value of the resources owned by households is what determines income, not the principle of equality, which drives a socialist economy. Each individual in society is free to pursue his or her monetary objectives through the improvement of his or her human capital and the accumulation of physical capital and land and the resulting increase in exchange-value in the resource market. And so, everyone should be taxed minimally, if at all.

The modern, mixed economy approach

In today's world, there exists neither a purely socialist economy nor a purely free market economy. In reality, all modern economies are mixed economies in which governments do much more than simply protect property rights, but do not go so far as to own and allocate all factors of production. The role of government in the distribution of income in today's economies is relegated to the collection of taxes and the provision of public goods and services and **transfer payments**.

Differences between progressive, regressive, and proportional effects taxation

Taxes can be proportional, regressive, or progressive in nature. This means that different taxes place different burdens on the rich and the poor.

Proportional tax

A **proportional tax** is a tax for which the percentage remains constant as income increases. The rich will pay more tax than the poor in absolute terms, but the burden of the tax will be no greater on the rich than it is on the poor.

A household earning €20,000 may pay 10% tax to the government, totalling €2,000. A rich household in the same country pays 10% on its income of €200,000, totalling €20,000 in taxes. There is a difference in total value but the proportional burden is the same on the rich household as it is on the poor household.

Proportional taxes are generally uncommon in advanced economies, with the exception of Russia and some former Soviet bloc countries who use the flat rate to encourage tax compliance. Although some payroll taxes (i.e. those collected to support social security or welfare programmes) are based on a percentage of employees' incomes up to a certain level. For instance, the US social security tax is 6.2% of gross income up to $108,000. Regardless of a person's income below $108,000, he or she will pay 6.2% to the government to support the country's social security programme.

Regressive tax

A tax that decreases in percentage as income increases is said to be regressive. Such a tax places a larger burden on lower income households than it does on higher income earners since a greater percentage of a poor household's income is used to pay the tax than a rich household's.

You may be wondering why a government would ever levy a tax that harms the poor more than it does the rich, but in fact almost every national government uses functionally regressive taxes to raise a significant portion of its tax revenues. Most indirect taxes are actually regressive, which may not make sense at first, since a sales tax is a percentage of the price of products consumed. The regressive nature becomes apparent when the amount of the tax is compared to the income of the consumer.

To demonstrate how a sales tax is regressive, imagine three different consumers who purchase an identical laptop computer for €1,000 in a country with a value added tax of 10% added to the price of the computer (Table 18.6).

Table 18.6 Indirect taxes are regressive because the tax paid is a smaller proportion of the income of a rich person than the income of a poor person

Income of buyer/€	Amount of tax paid/€	% of income taxed
10,000	100	1
50,000	100	0.2
100,000	100	0.1

The higher income consumer pays the same raw total of tax as the lower income consumer (€100), but the tax makes up a smaller percentage of the former's income (0.1%) than it does of the latter's (1.0%). Although they appear to be equitable since everyone pays the same percentage of the price of the goods they consume, indirect taxes such as value added tax (VAT), goods and services tax (GST), and sales taxes are in fact regressive taxes, placing a larger burden on those whose ability to pay is lower and a smaller burden on the higher income earners whose ability to pay is greater.

Progressive tax

This is a tax for which the percentage paid in tax increases as income increases. The principle underlying a progressive tax is that those with the ability to pay the most tax (the rich) should bear a larger burden of the nation's total tax receipts than those whose ability to pay is less. In this way, a progressive tax is the most equitable of the three types of taxes a government collects.

Lower income households not only pay less tax, but they pay a smaller percentage of their income in tax as well. Most nations' income tax systems are progressive, the most progressive being those in the Northern European countries which, not surprisingly, also demonstrate the most equal distributions of income. Of the various types of taxes, a progressive income tax aligns most with the macroeconomic objective of equity in the distribution of income.

Comparing tax systems

Figure 18.10 shows the relationship between an individual's income and the amount of tax the individual will pay under each of the three tax systems.

Assuming a proportional tax, for instance, each household will pay an identical proportion of its income in tax, so as income rises, the amount of tax paid rises at a constant rate.

Under a regressive system, on the other hand, lower income households pay a larger percentage of their income in taxes. Regressive taxes are mostly indirect, consumption taxes, so higher income households still pay more in tax (since they consume more), but the amount paid increases at a decreasing rate because at higher incomes the **marginal propensity to consume** becomes less and more income goes towards savings instead (thus left untaxed).

A progressive tax places very little burden on low-income households, since under most progressive income tax systems, the lowest income earners actually pay no tax at all. At higher income levels, a greater percentage of income is paid as tax, so the amount paid increases at an increasing rate as household income rises. The highest

Video suggestions:
You have read about it, now you can review what you have just learned by watching some videos by the author! Simply click here in your eBook for videos on the different tax systems' effect on income distribution.

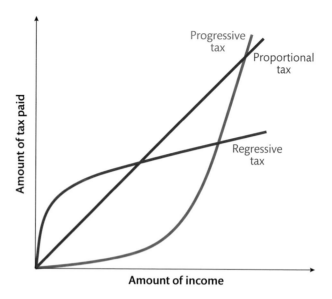

Figure 18.10 The relationship between tax paid and income differs between progressive, regressive, and proportional taxes

income earners in the economy pay the most tax in all three systems. However, only under a progressive tax system do the richest households also bear the greatest tax burden, meaning that they pay a higher proportion of their income in taxes than lower income households.

HL How are progressive tax rates calculated?

A progressive income tax typically consists of a marginal tax bracket in which the increasing tax rates apply to marginal income, rather than to total income. In such a system, the average tax a household pays increases less rapidly than the marginal tax because the higher marginal rate only applies to additional income beyond the upper range of the previous bracket. In other words, each successively higher tax rate is only charged on the income in excess of that already taxed at the previous level.

Table 18.7 shows a set of possible marginal tax rates. The third column shows the cumulative tax rate paid when tax on all the income in a given bracket has been calculated.

Few countries tax the most basic levels of income. The first portion of income earned in any period is not taxed, and then each successive level is taxed at a different rate, as the person graduates into a higher level or bracket.

Table 18.7   Income and marginal tax brackets

Tax level or bracket	Income (₡) (₡ is the symbol for colòn (plural colones), the currency of Costa Rica).	Marginal tax rate
A	0–6,000,000	0
B	6,000,001–18,000,000	20%
C	18,000,001–27,000,000	40%
D	27,000,001–36,000,000	50%

In the example above, a person who earns ₡21 million will have the following tax due:

From Level A, the first ₡6 million is not taxed = 0

From Level B, the whole ₡12 million is taxed at 20% = ₡2.4 million

From Level C, only ₡3 million is taxed (₡21 million − ₡18 million) at 40% = ₡1.2 million

Total tax due = ₡3.6 million

Another set of examples will be useful. With the table below, Diya is shown as earning лв50,000 and Maria earning лв100,000 (лв is the symbol for lev, the currency of Bulgaria). We can calculate the total tax due based on the tax brackets, as well as working out the average tax paid by each individual.

Diya's Income = лв50,000

Tax level or bracket	Income (лв)	Tax rate	Calculation	Tax amount (лв)
A	0–10,000	0	$10,000 \times 0$	0
B	10,001–30,000	20%	$20,000 \times 0.2$	4,000
C	30,001–45,000	40%	$15,000 \times 0.4$	6,000
D	45,001–60,000	50%	$5,000 \times 0.5$	2,500
E	60,001–100,000	60%	—	—
				Total tax: 12,500

Maria's Income = лв100,000

Tax level or bracket	Income (лв)	Tax rate	Calculation	Tax amount (лв)
A	0–10,000	0	$10,000 \times 0$	0
B	10,001–30,000	20%	$20,000 \times 0.2$	4,000
C	30,001–45,000	40%	$15,000 \times 0.4$	6,000
D	45,001–60,000	50%	$40,000 \times 0.5$	20,000
E	60,001–100,000	60%	$40,000 \times 0.6$	24,000
				Total tax: 54,000

Note that while Maria earned twice as much as Diya, she pays significantly more than twice the total tax. To calculate the average tax rate, take the total amount of tax paid by each and divide by their income.

Diya's average income tax rate: $\dfrac{12,500}{50,000} \times 100 = 25\%$

Maria's average income tax rate: $\dfrac{54,000}{100,000} \times 100 = 54\%$

There are two patterns worth observing. First, for workers in each of the income brackets above, the average rate of taxation is always lower than the marginal rate of taxation, since tax increases only apply to additional income earned beyond the previous bracket. Second, in a progressive system, this result would not necessarily be unusual. Because the higher marginal rates are rising, the average rate of a high-income earner will rise as well.

Practice exam questions – assessment tips (Paper 3)

For Paper 3, HL students may be asked to make a series of calculations, including total amount tax paid, average tax rate, total indirect tax from a set of data. Follow the worked example and then complete the exercise.

Worked example 18.1

The following table shows the marginal tax rates at each level for the USA.

Tax level or bracket	Income ($)	Tax rate
A	0–10,000	0
B	10,001–30,000	18%
C	30,001–45,000	25%
D	45,001–60,000	33%
E	60,001–75,000	39%
F	75,001–500,000	47%

In addition, VAT at the rate of 15% is charged on all purchases.

Donfor works in the USA and earns $47,000. He saves 10% of his disposable income.

Calculate the tax paid by Donfor as a percentage of his total income (the average overall tax rate).

a. First apply Donfor's $47,000 to each income tax bracket:
   Level A: $10,000 × 0 = 0
   Level B: $20,000 × 0.18 = 3,600
   Level C: $15,000 × 0.25 = 3,750
   Level D: $2,000 × 0.33 = 660
   Total income tax = $8,010

b. Calculate the disposable income (income – income tax paid):
   $47,000 – $8,010 = $38,990

c. Calculate the amount of disposable income spent:
   $38,990 × 0.90 = $35,091

d. Using the amount of disposable income spent, calculate the amount of indirect tax (in this example the VAT) paid by Donfor:

Donfor's $35,091 disposable income spent includes the price for all the goods and services purchased, as well as 15% VAT on top of those purchases, therefore:

Total spending = original spending + VAT at 15%

Total spending = 1.15x, where x is the original spending

$35,091 = 1.15x

$35,091 ÷ 1.15 = x

x = $30,514

To get the indirect tax (VAT) amount, take the total disposable income spent and subtract the original spending amount. What is left is the indirect tax payment total.

$35,091 − $30,514 = $5,039 total indirect tax paid by Donfor.

e. Calculate the amount of combined total tax paid:

Income tax + indirect tax = combined total tax

$8,010 + $5,039 = $13,049

f. Calculate the average overall tax rate:

Combined total tax ÷ income × 100 = average overall tax rate

$13,049 ÷ $47,000 × 100 = 0.277 × 100 = 27.7% average overall tax rate

Exercise 18.1

Udu also works in the USA, but earns a higher salary of $86,000. She spends 90% of her disposable income.

Complete the blank fields in the table below.

Worker	Total income tax ($)	Disposable income ($)	VAT paid (15% of disposable income spent, $)	Total combined tax amount ($)	Average rate of tax (%)
Donfor	8,010	38,990	5,039	13,049	27.7
Udu					

What are the arguments for and against a progressive income tax system?

Arguments for progressive taxation

The argument for progressive taxes rests on notions of fairness. Because the lower ranges of income are taxed relatively little, the poor are better able to meet basic needs of food, shelter, clothing, healthcare, and education. It is assumed, in countries with progressive systems that the marginal utility per dollar decreases with each dollar one earns, and so it is more fair to tax the billionth dollar (since it will certainly mean less) more severely than the first (which is essential for everyone). This tax revenue, very importantly, can be used to further address inequities by providing expensive merit goods like healthcare and education, as well as subsidies for child-rearing, social care, and unemployment. Countries that want more redistribution need only make their tax schemes more progressive and fund those programmes.

Arguments against progressive taxation

The main argument against progressive income taxes is that taxing higher incomes at higher rates creates a *disincentive* to work, in effect punishing any increase in productivity or effort. Supply-side economists would suggest the following example: suppose you are making $150,000 and you know that if you get a raise you may pay a higher marginal tax rate on that next amount. Economists debate the degree to which higher tax rates actually disincentivise working more hours, but it is reasonable to assume that there is some level of marginal tax that may act as a disincentive. Additionally, market-oriented views of progressive rates blame these rates for tax avoidance and evasion.

It is worth noting that the research provided in this chapter suggests that inequality has significant bad social effects. Moreover, it is not clear that low marginal tax rates paired with inequality actually raise the growth levels or even the happiness levels of the richest in those countries.

TOK

What are the key current open/unanswered questions in these discussions of inequality and poverty?

Case study – how do we know which countries levy the most progressive tax rates?

The degree to which a country's tax system is progressive depends a lot on how it is organised. An important distinguishing feature of a country is its tax structure; in other words the mix of taxation types that the country uses to raise revenue. For many, it is through a progressive income tax. However, as Figure 18.11 shows, some countries rely on pension or social security contributions for most funding, and others use sales taxes as their largest source of income.

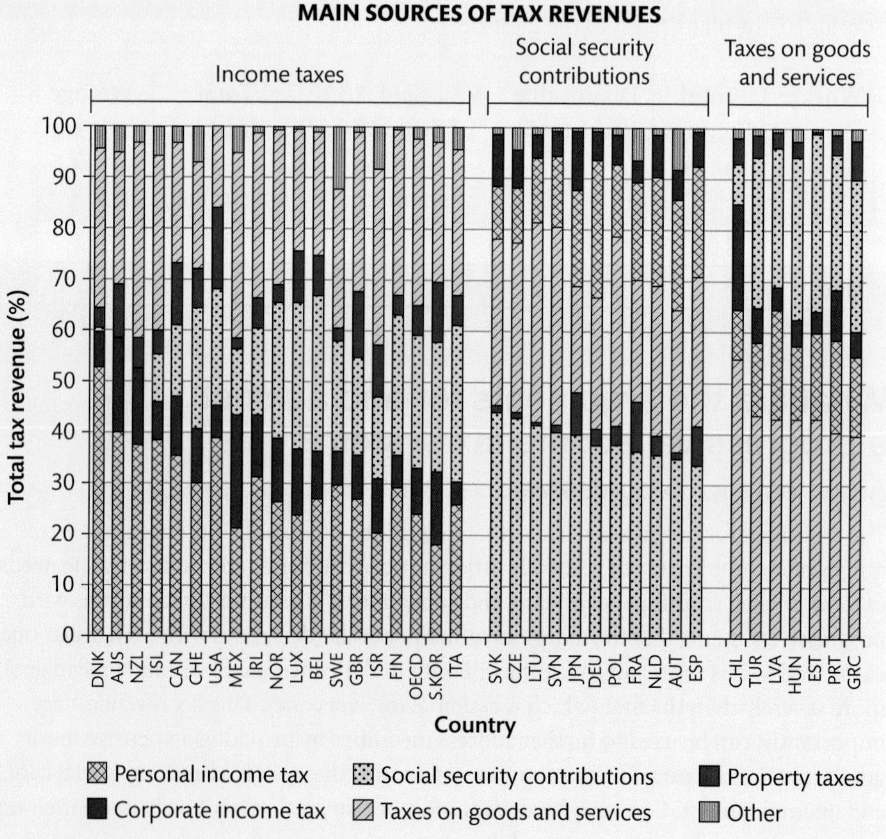

MAIN SOURCES OF TAX REVENUES

Figure 18.11 This graph, based on data from 2017, shows how tax structures vary from country to country

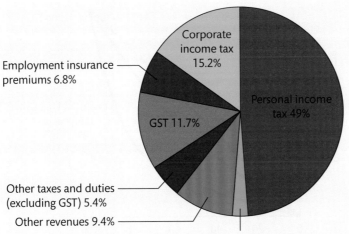

Figure 18.12 Almost 50% of Canadian tax revenues come from personal income tax

In many OECD economies, progressive income taxes typically account for the largest proportion of total tax receipts by the government. Canada, as shown in Figure 18.12 has an even higher top marginal tax rate than the USA and, rather than applying to people earning above $370,000, as it does in the USA, Canada's top tax rate kicks in for workers earning just $100,000 per year. In Canada, **personal income taxes** account for around 50% of total federal tax revenues, while the corporate tax and the national GST make up the next largest portions (Figure 18.12).

Who really pays the highest rates? Figure 18.13 shows the top income tax rates of selected OECD countries for 2019. In this showing, Sweden has the top marginal tax rate at 60%, while Turkey has the lowest top rate at 30%. However, to grasp the progressivity of a tax system it is also important to see the income level at which the highest rates take hold. The figure above expresses this as a multiple of the average wage in each country. For Sweden, the highest rate kicks in at only 1.5 times the average income, while for Japan, which has a similarly higher rate at 55%, that rate only takes hold when one has earned 8.5 times the average wage. Sweden, one can conclude, has a significantly more progressive income tax system than Japan. And one can also conclude that in Sweden, where the tax rates rise at lower income levels described above, the middle-class earners pay more to support the system.

Among the lower top-rate countries, Mexico and Turkey have a similar top rate at approximately 30%, but Mexico's will not take effect until one earns 25 times the average income, while Turkey's takes effect at merely three times the average income. Comparatively, Turkey has a much more progressive tax than Mexico. Therefore, one could conclude that among countries with lower top marginal tax rates, countries like Turkey may be more progressive than one might otherwise see.

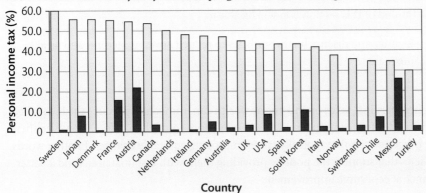

Figure 18.13 The highest marginal personal income tax rates (pale blue) are only part of the story. Here the darker blue bars show the variation in the threshold of the rate, given as a multiple of the average wage

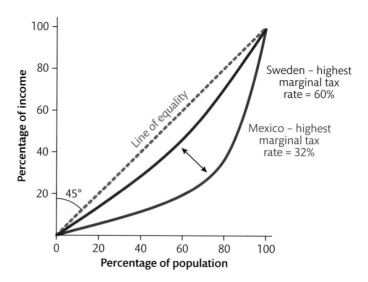

Figure 18.14 A more progressive income tax typically corresponds with more equal income distribution

Research and inquiry

Wait, what is a wealth tax?

The progressive taxes we have discussed so far have been taxes on income. And yet, research indicates that disparities of wealth are usually even greater than those of income. The returns to capital ownership, in particular, appear to be growing, while wages have stagnated by comparison. This reflects the critique of capital that goes back to Marx and continues with economists like Thomas Piketty, whose book *Capital in the Twenty-First Century* argued that returns to capital are higher than economic growth itself. Such a trend is bound to result in great inequality and very likely reduced equity as well. Piketty, as well as an increasing number of economists and politicians, have called for a tax on accumulated wealth rather than income.

Find countries that currently charge a wealth tax.

1 What are the assets being taxed?

2 Are wealth taxes popular with the public? Find out.

For discussion and debate:

3 Is a wealth tax more or less fair than an income tax?

How do tax rate changes affect income distribution?

Referring back to the Lorenz curve model for showing the distribution of a nation's income, it can be argued that the more progressive a nation's income tax, the closer the Lorenz curve is to the line of equality. It is no coincidence that some of the countries with the lowest Gini indexes (Sweden, Germany, and Belgium) also have some of the highest marginal tax rates in the world, while those with the lowest marginal tax rates (Mexico, Turkey) have a higher Gini index and a Lorenz curve further from the line of equality (Figure 18.14).

Taxes collected from higher income earners in a high marginal tax country like Sweden are used to provide goods, services, and transfer payments to those whose incomes would otherwise be much lower. The equity of such a progressive tax system is derived from the fairness behind making rich households bear a larger burden of the nation's tax system. Equity in the tax system leads to greater equality in the income distribution, as seen in the two Lorenz curves for Sweden and Mexico.

18.5 What are further policies to reduce poverty and income/wealth inequality?

Learning outcome

At the end of this section you will be able to:

* identify and discuss further policies to reduce poverty, income, and wealth inequality.

Higher marginal taxes on income or wealth can immediately reduce the inequality gap. In after-tax terms incomes are literally more equal than before. However, there are other policies that typically target improving equitable chances. In other words, policies that support the poor by providing them with essential needs and a better chance at economic improvement.

Policies that reduce inequalities of opportunity

Investment in human capital

The term human capital may sound sterile, but it conveys an important element of a productive society, one seeking ever higher degrees of health and education. It can be easy to simply promote 'more healthcare and education', without seeing that these goals can be self-reinforcing. More or better healthcare of certain kinds may allow more children to go to school rather than be sick at home. Every extra day of school counts. More and better education, in turn, helps people make more informed decisions about healthcare. Such improvements, reported in longer lives, more years of schooling, and other measures usually translate into higher productivity in the workforce as well, creating further economic benefits. These improvements may also increase social mobility for those previously disadvantaged by their systems.

To help quantify the value of human capital, the World Bank compiles its Human Capital Index (HCI) which estimates the value of a country's human capital in comparison to what it could be at full potential. The HCI uses indicators of child survival, education quality and quantity, adult survival rates, and healthy growth. As an example it finds that as of 2018, Tajikistan's children are estimated to be '50 percent as productive when they grow up as they could be if they enjoyed complete education and full health.' This suggests plenty of scope for improvement, but it is noteworthy that Switzerland, who scores well above average among countries in their region, only scores a 76%.

Health policies

- Nutrition and basic food provision programmes to food-insecure families will improve health for vulnerable people.
- Prenatal and postnatal care provision for all families will prevent early disease and death.
- Universal healthcare or insurance programmes to reduce costs for the poor will improve overall health because the poor will not avoid care because of costs.
- Social insurance and poverty reduction programmes for the elderly can be very effective at preventing penury in old age.

Education policies

- More pre-school years of care and education for the children of poor families can help bridge learning differentials that occur because some children do not have access to early years education.
- Improved resources and training for teachers, especially in disadvantaged areas, can support equity by improving opportunities.
- Programmes and attention for underperforming students who are more likely to be poor.
- Subsidies for post-secondary education can help ensure that successful students get access to further education.
- After school programmes for children with working parents allow workers to keep longer hours and stay on a career path.
- Finally, advocates of higher spending levels on human capital point out that such gains increase productivity and overall economic growth. This, in turn, can increase the tax base and make further investments in the country's well-being.

How can transfer payments reduce poverty and inequality?

Transfer payments refer to government programmes that shift tax revenues gathered from taxpayers and deliver them to various groups and individuals without an exchange of goods or services. Examples of transfer payments include unemployment insurance, financial aid, pensions for the elderly and sick, as well as government subsidies for firms.

The value of transfer payments may seem obvious because they are commonplace, and therefore taken for granted.

Pensions

Pension schemes for the elderly, for example, also known as 'social security', are relatively new, having been instituted after the Second World War in Western countries. These schemes have had powerful effects, and are credited with significantly reducing poverty for the old, and helping to increase life expectancy by lowering poverty-related health risks.

Unemployment insurance

Similarly to pensions, unemployment insurance builds a 'poverty floor' for those who are suddenly without a job by paying a portion of the salaries of the unemployed, or a simple flat rate, for a period of up to two years. In extraordinary circumstances, such as the financial crisis or the COVID-19 pandemic, countries will extend these programmes to negate the effects of mass cyclical unemployment.

Business subsidies

At times, business subsidies prevent mass layoffs and the consequent poverty, such as the rescue of a prominent industry. More commonly, agricultural sectors receive large subsidies to maintain a robust and independent food supply, and to prevent farm poverty, which was not unusual a century ago.

What is universal basic income?

A bold proposal that is gaining notoriety in recent years is that of universal basic income (UBI). It is also called an 'income guarantee' or 'citizen's income', and as the name suggests, UBI is a periodic payment delivered to all citizens of a population. The idea behind a basic income is that it would go a long way towards meeting the basic needs of any citizen. UBI levels would ideally be set somewhere near the poverty line.

One appeal of UBI plans is simplicity. Most current transfer payment programmes that involve unemployment or housing subsidies tend to require time-consuming administration, along with the bureaucracy designed to catch fraud and waste. UBI avoids those costs. Moreover, it reduces the disincentives sometimes attached to current programmes. Some of these are poorly designed so that taking work or earning beyond a particular level will eliminate the whole transfer, which effectively punishes the recipient for working. Basic income would avoid this by awarding the money to everyone, regardless of income. Getting a slightly better job would always be desirable and never a detriment to income.

One trend that has inspired more thinking around basic income is that leaps in information technology and automation can cause significant structural unemployment. If fast food workers, basic accountancy jobs, retail cash desk jobs,

and manufacturing are all replaced by artificial intelligence and automation, perhaps the modern economy simply requires fewer people to run efficiently.

Advocates of UBI cite the static trend in basic wages over the last several decades. As earnings to capital have risen, wages have fallen behind. The income gap, and costs associated with childcare and basic needs has led young people to be especially pessimistic about their standard of living. They tend to delay starting families, and also have lower home ownership than previous generations. A basic income can begin to correct this enduring wage inequity.

Of course, basic income tends to be very expensive. Most schemes would massively increase budget deficits unless offset by raising taxes, presumably on the wealthiest segments of society to make the redistribution effective. One could counter that inequality is expensive as well, costing society in terms of negative externalities and high social costs.

Arguments against a UBI

Another argument is the one that surrounds most transfer payment schemes, that of reduced incentive to work. Most hypothetical UBI plans keep the subsidy to a poverty line level, so work would be required to live a modestly acceptable lifestyle. However, the idea is that any 'free' income is expected to reduce the motivation to work.

Finally, some critics ask, 'Why everyone? Even the rich?' Universal programmes tend to be popular ones because of their common national purpose, with examples ranging from free university education to national health insurance. Testing for incomes would also raise bureaucratic costs, something basic income can avoid almost completely.

How might policies to reduce discrimination help reduce poverty?

Income disparities from gender and racial discrimination may be the result of active discrimination or of ingrained and subconscious cultural practices. Accrued over decades or longer, these deficits in opportunity and income from discrimination may account for much of the differences in wealth between genders and racial groups. Explicit policies and norms to combat it are readily available:

- anti-discrimination laws that bar discrimination on the basis of race or gender in areas of education, employment, and housing
- rigorous enforcement of existing anti-discriminatory laws
- equal pay for equal work laws to address gender pay gaps
- the implementation of target employment levels or quotas of underrepresented group
- target levels for management and company boards
- greater spending on housing and education for vulnerable groups in recognition of historical discrimination
- wealth taxes to correct the inequities and fund the programmes above.

TOK

This discussion of inequality has presented significant evidence of the harmful effects inequality can have on society. What responsibilities rest on you, the knower, as a result of your knowledge about inequality?

Case study – equity in the USA

'To be at 1970s levels of equity, workers should receive nearly double their current pay.'

In 2020, *New York* magazine reported that a RAND Institute research paper concluded that the median wage is $42,000 below what it would be, if the income distribution in effect in 1970 were still in effect today. Compared to current US median wages of $50,000, a worker today should earn $92,000 to keep up with the income gains that have accrued to the wealthiest segments of the US population.

Will a minimum wage help reduce poverty and inequality?

A minimum wage, as discussed in Chapter 9, is a legally required price floor for labour. As such, it has the potential to cause surpluses, like any price floor. However, in this case a higher than equilibrium wage may cause a surplus of workers. In other words, higher minimum wages may raise costs to firms, and firms may need to fire some workers. Notably, research to assess the effects of minimum wages on employment levels has not delivered clear answers for or against the policy. Some argue that the elasticity of supply for certain kinds of low-wage labour is not so sensitive to prices (elastic) that firms will fire very many workers. At the same time, minimum wage advocates point out that the higher incomes overall will raise demand for goods and services and negate whatever unemployment effects occur.

Research and inquiry

Is a minimum wage good or bad?

Many countries enforce a minimum wage. Conduct an internet search for real-world examples and information about a specific country's minimum wage. Try to find out the following.

1 The level of the wage floor, in either hourly, weekly, or monthly terms.

2 Whether there's any research on this country policy.

3 Whether the minimum wage level is across the entire country, despite variations in cost of living.

For discussion and debate:

4 Is a minimum wage a helpful way of addressing income inequality?

Practice exam questions

Paper 1, part (a) questions

1. Using a Lorenz curve diagram and examples, distinguish between a country with a high level of income equality and one with a low level of income equality. (10 marks)

2. Distinguish between progressive, regressive, and proportional taxation, providing examples of each.
   Explain the distinction between equality and equity.
   Identify and explain three causes of inequality.
   Explain the difference between relative and absolute poverty. (10 marks)

Paper 1, part (b) questions

3. Justify the claim that poverty's consequences make its elimination the most important objective of economic policy. (15 marks)

4. Evaluate the effectiveness of a progressive income tax at bringing about a more equal distribution of a nation's income. (15 marks)

5. **HL** Using real-world examples, evaluate the effects of a country making its tax system more progressive. (15 marks)

6. **HL** Using real-world examples, discuss the extent to which transfer payments can eliminate poverty. (15 marks)

4-mark questions from Paper 2 or HL Paper 3

7. Person A makes $100,00, while Person B makes $50,000. Each pays $10,000 in total tax. Identify and explain which person is paying tax in the more regressive system. (4 marks)

8. Using a Lorenz curve, show the effect of a change to a more progressive tax system on the distribution of income. (4 marks)

Real-world issue 2

How do governments manage their economy and how effective are their policies?

- **Government intervention** attempts to achieve macroeconomic objectives through a **choice** of policies.
- Political, economic, social, and environmental factors are **interdependent** and will influence the effectiveness of government policies.

Demand management: monetary policy

19

19.1 What is monetary policy?

Monetary policy refers to actions taken by a country's central bank that increase or decrease the supply of money in the economy in order to change interest rates and either expand or contract the amount of aggregate spending.

A *demand-side policy*, monetary policy aims to increase or decrease aggregate demand (AD) by changing the interest rate, which as you will recall from Chapter 14, is a determinant of both investment and consumption. A secondary objective of monetary policy is promoting trade objectives, since a change in the interest rate can affect a country's exchange rate, and thus a third component of AD, net exports.

What is a central bank?

To understand monetary policy, we must first have an understanding of what a central bank is and how central banks differ across countries. Defined simply, a central bank is the 'government's bank'. It is the institution that regulates all *commercial banks* (the for-profit institutions with which households and firms can save or borrow money). In addition to setting and overseeing bank regulations, central banks act as the bankers' banks. In other words, when commercial banks need to borrow money to extend credit in the economy, they can do so by borrowing from the central bank. Additionally, commercial banks' *reserves* (the share of total deposits that they do not lend out) are held by the central bank. In this regard, central banks act for commercial banks somewhat how commercial banks act for households and firms: they hold onto the assets of commercial banks and make loans to commercial banks, just as commercial banks do for the rest of the economy.

The most important function of a central bank, beyond regulating and offering services to commercial banks, is overseeing the process of **money creation** in the economy. It may seem odd, but the amount of money in an economy at any given time exceeds the size of the *monetary base* (the amount of actual cash and coins plus banks' reserves) by some multiple determined by the central bank's **minimum reserve requirement** – the proportion of total deposits the central bank requires commercial banks to keep in reserve. When this number is changed, the amount of credit, and thus the total supply of money in the economy, can be increased or decreased. Additionally, central banks have the ability to inject or withdraw money from the economy directly through **open market operations**, or the buying and selling of government securities (bonds) from commercial banks. Through the implementation of these and other tools, the central bank can control the interest rate in the economy and thus expand or contract the level of aggregate demand. The various tools of monetary policy will be explored in more detail later in this chapter.

A final note on central banks is to distinguish between the different roles they play across countries. In most Western democracies, such as in Europe and North America, central banks, while technically a part of the government, make monetary policy decisions independent of the other branches of government. They are not *political institutions*, in other words, and officials working for the central bank are neither elected nor are they expected to respond to the demands of elected officials. Central bank *independence* is necessary to promote certainty among all stakeholders in an economy that the levers of monetary policy will not be pulled for the political advantage of a particular elected official or political party, and instead will be harnessed solely for the promotion of the previously studied macroeconomic objectives.

There are many countries, however, in which central banks are not independent of the country's government, and instead act as *national banks*, promoting the objectives of whatever party controls the government. An example is China's People's Bank, which actively promotes aims laid out by the Chinese Communist Party, which might include the expansion of credit, inflation control, or intervention in the foreign exchange markets for its currency, the yuan, for the promotion of **international trade** objectives.

Before we dive deeper into the tools of monetary policy, which only HL students must know the details of, we will look more closely at monetary policy's goals.

19.2 What are the goals of monetary policy?

Learning outcomes

At the end of this section you will be able to:

- explain the goals of monetary policy, including:
    - inflation targeting
    - low unemployment
    - reducing business cycle fluctuations to promote stable, long-term growth
    - promoting **external balance**.

Inflation targeting

In Chapter 16, Macroeconomic objective: low and stable inflation, we use the story of Goldilocks as an analogy for the goal that economic policymakers pursue a low and stable rate of inflation. An inflation rate that is *too high*, recall, threatens to push the economy into an inflationary spiral, where too much demand chases too few goods, and prices are continually driven upward while wages struggle to keep up with increases in the consumer price index (CPI). An inflation rate that is *too low*, on the other hand, will dampen consumer and investor confidence and lead to delayed consumption and investment, possibly pushing the economy into the deflationary spiral described in Chapter 16, in which rising unemployment leads to falling consumption and investment, deflation, and further increases in unemployment. The resulting recessionary gap can be difficult to close as wages are slow to adjust to the depressed price level.

Thus, both deflation and high inflation are some of the most dreaded evils that monetary policymakers strive to avoid. *Inflation targeting* refers to the central bank's efforts to increase or decrease the supply of money and control interest rates with the aim of keeping inflation within a narrow range of values. In most developed economies this range is typically between 2% and 3%.

Low unemployment

While most central banks today explicitly target an inflation rate, a mostly unstated objective of doing so is to promote a low unemployment rate. The Phillips curve taught us that, at least historically, there has been a trade-off between inflation and unemployment in an economy. A very low inflation rate (or deflation) is typically accompanied by high levels of unemployment, as weak AD puts reduced pressure on price levels and also leads firms to reduce the size of their workforce. Very high inflation, on the other hand, is typically associated with very low unemployment, as high AD pushes prices up and leads firms to hire more workers to produce more output.

You will recall from Chapter 15 that high unemployment results in several consequences for society, including personal, social, and economic costs. Very low unemployment, evidence of an economy that is overheating, has consequences as well, first among which is the increased likelihood of an inflationary spiral. Therefore, an implicit objective of monetary policymakers is to promote a balance between low inflation and full employment with economic growth. The secondary objective of inflation targeting is low and stable unemployment.

Reduce business cycle fluctuations and promote long-term economic growth

In Chapter 13, Measuring economic activity, the business cycle model was introduced, showing how economies tend to fluctuate between periods of expansion and contraction, experiencing peaks and troughs over time. With these business cycle fluctuations come uncertainty and the resulting shocks to AD, rising and falling unemployment, and unstable inflation. Implicit in both inflation targeting and the promotion of low unemployment is the reduction in fluctuations in the business cycle. Because monetary policy influences AD, it is a powerful tool to moderate the business cycle.

Stable, long-term economic growth is evidence of a country's central bank practising responsible monetary policy. Not all fluctuations in the business cycle are the result of irresponsible monetary policies, but it has been argued that economic collapses like the Great Recession of 2008–10 were partly the fault of central banks in the USA and Europe. The property and stock market bubbles that burst in 2007 might have been checked at an earlier stage if interest rates had been increased in the mid-2000s. The 2007 collapse in asset values led to a drop in aggregate demand and pulled the world's economies into recession in 2008 and 2009. Figure 19.1 shows a business cycle for the world economy from 2000 to 2018.

The contractions in 2008 and 2014 each represent a period in which overall global output decreased. Many argue that the economic hardships experienced during recessions can be mitigated if responsible policymakers make decisions based on

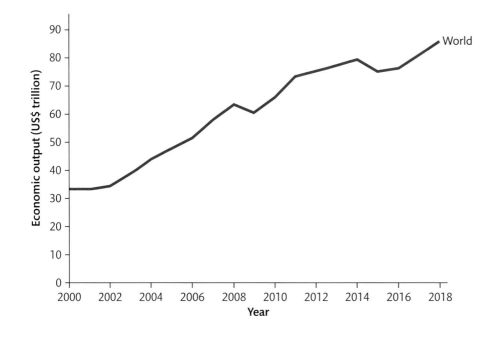

the best available evidence, and do not hesitate to take measures, even if they are unpopular, to constrain demand during periods of unsustainable economic growth. Of course, knowing when an economy's growth rate is unsustainable is a challenge that few can say they are able to achieve with 100% certainty.

External balance

A final goal of monetary policy is the promotion of international trade objectives, which might include the promotion of exports to other countries, increasing the availability of imported goods such as capital equipment or medical devices, or simply promoting stable, balanced trade with the rest of the world. A country's *external balance* refers to the flow of goods, services, and investments between the country and all other countries. External *imbalances*, such as when a country spends far more on imports than it earns from the sale of exports, have consequences that will be explored in later chapters, many of which are detrimental to the economy's health. Therefore, a goal of monetary policymakers is to promote some degree of balanced trade and investment with the rest of the world.

How does monetary policy affect external balances, you might ask? As we will see, a country's interest rate is a strong determinant of its exchange rate, or the value of its currency relative to other currencies on foreign exchange markets. You might recall from Chapter 14, on AD and aggregate supply (AS), that one of the determinants of net exports is the exchange rate. By raising or lowering interest rates, therefore, central banks can strengthen or weaken the value of their currencies relative to other currencies, and thereby either encourage or discourage exports or imports. If policymakers see their country's trade balance moving too far into the negative, for example (meaning imports are increasing and exports are decreasing), an interest rate cut can *devalue the currency*, which makes imports more expensive and exports cheaper. The result could be a reversal of the trade imbalance, as net exports increase, contributing to a boost in AD at home.

19.3 HL How do banks 'create' money?

Learning outcomes

At the end of this section you will be able to:

- outline how commercial banks operate using fractional reserve banking
- distinguish between required reserves and excess reserves
- analyse how excess reserves are the basis of expansion of the money supply by the banking system
- explain how the money multiplier is calculated and that the size of expansion of the money supply depends on the money multiplier.

To understand how central banks 'create' money in the economy, we first must explore the role that commercial banks play. Commercial banks are those that offer services to the general public and to businesses. By accepting deposits in checking/current and savings accounts, commercial banks protect households' and firms' financial assets, and by making loans banks provide money for investments in infrastructure, capital equipment, and housing for the economy. Banks act as the primary intermediary between households who wish to earn interest on their savings and businesses who want to borrow money for investment.

What is fractional reserve banking?

By accepting deposits from households, then lending out a proportion of those deposits to borrowers, which themselves end up being deposited and lent out again and again, banks *create new money* through their everyday activities. This is possible because banks only keep a fraction of their deposits in reserve; thus, the system of money creation described here is known as *fractional reserve banking*.

What are required reserves?

Commercial banks are required to keep a certain percentage of deposits in reserve. Required reserves are the portion of a bank's deposits the bank is required by the country's central bank to keep in reserve. A reserve requirement of 20% means that a bank with total deposits equalling ¥100 million (¥ is the symbol for yen, the currency of Japan) would have to keep ¥20 million on reserve at the central bank. This money may not be loaned out by the commercial bank.

With the other ¥80 million, the bank can make loans and charge interest on those loans. The bank's business model is to charge a higher interest rate to borrowers than it pays to households saving money with the bank.

What are excess reserves?

Excess reserves are a bank's actual reserves minus required reserves. Banks are allowed to make loans only from their excess reserves.

For example, assume Bank Y has €30,000 in total deposits, and that in the country in which Bank Y operates the minimum reserve requirement is 50% (or 0.5). We can calculate Bank Y's minimum required reserves by multiplying the reserve requirement by the bank's total deposits.

$$Minimum\ required\ reserves = 0.5 \times €30,000 = €15,000$$

Bank Y is required to keep €15,000 in its reserves. Let us assume that Bank Y's actual reserves equal €18,000. We can determine the bank's *excess reserves* by subtracting its required reserves from its actual reserves.

$$Excess\ reserves = Actual\ reserves - required\ reserves$$

$$= €18,000 - €15,000 = €3,000$$

Excess reserves are the money with which a bank is able to make new loans. Once a loan is made to a client and that money gets spent, earned, and deposited in someone else's bank, new reserves will be created, some of them required, some excess, which can once again be loaned out. Excess reserves, therefore, are the basis on which commercial banks can *create new money* in a fractional reserve banking system.

The fractional reserve system of banking described here, in which commercial banks are only required to keep a fraction of their total deposits in reserve and are allowed to loan out the excess reserves, forms the basis on which the supply of money in an economy can be increased or decreased via the central bank's interactions with commercial banks. Before we explore the tools through which central banks can expand or contract the money supply, we have to first understand more details about how fractional reserve banking works.

What is the money multiplier?

Whenever a bank makes a loan to a borrower, *new money is actually being created by the banking system*. It sounds crazy, but it really does happen.

Assume that Bank X receives a deposit of S/100 (S/ is the symbol for Peruvian nuevo sol, the currency of Peru) and that the central bank requires all commercial banks to keep 20% of their total deposits on reserve (the minimum reserve requirement is 0.2). Figure 19.2 illustrates how this S/100 deposit will lead to the creation of S/400 of new money across the banking system.

Money deposited in one bank creates excess reserves, which can be loaned out to borrowers, spent, and deposited in other banks, creating more excess reserves that can be loaned out again. In this way, an initial change in bank deposits will lead to a greater change in the overall money supply in an economy. The degree by which the money supply will be affected depends on the size of the money multiplier.

$$The\ money\ multiplier = \frac{1}{Minimum\ reserve\ requirement}$$

To determine the total impact on the money supply of an initial change in a bank's deposits, we can multiply the initial change in excess reserves by the money multiplier.

Video suggestion:
You have read about it, now you can review what you have just learned by watching a video by the author!
▶ Simply click here in your eBook for a video on money creation in a fractional reserve banking system.

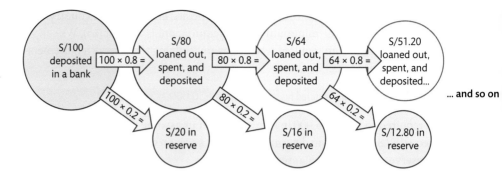

Figure 19.2 The expansion of money in a fractional reserve banking system

... and so on

Worked example 19.1

When S/100 is deposited in Bank X required reserves increase by S/20 and excess reserves increase by S/80. Assuming the bank loans out all of its excess reserves, we can multiply the change in excess reserves by the money multiplier:

$$S/80 \times \frac{1}{0.2} = S/80 \times 5 = \mathbf{S/400}$$

The initial deposit of S/100 will lead to the creation of S/400 of new money throughout the banking system.

Now that we have the mechanics of money creation in a fractional reserve banking system down, it's time to examine the ways central banks can pull levers to create or destroy money in an economy, and by doing so, stimulate or contract the level of aggregate spending to promote the macroeconomic objectives outlined earlier in this chapter.

19.4 **HL** What are the tools of monetary policy?

Learning outcomes

At the end of this section you will be able to:

- Outline the different tools monetary policymakers employ to either expand or contract the level of aggregate spending, including:
  - open market operations
  - minimum reserve requirements
  - changes in the central bank **minimum lending rate**
  - **quantitative easing**.

Monetary policy refers to the tools central banks use to increase or decrease the supply of money in an economy. By changing the money supply, a central bank can cause interest rates to change, which can then influence the level of aggregate expenditures in the economy. A central bank has three tools for increasing or decreasing the supply of money in an economy.

Open market operations

Open market operations refer to a central bank's buying and selling of bonds in the bond market and are the most commonly employed monetary policy tool. Every commercial bank will invest some of its depositors' money into government bonds. Bonds are not money. So if a central bank wishes to increase the supply of money in the economy, it can buy bonds from commercial banks using newly printed cash (which IS money!) If the goal is to reduce the money supply, a central bank can sell bonds to commercial banks, which results in less money in circulation and more government bonds on banks' balance sheets.

Open market operations can be employed as either an **expansionary monetary policy** (one that increases the money supply and reduces interest rates) or as a **contractionary monetary policy** (one that reduces the money supply and increases interest rates).

In order to reduce interest rates, a central bank will buy bonds from commercial banks and the public. An open market purchase of government bonds will cause the money supply to increase by a magnitude determined by the money multiplier.

Worked example 19.2

Assume the central bank that regulates Bank X from earlier in this chapter decides to reduce interest rates by increasing the money supply by S/10 billion. With a minimum required reserve ratio of 20%, the money multiplier equals 5 (for each sol deposited into the banking system, S/5 of new money can be created through banks' lending activities).

Therefore, in order to increase the money supply by S/10 billion the central bank must increase bank reserves by $\dfrac{S/10\ billion}{5}$, or S/2 billion. The central bank must purchase S/2 billion of bonds from commercial banks in order to increase the money supply by S/10 billion. Commercial banks will see an immediate increase in their excess reserves of S/2 billion, allowing them to make new loans that will eventually be multiplied until there is S/10 billion of new money in the economy.

As we will see in our next section, the initial increase in reserves will lead to a decrease in the equilibrium interest rate in the economy, stimulating consumption and investment, and boosting aggregate demand.

In order to raise interest rates, the central bank must reduce the money supply, requiring the central bank to sell bonds on the open market.

Worked example 19.3

Assume the central bank decides to decrease the money supply by S/15 billion. With a money multiplier of 5, a S/3 billion sale of bonds to commercial banks would be required.

$$Needed\ sale\ of\ bonds = \frac{Desired\ \Delta\ in\ money\ supply}{money\ multiplier}$$

$$\frac{-\$15\ billion}{5} = -\$3\ billion$$

In selling bonds to commercial banks, excess reserves in the banking system decrease by S/3 billion, leading to a decrease in the overall money supply of S/15 billion.

Open market operations, involving the purchase or sale of government bonds by the central bank, are the most commonly pulled lever of monetary policy, but not the only one. A more powerful, albeit less frequently used tool of monetary policy is changing the minimum reserve requirement itself.

Minimum reserve requirements

When a central bank changes the minimum reserve requirement itself, the size of the money multiplier changes, and banks will find that they either have more excess reserves with which to make loans (when the reserve requirement is decreased) or smaller excess reserves (when the reserve requirement is increased). Lowering the reserve requirement would increase the size of the money multiplier, while raising the reserve requirement would cause less new money to be created whenever a loan is made.

Despite the immediate and dramatic effect changing the minimum reserve requirement can have on the money supply, central banks rarely do so. This is likely because so many commercial banks operate with very low levels of excess reserves; therefore, any increase in the reserve requirements would create *liquidity problems* for commercial banks (in other words, they would not have the cash on hand to meet the increased requirement). Reducing the reserve requirement could create new money immediately and lead to more lending activity in the economy, but once lowered, banks would be strapped for cash once the central bank inevitably tried to raise the reserve requirement in the future to constrain aggregate demand.

Changes in the central bank minimum lending rate (base rate/discount rate/refinancing rate changes)

Recall from earlier in this chapter that in addition to regulating commercial banks and acting as the reserve bank to the commercial banking system, central banks also make loans to commercial banks when they are in need of liquidity. If a central bank wishes to increase the money supply, one way it can do so is by reducing the interest it charges commercial banks on these loans.

The central bank's lending rate goes by different names in different countries, including the 'base rate', the '**discount rate**', and the 'refinancing rate'. If this rate is lowered, commercial banks will be more willing to make loans to private borrowers and interest rates will fall; thus a decrease in the central bank's lending rate is an expansionary monetary policy. If the central bank's lending rate is increased, commercial banks will be less willing to loan to private borrowers and the interest rate will increase, a contractionary monetary policy.

Quantitative easing

A final tool of monetary policy is one that was only recently added to central banks' policy quiver: quantitative easing (QE). QE is the process of the central bank loaning money *directly to the government* by purchasing government bonds. The difference between QE and an open market bond purchase is that in open market operations the central bank buys bonds that have already been bought by the public and are held by commercial banks in a secondary market. In QE, on the other hand, a central bank buys bonds directly from the government, essentially financing government deficits and debt with *newly printed money*.

QE increases commercial bank reserves as they sell bonds to the central bank. By financing government debts directly, QE increases the overall money supply in the economy and allows the government to spend money that might not have been made available by the private sector, keeping interest rates low in the economy. Lower interest rates lead to reduced debt payments of those who have already borrowed, freeing up funds for consumption and investment. A secondary effect of QE is downward pressure on the exchange rate, which adds the additional stimulus of increased net exports. Chapter 25 will explain the relationship between interest rates and exchange rates in more detail.

QE was introduced during the global financial crisis of 2007 and the subsequent Great Recession of 2008–10, when private investor confidence hit an all-time low and government deficits across the developed world hit all-time highs. The US Federal Reserve Bank and the European Central Bank (the central banks of the two respective economies), along with the Bank of Japan turned to QE as a way of massively increasing the amount of money in the economy, keeping interest rates low, but also financing actual spending, rather than pumping money into the private sector where it would only be saved due to uncertainty and low consumer and business confidence.

One of the shortcomings of traditional monetary policy tools (open market operations, changing the reserve requirement, and changing the central bank's lending rate) is that pumping money into the banking system and lowering interest rates only stimulates AD if households and firms are confident enough to borrow money and spend it. When private sector confidence is very low, as it tends to be during deep recessions, QE can be employed to lend money not to the private sector, but to the government, who can pump newly minted money into the economy through infrastructure projects, education, and health spending, increased transfer payments to unemployed or low-income households, or other public spending programmes that promise to prop up aggregate demand during a downturn in the business cycle.

Video suggestion:
You have read about it, now you can review what you have just learned by watching a video by the author!
▶ Simply click here in your eBook for a video on the tools of monetary policy.

Case study – experiments in monetary policy

During the summer of 2020 the US Federal Reserve Bank invented yet another tool of monetary policy. For the first time the 'Fed' began intervening in the market not only for government bonds, but for *corporate bonds* as well. A corporate bond is a certificate of debt issued by a private business, or corporation. When the COVID-19 pandemic struck and the world's economies began shutting down in spring 2020 the markets for private corporate debt began to shudder, as investors feared that with their consumers trapped in their homes large companies would struggle to pay the interest on their past debts and possibly even default on their bonds, leaving bondholders stuck with worthless investments.

In mid-May 2020 the Fed began purchasing shares in 'broad-based exchange-traded funds', which are basically bundles of lots of different corporations' bonds. Much like an open market purchase of *government bonds* injects money into the banking system and drives interest rates down, a central bank purchase of corporate bonds helps keep borrowing costs for businesses low and instils confidence among investors in bonds and in equities (also called stocks, equities represent ownership shares in businesses) that large firms will not go bust even as aggregate demand falls across the economy.

Discussion questions:

1 How does the Fed's intervention in the corporate bond market affect the level of household wealth in the USA?
2 Why is it important to protect wealth during recessions?
3 What are the risks of a government bank buying up the bonds of private companies?
4 Should a central bank take steps to keep interest rates for private firms lower than they would be otherwise without central bank intervention? Why or why not?

19.5 HL How are equilibrium interest rates determined?

Learning outcome

At the end of this section you will be able to:

• explain, using a demand and supply of money diagram, how equilibrium interest rates are determined, outlining the role of the central bank in influencing the supply of money.

With the tools of monetary policy behind us, it is time to employ a model of the *money market* to show *how* changes in the money supply and money demand affect the equilibrium interest rate in an economy.

Money demand

The demand for money shows the inverse relationship between the nominal interest rate and the quantity of money people want to hold. People demand money for one of two reasons: either as an asset or to purchase goods or services.

Asset demand

The asset demand for money is inversely related to the interest rate. At higher interest rates less money is demanded as an asset, because the opportunity cost of holding cash is higher due to the interest income foregone by holding money instead of investing it in savings accounts, government bonds, or other interest-earning assets. At low interest rates the asset demand for money is greater since there is less opportunity cost of holding cash since alternative financial assets (savings accounts, bonds) would earn less interest income.

Transaction demand

The transaction demand for money depends on the level of output produced in the nation and the interest rate. At lower interest rates households are more willing to spend money on goods and services due to the lower opportunity cost of spending rather than saving. At higher interest rates the public demands less money for transactions, since the opportunity cost of buying stuff is higher when more interest can be earned in financial assets.

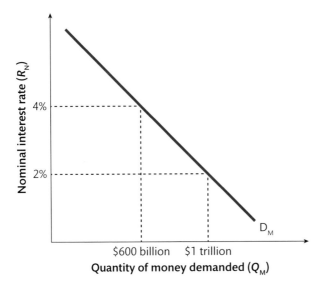

Figure 19.3 Money demand drops as the nominal interest rate rises

As national income rises, the demand for money for transactions increases at every interest rate, as people wish to consume more when their incomes are higher. During recessions, when national income falls, the transaction demand for money decreases at every interest rate due to the fall in income and consumption.

The inverse relationship between the demand for money as an asset and for transactions and the nominal interest rate is illustrated in a money demand curve. Figure 19.3 shows an economy's money demand curve.

Figure 19.3 shows that at a 4% interest rate, households wish to hold $600 billion as an asset and for transactions, while at 2%, $1 trillion is demanded.

A change in national income and consumption would cause a shift in the money demand curve. Assume, for instance, the economy enters a recession and household incomes fall, leading to a fall in consumption of goods and services. Now, at every interest rate, consumers demand less money for transactions. The decrease in money demand is shown as an inward shift of the D_M curve in Figure 19.4.

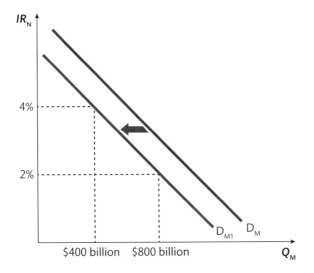

Figure 19.4 A recession leads to a decrease in money demand at every interest rate

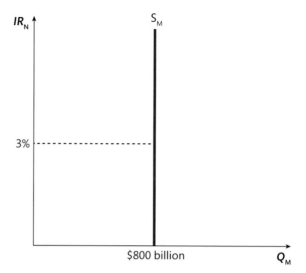

Figure 19.5 Money supply is determined by the central bank and is therefore vertical ▶

Owing to falling income and consumption, money demand has decreased. Now, only $400 billion is demanded at an interest rate of 4% and $800 billion at 2%.

Money supply

The money demand curve is just one side of the money market model. Any demand curve is lonely without its counterpart, the supply curve. Money supply is determined by a country's central bank and is independent of the nominal interest rate. As we have learned, the central bank can increase or decrease the money supply in order to influence the equilibrium interest rate and promote its macroeconomic objectives, the primary one being low and stable inflation.

The money supply curve is vertical at the central bank's desired quantity of money. If, for example, the central bank sets the money supply (cash and demand deposits) at $800 billion, the money supply curve is as shown in Figure 19.5.

The money supply, established by the central bank's monetary policy, is vertical at $800 billion.

Equilibrium in the money market

The interest rate does not affect the supply of money; rather, the equilibrium interest rate is achieved where the quantity of money demanded is equal to the quantity supplied by the central bank. In order to determine what the equilibrium interest rate is in Mongolia, in other words, we must consider both the money supply and money demand, as in Figure 19.6.

By including money demand and money supply in the same graph we can see the equilibrium interest rate is 3%. At this rate households demand ₮800 billion (₮ is the symbol for tögrög, or tughrik, the currency of Mongolia) for transactions and as cash to hold onto as an asset. At 3% the quantity of money demanded is equal to the quantity supplied.

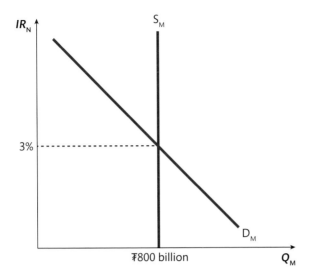

Figure 19.6   The equilibrium interest rate is where money demanded is equal to money supplied

Disequilibrium in the money market

Disequilibrium nominal interest rates create surpluses and shortages in the money market. For example, assume commercial banks attempted to charge borrowers and offer savers 4% instead of 3%. The impact on the market can be seen in Figure 19.7.

At 4%, there is a surplus of money in the system; the quantity supplied (₮800 billion) exceeds the quantity demanded (₮600 billion). Market forces would drive nominal interest rates towards equilibrium, as banks must lower rates to incentivise borrowers to take out and spend the extra ₮200 billion that banks have in their reserves.

At a rate below equilibrium, a shortage of money arises and market forces would drive nominal interest rates up as banks would be unable to meet the demand from households and firms that wish to hold more money for transactions or as an asset

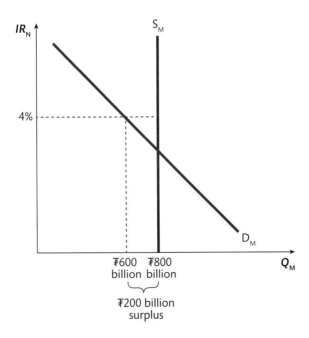

Figure 19.7   An interest rate above equilibrium creates a surplus of money

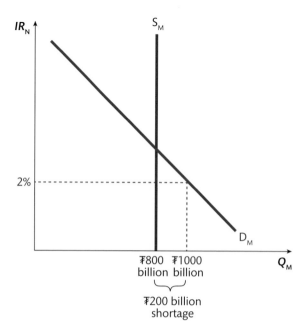

than there is available. At 2%, for example, a shortage of ₮200 billion would exist, as seen in Figure 19.8.

Shortages and surpluses in a country's money market exist when either the quantity of money demanded by households and firms is greater than or less than the quantity supplied. As in the market for anything (cars, toys, food, houses), market forces tend to drive the money market towards equilibrium, where the quantities of money demanded and supplied are equal. The equilibrium nominal interest rate is where households and firms demand just as much money as the central bank supplies.

Changes in equilibrium

Factors that shift the demand for money, such as changes in national income or the price level, and supply of money, such as monetary policy, change the equilibrium nominal interest rate.

Previously we explained how a change in national income can shift the demand for money. Recessions cause money demand to fall, while expansions cause it to rise. Changes in the price level can have similar effects on money demand. Inflation, which occurs when there is an increase in the price of consumer goods and services, causes money demand to increase and drives up the nominal interest rate (when things cost more, more money is needed to buy them). Deflation, on the other hand, causes money demand to fall and nominal interest rates to decrease.

Figure 19.9 shows the effect of recession or deflation (a) and economic expansion or inflation (b) on the equilibrium interest rate. In both cases, we assume the central bank holds the money supply constant at ₮800 billion.

A decrease in money demand caused by falling income or falling prices causes the nominal interest rate to fall. Banks must lower interest rates in order to maintain the quantity demanded at the same level as the quantity supplied. Without a drop in interest rates, excess money would be available in the system and banks would not be able to loan out all the money they have in reserve.

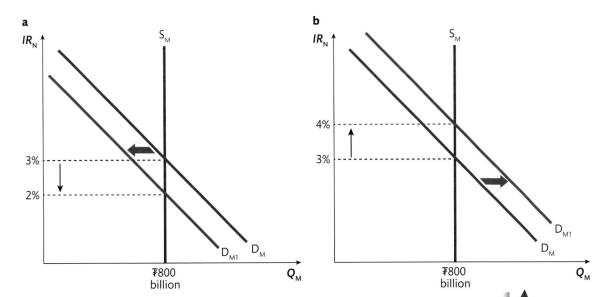

An increase in money demand caused by rising incomes or rising prices causes the nominal interest rate to increase. Banks must raise interest rates in order to maintain the quantity demanded at the same level as the quantity supplied. Without a rate hike, there would be a shortage of money in the system and borrowers would not be able to access the money they demand for transactions and as an asset.

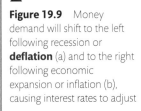

Figure 19.9   Money demand will shift to the left following recession or **deflation** (a) and to the right following economic expansion or inflation (b), causing interest rates to adjust

Monetary policy's effect on the equilibrium interest rate

A change in a central bank's monetary policy causes the money supply to shift and leads to a change in the equilibrium interest rate. When the supply of money in an economy increases as the result of expansionary monetary policy, the nominal interest rate falls in order to maintain equilibrium in the market. A decrease in the money supply resulting from a contractionary monetary policy causes interest rates to rise as money becomes scarcer thus the cost of borrowing it or the reward for saving it increases. Figure 19.10 shows the effect of expansionary and contractionary monetary policies on the money market.

Figure 19.10   Interest rates also respond to expansionary monetary policy (a) and contractionary monetary policy (b)

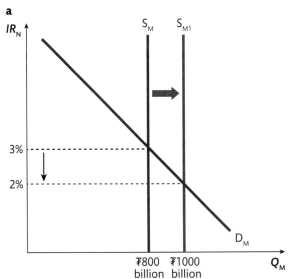

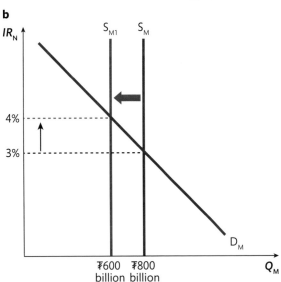

Video suggestion:
You have read about it, now you can review what you have just learned by watching a video by the author!

▶ Simply click here in your eBook for an introductory video on the money market.

Changes in the money supply are the result of a central bank's deliberate intervention in the money market through the use of monetary policy. Expansionary monetary policies (including buying bonds on the open market, lowering the minimum reserve requirement, lowering the central bank's borrowing rate, and QE) increase the money supply and cause the equilibrium interest rate to decrease. Contractionary policies (selling bonds, raising the reserve requirement, or increasing the central bank's borrowing rate), cause money supply to decrease and result in a higher equilibrium interest rate.

19.6 What is the difference between real and nominal interest rates?

Learning outcomes

At the end of this section you will be able to:

- describe the nominal interest rate as the rate of interest paid for a loan, unadjusted for inflation
- explain that lenders and borrowers establish nominal interest rates as the sum of their expected real interest rate and expected inflation
- calculate a real interest rate in hindsight by subtracting the actual inflation rate from the nominal interest rate.

The nominal interest rate is the annual rate a borrower must pay back a lender for the use of borrowed money or the annual rate a lender receives in payment for their investment. The real interest rate is the nominal interest rate adjusted for inflation.

Lenders and borrowers will establish nominal interest rates based on their desired rate of return and the expected rate of inflation. For example, if a bank is lending money to Rahim, and the two agree that the bank should earn a real return of 5% each year the loan is paid back, then the bank and Rahim must establish a nominal interest rate that takes into account the expected inflation rate. Let us assume both parties expect an inflation rate of 3%. If the bank's desired return on a loan to Rahim is 5%, then the bank must factor in inflation of 3% and charge Rahim 5% + 3%, or 8%.

Inflation will reduce the value of money a borrower repays, so lenders must add the expected inflation rate to the real rate in order to establish a nominal interest rate.

Nominal interest rate = Real interest rate + Expected inflation rate

A real interest rate can be calculated in hindsight by subtracting the actual inflation rate from the nominal interest rate:

Real interest rate = Nominal interest rate − Inflation rate

Lenders charge an inflation premium by adjusting the nominal interest rates they charge borrowers by the anticipated inflation rate. Higher expected inflation will lead banks to raise the inflation premium and increase the nominal interest rate on new loans. This way, banks are protected from the diminished purchasing power of the money they are repaid. The nominal interest rate established is the expected real interest rate plus the expected inflation rate.

19.7 How can monetary policy be used to close output gaps?

Learning outcomes

At the end of this section you will be able to:

- explain how changes in interest rates can influence the level of AD in an economy
- describe the mechanism through which monetary policy can help an economy close a deflationary or an inflationary gap
- construct diagrams to show the potential effects of expansionary and contractionary monetary policy.

Expansionary or contractionary monetary policies are used to restore full employment when the economy is in a negative or positive output gap.

Expansionary monetary policy

Assume, for example, that the economy is experiencing a recession with lower than desired inflation; because output is falling and prices are rising more slowly than usual, business investment has declined and household savings has increased as business and consumer sentiment are low. In an effort to stimulate spending and restore full employment the central bank engages in an expansionary monetary policy, which reduces interest rates and stimulates consumption and investment.

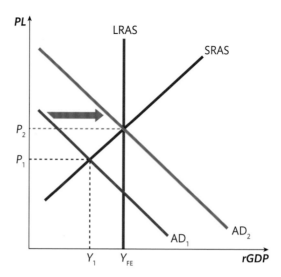

Figure 19.11 Expansionary monetary policies close a negative output gap by stimulating an outward shift in AD

In Figure 19.11, monetary 'stimulus' has lowered interest rates, increased AD, and closed a recessionary gap in the economy. Notice that before the expansionary monetary policy this country had a recessionary gap of $Y_{FE} - Y_1$. However, after the stimulus, AD has increased to the full employment level.

Contractionary monetary policy

A contractionary monetary policy will have the opposite effect on output, employment, and the price level. Assume that rather than a recession, the economy is facing high inflation. The central bank can contract AD and reduce inflation by reducing the money supply, causing interest rates to increase, leading to less consumption and investment. Figure 19.12 shows the effect of a contractionary monetary policy.

A 'tight' monetary policy has increased interest rates, reduced AD, and closed an inflationary gap of $Y_1 - Y_{FE}$. Inflation is brought within its target range, consistent with the full employment level of output and a natural rate of unemployment.

Figure 19.12
Contractionary monetary policies shift AD inwards to close an inflationary gap

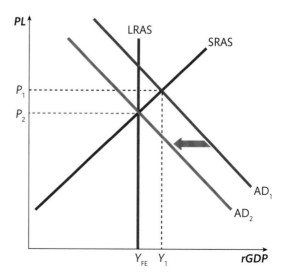

19.8 How effective is monetary policy?

This chapter has gone deep into monetary policy: its aims, the role of central banks, the different tools at central banks' disposal, the money market, and how it can be used to close output gaps. With its mechanics understood, we can now consider the effectiveness of monetary policy at achieving its desired objectives, which as we have seen include low and stable inflation, full employment, and other desired outcomes.

Constraints on monetary policy

While effective in some circumstances, there are situations in which monetary policy will prove inadequate or have only limited effect, particularly during deep recessions when interest rates have been lowered close to zero and when consumer and business confidence are depressed.

Limited scope for reducing interest rates when close to zero

Here is the thing about interest rates: when they are high, lowering them makes new spending by households and firms really attractive. Money becomes 'cheap', savings becomes less attractive, and therefore consumption and investment are likely to take off.

Free money!

But what about when interest rates are *already low*, or even *close to zero percent?* Economists have a term for such a situation: the 'zero-bound'. Zero percent is logically as low as interest rates can go; at this level the cost of borrowing money is, well, FREE, and the benefit of saving money is, well, nothing. There is no return on savings and no cost to borrowing. In normal economic times, when an economy is close to full employment, zero percent interest rates would likely lead to a spending spree that pushes the economy into an inflationary spiral.

However, during deep recessions zero percent might not be enough to incentivise the level of spending needed to pull the economy back to full employment. Such a situation is known as a *liquidity trap*; even when money is 'free', private stakeholders prefer to hold onto it as an asset rather than spend it. Alternative monetary policy tools, such as quantitative easing, are needed, when faced with a liquidity trap.

Some central banks, such as Switzerland's and Japan's, have experimented with *negative nominal interest rates* to stimulate spending when faced with a liquidity trap. The idea is by saving money, households and firms will actually see their savings *lose value* over time. A CHF100 savings account in a bank with -1% interest rates will have only CHF99 in it a year later. Negative rates give individuals motivation to spend now before their money loses value in the future. Of course, referring back to the section of this chapter that distinguished between nominal and real interest rates, we realise that individuals do not make decisions based only on the nominal rate, and will consider the effect inflation will have on the value of their money as well. A negative nominal interest rate will, in fact, translate to a positive real rate if there is *deflation* in the economy. To illustrate, consider a Swiss individual facing a -1% interest rate on her savings. If inflation is -2%, then the real interest rate can be calculated by subtracting the inflation rate from the nominal interest rate.

$$Real\ interest\ rate = -1\% - (-2\%) = -1\% + 2\% = 1\%$$

Whereas the Swiss central bank is trying to push households to spend by driving nominal rates below zero, in a deflationary environment there may still be an incentive to save.

The zero lower bound of nominal interest rates poses a limitation on monetary policy's effectiveness at stimulating aggregate demand during deep recessions.

Low consumer and business confidence

As we hinted above, low consumer and business confidence can create a *liquidity trap*, in which households and firms prefer to hold onto cash for the future rather than spend it now, no matter how low interest rates get. Money is an asset that becomes *more valuable over time* when there is deflation in the economy. In such a situation monetary policy becomes almost useless at stimulating consumption and investment.

Strengths of monetary policy

Monetary policy is usually the first line of defence against high inflation or rising unemployment and deflation. This is because it has several strengths over the other two types of policies the government has to choose from: fiscal and supply side, both of which will be explored in the following two chapters.

Video suggestion:
You have read about it, now you can review what you have just learned by watching a video by the author!
▶ Simply click here in your eBook for a video on evaluating the effectiveness of monetary policy during recessions.

Incremental

First of all, monetary policy can be enacted relatively quickly and in small increments. Central bankers refer to changes in interest rates in 'basis points'. One basis point is equal to 1/100th of 1%. That is SMALL! Typically, when expansionary or contractionary policies are enacted, central bankers will announce their changes in terms of how many basis points by which they are changing the nominal interest rate, and in most developed economies these changes rarely happen in increments larger than 25 basis points. In other words, a monetary stimulus might lower the nominal interest rate by 1/4th of 1%: for example, from 3.75% to 3.5%.

Flexible with short time lags

Compared to fiscal policies and supply-side policies, which require the national government to convene and agree upon a set of spending and taxation changes that will help promote the government's macroeconomic objectives, monetary policy is typically able to be enacted quickly and with more flexibility. Recall from earlier in this chapter that central banks and the officials who work at them are typically *independent* from the elected politicians in government.

Central bankers are considered *technocrats,* meaning they make decisions based solely on available scientific evidence, not political priorities or social expectations. In addition, when a central bank announces an expansionary or contractionary policy change, the impact on the markets is instantaneous. Interest rates fluctuate thousands of times each day based on market conditions, and when an interest rate hike is announced by the central bank, its effect will be felt immediately, leading investors and consumers to respond within minutes or hours. There are short *time lags*, in other words. In contrast, a government spending package or tax increase will take months to be enacted and their effects will only trickle down into the real economy over a very long period of time.

Easily reversible

Finally, monetary policy changes are *easily reversible*. Interest rates, once lowered, can be raised within days if necessary, and vice versa. Technically, the same could be said for changes governments make to spending and taxation. But in reality, government fiscal policies (Chapter 20) are far harder to reverse once enacted. For example, if a government lowers taxes on the middle class to stimulate AD, but then a couple of years later high inflation is threatening economic stability, it is almost impossible for elected politicians to stand up and tell their voters that 'I promise to raise your taxes to bring down inflation.' A tax cut, it turns out, is very hard to reverse once put in place. Same with government spending: once a government has increased spending in some sector of the economy, stakeholders become accustomed to the increased income from government sources and any elected official would be risking his or her career by threatening to roll the government's spending back.

Once again, because of their independence from political influence and their tendency to act as technocrats, central bankers are able to do what is *best* for the economy at any given time, responding with flexibility and speed to macroeconomic shocks. For these reasons, monetary policy is typically the first line of defence against unwanted fluctuations in the business cycle.

Practice exam questions

1a. Explain how an increase in interest rates might affect the level of aggregate demand in an economy. (10 marks)

b. Evaluate the effectiveness of monetary policy when an economy is in deep recession. (15 marks)

2. **HL** Using appropriate diagrams, explain how a central bank's sale of government bonds to commercial banks will affect the equilibrium interest rate and level of aggregate demand in the economy. (8 marks)

3. How does an increase in the inflation rate affect the real interest rate in the economy, assuming all else is held constant? (4 marks)

4. **HL** Outline two monetary policy tools a central bank could employ to help close a recessionary gap. (4 marks)

5. **HL** Compare and contrast quantitative easing with an open market purchase of bonds by the central bank. (10 marks)

6. What is inflation targeting and why is it a worthwhile goal of monetary policymakers? (8 marks)

7. **HL** Using a money market diagram, explain what would happen if commercial banks attempted to charge borrowers an interest rate higher than the equilibrium interest rate. (8 marks)

8. **HL** Country Y is currently experiencing a negative output gap. Assume the minimum reserve requirement is 0.4 and the central bank engages in a $15 billion purchase of government bonds on the open market.

a. Calculate the maximum change in the money supply that might result from the central bank's open market operations. (2 marks)

b. Using a money market diagram, illustrate the effect the government bond purchase will have on the equilibrium nominal interest rate. (2 marks)

c. Using an AD/AS diagram, illustrate and explain the effect the central bank's open market operation will have on equilibrium output, employment, and the price level in the short run. (4 marks)

Demand management: fiscal policy

20

20.1 What is fiscal policy?

Learning outcomes

At the end of this section you will be able to:

- outline the sources of government revenue
- explain how government spending can be classified into current expenditures, capital expenditures, and transfer payments, providing examples of each
- distinguish between a budget deficit, a budget surplus, and a balanced budget.

In Chapter 19, Demand management: monetary policy, we learned all about how central banks, which are the government-affiliated, but usually politically sheltered institutions that control the money supply and set interest rates, can promote macroeconomic objectives by harnessing the various tools at their disposal. Monetary policy, we explained, is typically deployed as the first line of defence against fluctuations in the business cycle.

Because it is relatively nimble and has short time lags, monetary policy can be put into action quickly to fend off recessions or dampen inflation. However, when it fails, either due to the economy already having very low interest rates or due to depressed consumer and business confidence, the government often brings out the 'big guns' of *fiscal policy*. Fiscal policy refers to the central government's use of taxation and government spending to either directly or indirectly stimulate the level of aggregate demand (AD) in the economy.

Like monetary policy, fiscal policies are **demand-side policies**, meaning they are primarily used to target aggregate expenditures. Therefore, fiscal policy can be used to close output gaps with a view to promoting the macroeconomic goals of:

- low and stable inflation
- low unemployment
- a stable economic environment for long-term growth
- reduced business cycle fluctuations
- equitable distribution of income
- external balance.

As we will see, fiscal policy has several strengths and weaknesses, as well as potential long-run consequences that must be considered before government officials decide the extent to which it should be employed, particularly during recessions or periods of stagnation. Before we get into its evaluation, however, we will lay some groundwork for understanding what makes up the government *budget*, because fiscal policy is all about the flow of money into and out of government coffers.

What are the sources of government revenue?

Governments, like businesses and households, earn money and spend money. (Unlike households, many governments can also *create money*, which will be explored later in this chapter.) While households earn income by providing resources, most notably labour, to factor markets, and firms earn money through the sale of goods and services

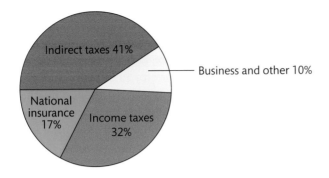

Figure 20.1 Most of the UK government's £873 billion total revenue for fiscal year 2020 is from direct and indirect taxation

in product markets, governments earn revenue through various sources, but most notably *taxes*. Together, direct taxes (taxes on income) and indirect taxes (on goods and services) are the primary source of government revenues in every country. Figure 20.1 depicts the sources of government revenue in the UK in fiscal year 2020, when the UK government's total revenues equalled £873 billion.

The 17% of UK tax revenue that comes from 'national insurance' is, in fact, another form of direct tax, as all UK workers pay 12% on weekly income of between £183 and £962 and 2% on earnings over £962 into the national insurance programme. Other direct taxes include the 32% of the UK's tax revenue that comes from income taxes paid both by households and firms.

The 41% of revenue generated by indirect taxes includes consumption taxes such as the value added tax (applied to all goods) and excise taxes (applied to specific goods, such as cigarettes, alcohol, and certain imports).

Finally, 10% of the UK's revenue comes from 'other' sources, which may include sales of businesses owned by the UK government or the sale of government property or other assets.

Case study – do taxes really 'pay' for government spending?: an introduction to modern monetary theory

It should be noted that while the £873 billion generated by the UK government through taxation and other sources is typically thought of as income for the government, it is not necessarily the case that the government *relies on this money* to pay for its expenditures (which we'll examine in a moment). In reality, the UK, as a country with its own currency, finances government spending through its treasury, which credits bank accounts with 'new money' whenever the government orders an expenditure.

According to *modern monetary theory* (MMT), the role of taxation in a country with its own currency (like the UK) is to create a demand for currency (if everyone has to pay taxes in British pounds, there is guaranteed to be demand for the pound), to control inflation (money can be taken out of the economy when too much demand threatens higher prices), to address income inequality (money can be redistributed from one group to another through transfers), and to discourage bad behaviour (*Pigouvian taxes*, Chapter 10, are those that discourage the consumption of harmful goods), but NOT to finance government spending.

Governments in countries with their own currencies (in contrast to countries that are in a **monetary union**, such as the eurozone) coordinate and execute government expenditures through their treasury departments or ministries. For example, when the government goes to pay for an infrastructure project such as a new highway, the treasury deposits newly 'printed' money into the accounts of the private sector contractors doing the work for the government (in reality, these transactions are mostly electronic, as paper money forms only a small fraction of the reserves in the banking system).

According to proponents of MMT, the idea that the government keeps tax revenues collected from households and firms in some account that it then uses to pay for new expenditures is a misunderstanding of how government finances actually work. While it is true that individuals and firms set income earned aside for expenditures or savings, the government collects taxes not in order to spend money, but to *destroy it*. Taxes are a means of 'de-circulating' currency that, if allowed to remain within the circular flow, would create inflation when added to new money the government injects into the economy through its current and capital expenditures.

MMT, described above, is a relatively new and somewhat controversial take on macroeconomic theory that we will explore further throughout this chapter. For now, let us assume that orthodox, mainstream, Keynesian economics is correct, and that a pound spent by the British government must either be collected as taxes or borrowed through the issuance of bonds.

What are the types of government expenditures?

Revenues represent the money taken out of the economy by the government. Expenditures are the money the government injects into the circular flow of the economy. Government spending takes three forms: current expenditures, capital expenditures, and transfers.

Current expenditures

Spending that keeps government institutions operating year after year is classified as *current expenditures*. This includes spending on education and healthcare, defence, general government operations, and public transportation, among other things. Current expenditures include the wages for all public sector employees plus other costs of 'keeping the lights on' at public institutions, such as utilities, rent, interest expenses, and so on.

Capital expenditures

When the government spends money on *new capital* or *infrastructure* it is considered a capital expenditure. Any spending that adds to the economy's stock of public capital is a capital expenditure, including new roads, bridges, airports, schools, hospitals, or military bases paid for by the government. In contrast to current expenditures, capital spending does not have to be renewed each year as projects are likely to have a start and an end date. Current expenditures, on the other hand, must be renewed each year just to keep public services functioning.

Transfers

Transfers are payments from the government to individuals or businesses for which no goods or services are provided. The term 'transfer' implies that money is being taken from one set of stakeholders in the economy (higher income earners, who pay more taxes, for example) and transferred to another group (families earning lower incomes, who may receive a wage subsidy, for instance). Transfers include spending on unemployment insurance, social security (old age pensions), subsidies for producers, and welfare payments to the poor.

Pensions and welfare are transfers, while healthcare, education, defence, protection, interest, transport, and general government are current expenditures. We can assume that a share of 'other spending' is made up of capital expenditures by the UK government.

The budget balance, deficits, and surpluses

You may have noticed that in 2020 UK government spending (£928 billion) exceeded government revenues (£873 billion). When a government spends more than it collects in revenues the government has a *budget deficit*. When in deficit, the government is injecting more into the economy in the form of spending than it is subtracting through taxation. On the other hand, a government may collect more revenue than it spends, a situation known as a *budget surplus*. When in surplus, the amount of money subtracted from the circular flow is greater than the amount the government injects.

Budget deficits are *expansionary*, since injections are greater than subtractions. Surpluses, which may sound like something to be pursued, are *contractionary*, since more money is withdrawn from the economy than is injected. An *expansionary fiscal policy*, therefore, typically requires the government to reduce taxes and increase government spending, increasing the size of its budget deficit in order to stimulate the level of AD and close a recessionary gap. A *contractionary fiscal policy*, which may be employed to close an inflationary gap, requires raising taxes and/or reducing government expenditures, which moves the budget towards surplus.

20.2 　HL　 What is the government debt?

Learning outcome

At the end of this section you will be able to:

- analyse the relationship between budget deficits/surpluses and the public (government) debt.

You will recall from Chapter 14 that debt is defined simply as 'what one owes'. Debt is a liability incurred when an individual, a business, or, in this case, a country's government, borrows money to pay for something. According to mainstream Keynesian economic theory, the government debt is the means by which governments finance their deficits; when expenditures are greater than revenues, government must borrow to make up the difference.

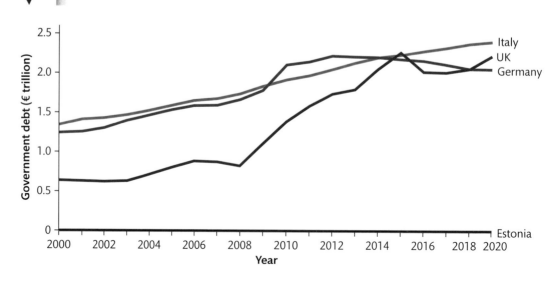

US government bonds

Video suggestion:
You have read about it, now you can review what you have just learned by watching a video by the author!

▶ Simply click here in your eBook for an introductory video on bond markets and interest rate determination.

How does the government 'borrow' money?

While an individual may have several channels through which money can be borrowed (credit cards, commercial banks, family or friends) governments typically borrow money from the *public* by issuing and selling *government bonds*. A government bond (called a *security* by some countries) is essentially a certificate of debt; it is an 'IOU' that promises whoever buys the bond that at some point in the future (1 year, 5 years, 10, or even 30 years later) the government that issued it will pay back its full face value. The reason individuals might wish to buy a government bond today, and thereby lend a government money, is that in addition to being paid back once the bond has 'matured', the buyer also receives a 'coupon rate', which is an annual payment made to the bond holder.

What is the relationship between budget deficits, surpluses, and the national debt?

Figure 20.2 Rising national debt indicates a budget deficit

▼

Figure 20.2 shows the national debts, in euros, of four European countries between the years 2000 and 2020.

408

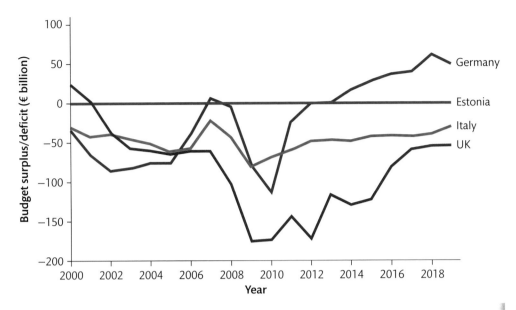

Observe from Figure 20.2 that Italy, the UK, and Germany all have large national debts that increased over the 18 years following 2000, and by 2019 were all between €2 trillion and €2.5 trillion. Estonia, meanwhile, has a national debt that appears close to zero (in fact, it was around €2.4 billion in 2018).

Why do each of these countries have any debt at all? The answer is that, at least for the three heavily indebted countries, they ran *budget deficits* for most of the first two decades of the 21st century. Every year the national debt increases for a country we can assume that country's government ran a budget deficit that added to the total debt level.

In years in which governments have budget surpluses, the national debts decrease. Figure 20.3 shows the actual budget balances of our four countries over the same time period, allowing us to more easily identify years when budget surpluses and deficits were experienced.

Once again Estonia stands out; we can see that the smallest of the European economies ran a nearly 'balanced budget' during most of the two decades represented. In fact, until 2016 Estonia ran small budget surpluses, and then small deficits from 2016 to 2018. Our big three economies, on the other hand, experienced sometimes sizeable deficits as large as −€175 billion in the UK in 2009. Germany stands out as being the only big economy to experience budget surpluses, which it had briefly in 2006, then again from 2013 onward.

What is meant by 'debt to GDP ratio'?

It is a bit unfair to compare the big three economies of Europe to tiny Estonia on the same charts. Estonia looks like a shining example of fiscal responsibility, after all, because its lines are quite nearly 0 for every year represented. To provide a more relevant comparison of deficit and debt situations, therefore, we can look at the size of each country's budget deficits/surpluses and national debts relative to each country's gross domestic product (GDP). After all, if I were to tell you that I personally had debts equal to half a million dollars, you might think, 'Wow, this

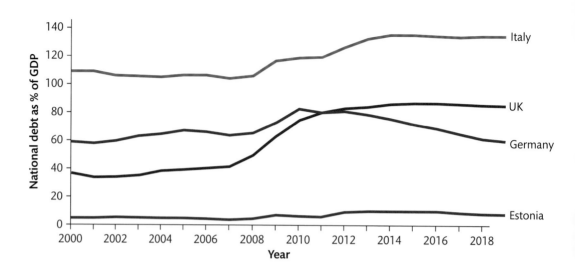

▲

Figure 20.4 Debt to GDP ratios compare the size of the national debt to national income

textbook author is in some deep trouble financially!' But then if you learned that I am also a billionaire, that half a million would not seem like such a big deal. (Editor's note: the author of this textbook is most definitely *not* a billionaire!) Like individuals, a country's debts are significant in relation to their *national incomes*, or their real GDPs.

Figure 20.4 shows us the sizes of each country's national debts expressed as a percentage of their GDP.

Once again we can see that Estonia is, in fact, the country that has relied least on debt as a means of financing its government expenditures. Italy, meanwhile, has accumulated debts equal to 130% of its national income. This is equivalent to an individual who earns €100,000 each year in his or her job owing the bank, his or her credit card company, and other lenders €130,000. This is not a financial situation most individuals would wish to find themselves in. Later in this chapter, we will explore the consequences of large national debts on whole economies.

Finally, we can observe the relationships between our four countries' annual budget deficit/surplus and their GDPs. Figure 20.5 does just that.

Finally, Estonia begins to blend in a bit more with the other countries, following a very similar track to its fellow fiscally responsible European neighbour, Germany. Both countries have managed to maintain budget deficits of no greater than −3% of their GDPs for almost the entirety of the two decades. The exception is in 2010, when Germany had to borrow an amount equal to about −4% of its GDP to support its economy in the midst of the Great Recession. Italy and the UK, on the other hand, have experienced deficits as large as −5% of their GDP (in Italy's case) and as large as −10% of its GDP (the UK in 2009).

Later in this chapter we will put our knowledge of government debt to use in our evaluation of fiscal policy, when we will explore whether using deficit spending to promote macroeconomic objectives is sustainable in the face of an ever increasing national debt.

Video suggestion:
You have read about it, now you can review what you have just learned by watching a video by the author!

▶ Simply click here in your eBook for a video on the relationships between budget deficits, surplus, and the national debt.

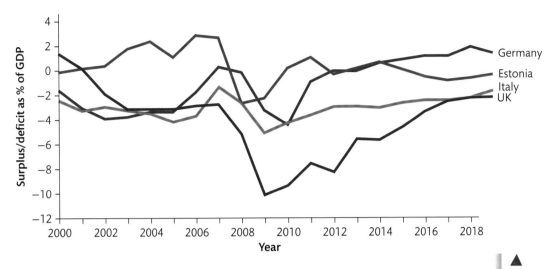

Figure 20.5 This graph looks at government surplus/deficit as a percentage of GDP

20.3 Expansionary and contractionary fiscal policies in order to close deflationary/recessionary and inflationary gaps

Learning outcomes

At the end of this section you will be able to:

- examine how changes in the level of government expenditure and/or taxes can influence the level of AD in an economy
- evaluate the mechanisms through which fiscal policy can help close deflationary and inflationary gaps
- draw diagrams to show the potential effects of expansionary and contractionary fiscal policies.

As a demand-side policy, fiscal policy can be used to manage the level of AD in an economy and therefore help to close output gaps.

How can fiscal policy help close a negative (recessionary) output gap?

An economy experiencing a negative output gap has seen AD decrease, unemployment increase, and either **disinflation** or deflation. The government can counteract the negative consequences of weak AD by engaging in an **expansionary fiscal policy**, which requires the government to run a **budget deficit**. A reduction in the income tax rate will increase households' disposable incomes, leading to increased consumer spending. Increases in government expenditures will lead to a direct injection into the economy due to the government's 'fiscal stimulus'.

Video suggestions:
You have read about it, now you can review what you have just learned by watching some videos by the author! Simply click here in your eBook for videos on expansionary and contractionary fiscal policies.

411

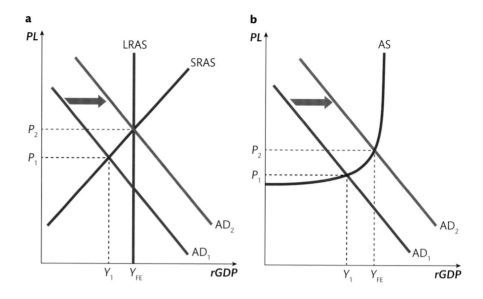

Figure 20.6 Fiscal stimulus pulls equilibrium national output back to the full employment level by increasing AD in both the new classical model of AD/AS (a) and the Keynesian model (b)

Figure 20.6 illustrates the effect of expansionary fiscal policy in an economy experiencing a negative output gap. Figure 20.6(a) takes the monetarist/new classical approach, which assumes that short-run aggregate supply (SRAS) is upward sloping. Figure 20.6(b) looks at the effect of fiscal stimulus from the Keynesian perspective.

In both interpretations of the economy, fiscal stimulus has achieved an increase in AD and equilibrium national output from a level that was below full employment back to the full employment level.

Expansionary fiscal policy, while an effective tool for closing a negative output gap, is not necessarily a means of increasing the rate of long-run economic growth in an economy already producing at full employment. Figure 20.7 shows the effect of fiscal stimulus.

Expansionary fiscal policy has resulted in an increase in real GDP from Y_{FE} to Y_1 in both models. However, due to the limited spare capacity in the economy, these gains are only temporary, as in the long run labour and resource shortages will drive wages and other costs of production up, leading to higher inflation and reductions in aggregate supply (AS) and output.

Expansionary fiscal policy, in other words, may be an effective means of stimulating demand in an economy experiencing a recession, but it is not in all cases an effective means of promoting long-run economic growth in an economy producing its full employment output. In Chapter 21, Supply-side policies, we will explore the types of government expenditures and tax policies that might actually encourage long-run economic growth, but by targeting AS rather than AD.

How can fiscal policy help close a positive (inflationary) output gap?

While tax cuts and increases in government spending can stimulate demand and help an economy experiencing a recession get back to full employment, an overheating

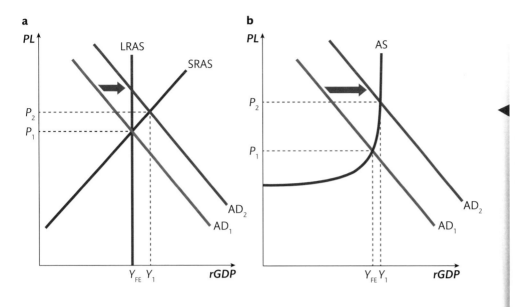

Figure 20.7 Fiscal stimulus in an economy already achieving full employment leads to inflation in both the new classical model of AD/AS (a) and the Keynesian model (b)

economy with high inflation might require a *contractionary fiscal policy*, such as an increase in taxes or a decrease in government expenditures.

Figure 20.8 shows the effect of a tax increase, which would reduce households' and firms' disposable incomes and therefore cause consumption and investment to fall, or a government spending cut, which would directly reduce the amount of spending in the economy.

In both models, inflationary gaps $(Y_1 - Y_{FE})$ have been eliminated due to falling AD.

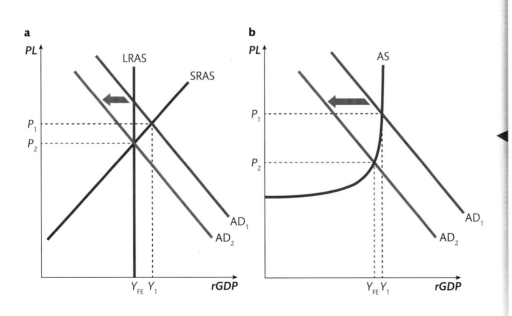

Figure 20.8 Contractionary fiscal policies reduce AD and close an inflationary gap in both the new classical model (a) and Keynesian model (b)

John Maynard Keynes believed that private individuals are driven as much by their *animal spirits* as they are by rational thought. He therefore believed that free market theory was flawed because it assumed humans always act rationally.

'Even apart from the instability due to speculation, there is the instability due to the characteristic of human nature that a large proportion of our positive activities depend on spontaneous optimism rather than mathematical expectations, whether moral or hedonistic or economic. Most, probably, of our decisions to do something positive, the full consequences of which will be drawn out over many days to come, can only be taken as the result of animal spirits – a spontaneous urge to action rather than inaction, and not as the outcome of a weighted average of quantitative benefits multiplied by quantitative probabilities.'
– John Maynard Keynes, *The General Theory of Employment, Interest and Money*, 1936

Discussion questions:

1 What are some examples of decisions you or people you know have made that were decided more by emotion than by rationality?

2 How can the actions of society as a whole, when driven by emotion and irrationality, result in economic instability and ultimately recession and unemployment?

20.4 HL Multiplier effects

Learning outcomes

At the end of this section you will be able to:

- explain, with reference to the concepts of leakages (withdrawals) and injections, the nature and importance of the **Keynesian multiplier**
- calculate the multiplier
- use the multiplier to calculate the effect on GDP of a change in fiscal policy.

An open question is just how much stimulus to AD is required to fill an output gap? Is it $1-for-$1, more than that, or less? In reality, in order to achieve a particular change in real GDP, a smaller change in expenditures or taxes is required, due to what are known as the *multiplier effects*. When any component of AD (consumption, investment, government spending, or net exports) changes, the ultimate change in real GDP will be greater by some multiple determined by the proportion of the resulting change in household income that is spent on domestic goods and services. This is true for both expansionary and contractionary fiscal policy. The more of their income households tend to spend on domestic output, the greater the multiplier effect will be.

What is the spending multiplier?

A $1 change to one of the components of AD leads to a greater change in total expenditures and total output. The *Keynesian spending multiplier* quantifies the size of the change in total spending as a result of a change in any one of the components of AD.

Let us consider how a change in government spending will impact total spending and total output in a fictional country, Snowlandia. Assume the government increases spending on infrastructure by ❆1 billion (❆ is the symbol for flake, the currency of Snowlandia). Assume also that there is no increase in taxes to 'pay for' the new government spending. The ❆1 billion of new spending in the economy will lead to an increase in household incomes of ❆1 billion. As their incomes rise, households will increase their spending on goods and services (remember, incomes are a determinant of consumption.) Owing to increasing consumption, the economy's AD is stimulated by more than the initial ❆1 billion increase in government spending.

While a portion of income is typically saved from each round, the spending and income process continues: More spending leads to more income which leads to more spending. Ultimately, the initial change in expenditures is 'multiplied' throughout the economy by a factor determined by the amount by which households increase their consumption in response to a particular increase in income (this is called marginal propensity to consume, and will be explained further below). The Keynesian spending multiplier quantifies the size of the change in AD as a result of a change in any of the components of AD.

What is the tax multiplier?

The multiplier concept can be applied to the taxation side of fiscal policy as well. Assume that instead of increasing spending on infrastructure by ❄1 billion, Snowlandia's government instead lowers taxes on the country's households by ❄1 billion. Snowlandians now see an immediate increase in their disposable incomes, which in turn will lead them to increase their consumption by some amount less than ❄1 billion (assuming they choose to save, buy imports with, or pay more tax on some of their newly disposable income).

The initial tax cut will lead to an increase in consumption, which leads to an increase in incomes and a further increase in consumption. The process continues: lower taxes leads to more income which leads to more consumption and more income. Ultimately, the initial change in taxes is 'multiplied' throughout the economy by a factor determined by the amount by which households increase their consumption in response to a particular increase in disposable income. The *tax multiplier* quantifies the size of the change in AD as a result of a change in taxes.

What are the 'marginal propensities'?

To estimate the size of the spending and tax multipliers, we must know how much of any change in income the typical household will use to buy domestic goods and services, how much will be saved, how much will go to paying taxes, and how much will be spent on imports. The **marginal propensities** measure the change in different variables divided by the change in disposable income experienced by a country's households.

$$\text{Marginal propensity to consume}\left(MPC\right) = \frac{\text{Change in consumption spending }(\Delta C)}{\text{Change in income }(\Delta Y)}$$

$$\text{Marginal propensity to save}\left(MPS\right) = \frac{\text{Change in saving }(\Delta S)}{\text{Change in income }(\Delta Y)}$$

$$\text{Marginal propensity to tax}\left(MPT\right) = \frac{\text{Change in taxation }(\Delta T)}{\text{Change in income }(\Delta Y)}$$

$$\text{Marginal propensity to buy imports}\left(MPM\right) = \frac{\text{Change in import spending }(\Delta M)}{\text{Change in income }(\Delta Y)}$$

The sum of the marginal propensities is equal to one. Any new income earned by households that is not spent on domestically produced goods, in other words, is saved, paid in taxes, or used to buy imports.

$$MPC + MPS + MPT + MPM = 1$$

Let us assume that in Snowlandia the typical household spends ❄0.80 of every ❄1 increased income, saves ❄0.10, pays ❄0.05 in taxes and buys ❄0.05 of imports. The marginal propensities can be calculated:

$$MPC = \frac{0.8}{1} = 0.8$$

$$MPS = \frac{0.1}{1} = 0.1$$

$$MPT = \frac{0.05}{1} = 0.05$$

$$MPM = \frac{0.05}{1} = 0.05$$

How do we calculate the size of the multipliers?

The sizes of the spending and tax multipliers depend on the marginal propensity to consume. To estimate the magnitude by which a particular change in expenditures will affect AD, we can determine the expenditure multiplier as a function of the marginal propensity to consume (MPC):

$$Keynesian\ spending\ multiplier = \frac{1}{1 - MPC}\ or\ \frac{1}{MPS + MPT + MPM}$$

With an MPC of 0.8, Snowlandia's spending multiplier can be determined:

$$\frac{1}{1 - 0.8} = \frac{1}{0.2} = 5$$

This multiplier indicates the amount by which any initial change in expenditures (*C, I, G, or Xn*) must be multiplied to determine the final change in total spending in the economy. We can calculate how much the government's ❄1 billion increase in infrastructure spending will increase overall AD using the multiplier:

Δ *in AD = initial* Δ *spending* × *spending multiplier*

Δ *in AD =* ❄*1 billion* × *5 =* ❄*5 billion*

Given an MPC of 0.8, an initial increase in spending of ❄1 billion can ultimately expect to see increased AD in Snowlandia of ❄5 billion.

The lower the MPC, the smaller the spending multiplier will be, explained by the fact that consumers will not spend as much of any increase in income they experience, choosing to save instead. Table 20.1 shows the multiplier calculations for different marginal propensities to consume.

Table 20.1   The spending multiplier decreases as the MPC decreases

MPC	Spending multiplier	Effect on GDP of $1 billion increase in AD
0.9	$\dfrac{1}{0.1} = 10$	$\$1b \times 10 = \$10b$
0.6	$\dfrac{1}{0.4} = 2.5$	$\$1b \times 2.5 = \$2.5b$
0.5	$\dfrac{1}{0.5} = 2$	$\$1b \times 2 = \$2b$
0.4	$\dfrac{1}{0.6} = 1.67$	$\$1b \times 1.67 = \$1.67b$
0.2	$\dfrac{1}{0.8} = 1.25$	$\$1b \times 1.25 = \$1.25b$

The tax multiplier is also a function of the marginal propensities to consume and save. The magnitude by which a particular change in taxes will impact AD is found using the formula:

$$Tax\ multiplier = \frac{-MPC}{1 - MPC}$$

Worked example 20.3

With its MPC of 0.8, Snowlandia's tax multiplier can be calculated:

$$\frac{-0.8}{0.2} = -4$$

Every ✳1 decrease in taxes will *increase* AD in Snowlandia by ✳4. We can estimate the impact of a ✳1 billion tax cut given to Snowlandian citizens using the tax multiplier.

Δ in AD = initial Δ taxes $\times$ tax multiplier

$= -$✳$1\ billion \times -4 = $✳$4\ billion$

Notice that the tax multiplier is negative, explained by the fact that there is an inverse relationship between taxes and spending. Tax cuts (a negative change in taxes, like that experienced in Snowlandia) cause disposable incomes and consumer spending to increase while tax increases cause spending to fall.

Notice also that the tax multiplier effect is smaller than the spending multiplier effect. Consider Snowlandia's two government policies: a ✳1 billion increase in infrastructure spending versus a ✳1 billion tax cut. The first option would result in a ✳5 billion increase in total spending while the second would only result in ✳4 billion of new spending. The difference is explained by the fact that government spending is a *direct injection* into the circular flow of income, while a tax cut is an *indirect injection*. Before Snowlandians saw their incomes rise, AD had already been boosted by ❄1 billion in the case of new infrastructure spending. On the other hand, no jobs are directly created or output actually produced by a tax cut; the stimulus only occurs after households who receive it have saved, paid taxes, or bought imports with 20% of their increase in income.

How do we calculate the effect of a change in government spending or taxation on GDP?

The ultimate impact of any change in aggregate expenditures or taxation is determined by the spending muliplier or the tax multiplier, both of which are a function of the marginal propensities to consume, save, pay taxes, and buy imports. The larger the proportion of any change in income households use to buy domestic goods and services, the larger the multipliers will be. If consumers tend to save more of the new income they earn, the multiplier effects will be smaller, meaning a particular change in spending or taxation will result in a smaller change in total output.

Worked example 20.4

Assume the MPC in a country is 0.6. With this value we can calculate the multipliers:

$$The\ spending\ multiplier = \frac{1}{1 - MPC} = \frac{1}{0.4} = 2.5$$

$$The\ tax\ multiplier = \frac{-MPC}{1 - MPC} = \frac{-0.6}{0.4} = -1.5$$

With these values we can calculate the impact of a change in government spending or taxation. For example, assume the government reduces spending on defence by $10 billion. The impact on overall AD can be calculated:

$$Total\ \Delta\ in\ AD = Initial\ \Delta\ in\ spending \times Spending\ multiplier$$

$$= -\$10\ billion \times 2.5$$

$$= -\$25\ billion$$

A $10 billion decrease in government spending will result in a $25 billion decrease in AD.

Next let us consider the impact of a $10 billion increase in taxes.

$$Total\ \Delta\ in\ AD = Change\ in\ taxes \times Tax\ multiplier$$

$$= \$10\ billion \times -1.5$$

$$= -\$15\ billion$$

Video suggestions:
You have read about it, now you can review what you have just learned by watching a few videos by the author!

▶ Simply click here in your eBook for videos on the government spending multiplier, the tax multiplier, and the multiplier effect in the AD-AS model.

Notice that a $10 billion dollar decrease in government spending has a larger impact on total spending than a $10 billion increase in taxes. Again, this reflects that a change in government spending affects AD directly while a change in taxes affects AD indirectly. Of course, this holds true when fiscal policy is used to close negative output gaps as well. For example, if there is a $25 billion negative output gap, then a $10 billion increase in spending should be enough to restore full employment (assuming an MPC of 0.6), but a $10 billion decrease in taxes would not be adequate.

20.5 How effective is fiscal policy?

Learning outcomes

At the end of this section you will be able to:

- discuss the constraints on fiscal policy, including:
  - political pressure
  - time lags
  - the sustainability of government debt
  - **HL** **crowding out**
- evaluate the strengths of fiscal policy including:
  - the ability to target sectors of the economy
  - the direct impact on AD
  - the effectiveness of promoting economic activity in a recession
- **HL** examine how progressive taxes and **unemployment benefits** automatically help to stabilise short-term fluctuations in output.

What are some of the constraints on fiscal policy?

Political pressure

A potential shortcoming of fiscal policy is the fact that policy decisions rest in the hands of politicians whose incentives may not lie entirely in the best interest of the nation's economy. Politicians may promote and push through fiscal policies that are popular among voters, even if they are economically irresponsible.

Political hijacking of fiscal policies may lead to what economists refer to as *political business cycles* in which total spending in the economy fluctuates depending on politicians' desire to enact popular tax breaks and government handouts even when an economy is close to or at full employment. The goal of such irresponsible policies, of course, is to maintain political support and earn votes in the next national election, while the effect is often prolonged periods of expansion and inflation.

For example, in 2017, during Donald Trump's first months as the president of the USA, he signed the 'Tax Cuts and Jobs Act', which reduced the corporate and individual tax rates in the USA: a fiscal stimulus at a time when US unemployment was already at the lowest rate it had been in decades. The resulting budget deficits helped grow the US national debt while doing little to stimulate economic growth in an already fully employed economy.

Compared to its central bank-enacted sibling, monetary policy, fiscal policy is likely to be subject to the political agendas of the elected leaders who are charged with enacting it, therefore, as was the case of the 'Trump tax cuts', it can actually exacerbate macroeconomic problems rather than alleviate them.

'The government is best which governs least.'

This aphorism is sometimes used to argue against the active role of government in an economy. Do you agree that society is better off with less government? Would we all be better off without any government in our lives? What do governments do that contributes to our well-being? What do they do that detracts from our well-being?

What practical problems can be solved through the application of knowledge from macroeconomics?

Time lags

Recall from our evaluation of monetary policy that one of its strengths is the short *time lags*. Central bank officials meet at regular intervals to discuss possible interventions in the money markets, and once announced, central bank actions have immediate effects on the interest rate, meaning they can begin to influence economic activity relatively quickly in response to a macroeconomic shock.

Fiscal policy, in contrast, demonstrates much longer time lags. Often, by the time policymakers have identified a macroeconomic problem (a recession or an overheating economy), quantified it (determined the size of the output gap), determined the size of the multipliers and debated the appropriate policy response in the halls of congress or parliament, the economy will have already self-corrected or demand may have recovered on its own. A real economy is a dynamic machine that is always changing. Time lags refer to the fact that in the time it takes policymakers to figure out how to respond, everything could have changed in the economy.

For this reason, some government policymakers prefer to wait for an economy to self-correct from recessions or from demand-pull inflation. The laissez-faire approach to economic policy is often to 'wait and see' how an economy will respond to macroeconomic shocks.

HL Sustainable debt

Earlier in this chapter we discussed the relationship between government budget deficits and the national debt. Fiscal policies, most likely to be used to close negative output gaps, necessitate budget deficits, which by definition mean the national debt increases following the use of fiscal policy.

The question is, is there such a thing as *too much debt*? Why should governments care about the size of the national debts, and what would it mean for the national debt to become *unsustainable*?

The answer to these questions lies in our earlier explanation of how bond prices and bond yields can be affected by the basic principles of supply and demand. In years when a government must borrow a significant amount of money to finance a deficit it must increase the supply of its bonds, and in order to attract new lenders (bond buyers) the government may have to increase the coupon rate as well. As bond supply increases, bond prices fall, and the government's cost/benefit ratio shifts towards costs, away from benefits, as the government gets less money for each bond sold and has to pay a higher effective yield to whoever bought it. The *cost of borrowing* literally increases as the government needs to borrow more. The amount the government must pay back its bondholders increases as the size of the national debt increases.

To make matters worse, a government with a level of debt that is very large relative to its GDP may see its **credit rating** downgraded and risk losing the faith of bond buyers who might begin to question whether the country's large debt burden will make it difficult for the country to continue servicing its debt in the future. If this happens, demand for that country's bonds could decrease, lowering bond prices and shifting the cost/benefit ratio even further towards costs, as effective bond yields continue to grow relative to the amount of money borrowed.

In short, a country that runs persistent budget deficits will see its national debt grow year after year after year. If its GDP also grows, and at a rate equal to or greater than the rate of growth in its national debt, then the *debt burden* (the debt to GDP ratio) will actually shrink over time, and there is little to worry about with regards to a growing debt number. However, if debt grows faster than GDP, then the cost to the government (and taxpayers) of servicing that debt (paying the yield on its bonds and repaying bondholders the face value when the bonds mature) increases over time, requiring the country's limited tax revenues to be increasingly allocated towards **debt servicing** and away from the provision of important public goods such as education, infrastructure, defence, and healthcare.

We can conclude that, according to mainstream economic theory at least, one objective of government policymakers is to maintain a 'sustainable' level of national debt. For most developed countries, this means keeping annual budget deficits below 3% of GDP and keeping the overall debt below 60% of GDP.

Again, just as target inflation rates vary widely depending on countries' income levels and their levels of economic development, the same can be said for debt to GDP ratios. Some countries may be able to sustain far larger national debts relative to their GDPs than others. Japan, for instance, has maintained a debt to GDP ratio of well over 200% for over 20 years. Greece, on the other hand, experienced a complete economic collapse in 2011 when its debt grew to nearly 160% of its GDP. There is no 'one size fits all' rule for inflation, debt, or other macroeconomic indicators including the level of unemployment, the rate of economic growth, or the degree of income inequality in society.

MMT revisited

According to MMT, a sovereign government in a country with its own currency is not financially constrained in its ability to spend. There is no level of debt, in other words, that is unsustainable, because government spending is not financed by debt, it is financed by the treasury, which issues the currency that the government uses to finance its spending.

HL Crowding out

When a government engages in an expansionary fiscal policy, it either increases spending or decreases taxes or does both simultaneously. The resulting budget deficit, financed by government borrowing, could drive up interest rates in the economy and therefore 'crowd out' private sector spending.

Recall that both consumption and investment are interest sensitive, meaning that at higher interest rates, both households and firms will constrain their spending and opt to save more instead. When a government issues new bonds to finance a fiscal stimulus, the result is an increase in bond yields, which attracts investors who might otherwise have made their funds available to the private sector. The theory of the crowding out effect argues that in an economy with limited funds available for loans, government borrowing reallocates money away from businesses and households who might have spent it and puts it in the hands of the government.

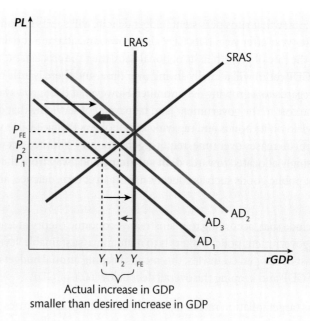

Figure 20.9 Fiscal stimulus is 'crowded out' by a decrease in private sector spending

In short, government borrowing *might* cause higher interest rates, due to the increased yields on government bonds needed to attract investors to the bond market. If this happens, then the resulting signal to households and firms is to 'spend less, save more'. The intent of a fiscal stimulus is to increase AD, but the unintended consequence may be to *constrain* AD through reduced consumption and investment. The multiplier effect of a tax cut or increase in government spending might, therefore, be smaller than anticipated due to the decreased private consumption and investment.

Figure 20.9 shows the effect of crowding out. A government that enacts a fiscal stimulus aimed at increasing AD from AD_1 to AD_2 might find the economy only achieves AD_3, assuming the resulting budget deficit drove interest rates up and led households to increase their savings and firms to reduce their investment. The government's stimulus was 'crowded out' and AD increased by less than desired.

There are many problems with the crowding-out theory. First of all, there is almost no evidence that it happens in the real world. During the 2010s, as the developed economies of the world climbed out of the trough created during the Great Recession of 2008–10, many countries ran persistent budget deficits and saw their national debts grow year after year. According to mainstream theory, such a scenario should have seen higher interest rates lead to falling investment by the private sector. Neither happened, however. Even as government spending increased and public debts grew (see Figure 20.2), interest rates in the developed economies remained low and private investment grew as well.

The Keynesian explanation for why crowding out has not occurred in the last decade is that much of the developed world might have been in what Keynesian economists call a 'liquidity trap'. The government is most likely to engage in expansionary fiscal policies only when the economy is producing below its full employment level of output. During deep recessions, crowding out is less likely to be a concern than when fiscal stimulus is applied in an economy already producing at full employment since, due to low consumer and business confidence, investment demand is weak during recessions, while due to uncertainty about future employment opportunities and the expectation of disinflation or deflation, household savings is higher during recessions.

When investment demand is very weak and the level of household savings is very high, a country may experience what is called a liquidity trap, which occurs when the equilibrium interest rate actually falls below 0%. When the amount of savings exceeds the amount of investment by the private sector, there is room for the government to borrow from the public without actually driving up interest rates and depressing private investment and consumption. Think of it this way, during deep recessions, when private consumption and investment are already depressed, government spending does not crowd out private spending, rather it 'picks up the slack' created by decreased expenditures by the private sector. It quite literally picks up the extra funds that everyone in the economy is saving and turns those idle funds into active expenditures, injecting money into the economy that otherwise would have been leaked through savings.

Thus, crowding out is highly unlikely to occur following a fiscal stimulus during a deep recession. On the other hand, when private sector spending is healthy and strong and the economy is producing close to or at its full employment level, it is more likely that a deficit financed fiscal stimulus will create incentives for the private sector to cut back on their own spending and allocate more funds towards government debt.

Case study – the MMT view of crowding out

According to MMT, crowding out does not occur because sovereign governments with their own currencies do not, in fact, have to borrow to finance deficits. As we have stated, government spending is paid for by the treasury depositing currency into private banks when ordered to pay for a particular government expenditure. In this regard, the opposite of crowding out should occur when government spends: private sector spending might in fact be 'crowded in', as bank deposits increase due to more money flowing through the system following an increase in government spending or a tax cut.

According to MMT, *deficit spending should drive down interest rates*, encouraging investment and 'crowding-in' economic activity. This may just be another way to describe the multiplier effect outlined earlier in this chapter; but either way, there is plenty of evidence from the post-Great Recession era to support the view that increased deficit spending might stimulate, rather than crowd out, private sector spending.

What are the strengths of fiscal policy?
Targeting of specific economic sectors

Unlike monetary policy, which increases or decreases the money supply to influence interest rates and the level of consumer and business spending in general, fiscal policy has the potential to be far more specific and targeted in its application. For example, a 'tax cut' does not mean that *all taxes are cut equally*. The government may choose to reduce the value added tax, an indirect tax, in order to free up income among the country's poorer households, who tend to spend a larger proportion of their income on goods and services compared to the rich, who save more. Lowering consumption taxes, a fiscal stimulus, will also achieve the objective of reducing income inequality in society since the greatest beneficiaries will be lower income earners.

Likewise, there are countless sectors towards which an increase in government expenditures could be targeted. In the USA there is growing support among elected officials for a 'Green New Deal', a proposed multi-trillion dollar federal government programme that would massively increase spending on renewable energies and improve the country's energy infrastructure. In contrast, there are some in government who prefer to see more government spending on healthcare or simply prefer to cut taxes on the rich or corporations. Each of these proposed fiscal policies would have varying effects depending on the sector or the population towards which the policies are targeted.

Government spending may be more effective in deep recessions

For reasons already explained throughout this chapter, fiscal policy is a highly effective alternative to monetary policy during deep recessions. The 'zero lower bound' described in Chapter 19 limits the effectiveness of monetary stimulus in an economy where interest rates are already close to 0%. The 'liquidity trap' experienced when household savings increase while private investment is depressed allows the government to borrow money at almost no cost and stimulate AD during deep recessions, 'picking up the slack' left by depressed consumption and investment. In short, the government can be the 'spender of last resort' in an economy in which consumer and business confidence are extremely low and in which the business cycle is on a precipitous downward slope.

HL What are 'automatic stabilisers'?

When government policymakers get together and decide to take fiscal actions to either contract or expand AD, they are implementing *discretionary fiscal policies*. However, when changes in output or employment trigger automatic increases or decreases in spending and taxation, an economy is employing *automatic fiscal stabilisers*.

Automatic stabilisers are the built-in changes in transfers and taxation that happen when an economy's output and employment increase or decrease. Consider what happens after a fall in AD results in rising unemployment and decreased output. Unemployed workers who have lost their income stop paying income taxes, so there is an automatic decrease in the amount of tax collected by the government. Additionally, as they lose their jobs workers become eligible for unemployment insurance, a transfer payment by the government to people who are unable to find work. In other words, government spending increases automatically following a decrease in aggregate output.

During a demand-deficient recession tax revenues decrease *automatically* as GDP falls, preventing consumption and the economy from falling further. At the same time, transfer payments increase, helping maintain consumption among those who have lost their jobs. The effect of these automatic stabilisers is to, well, *stabilise* AD and prevent it from falling as much as it would if these effects did not kick in.

Next consider what happens when an economy already producing at full employment experiences an increase in AD. Workers who were structurally or frictionally unemployed will be hired, causing unemployment to fall below its natural rate. Newly employed workers start paying income tax, which automatically increases tax revenues for the government, and since they are no longer unemployed, the same workers will stop collecting unemployment benefits from the government, automatically reducing government spending on transfers.

Furthermore, rising output and employment drives wages upwards, pushing some workers into a higher income bracket, at which they are likely to pay a higher tax rate. A *progressive income tax* is one that increases in percentage as incomes rise. Progressive taxation acts as an automatic stabiliser as rising incomes automatically trigger higher tax rates for those earning them.

During an expansion, tax revenues increase automatically as GDP rises, slowing consumption and preventing the economy from overheating. At the same time, transfer payments decrease, helping prevent consumption from rising more than it otherwise would. The effect of these automatic stabilisers is to prevent an economy from overheating that otherwise might follow an increase in AD.

While discretionary fiscal policies (those that require the government to come to some agreement and put new spending or tax policies into action) can fairly be criticised for the associated time lags, automatic fiscal policies like unemployment benefits and progressive taxes do not suffer this shortcoming. The changes happen automatically, thus there is little or no time lag. However, when the economy is threatened with more than just minor inflationary or recessionary gaps, the automatic stabilisers described here will fall short of helping an economy restore its full employment output.

Practice exam questions

1a. Explain the impact of automatic stabilisers on an economy. (10 marks)
  b. Evaluate the effectiveness of fiscal policy in achieving economic growth. (15 marks)
2. Explain how expansionary fiscal policy can be used to close a deflationary gap. (10 marks)
3. **HL** Using an AD/AS diagram, explain the implications for government policymakers if the crowding out effect is more powerful than the multiplier effect of an expansionary fiscal policy. (10 marks)
4. Using an AD/AS diagram, explain the effect of contractionary policy on a positive output gap (demand-pull inflation). (10 marks)
5. Assume the marginal propensity to consume is 0.75. Calculate the effect the fiscal policies below would have on AD:
  a. A $6 billion increase in infrastructure spending. (2 marks)
  b. A $8 billion increase in income taxes. (2 marks)
  c. A $5 billion increase in transfer payments. (2 marks)
6. Outline the strengths and weaknesses of expansionary fiscal policy as a tool for combatting deep recessions. (10 marks)
7. Discuss whether fiscal policy is effective at promoting long-run economic growth in an economy already producing at its full employment output level. (10 marks)

Supply-side policies

21

21.1 What are supply-side policies and what is the goal of such policies?

Learning outcomes

At the end of this section you will be able to:

- explain that supply-side policies aim to positively affect the production side of an economy by shifting the LRAS curve to the right
- distinguish between market-based and **interventionist supply-side policies**
- analyse the goals of supply-side policies including:
  - increasing long-run growth
  - improving competition
  - improving **labour market flexibility**
  - reducing inflation
  - creating incentives for firms to innovate.

Supply-side policies aim to positively affect the production side of an economy by improving the quantity or the quality of the factors of production. These policies attempt to develop a healthier institutional framework for production to occur. On an aggregate diagram, successful supply-side policies shift right the short-run aggregate supply (SRAS) curve (Figure 21.1a), and ideally a long-run aggregate supply (LRAS) curve to the right, increasing the overall **productive capacity** of the economy (Figure 21.1b). This pushes future full employment income, Y_{FE1}, out to the right to Y_{FE2}. This shift of LRAS would correspond to a shift outward of the production possibility frontier (PPC), which suggests an increase in overall potential capacity in the economy.

Supply-side policies fall in to two categories: government based and market based. Governments can act directly to improve the economy's capacity to produce. Government intervention seeks to provide capital goods or services where, it is believed, the market itself has failed to provide them. In contrast, market-based policies seek to unleash the full power of open markets to improve incentives, open labour markets, and create competition.

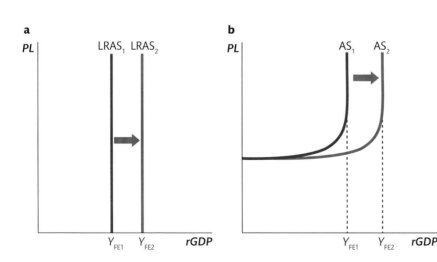

Figure 21.1 A successful supply-side policy will shift both long-run AS (a) and short-run AS (b) to the right

The primary goals of supply-side policies are:

1   long-term growth by increasing the economy's productive capacity

2   improving competition and efficiency

3   reducing labour costs and unemployment through labour market flexibility

4   reducing inflation to improve international competitiveness

5   increasing firms' incentives to invest in innovation by reducing costs.

21.2 What are market-based supply-side policies?

Learning outcomes

At the end of this section you will be able to:

- analyse the use of market-based policies including:
  - deregulation
  - **privatisation**
  - **trade liberalisation**
  - anti-monopoly regulation
- explain the effects of labour market policies such as:
  - reducing the power of labour unions
  - reducing unemployment benefits
  - abolishing minimum wages
- outline the idea behind **incentive-related policies** such as cuts in personal income tax, business tax, and **capital gains tax**
- evaluate the effectiveness of **market-based supply-side policies** in terms of their effects on:
  - employment
  - inflationary pressure
  - economic growth
  - the government budget
  - equity
  - the environment.

Market-based supply-side policies generally act to reduce government intervention with the goal of unleashing market forces to improve macroeconomic efficiency and capacity. More specifically, market-based supply-side policies try to improve incentives, open labour markets, and create more competition in the market.

What are the origins of market-based supply-side policies?

The impetus behind the criticism of Keynesian policies came from an influential group of new classical economists. Among the most prominent was Milton Friedman, who also became renowned for contributions to thinking about the money supply.

Friedman and the other new classical economists followed in the tradition of Friedrich von Hayek, an Austrian economist who had openly clashed with Keynesian approaches since the 1940s. The term 'new classical' implied a harking back to old, accepted classical economics precepts. Energised by the economic crises of the 70s, new classical economists fiercely criticised the heavy regulation of markets and government ownership of major industries that had become emblematic of Keynesianism.

Their protests took root as politicians in the UK and USA began to advocate freer markets and less government control. Most notably, UK Prime Minister Margaret Thatcher privatised and shrank the coal industry in the UK, causing large-scale strikes and subsequent unemployment in the industry during the 1980s. Ronald Reagan, meanwhile, crushed a prominent strike by US air traffic controllers in 1981, sending a signal that the days of trade union ascendancy were over.

These policies aimed to open up competition, free up markets from government involvement, and return influence to the private sector. At the same time, the countries that implemented them likely suffered some of the negative effects that the policies can bring.

What are incentive-related policies?

Reducing personal income tax

Lowering marginal tax rates increases the after-tax income of those affected. It should, therefore, increase the incentive to work since every hour of work results in greater pay. At some level of marginal tax, a worker may find that the diminished value of the disposable income derived from that hour is less valuable than an hour of leisure or childcare. Lowering the rate tips the cost–benefit calculation in favour of the benefits of extra work. In theory, this will cause workers to seek more work, and become more productive and the value of labour as a factor of production will rise, contributing to the aggregate supply (AS) of a country.

Reducing business and capital gains tax

A tax on business profits obviously diminishes profits. Cutting corporate taxes, it is said, encourages firms to produce more by reducing the costs of production. It is also possible that this extra profit will be ploughed back into the business in the form of investment if it is not simply taken as dividend/income by the owners. If it encourages more production and investment, lower corporate taxes will shift AS to the right. The taxes on capital gains work in a similar way. First a capital gain is a profit made on the sale of an asset, which could be profit from the sale of property or company shares. The idea is that reducing these taxes encourages entrepreneurial investment spending in property and companies, which helps keep firms well-capitalised.

Labour market policies

Supply-side economists see government efforts to regulate and manage labour relations as an intrusion into the operation of free markets, and believe that inefficiencies result. Reforms in this area are intended to make labour markets more responsive to supply and demand.

Reducing trade union power

This could be viewed as the counterpart to anti-monopoly rules, if one takes the view that trade unions attempt to assume a collusive or monopolistic control over the market for their work. Trade unions generally seek to raise wages for their members, as well as to improve working conditions. Where successful, unions keep wages above the market level and raise non-wage costs for firms, reducing the supply of goods produced by firms. On a macroeconomic level, this translates into a diminished aggregate supply. Restricting trade union power to organise and bargain collectively with employers would decrease their wage-setting power and condition-setting power. In theory, firms produce more at lower costs, and the economic growth that results will result in more overall employment.

Reducing unemployment benefits

Unemployment benefits, according to supply-side economists, reduce the incentive to find employment. The supplementary income received creates a disincentive for workers to accept jobs at lower wages during periods of unemployment, and thus prolongs the economy's return to full employment. For a measure of comparison, some countries offer up to 80% of wages for two years, whereas some offer a low flat rate far below median wage levels for a shorter time. Supply siders argue for benefits that are smaller and shorter in duration.

Ending the minimum wage

The minimum wage sets a price floor for labour, which raises costs for firms and reduces overall supply of goods and services. Moreover, such price floors are believed to create a surplus of workers who will not be hired at the government-enforced wage rate, and so require more unemployment benefits, which require more tax revenue. Figure 21.2 shows a binding $15 minimum wage, one which has increased the quantity supplied of labour and reduced the quantity demanded, causing a surplus of unemployed people. Eliminating that minimum wage would allow the price to drop back to W_E at $12, where the market clears and there is no unemployment. Repealing minimum wage laws would reverse the surplus of workers, keeping costs low for firms, freeing up government revenue, and allowing the AS to grow.

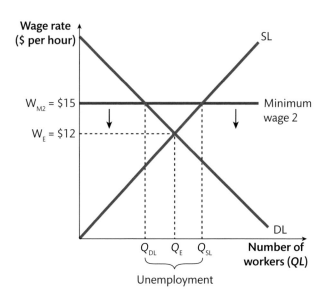

Figure 21.2 Effect of ending a binding minimum wage

Fast food workers stage a one day strike in 2016, calling for $15 minimum wage, paid sick days, and union rights

What are policies that encourage competition?

Another group of supply-side policies aim to open the market to greater competition. They flow from the free market philosophy that greater competition encourages harder work, more innovation, lower prices, and better quality in an attempt to earn money and win customers.

Deregulation

Supply siders argue that governments discourage business by applying stringent or unnecessary regulation to markets. Rules about professional qualifications, products standards, worker health, and safety requirements may be well justified by public concerns, but they impose costs on firms. Deregulation can be applied to a variety of situations in order to reduce bureaucracy as well as the required costs of complying with government rules. Tearing away the rules should therefore automatically reduce costs and encourage greater production.

Privatisation

One legacy of the Second World War **industrial policies** in many countries has been government control of the 'commanding heights' of the economy. In many otherwise free market economies in the Cold War West, the industries of steel and iron, energy, and transportation industries were under government ownership and control. Supply siders believed that most of these had become bloated with unnecessary employees and operated inefficiently because they lacked the right incentives. Privatisation, it was argued, would encourage owners to lower costs and thus prices to the public if they were run more like private businesses. Prominent examples of implementation include the coal industry in the UK, as well as telecommunications and airlines in many countries.

Trade liberalisation (free trade)

Supply-side economists applied the free market principle to international trade as well. They opposed tariffs, quotas, and subsidies that encouraged dependence on the government.

431

They encouraged free trade, reduction of trade barriers, and open competition. Such competition, according to the idea of comparative advantage, would encourage countries to work to their relative strengths and improve global macroeconomic efficiency.

Anti-monopoly regulation

Where monopoly power exists, it gives producers the ability to restrict output and increase prices. Monopolies therefore extract extra producer surplus, and profits, from consumers without necessarily adding extra value to the market. Anti-monopoly laws (also called antitrust laws) seek to prevent or dismantle monopolies. It is thought better for most industries to have competition, as Adam Smith suggested, to keep firms from exploiting customers with simple control of the market. Antitrust laws prevent monopolistic mergers and seek to break up monopoly firms that harm consumers. Fewer monopolies make for more competition, greater innovation, and lower costs and prices, all of which contribute to aggregate supply. Chapter 12 explores the problems and solutions for monopoly power in more detail.

What are the advantages and disadvantages of market-based supply-side policies?

Advantages

- In labour markets, the withdrawal of government intervention in the forms of minimum wages, trade union rights, and unemployment benefits may indeed make the labour market more flexible and responsive to market forces.
- By reducing monopolies and improving competition, a country benefits from lower costs, more innovation to win customers, and greater corporate integrity. The gains to output are at no cost to the government, and require no extra expenditure of resources. The allocation of resources in the market becomes more efficient, as determined by the forces of supply and demand.

Disadvantages

- Labour market reforms such as eliminating the minimum wage and reducing union power, and cutting unemployment benefits expose vulnerable people to the quixotic consequences of the market. Workers paid below minimum wage would be ever more dependent on their employers, and therefore at more risk of exploitation.
- While trade unions explicitly and openly exist to drive up wages, they also help to protect workers from illegal and coercive treatment by employers. This could worsen if unions are further diminished.
- Dropping unemployment benefits may inspire the jobless to take whatever work is available. However, those out of work for structural reasons need time to retrain or even relocate to new jobs.
- Privatised firms can be bought on the cheap by politically connected elites, robbing the public of their true value, while firms charging free market prices may harm the public interest by overcharging for essential services like power and water.
- It is not clear that policies to lower taxes actually result in more or better work. Cutting corporate and capital gains taxes may merely be taken as extra income rather than being used to invest and grow the company.
- Deregulation can expose natural environments and delicate ecosystems to the risk of ruin. Eliminating or loosening these rules allows firms to externalise their costs and the public will eventually pay through taxes to clean up the problem or simply through diminished quality of life.

In an attempt to quantify the level of a country's labour market flexibility, a consortium of free market non-profit groups headed by the Lithuanian Free Market Institute using World Bank data compiled the *Labour Market Flexibility Index 2020.* Using criteria such as minimum wage levels, mandatory work hour rules, redundancy regulations, and costs, the group ranks EU and OECD countries. At the top for flexibility were the USA, Japan, and New Zealand. At the bottom were Mexico, Luxembourg, and France. Where did your country rank, and why? Find this publication online and see if you agree with these results.

21.3 What are interventionist supply-side policies?

Learning outcomes

At the end of this section you will be able to:

- explain how investment in:
  - education and training
  - research and development
  - improved infrastructure
  will raise the levels of 'human capital', result in new technologies and have a short-term impact on AD, as well as increasing LRAS
- comment on the effects of targeting specific industries through tax cuts, tax allowances and subsidised lending, in terms of promoting growth in key areas of the economy and increasing AD in the short term, as well as increasing LRAS
- evaluate the effectiveness of interventionist supply-side policies with regard to:
  - time lags
  - creating employment
  - reducing inflationary pressure
  - economic growth
  - impact on the government budget
  - effect on equity
  - the effect on the environment.

Interventionist supply-side policies require some kind of government action to improve the factors of production. Note that most of these require immediate spending, which will initially stimulate aggregate demand (AD). However, well-crafted policies should create an enduring expansion of LRAS. Such policies include:

- investment in human capital
- investment in research and technology
- investment in infrastructure
- direct support to specific industries.

Investment in human capital

Labour and entrepreneurship are two of the four factors of production, and can collectively (if somewhat coldly) be called human capital. Enhancing the productivity of that capital is likely to require significant government investment.

Education spending

Public education is a common policy in most countries. This has not always been true, but has gradually become accepted as a necessary ingredient of a modern economy. Learning basic literacy and numeracy, in particular, is rewarded with large jumps in the incomes of those so educated. Education improves the skills and productivity of the workforce as well. High levels of educational achievement are highly correlated with national income.

Investment in worker training schemes

Specific training for some jobs may not be offered in schools, and may be offered by special job training centres established by the government. This helps businesses find productive employees and thus should enhance economic growth.

Improving and extending health services

In countries where public health is poor, it is difficult for children to regularly attend school, and worker absenteeism is chronic. Government efforts to improve healthcare can improve labour productivity in these situations. For example, at a basic level, prenatal care and inoculations can help ensure healthy births and childhoods. Most governments recognise this benefit, although some developing countries find the costs difficult to manage. Investing in education, training, and health services will, by the building and staffing of these institutions stimulate AD. However, the lingering effects of a well-trained, educated, and healthy workforce should endure into the future, pushing LRAS outwards by improving labour and entrepreneurship.

Investment in research and technology

Policies that encourage research and development have an immediate impact on AD. However, the more enduring effect should come through the resulting new technologies and knowledge that will increase LRAS. When the government hires or sponsors the hiring of scientists and engineers to work in a particular area, this government spending stimulates AD in the immediate term. When their work results in new life-enhancing drugs, increased food production, and safer or cleaner technologies, the entire productive capacity is enriched, pushing LRAS outwards. This can be accomplished by public/private sector partnerships, as well as tax incentives for research and development.

Investment in infrastructure

Infrastructure is the building of large-scale public projects such as ports, highway systems, bridges, communications networks, as well as power and water systems. This kind of spending most certainly increases AD in the short run, but should also expand the capital base of the country in the long term, increasing LRAS in the process. The creation of a port, for example, makes it easier for the country to import goods, which may enhance the capital base of that country. At the same time, exports of goods will also be improved. The expanded market for domestic goods spurs investment to produce for overseas markets.

Direct support to specific industries

Governments may support specific industries; perhaps an industry where the country has comparative advantage fulfils a strategic need, or one with good long-term prospects. The government can support the industry with reduced taxes, subsidised loans, and even direct subsidies. These all reduce the costs to the firms, and encourage more production. Industries believed to be potentially competitive in the world market may get this special treatment. Compared to their global competitors, they may currently be too small to enjoy the benefits of economies of scale. Governments can put down protective tariffs or quotas to keep foreign competition out until the firm is sufficiently large and developed.

What are the advantages and disadvantages of interventionist supply-side policies?

Advantages

- In many of the above policy situations, the government is providing for goods that are underprovided in the free market. Education, training, healthcare, research, and infrastructure are *merit goods* that the free market finds little profit in providing at sufficient levels. Where economics defines these goods as providing significant economic benefits, such support is well justified on its own terms.

Disadvantages

- Interventionist policies come with considerable expense. Countries weighing the costs and benefits of interventionist policies worry that the budget expense will not yield the desired economic benefits. Budget deficits can be excused if the spending brings enough economic growth that paying them off is affordable. Prioritising such expenses poses a major challenge to any country, especially developing ones for whom tax revenues are especially precious.
- Interventionist policies take time to implement and bear results. Building a road system, for example, in the name of greater infrastructure, can take a decade. Improvements to education can take even longer to show up. Therefore, a balance between short-term and long-term achievable goals is desirable.
- Because interventionist policy requires government decision making and action, as well as money, they are inherently political decisions. They are subject to political debate, controversy, and opposition. This may make long-term commitment to particular goals difficult to sustain.

21.4 How are demand and supply-side policies related?

Learning outcome

At the end of this section you will be able to:

- analyse how supply-side and demand-side policies are interconnected.

Research and inquiry

Often a country's bureaucracy has departments that are designed to both regulate and promote the industries under their supervision. These can include a department of agriculture, or a ministry of energy, for example. Conduct an internet search of your home country's major agencies and find an industry-specific ministry.

1 Identify which groups it represents.
2 List its recent actions in the news with regard to promotion and regulation.

TOK **Ethics**

Having learned so much about macroeconomics so far, it is fair to question how you may have changed your thinking. And if this is true for you, that you think differently now that you have learned more about this subject, is it true for people in general? Do established values change in the face of new knowledge?

Video suggestion:
You have read about it, now you can review what you have just learned by watching a video by the author!
 Simply click here in your eBook for an introductory video on supply-side policies.

435

It is important to see the distinction between supply-side and demand-side policies as the different areas where government policy takes hold. However, such policies can have different longer term effects that result in outcomes in the opposite area. For example:

What are the demand-side effects of supply-side policies?

Supply-side policies can affect AD in the short run, even if they are intended to influence LRAS. Market-based policies that reduce union power or minimum wage laws may reduce income in the short run, reducing AD, while reductions in tax rates at all levels could increase AD.

Interventionist policies, because they require increased government spending, will immediately increase AD, and then eventually long-run supply. Increased spending on company subsidies, education, infrastructure, and healthcare will all stimulate the economy, providing short-run AD-based growth before growing the supply capacity of the country.

What are the supply-side effects of fiscal policies?

It is possible that the reduction of taxes that are intended to have short-run AD effects (to fill an output gap, for example) may also increase supply through boosting the labour and entrepreneurship factors of production.

Expansionary fiscal policy that involves increased government spending, perhaps to meet short-run recessionary policy goals, will boost AD. However, spending on power grids and road projects, mainly intended to increase employment and spending, could also result in long-run supply improvements.

21.5 What is the appeal of supply-side policies in terms of growth, employment, and inflation control?

Learning outcome

At the end of this section you will be able to:

- evaluate the effectiveness of supply-side policies in achieving growth, full employment, and stable price levels.

In theory, supply-side policies are especially desirable because they improve the overall macroeconomic environment in which individual actors operate. Good policies would encourage productivity as well as create more and better factors of production. In this environment of productive surplus, growth is the logical outcome. Furthermore, increasing LRAS manages to expand the economy without generating inflation, a typical problem with expansionary demand-side policies.

In particular, supply-side policies appear to address one of the most serious challenges of macroeconomic policies – stagflation. This is a loathsome combination of economic recession with rising inflation that is unresponsive to demand-side approaches. The economies of many Western nations were widely seen as locked into a period of stagflation in the 1970s, where the equilibrium price levels were high and increasing, while output was below full employment. Movement of AD would have either (in the case of expansionary policy) increased inflation further or (in the case of deflationary policy) driven the country into deeper recession.

In practice, some supply-side policies are criticised for hurting the economically vulnerable. In particular, those labour market reforms designed to reduce union power and eliminate the minimum wage, while they may increase employment, will also create more jobs that are poorly paid, and that put workers in situations where they have little legal protection against various kinds of exploitation and mistreatment. For some, this approach does little to increase general economic well-being but instead increases employer power at the expense of workers.

Both problems can be eased, however, by increasing AS. Successful supply-side policies would push SRAS to the right, reducing inflation and encouraging recovery to full employment.

Practice exam questions

Paper 1, part (a) questions

1. Using examples, distinguish between market-based and interventionist supply-side policies. (10 marks)
2. Explain the difference between demand-side policies and supply-side policies. (10 marks)

Paper 1, part (b) and Paper 2, part (g) questions

3. Evaluate the view that demand-side policies are more effective than supply-side policies in reducing the level of unemployment. (15 marks)
4. Using real-world examples, discuss the effectiveness of three interventionist policies that might be used to increase aggregate supply. (15 marks)
5. Using real-world examples, discuss the effectiveness of labour market reforms that may be used to increase aggregate supply. (15 marks)

4-mark Paper 2 and HL paper 3 questions

6. Using an appropriate diagram, explain how supply-side policies are expected to affect national income. (4 marks)

The global economy

Benefits of international trade

22

22.1 Introduction to international trade

Learning outcomes

At the end of this section you will be able to:

- analyse the various benefits of international trade
- draw diagrams to show imports and exports when world prices are lower/higher than domestic prices
- **HL** calculate the quantity of imports/exports and expenditure/revenue from a diagram.

International trade involves the exchange of goods and services between two countries. In recent years, the debate around free trade has inspired economists to revisit both the theoretical principles and the real-world evidence of its benefits. This chapter will explain and explore the benefits of trade, and Chapter 23 will discuss protectionism and look deeper at the debate around the role of trade in the world today.

What are the benefits of international trade?

One idea on which the vast majority of economists tend to agree is the axiom that 'trade is good'. The market economic system, after all, is based on the *free exchange of goods, services, and resources* all the way down to the level of individual households and firms. On the global scale, the same benefits from free trade experienced between individuals apply to entire nations, therefore, *free international trade* is an ideal towards which most economists would agree societies should strive.

The benefits economists see in international trade are outlined below.

Increased competition

Free trade will expose domestic firms to international competition. This gives domestic firms a further incentive to improve quality, lower price, and improve efficiency. Under competition, companies are pressed into lowering prices and improving service, or they suffer from their rivalry with the foreign firms.

Lower prices

Countries, just like individuals, can specialise in particular areas of expertise. This means they produce more efficiently than if each country tried to produce enough of everything for all its needs. Thus, a global division of labour takes place, where these multiplied efficiencies add to the overall wealth of consumers everywhere. In short, we get more output for less resources. Trade should therefore drive down real prices of the goods and services we all want.

Increased variety/choice

More sellers will lead to greater variety in the products available in all countries. A brief check around your room or class will reveal an array of goods from many places:

for example, a computer assembled in China, a glass from Russia, and clothes from Cambodia, Egypt, and the Dominican Republic. As the number of countries in the global market has grown, so has the amount of choice. Even a simple desk lamp is now available in nearly any size, colour, design, and wattage. While some find these choices overwhelming, others enjoy the power it gives to consumers to make decisions about their own purchases.

Acquisition of needed resources

Some countries lack critical goods to improve their standard of living. In some cases, production of a needed good is simply impossible. Trade is the only way to get it. This need can range from a vital natural resource like natural gas for heating, to the need to import capital goods that might improve industry or agriculture. Adding these imported goods can improve production or improve everyday life for buyers.

More foreign exchange earnings

Exporters generally want to be paid in their home currency. So, when foreign consumers buy a country's exports they must also buy their currency to pay for it. In doing so, the exporting country accumulates larger amounts of the foreign currency. For example, when Guatemala exports commodities like bananas and coffee to the USA, it earns US dollars that it can use to buy cars and capital goods from the USA and elsewhere because the dollar is easily exchanged for other currencies. For smaller and developing countries, in particular, an important feature of trade is getting access to foreign exchange that can be used to buy goods and services from other countries.

Access to larger markets

Often countries find that they are so productive in a particular product that their own country's market is too small to satisfy all the supply available. When supply is much greater than demand, prices are low, and incomes stay low as well. For example, if Paraguay were to sell its soybeans only in Paraguay, with its population of just 7 million people, a massive surplus and a drop in price would result. Instead, Paraguay trades with the neighbouring countries in the MERCOSUR trade area (which includes Brazil and Argentina with combined 260 million people). Because of their access to larger markets, soybeans are a leading export.

Economies of scale

Firms that trade internationally experience larger markets, as noted above, and so their production levels grow ever larger. Because they are producing such large runs of output, firms can now enjoy bulk buying power, as well as the specialisation of managers and the introduction of expensive technology to improve the productivity of a given business sector. The benefits of extreme specialisation bring lower and lower average costs. These low costs drive down prices, which benefit consumers as well as making the firms more internationally competitive. But these gains come from large-scale production and would not be likely to occur if production were limited to the domestic market.

Taking advantage of different factor endowments

No two countries share exactly the same resource base. Some are by the sea, some blessed with fertile farmland, some with ample deposits of minerals, and others placed well to act as a hub to facilitate trade between other countries. Trade takes advantage of these differences between countries. For example, Saudi Arabia, flush with oil deposits, buys technology from South Korea, which has few natural resources but a very skilled technical and technology sector. Both are better off.

More efficient production

Firms are both pressed to develop more efficiencies but at the same time have greater opportunities to increase productivity. By facing competition, local firms have greater incentives to innovate and cut costs. But they also enjoy the benefits of a larger market and so can vastly increase their economies of scale as a global competitor. Also, by having access to a large international market for resources, producers will be able to have reliable, appropriate quality inputs at competitive prices.

Taken together, the above benefits of trade suggest that there are enormous gains to be enjoyed by trading internationally. After exploring the theory that supports this premise in more detail for the remainder of the chapter, we will turn to arguments against free trade in Chapter 23.

How did theories of free trade develop over time?

The Scottish economist and moral philosopher Adam Smith first developed our view of the division of labour at the village level with his analogy of the pin maker:

> '… a workman not educated to this business, nor acquainted with the use of the machinery employed in it, could scarce, perhaps, with his utmost industry, make one pin in a day, and certainly could not make twenty. But if they had all wrought separately and independently, and without any of them having been educated to this peculiar business, they certainly could not each of them have made twenty, perhaps not one pin in a day; that is, certainly, not the two hundred and fortieth, perhaps not the four thousand eight hundredth part of what they are at present capable of performing, in consequence of a proper division and combination of their different operations …'

– Adam Smith, *The Wealth of Nations* (Book 1), 1776

To Smith, the benefits of specialisation were obvious. Everyone develops special efficiency, and auctions off that efficiency in the free market. Thus, through self-interest and trade, prosperity is made possible.

Smith's observations were seconded by the work of David Ricardo just a few decades later. Ricardo, a banker and member of parliament, wrote an essay in 1815 entitled *Essay on the Influence of a Low Price of Corn on the Profits of Stock* in which he argued that the British Corn Laws protected wealthy landowners and drove food prices up for everyone else. In particular, he viewed the laws as a redirection of income and resources away from relatively new and dynamic industries. In the process of fighting the Corn Laws, Ricardo developed the theory of comparative advantage. The theory holds that even countries that are more productive in all aspects should still trade with their otherwise inferior partners.

The French economist and philosopher Frédéric Bastiat took up the theme on the national level. In his 'Petition of the Candlemakers', first published in 1845 in the French *Journal des Économistes*, Bastiat satirises the impulse to protect this or that market.

The candlemakers in this work see the Sun as a rival and propose that the illumination of buildings with natural light be made illegal, as this would benefit the candle trade. Furthermore, by protecting candlemakers, all suppliers of candle-related goods would benefit: tallow producers, whale hunters who sell the blubber, the shipping industry, by extension all of France would benefit from the new rule. However, Bastiat's ridicule did not end the impulse to restrict markets.

More recently, James Ingram presented another way to demonstrate the benefits of trade, with the story of Mr X. This secretive and mysterious businessman tells the world he can turn simple primary goods like grain, coal, and cotton into TVs, radios, and cars, very cheaply. Mr X opens his factory, and the results stun the world. True to his word, the basic goods go in and the relatively advanced ones roll out. Consumers love the cheaper prices, competitors loathe the competition. Mr X jealously guards his trade secrets but a little boy wanders onto the property one day and discovers the truth: there are no miraculous manufacturing techniques, no special processes. The company, it turns out, is one big import–export business. The gains Mr X produced were made by trade alone.

Case study – a battle over free trade inspires the founding of *The Economist*

The Corn Laws were protectionist tariffs placed on imported grain to protect British landowners from foreign competition. Most British members of parliament were aristocratic landowners, who staunchly supported high prices and high tariffs on agriculture. A member of the anti-Corn Law lobby, James Wilson, founded *The Economist* to offer succinct and persuasive arguments in favour of free trade and in particular cheaper food for the residents of Britain's growing cities. The repeal of the Corn Laws in 1846 marked a significant shift towards freer trade by the British Empire, which had previously pursued mercantilism. While the players are not the same today, and mercantilism has faded, many of the free trade and protectionist disputes today resemble that over the Corn Laws, with vested interests arguing against competition and lower prices from foreign competition.

James Wilson (1805–60) campaigner for free trade and founder of *The Economist*

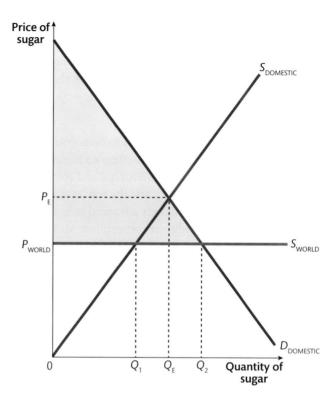

Figure 22.1   Sugar imports result in an expansion of consumer surplus compared to when the market is closed

How can the benefits of trade be shown with diagrams?

Basic supply and demand graphs can demonstrate the benefits of trade from the import and export sides. Figure 22.1 shows a domestic sugar market that is opened up to trade. The closed market price P_E is determined by the domestic suppliers and buyers. If this country is suddenly allowed to trade, all the world's sugar is now available at whatever the free market price is, here shown as P_{WORLD}. No matter how much the country wants, the price will be P_{WORLD} and so the global supply S_{WORLD} is shown as a flat line: any amount will be sold at that price. Because global sellers offer at a much lower price, domestic buyers get a much lower price (P_{WORLD} instead of P_E) and enjoy a much larger market ($0 - Q_2$ compared to $0 - Q_E$). We could further show the benefit in terms of expanded consumer surplus, the shaded blue area.

From the perspective of an exporting country, the view is reversed. In Figure 22.2, we can observe a country that produces cotton very competitively. Domestic cotton suppliers have a low domestic equilibrium price at P_E, compared to the higher P_{WORLD} price. At a price of P_{WORLD}, this country will increase its domestic supply, causing a movement along its supply curve to where it is offering Q_2 for sale. It will then export the quantity between Q_1 and Q_2.

This increases the size of the market for firms, increasing revenues, and expanding producer surplus, shown in yellow. Note an interesting side effect: the higher prices paid for cotton at home. This could raise prices for cotton-using firms inside the country. Overall, however, this shows the expanded markets benefiting some sellers, which may in turn lead them to develop economies of scale in the expanded industry.

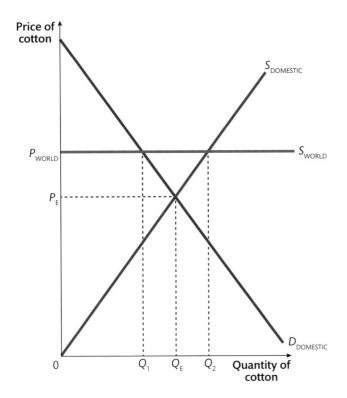

Price of cotton

$S_{DOMESTIC}$

S_{WORLD}

P_{WORLD}

P_E

$D_{DOMESTIC}$

0 Q_1 Q_E Q_2 Quantity of cotton

Figure 22.2 A higher global price for cotton means domestic suppliers can increase their output, enjoying greater producer surplus

How does free trade come about?

The term 'free trade' describes the process of lowering protectionist barriers and thereby realising those gains from trade. Countries work out these agreements through tedious negotiation at the global level through the World Trade Organization (WTO) and on the regional level through trade blocs such as the EU, the US–Mexico–Canada Agreement (USMCA) or Mercado Común del Sur (MERCOSUR), also known as the Common Market of the South. How the WTO works and how countries form such trade blocs is discussed in more detail in Chapter 24.

HL   Exercise 22.1

From a diagram, you should be able to calculate the quantity of exports, the quantity of imports, import expenditures, and export revenue. These calculations use your understanding of supply and demand, as well as the calculations of total revenue we have already learned. Try the examples below to test your understanding.

Calculate the following based on the import diagram:

1   domestic revenue before trade
2   quantity of exports after trade
3   domestic quantity after trade
4   export revenue after trade
5   domestic revenue after trade.

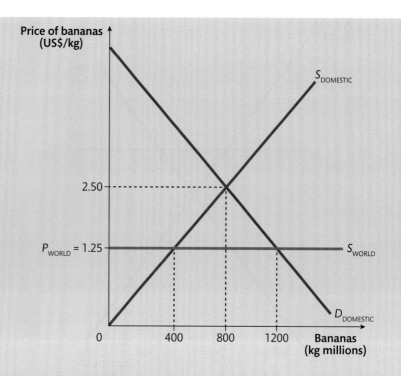

Calculate the following based on the export diagram:

6   domestic revenue before trade
7   quantity of exports after trade
8   domestic quantity after trade
9   export revenue after trade
10 domestic revenue after trade.

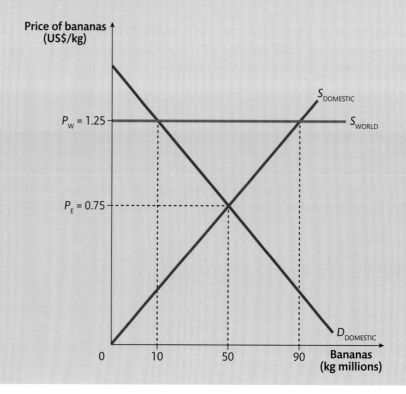

Case study – does trade lead to peace?

'Merchants have no country. The mere spot they stand on does not constitute so strong an attachment as that from which they draw their gains.'

– Thomas Jefferson, 1814

Trade requires relationships and attachments. Merchants want predictable supply of their imported resources and hope to maintain steady and reliable output to customers abroad. They abhor disruptions to everyday business and future planning.

This, economists believe, helps discourage conflict and helps keep the peace. A playful metaphor for this was popularised by Thomas Friedman as 'the golden arches theory of conflict resolution', which holds that no two countries with a McDonald's have ever fought a war, nor are they likely to do so because it goes against their mutual interests.

The updated version of this analogy suggests the same sort of pacifying effect to countries who are part of Apple's or Huawei's phone supply chain.

However, more profound examples may offer evidence as well. After hundreds of years of conflict, reaching an apex of destruction and misery in two world wars in the 20th century, most of Western Europe has since enjoyed a period of relative quiet and peaceful relations. They have also, not coincidentally, embarked on an extraordinary experiment in economic integration. Decade by decade, the six founding countries of the original European Economic Community (EEC) (created in 1957, and often referred to as the European Common Market) have been joined by 21 others while lowering barriers and opening borders to goods, services, and now workers. While this period of calm may seem small compared to the ages of bloody rivalry that preceded it, economists and political thinkers generally agree that trade and integration have consistently encouraged compromise and resolution over conflict and antagonism.

For discussion:

1   Is this notion still alive today? How has the Golden Arches theory held up?
2   Have the trade wars of the 2010s significantly affected trade flows?
3   Have nationalist movements succeeded in breaking up trade relationships?
4   What kind of trends could jeopardise the apparent correlation between trade and peace?

22.2 HL Absolute and comparative advantage

Learning outcomes

At the end of this section you will be able to:

*   explain the theories of absolute and comparative advantage, giving examples
*   suggest the sources of comparative advantage

- use a PPC diagram to show the gains from trade from comparative advantage
- calculate opportunity costs from a set of data in order to identify comparative advantage
- discuss the real-world relevance and limitations of the theory of comparative advantage.

What is absolute advantage?

It is important to acknowledge what may be obvious: some countries are simply more efficient at some forms of production than other countries. Called **absolute advantage**, this is where a country is able to produce more output than other countries using the same input of factors of production.

Table 22.1 shows two fictional countries trading two goods. This theory assumes that each country uses the same amount of resources to produce wheat and oil. This table shows the limits of production for these countries: Maleyland produces thirty units of oil or ten units of wheat; Welkeria can produce three units of oil or six units of wheat. Maleyland is far superior to Welkeria in both oil production and wheat production.

Maleyland clearly has an absolute advantage in both goods. Based on this information, should the two countries specialise and trade? In fact, should more efficient countries ever trade with less efficient ones? It would appear that the answer is 'no', but if we employ the concept of comparative advantage, we will see that the answer is usually 'yes'.

What is comparative advantage?

Comparative advantage is where a country is able to produce a good at a lower opportunity cost than another country. Comparative advantage theory says that even countries that are much more productive in all industries should trade with less productive ones. This sounds illogical, so why does it make sense?

To better grasp the problem, imagine the following example. Lawyer J worked her way through school doing accounting, and became quite good. After establishing a successful law practice, J thought to save some money by doing her own accounting. Is this a good idea? In economic terms, let us assume that Lawyer J possesses an absolute advantage in both accounting and lawyering. (She is good at both.)

However, she is rewarded very differently for each activity. When she does her own accounting, she saves the $40 per hour she would normally pay her accountant. When she is working as a lawyer, she is paid an average of $300 per hour. If the answer seems a little clearer now, let us clarify the reasons why.

Table 22.1 **One country can produce more of a good using the same resources and is said to have an absolute advantage**

Country/Product	Oil	Wheat
Maleyland	30	10
Welkeria	3	6

Table 22.2   A simple production possibility matrix enables us to work out the opportunity costs of production

Country/Product	TVs (thousands)	Smartphones (thousands)
Siliconia	15	5
The Solid States	20	15

Because she earns so much more as a lawyer (and would not earn that if she chose to do accounts for that hour), it is logical to conclude that she should always work as a lawyer. This is the activity with the *lower opportunity cost*. Therefore, even though she has an absolute advantage in both jobs, her comparative advantage lies in lawyering because she loses less by doing it.

The same principle applies to countries. Comparative advantage theory says that countries should specialise in the production of whatever has the lowest opportunity cost (saying something has the lowest opportunity cost naturally implies that it is the good whose production has the most value). Countries that specialise produce more efficiently and should trade their output with other countries to enjoy a higher standard of living.

David Ricardo was the first to show the benefits of comparative advantage mathematically, in the early 1800s. With countries, the theory assumes a simplified example involving just two countries producing only two goods each. For a country to produce more of Good A, it must shift resources away from Good B and sacrifice some amount of Good B. Whatever is lost is the opportunity cost of more of Good A, and the reverse holds true for shifting resources to more of Good B.

Table 22.2 shows the output possible for each product and each country, if each produced only that good. For example, if Siliconia produced only TVs, it could produce 15,000 TVs and no smartphones. If the Solid States produced 15,000 smartphones, it could not make any TVs. If either country wanted to produce more of one, it would need to sacrifice some of its production of the other. In this regard, Table 22.2 represents the countries' production possibilities.

Based on their output, it is rather easy to determine who has the absolute advantage. Which country produces more efficiently? The Solid States produces more TVs, as well as more smartphones. Therefore, the Solid States has the absolute advantage in both industries. Like Lawyer J, the Solid States is better at both tasks. However, the Solid States may still benefit from trade with the clearly inferior producer, Siliconia.

Domestic opportunity cost

To find out who has the comparative advantage, we need to calculate the domestic opportunity costs in each country for both TVs and smartphones. In other words, what is the trade-off for production inside Siliconia and the Solid States?

Worked example 22.1

In calculating domestic opportunity cost for an output problem, we use the equation:

Opportunity cost of x = Output Y/Output X

For Siliconia:

Opportunity cost of producing 1 TV = 5 smartphones/15 TVs = 0.33 smartphone

Opportunity cost of producing 1 smartphone = 15 TVs/5 smartphones = 3 TVs

For the Solid States

Opportunity cost of producing 1 TV = 15 smartphones/20 TVs = 0.75 smartphone

Opportunity cost of producing 1 smartphone = 20 TV15 smartphones = 1.33 TV

Cross-market comparison

To more easily compare these values, we can place opportunity cost values inside the table to clarify the choices. Table 22.3 shows the trade-offs for making one good, in terms of another. For example, for Siliconia, to produce 1 TV would require the sacrifice of 0.33 of a smartphone, and for Siliconia to make one smartphone, it would lose three TVs.

In the market for TVs, Siliconia has the lower opportunity cost, giving up only 0.33 of a smartphone for every TV made, whereas the Solid States gives up 0.75 of a smartphone for every TV made. Thus, Siliconia has the comparative advantage in TVs, because it has the lower opportunity cost.

In the market for smartphones, the Solid States has the lower opportunity cost, giving up only 1.33 of a TV for every smartphone made, whereas Siliconia gives up three TVs for every smartphone made. Thus, the Solid States has the comparative advantage in smartphones, because it has a lower opportunity cost.

Specialise and trade

With comparative advantage determined, it is rational for each country to specialise in the production of the good for which it has the lowest opportunity cost. This maximises production between the two countries, which then trade their goods with each other. The Solid States may consume the number of smartphones it likes, then trade the rest for TVs. Siliconia can consume their own TVs, and trade any surplus to the Solid States.

The situation described in Table 22.2 can also be shown with production possibilities. In Figure 22.3, you can see the limits of each country's production, as well as the rate

Table 22.3   The addition of opportunity costs reveals which country has a comparative advantage

Country	Output of TVs (thousands)	Opportunity cost of producing 1 TV	Output of smartphones (thousands)	Opportunity cost of producing 1 smartphone
Siliconia	15	0.33 smartphone	5	3 TV
The Solid States	20	0.75 smartphone	15	1.33 TV

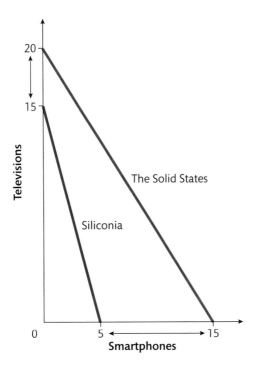

Figure 22.3 Absolute and comparative advantages can be inferred from these straight-line PPCs

of opportunity cost as you move from one output combination to another. The PPC demonstrates the Solid States' possession of absolute advantage in both industries by having a PPC that goes beyond Siliconia's in every direction.

It may also be possible to infer the comparative advantage from these PPCs. If the scale of the axes is the same, and there is a country with clear absolute advantage, the comparative advantages for the more efficient country is where the gap between the two PPCs is greatest, in this case shown by the lower arrows. The comparative advantage for the less efficient country is where the gap is the smallest, in this case shown with the upper arrows. This is a handy double check on your opportunity cost calculations. Another way to view it is that Siliconia's line is steeper, suggesting that it probably gives up TVs more rapidly as it tries to increase its production of smartphones. We could then infer that the Solid States had the lower opportunity cost of smartphones. Logically, Siliconia would then have the better opportunity cost of TVs. Straight-line PPCs will always show the rate of trade-off, and therefore the relative domestic opportunity cost, enabling you to make this assessment.

How can one show the gains from trade using a PPC?

It is possible to show the gains from trade using a PPC. Looking at Figure 22.4, let us assume a trade rate of two TVs for one smartphone. Next, assume that the Solid States is currently consuming along their own PPC at point *x*, which provides 10,000 TVs and 7500 smartphones. The Solid States will specialise in smartphones and use all their resources to produce 15,000 phones. The Solid States can now trade at a rate of one phone for two TVs. By trading 6000 of the 15,000 phones, keeping 9000, they gain 12,000 TVs, a combination shown as point *y*. By specialising and trading the good in which they have a comparative advantage, the Solid States now enjoys more of both goods (an extra 2000 TVs and 1500 smartphones).

Video suggestion:
You have read about it, now you can review what you have just learned by watching a video by the author!
Simply click here in your eBook for a video on determining absolute and comparative advantage.

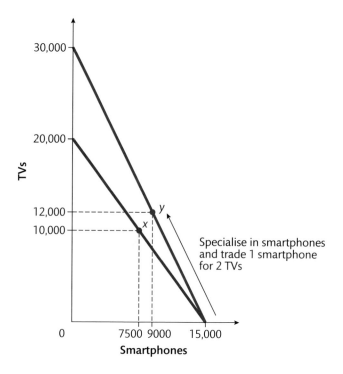

Figure 22.4 Gains in
two goods are made by
specialising in the good
that offers a comparative
advantage and trading some
units away in return for the
other good

For Siliconia, assume the same trade rate of two TVs for one smartphone. Next,
assume that Siliconia is currently consuming along their own PPC at point *x*, which
provides 7500 TVs and 2500 smartphones. Siliconia will specialise in TVs and uses all
their resources to produce 15,000. Siliconia can now trade at a rate of two TVs to buy
every phone. By trading 7500 TVs they gain 3750 smartphones, a combination shown
as point *y*. By specialising and trading the good in which they have a comparative
advantage, Siliconia now enjoys 1250 more smartphones.

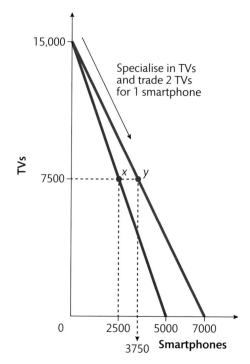

Figure 22.5 Despite not
having an absolute advantage,
Siliconia also gains by
specialising and trading

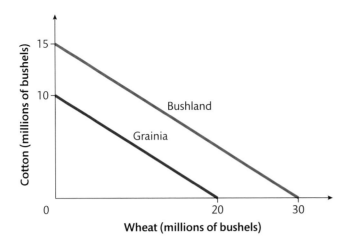

Figure 22.6 The equal gradient of two countries' PPCs indicates identical opportunity costs and therefore no comparative advantage

While it is important to know the specifics of this method, a larger point is demonstrated here as well. According to comparative advantage theory, *a country can consume beyond its means*, as measured by the limits of a PPC. Levels of consumption that appear 'impossible' because they are beyond the PPC are made possible by the gains from trade, and this is possible for both countries.

An important exception to the principle of comparative advantage is when both countries have the same opportunity cost. In that event, neither country will possess a comparative advantage and there will be no observed gains from trade. In Figure 22.6, note that the PPCs have exactly the same gradient, which means the rate of trade-off between one product and another is exactly the same for each country.

Figure 22.6 shows the respective production possibility curves for cotton and wheat in Bushland and Grainia. For Bushland, the trade-off shown is 15 bushels of cotton for every 30 bushels of wheat, or one cotton for two wheat. For Grainia, the trade-off is between 10 bushels of cotton and 20 bushels of wheat, still a one cotton for two wheat trade-off. With exactly the same domestic opportunity costs, neither country stands to benefit from trade.

What are the sources of comparative advantage?

It might be easy to say a country with more of one resource than another has the comparative advantage. If a country has an abundance of oil, for example, do they have a comparative advantage? Not necessarily. Such a situation may only be a source of reciprocal absolute advantage because it trades something it has in abundance with a country that has much more of something else, like manufacturing labour, for example.

Comparative advantage is more subtle than this. Let us imagine two countries that both produce corn and soybeans. Country Z is more productive than Country A at both. Country A makes fewer of both crops, but is still a good producer. If their opportunity cost is different, then there will be a comparative advantage in each country, and trade will be beneficial. Comparative advantage does not mean necessarily being the 'best' at anything, it just means having a lower opportunity cost in a product compared to your trade partner.

Video suggestions:
You have read about it, now you can review what you have just learned by watching a few videos by the author!

▶ Simply click here in your eBook for videos on the gains from international trade in the PPC and demand and supply models, and on whether two countries can benefit from trade if neither has a comparative advantage.

Exercise 22.2

The following table gives output figures of two countries, Podland and Canesia, for two commodities, sugar and cocoa. The countries have the same quantities of resources for production.

Podland		Canesia	
Cocoa (million kg)	Sugar (million kg)	Cocoa (million kg)	Sugar (million kg)
60	0	80	0
50	5	60	40
40	10	40	80
30	15	20	120
20	20	0	160
10	25		
0	30		

1 Calculate the opportunity costs of producing cocoa and sugar for:
   a. Podland
   b. Canesia.

Assume the two countries exchange cocoa and sugar at a rate of 1 : 1, 1 kg of sugar to 1 kg of cocoa.

2 Draw a PPC diagram for Podland at its current domestic opportunity costs; add the trade line of 1 : 1.
   a. Mark with an X the point where Podland would be consuming 40 million kg cocoa and 10 million kg sugar.
   b. Using the diagram, show and explain what happens if Podland specialises in cocoa and consumes 40 million kg cocoa and trades the extra cocoa to Canesia at the 1 : 1 ratio. Label this point Y.
3 With a new diagram, draw a PPC diagram for Canesia at its current domestic opportunity costs; add the trade line of 1 : 1.
   a. Mark with an X the point where Canesia would be consuming 120 million kg of sugar and 20 million kg of cocoa.
   b. Using the diagram, show and explain what happens if Canesia specialises in sugar and trades the rest in exchange for cocoa at the rate of 1 : 1. Label this point Y.

What are the limitations of comparative advantage theory?

While recognised as essentially valid in theoretical form, the theory of comparative advantage is heavily criticised for not being an accurate representation of real trade.

Overspecialisation

In theory, a country might devote its entire resources to the production of a single good. This makes the relative prosperity of the country dependent on the value of that good. If the good is a commodity, the country's entire income is bound to the price of the commodity. A long-term concern is whether a country will be trapped in a certain type of production, thus limiting its potential for full development.

Transportation costs

Transport costs, assumed to be irrelevant in theory, cannot be ignored in practice. They can raise costs enough to eliminate a comparative advantage.

Assumption of homogeneity

Goods are assumed to be identical. Wheat is wheat, whether from the USA or Ukraine. However, goods often have some differentiation, especially in the world of manufactured goods. It is difficult to assess true comparative advantage when the goods are not the same.

Imperfect information

Perfect information about the availability and prices of all available goods is assumed, but given the vast nature of global markets such knowledge is not easy to find.

Constant costs

The theory assumes relatively constant costs. This is reflected in the PPCs with constant slopes. However, one would expect improvements in production that may lead to significant economies of scale.

Bilateral versus multilateral trade

The two-country model is unrealistic, making the determination of comparative advantage difficult in a multinational world. However, multi-country analysis is possible with appropriate mathematical modelling.

Migration and cross-border investment

It is assumed that the factors of production stay in-country. However, people migrate from country to country, and capital (either financial or physical) can move between countries as well. The relocation of a factory from one country to another is just one example of this.

Barriers to trade

Finally, the assumption that countries practise free trade is highly debatable. While tariffs and other forms of protectionism have been significantly reduced in recent decades, many countries still protect markets with tariffs, subsidies, quotas, and bureaucratic barriers. These practices distort the market, making the gains from comparative advantage difficult to discern, and even harder to realise.

In summary, comparative advantage is a drastically simplified model, used to explain the likely benefits of trade between countries. While the reality may be quite different at times, the theory helps justify the general principles of free exchange and the gains from trade.

Practice exam questions

Paper 1 part (a) questions

1. Using examples, explain three gains from international trade. (10 marks)
2. Using real-world examples, explain the theory of comparative advantage. (10 marks)

Paper 2, part (b) question

3. Using real-world examples, discuss the extent to which comparative advantage theory accurately describes international trade. (15 marks)

Paper 2 Questions

4. Define absolute advantage. (2 marks)
5. Using two-country PPC diagrams with different domestic opportunity costs for coal and steel, explain how to determine comparative advantage using the gradient of the PPCs. (4 marks)

Trade protection

23

Despite the obvious gains made possible by trade, most countries try to protect at least some industries from unpredictability and the threat of foreign competition, a practice known as trade protection – or protectionism. Protectionism can take many forms and is practised to varying degrees by every country. Some of the most ardent free trade countries still shelter or support large portions of their economies with a variety of protectionist methods. Other countries openly promote protectionism as their fundamental economic growth policy. Why is protectionism so popular? This chapter explores the arguments around protectionism and evaluates the effects of protectionist policies.

23.1 What are the arguments for and against protectionism?

Learning outcomes

At the end of this section you will be able to:

- discuss the various arguments in favour of the use of **trade protection** measures, including:
  - for the protection of infant industries, domestic employment, national security, and health and safety and environmental standards
  - as an **anti-dumping** measure
  - to combat unfair competition
  - to correct the balance of payments
  - to raise government revenue
  - to diversify a **less economically developed country (LEDC)**
- examine the disadvantages of protectionism, including:
  - the misallocation of resources
  - retaliation
  - increased costs
  - higher prices
  - less choice
  - poor incentives
  - reduced export competitiveness.

The proponents of protectionism argue that their vulnerable domestic markets face unfair and damaging foreign competition. As global trade has expanded dramatically in recent decades, many of the following arguments continue to be raised, especially in the wake of economic crises like the Great Recession of 2008–10 and the COVID-19 pandemic of 2020–21.

What are the arguments for protectionism?

To protect infant (sunrise) industries

Many countries, perhaps especially less economically developed countries (LEDCs), believe they have industries that are future champions. Countries can argue that their industries are as yet underdeveloped, and have not grown large enough to achieve lowered costs through economies of scale. These industries should therefore be sheltered until they can face *on more equal terms* the powerful multinational corporations and highly developed industries of rich countries. The strategy is to block imports with tariffs, subsidise, and offer industries administrative support until the 'infant' has grown into 'adulthood', being large enough to enjoy economies of scale. In theory, these firms will eventually grow strong enough to compete without such assistance.

Advocates of the sunrise industry perspective point to the success of countries that have developed dramatically in a relatively short period, citing the Asian tigers of South Korea, Singapore, Taiwan, and Hong Kong. Major industrial powers like the USA, Germany and others have histories of protecting their heavy industries as they grew. These countries identified potential growth industries and supported them with state subsidies, as well as discouraging domestic consumption by levying high import tariffs. Critics take issue with these results, citing evidence of higher education levels and lower wages as the drivers of productivity in the tiger economies in particular. At the same time, critics of the sunrise industry view also note that most sunrise industries never grow up fully, and often require state support long after their infancy or even adolescence has passed. These dependent firms, they argue, will continue to draw government subsidies and will cry out for protectionism long into the future.

Case study – modern economists – is industrial policy a good idea?

A number of economists have developed lines of thinking that run counter to the orthodox view of free trade as explained by David Ricardo. Those critics, like Ha-Joon Chang, point out that the theory of comparative advantage is only a theory, and does not take into account the different starting points of each country. Chang points out that the government should and must 'pick winners' by directing industrial policy towards promising, high-value fields. Britain waited to open its markets, he argues, until well after it was a global empire, as did the USA, which advanced free trade in earnest only after the Second World War. In *23 Things They Don't Tell You About Capitalism*, Chang challenges the notion that governments are necessarily bad at identifying and supporting industries in the economy. They are no worse and can be better than, he says, private firms in some cases. 'The reality is that winners are being picked all the time both by the government and by the private sector, but the most successful ones tend to be done in joint efforts between the two.'

To protect national security

Plausible arguments can be made that military or defence-related goods should be produced domestically for national security reasons. Buying sophisticated telecommunications equipment from foreign suppliers, for example, could make a country vulnerable to information theft (for example, the concerns the USA raised over purchasing 5G technology from the Chinese manufacturer Huawei in 2020). Or it may leave a country vulnerable to supply problems if relations between partners deteriorate. This could also be true of any strategic commodity, like food and medical equipment as well.

To enforce product standards

Product standards exist to protect consumers from hazardous products as well as to ensure a reputation of quality production across an industry. These standards are likely to raise the cost of production. In recent years, countries have used product standard rules to challenge some imports on the basis that those products threaten national safety or health. These claims can be derived from scandals in the news, or they can be based on disputed scientific claims about new methods of production, such as the long-running conflict over US hormone-injected beef. Several European countries, as well as Japan, have restricted such imports from the USA, citing public health concerns. And in recent years, the EU has allowed small quotas of hormone-injected beef, which may come from any country, not just the USA. All such disputes must be arbitrated by the World Trade Organization (WTO) as well as associated agencies, like the World Bank and the World Health Organization, and be based on science-based concerns. The standards may be difficult and very costly to comply with. Developing countries, in particular, will struggle to achieve and prove compliance.

To protect against product dumping

To prevent the **dumping** of foreign goods onto the domestic market. Dumping is the selling of a good in another country at a price below its unit cost of production. This implies that exporters are losing money on these goods and hoping to steal away domestic consumers with unsustainably low prices. In the short term the foreign firms may lose money, but can raise prices after driving domestic firms out of the market. Dumping in this way might be seen as a form of predatory pricing.

Dumping firms might also be selling off surplus goods, having extracted higher prices for them in their domestic markets. For example, in recent years, the sell-off of excess clothing and textiles to African countries has prompted objections to dumping from domestic clothing makers there. If this were only an occasional instance, there would be little harm done. But when the practice is sustained over time, long-term damage to domestic sellers can occur. The benefit to domestic consumers, in the form of cheaper clothes in the long run, is debatable if the practice prevents the development of higher value industries that would bring higher incomes.

Countries that believe they are victims of dumping can take their case to the WTO.

Allegations of dumping, however, have proven difficult to prove. Wide differences in cost structures, as well as a lack of transparency and uniform accounting procedures, can make the calculation of relative costs exceptionally complicated. If one country wins a dumping complaint against another in the WTO, it can establish peremptory protectionist measures against the offender. However, this approach, as with any escalation of protectionist barriers, can lead to bitter and counterproductive trade wars.

To protect against unfairly low labour costs

A popular argument among wealthy countries is that many imported goods are produced at wage rates far below those paid in their own domestic industries. This argument can be further extended to include hiring and working conditions that would be considered unacceptable at home. The combination of lower wages and reduced labour standards makes it impossible for industries at home to pay a living wage to their workers and provide them with safe and reasonable work environments.

However, for many countries a surplus of labour is their primary comparative advantage, allowing them to produce competitively in industries where they may lack technological knowledge or the latest capital equipment. The Chinese coastal town of Datang has become known as Sock City for its massive share of the global sock market. Many of Datang's workers sewed socks by hand in the 1970s, and the industry grew in large part because of its labour-cost advantage. All the while, China and other low-cost labour markets have won this share from Europe and the USA – countries with a high labour cost.

To overcome a balance of payments deficit

The balance of payments measures the flow of money into and out of a country. The overall system of balance of payments will be covered in more detail in Chapter 26. For now, it is important to know that the export and import of goods and services, called the *trade balance*, is normally a major part of that accounting. In national income accounting for gross domestic product (GDP), this would be recorded via the expenditure approach as net exports $(X - M)$ from the equation for aggregate demand, $AD = C + I + G + (X - M)$. Therefore, countries that find they are spending excessively on imported goods are worsening their trade deficit. More money flows out to buy imports than is flowing in from exports. In response, governments may enact protectionist policies to address this imbalance.

This approach, called **expenditure-switching**, is regarded by most economists as only a temporary solution. While it may lower imports for a short time, the causes of the imbalance are not addressed by this policy. In the meantime, higher tariffs or stricter trade barriers continue to distort trade and deny the potential gains from comparative advantage.

To raise government revenue

A nation can raise revenue through a variety of tax methods. In developing countries, where income tax compliance is low, customs duties can provide a vital source of money. Nevertheless, the additional taxes still distort the market by taxing goods that are wanted or needed by the domestic population. By raising import prices, they may also limit the importation of important resources needed for growth and development to flourish by taxing needed capital goods or health products. Table 23.1 shows selected countries and their reliance on tariffs for tax revenue.

Table 23.1   Tariffs may raise a significant proportion of tax revenues in developing countries

Country	Total tax revenues from tariffs (%)
Somalia	36.5
Bangladesh	24.5
Ethiopia	21.9
Philippines	20.9
Nepal	16.0

To protect domestic employment

A prominent argument among protectionists is the desire to preserve employment and save jobs. It is most likely to be heard from industries that are in a 'sunset' stage of relative decline compared to their international competition. The vested interests here include the company itself, the workers and any unions associated with them, as well as related industries that rely on the business. When the USA rescued its automobile industry from bankruptcy in 2008, the jobs at stake were estimated to be 3 million, of which more than one-half were not directly employed by the automobile industry itself. Clearly, this kind of government subsidy was granted to protect domestic employment.

Firms making the employment argument typically vie for more time to adjust to the market, to modernise and improve efficiency. Rather ironically, this kind of modernising would usually eliminate many of the jobs these industries profess to want to save. However, in most situations, these firms are in long-term decline and protectionist measures merely delay an inevitable loss of market share.

Nevertheless, industries threatened in this manner will often see management and labour unions join forces to press parliament or congress for protectionist advantages.

To diversify the economy of a less economically developed country

Many developing countries export a limited range of goods, and typically these goods are basic commodities. Because commodity prices tend to be volatile, some LEDCs go quickly from an excellent year of export revenues to near-collapse when prices fall. At the same time, developing countries generally do not have higher value production that drives up national income. So, it is argued that some developing countries would benefit from selectively protecting some domestic markets in an attempt to diversify the economic base. With such protection, perhaps for sunrise industries, the country would be less vulnerable to wide swings in global market prices for their goods.

This argument draws strength from the worries about over-specialisation when countries trade based solely on comparative advantage. The expression 'a one crop economy' used to be used to describe countries that were centred on a single good.

The same could be true of those reliant on a metal or another primary commodity. It is understandable that a country would not want its entire economic future to be dependent on one industry. Brazil in the 1960s feared that coffee would be its only viable export, a situation that currently concerns Ethiopia. Tobacco makes up 69% of Malawi's exports, and Burkina Faso's exports rely almost exclusively on gold mining. Furthermore, where these countries rely on extraction industries like mining, the worry can become rather acute as the resource is gradually depleted. Many sub-Saharan African LEDCs (Cameroon, Congo, Angola) are hugely dependent on oil production. For all of these countries, protecting a new industry may help it grow and help the country diversify its exports.

What are some arguments against protectionism?

The arguments against protectionism are closely related to the advantages of free international trade explained in Chapter 22. After reading the arguments in favour of protectionism, it is worth another look at these arguments.

Misallocation of resources

Countries that protect declining industries compel their consumers to pay higher prices. This is an unnecessary misallocation of income to inefficient producers. Furthermore, because such industries are larger than they would otherwise be, they draw more workers and capital than would occur under free trade conditions. It follows that industries with the potential to realise their comparative advantage do not get these workers, nor the benefit of access to capital. It all goes to the inefficient but politically connected 'dinosaur' firm.

The risk of retaliation and a trade war

What might start out as a dispute over subsidies or unfair bureaucratic barriers can degenerate quickly into a damaging trade conflict. When this occurs, trade can grind to a halt and economic growth is put at risk. This kind of escalation took hold during the Great Depression, as desperate governments resorted to protectionism as a way to prevent unemployment from deepening. Many economists have blamed this rapid shutdown of world trade as a major factor in the entrenchment of the crisis.

During the Great Recession of 2008–10, trade complaints grew rapidly, while many governments and the WTO urged everyone to stay calm and avoid sparking a round of retaliatory policies. Despite a few isolated incidents of a tariff or quota, trade remained largely as free as it was before the crisis.

However, after the US Trump administration raised US tariffs on many European, Canadian, and Chinese imports many countries retaliated with their own charges, resulting in an escalating trade conflict that some labelled a 'trade war'. The conflict hurt several industries quite hard on both sides. When China responded to tariffs on its goods with retaliatory action against American soy farmers, the US government agreed to pay $28 billion in subsidies to farmers. Trade disputes like these can lead to growth-strangling trade wars.

TOK

Ethics
Free trade is advocated on the grounds that it leads to greater efficiency. Yet it results in both winners and losers. Do economists have a moral responsibility towards the losers when they advocate free trade?

Trump trade conflict

World markets dip as Trump ratchets up China trade war

Richard Partington
Economics correspondent

we are unlikely to see tariffs averted by simply promising to resume talks." In a development likely to have severe ramifications for global growth, Trump said Washington would impose tariffs on $300bn of Chinese...

havens amid global turmoil, with the yield on 10-year US treasuries falling to 1.832%, the lowest since November 2016. Trump said the fresh tariffs were a punishment for Chinese noncompliance with agreed measures. In a flurry of tweets, he said: "We thought we had ... three months ago...

Trump, the trade wars, and China

Starting in 2018, the USA initiated a series of tariffs against Chinese industries, as well as EU, Canadian, Mexican, and other producers. Conduct an internet search to see what some of the main issues were. Suggested search terms include: 'Trump Trade Wars', 'China steel tariffs', and 'US tariffs on European goods'.

For discussion and debate:

1 Identify the main rationales supplied by the countries levying tariffs.

2 Discuss whether those claims, based on your knowledge now, are justified.

3 List the pieces of information you would like to know to be more sure of your answer to question 3.

4 Check in on the status of these trade disputes today. Are they still in effect, or has there been a change over time?

Government protection creates bad incentives for domestic firms

Protected firms quickly understand that their real profits come from staying protected, and thus put more energy into persuading the public and politicians of their case. They have less of an incentive to actually modernise or innovate for greater efficiency. After all, that would weaken their case for assistance the next time the laws are up for renewal. With such poor incentives, firms tend to be complacent and resist change. Thus, consumers and firms that buy from the protected firm pay higher prices, and often for worse products.

Increased import prices to consumers and higher costs to firms

Protectionist measures directly affect the consumers and firms who buy imported goods. These higher prices might drive some imports out of the market entirely, relegating domestic producers and consumers to pay higher prices for possibly inferior quality goods. This reduces the real income for families and the higher costs of production reduce the supply of domestically made goods and services.

Less variety and choice of goods

The more stringent the protectionism, the greater the impact on the choice and variety of goods offered on the domestic market. This undermines a core tenet of capitalism, that consumers vote with their spending and lead the market to more efficient outcomes.

Reduced export competitiveness

Those domestic firms that use imported resources will pay higher costs, and firms that hope to export suffer reduced competitiveness on the world market. They endure the indirect harm of having workers and resources (capital) drawn away by inefficient domestic producers. For example, if a country protects its domestic lumber industry with high tariffs, then its domestic furniture makers will pay higher input costs and be at a disadvantage compared to foreign furniture manufacturers. In 2018, the US Trump administration was opposed by many US firms whose costs were expected to rise after ever higher tariffs were announced, including firms in the retail, automobile, furniture, and building materials industries.

At the end of this section you will be able to:

- discuss, using a tariff diagram, the various effects of imposing a tariff on imported goods
- examine, using a diagram, the effects of setting a quota on foreign producers
- explain, using a diagram, the effects of subsidies
- describe and discuss the effects of **administrative barriers** that may be used as a means of trade protection
- **HL** calculate from diagrams the effects of imposing tariffs, quotas, and subsidies on different stakeholders.

Protectionist policies have different approaches but the same goal: promote selected domestic industries at the expense of foreign ones. These policies might seek to expand the market for a successful domestic industry or merely defend a less competitive one from global competition.

What is a tariff?

A tariff is a duty (tax) that is placed upon imports to protect domestic industries from foreign competition and to raise revenue for the government. To understand the effect of a tariff, recall the basic free trade diagram from the perspective of the importing country, which was explained in Chapter 22. The domestic producer's equilibrium price, P_E, is much higher than the world price P_{WORLD}. The global market can supply all the domestic market could want at P_{WORLD}, so global supply is perfectly elastic at S_{WORLD}.

Remember that taxes are viewed as an added cost of production by firms, so a tariff shifts the supply curve to the left or backwards. Take for example a widely produced commodity, in this case rice, and examine the various effects of a tariff on the market. In Figure 23.1, a tax on imported rice shifts the supply curve S_{WORLD} upwards, reflecting higher costs imposed by the tax.

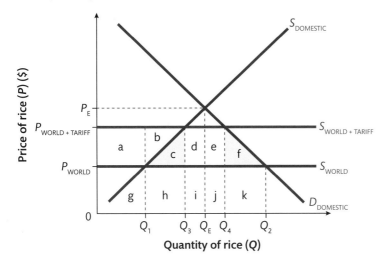

Figure 23.1 A tariff designed to reduce the quantity of imported rice has a variety of effects

Effect on domestic producers

Before the tariff, the domestic quantity supplied was $0 - Q_1$, from which the revenue earned is shown by taking $P_{WORLD} \times Q_1$, or the area of box 'g'. Now at the new tariff price of $P_{WORLD + TARIFF}$, domestic producers can afford to produce more, and so increase production to $0 - Q_3$, and earn greater revenue at $a + b + c + g + h$.

Effect on foreign producers

Before the tariff, foreign production (imports) was $Q_1 - Q_2$ and earned revenue $h + i + j + k$. At the higher tariff price, domestic producers take the share of the market shown by $Q_1 - Q_3$, and the consumer quantity demanded decreases from $0 - Q_2$ to $0 - Q_4$. So now foreign production (imports) drops to $Q_3 - Q_4$ and import revenue declines to $i + j$. Foreign producers do not, however, enjoy the benefit of the higher prices, as the government collects the difference between the world import price and the new tariff price, shown by $d + e$.

Effect on government

Government collects the import tax, which can be a substantial benefit to the country's revenue base. This tariff revenue is shown in the areas $d + e$.

The effect on consumers

Consumers pay higher prices, from P_{WORLD} to $P_{WORLD + TARIFF}$ and now buy less of the product, from $0 - Q_2$ to $0 - Q_4$.

Welfare loss

The new market share enjoyed by domestic producers only occurs because of the artificially high tariff price. The area of the blue triangle c represents an inefficiency form of welfare loss, because that amount would already be produced at the world price, but now consumers must pay more for domestic producers to supply it. This other lost surplus is represented by the blue area f. Because of the higher prices, consumers reduce their overall quantity demanded from $0 - Q_2$ to $0 - Q_4$ as a result of the tariff price, and so consume less. The reduced consumption overall represents another welfare loss, the loss of consumer surplus enjoyed before the tariff raised prices.

In sum, the tariff causes the price of the affected good to rise. If this product were a factor cost in other products (e.g. tyres for cars) then the price of the final goods (cars) would rise as well. Smaller quantities of the good are consumed, harming domestic consumers and reducing their welfare. Domestic producers enjoy the benefits of this protection, earning more revenue and producing more output, but they do so inefficiently and at the expense of consumers paying the higher tariff prices. Meanwhile, the government can gain some tax revenue that was not possible before imposing the tariff.

It is logical to conclude that domestic producers have a strong incentive to keep the tariff in place, while the government also enjoys the benefit of the tariff. Consumers, however, may not be aware of the impact of the tariff. If consumers are conscious of the tariff, it still represents a relatively minor impact on their welfare in terms of higher prices when measured against the gains made by the producer, which can be very large. The result is that consumers feel a relatively smaller incentive to fight the tariff politically. Foreign producers, while not having a political voice on the issue, can urge their governments to retaliate against the country imposing the tariffs. This can result in arbitration with the WTO or an outright trade war should the matter escalate beyond this dispute.

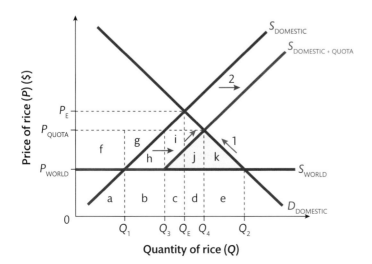

Exercise 23.1

Assume that Brazil, seeking to protect its domestic electronics industry, decides to place a large tariff on South Korean TVs. Create an appropriate diagram to show this situation from the Brazilian television industry perspective. To the left of your diagram list the beneficiaries of this policy under the heading of 'helped', and to the right of the diagram make a list of the injured parties under the heading of 'hurt'. Be prepared to explain the reasons for each item on your list.

What is a quota?

A quota is an import barrier that sets limits on the quantity or value of imports that may be imported into a country. For example, in the recent past, the US has placed strict quotas on imported textiles, a limit that most profoundly affected Taiwan and, more recently, China. Like a tariff, a quota tends to raise both domestic and import prices, but in ways that are unusual compared to the other protectionist diagrams.

In a closed market (Figure 23.2), producers will produce Q_E at a price of P_E. If that market is open to trade, world producers can sell at a much lower price, P_{WORLD}. Among domestic producers, relatively few can produce at P_{WORLD}, and they produce only the amount $0 - Q_1$. World producers can sell the rest, $Q_1 - Q_2$. Note that the world supply is perfectly elastic at that price, reflecting the fact that for most commodities, the size of the market is quite large compared to the demand of any single country. Therefore, the world market can supply as much as this country is willing and able to buy, represented by domestic demand, at the market price P_{WORLD}. For domestic producers, this marks a dramatic fall in revenue. Now they only receive a, where the foreign sellers receive $b + c + d + e$.

TOK Is it ethically sound for economically developed countries to demand that less developed countries remove their trade barriers in the interests of free trade when they continue to provide income support to their farmers? Can one country know what is right for another to do?

Video suggestion:
You have read about it, now you can review what you have just learned by watching a video by the author!
▶ Simply click here in your eBook for a video on protectionist tariffs.

Figure 23.2 A quota is designed to reduce rice imports

At this point, domestic rice producers are likely to call for protection from the overwhelming competition of foreign suppliers. If they convince the government to implement a quota, world producers will be limited to a specific amount, $Q_1 - Q_3$. So, at P_{WORLD}, the domestic market still supplies only $0 - Q_1$, and $Q_1 - Q_3$ is imported. From this point onwards, there is a gap between the amount demanded, $0 - Q_2$, and the amount supplied, which has stopped at $0 - Q_3$. This shortage will cause producers, including foreign ones, to start raising prices. Producers begin to supply more to the market at higher prices, and consumers reduce their quantity demanded along the demand curve.

This process, denoted by the two green arrows, continues until the market is cleared at P_{QUOTA} and Q_4. As producers supply more, this creates a new extension of the domestic supply curve, $S_{DOMESTIC + QUOTA}$, shown by the red arrows. Therefore, the market settles at a price below the domestic equilibrium P_E, but above the free trade price P_{WORLD}. This situation creates clear winners and losers, as well as market inefficiencies and deadweight losses.

Effect on domestic producers

Before the quota, domestic producers earned revenue represented by area a. After the quota, they earn a + f, and i + j + c + d where domestic suppliers resumed production.

Effect on foreign producers

Before the quota, foreign producers earned revenue represented by areas b + c + d + e. After, foreign producers sell fewer units, but get a higher price (P_{QUOTA}) for each of them. Their new revenue is shown by areas b + g + h. This could be viewed as an improvement over the alternative of a similar tariff, where the increased revenue from higher prices (g + h) would all go to the government. Here, the foreign producer receives that revenue.

Effect on consumers

Before, consumers paid the lower price P_{WORLD} and could buy more on the market, $0 - Q_2$ rather than $0 - Q_4$. The quota causes higher prices and less consumption.

Effect on government

Government gains no obvious advantage from a quota, although it is possible that overall sales tax receipts would be lower with fewer goods on the market.

Effect on market efficiency

Where domestic supply resumes and begins to rise again, at Q_3, domestic producers only supply more with the incentive of higher prices. Before the quota, that same quantity was produced at the lower world price. This unnecessary increase in prices marks a global market inefficiency, where consumers pay more than the market would otherwise require, and is denoted by the blue area j.

Welfare loss

When the post-quota quantity demanded decreases to Q_4, it represents a loss of consumer surplus previously enjoyed by buyers of the good. This loss is marked by the blue area k. Over the long term, like all forms of protectionism, quotas can lead to the dependence of domestic industries on government assistance rather than their own efforts.

What is a voluntary export restraint?

When a trade dispute is looming, the exporting country can offer to voluntarily limit the amount of their exports. This has the exact same effect as a quota of a similar size. This may pre-empt a worse outcome for the foreign producer, and may satisfy the protectionist demands of the domestic industries. A voluntary export restraint has advantages for the exporting country. Like a quota, any increase in market prices goes to the foreign producers. Politically, it prevents a tariff or quota from becoming law, and as a result is more likely to be flexibly applied in the future.

Video suggestion:
You have read about it, now you can review what you have just learned by watching a video by the author!

▶ Simply click here in your eBook for a video on protectionist quotas.

Exercise 23.2

In the 1900s and early 2000s, the US imposed quotas on imports of textile goods from Taiwan and China. Create a diagram that shows an active quota on US imports of Chinese textiles. To the left, list beneficiaries of this policy; to the right, list injured parties. Be prepared to explain the reasons for your lists.

What are international trade subsidies?

A country can also choose to protect domestic producers by subsidising them. Subsidies are sums paid to firms by the government to produce a particular good. A review of simple, closed-economy subsidies is found in Chapter 9. In the international trade context, subsidies are designed to defensively protect firms against foreign competition and to perhaps aggressively help an industry earn export revenue overseas. Subsidies can be of two types: lump sum or per unit. A lump-sum subsidy has the effect of lowering overall costs and encouraging production. Per-unit subsidies are payments made for every extra unit produced. We will consider protectionist subsidies from the per-unit perspective. If the country in question were to subsidise its rice market, it would pay a specific amount for each level of output (number of bushels, kilograms, or tonnes).

Figure 23.3 demonstrates the effects of a subsidy intended to reduce the amount of imported rice. Facing open competition before the subsidy, domestic production only measures $0 - Q_1$. The rest of the market is satisfied by foreign producers selling $Q_1 - Q_2$ at a market price of P_{WORLD}. Domestic producers earn far less, represented by box a, whereas foreign producers earn $b + c + d$. This kind of potent competition could devastate local production, so domestic rice farmers request government help.

If that help takes the form of a subsidy, the government would pay a subsidy that can be seen as the distance between the two supply curves, or as the distance between P_{WORLD} and $P_{WORLD + SUBSIDY}$. That amount would be paid for each unit of production and has the following effects on stakeholders.

Effect on domestic producers

This has the effect of lowering the production costs for local rice farmers, increasing supply to a new level of production, $0 - Q_3$. Imports of rice drop to $Q_3 - Q_2$.

Figure 23.3 A subsidy could be intended to reduce the quantity of imported rice ▶

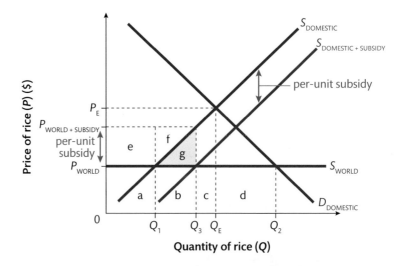

Note: the price of rice has not changed. Domestic producers are merely now able to produce more at the world price than before. Domestic producers now earn a + b + e + f + g.

Effect on foreign producers

Foreign imports go from $0 - Q_2$ to $Q_1 - Q_3$, while foreign revenue drops from b + c + d to just c + d.

Effect on the government

The total amount of government expenditure on the subsidy is shown by the amount of the per-unit subsidy multiplied by the amount produced domestically, which is ultimately $0 - Q_3$. So, the government spends e + f + g on rice subsidies.

Welfare loss

Just as with tariffs and quotas, this form of protectionism ignores comparative advantage and distorts the market. In the market for rice, the amount $Q_1 - Q_3$ switches from foreign, low-cost production, to domestic higher cost production. Foreign producers would have produced that amount without a subsidy, but domestic producers could only enter the market because they were paid the subsidy. The triangle g shows the area of inefficiency, where resources are being misallocated.

What are export promotion subsidies?

If a country is already exporting a good, and the government decides to subsidise its exporters, then a subsidy acts as a means to promote exports, rather than restrict imports as described above. Figure 23.4 shows how an industry that is already producing and exporting at the world price can be further helped by an **export subsidy**.

In this case, domestic producers are already competitive, and already exporting $Q_1 - Q_2$. The government grants a large subsidy so that they can produce even more at P_{WORLD}, pushing exports to $Q_1 - Q_3$. Domestic export revenue soars. The extent of market inefficiency grows, as resources are more pervasively misallocated.

This policy is part of a programme called 'export-led growth' that requires governments to select likely export 'winners' from their domestic industries.

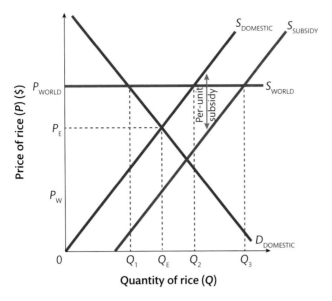

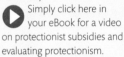

Figure 23.4 In some cases a subsidy can be used to promote exports

Ideally, such winners would be somewhat competitive on world markets and need only a relatively small subsidy to become export competitive. It is worth noting that such subsidies will come at significant cost to taxpayers, and mark a major redistribution of resources from those taxpayers to the favoured industries.

What are administrative barriers?

Bureaucratic barriers or 'red tape'

Countries may impede the penetration of their markets with waves of paperwork and legal requirements that raise the cost of importing. While any imported good must clear appropriate customs checks for health, safety, and valuation, it is possible to extend and amplify these requirements so as to frustrate potential importers. Compliance with bureaucratic demands raises costs to producers. Eventually, the time and energy required may prevent potential importers from making the attempt, so imports are effectively reduced.

Product standards

Health, safety, and environmental considerations can also be used to exclude goods from the local market. Imports may be expected to meet specific technical standards, and importers may be required to test and prove the safety and quality of their goods. This may raise costs to the point where many importers decide the extra cost is not worth it, and thus quit their attempt to enter the market. Where domestic producers and government regulatory agencies create these import standards with the primary goal of limiting imports, they are engaging in protectionism.

Environmental standards

Environmental standards provoke passionate debates in trade matters. The depletion of common access resources sparks fierce argument, with endangered species being particularly controversial. Japanese whalers, for example, have long argued that theirs is a legitimate activity, based on the use of available resources, and that restrictions against it are disguised protectionism. In these cases, the WTO is asked to rule on the legitimacy of the claims.

Video suggestion:
You have read about it, now you can review what you have just learned by watching a video by the author!

▶ Simply click here in your eBook for a video on protectionist subsidies and evaluating protectionism.

Embargoes

Embargoes are extreme quotas that completely stop some or all trade with a particular country. They can be applied unilaterally or multilaterally, by a trade block. Embargoes on the dealing of weapons and arms is fairly common. Typically, embargoes are organised to achieve strategic or political aims. In recent years, the EU and US maintained an embargo on the Republic of Iran, forbidding Iran's oil imports and denying consumer goods exports from the two largest economies. Here the stated aim was not to bargain about further trade rules but to constrain the Iranian nuclear programme.

What is a nationalistic campaign?

Governments can also resort to campaigns of persuasion designed to promote more conscious consumption. 'Buy American' and 'Buy British' advertising campaigns, for example, exhort consumers to buy local goods whenever possible. These efforts appeal to national pride and hope to make a marginal difference in buying patterns, ideally supporting domestic firms and employment.

HL Worked example 23.1

For HL Paper 3, you may be asked to use diagrams to calculate the effects of tariffs, quotas, or subsidies on the different stakeholders. Here is an example of the kind of question you may face, with solutions worked throughout.

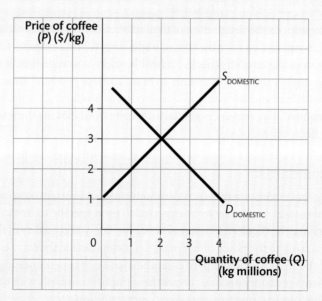

1   Show the domestic equilibrium price and quantity on the diagram.
2   Coffee may be imported at the world price of $2/kg. Draw world supply on the diagram.
3   How much coffee will be supplied by local (domestic) producers and how much will be supplied by foreign producers (imports)?
4   If the government imposes a subsidy of $.50/kg, show the effect of the international trade subsidy on the diagram.
5   Calculate the change in producer revenue from before and after the subsidy.

6 Calculate the change in consumer spending before and after the subsidy.
7 Calculate the change in government spending on the subsidy before and after.
8 Explain the impact of the subsidy on any three stakeholders in the market
   for coffee.

Worked example 23.2

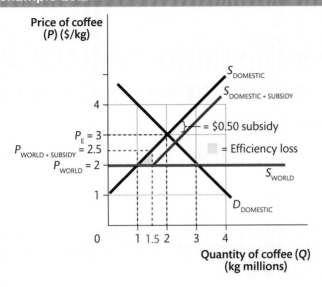

1 The equilibrium price and quantity are shown as $3 and 2 million kg.
2 The world supply curve (S_{WORLD}) is shown above.
3 In a closed economy before trade, domestic firms produced 2 million kg. After
   trade they produced only 1 million. Foreign producer quantity is equal to the
   total quantity supplied of 3 million − 1 million domestic quantity supplied =
   2 million kg.
4 With the subsidy, the domestic supply curve has shifted down (right) by $0.50 at
   all price levels. Domestic production rises to 1.5 million kg, still at a price of $2.
   Foreign production has been reduced to 1.5 million.
5 Producer revenue before the subsidy was $2 × 1 million = $2 million. Producer
   revenue after the subsidy was $2.5 × 1.5 million = $3.75 million.
6 Consumer spending before the subsidy was $2 × 3 million = $6 million.
   Consumer spending after the subsidy was $2 × 3 million = $6 million.
7 Government spending before the subsidy was 0. Government spending on the
   subsidy is $.50 × 1.5 million = $.75 million or $750,000.
8 Stakeholders in this event are domestic producers, foreign producers,
   consumers, the government, and market efficiency. The question requires a
   discussion of any two of the following.
   a. Domestic firms who were harmed by free market imports before the subsidy
       are now able to produce and sell more at the P_{WORLD} market price. This
       increases their revenues to nearly double the free market level. Domestic
       profits and employment will rise.
   b. Foreign firms lose a share of the market to the subsidised domestic firms.
       They sell less quantity and suffer lower revenue. This is likely to reduce
       profits and employment in that industry.

473

c. The government suffers the loss of $750,000, which is tax revenue that could have been spent on infrastructure, housing, healthcare, education, or any other government priority.

d. Market efficiency suffers a welfare loss, as shown by the blue triangle above. After the subsidy, the market stays the same size of 3 million kilograms and at the same price of $2. However, a large amount of production (500,000 kg) is paid for through subsidies, a quantity that would have been supplied to the market without the subsidy.

e. Consumers are equally well off as before, getting the same quantity and price as before the subsidy. However, they are likely to be indirectly paying the cost of the subsidy through their own tax payments.

Practice exam questions

Paper 1, part (a) questions

1. Explain, using a diagram, the effect of the imposition of a tariff. (10 marks)
2. Explain, using a diagram, the effect of the payment of an international trade subsidy. (10 marks)
3. Explain, using a diagram, the effect of the imposition of a quota in the market for an imported good. (10 marks)
4. Explain three arguments in favour of protectionism. (10 marks)
5. Explain three arguments against protectionism. (10 marks)

Paper 1, part (b) questions

1. Using real-world examples, discuss the advantages and disadvantages of free trade versus protectionism. (15 marks)
2. Using real-world examples, evaluate the case for protectionism. (15 marks)

Paper 2: two-mark and four-mark questions

Anti-dumping worries prompt Thailand to enact tariffs

The US-China trade war has left Asia flooded with an oversupply of steel, and importing countries are fighting back with more than a dozen anti-**dumping** accusations in recent months.

Among those countries was Thailand, who alleged that China was dumping a range of steel products on its market. Motivated by these concerns, Thailand placed a **tariff** of nearly 40% on two Chinese steel products.

China is the world's largest producer of steel, producing over half of the world's output. It has frequently been accused of distributing cheap and **subsidised** steel to global markets.

The recent pandemic has dampened demand for industrial products across the world, and Thai manufacturing sectors have suffered. Decreased domestic demand for steel in Thai industries has hurt steel sales at home, and prompted calls for retaliatory measures against China.

2-mark questions

Define the following terms, indicated in bold in the data:

1. tariff   (2 marks)
2. subsidised   (2 marks)
3. dumping   (2 marks)

4-mark questions

4. Using an international trade diagram, show the effect of Thailand's tariff on China's steel imports.   (4 marks)
5. Using an AD/AS diagram, show the effect of 'dampened demand for industrial products across the world' on the Thai economy.   (4 marks)
6. Using a labour market diagram, show the effect of China's steel subsidies on the wage rates of steel workers in Thailand.   (4 marks)

HL Paper 3 Questions

Below is a market for bananas in a country:

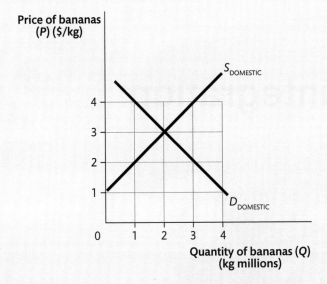

1. Show the domestic equilibrium price and quantity on the diagram.
2. Bananas may be imported at the world price of $1.5/kg. Draw world supply on the diagram.
3. How much coffee will be supplied by local (domestic) producers and how much will be supplied by foreign producers (imports)?
4. If the government imposes a tariff of $1.00/kg, show the effect of the tariff on the diagram.
5. Calculate the change in producer revenue from before and after the tariff.
6. Calculate the change in consumer spending before and after the tariff.
7. Calculate the change in government revenue after the tariff.
8. Explain the impact of the subsidy on any three stakeholders in the market for coffee.

Economic integration

24

24.1 What is 'economic integration'?

Learning outcome

At the end of this section you will be able to:

- define economic integration as a staged process of working towards free trade through negotiated trade agreements between countries.

Chapters 22 and 23 introduced the theories of free trade and protectionism. You learned about the theory of comparative advantage and the principle that when countries engage in free trade, there are mutual benefits enjoyed by many stakeholders, such as lower prices, greater variety of goods and services, greater efficiency, and larger markets for producers. Of course, there are always losers whenever nations engage in trade but, in most cases, the gains of trade for society outweigh the costs.

Free trade based on the principle of comparative advantage is an ideal that would promote maximum allocative efficiency of the world's scarce resources. Unfortunately, it is an ideal that is far from being achieved in the real world today. Since the Industrial Revolution and the end of colonialism, the status quo for most of the world's nations has generally been protectionist and anti-trade. During much of the 20th century, many of the world's economies were ideologically aligned in opposing camps; divided by the Iron Curtain into capitalist and communist systems. With the break-up of the Soviet Union and the reduction of its influence of the Eastern Bloc, the ideological battle seemed to end as the vast majority of nations pursued free market reforms in an effort to promote long-run economic growth and development in their economies.

However, while free market reforms have prevailed within nations and trade has flourished among the citizens of the emerging market economies, free trade between nations has grown more slowly than many would have hoped it would. Nations often act out of the fear of losing current industry, rather than seeing the opportunities and benefits of open trade. And so, they resist further economic integration.

The hesitancy among nations to open their borders to international trade has led to the need for clearly articulated agreements between nations as a precursor to economic integration. **Trading blocs** are arrangements between two or more nations through which tariffs, quotas, and other barriers to trade of most goods and services are either reduced or eliminated altogether. Trading blocs may take several forms and can be categorised by the stages of economic integration achieved. The lowest stage represents the first steps between two or more nations at integrating their economies, while the highest stage is complete economic integration.

24.2 What are the different levels of economic integration?

Learning outcomes

At the end of this section you will be able to:

- define **preferential trade agreements**
- distinguish between bilateral and multilateral (WTO) trade agreements
- distinguish between a **free trade area**, a **customs union**, and a common market
- evaluate the advantages of trading blocs, including **HL** **trade creation**, greater access to markets, freedom of labour, stronger bargaining power, and political stability and cooperation
- examine the disadvantages of trading blocs, including **HL** **trade diversion**, loss of sovereignty, and challenges to multilateral negotiations
- distinguish between a common market and a monetary union
- **HL** analyse the possible advantages and disadvantages of a monetary union for its members.

Completely free trade between nations is the outcome many economists dream of, but, in reality, countries tend to take small steps towards eliminating barriers to trade between one another. The types of trading bloc nations may enter into with other nations, in order of the degree to which member countries' economies are integrated with one another, from least to most integrated are:

1 preferential trade agreement

2 free trade area

3 customs union

4 common market

5 monetary union.

Trading blocs can be either bilateral (between two nations) or multilateral (between more than two nations). Typically, preferential trade agreements are agreed between two nations or between a group of nations that are part of a free trade area and another nation. At the other end of the spectrum, there is only one major monetary union in the world today – the eurozone: European nations using a common currency, the euro. However, several economic and monetary unions are in various stages of proposal and development.

Preferential trade agreements

A preferential trade agreement (PTA) is when two or more countries reduce or remove tariffs on particular goods or services produced in participating countries, or make other agreements reducing the barriers to free trade between the nations. A PTA is the first stage of economic integration, and differs from higher stages in that not all goods are necessarily exempt from tariffs, nor must tariffs be eliminated completely on the goods included.

A bilateral agreement is between two countries. A multilateral agreement is between three or more countries. Multilateral agreements can include as few as three, but as many as 186 countries, which is how many countries are members of the World Trade Organization (WTO) as of 2020. The WTO will be examined in more detail later in this chapter.

The term 'preferential' points to the fact that when nations sign up to such an agreement, the result is that one nation ends up preferring to buy goods and services from the other rather than from countries not included in the agreement. Preferred trade differs from free trade in that tariffs are not completely eliminated on all goods and services, and tariff reductions only apply to select nations, not all of a country's trading partners. Therefore, PTAs result in increased trade between participating nations at the expense of trade with the rest of the world. PTAs fall short of achieving an efficient allocation of resources, even between their members.

PTAs can be either bilateral or multilateral. Table 24.1 shows some contemporary PTAs.

Table 24.1 Preferential trade agreements

Name of PTA	Countries involved	Coverage	Year created
Asia Pacific Trade Agreement	Bangladesh, China, India, Lao People's Democratic Republic, Republic of Korea, Sri Lanka	Goods only	1976
Latin American Integration Association (LAIA)	Argentina, Bolivarian Republic of Venezuela, Bolivia, Brazil, Chile, Colombia, Cuba, Ecuador, Mexico, Paraguay, Peru, Uruguay	Goods only	1981
Lao PDR–Thailand	Lao People's Democratic Republic, Thailand	Goods only	1991
Economic Cooperation Organization (ECO)	Afghanistan, Azerbaijan, Islamic Republic of Iran, Kazakhstan, Kyrgyz Republic, Pakistan, Tajikistan, Turkey, Turkmenistan, Uzbekistan	Goods only	1992
Melanesian Spearhead Group (MSG)	Fiji, Papua New Guinea, Solomon Islands, Vanuatu	Goods only	1994
South Asian Preferential Trade Arrangement (SAPTA)	Bangladesh, Bhutan, India, Maldives, Nepal, Pakistan, Sri Lanka	Goods only	1995
Chile–India	Chile, India	Goods only	2007

Two of the agreements in Table 24.1 are bilateral (Lao PDR–Thailand and Chile–India), others are regional (such as the Economic Cooperation Organization (ECO), which includes countries in the region of Central Asia), while one includes nations that are in very different geographical locations (Chile–India). All the agreements involve reductions in or removal of tariffs on selected goods. Services are not included in any of these PTAs.

A PTA represents a step towards free trade, but it must be noted that it is a rather small step. Such a pact between two or more nations promotes increased integration of the small number of countries involved, but only on selected goods and at the expense of increased integration with the rest of the world's economies.

For example, when Chile and India enter into a PTA, the reduction in tariffs on Indian goods in Chile will certainly increase the demand for Indian imports in Chile, but possibly also a decrease in demand for other countries' goods. Indian rice is cheaper for Chilean consumers because of the PTA between the nations. This may mean that Chile imports more Indian rice, but it also means that Chile imports less Thai rice. PTAs, in other words, are *preferential*, but not *free trade* agreements. Under totally free trade, Chile would import rice from the country that has the lowest opportunity cost in rice production, which may not actually be India. Under a PTA, Chile imports more rice from India, even if India does not have the lowest opportunity cost, simply because the tariff on Indian rice is lower than that on rice from other countries.

Free trade areas

A free trade area (FTA) is formed when two or more nations make an agreement to *completely eliminate trade barriers* on most (if not all) goods and services traded between them. FTAs are at the second level of economic integration, closer to truly free trade than a PTA where tariffs are reduced or eliminated only on certain goods.

Countries in an FTA agree to eliminate tariffs on goods and/or services produced in other member countries, but maintain the right to set their own tariffs on non-member countries.

There are hundreds of separate **free trade agreements** in the world today, some bilateral, some multilateral. The USA alone is involved in 14 separate FTAs with 20 countries, including Australia, Bahrain, Canada, Chile, Costa Rica, South Korea, Mexico, Morocco, Peru, and Singapore (plus ten more!).

Some examples of FTAs are shown in Table 24.2.

Each of these FTAs requires the removal of tariffs in the member countries on goods and/or services produced in and imported from all other member countries. The intended effect of such an agreement, of course, is to allow for a more efficient allocation of resources based on the principle of comparative advantage among the member states.

Customs unions

Next on the spectrum of economic integration is the customs union. A customs union is an agreement between two or more countries to phase out or eliminate tariffs and

Table 24.2 Free trade areas

Name of FTA	Countries involved	Coverage	Year enacted
Australia–New Zealand (ANZCERTA)	Australia, New Zealand	Goods and services	1989
Ukraine–Russian Federation	Ukraine, Russian Federation	Goods only	1994
United States–Mexico–Canada Agreement (USMCA)	Canada, Mexico, US	Goods and services	1994
EC–Egypt	Austria, Belgium, Bulgaria, Cyprus, Czech Republic, Denmark, Estonia, Finland, France, Germany, Greece, Hungary, Ireland, Italy, Latvia, Lithuania, Luxembourg, Malta, Netherlands, Poland, Portugal, Romania, Slovak Republic, Slovenia, Spain, Sweden, Egypt	Goods only	2004
South Asian Free Trade Agreement (SAFTA)	Bangladesh, Bhutan, India, Maldives, Nepal, Pakistan, Sri Lanka	Goods only	2006
US–Morocco	US, Morocco	Goods and services	2006
ASEAN–Japan	Brunei Darussalam, Myanmar, Cambodia, Indonesia, Lao People's Democratic Republic, Malaysia, Philippines, Singapore, Vietnam, Thailand, Japan	Goods only	2008
China–New Zealand	China, New Zealand	Goods and services	2008
Canada–Peru	Canada, Peru	Goods and services	2009
Japan–Switzerland	Japan, Switzerland	Goods and services	2009

other trade barriers and establish common external barriers towards non-member countries. Thus, a customs union differs from a free trade agreement in that:

- in a free trade agreement, each member nation maintains the freedom to determine the barriers to trade it will impose on imports from nations that are not part of the FTA
- in a customs union, member nations adopt common tariffs on non-member nations' goods and services.

Table 24.3 Customs unions

Name of customs union	Countries involved	Coverage	Year enacted
East African Community (EAC)	Burundi, Kenya, Rwanda, Tanzania, Uganda	Goods only	2000
Economic and Monetary Community of Central Africa (CEMAC)	Cameroon, Central African Republic, Chad, Congo, Equatorial Guinea, Gabon	Goods only	1999
Gulf Cooperation Council (GCC)	Bahrain, Kuwait, Oman, Qatar, Saudi Arabia, United Arab Emirates	Goods only	2003
Eurasian Economic Community (EAEC)	Belarus, Kazakhstan, Kyrgyz Republic, Russian Federation, Tajikistan	Goods only	1997
Southern Common Market (MERCOSUR)	Argentina, Brazil, Paraguay, Uruguay	Goods and services	1991 (goods) 2005 (services)

In 2020, there were 15 customs unions in effect worldwide – a selection is shown in Table 24.3.

Common markets

The fourth type of trading bloc is the common market. This is like a customs union in that goods and services are traded without tariffs but, in addition, member countries agree not only to free trade of goods and services but also to free movement of capital and labour. In other words, the barriers to the flow of labour, land, capital resources, and entrepreneurial talent are also reduced or eliminated. The aim is to improve the allocation of resources within member nations and between them. In order to facilitate the flow of productive resources between nations in a common market, shared regulations and policies regarding labour and capital employment must be adopted by member nations.

The most successful example of a common market is the European Economic Area (EEA), which includes the 27 countries in the EU plus Switzerland, Norway, and Liechtenstein. Another example is the East African Community (EAC), a common market formed in 2010, which includes six partner states: Burundi, Kenya, Rwanda, South Sudan, Tanzania, and Uganda.

One fact worth pointing out is that each type of trading bloc *includes* the characteristics of the trading blocs lower down on the integration ladder. For example, a customs union *is an* FTA, but one in which member nations also share common external tariffs. A common market *is a* customs union, but one in which member nations also allow the free flow of labour and capital. In other words, as we move up the ladder of economic integration, each level of trading bloc builds on the lower levels (for example, the EAC which was a customs union of five nations formed in 2000, and later became a common market in 2010 of six nations). Increased integration increases the level of competition across member nations' producers and within labour markets.

Research and inquiry

Nearly every country in the world is part of at least one trade bloc. Using a search engine, enter the name of your country, followed by 'trade agreements' to investigate the various trade blocs of which your country is a part.

For discussion and debate:

1 How many trade agreements is your country currently in with other countries?

2 Of these, how many are bilateral? How many are multilateral?

3 Is your country part of any customs unions? Common markets? Monetary union?

Choose one of the agreements you uncovered in your investigation. Dig a little deeper by looking for a website for the trade bloc or agreement. Answer the questions that follow.

4 Does the trade bloc cover specific goods or all goods? If it only covers specific goods, what are three categories that are covered?

5 Does the agreement reduce or eliminate tariffs?

6 Which producers in your country benefit from membership in the selected trade bloc? How do they benefit?

7 How do consumers in your country benefit from membership in the selected trade bloc?

8 Who are the potential losers of your country's membership in the selected trade bloc?

Advantages and disadvantages of trading blocs

Trading blocs represent a step towards economic integration, and within common markets the economies of member nations are all but fully integrated, with only monetary and fiscal policies remaining under the control of each sovereign nation. While the trend over the last century has been towards greater economic integration globally, the free trade ideal that economists imagine is still largely one that only exists in their imaginations. Economic integration has advantages and disadvantages for countries that pursue it, and the consequences of increased integration with other economies are felt across all levels of society, from businesses to households and the government.

Advantages

HL Trade creation

Trade creation occurs when the formation of a trading bloc, whether bilateral or multilateral, shifts production from a higher cost country to a lower cost country, increasing the level of efficiency by assuring that goods are produced where the least amount of resources are required for their production.

Let us consider a possible outcome of the Asia Pacific Trade Agreement as an example. The APTA includes, among other nations, India and South Korea. Prior to joining one another in a trade bloc, the two countries likely had tariffs on most imports between them. However, over several rounds of negotiations tariffs on over 4000 items traded between the two countries have been reduced or eliminated, increasing the flow of goods between them.

South Korea, a country with an advanced automobile industry, exports more cars and car parts than any other country in APTA. India, on the other hand, has a relatively undeveloped automobile sector and likely faces higher average costs in car manufacturing than South Korea. If, as a result of their membership of APTA, India ends up importing more cars from South Korea and producing fewer cars domestically, then trade has been *created* as a result of the FTA. Production has shifted from a higher cost country (India) to a lower cost country (South Korea).

A Hyundai Motor assembly line at Asan, South Korea

Meanwhile, India, which has a large and productive agricultural sector, is likely to see its production of grain and other food products increase because of its trade with South Korea, where land is scarcer and food production less efficient. Trade is once again created because of the two countries' membership in an FTA; agricultural production shifts from South Korea (a higher cost country) to India (a lower cost country).

Unfortunately, not all trade blocs result in trade creation. In our next section we'll look at examples of where trade is *diverted*, which occurs when a trade bloc causes production to shift from a lower cost country to a higher cost country.

Greater access to markets

When two or more countries enter into a trade bloc the producers in each country enjoy access to a larger customer base than they would have without economic integration. Producers that are able to compete with foreign firms on price and quality will see demand for their products grow, allowing them to achieve *economies of scale*, which are the cost advantages firms experience when they produce a larger quantity of output for more consumers. Economies of scale result from things like bulk buying of inputs, greater specialisation of labour as more workers are hired to do specific tasks within an industry, and the cost savings from producing and shipping products in bulk rather than in the smaller quantities firms might have produced at for their domestic markets alone.

Freedom of labour

Free movement of labour, a characteristic of common markets but not the lower levels of the trading bloc, provides increased employment opportunities and a larger pool of available workers for the households and firms of the partner nations. For example, in Germany, where labour markets are notoriously tight (the natural rate of unemployment is around 3.5%), firms are more likely to maintain domestic production facilities if workers from other EEA member nations are able to migrate to Germany to meet the demand for labour when it arises. Workers from Poland, the Czech Republic, Estonia, and other nations are available to fill the jobs that German workers may be unable or unwilling to complete.

From the households' perspective, joining a common market can provide for opportunities that might not be available in the domestic economy. Unemployment rates across member countries should converge on one another as excess labour in one country migrates to where there are labour shortages. The result is greater efficiency in labour markets, higher employment overall, and lower production costs for the firms that would find themselves at a competitive disadvantage without the common market in the face of lower wages abroad.

Stronger bargaining power

Another advantage to workers of trading blocs is the ability to leverage increased employment opportunities abroad to negotiate higher wages at home. Take our example of Estonian workers, who as part of the EEA have the freedom to emigrate to Germany or any other EU nation in search of work. When domestic firms go to negotiate wages with labour unions in Estonia, their position is strengthened due to the ease with which workers could take jobs in the rest of Europe. The outcome is higher wages for workers in Estonia.

This outcome is reversed from the perspective of higher wage countries, however. German firms gain bargaining power because of the availability of lower wage workers who could come from Estonia or elsewhere in the EEA to do jobs that German workers might otherwise have taken. Employers now have the upper hand in wage negotiations with German labour unions, as German workers find themselves competing not just with one another, but with workers from lower wage countries within the EEA.

In both cases, the outcome is greater efficiency in labour markets, once again, as both employment rates and wage rates converge across countries within a common market agreement.

Political stability and cooperation

When countries' economies become integrated with one another, the consequences of a conflict become much greater than if no economic ties exist. As economists, we always think in terms of costs and benefits. At least for the countries within a trading bloc, the economic costs of conflict (in terms of lost revenues or decreased access to resources or goods through trade) often outweigh potential benefits. The result is increased political stability and cooperation between nations whose economic fortunes are tied together through trade agreements or other forms of economic integration.

Disadvantages

HL Trade diversion

Trade diversion occurs if the formation of a trading bloc between two or more nations results in the production of a good shifting from a nation with a lower opportunity cost to one with a higher opportunity cost. Such a scenario may seem unlikely, but it occurs rather commonly at the higher levels of economic integration, such as in a customs union. When two or more nations agree to eliminate barriers to trade between themselves, but to maintain common external tariffs on all other nations, it is possible that the result will be the diversion of trade from low-cost producers to high-cost producers.

Take, for instance, the EEA, which includes the 27 countries of the EU plus Norway, Switzerland, and Liechtenstein. All 30 countries in the EEA are middle- or high-income nations that have agreed to eliminate tariffs between all member nations. However, the EEA has common tariffs on non-member imports, many of which are low-income countries that may have a comparative advantage in the production of certain goods over high-income EEA nations. Owing to the agreement between member nations, the existence of external tariffs could increase trade between European economies at the expense of trade with lower cost economies outside of Europe.

For example, Poland, a middle-income country with a comparative advantage in the production of intermediate manufactured goods such as automobile parts, joined the EEA in 2004. As a member of the EEA, Poland enjoys duty-free exports to Germany, its largest trading partner, also a nation with a large automobile industry.

When the UK voted to leave the EU, the vote surprised many observers and even 'leave' voters who expected to stay in the EU, but wanted to register a vote of protest. No country had ever voted to leave the EU since its founding in 1993. To better understand the issues at stake over 'Brexit', conduct an internet search for articles published before the referendum on 23 June 2016.

For discussion and debate:

1 Seek out reliable sources for the 'leave' side of the debate.

2 Seek out reliable sources for the 'remain' side of the debate.

3 Discuss and debate with your class the trade-offs suggested by these points, and a decision to leave.

Germany most likely began importing more auto parts from Poland after its entry into the EEA in 2004 than it had before, since these goods could now be obtained duty free, whereas goods from countries outside the EEA would be subject to tariffs. But if this increase in trade with a middle-income European neighbour came at the expense of trade between Germany and a lower cost non-European nation, such as China, then trade was not created, it was diverted. When trade is diverted due to the formation of a trade bloc, overall efficiency is reduced.

Loss of sovereignty

Some degree of national sovereignty is by definition sacrificed when a country joins a trade bloc. The freedom to set tariff rates on other countries is abandoned when joining a customs union, for instance, as common external tariffs must be shared with other members of the union. When joining a common market each member nation's ability to set not only tariff rates, but minimum wage rates and other labour market policies, is undermined. A minimum wage in one country is only effective if businesses cannot easily move across the border to a neighbouring country and set up shop where wages are lower.

The nationalist inclinations of many countries' citizens make economic integration with other nations politically unpopular, even while the potential economic benefits are understood. The UK's 2016 referendum on whether or not to remain in the EU, known as the 'Brexit' vote, showed that, after decades of ever increasing integration between the UK and European economies, the majority of British citizens ultimately preferred more sovereignty over more integration. On 31 January 2020, the UK officially withdrew from the EU common market, marking a new era of economic dis-integration for 66 million British citizens, now free to determine their own economic future.

Challenges to multilateral trading negotiations

When countries lock into their respective trade blocs, it may interfere with the work of the WTO to create a broader coalition of global trade rules and partners. Since the last WTO global round of negotiations started in 2001, dozens of **regional trade agreements** have been negotiated. Some of them, like the Comprehensive and Progressive Agreement for Trans-Pacific Partnership (once known as just the TPP) are large multilateral agreements that are being negotiated in place of a larger global agreement with the WTO. Frustrated by a lack of progress there, countries are finding the best trade deals they can in lieu of a bigger deal.

Negotiating the terms of trading blocs can be a several year process and in many cases may fail altogether, as various industry representatives are consulted, who may have competing desires that stall progress towards an ultimate agreement.

Case study – is the USMCA just a 'Trump' branded version of NAFTA?

When Canada's Prime Minister Brian Mulroney, Mexican President Carlos Salinas, and US President George H.W. Bush agreed the North American Free Trade Agreement (NAFTA) which came into force on 1 January 1994, the world's largest free trade area was formed. In the decades that followed, all three countries enjoyed increased trade, economic growth, and rising living standards, in no small part as a result of the benefits the agreement provided both producers and consumers in North America.

When President Donald Trump came into office in January 2017, he planned to remove NAFTA and replace it with a new trade agreement that would benefit American producers, who he argued had been suffering for decades under NAFTA; losing out to lower cost producers in Mexico and Canada. Over the next year and a half the Trump administration engaged in negotiations with trade representatives from Mexico and Canada to work out the details of what many have called the 'new NAFTA', but what was officially called the United States–Mexico–Canada Agreement (USMCA).

So, what changed from NAFTA to USMCA? To find out, conduct a web search using the term 'NAFTA USMCA trade deal differences'. One of the top results should direct you to an article with information about the difference between these two free trade agreements.

Discussion questions:

1 Is the new rule that requires 75% of a car's parts to be made in one of the three countries in order to be traded tariff free likely to result in trade creation or trade diversion? Explain.
2 How will the requirement of workers making car parts most likely affect where car parts are manufactured in North America? Do 'minimum wage' requirements increase or decrease efficiency of resource allocation between trading partners?
3 Which country's farmers are most likely to benefit from the changes to USMCA compared to NAFTA?
4 Overall, do free trade agreements like USMCA represent 'free trade' or 'preferential trade'? What is the difference between these two concepts?

Monetary unions and complete economic integration

Monetary unions

The final stage of economic integration is the monetary union, which comprises a common market in which member states also adopt a common currency managed by a single central bank. A monetary union, for all intents and purposes, joins the economies of member states into *one single economy*. The only thing that distinguishes a monetary union from *complete economic integration* (which is when different states or provinces are united under a single national government) is that the governments of member states in a monetary union still control their own national fiscal policy.

Two examples of monetary unions are the USA (which essentially combines the economies of America's 50 states under one central bank sharing one currency, the US dollar) and the eurozone, which includes 19 European nations that adopted the euro.

Monetary unions share all the characteristics of lower stages of economic integration:

- tariffs between member states are eliminated
- common tariffs on non-member nations are adopted by member states

- land, labour, and capital resources may flow free of intervention between member states
- regulations regarding labour and capital are shared between member states.

In addition, members adopt a single currency, thereby foregoing their ability to control the money supply in their own economies. Commercial bank regulations and monetary policies, such as changes in the interest rate and foreign exchange market interventions, are determined by a shared central bank rather than by each individual state or country's government.

The states in the USA began sharing a single currency almost immediately after declaring independence from Great Britain, and since 1913 the US money supply has been managed by the country's central bank, the Federal Reserve. When the euro was launched in 1999, the 11 original eurozone economies each switched from their own currencies (the deutschmark, the franc, the lira, and so on) and thereby lost the ability to independently determine their own monetary policies. Today, the European Central Bank controls the money supply in the 19 nation eurozone economy, setting interest rates across the monetary union.

While a monetary union represents nearly complete economic integration, the states in such an arrangement maintain much of their fiscal sovereignty, albeit with strict guidelines established by the central bank. In Chapter 20, Demand management: fiscal policy, we learned why member states in a monetary union are held to strict standards regarding deficit and debt levels: by limiting the sizes of annual deficits of members states, a central bank protects the value of the currency on foreign exchange markets and prevents individual governments from undermining its ability to set interest rates across the union. Large deficits and high levels of national debt tend to drive interest rates up and threaten to turn international investors away from a currency, which could cause it to weaken on foreign exchange markets, an outcome that may not be compatible with the central bank's desired policy outcomes.

Complete economic integration

Beyond countries joining one another in a monetary union lies complete economic integration, in which member states completely abandon independence of both monetary and fiscal policies. The difference between the USA and the eurozone is that the 50 states in the US are subject to the monetary *and* fiscal policies of the US federal government, while the eurozone nations are subject only to the monetary policies of the European Central Bank.

The USA therefore represents an example of complete economic integration; but since each nation in the eurozone is free to determine its own government budget and allocate government tax revenues as it sees fit, the eurozone is not a completely integrated economy. The 19 euro nations are integrated economically and monetarily, but not fiscally. Each nation's government can decide its own fiscal policies, unlike each US state government. A group of states joined in complete economic integration essentially become one nation, foregoing economic sovereignty over the majority of the economic policies and activities in the integrated economy.

The loss of fiscal sovereignty may explain why the euro countries have thus far avoided complete economic integration; it is not yet politically viable to the culturally and socially diverse citizens of Europe to accept the sacrifice of fiscal sovereignty and hand over control of their governments' budgets to a federal European government.

HL Advantages and disadvantages of monetary union

Advantages

The benefits of joining a monetary union are clear for prospective members: sharing a currency with other countries vastly smooths the process of trade between economies. In addition to sharing a currency, countries in a monetary union have no trade barriers between them and investment can flow freely across borders; even labour can migrate as if there is only one economy across all countries, which, essentially, is the case.

Producers in member countries find the markets for their products vastly expanded within a monetary union, and since consumers in other countries even share a currency, the demand for firms' output is higher than it would be without a shared currency. Workers who take jobs in another country and send money home will find the lack of exchange rate fluctuations provides more stable income and eliminates the resulting uncertainty of moving to another country to find work.

Finally, increased macroeconomic stability is a likely result for smaller countries that join a monetary union in which larger economies are already a part. Greece, one of the smaller members of the eurozone, has benefited from bailouts during periods of financial uncertainty in the past decade thanks to its membership in the eurozone economy. A member of a monetary union will not be left to default on its national debt by other members, as doing so would undermine the stability of the currency across the common market. The downside to this, of course, is a sort of moral hazard where smaller countries within a monetary union may lack the fiscal discipline required to assure monetary stability, and therefore strict oversight might be needed to protect the value of the currency on foreign exchange markets.

Disadvantages

Nations in a monetary union must give up the ability to control their own monetary policies, reducing each country's ability to manage aggregate demand in its domestic economy by raising or lowering interest rates or manipulating the exchange rate of its currency relative to its trading partners' currencies. Since no single nation in a monetary union can determine the level of interest rates or the exchange rate on its own, control of the nation's macroeconomy is to some extent essentially handed over to a multinational central bank, a sacrifice many nations are not eager to make.

This explains why some of the nations in the EU (in which there are 27 countries) are not currently seeking to become a part of the eurozone (in which there are only 19 countries). Giving up its own currency prevents a country from increasing its attractiveness to foreign consumers and investors by keeping domestic interest rates low and the value of its currency weak.

To what extent would increased economic integration ever be considered undesirable?

TOK

Video suggestion:
You have read about it, now you can review what you have just learned by watching a video by the author!

▶ Simply click here in your eBook for a video on the six stages of economic integration.

24.3 What is the World Trade Organization?

Learning outcomes

At the end of this section you will be able to:

- describe the objectives and functions of the WTO
- explain what factors affect the WTO's influence, including the difficulties in reaching agreement and the unequal bargaining power of its members.

The largest **multilateral trade agreement** in the world is the WTO, which advertises itself as the 'only international organisation dealing with the global rules of trade between nations. Its main function is to ensure that trade flows as smoothly, predictably and freely as possible'. In 2020, there were 159 countries in the WTO.

How and when was the WTO formed?

The WTO originated from negotiations on trade that followed the Second World War. It was generally thought that a wave of protectionism in the 1930s drew countries closer to the war that followed. Thus, in 1948, 23 countries signed the General Agreement on Tariffs and Trade (GATT).

During the same negotiations, held in Bretton Woods, New Hampshire, USA, the **International Monetary Fund (IMF)**, the World Bank, and the Bretton Woods exchange rate system were also established with the aim of creating stability and order to world trade and income flows. In time, the GATT developed from an agreement to a forum for future negotiations, and eventually an organisation in its own right.

Every few years, GATT negotiations were staged with the goal of creating standardised trade rules. After holding seven rounds of negotiations, the final round culminated in the creation of the WTO in 1993. The WTO extended and expanded the GATT mission, with greater scope over services and capital flows, as well as increased authority. It is based in Geneva, Switzerland, and has a staff of over 600.

The main barriers faced by the WTO in achieving increased economic integration between member states surround reluctance of rich countries to reduce their heavy subsidies and protection of agricultural markets. In turn, rich countries are seeking reductions in allowable tariffs on developing country protectionist measures. At stake are hundreds of billions of dollars in new markets for developing countries.

What are the WTO's aims?

The WTO seeks to expand international trade by lowering trade barriers and improving the flow of trade. It has specific objectives that enhance this overall goal.

Trade without discrimination

WTO members are all asked to subscribe to 'most favoured nation' status. This means that goods from all WTO member countries are treated equally. A tariff applied to one is applied to all, and there are thus no real favourites. At the same time, foreign goods should be treated the same as domestic goods.

Freer trade through negotiation

The success of each trade round is attributed to the combined efforts of continuous negotiation. This ensures that changes to trade policy are done by direct dealing, and also that they are done gradually. This allows affected countries to prepare for the adjustments that will probably be enacted when the new agreement comes into force.

Predictability through binding agreements and transparency

Binding refers to the commitment among members to keep tariffs at or below certain rates. This allows importers to assess markets more accurately and make better decisions about trade. Openness about trade rules also encourages more trade.

Promoting fair competition

While devoted to free trade, the WTO also claims to seek trade that is more fair. Rules against dumping and intellectual property theft, for example, are aimed at increasing fair competition. More generally, the creation of a system of trade rules promotes fair play by establishing some fundamental guidelines for most trade.

Encouraging development

Nearly two-thirds of WTO members are developing countries. These countries are granted special trade concessions because it is assumed that their industries need time and space to grow to a level of direct global competition.

What functions does the WTO perform?

With the above objectives in mind, the WTO performs the following functions:

- provides a forum for trade negotiation
- executes WTO agreements
- evaluates and rules on trade complaints by member countries
- provides technical assistance to developing countries on trade issues
- tracks changes in member trade policies.

What factors affect the influence of the WTO?

The WTO had a tough decade following the Great Recession of 2008–10. As the world's economies recovered from the deepest slump since the 1930s Great Depression, global trade struggled to resume the pace of expansion that occurred in the 1990s and early 2000s. In their efforts to restore output and employment to pre-recession levels, many governments embraced import substitution and export promotion policies that required the erection of trade barriers, undermining much of the progress the WTO had made pre-recession towards increased economic integration and reduced protectionism among its member countries.

Then came 2016. The election of Donald Trump as the 45th president of the USA immediately called into question the future of the WTO. A key message of the Trump campaign had been 'America First', and during his campaign rallies one of his go-to messages was that China was partly responsible for America's sluggish recovery and loss of jobs in manufacturing over the previous decade. Trump proudly called himself a 'tariff man' and promised new taxes on foreign imports once he took office.

As the world's largest economy by gross domestic product (GDP), the largest importing nation and the second largest exporter (after China), America's embrace of protectionism under president Trump put a halt to decades of increased global economic integration. In response to new tariffs on steel and other metals, lumber, agricultural commodities, automobile parts, and thousands of other items, America's largest trading partners, including China, Mexico, Canada, Germany, and other EU economies all began raising tariffs on goods from the USA and from other countries. The era of WTO progress had come to an end.

While the Trump administration may have struck a death blow to the WTO's progress (perhaps temporarily, as we have yet to see what will occur now Trump has left office; Joe Biden the 46th president as already indicated he intends to unpick a lot of what Trump undertook), the organisation had been struggling to meet its objectives for some time. One of the factors affecting the influence of the WTO was its inability to effectively influence non-market economies like that of China, which since its accession into the WTO in 2003 had made little progress in the liberalisation of its markets, resulting in an unequal playing field as state-run and subsidised industries increasingly competed on a global market in which free trade rules assume a limited role of government. The backlash among China's trading partners, notably the USA, to the perceived unfair trade with China, contributed to the rise of nationalistic economic policies in the two decades following China's accession.

Another factor limiting the effectiveness of the WTO in the 21st century was its inability to find a balance between its legislative and its judicial functions. As a legislative body, the WTO is expected to make rules that govern free and fair trade between its member nations. The development of these rules is supposed to take place through regular meetings, or 'summits', during which trade representatives negotiate agreements about what freer trade might look like, establishing rules that can later be enforced through the WTO's judicial branch. When a member country is thought to be violating a WTO rule, another member can take the dispute to the WTO, which will make a decision and impose penalties if a rule is determined to have been broken (often allowing tariffs to be erected against the violator nation).

However, in the 1990s and early 2000s, the legislative branch of the WTO repeatedly failed to establish agreed upon rules for the judicial branch to enforce, leaving member countries with outdated rules established decades earlier, which were often irrelevant in 21st-century trade disputes surrounding issues such as intellectual property theft, which was not covered in the earlier rounds of legislation. As a result, the judicial branch of the WTO had no means for settling many of the disputes that arose among member countries in the 2000s and 2010s, meaning the WTO overall became less effective as a forum for promoting and facilitating free trade.

Agreements on intellectual property rights were not the only rules lacking; the WTO also struggled to establish rules for trade in services, which by the 2000s was expanding rapidly thanks to the growth in broadband internet, which increasingly allowed skilled workers to provide services to customers around the world. Primary commodities, the most basic of exports, also proved controversial, as member nations often favoured domestic producers over imports for strategic and political reasons, making it difficult for the WTO to establish rules governing the liberalisation of trade in primary commodities.

A final factor limiting the effectiveness of the WTO, and a criticism economists have had of the organisation going back to the GATT days of the 1950s, is the unequal bargaining power of member nations. As WTO membership has expanded to include three-quarters of the countries in the world, the voices of the least developed, lowest income countries have largely gone unheard. Global trade rules, it turns out, have been largely written by the dominant players in global trade, often ignoring the interests of the developing countries for whom free trade is supposed to bring the greatest benefits. Without creating a level playing field on which less developed economies can feel like they are given equal bargaining power to the rich countries of the world, buy-in among member nations will continue to be limited and countries of all income levels will continue to favour inward oriented growth and development strategies over the idealistic, open border, free **market-oriented approach** envisioned by the WTO.

Is the WTO making a difference?

Free trade, in theory and in practice, is among the more hotly debated international topics of our time. Research continues to inform this debate, with more and more data employed to establish some reliability to its conclusions. We will conclude our chapter on economic integration with a few observations by the Indian economist Arvind Panagariya, who addressed some popular notions surrounding the role of free trade in an article for *Foreign Policy* in November 2003:

> '*Notion 1: Economies that are open to trade grow faster.* Poor countries grow richer when more open to trade, as recent successes in India and China have helped to demonstrate.
>
> *Notion 2: Rich countries are more protectionist than poor ones.* Not true, since poor countries tend to have higher average tariffs than rich ones. This does not address the problem of tariff escalation.
>
> *Notion 3: Agricultural protectionism in the rich world worsens global poverty.* If subsidies were removed, food prices would rise. These increases could hurt nutrition levels in some poor countries that rely on food imports.'

> – Arvind Panagariya, 'Think again: international trade', *Foreign Policy*, 1 November 2003

According to Panagariya, trade plays an important role in the continued growth and development of the world's economies, but our notions about that role must continually be challenged and refined. In the chapters that come we will further explore the role of international trade, including the mechanics of how it actually takes place, and later, the impact it can have on economic growth and development.

Practice exam questions

Paper 1, part (a) questions

1. Distinguish between a customs union and a common market, and monetary union. (10 marks)
2. Outline the advantages and disadvantages of a smaller, less developed economy joining a monetary union with larger, more developed economies. (10 marks)

Paper 2 questions

1. The United States, Mexico, and Canada entered into the North American Free Trade Agreement in 1994. Study the following charts and answer the questions that follow.

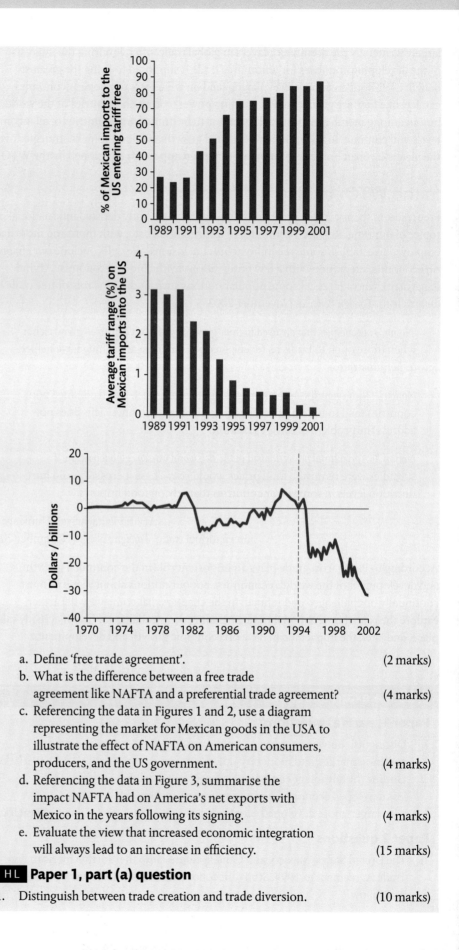

Figure 1 The share of US goods imported from Mexico entering tariff free

Figure 2 Average US tariff on taxable goods imported from Mexico

Figure 3 US trade balance with Mexico before and after NAFTA

a. Define 'free trade agreement'. (2 marks)

b. What is the difference between a free trade agreement like NAFTA and a preferential trade agreement? (4 marks)

c. Referencing the data in Figures 1 and 2, use a diagram representing the market for Mexican goods in the USA to illustrate the effect of NAFTA on American consumers, producers, and the US government. (4 marks)

d. Referencing the data in Figure 3, summarise the impact NAFTA had on America's net exports with Mexico in the years following its signing. (4 marks)

e. Evaluate the view that increased economic integration will always lead to an increase in efficiency. (15 marks)

HL Paper 1, part (a) question

1. Distinguish between trade creation and trade diversion. (10 marks)

Currencies	Per	We Buy	We Sell
AUSTRALIA	1	5.76510	6.70840
CANADA	1	6.82840	7.79440
CHINA	1	1.06130	1.19880
EURO	1	10.0154	11.3947
JAPAN	1	0.06840	0.07780
KOREA	1	0.00640	0.00790
PHILIPPINES	1	0.14800	0.19130
NEW ZEALAND	1	4.80760	5.49830
SINGAPORE	1	5.10260	5.83300
SWITZERLAND	1	6.38630	7.22410
TAIWAN	1	0.22530	0.27530
THAILAND	1	0.21090	0.26380
UNITED KINGDOM	1	12.8576	14.6689

Exchange rates

25

In Chapters 22–24 you have been introduced to the theories of international trade and protectionism and you have learned about the different stages of economic integration that countries might pursue as they open their economies to trade with the rest of the world. In Chapters 25 and 26 we are going to get into the details of *how trade actually works*, starting with the role of foreign exchange markets in determining the values of currencies relative to one another.

The reality is that, despite the trend towards increased international cooperation and economic integration, there are still roughly 180 different currencies being used around the world today. Whenever a consumer or producer in a country with its own currency wishes to buy or sell something from another country, or an investor wishes to purchase capital, real estate, or financial assets from abroad, an exchange of foreign currency must take place.

This chapter will explore the role of *exchange rates* in international trade, the causes and consequences of changes in a currency's exchange rate, and the different systems countries employ to manage their currencies' values on foreign exchange markets.

25.1 What are exchange rates?

Learning outcomes

At the end of this section you will be able to:

- explain that the value of an exchange rate in a floating system is determined by the demand for, and supply of, a currency
- distinguish between a depreciation of the currency and an **appreciation** of the currency
- draw a diagram to show determination of exchange rates in a floating exchange rate system
- calculate the value of one currency in terms of another currency
- calculate, using exchange rates, the price of a good in different currencies.

How are exchange rates determined?

Imagine you have just landed in New Delhi. You have big plans to see the sights, visit museums, try new foods, and generally make the most of your time in India. As your plane begins to land, you wonder how much money you will need. As you enter the terminal, you observe that the banks are charging different rates from those back home. Are the banks making big profits at your expense, or did something happen to change the value of the currency while you were travelling?

An exchange rate shows the price of one currency in terms of the amount of another. For example, if the £1 is valued at ₹100 (₹ is the symbol for the rupee, the currency of India), then the exchange rate between the pound and the rupee is £1 = ₹100. This valuation can also be expressed in reverse, as the number of pounds needed to buy ₹1. To determine this number, take the reciprocal of the original ratio. In this example, ₹100 would be needed to buy £1.

Research and inquiry

Many websites provide information on current exchange rates, including XE.com. Using this or a similar site, answer the questions that follow.

1 Determine the current exchange rates for the following currencies:

a. the US dollar (USD) in terms of Indian rupee (INR)

b. the euro (EUR) in terms of Japanese yen (JPY)

c. the British pound (GBP) in terms of Chinese yuan (CNY).

2 Using the value you found in part (c) above, determine how much a hotel room that costs ¥2,000 (¥ is the symbol for the Chinese yuan, the currency of China) per night would cost a British businessman arriving in Beijing for a meeting in terms of British pounds.

Tourists at Humayun's Tomb, Delhi, India

What is the foreign exchange market?

Currency as a market commodity is relatively new. At the close of the Second World War, in an attempt to organise the post-war global financial system, the Allied nations created a fixed rate system of foreign exchange. In this system, the value of each currency was pegged in relation to other currencies, and that rate was backed up by the country's gold reserves. Since the 1970s, countries have increasingly freed their currency exchange rates to float with supply and demand.

The foreign exchange market, also known as the *forex* market, is said to be the closest to a perfectly competitive market that there is. Information about prices is immediately discoverable through apps and websites like XE.com, the 'products' (which are really just currencies) are perfectly homogeneous, and there are millions upon millions of buyers and sellers in the market at all times (since anyone can exchange a currency for another one online, at an airport, or at a money changer anywhere in the world).

Additionally, forex markets span the globe and operate 24 hours a day. As is characteristic of perfect competition, profit margins for sellers tend to be low, due to the single price and the ease with which buyers (people trading their currency) can access the market. Countless mobile apps are available that allow individuals and businesses to convert their dollars or lira or pesos to yen or rand or pounds right on their smartphone.

Because of its size and broad access to it across every economy in the world, the global forex market is gigantic, accounting for over $6.6 trillion in transactions *every day*. The market's size is a testament to the role that international trade plays in the global economy today. While in macroeconomics we examined the output of individual nations, made up mostly of the interactions between domestic buyers and sellers, international transactions contribute no small part to the amount of economic activity in the world every day.

Forex markets cater to a variety of stakeholders, from the smallest retail currency trader and the backpacking tourist looking for a cheap hostel during their travels to central banks and multinational investment firms, which may exchange billions of dollars' worth of foreign currency in a single transaction as they build their portfolios of foreign assets. Figure 25.1 presents some of the stakeholders who engage in forex transactions.

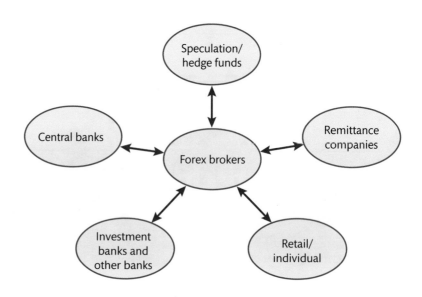

Figure 25.1   Stakeholders in the forex market

An individual buying currency on the streets of Delhi is probably buying at the retail level, from a small trader who buys from a forex broker. These brokers, at the highest levels, buy and sell currency to nearly all the other actors on the market. The brokers normally make profits from charging an explicit service fee of some fixed or percentage amount. They can also create spread (a gap) between the buying and selling prices, from which they take their profit.

Central banks buy and sell currency to influence the exchange rate, but sometimes have less power over the rate than the brokers themselves. Remittance companies exchange money for foreign workers who are sending money back home, and therefore need it to be converted to their home currency. Investment banks and hedge funds account for a very large share of forex trading, and often do so with pure **speculation** in mind. In other words, they buy currency with the specific intent of trading it later at a higher value. At its most dynamic, the forex market is highly speculative and subject to wide swings in values, as well as to panic selling and runs on a currency when the value of one currency suddenly drops.

What is a 'floating' exchange rate?

A floating exchange rate is one where the value of a currency is determined by the free market fluctuations in the demand for and supply of that currency on the foreign exchange market. A currency floats freely when the country's government and central bank refrain from intervening in its overseas markets.

Figure 25.2 shows the market for the most heavily traded currency, the US dollar, in terms of the second most heavily traded currency, the euro, using the market exchange rate as of October 2020.

The price axis in a forex market diagram shows the price of one currency in terms of the other. The market in Figure 25.2 is that for US dollars in Europe, therefore the price represents how much $1 costs in terms of euros: in this case, €0.85. The price of a euro in the USA can be determined by calculating the reciprocal, or the inverse, of the dollar price in Europe.

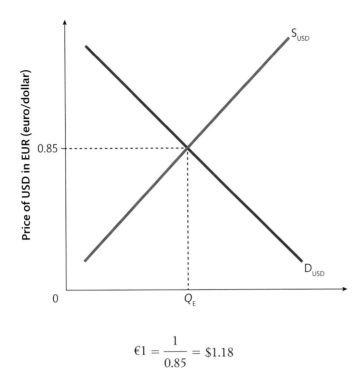

$$\text{€}1 = \frac{1}{0.85} = \$1.18$$

Figure 25.2 The market for US dollars in Europe

One US dollar costs a European €0.85 while €1 costs an American $1.18.

Just as with the demand for any commodity, currency demand is downward sloping and supply is upward sloping. Europeans who demand dollars will want more of them as the exchange rate decreases, since American goods and investments will be more attractive when dollars can be gotten more cheaply. On the other hand, as the dollar price increases in terms of euros, Europeans will demand less dollars while Americans will supply more. A stronger dollar makes European goods and investments more affordable to Americans, who will therefore supply a greater quantity as the exchange rate rises.

Equilibrium in the forex market occurs where the quantity supplied and demanded are equal. Any exchange rate higher or lower than the equilibrium rate will create shortages or surpluses in the forex market. Assume, for example, that the European Central Bank were to announce that the exchange rate of the dollar was fixed at €1, rather than the equilibrium of €0.85 per dollar. Figure 25.3 shows what happens when a rate higher than equilibrium is established in the market.

At an exchange rate higher than €0.85 per dollar, Americans will supply more dollars to Europe than Europeans demand. Americans find that when $1 dollar can buy €1 worth of goods or assets, instead of just €0.85, European goods and investments become much more attractive, leading Americans to supply more dollars to the European market. From the European perspective, however, the stronger dollar has made American imports and investments less attractive, so fewer dollars are demanded.

As in any market, when a disequilibrium exists market forces will drive the price back to equilibrium. In this case, an exchange rate of €1 per dollar is *too high*, resulting in excess dollars flooding onto the forex market. The exchange rate should fall until it occurs where demand equals supply.

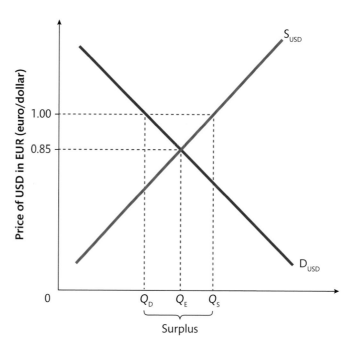

Figure 25.3 Disequilibrium in the foreign exchange market would occur if an exchange rate were fixed (i.e. a **fixed exchange rate**)

An exchange rate set below equilibrium will create a shortage of a currency, as domestic stakeholders will wish to buy more foreign goods and invest in more foreign assets than foreigners are willing to allow at the lower exchange rate. Market forces will drive the exchange rate up until equilibrium is restored where supply equals demand.

Appreciation and depreciation

When floating exchange rates change, the increase in the value of one currency against another is called appreciation. It follows that the relative decrease in value of the other currency is called depreciation. Using our dollars and euros example, let us assume European demand for US dollars decreases. Figure 25.4 shows the effect of a decrease in demand to D_1.

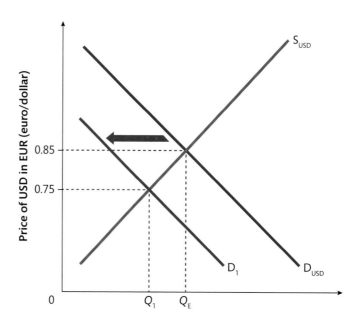

Figure 25.4 A decrease in demand causes depreciation of the dollar

At the new euros-for-dollars exchange rate, it takes €0.75 to buy $1, rather cheaper than before. The price of dollars, in euro terms, has decreased, and we can say that the dollar has depreciated against the euro. From the perspective of Americans, the weaker dollar corresponds with a more expensive euro. The price of a euro can be calculated by determining the reciprocal of the dollar price.

$$\$1 = €0.75$$

$$€1 = \frac{1}{0.75} = \$1.33$$

A dollar costs Europeans €0.75 and a euro costs Americans $1.33. The depreciation of the dollar corresponds with an appreciation of the euro.

A currency depreciation can occur as the result of a decrease in demand, as in Figure 25.4, or as the result of an increase in supply. For example, if Americans were to begin supplying more dollars to the European forex market for dollars, the supply would increase and the dollar would depreciate.

Appreciation has the opposite causes, naturally. An increase in demand for dollars or a decrease in supply of dollars in the European forex market would cause the dollar to appreciate. Figure 25.5 shows the result of a decrease in supply of dollars.

Dollars are scarcer in Europe following a decrease in supply (which could result from anything that led Americans to do less business in Europe, such as reduced demand for European exports or reduced investment in Europe by American investors). At the new exchange rate euros and dollars have achieved *parity*, or a 1 to 1 exchange rate. The dollar has *appreciated*, or gotten stronger against the euro, and euros have depreciated against the dollar.

Of course, a decrease in supply is not the only change that can cause appreciation; if demand for dollars by Europeans had increased, dollars would have become scarcer and appreciated on the forex market. In the next section we will examine all the

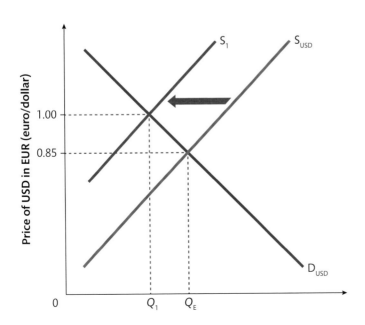

Figure 25.5 A decrease in supply causes appreciation of the dollar

Table 25.1 The dollar exchange rate and the price of a $1,000 product in different currencies

1 USD	Euro	British pound	Indian rupee	Australian $
1 US $ =	0.85	0.77	73	1.45
Price of a $1,000 American product in each currency	$1,000 \times 0.85$ = €850	$1,000 \times 0.77$ = £770	$1,000 \times 73$ = ₹73,000	$1,000 \times 1.45$ = AU$1,450

Research and inquiry

Let's plan a vacation!

Who doesn't love a great beach vacation? For this activity, you are going to price out a beach vacation to the Maldives, a lovely island nation in the Indian Ocean. To do so, use a travel website like Kayak.com or Expedia.com (one where you can book both flights and a hotel).

Determine how much a plane ticket would cost from the closest major city to where you live to Malé, the capital of the Maldives, leaving one week from today and returning two weeks from today. Depending on which currency your travel website displays prices in, convert the price of your plane ticket to either USD or, if it is already expressed in dollars, to your home country's currency, using XE.com to find the latest exchange rate.

Finally, calculate the price of the plane ticket in terms of Maldivian rufiyaa, again using XE.com to determine the current exchange rate.

Next, book a hotel! How much would it cost in US dollars, your home country's currency, and in Maldivian rufiyaa to stay seven nights at a high end resort in the Maldives?

For discussion and debate:

1 Which of the currencies you found prices for is the 'strongest'? Which is the 'weakest'?

2 What would most likely happen to the US dollar price of a week's hotel stay in the Maldives if the Maldivian rufiyaa were to *depreciate*? Explain your answer.

3 What would happen to the demand by foreigners for beach vacations in the Maldives if the Maldivian rufiyaa were to *appreciate*?

factors that can cause a change in a currency's demand or supply and therefore an appreciation or a depreciation in a floating exchange rate system.

Not all currencies are allowed to 'float freely' on the forex market. Later in this chapter we will look at two alternative exchange rate systems: fixed (or 'pegged') exchange rates and managed floats, both cases in which a government or central bank intervenes in the forex market to control the currency's value against one or more foreign currencies.

How do you calculate prices in different currencies?

With knowledge of exchange rates, we can calculate how much a good produced abroad in one currency will cost a foreign consumer who is spending another currency. Table 25.1 shows the dollar's exchange rate in terms of four currencies in the first row and the price of a $1000 product to a consumer from each of the four countries in the second row.

To calculate the price of a good in different currencies, we must multiply the price of the good in US dollars by the exchange rate of the dollar in each country.

Even if we do not know the value of one currency against another, but we know the value of both against a common third currency, we can determine prices. For example, while our table does not show the euro/pound exchange rate, we do know the euro/dollar and the pound/dollar rates.

Worked example 25.1

For example, using the information in the table, we can calculate how much a £150 theatre ticket in London would cost a German tourist in terms of euros.

First we can convert the £150 to US dollars by taking the reciprocal of the dollar exchange rate and multiplying it by 150.

$1 = £0.77, therefore:

$$£150 \times \frac{1}{0.77} = \$194.80$$

Next we can determine how many euros the $194.80 costs our German tourist.

$1 = €0.85, therefore:

$194.80 × 0.85 = €165.58

A £150 theatre ticket would cost a German tourist the equivalent of €165.58.

25.2 What are the determinants of exchange rates?

Learning outcomes

At the end of this section you will be able to:

- analyse the factors that lead to changes in currency demand and supply, including foreign demand for a country's exports, domestic demand for imports, foreign investment, **remittances**, speculation, relative inflation rates, relative interest rates, relative growth rates, and central bank intervention
- calculate changes in the value of a currency from a set of data.

When you go to the grocery store or to the movie theatre, you expect to see roughly the same prices you saw the last time you were there. Sure, once in a while the price of a dozen eggs or a ticket to a matinee will be adjusted upwards or downwards, but it is not like these prices change every hour or even every minute. Currencies with floating exchange rates, on the other hand, are *constantly* fluctuating in price throughout every minute of the day, as investors and retail traders buy and sell currencies to facilitate their cross-border transactions.

A currency's exchange rate changes whenever one of the determinants of supply or demand changes. Given the dynamic nature of international trade and investment, currency demand and supply are always changing, therefore floating exchange rates will rise and fall (usually within a fairly narrow range) repeatedly throughout any given day. Figure 25.6 shows the dollar exchange rate in the UK on a single day, 2 October 2020.

Video suggestion:
You have read about it, now you can review what you have just learned by watching a video by the author!
▶ Simply click here in your eBook for a video on calculating prices in different currencies using exchange rates.

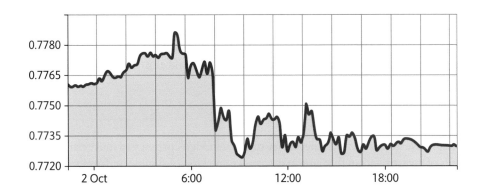

Figure 25.6   Floating exchange rates fluctuate throughout the day; this data shows the dollar exchange rate in the UK on the 2 October 2020

Notice that between midnight and 6 a.m. the dollar was steadily appreciating, from £0.775 to £0.778. When the UK forex markets opened in the morning, however, the dollar took a sharp plunge, from more than £0.778 at 4 a.m. to £0.772 by 8 a.m. Throughout the rest of the day the dollar continued to fluctuate, but at a weaker level than it started the morning at.

Case study – what happened on 2 October 2020?

In case you are wondering what happened that may have caused the steep drop in the dollar exchange rate in the UK on 2 October 2020, it might help to know that that was the day that then US President Donald J. Trump announced that he had tested positive for the coronavirus and was therefore sick with COVID-19.

Without reading further in this chapter and learning what the determinants of exchange rates are, do you have any hypotheses about why the news of President Trump's illness might have caused the dollar exchange rate to fall on the forex market? Who demands dollars, and why might demand have suddenly dropped on the morning of 2 October 2020?

So, what might explain the constantly changing values demonstrated by floating currencies like the US dollar? There are several determinants of exchange rates, each of which will be explained below.

Demand for exports and imports

The relative demand for imports and exports can directly influence the purchase of currencies, and so alter the exchange rate. When demand for a country's exports increases, it increases demand for the currency itself. To buy the exports, importers first need to buy the exporting country's currency to pay for them. To import Canadian maple syrup, for example, the importer first needs to buy Canadian dollars.

Thus, demand for a country's currency is partially derived from the relative demand for its exports compared to that of the trading country. For example, an increase in European demand for Thai goods should increase the demand for the Thai baht and cause an appreciation of the baht in euro terms. Correspondingly, it would result in a depreciation of the euro versus the Thai baht.

Furthermore, the interaction of imports and exports with the exchange rate can be self-correcting. As the Thai baht climbs, the price of Thai goods in euro terms rises and makes them less attractive. European consumers, if sensitive to the price change caused by the new exchange rate, may reduce overall Thai imports and their demand for baht will decrease again. Thus, extreme levels of appreciation and depreciation can be balanced out by the export price and demand changes that are the result. This can have implications for the balance of payments and specifically the **current account** (which will be introduced in Chapter 26).

Foreign investment

Foreign investors may find it necessary to buy a foreign currency to make particular kinds of investments in that country. To make any kind of significant **foreign direct investment (FDI)** by opening a branch location, starting a new firm, or creating a joint venture in another country, that country's currency is required to buy capital equipment, rent space, pay salaries, and purchase materials. Increases in FDI appreciate a currency, and the loss of FDI depreciates it.

Financial investments such as the buying of foreign company shares, or interest-earning deposits in a foreign bank, are also likely to require the purchase of foreign currency. In other words, greater demand for a country's financial investments appreciates the currency. The same applies to cross-border real estate purchases; if a national of one country buys property in another country, demand for the country's currency where the investment takes place increases, causing it to appreciate, while supply of the buyer's currency increases, leading it to depreciate.

Remittances

When a worker from one country earns income in a foreign country, inevitably a portion of the foreign income will be 'remitted' to the worker's home country. Foreign remittances refer to money earned by a foreign worker that is sent to family or to other individuals in their home country. Consider the example of a British banker working in Hong Kong. The banker, a British citizen, saves for retirement in British accounts and also owns a house in the UK, for which a monthly mortgage payment must be made. Therefore, the banker transfers a significant share of his weekly earnings back to the UK. The act of remitting income home increases the demand for British pounds on the forex market in Hong Kong, and increases the supply of Hong Kong dollars on the forex market in the UK. The more remittances flow from Hong Kong to the UK, the more the British pound will appreciate and the Hong Kong dollar will depreciate.

Speculation

Foreign exchange market investors regularly speculate on currencies' future values. As with the buying and selling of shares, speculators may buy a currency hoping it will appreciate, sell it when they believe it has reached peak value, and take the resulting profits. The exact portion of forex trading devoted to speculation is unknown, but it is believed to make up the majority of the daily transactions in the $5 trillion market.

The actions of speculators can cause large swings in exchange rates, particularly during periods of macroeconomic uncertainty. During the summer of 2011, for example, demand for the Swiss franc in European forex markets skyrocketed as uncertainty over the ability of certain European nations to remain solvent in the face of huge national debts and contracted economic output during the Great Recession led investors to dump their euro-denominated assets (such as government bonds) and invest in 'safe' Swiss assets, namely the Swiss franc itself, which along with gold was considered one of the safest investments in 2011. Figure 25.7 shows the effect of the 'run' on the Swiss franc in the summer of 2011.

For months the franc had hovered around 0.80 euros per franc, then in mid-July 2011 international investors began to buy the franc due to uncertainty over the value of the euro. As demand for the franc increased, the franc appreciated, making it an even more attractive asset for investors to buy. Very rapidly the franc appreciated from 0.80 euros to 0.97 euros, a 21% increase in value in just a month.

For Switzerland, an economy for which trade with its European neighbours provides the life blood, the sudden and unexpected appreciation of its currency posed a dire

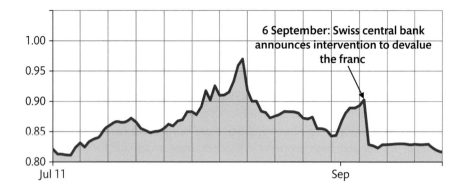

Figure 25.7 Swiss franc exchange rate in euros from July to September 2011

threat to macroeconomic stability, as demand for Swiss exports would undoubtedly begin to fall as a result of the franc's appreciation and Swiss products become more expensive to consumers in other countries. Fortunately, the peak of 0.97 euros per frank was short lived, but by early September a second run on the franc appeared to be underway as its value began climbing once again.

On 6 September, Switzerland's central bank announced it would begin intervening in the forex markets to *devalue* the franc, capping its value at 0.83 euros per franc. The effect of this announcement can be clearly seen in Figure 25.7 as the franc's second climb is instantly interrupted and its value plummets to 0.83 euro overnight on 7 September. The effect of a central bank's forex market interventions to either devalue (as the Swiss national bank did) or revalue a currency will be explored later in this chapter.

Defenders of currency speculation have pointed out that speculators provide a service because they have an interest in rationally assessing a currency's true value. Speculators, they argue, merely accelerate a process that would otherwise take much longer. With this in mind, it is important to remember that speculators not only make their bets on a variety of purely economic factors such as the balance of payments situation and relative budget deficits, but also on political events and other less tangible factors.

Relative inflation rates

As the average price level in one country rises faster than it does in the economies of its trading partners, the higher inflation country's exports become more expensive and, therefore, less desirable to foreign consumers. At the same time, imports from other countries where inflation is lower will be cheaper than before and more attractive.

If Paraguay's prices were to soar relative to its neighbour Argentina, the demand for Paraguayan exports in Argentina and the corresponding demand for Paraguay's currency would decrease, causing it to depreciate. At the same time, Paraguay's consumers would demand more imports from Argentina, causing the Argentinian peso to appreciate.

All else equal, an increase in domestic inflation will cause a country's currency to depreciate (as net exports decrease), while disinflation or deflation will cause the currency to appreciate (as net exports increase).

Relative interest rates

A change in a country's interest rate can attract or repel foreign financial investors. Should the interest rates offered in one country increase, overseas investors would be attracted to the higher relative interest rate and buy the local currency to deposit in the bank or invest in bonds, an outcome referred to as a *capital inflow*.

The reverse is also true: a decrease in relative interest rates in one country will cause some international investors to withdraw money from that country's banks and other interest-bearing assets and search for a better rate of return in other economies, an outcome referred to as a *capital outflow*.

Capital inflows cause a country's currency to appreciate, while outflows cause a depreciation. If the Bank of Turkey were to raise interest rates relative to other countries, foreign investors would buy Turkish lira and put it into Turkish banks or invest it in Turkish bonds, causing a capital inflow that would raise the exchange rate of the Turkish against other currencies.

Relative growth rates

It may sound counterintuitive, but assuming, all else is held constant, an increase in a country's gross domestic product (GDP) growth rate should cause its currency to *depreciate*. The logic is straightforward enough: higher GDP means higher incomes, and as household incomes rise, consumption increases, not just of domestic goods and services, but also of imports. Higher demand for imports increases the supply of the domestic currency on forex markets, causing it to depreciate, and increases demand for foreign currencies, causing them to appreciate.

As an example, consider the effect of a booming economy in Canada while the economic growth rate in the USA remains constant. Canada's largest source of imports is the USA, so as Canadian incomes rise, demand for US exports will increase, causing demand for the US dollar to increase and its value to rise. To buy all those new American imports, Canadians must supply more of their own currency to the forex market, causing the Canadian dollar to depreciate.

Central bank intervention

Last, but most definitely not least in our list of factors that determine the exchange rate is central bank intervention. We learned in Chapter 19, Demand management: monetary policy, that one of the roles of a central bank is to manage the value of its currency to promote domestic macroeconomic and international trade objectives. A central bank can intervene in the forex market in two ways.

1   Raising or lowering domestic interest rates to attract capital inflows or promote capital outflows.

2   Directly intervening in the forex market by buying or selling its own currency, either adding to or drawing down its official reserves of foreign currency, in order to *devalue* or *revalue* its currency.

When a central bank intervenes in the forex market to strengthen its currency, it is known as a **revaluation** (distinct from an *appreciation*, which results from free market forces). A forced depreciation by the central bank is known as a **devaluation** of the exchange rate. Later in this chapter we will explore the means by which and reasons behind why a central bank might revalue or devalue its currency.

How do you calculate the change in exchange rates from a set of data?

Given a set of data, we can calculate the change in a currency's exchange rate between two periods of time.

Worked example 25.2

Below we are given hypothetical exchange rates of a Mexican peso in terms of US dollars over three years:

- January 2020: Mex$1 = US$0.03
- January 2021: Mex$1 = US$0.04
- January 2022: Mex$1 = US$0.05

Using these values, we can calculate the changes in the value of the US dollar in terms of pesos for the three years. To do so, we take the reciprocal of the peso exchange rate for each period:

- January 2020: US$1 = $1 \div 0.03$ = Mex$33.33
- January 2021: US$1 = $1 \div 0.04$ = Mex$25
- January 2022: US$1 = $1 \div 0.05$ = Mex$20

The data reveals that over the two years from January 2020 to January 2022 the peso appreciated against the dollar, increasing in value by 66.6% (US$0.05 per peso is 66.6% stronger than US$0.03 per peso). The peso's appreciation corresponded with a 40% depreciation of the US dollar (the 2022 exchange rate of Mex$20 per dollar is 40% below the 2020 exchange rate of Mex$33.33 per dollar).

25.3 What are some consequences of a change in the exchange rate?

Learning outcome

At the end of this section you will be able to:

- evaluate the possible economic consequences of a change in the value of a currency, including the effects on a country's inflation rate, economic growth, employment, the current account balance, and the effect on living standards.

Effect on inflation

When a currency appreciates on forex markets the price of imports goes down. Consumer goods, capital goods, imported energy, and raw materials all become cheaper, causing an increase in short-run aggregate supply (SRAS) and disinflation.

At the same time, a stronger currency will cause foreign demand for the country's exports to fall, reducing the level of aggregate demand (AD) at home and further bringing inflation down.

A depreciated currency has the opposite effects. All imports become more costly to domestic consumers, while exports become cheaper to foreigners. SRAS could decrease as imported energy, raw materials, and capital goods become more expensive, and AD is likely to increase as net exports rise. Depreciation therefore leads to higher inflation, while appreciation leads to lower inflation or perhaps even deflation.

Effect on economic growth

Once again we encounter a situation that may seem counterintuitive at first: a weaker currency is *good for economic growth*, and a stronger currency is *bad for economic growth*. There are some exceptions to this idea, but let us first review why this is usually the case. Depreciation will increase AD in a country as net exports increase. In the short run, more demand means more jobs, more income, and a higher level of output. The result is an increase in real GDP.

However, in the long run a weaker currency alone will not drive economic growth, since it stimulates demand while simultaneously limiting the potential increase in aggregate supply (AS). Most countries depend at least to some extent on imported capital, energy, and raw materials to drive economic activity; a weaker currency therefore makes inputs more expensive and could slow increases in SRAS. In other words, while a weaker currency could fuel short-run economic growth, it could also limit long-run growth and lead only to inflation as potential output is limited by constraints on inputs.

A currency appreciation has similarly conflicting outcomes in the short run and in the long run. From the perspective of producers, a currency appreciation is undesirable in the short run, as imports become more attractive and exports less attractive. Domestic consumers will shift some of their consumption to foreign goods, reducing AD in the home economy. However, in the long run a stronger currency will make imported capital and other inputs cheaper for domestic firms. Additionally, domestic firms that are able to might shift some of their production overseas, where costs are lower thanks to the stronger home currency. In other words, currency appreciation can help firms in the long run, making production cheaper and increasing the country's AS, contributing to economic growth.

The effect of a change in the exchange rate on economic growth is therefore dependent on whether we are looking at the short run or the long run: in the short run depreciation increases output as AD shifts outward, but in the long run a weaker currency only leads to inflation, while appreciation creates more opportunities for the country's aggregate output to increase. Generally, therefore, exchange rate stability is a more desirable outcome for most economies than a constantly appreciating or depreciating currency.

Effect on unemployment

You might start to notice a pattern here; as with economic growth, the effect of changes in the exchange rate on employment and unemployment may vary depending on whether we are considering the short run or the long run. Obviously, a depreciation of the currency is beneficial for employment in the short run, as AD will increase thanks to higher net exports, increasing demand for labour in return. However, if the weaker currency creates inflation, then in the long run employment gains will be limited due to rising wages and the constraints imposed by scarcity in the economy.

Since a stronger currency is more likely to increase AS, there may be benefits to employment from a supply-side perspective; however, appreciation also causes net exports to fall, leading to less aggregate demand and therefore less demand for labour.

In the short run, currency depreciation will reduce unemployment, while in the long run, exchange rate stability is most likely to result in stable levels of employment consistent with the economy's full employment level of output.

Effect on the current account balance

In Chapter 26, Balance of payments, we will explore in great detail the components of a country's *current account*, but for now you need to know this: the *current account balance* is where a country measures the flow of money between the home country and all other countries for the purchase of exports and imports. When a country's currency depreciates on the forex markets, its exports will increase and its imports will decrease, and money will flow *into* its current account. We refer to this as a move towards *surplus in the current account*.

An appreciation of the currency, on the other hand, will lead to an increase in imports and a decrease in exports, causing money to flow *out* of the current account. When net exports decrease, we call it a move towards *deficit in the current account*.

Depreciation moves a country's current account towards *surplus*, and appreciation moves the current account towards *deficit*.

Effect on living standards

Finally, let us think about how the living standards in a country are affected by changes in the exchange rate. You may say that a stronger currency is likely to increase living standards, and you would not be incorrect in assuming so: When your currency appreciates you will find imported goods to be cheaper, allowing you to afford more output on the same income, thereby increasing your standard of living. Additionally, if you are the kind of person who enjoys international travel, an appreciation of your currency will make such adventures cheaper and allow you to enjoy more comfort and luxury while abroad than before your currency strengthened.

On the other hand, a stronger currency also threatens domestic households through the negative effects on domestic employment in the short run. If you are a worker in an export-oriented industry, an appreciation of your currency might cost you your job as foreign demand decreases due to higher prices. In this case, a depreciation might mean more demand for workers in your industry and therefore higher wages as export-oriented firms scramble to hire workers. While a weaker currency might mean more employment in the short run, which will increase living standards for those who get jobs, a depreciation could also be inflationary, reducing real incomes of everyone in the economy as imported goods, capital, and raw materials become more expensive.

Unfortunately, the consequences of a change in the exchange rate, like so much else in economics, are not clear-cut. There are advantages and disadvantages to both a currency appreciation and a depreciation. Whether an economy is better off or worse off following a change in its exchange rate depends on whether we are looking at the short run or the long run, producers or consumers, or the level of unemployment or inflation. We can predict likely outcomes, but ranking their desirability by assigning a value to any particular outcome is an exercise in *normative economics*.

25.4 What are fixed exchange rates?

Learning outcomes

At the end of this section you will be able to:

- describe a fixed exchange rate system involving commitment to a single fixed rate
- distinguish between a devaluation of a currency and a revaluation of a currency
- explain, using a diagram, how a fixed exchange rate is maintained.

In a fixed exchange rate system, the value of a currency is locked in (pegged) to the value of another currency. The central bank determines a desirable value and enacts intervention to maintain the established rate. Forex market intervention can take the form of the central bank buying and selling currency reserves, or raising or lowering interest rates to encourage capital inflows or outflows. The latter form is the more benign means of manipulating the market.

What does it mean to 'devalue' or 'revalue' a currency?

Let us imagine that Argentina's central bank decided that its currency (the peso ($ is the symbol for the Argentine peso, the currency of Argentina)) is overvalued at the rate of $77 required to buy a single US dollar. The exchange rate of the peso is the reciprocal of the dollar exchange rate, or $\frac{1}{77}$, which equals US$0.013 per peso. The central bank decides to *devalue* the peso, or make it weaker against the dollar. A devaluation requires reducing the peso exchange rate, so that a single US dollar could buy more than $77. Assume the central bank wishes to devalue the peso to a level where US$1 could buy $100.

Devaluing the peso would increase the dollar exchange rate and decrease the peso exchange rate. If it achieved its goal, $100 would be required to buy a dollar, but only US$0.01 dollars would be required to buy a peso. In other words, the peso exchange rate would fall from its current rate of US$0.013 to US$0.010.

In a fixed exchange rate system, Argentina's central bank would first devalue its currency, then actively intervene in the forex markets to maintain it at the desired level. If market pressures caused the peso to appreciate, the central bank would intervene to devalue it again. If market pressures pushed the value of the peso down, the central bank would have to *revalue* the peso, or intervene to strengthen it against the dollar.

The power of language

Strong is good, weak is bad. Appreciation is good, depreciation is bad. Surplus is good, deficit is bad. In each of these statements a value is placed to a word. It would be a rare occasion in which a political leader would argue for the 'weakening' of the home country's currency, or to claim that a 'deficit' could be desirable, or that 'depreciation' is better than 'appreciation'. As an example, in May 2020 then US President Donald Trump told reporters that 'It is a great time to have a strong dollar', and that 'strong dollars are overall very good'.

How does language influence our interpretation of economic concepts? Why might leaders favour a 'strong' currency over a 'weak' currency? What are the economic effects of a strong currency compared to a weak currency? Is it necessarily true that 'stronger' is 'better' when it comes to exchange rates?

Later in the chapter we'll examine the reasons *why* a central bank may wish to peg its currency in the forex markets, and evaluate the advantages and disadvantages of a fixed exchange rate compared to a floating exchange rate. First, however, we'll look at *how* fixed exchange rates are maintained.

How are fixed exchange rates maintained?

Let us look more closely at our example from above, and examine the market for Argentinian pesos before and after the central bank's decision to peg it against the dollar.

Figure 25.8 shows the market for US dollars in Argentina before the fixed exchange rate has been enacted, with US$1 costing $77.

The central bank wishes to *devalue* the peso, which would mean increasing the number of pesos a single dollar could buy on the forex market, to $100 peso per US dollar. Figure 25.9 shows what would happen if the central bank were to simply set a price floor on the dollar at $100.

As we can see, without intervention a $100 price floor would simply create a disequilibrium in the dollar market in which the quantity supplied exceeded the quantity demanded. Americans would wish to buy more Argentinian products and Argentinians would demand less American output, but because no actions were taken to actually achieve the higher exchange rate of the dollar, there is a surplus of dollars on the forex market.

Because simply setting an exchange rate higher or lower than the market rate will just create a disequilibrium in the market, a fixed exchange rate system requires the central banks to actually intervene to establish the desired exchange rate. The two means of forex market intervention are raising or lowering interest rates and buying or selling currency directly on the market.

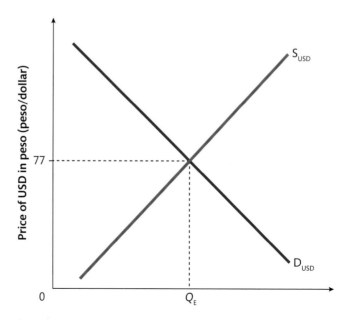

Figure 25.8 The market for US dollars in Argentina under a floating exchange rate

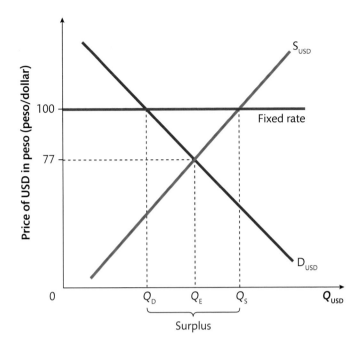

Figure 25.9 Without intervention a price floor creates disequilibrium in the dollar market

Raising and lowering interest rates

Now let us examine what happens when the central bank actually intervenes in the market for dollars to achieve the desired exchange rate of $100 per dollar (or US$0.010 per peso). By reducing domestic interest rates, Argentina's central bank will make dollar-denominated assets more attractive to Argentinian investors, and there will be a capital outflow in Argentina and a capital inflow to the USA. In order to put their money into higher-yield interest-bearing US assets (savings accounts, government bonds, etc.), Argentina's investors will demand more dollars. Figure 25.10 shows the effect of an expansionary monetary policy in Argentina on the forex market for US dollars.

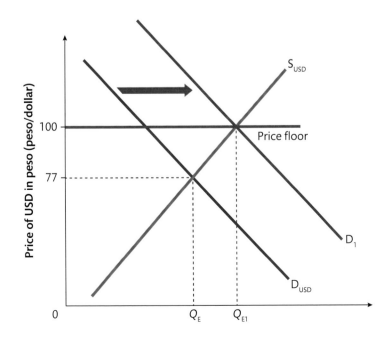

Figure 25.10 Lower interest rates in Argentina would cause an increase in demand for US dollars

The surplus of dollars is eliminated because now there is more actual demand for dollars thanks to the relatively higher interest rates US investments are offering Argentinian investors. An expansionary monetary policy in Argentina has caused an appreciation of the dollar, and a *devaluation* of the peso. We can look at the effect of the central bank's actions in the peso market as well, which we do in Figure 25.11.

Lower interest rates in Argentina have led to a capital outflow, increasing the supply of pesos on the forex market in the US as Argentinian investors scramble to put their money in higher-yield interest-bearing assets in the USA. The peso has been *devalued* from its market exchange rate of US$0.013 to the pegged value of US$0.010.

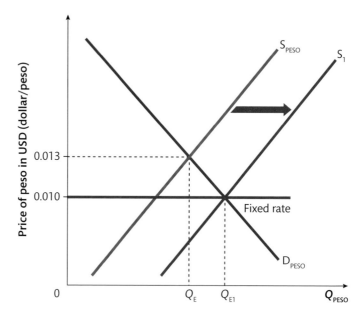

Figure 25.11
An expansionary monetary policy in Argentina would increase the supply of pesos on the forex market in the USA

Direct intervention in the forex market

In order to maintain its pegged exchange rate, Argentina's central bank must actively intervene in the market for peso and the market for dollars to devalue or revalue the peso. If free market pressures lead to the peso's appreciation, the central bank will have to either reduce interest rates further (keeping demand for pesos low and supply of pesos high) or directly intervene in the market by buying US dollars and adding them to its foreign exchange reserves. Foreign exchange reserves are held by every central bank in the world, and serve as a means for managing their exchange rate.

Let us consider what would happen if the market exchange rate of the peso were to fall below US$0.010, forcing the central bank to *revalue* the peso against the dollar in order to maintain its fixed rate or 'peg'.

Decreased demand for Argentinian goods in the US is causing the peso to depreciate below the central bank's peg. In order to maintain the peg, Argentina's central bank must now *revalue* the peso. Let us assume it does so by using some of its foreign exchange reserves of US dollars to buy up pesos in the forex market. The result is an increase in demand for pesos and an increase in supply of US dollars. In Figure 25.12, the D_1 would increase back to D_{PESO}, while in the dollar market the supply would increase bringing the dollar back down to the desired exchange rate of $100 per US dollar.

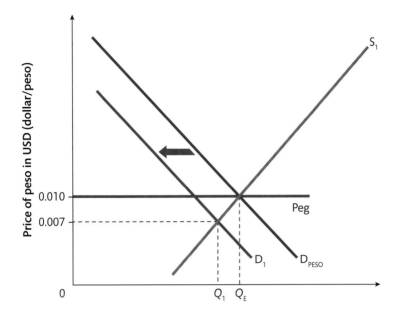

Figure 25.12 Falling demand for peso puts downward pressure on the exchange rate

Foreign exchange controls

A nation's government can also manipulate its currency's exchange rate without depending on central bank policymakers. Foreign exchange controls are legal limits on how much of a country's currency foreign investors are allowed to buy or sell in any single transaction. Under a floating exchange rate system, governments are unlikely to have any foreign exchange controls whatsoever, since they are comfortable leaving the exchange rate up to the free market. However, if a government wishes to devalue its currency, one way it could do so is setting strict limits on how much of the currency foreign investors and forex traders are allowed to buy in a single day or for a single transaction.

Tighter limits on foreign holdings of the domestic currency will limit demand and put downward pressure on the exchange rate; in other words, foreign exchange controls will devalue the currency. Loosening foreign exchange controls will revalue the currency, that is, assuming they were effective at limiting demand in the first place. If the market demand for the currency was already less than the limit imposed by the government, then loosening exchange controls will have no effect on the exchange rate, of course.

25.5 What are managed exchange rates?

Learning outcomes

At the end of this section you will be able to:

- explain how a **managed exchange rate** operates, with reference to the fact that there is a periodic government intervention to influence the value of an exchange rate
- analyse the possible consequences of overvalued and **undervalued currencies**.

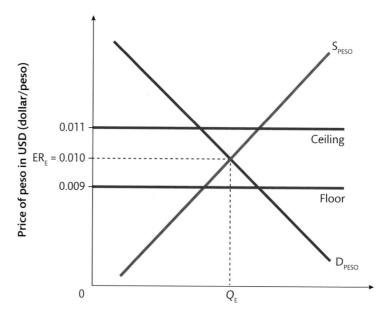

Figure 25.13 A managed floating exchange rate establishes a range of acceptable exchange rates

Now that we have covered the tools that policymakers can use to revalue or devalue a currency, we'll look at another exchange rate system that is commonly used by countries to promote stability in international trade and investment flow: the *managed exchange rate system*. A managed exchange rate is one that floats in the foreign exchange market but is subject to intervention from time to time by domestic monetary authorities, in order to resist fluctuations that they consider to be undesirable.

In our peso–dollar example above we assumed the central bank was 'pegging' the peso against the dollar at US$0.01 per peso and $100 per dollar. Let us assume instead that Argentina adopted a managed float, and rather than a fixed exchange rate, the central bank set up a range of acceptable exchange rates between which the peso could fluctuate. Figure 25.13 illustrates how a managed float might look in a forex market diagram for the peso, with a maximum exchange rate of US$0.011 and a minimum exchange rate of US$0.009 per peso.

At the current equilibrium of US$0.010 neither the ceiling price nor the floor price are binding; therefore, the central bank needs not take any policy action to maintain the exchange rate.

How do policymakers correct an overvalued currency?

Assume now that there is capital inflow into Argentina, as foreign investors demand more Argentinian assets. The inflow puts upward pressure on the peso as demand increases, driving the equilibrium exchange rate up to US$0.012. Figure 25.14 shows the effect of the capital inflow on the value of the peso.

Greater peso demand has pushed the equilibrium rate above the ceiling rate of US$0.011, creating a shortage of pesos. In order to maintain the ceiling rate of US$0.011 per peso, Argentina's central bank must intervene in the market. It can do so by either reducing interest rates, which would make investments in Argentina less attractive and stem the capital inflow, or by using pesos to buy US dollars on the forex

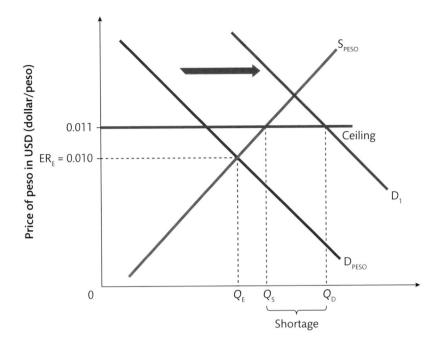

Figure 25.14 A capital inflow would cause the domestic currency to appreciate

market, increasing its foreign exchange reserves. A direct intervention would require the central bank to increase the supply of pesos, which would bring the exchange rate back below the ceiling rate. A decrease in interest rates would reduce demand from foreign investors, also bringing it back within the target range.

Figure 25.15 shows the effect of a decrease in interest rates in Argentina on the peso market and the equilibrium exchange rate.

Expansionary monetary policy has made investments in peso-denominated assets less attractive, stemming the capital inflow that caused the initial appreciation of the peso. The exchange rate has settled at an equilibrium within the central bank's desired range, at US$0.011 per peso.

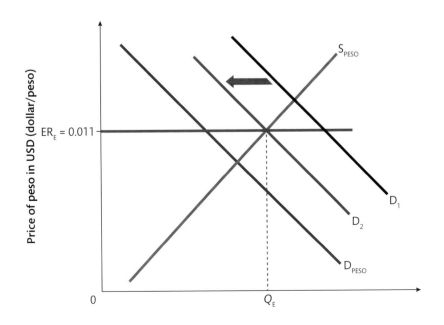

Figure 25.15 If Argentina lowers interest rates, demand for pesos on the forex market will go down

Video suggestions:
You have read about it, now you can review what you have just learned by watching some videos by the author! Simply click here in your eBook for videos on managed exchange rates.

How do policymakers correct an undervalued currency?

When the market exchange rate falls below the floor price set by the central bank, an intervention is required to restore the rate to within the acceptable range. For example, if a capital outflow has pushed the exchange rate to US$0.008, then Argentina would have needed to either increase demand for peso or reduce its supply to keep the rate above the floor rate of US$0.009.

The two ways it could *revalue* the peso include enacting a contractionary monetary policy, which would have stemmed the capital outflow as international investors would find peso-denominated assets more attractive, or an intervention in the forex market where Argentina buys its own currency, increasing peso demand and increasing dollar supply. The result would be a revaluation of the peso, bringing its exchange rate back within the acceptable range.

Managed exchange systems offer policymakers an option that lies between the free market float and the hard peg described by a fixed exchange rate regime. The map in Figure 25.16 below shows the predominant exchange rate systems of every country in the world in 2013, according to the International Monetary Fund (IMF).

As we can see, fixed exchange rates are quite rare, while managed and floating systems are used by most countries.

Figure 25.16 As this map of exchange rate regimes around the world in 2013 shows, few countries fix their currencies

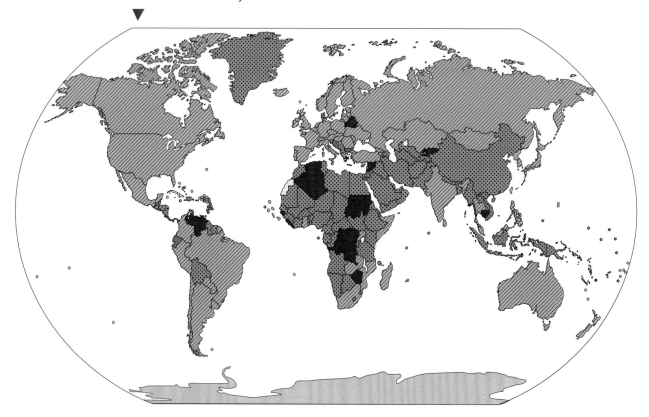

- Floating
- Managed (within horizontal bands)
- Fixed
- Other managed arrangement

Learning outcomes

At the end of this section you will be able to:

- compare and contrast a fixed exchange rate system with a floating exchange rate system
- evaluate the merits of floating versus fixed exchange rates with reference to the degree of certainty for stakeholders, ease of adjustment, the role of international reserves in the form of foreign currencies and flexibility offered to policymakers.

As we saw in Figure 25.16, the world is split about 50/50 between floating exchange rates and managed or fixed exchange rates. There are advantages and disadvantages to each type of system. The range in which an exchange rate is managed might be very narrow, meaning the system is close to a peg, or broad, allowing for more market fluctuations. However, in all cases, some degree of intervention is expected. Therefore, both fixed and managed exchange rates share some characteristics when compared to the free float.

What are the arguments for floating exchange rates (and against fixed/managed)?

Domestic policy freedom

Overall growth and inflation management is enormously difficult even under normal conditions, without the need to factor in the management of exchange rates as well. Allowing the exchange rate to float freely means that central bankers are free to manipulate monetary policy, specifically interest rates, to manage domestic AD towards the objectives of price level stability, full employment, and economic growth.

Exchange rate management as a goal might create conflicts with the other goals of monetary policy. Therefore, saving monetary policymakers this task allows them to focus on domestic policy objectives.

More balanced trade

A surge in demand for exports can lead to a surplus in the current account of the balance of payments (more on this in Chapter 26). Under a floating exchange rate system, the increased demand for the currency that accompanies an increase in demand for exports leads to currency appreciation, which in turn should make exports less attractive and counteract the move towards a trade surplus. In this way, a floating exchange rate will lead to a self-adjusting trade balance, reducing surpluses and deficits in trade between nations.

On the flip side, when exports are falling, reduced demand for the currency will cause depreciation, which should make exports attractive again and counteract the decline in net exports that would otherwise occur if the exchange rate were fixed.

Under a fixed exchange rate system, persistent trade imbalances are more likely to occur, as a consistently undervalued currency will lead to long-run **current account surpluses** while an **overvalued currency** will contribute to long-run current account deficits.

No surplus currency reserves

As floating exchange rate schemes do not require the stockpiling of currency reserves to prop up or devalue a currency, financial resources are allocated more efficiently. Foreign exchange can then be used to more productive ends, such as purchasing capital goods or imported resources, rather than held in reserve for the time when they are needed to intervene in the forex market to revalue or devalue the currency.

Flexible response to external shocks

Sudden disruptions to the economy can be managed without the need to devote resources to fixing an exchange rate. In the event of a massive **debt relief** package, such as that agreed by the EU for some of its members in 2010, countries would normally see their currency depreciate as faith and expectations for growth fall. This depreciation would allow for greater exports, and for growth to return, helping the debtor countries pay off their debts.

What are the arguments against floating exchange rates (and for fixed/managed)?

Uncertainty for investors

When entering new or unfamiliar markets, foreign investors put a priority on holding as many factors as possible stable and predictable. Exchange rates are very important here because the foreign company may need to import materials and capital equipment. Simultaneously, it will be paying wages and property costs in local currency; this is also true for domestic companies with foreign sales or investment aspirations. Navigating wide fluctuations in the exchange rate adds administrative cost and makes both predicting costs and setting product prices very difficult.

Therefore, a developing country hoping to attract foreign investment to increase its capital stock and to create jobs may favour a managed or fixed exchange rate to calm the nerves of foreign firms that may be turned away due to exchange rate uncertainty.

Influence of random events prevent automatic adjustment

While floating rates permit a flexible response to economic crises, not all shocks can be solved by exchange rate self-adjustment. Severe international political tension, domestic social turmoil, and other random events can depress markets and limit growth, despite any self-adjustment in exchange rates. By managing its currency, therefore, a central bank can promote the objective that if left to the free market may be less likely to be achieved.

Risk of imported inflation

Countries that rely heavily on foreign-sourced factors of production (energy resources, raw materials, capital equipment, medical equipment, etc.) may find themselves with a persistently low exchange rate due to the high demand for foreign currencies. When imports consistently outpace exports, currency depreciation causes creeping inflation. In such a situation, a revaluation of the currency might be necessary to promote continued economic development and growth.

However, just because a country *wants* its currency to be stronger does not mean it is *able* to make it stronger. Revaluation requires a credible central bank that can assure foreign investors that buying its currency, even when higher interest rates are offered, is a safe bet.

Additionally, direct intervention on the forex market requires a central bank to have substantial reserves of foreign currency, which can only be acquired through money earned from exports, or, in the case of countries experiencing financial crises, from development agencies like the IMF, which extends loans to developing countries to help them stabilise the value of their currencies on forex markets. In other words, as much as a managed exchange rate might help poor countries achieve their development objectives, it is poor countries with few exports that will have the toughest time establishing a successful managed exchange rate regime due to their lack of foreign exchange reserves.

Volatility

Wide swings in currency values make doing business much more difficult, especially for those who import or export on a regular basis. With this in mind, developing countries often seek to peg their currency to a large trading partner. In extraordinary circumstances of great volatility, a rescue of the currency is required. Typically administered by the IMF, these rescue plans can come with significant conditions that may dictate the management of domestic fiscal policy.

Practice exam questions

Paper 1 questions

Part (a) questions

1. Explain three factors that might lead to a decrease in demand for a country's currency. (10 marks)
2. Explain three factors that might lead to a decrease in supply of a country's currency. (10 marks)
3. Explain two methods a central bank might use to revalue its currency. (10 marks)

Part (b) questions

1. Using real-world examples, discuss the consequences of the depreciation of a country's currency. (15 marks)
2. Using real-world examples, discuss the consequences of an appreciation of a country's currency. (15 marks)
3. Using real-world examples, evaluate the effect of using fixed exchange rates on a country's economic well-being. (15 marks)

Paper 2 and Paper 3 questions

The chart below shows the euro exchange rate in dollars ($/€) from 2014 to 2016. Use the chart to answer the questions that follow.

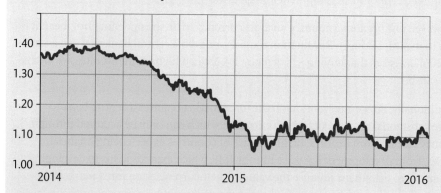

1. Calculate the euro per dollar exchange rate:
   - at the beginning of 2014 (when €1 = $1.4)   (1 mark)
   - at the beginning of 2015 (when €1 = $1.05).   (1 mark)
2. Using economic terminology, describe what happened to the exchange rates of the euro against the dollar and the dollar against the euro between 2014 and 2016.   (2 marks)
3. Outline two possible causes for the change you described in question (2).   (4 marks)
4. Using a forex market diagram for the euro in the United States, illustrate the effect of one of the causes you described in question (3). Use values from the chart to label the equilibrium exchange rates on your graph before and after the change.   (4 marks)
5. Using information from the text/data and your knowledge of economics, discuss the possible consequences for eurozone economies of the change in the euro's value between 2014 and 2016.   (15 marks)

Assume that the exchange rate for British pounds and USD is 1.60 USD per GBP.

1. Calculate the value in GBP for 1 USD.   (2 marks)
2. From the information given above, calculate how many pounds would be received in exchange for 1,200 USD.   (2 marks)
3. Calculate in USD the price of a Manchester United football jersey that costs 45 GBP.   (2 marks)
4. Assume that large pack of US writing pens costs 10 GBP. A change in the exchange rate raises their price to 11 GBP. Calculate the value of the new USD per GBP exchange rate.   (2 marks)

More Paper 2 and Paper 3 questions

1. Last year, Japan could import athletic jerseys from China costing ¥60 (yuan, China's currency), which cost 720 JPY (yen, Japan's currency) at current exchange rates. Now the same ¥60 jersey costs 780 JPY. What is the current exchange rate?   (2 marks)

2. Distinguish between currency appreciation and currency revaluation. (4 marks)

3. Using an appropriate diagram, illustrate the effect of an increase in domestic interest rates on the value of the Japanese yen on the forex market in the United States, assuming all else is held constant. (4 marks)

Paper 1, part (b) questions

1. Discuss the consequences of a currency appreciation for various stakeholders in an economy. (15 marks)

2. Evaluate the decision by a country's central bank to go from a floating exchange rate to a fixed exchange rate, and in doing so devaluing its currency on the foreign exchange market. (15 marks)

Balance of payments

26

26.1 What is a nation's balance of payments?

Learning outcomes

At the end of this section you will be able to:

- explain the role of the balance of payments
- distinguish between **debit items** and **credit items** in the balance of payments
- distinguish between a surplus and a credit on an account.

When you hear the word 'balance' what do you imagine? A scale in an old fashioned spice store, perhaps, with an even amount of spice on both sides, teetering over its fulcrum, gently swaying from side to side. Add just a pinch of spice to one side, and the scale becomes unbalanced.

As one side of a balance scale rises the other side falls. So it is with the components of an economy's balance of payments

Now imagine a scale of massive proportions, one so large that it could hold all the goods and money that flow into and out of a country as it trades with other countries. On one side of the scale would be the goods a country *exports*, the money its overseas residents send home, money invested by foreigners in its domestic assets, and other inflows of foreign spending or investment. On the other side would be the goods it imports and the money that flows out of the country for investments abroad. The scale that measures the flows of goods, services, and financial and real capital between a country and all other countries has a name, it is called the *balance of payments*.

One side of the scale representing a nation's balance of payments measures the *credit items*, or money that flows *into the economy* because of international trade and investment. The other side of the scale measures *debit items*, or money that flows *out of the economy* through international trade and investments. If credits and debits are equal in one of the accounts included in the balance of payments, then a country has a *zero balance* in that account. If credits exceed debits within an account measured by the balance of payments, then the country has a *surplus* in that account. And, finally, if debits exceed credits in any account, then a *deficit* exists.

A scale is used by spice traders to assure that an accurate measurement of how much spice is being sold can be determined in order to assure that the customer pays the correct amount. If a scale were imbalanced in the favour of the seller, then she would earn more money than the value of the spices being sold. If imbalanced in favour of the buyer, then the trader would receive an amount of money lower than the value of the spices sold. Likewise, whole economies can experience imbalances in the accounts included in their balance of payments, in which more money flows into or out of a country through either trade in goods and services, income transfers, **capital transfers**, or international investment. Surpluses and deficits in the different accounts of balance of payments have consequences that we will explore in detail within this chapter.

First, we must look more closely at each of the *accounts* that are included in a country's balance of payments. These are the components of the scale that measures all the international transactions a country can possibly engage in with other countries. Within each of the accounts, we will break down the different transactions and indicate whether they result in a credit (which moves the account towards surplus) or a debit (which moves the account towards deficit).

26.2 What are the components of the balance of payments?

Learning outcomes

At the end of this section you will be able to:

- explain the four components of the current account, specifically the **balance of trade in goods**, the **balance of trade in services**, income and **current transfers**
- calculate elements of the balance of payments from a set of data
- distinguish between a current account deficit and a current account surplus
- explain the two components of the **capital account**, specifically capital transfers and transactions in **non-produced, non-financial assets**
- explain the three main components of the financial account, specifically: direct investment, **portfolio investment**, and **reserve assets**.

A nation's balance of payments measures all the international exchanges it engages in with other countries in three separate accounts.

- The *current account* measures the balance of trade in goods and services and the flow of income between a nation and all other nations. It also records monetary gifts or grants that flow into or out of a country.
- The *capital account* measures the transfer of ownership of capital goods between a nation and all other nations and the transfer of ownership of non-produced, non-financial assets.
- The *financial account* measures the flow of funds for investment in real assets (such as factories or office buildings) or financial assets (such as stocks and bonds) between a nation and the rest of the world. The financial account also measures official borrowing and the official reserves of foreign currencies held at a country's central bank.

How do you calculate the elements of the balance of payments?

The balance of payments is the sum of the three accounts included in it. In other words, when we add the current account balance, the capital account balance, and the financial account balances together we arrive at the balance of payments.

Current account + capital account + financial account = balance of payments

The balance of payments will always equal zero; in other words, our metaphorical scale must be balanced. This means that if we know the value of any two of the accounts, we can calculate the value of the third account.

Worked example 26.1

Assume that the fictional country of Cranville currently has international balances as follows:

Current account balance = −$55 billion

Capital account balance = −$2.5 billion

Financial account balance = _____

We are not given Cranville's financial account balance, but it can be calculated by plugging it into our balance of payments equation:

Current account (− $55 billion) + capital account (−$2.5 billion) + financial account (?) = balance of payments ($0)

−$55 billion − $2.5 billion = −(financial account)

−$57.5 billion = −(financial account)

Financial account = $57.5 billion

Cranville's financial account balance is $57.5 billion, calculated by determining the size of the surplus necessary to offset the combined deficits in the current and capital accounts.

Throughout the rest of this chapter we will use a hypothetical model of New Zealand's balance of payments as an example of how flows into and out of a country through trade and investment affect the different accounts in the balance of payments.

Figure 26.1 provides an overview of the credits and debits that may occur in each of New Zealand's balance of payments accounts.

A green arrow in Figure 26.1 represents a *credit* in New Zealand's balance of payments, or money flowing into the economy because of international trade and investment. A red arrow represents a *debit*, or money flowing out. The balance of payments must always have a total balance of *zero*. This means that the money flowing into New Zealand is equal to the money flowing out. This does not mean that each of the accounts is always balanced, however.

For instance, in a given year, New Zealand's balance in its current account could be negative (meaning the country has spent more on imports than it earned from exports); therefore, the balance in the financial and capital accounts must be positive.

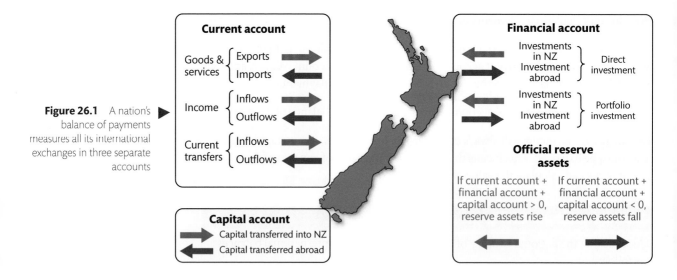

Figure 26.1 A nation's balance of payments measures all its international exchanges in three separate accounts

The reason for this is simple. Every dollar New Zealanders spend on foreign goods and services ultimately ends up being spent again on something from New Zealand or held as an asset by foreign countries with which New Zealand has a trade imbalance.

What is measured in the current account?

A nation's current account has four components measuring transactions between the residents of one nation and the residents of all other nations. The account measures the flow of goods, the flow of services, the flow of income (also called remittances), and the flow of transfers.

Sometimes a nation's current account balance is referred to as the *balance of trade* because it records the transactions involving goods and services actually produced by workers in one country and sold to or bought from consumers in another country. To be clear, however, the balance of trade only includes two of the four components: the flow of goods and services.

If the sum of the four components of the current account is greater than zero, then a nation has a *current account surplus*, which means the total income from remittances into the country and foreign spending on domestic output is greater than remittances out of the country and spending on foreign-produced goods and services. On the other hand, a current account deficit results when the amount that residents of a nation spend on imported goods and services and send overseas as income remittances is greater than foreign spending on exports and remittances from abroad.

Balance of trade in goods

The balance of trade in goods measures the spending by consumers and firms in one nation on another nation's goods (both consumer and capital goods) as well as spending by consumers in the rest of the world on the recording nation's goods.

- **Goods credits (+).** Goods exports count as a credit in the current account because they require that foreigners make payments to the exporting nation. Exports, as a component of aggregate demand (AD), also contribute to employment and output of a nation. However, the level of exports depends primarily on economic conditions abroad, such as foreign incomes and growth in foreign consumer and capital markets. Note that the export of both consumer and capital goods counts as a credit in the current account.

- **Goods debits (−).** Spending by domestic consumers on goods produced in foreign nations counts as a debit in the current account, since it requires a payment to foreign producers. Spending on imports subtracts from domestic AD, since it is a leakage of national income from the importing nation. The main determinant of imports is the level of income of domestic households; as incomes rise, domestic consumers and firms spend more on both imported consumer and capital goods, as well as on domestic output.

Balance of trade in services

Services refer to non-tangible purchases such as tourism, banking, consulting, legal services, and transportation. Services can be imported and exported, although there is no physical movement of a product involved. Many services can be bought and sold remotely thanks to the high-speed communication made possible by broadband internet.

- **Services credits (+).** Services bought by foreigners, either within the nation or from abroad, count as a credit in the current account, since they require that a foreign consumer makes a payment to a domestic producer. Earnings from the tourist industry in Thailand are a credit in Thailand's current account because foreigners are spending on transport, accommodation, entertainment and leisure services within Thailand. On the other hand, an X-ray examination of a patient in the US analysed overnight by a medical student in Mumbai, India, is a service export for India that did not require the presence of a foreign consumer within India's borders.
- **Services debits (−).** Services purchased from foreigners and consumed by domestic households are a debit in the current account because they require a payment to a foreign producer. The spending by a German tourist travelling in Thailand and spending income earned in Germany on Thai services, counts as a debit in Germany's current account. The Chicago hospital that outsources its X-ray analysis to India has imported the service from India, so the US experiences a debit in its current account.

The term 'balance of trade' usually refers to a nation's goods and services balance in the current account. However, these are not the only flows that are measured in this account.

Income

When citizens of one country earn income from activities in another country, the transfer of income back to the income earners' country of origin is also measured in the current account. This includes the wage income earned by a country's citizens from employment by foreign companies abroad.

For instance, an American teacher working at an international school in Germany may send home a portion of his or her wages to the USA; this would be measured in both the USA and Germany's current accounts. Income also refers to investment income, such as interest and dividends earned on investments in foreign bonds or stocks. If a British citizen living in the UK has a savings account in a Swiss bank, the interest earned on his savings counts as a credit for the UK current account and a debit for Switzerland's.

- **Income credits (+).** This includes wages earned by a country's workers employed abroad which are sent home, interest on a country's residents' savings and investments in foreign banks and financial markets, and dividends earned abroad from domestic investors purchasing stocks in foreign firms. Each of these transactions requires that foreigners make payments to residents in the country in question, so they are counted as a credit in that country's current account.
- **Income debits (−).** Wages that are paid by firms in one country to foreign workers in that country and which are then sent abroad count as a debit in the current account. In addition, interest paid to foreign savers in domestic banks and dividends paid to foreign shareholders in a domestic company are all considered 'leakages' and therefore are counted as a negative (debit) in the current account.

Current transfers

A transfer refers to a payment made from one nation to another that is not in exchange for any good or service, such as a gift or a grant. New Zealand's central bank explains why such monetary, non-production transfers are measured in the balance of payments: 'Current transfers directly affect the level of disposable income and influence the consumption of goods and services for the donor and the recipient economies.'

Transfers are divided into two categories: official transfers are payments from one government to another, sometimes known as 'aid'. Private transfers are payments made by citizens of one country to residents of any other country.

Current transfers can be recorded as either a credit or a debit in the current account.

- **Transfer credits (+).** Official and private transfers from foreign governments or households to the government or individuals in a country count as a credit in the current account. All such transfers require a payment from foreigners to domestic stakeholders, increasing the level of disposable income at home and reducing it in the foreign country.
- **Transfer debits (+).** Official and private transfers by the government or individuals within a nation to foreign governments or households count as a debit in the current account. Both transfers require a payment from domestic stakeholders to interests abroad, and increase disposable income abroad while reducing it at home.

To calculate the components of the current account for New Zealand, we must add together the credits (+) and debits (−) for each of the sub-accounts in the current account. Table 26.1 shows hypothetical values for New Zealand's current account, expressed in New Zealand dollars (NZD).

New Zealand has a current account balance of 4.5 billion NZD, meaning the country's current account is in *deficit*. By examining the credits and debits in the sub-accounts we can see why the country has a deficit.

- While it spends more money on imported goods than it earns from its exports, the country actually earns more from service exports than it spends, giving New Zealand a combined trade balance of 1 billion NZD (the −$1 billion goods balance plus the $2 billion services balance).

Table 26.1 Current Account Balance by Category, New Zealand

Sub-account	Credits / millions of NZD	Debits / millions of NZD	Balance / millions of NZD
goods	30,000	−31,000	−1,000
services	12,000	−10,000	2,000
income	3,000	−8,700	−5,700
transfers	1,300	−1,100	200
Total:	+46,300	−50,800	−4,500

- Income transfers out of New Zealand by foreigners to other countries far outweigh income flowing back to the country from abroad, giving New Zealand a −3 billion NZD income balance.
- The transfer balance is positive, although very small relative to the other sub-accounts, with 200 million NZD more being transferred to New Zealand than to other countries from New Zealand.

On the whole, New Zealand has a current account deficit of 4.5 billion NZD, meaning there are more New Zealand dollars flowing out of the country for trade, income, and current transfers than foreign exchange flowing into the country. As we will see, the current account deficit will be made up for through surpluses in the other accounts in New Zealand's balance of payments.

What is measured in the capital account?

The capital account measures the transactions involving ownership of capital, forgiveness of debt, or the acquisition and disposal of non-produced, non-financial assets between a nation and all other nations.

Capital transfers

When a nation's government or private sector gives money to another nation for the purchase of fixed assets or directly donates capital goods to residents of another country, this is recorded as a debit by the donor country and a credit for the recipient country. The capital account does not measure the purchase or sale of capital between nations, rather the actual transfer of fixed assets from one nation to another.

- **Capital transfer credits (+).** If the Canadian government were to make a $2 million donation to the Ministry of Education in Tanzania to build schools in rural areas, the transaction would involve the transfer of money from Canada to Tanzania for the purpose of helping Tanzania acquire fixed assets in the form of new school buildings. Tanzania would record this as a capital account credit.
- **Capital transfer debits (−).** If the US Agency for International Development, USAID, were to finance the construction of a new port facility in Liberia's capital city, Freetown, the money provided would be recorded as a debit for the USA, because it would require transfer of income from the USA to a foreign country

Debt forgiveness

Besides the transfer of cash to acquire new capital or of capital itself, the capital account also measures the forgiveness of debt from lenders in one country to debtors

Video suggestion:
You have read about it, now you can review what you have just learned by watching a video by the author!

Simply click here in your eBook for a video on the current account of the balance of payments.

TOK

Economics as a science generally focuses on positive analysis. That is to say, it examines the world through an objective lens aimed at examining what is, rather than what should be. An example of a positive statement is: New Zealand spent more on imports in 2020 than it sold in exports to the rest of the world.

Normative statements are more subjective in nature, expressing an opinion or arguing for what should be, rather than what is. For instance, it would be a normative statement to say: New Zealand would be better off with greater balance in its current account.

To what extent is it appropriate for economists to make normative statements such as this? Should economics stick to analysis of what is and leave what should be up to politicians and the media? Or is it appropriate for economists to determine what should be based on their analysis of data such as that of a nation's balance of payments?

in another. Debt owed by one nation to a lender in another nation, if forgiven by the lender, counts as a credit for the debtor's nation and a debit for the lender's nation in their capital accounts.

- **Debt forgiveness credit (+).** If the government of Rwanda were to be relieved of its debts on a loan made to the previous government by the African Development Bank, this would be recorded as a credit in Rwanda's capital account.
- **Debt forgiveness debit (−).** If a bank in Switzerland which made a loan to the government of Sierra Leone ten years ago were to decide to forgive the debt still owed by the Sierra Leonean government, the balance owed to the Swiss bank would be measured as a debit for Switzerland.

Transaction in non-produced, non-financial assets

Finally, the capital account measures the flow of non-produced, non-financial assets. This includes the purchase or sale of intangible, non-financial assets, such as patents, copyrights, trademarks, franchises and licences and the acquisition of land by a government or international organisation or the disposal of such land.

- **Non-produced, non-financial assets credit (+).** An American tech company sells the copyright on a 3D printing technology to a Chinese investment firm. Money flows into the US capital account as ownership of the copyright is transferred to China.
- **Non-produced, non-financial asset debit (−).** A Chinese energy company buys the mineral rights to a large off-shore oil field off the coast of Ghana. The money it spends for the rights to this 'non-produced, non-financial' natural resource is a debit for China's capital account.

Table 26.2 shows hypothetical values for New Zealand's capital account, summing the credits and debits of the different sub-accounts.

New Zealand has an 800 million dollar surplus in the capital account of its balance of payments. More money has flowed into the country from the acquisition or disposal of non-produced, non-financial assets than has flowed out of New Zealand.

Table 26.2   Capital account, New Zealand

Account	Credits / millions of NZD	Debits / millions of NZD	Balance
Capital account	1,600	−800	800

What is measured in the financial account?

A nation's financial account measures the exchanges between a nation and the rest of the world that involve ownership of financial and real assets. Foreigners may buy and sell a country's real assets, including real estate, factories, office buildings and other factors of production. Such transactions are recorded in the financial account because they involve the ownership of assets, not the purchase of the nation's output of goods or services. If an office building in Auckland were sold to a Chinese electronics manufacturer, none of New Zealand's output would actually be consumed by China; this explains why such an investment is not measured in the current account. Ownership would be transferred, and there would be a flow of money into New Zealand, moving the country's financial account towards surplus.

In addition to real assets, much of the activity measured in the financial account is the buying and selling of financial assets such as company stocks and government bonds. If an investment bank in New Zealand were to invest in Spanish government bonds, the transaction would require a payment from New Zealand to the government of Spain, but no goods or services would be exchanged, so the transaction is purely financial. Such a bond purchase would be recorded as a credit for Spain and a debit for New Zealand.

The financial account measures two broad types of investment: direct investment and portfolio investment.

Foreign direct investment

Foreign direct investment (FDI) occurs when a foreign firm acquires a significant ownership stake in a domestic business, or vice versa. To be considered FDI a minimum of 10% of a company's shares must be owned by a foreign investor in the domestic economy or by a domestic investor in another nation's economy. Whether direct investment counts as a positive or a negative in the financial account depends on who is buying what.

When investors in the home country buy or sell ownership stakes in foreign firms the following applies.

- **Credits (+).** Domestic investors sell shares in foreign firms, causing an inflow of financial capital, moving the financial account towards the positive.
- **Debits (−).** Domestic investors acquire an ownership stake in foreign companies, causing an outflow of financial capital, moving the financial account towards the negative.

When foreign investors buy or sell ownership stakes in domestic firms the following applies.

- **Credits (+).** Foreign investment in shares of domestic firms increases, causing a net inflow of financial capital, moving the financial account towards the positive.
- **Debits (−).** Foreigners sell their ownership stake in domestic firms to domestic investors, causing an outflow of financial capital, moving the financial account towards the negative.

The dividends and interest income earned from direct investments abroad or paid to foreign investors at home are counted in the income section of the current account of the balance of payments. But the flow of financial capital into or out of a country for the acquisition of ownership of firms as described above is part of the financial account.

Portfolio investment

Portfolio investment consists of small investors buying and selling equity shares of companies abroad as part of their portfolio of assets. It also includes ownership of foreign debt, issued either by governments or private firms. The difference between portfolio investment and FDI is that portfolio investment includes relatively small investments (less than 10% of a foreign company), while larger ownership purchases qualify as FDI.

In addition to stocks, portfolio investment includes the buying and selling of bonds (debt certificates), both public and private. Portfolio investment measures the investments of foreigners in domestic equities and debt and of domestic investors in foreign equities and debt.

Portfolio investment abroad: the money spent by domestic investors on foreign equity and debt counts as an asset to the investor's home country. Since domestic investors own equity or debt in a foreign firm or government, such investment is considered an asset to the home country and a liability to the foreign firm or government.

- **Credits (+).** Domestic investors sell foreign assets, resulting in a payment to the domestic investor, which causes an inflow into the financial account.
- **Debits (−).** Domestic investors buy foreign assets, resulting in a payment to foreign shareholders or bondholders, which causes an outflow from the financial account.

Portfolio investment at home: the money spent by foreigners on domestic stocks, shares and bonds counts as a liability for the home country. Since a share of a domestic firm or government's debt is transferred to a foreign stakeholder, such investment is considered a liability to the home country, an asset to foreigners.

- **Credits (+).** A foreign investor buys domestic stocks and bonds, resulting in a payment to the home country, creating a positive entry in the financial account.
- **Debits (−).** A foreign investor sells domestic stocks and bonds back to a domestic investor, resulting in a payment to the foreign investor, creating an outflow in the financial account.

Just as the profit income earned from direct investment is measured in the current account, so are the interest and dividend incomes earned from portfolio investments. However, the financial flows involved in the acquisition of private and public securities and debt are not considered income, so they are measured by the financial account.

Other investment

Other investment includes loans made by banks to foreign borrowers or money saved in banks across national borders.

Loans from domestic banks to foreign borrowers and savings by domestic households in foreign banks count as assets for the home country, since foreign interests owe money to domestic interests.

- **Credits (+).** A foreign borrower pays back a loan to a domestic bank, resulting in a payment from abroad into the country's financial account.
- **Debits (−).** A domestic bank makes a loan to a foreign borrower, resulting in money flowing out of the financial account.

Domestic borrowing from foreign banks and foreign savings in domestic banks are considered liabilities for the home nation and an asset for the foreign nation.

- **Credits (+).** A domestic borrower takes out a loan from a foreign bank, resulting in money flowing into the home country's financial account.
- **Debits (−).** A domestic borrower pays back a loan taken from a foreign bank, resulting in money flowing out of the home country's financial account.

As with direct investment and portfolio investment, incomes earned or interest paid from other investments are measured in the current account under income, but the money transferred for a loan or as savings abroad is measured in the financial account.

Reserve assets

Foreign exchange reserves refer to the assets of other nations held by a country's central bank. Reserves consist primarily of foreign financial assets such as government bonds and foreign currency. In a given year, if the flow of money into a country due to its exchanges in the current and financial accounts exceeds the flow of money out of the country, the difference is added to the central bank's official reserves of foreign exchange. If there is a net outflow of money in a year, the difference is made up by a withdrawal from the central bank's reserves of foreign exchange.

Domestic currency held in foreign central banks.

- **Credits (+).** Domestic currency reserves held by foreign central banks increase due to deficits in the home country's current and capital accounts, leading to an accumulation of domestic exchange abroad. An increase in domestic currency held by foreigners counts as a credit in the financial account.
- **Debits (−).** Domestic currency reserves held by foreign central banks decrease due to surpluses in the home country's current and capital accounts, leading to diminished reserves of the domestic currency abroad. A decrease in domestic currency held by foreigners counts as a debit in the financial account.

Foreign currency held in the domestic central bank.

- **Credits (+).** Foreign currency reserves held in the domestic central bank decrease due to a deficit in the current and capital accounts, leading to decreased ownership of foreign assets by the domestic economy.
- **Debits (−).** Foreign currency reserves held in the domestic central bank increase due to a surplus in the current and capital accounts, leading to increased ownership of foreign assets by the domestic economy.

It should be pointed out that, contrary to common sense, a deficit in the current and capital accounts actually results in an inflow (thus, a positive sign) in the official reserves account, since the reserves of foreign currency must be drawn down to finance the current and capital account deficits (since more is being spent than is being earned). On the other hand, if a country has a current account surplus, then the change in foreign exchange reserves is recorded as a negative since the ownership of assets denominated in foreign currencies actually increases.

From an accounting standpoint, running a current account surplus results in a deficit in the financial account, since the accumulation of foreign exchange due to trade creates a liability for the surplus country. A current account deficit, on the other hand, reduces liabilities in the financial account as foreign exchange reserves are drawn down to pay for the excess of imports in the current account.

In addition to financing trade deficits, having reserves of foreign exchange in the central bank allows the government to draw on these reserves to intervene in the market for their nation's currency to influence the exchange rate, as described in Chapter 25, Exchange rates.

Official borrowing

Table 26.3 presents hypothetical figures for New Zealand's financial account, including each of the sub-accounts.

Table 26.3   Financial account balance by category, New Zealand

Sub-account	Credits / millions of NZD	Debits / millions of NZD	Balance / millions of NZD
Direct investment	3,900	−1,300	2,600
Portfolio investment	3,900	−6,600	−2,700
Other investment	1,800	−300	1,500
Reserve assets	4,500	−2,200	2,300
Total	+14,100	−10,400	3,700

On the whole, New Zealand has a surplus in its financial account, meaning more money has flowed into the country for investments in real and financial assets, and its reserve assets held by foreign banks have increased due to its current account deficits for a total financial account balance of 3.7 billion NZD.

Video suggestion:
You have read about it, now you can review what you have just learned by watching a video by the author!

▶ Simply click here in your eBook for a video on the capital and financial accounts of the balance of payments.

26.3 How do the accounts in the balance of payments relate to one another?

Learning outcomes

At the end of this section you will be able to:

- explain that the current account balance is equal to the sum of the capital account and financial account balances
- explain that the overall balance between accounts should be zero
- explain that credits should be matched by debits, and deficits should be matched by surpluses
- examine how the current account and the financial account are interdependent.

Why is there a zero balance in the balance of payments?

America's founding father, Benjamin Franklin, once said, 'A dollar saved is a dollar earned.' The axiom makes sense on an individual level, but it also has some application when considering an economy's balance of payments. Recall, the balance of payments records all transactions between one country and all other countries, including trade in goods and services, income transfers, foreign investment, changes in official reserves, and more.

When we think about Franklin's quote, we can tweak it slightly to apply to a country's balance of payments. 'A dollar *spent* is a dollar earned.' That is right, when a country spends money on foreign goods or invests in foreign assets, it will ultimately earn that money back through increased trade or investment from abroad.

To illustrate, let us look at things from the perspective of the USA. A dollar spent by an American consumer on a foreign good is a dollar earned by a foreign producer. That dollar is an American asset owned by a foreign person or company, and when foreign ownership of American assets increases, it automatically moves America's financial account towards surplus. What has happened to America's balance of payments following a dollar of spending on an import? The current account has moved $1 towards deficit and the financial account has moved $1 towards surplus. Before the foreign person or company even decides what to do with their new $1 of income, the US balance of payments has reached a *zero* balance: −$1 in the current account, +$1 in the financial account.

Of course, our foreign exporter will be unlikely to hold onto his or her newly earned dollar for long. In the short term he or she will convert it to his or her domestic currency at a commercial bank in their country in order to pay his or her workers. The commercial bank will exchange the dollar for domestic currency at the country's central bank, increasing the country's official reserves of foreign exchange (keeping America's financial account in surplus). The central bank might then make that dollar available to importers within its country who wish to buy pharmaceuticals or airplane parts or software from an American firm, which will mean the dollar comes back to the USA in its current account. In such a case, when US exports increase by $1, the US financial account moves back towards deficit and the current account back towards surplus. Overall, the balance of payments remains at zero. A dollar *spent* by the USA is a dollar *earned* by the USA.

Whichever way you start the story, the outcome is going to be the same. Credits are matched by debits and deficits are matched by surpluses. When a Korean electronics manufacturer builds a factory in Vietnam, Korea's financial account is debited (money flows out) and Vietnam's is credited (money flows in). Korea's financial account has moved towards a deficit and Vietnam's towards a surplus. Vietnam now has Korean currency which it can either invest in Korea or buy Korean goods with. If imports from Korea rise, then Korea's current account moves towards a surplus and Vietnam's towards a deficit.

We come back to our scale analogy once again: the balance of payment must always be *balanced*. A deficit in one account is offset by a surplus in the other, and every debit is offset by a credit.

What we discover is that at any given time, every country's balance of payments will have a net balance of *zero*. (In reality, accounting errors will occur and the value reported by each country for its balance of payments may reflect a slight overall surplus or deficit.) Let us put the three accounts in New Zealand's hypothetical balance of payments together to illustrate. Table 26.4 summarises the current account, the capital account, and the financial accounts for New Zealand, adding their balances together to determine the balance of payments.

New Zealand's current account deficit of −4.5 billion NZD means more money is leaving New Zealand through trade and income transfers than is coming into the country. Its capital and financial accounts are in surplus by a combined 4.5 billion

Table 26.4   New Zealand's balance of payments, credits and debits

Balance of Payments account	Credits (+) / millions of NZD	Debits (−) / millions of NZD	Balance
Current account	46,300	−50,800	−4,500
Capital account	1,600	−800	800
Financial account	14,100	−10,400	3,700
Total	+62,000	−62,000	0

Video suggestion:
You have read about it, now you can review what you have just learned by watching a video by the author!

▶ Simply click here in your eBook for a video on the relationship between the accounts in the balance of payments.

NZD, providing the counterbalance to its current account deficit. A dollar spent is a dollar earned for New Zealand. While it spends, transfers, or invests 62 billion NZD in other economies (the combined debits in its three accounts) it earns or receives investments from abroad of the same amount.

The difference between its export income, income transfers, current and capital transfers, and financial investment income from abroad and the size of its current account deficit is made up for by foreign holding of New Zealand dollars as official reserves; which again, count as a credit in New Zealand's financial account since NZD are an asset of the country held abroad.

26.4 HL What is the relationship between the current account and the exchange rate?

Learning outcomes

At the end of this section you will be able to:

- explain why a deficit (surplus) in the current account of the balance of payments may result in downward (upward) pressure on the exchange rate of the currency
- use an exchange rate diagram to show the relationship between the current account balance and the exchange rate.

In Chapter 25, Exchange rates, you learned the determinants of exchange rates, one of which is the demand for a country's exports relative to the demand for imports from other countries. With this in mind, let us examine the likely effects of a current account deficit on a nation's currency's exchange rate.

When households and firms in one nation demand more of other countries' output than the rest of the world demands of theirs, there is upward pressure on the value of trading partners' currencies and downward pressure on the importing nation's currency. In this way, a movement towards a current account deficit should cause a country's currency to weaken.

Figure 26.2 shows the effect on the Korean won (KRW, ₩) and the Vietnamese dong (VND, ₫) of an increase in exports from Korea to Vietnam, which results in a deficit in Vietnam's current account and a surplus in Korea's current account.

As Korea moves towards a current account surplus, the won appreciates. As Vietnam moves towards a deficit, the dong depreciates. The stronger won results from increased demand for Korean exports in Vietnam, and the weaker dong results from the increased supply of dong in Korea.

All else equal, when the current account balance moves towards (or further into) deficit, a country's currency will depreciate on forex markets. A move towards (or further into) current account surplus causes the currency to appreciate.

In the long run, the depreciation resulting from a current account deficit should be self-correcting, slowing the move into deficit and helping restore balance in the current account. Consider our Vietnam/Korea example again. As the dong depreciates due to

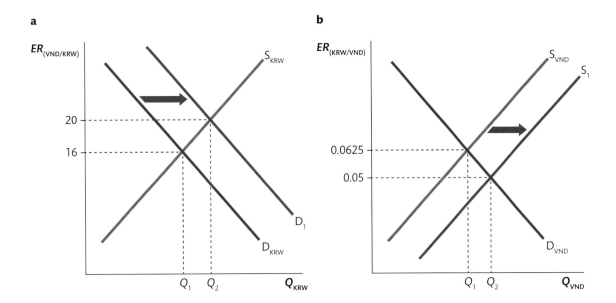

a

ER(VND/KRW)

b

ER(KRW/VND)

increased demand for Korean goods in Vietnam, Korean goods start to become more and more expensive to Vietnamese households (since their currency buys less won than before). The simple law of demand will lead Vietnamese consumers to begin demanding fewer Korean goods as the dong depreciates, and over time Vietnam's current account deficit will move back towards surplus.

From the perspective of Korea, the move towards surplus caused the won to appreciate, which over time will make Vietnamese goods more attractive to Korean consumers, leading them to import more from Vietnam. In other words, the metaphorical scale representing the current account, once tipped into deficit or surplus, will right itself over time due to the effect of exchange rate appreciation or depreciation.

As we learned in Chapter 26, Exchange rates, not all countries have floating exchange rate systems (in fact, about half the countries in the world have managed or fixed exchange rates). When currencies are not allowed to float on forex markets, the self-correcting mechanism described here is less likely to occur, since a currency that is *devalued* will not appreciate when a current account surplus arises, and an artificially strong currency cannot depreciate to correct a deficit. Therefore, countries with fixed or managed exchange rate systems are more likely to experience *persistent imbalances in their current and financial accounts.*

▲

Figure 26.2 A surplus in Korea's current account would strengthen the won (a), while a Vietnamese **current account deficit** would weaken the dong (b)

Video suggestion:
You have read about it, now you can review what you have just learned by watching a video by the author!
 Simply click here in your eBook for a video on the relationship between the current account and the exchange rate.

26.5 ⬛HL⬛ What is the relationship between the financial account and the exchange rate?

Learning outcome

At the end of this section you will be able to:

- explain why a surplus (deficit) in the financial account of the balance of payments may result in downward (upward) pressure on the exchange rate of the currency.

All else equal, as a country's ownership of foreign assets increases, its financial account moves towards deficit and its currency depreciates. Consider an example: A Switzerland-based investment bank wishes to invest in a Hong Kong-based real estate company, and so it acquires a 25% ownership stake in the Hong Kong firm. The FDI from Switzerland into Hong Kong moves the Swiss financial account towards deficit: essentially Switzerland is 'importing' ownership shares of a foreign company.

Investment funds flow out of Switzerland, exerting downward pressure on the Swiss franc. In Hong Kong, investment funds flow into the country, exerting upward pressure on the exchange rate of the Hong Kong dollar. Hong Kong's financial account moves towards surplus.

While we do not use the terms 'export' and 'import' when referring to financial investments, one useful way to think about financial account flows is that foreign investment into a country's domestic firms amounts to 'exporting' ownership shares of a domestic firm. Since exports count as a credit, the financial account moves towards surplus when foreign investors buy shares in domestic firms.

In the forex markets, the capital inflow in Hong Kong causes the Hong Kong dollar to appreciate, adversely affecting the current account as Hong Kong's exports to Switzerland become less competitive due to the stronger currency. The financial account surplus is therefore countered by a current account deficit.

In summary, a capital inflow moves the financial account into surplus and causes the currency to appreciate, while a capital outflow has the opposite effect. Under managed or fixed exchange rate systems, these adjustments do not occur, therefore persistent imbalances in the financial and current accounts are more likely to result.

26.6 HL What are the implications of persistent current account deficits?

Learning outcome

At the end of this section you will be able to:

- discuss the implications of a persistent current account deficit, referring to factors including foreign ownership of domestic assets, exchange rates, interest rates, indebtedness, international credit ratings, and demand management.

We have hinted repeatedly at the likelihood that under managed or fixed exchange rate systems, the self-adjusting mechanism of exchange rate appreciation and depreciation described in the above sections does not occur, therefore *persistent imbalances* in the balance of payments are likely to arise. A persistent current account deficit is experienced when year after year the debits in a country's current account exceed the credits. The most likely cause of persistent current account deficits is that a country spends more on imports than it earns from the sale of exports, although it is also possible that income outflows are greater than income inflows (as was the case with New Zealand earlier in this chapter).

Persistent trade deficits have implications for countries. We have already outlined the effect on the exchange rate (a weaker currency), but the consequences can go much further than exerting downward pressure on the currency.

The effect on interest rates

A persistent deficit in the current account can have adverse effects on the interest rates and investment in the deficit country. A current account deficit can put downward pressure on a nation's exchange rate, which causes inflation in the deficit country because imported goods, services and raw materials become more expensive. In order to prevent sustained currency depreciation, the country's central bank may be forced to tighten the money supply and raise domestic interest rates to attract foreign investors and keep demand for the currency and the exchange rate stable.

Additionally, since a current account deficit must be offset by a financial account surplus, the deficit country's government may need to offer higher interest rates on government bonds to attract foreign investors. Higher borrowing rates for the government and the private sector can slow domestic investment and economic growth in the deficit nation.

Trade deficits may drive up interest rates as central banks take measures to slow the inflationary effects of the weaker currency. Higher interest rates attract foreign capital inflows, but also slow domestic investment and economic growth.

The effect on foreign ownership of domestic assets

By definition, the balance of payments must always equal zero. For this reason, a deficit in the current account must be offset by a surplus in the capital and financial accounts. If the money spent by a deficit country on goods from abroad does not end up returning to the deficit country for the purchase of goods and services, it will be re-invested into that country through foreign acquisition of domestic real and financial assets, or held in reserve by surplus nations' central banks.

Essentially, a country with a large current account deficit cannot export enough goods and services to make up for its spending on imports. Instead, it ends up 'exporting ownership' of its financial and real assets. This could take the form of FDI in domestic firms, increased portfolio investment by foreigners in the domestic economy, and foreign ownership of domestic government debt, or the build-up of foreign reserves of the deficit nation's currency.

While it is not necessarily a *bad thing* for foreign investors to own domestic assets, some stakeholders may worry about the threat to domestic economic sovereignty and control that increased foreign ownership of the economy's factors of production (land and capital) poses.

The effect on the country's debt level

One source of credits in the financial account is foreign ownership of domestic government bonds (i.e. debt). When a central bank from another nation buys government bonds from a nation with which it has a large current account surplus, the deficit nation is essentially going into debt to the surplus nation.

In September 2020 the US national debt stood at $26 trillion; of that around 40% was held by foreigners, meaning that the interest payments that the US government pays on that debt 'leak' from America's circular flow, and represent a transfer of income from the American taxpayer to foreign owners of America's debt. Why do foreigners own so much of the US national debt? Simple: the USA is a country that runs persistent current account deficits, meaning hundreds of billions of dollars are earned by foreigners each year that are not spent on US exports. This money represents a credit in America's financial account, but rather than holding the dollars as cash, foreign investors prefer to put them in interest-earning assets from the USA, specifically US government bonds.

On the one hand, foreign lending to a deficit nation benefits the deficit nation because it keeps demand for government bonds high and therefore allows the deficit country's government to finance budget deficits without raising taxes on domestic households and firms. On the other hand, every dollar borrowed from a foreigner has to be repaid with interest. Interest payments on the national debt were $240 billion in 2014, or 1.3% of gross domestic product (GDP), but they are expected to rise to $800 billion by 2024, or 3% of GDP. With 40% of the country's debt held overseas, this means that over 1% of the national income could be transferred to foreign bondholders by 2024, representing a significant leakage in spending power from the American economy.

In other words, current account deficits do not come cheap. The resulting financial account surpluses mean foreigners own a larger share of the domestic economy's assets, including debt, and a meaningful share of national income must be transferred overseas each year.

The effect on the country's credit rating

A large current account deficit requires a nation to run a financial account surplus. As explained above, a surplus in the financial account may consist of foreign ownership of the deficit nation's government debt. Over time, budget deficits financed through foreign borrowing reduce the attractiveness of the deficit country's government bonds to foreign investors, harming its international credit rating, forcing the government to offer ever increasing interest rates to foreign lenders.

The effect on the country's ability to manage domestic AD

Owing to the negative consequences arising from persistent current account deficits outlined above, government and central bank policymakers might find themselves distracted in their efforts to reduce deficits in the current account from the pursuit of the other macroeconomic objectives of full employment, price level stability, and economic growth. Later in the chapter we will outline methods that can be used to correct a current account deficit, and we'll see that some of these include fiscal and monetary policies that once enacted might have undesirable effects on domestic AD.

The effect on economic growth

Deficits in the current account mean there is more spending on foreign goods and/ or income transfers abroad than there is spending on domestic output or income transfers into the economy. The less income and spending there is at home relative to overseas, the slower the rate of economic growth, due to weaker AD. On the other hand, the financial account surpluses that arise when a country has persistent current account deficits might mean increased international investment, which could have a positive supply-side effect in the economy. Therefore, it is not necessarily the case that deficits in the current account will slow economic growth, but they do limit the extent to which AD can keep up with aggregate supply.

TOK

Some argue that personal debt is higher in countries with higher levels of national debt because the government sets an example for the nation's households. If a government accumulates large amounts of foreign debt, are individuals in society more likely to accumulate debt themselves? To what extent is the behaviour of individuals in society modelled after the behaviour of the government?

26.7 `HL` What methods can be used to correct a persistent current account deficit?

Learning objectives

At the end of this section you will be able to:

- explain the methods that a government can use to correct a persistent current account deficit, including expenditure-switching policies, **expenditure-reducing** policies and supply-side policies, to increase competitiveness
- evaluate the effectiveness of the policies to correct a persistent current account deficit.

The existence of a persistent current account deficit can have many detrimental effects on a nation's economy. For this reason, a government or central bank may find it necessary to intervene to promote greater balance in the nation's current account. At the very least, reducing a current account deficit promotes domestic employment as it leads to an increase in the nation's net exports, meaning more demand for the nation's output and a reduction in unemployment.

Expenditure-switching policies

Any policy by a government aimed at reducing domestic spending on imports and increasing spending on domestically produced goods and services is known as an expenditure-switching policy. Such policies could also be called protectionist since essentially they are aimed at reducing demand for imports and increasing domestic employment, albeit in the name of promoting a balanced current account.

Exchange rate manipulation

As you know, it is possible for governments and central banks to intervene in foreign exchange markets to manipulate the value of their own currency relative to their trading partners (Chapter 25). A central bank may supply a greater quantity of its own currency on forex markets by demanding more of other currencies so as to devalue its currency and make imports less attractive to domestic consumers. Alternatively, it may lower domestic interest rates to make foreign investment less appealing, reducing demand for its currency and lowering the exchange rate.

Either of these policies will make imports more expensive to domestic households, who will switch their expenditures to domestically produced goods and services. Likewise, foreign consumers will find the nation's output more affordable.

Protectionism

Another method for switching expenditures from imports to domestically produced output is to increase the barriers to trade with other nations. Import tariffs or quotas, or subsidies to domestic producers will all make domestically produced goods more attractive to consumers at home and reduce demand for imports.

In the short run, net exports may rise and the current account move towards surplus, but in the long run, such policies promote inefficiency among domestic producers who enjoy artificially high prices due to government protection. Over time, the comparative advantage of foreign producers is likely to increase as domestic firms can get away with being productively inefficient. Instead of focusing on efficiency, domestic producers have strong incentives to devote resources to preserving or expanding protectionist laws. In the meantime, foreign producers grow stronger and more efficient by competing in the world market. Protectionism leads only to a misallocation of resources and ultimately the costs it imposes on society are greater than the benefits it brings.

Expenditure-reducing policies

A second set of policies available to governments hoping to reduce a current account deficit involves the reduction of overall expenditures by firms and households in the nation. This reduces spending on imports and thus restores balance in the current account. Clearly, expenditure-reducing policies have adverse effects on domestic output and employment, and are thus not desirable except as a last resort.

Contractionary fiscal policies

Raising taxes on domestic households and firms reduces disposable income and reduces overall AD, including demand for imports. Reductions in government spending would also reduce disposable incomes and overall AD in the nation. In addition, the fall in import demand, the lower rate of inflation (or, if the decline in AD is great enough, the deflation) that occur as a result of contractionary policies actually make the country's exports more attractive to foreign consumers, further improving the current account deficit.

Contractionary monetary policies

Another means of reducing overall demand for imports in a nation is to raise interest rates to discourage consumption of imported durable goods (financed by borrowing) and firms' investment in imported capital goods. Higher interest rates also have a disinflationary (or deflationary) effect, making the nation's exports more attractive to foreign consumers. On the other hand, higher interest rates may attract foreign investors, shifting the nation's financial account further towards surplus and appreciating the currency as foreign demand for domestic assets rises. This could have the opposite effect of that intended by the central bank, as a stronger currency might make imports even more attractive, offsetting any improvement in the current account achieved by reducing consumption of durable goods and investment in foreign capital goods.

Supply-side policies

Contractionary fiscal and monetary policies will surely reduce overall demand in an economy and thereby help reduce a current account deficit. But the costs of such policies are likely to outweigh the benefits, as domestic employment, output and economic growth suffer due to reduced spending on the nation's goods and services. A better option for governments worried about their trade deficit is to pursue supply-side policies that increase the competitiveness of domestic producers in the global economy.

In the long run, the best way for a nation to reduce a current account deficit is to allocate its scarce resources towards the economic activities in which it can most effectively compete in the global economy. In an environment of increasingly free trade between nations, countries like the USA and those of Western Europe will continue to confront structural shifts in their economies that at first seem devastating. However, over time, such shifts are likely to be seen as both inevitable and beneficial to the overall level of efficiency and welfare in the global economy.

The automobile industry in the USA has changed forever due to competition from Japan. The textile industry in Europe long since passed its apex of production, and the UK consumer will probably never again buy a TV or computer monitor made in the UK. The reality is, much of the world's manufactured goods can and should be made more cheaply and efficiently in Asia and Latin America than they ever could be in the US or Europe.

The question Europe and the USA should be asking, therefore, is not 'How can we get back what we have lost and restore balance in our current account?' but 'What can we provide for the world that no one else can?' By focusing their resources towards providing the goods and services that no Asian or Latin American competitor is capable of providing, the deficit countries of the world should be able to reduce their current account deficits and at the same time stimulate AD at home, while increasing the productivity of the nation's resources and promoting long-run economic growth.

That may be easy to say, and it is fair to ask 'How can they achieve this?' This is where supply-side policies come in. Smart supply-side policies mean more than tax cuts for corporations and subsidies to domestic producers. Smart supply-side policies that would promote more balanced global trade and long-run economic growth include the following.

Investments in education and healthcare

Nothing makes a nation more competitive in the global economy than a highly educated and healthy workforce. Exports from Europe and the USA will increasingly come from the highly skilled service sector and less and less from the manufacturing sector. Highly educated and skilled workers are needed for future economic growth and global competitiveness, particularly in scientific fields such as engineering, medicine, finance, economics, and business.

Public funding for scientific research and development

Exports from the USA and Europe have increasingly depended on scientific innovation and new technologies. Copyright and patent protection ensure that scientific breakthroughs achieved in one country are allowed a period of time during which only that country can enjoy the sales of exports in the new field. Green energy, nano-technology, and biomedical research are emerging technologies that require sustained commitments from the government sector for dependable funding.

Investments in modern transportation and communication infrastructure

To remain competitive in the global economy, the countries of Europe and North America must ensure that domestic firms have at their disposal the most modern and efficient transport and communication infrastructure available. High-speed rail, well-maintained inter-state or international highways, modern port facilities, high-speed internet and telecommunications; these investments allow for lower costs of production and more productive capital and labour, making these countries' goods more competitive in the global marketplace.

What are the benefits of reducing a current account deficit?

Reducing a current account deficit will have many benefits for a nation like the USA, Spain, the UK or Australia. A stronger currency ensures price stability, low interest rates allow for economic growth, and perhaps most importantly, less taxpayer money has to be paid in interest to foreign creditors. Governments and central banks may go about reducing a current account deficit in many ways: exchange rate controls, protectionism, contractionary monetary and fiscal policies, or supply-side policies may all be implemented to restore balance in the current account. Only one of these options promotes long-run economic growth and increases the efficiency with which a nation employs its scarce factors of production.

Supply-side policies are clearly the most efficient and economically justifiable method for correcting a current account deficit. Unfortunately, they are also the least politically popular, since the benefits of such policies are not realised in the short run, but take years, maybe decades, to accrue. For this reason, time and time again governments turn to protectionism in response to rising trade deficits.

26.8　HL　Does currency depreciation always reduce a trade deficit?

Learning objectives

At the end of this section you will be able to:

- state the **Marshall–Lerner condition** and apply it to explain the effects of depreciation/devaluation
- explain the **J-curve** effect, with reference to the Marshall–Lerner condition.

When a nation runs a persistent deficit in its current account it should put downward pressure on the country's exchange rate. In a system of floating exchange rates, such fluctuations between the currencies of deficit and surplus countries should correct the imbalances by altering relative prices of imports and exports in a way that moves both deficit and surplus countries towards a more balanced current account. However, such shifts do not always occur.

The Marshall–Lerner condition

Whether or not depreciation of a nation's currency reduces a trade deficit depends on the combined price elasticity of demand (PED) for imports and exports. If $PED_X + PED_M > 1$, then depreciation in the currency will move a country's current account towards surplus. This is known as the Marshall–Lerner condition (MLC).

If the MLC is not met, then depreciation of a nation's currency will worsen a country's current account deficit.

Common sense might indicate that if a country's currency depreciates relative to other currencies, this should lead to an improvement in the country's balance of trade. For Country Z whose currency is the dollar, the reasoning is as follows.

- A weaker dollar means foreigners have to give up less of their money in order to get one dollar's worth of Country Z's output.
- At the same time, since Country Z's dollar is worth less in foreign currency, imports become more expensive, as Country Z's residents have to spend more dollars for a certain amount of another country's output; hence, imports should decrease.
- The decrease in imports and increase in exports should reduce Country Z's current account deficit.

Fewer imports and more exports should mean an improvement in the country's balance of trade, but this is not necessarily the case. What matters is not whether a country is importing less and exporting more, but whether the increase in revenues from exports exceeds the decrease in expenditures on imports. Here is where the MLC can be applied.

The following is an example of a situation in which the MLC is met and depreciation of Country Z's dollar results in an improvement in the current account.

- Import spending exceeds export revenues in Country Z, causing depreciation of Country Z's dollar.
- If foreigners' demand for Country Z's exports is relatively elastic, then a slightly weaker dollar should cause a proportionally larger increase in foreign demand for Country Z's output, causing export revenues in Country Z to rise.
- Likewise, if Country Z's residents' demand for imports is relatively elastic, then a slightly weaker dollar should cause their demand for imports to decrease proportionally more than the increase in price of those imports, reducing overall expenditures on imports.
- If the combined **elasticity of demand for exports and imports** is elastic (i.e. the coefficient is greater than 1), then depreciation of Country Z's currency will shift its current account towards surplus. In this case, the MLC is met.

So, what if the MLC is not met? Demand for exports and imports may not always be so responsive to changes in prices brought on by changes in exchange rates. Imagine a scenario in which a weaker dollar does little to change foreign demand for Country Z's output. In this case, income from exports may actually decline (since it now takes fewer units of foreign currency to buy Country Z's exports) as Country Z's dollar depreciates.

Likewise, if Country Z's residents' demand for imports is highly inelastic, then more expensive imports have a proportionally small effect on import demand. In which case, expenditures on imports may actually rise as they become more expensive. If the combined price elasticity of demand for exports and imports is inelastic, depreciation of the currency actually worsens a trade deficit. Country Z's import expenditures rise while export revenues fall, worsening the current account deficit.

The MLC is basically an application of the total revenue test of elasticity (Chapter 4). If demand for a country's exports is inelastic, a fall in price leads to a decrease in total revenues from the sale of exports. The same depreciation that caused the price of

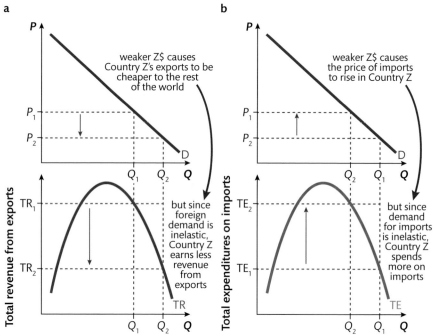

Figure 26.3 The effect of depreciation on imports and exports depends on their PED: if demand is inelastic, depreciation may worsen a current account deficit. (a) Market for Country Z's exports; (b) market for imports in Country Z

exports to fall causes the price of imports to rise, and if demand for imports is inelastic, then their higher prices causes total expenditures on imports to rise. Thus, the MLC is not met (Figure 26.3).

If the MLC is met, depreciation of a nation's currency causes revenues from export sales to rise and expenditures on imports to fall, moving the country towards a trade surplus.

A comparison of Figures 26.3 and 26.4 show how price elasticity is a critical element in any decision to devalue a currency. In reality, the MLC can be met even when the elasticities of demand for exports and imports are separately somewhat inelastic. For example, a PED_X of 0.5 and a PED_M of 0.6, both relatively inelastic by themselves, combine to have a value of 1.1, enough to satisfy the MLC.

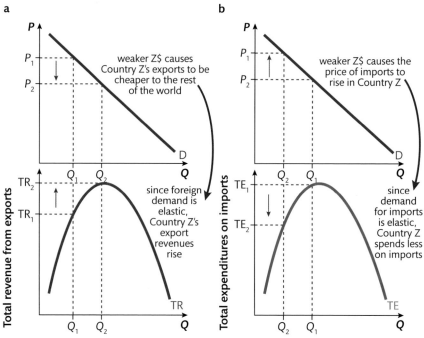

Figure 26.4 The effect of depreciation on imports and exports depends on their PED: if demand is elastic, depreciation may move a country towards a current account surplus. (a) Market for Country Z's exports; (b) market for imports in Country Z

The J-curve

The MLC analysis above suggests that a country with an inelastic import and export demand combination would never want to devalue its currency, because that would lead to a worsening of its current account. However, PED changes over time. As consumers have time to adjust to changes in the price of particular goods, they are able to change their behaviour to consume either more or less of the good in question depending on how the price changed.

For example, when the price of a particular brand of toothpaste goes up, consumers who are used to buying that toothpaste may continue to do so for a while until they have found a suitable substitute. Over time, the responsiveness of consumers to a change in price increases as consumers can alter their decisions about what and where to buy.

Fine chocolate shop, Geneva, Switzerland

When the exchange rate between two nations changes, consumers in both nations will be more responsive to the changing price of imports as time goes by. For example, if the value of the Swiss franc were to fall relative to the British pound, British consumers would not immediately notice that Swiss goods were getting cheaper in the UK. Chocolate consumers in the UK would continue to buy, say, French and Belgian chocolate in the short run. However, over time, they would begin to take notice of the relatively cheaper Swiss chocolates, and therefore become more responsive to the lower price of Swiss imports in the long run. Likewise, Swiss consumers would find British goods more expensive, but Swiss consumers who are used to buying British beers would be more responsive to the higher prices over time, once they have been able to find suitable substitutes, such as Belgian and German beers.

The PED for both imports and exports increases over time. Therefore, following depreciation of a nation's currency, it is likely that in the short run, demand for imports and exports will be inelastic, the MLC will not be met, and therefore the weaker currency actually moves a country towards a current account deficit. As time passes, however, and the currency remains weak, consumers at home and abroad begin to alter their demand based on the changing price of imports and therefore

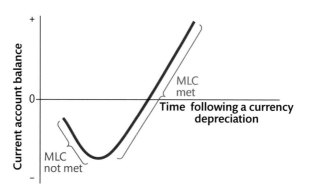

PED becomes more elastic, the MLC is met, and the nation whose currency weakened moves towards a current account surplus.

The implication is that in the short run, depreciation of a nation's currency is likely to move its current account towards a deficit, whereas in the long run, the current account balance should begin to improve. This is illustrated in a simple diagram known as the J-curve, as seen in Figure 26.5.

Research and inquiry

Looking for evidence of the MLC

The MLC states that a country's current account balance will improve if its currency depreciates as long as the combined elasticity of demand for exports and imports is greater than one, or *elastic*. While calculating the PEDs for imports and exports would require a huge trove of data on export and import prices and quantities, finding *evidence* of whether demand for exports and import is elastic or inelastic should be relatively easy: all we need to do is look at what happens to a country's current account balance following a depreciation of its currency.

Using publicly available data we should be able to determine whether the MLC is met for a particular country in a particular period. To do so, we must find a period over which a country's currency depreciated and look at the effect the depreciation had on its trade balance with the country against whose country it depreciated.

The chart below shows the exchange rate of the US dollar in terms of Chilean pesos between April and June of 2020.

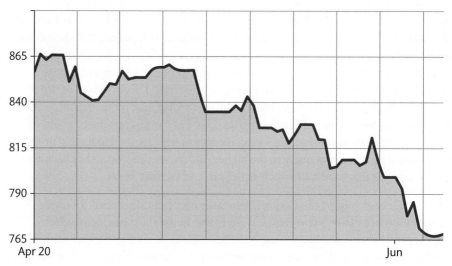

Note that the dollar *depreciates* from $865 ($ is the symbol for the Chilean peso, the currency of Chile) peso to $765 pesos over the two-month period.

The table below shows US exports and imports with Chile over the same two-month period.

Month	Exports to Chile (millions of US$)	Imports from Chile (millions of US$)	Trade balance (millions of US$)
April 2020	861.8	883.2	−21.3
May 2020	861.7	679.1	182.6

Notice that while exports remain steady in April and May, imports decrease precipitously. Therefore, the trade balance moves from a deficit in April to a surplus in May.

Given the evidence above, we should be able to draw some conclusions about how trade flows responded to the depreciation of the dollar in 2020 and from those determine whether the MLC was met between the US and Chile.

The dollar depreciated between April and May while the US trade balance moved from deficit to surplus. Based on this, *is the MLC met between April and May? Explain your answer.*

26.9 [HL] What are the implications of a persistent current account surplus?

Learning objectives

At the end of this section you will be able to:

* explain why a surplus in the current account of the balance of payments may result in upward pressure on the exchange rate of the currency
* discuss the possible consequences of a rising current account surplus, including lower domestic consumption and investment, as well as the appreciation of the domestic currency and reduced export competitiveness.

The effect on the exchange rate

If a nation consistently sells more of its output to foreigners than it demands of foreign output, demand for the exporting nation's currency will eventually rise and appreciate. In addition, since the surplus nation demands relatively little of foreign goods, the supply of its currency in foreign exchange markets will fall, contributing to the currency's appreciation.

Over time, an appreciating currency will reduce the export industry's competitiveness with the rest of the world and force domestic producers to become more efficient or shut down as foreign demand for their goods eventually falls.

This adjustment assumes, of course, that exchange rates are floating and the currency is allowed to appreciate. China, the country with the third largest current account surplus in 2017 (the year for which most current data is available, behind Germany and Japan) prevents its currency from appreciating as it would under a floating exchange rate system by intervening in the forex market to peg the exchange rate to the US dollar. By closely managing the RMB's value through its use of its foreign exchange reserves to buy and sell dollars and RMB in the forex market, the Chinese government ensures that the country's large trade surplus does not cause an appreciation of its currency, which would reduce demand for Chinese exports and slow the country's economic growth.

Under a system of floating exchange rates, current account surpluses should be kept in check by the appreciation of the surplus nation's currency and the corresponding decrease in demand for its exports and the increasing appeal of imports among domestic consumers. However, in a global economy in which governments actively intervene in foreign exchange markets to devalue their own currencies, massive imbalances can persist for years and even decades.

The effect on domestic consumption and savings

Persistent current account surpluses imply that households in the surplus nation are consuming at a lower level over time than households in countries with current account deficits. The reason for this may not be immediately clear. Essentially, the high levels of investment in foreign assets, plus the large reserves of foreign exchange held in the central bank of a surplus nation add up to a form of forced savings among the surplus country's households.

Think of it this way: money earned from the sale of exported goods but not spent on imported goods is money saved by the nation with the trade surplus. The financial account deficit needed to maintain a current account surplus reduces households' consumption by re-investing money earned from export sales in foreign assets rather than spending it on goods and services.

China's national savings rate is around 45%. This does not mean that the average Chinese household saves 45% of its income earned in the workplace. It means that of the Chinese GDP of $12 trillion, nearly half is invested in real and financial assets at home or abroad. Only around 40% of China's GDP is accounted for by household consumption. Compare this to the USA, where 12% of GDP is accounted for by savings and investment, and 70% was made up of household consumption.

The high levels of savings and investment at home and abroad necessary to maintain China's massive current account surplus result in less of the country's hard-earned income going towards domestic consumption or spending on imports. Another way to think about this situation is as follows. Nearly half of the goods produced in China is exported to and consumed by the rest of the world, but China imports far less than it exports, meaning nearly half of China's output is not consumed by Chinese households, but by foreigners. A trade deficit nation, on the other hand, may actually be able to consume more than it produces, since many of the goods and services its households enjoy are produced abroad and are imported using money borrowed from foreigners in the financial account.

The effect on inflation and employment

In contrast with deficits, current account surpluses can be inflationary and are likely to increase employment in the short run. An excess of exports over imports stimulates AD, driving up the domestic price level and the level of employment. Foreign demand for domestic output competes with that of domestic consumers, putting upward pressure on prices and tightening labour markets.

Paper 1 questions

Part (a) questions

1. Explain three reasons why a country might experience a current account deficit. (10 marks)
2. Explain three reasons why a country might experience a current account surplus. (10 marks)
3. Explain why a country that experiences a surplus on the financial account will have a deficit on the current account. (10 marks)

Part (b) questions

1. Using real-world examples, evaluate the view that countries should enact policies that help maintain a surplus in the current account of their balance of payments. (15 marks)
2. Using real-world examples, discuss the consequences of a persistent current account deficit. (15 marks)
3. Using real-world examples, discuss the consequences of a persistent current account surplus. (15 marks)

Paper 2 questions

Read the excerpt below and answer the questions that follow:

Item 1:

A reduction in inflationary pressures because of slow growth of international demand, and a deceleration of the world economy, has allowed the Central Bank of Chile to cut interest rates to their lowest level for 14 years. The low interest rates have in turn contributed towards the peso (the Chilean currency) hitting a record low; and the **depreciation** of the peso is raising import prices.

The Chilean government would like to see foreign trade add to growth, and is planning to eliminate its remaining controls on **capital flows** to stop the decline in FDI, and to provide funds for businesses.

A bilateral free trade agreement with the USA will help in the long run, but Chile's economy could use a boost now, which may leave expansionary monetary policy as the main instrument available. Adapted from Business Week.

Item 2: Chile's real GDP and current account balance

Real GDP (annual % change)			Current account balance (% of GDP)		
2015	2016	2017	2015	2016	2017
2.3	1.67	1.27	−1.32	−1.58	−2.15

1. With reference to Item 1, explain the following terms which are in bold in the passage:
   i. depreciation (2 marks)
   ii. capital flows. (2 marks)

2. With reference to Item 2, briefly describe what has happened to the current account balance since 2015. Using any of the data provided, give one possible reason for this change.   (4 marks)

3. Explain the relationship between low interest rates and the depreciation of the peso.   (4 marks)

4. Use the data and your knowledge of economics to evaluate the decision of the Chilean government to enter trade agreements and reduce controls on capital flows.   (15 marks)

Country X has a flexible exchange rate and international capital mobility. Political turmoil outside of Country X generates capital flow into Country X.

1. Using a correctly labelled foreign exchange market graph, explain the impact of the capital inflow on the international value of the currency of Country X.   (4 marks)

2. For Country X, explain the effect of the change in the international value of its currency on each of the following:
   i. exports   (2 marks)
   ii. imports   (2 marks)
   iii. the balance of payments (both the current and financial accounts)   (2 marks)

3. **HL** With reference to the Marshall–Lerner condition, explain why a depreciation of a country's currency may not improve its current account balance.   (15 marks)

Real-world issue 2

Why is economic development uneven?

- Perceptions of the meanings of development and **equity** change over time and vary across cultures.
- Governments and other economic agents may intervene in an attempt to promote **economic well-being** and **equity** in societies.
- The pursuit of **sustainability** is subject to various constraints.
- Effective strategies should take account of the relevant social, economic, and political context.

Sustainable development

27

27.1 What is economic development?

What is meant by economic development?

'Remember: things can be bad, and getting better.'

– Hans Rosling

For as long as humans have organised into small groups, village councils, city-states then national governments, their reason for being has been to answer the question: how can we improve our lives? Economic development is a broad concept involving efforts to improve standards of living, reduce poverty, improve health and education, and increase freedom and economic choice. The purpose of development economics is to better understand the barriers countries face in pursuing these goals and the strategies that can be used to achieve them.

The benefits of development may be obvious: our modern era of globalisation has made it possible for more people to live lives of greater wealth, and in better health and comfort than at any time in history. Globally speaking, people have longer life spans and enjoy comforts and conveniences only imagined by people living as recently as 100 years ago. However, this obvious fact runs alongside another, very unpleasant one. Across 47 countries, 880 million people suffer extreme poverty. Approximately 12% of the world's population live in the less economically developed countries (LEDCs), many of them in gruelling conditions. Furthermore, LEDCs account for less than 2% of total world income. Expand the view more widely and one sees that it is not simply a matter of 'developing countries and rich countries'. Significant pockets of underdevelopment exist in developing countries as well.

However, there is cause for optimism. The World Bank reports that in 1990, more than one-third of the world lived in extreme poverty – living on $1.90 a day or less. By 2015, that figure had dropped to 10%, the 'lowest level in recorded history'. And that in the last few decades, more than 1 billion people have risen out of extreme poverty. It is enormously encouraging to see the progress made by so many so quickly. Surely something can be learned of this success, and surely these lessons can be applied in service to the unlucky billions who are just getting by?

Figure 27.1 shows relative development levels geographically. Its findings are based on scores for countries on the **Human Development Index (HDI)**, a composite indicator of development (more on the HDI in Chapter 27). This map shows where some of the biggest challenges currently lie, where the problems may appear to be interlocking and overwhelming. Remember, though, that many countries were much less developed 50 years ago. If a better life is possible for 1 billion people in a relatively short time, why not for the next billion?

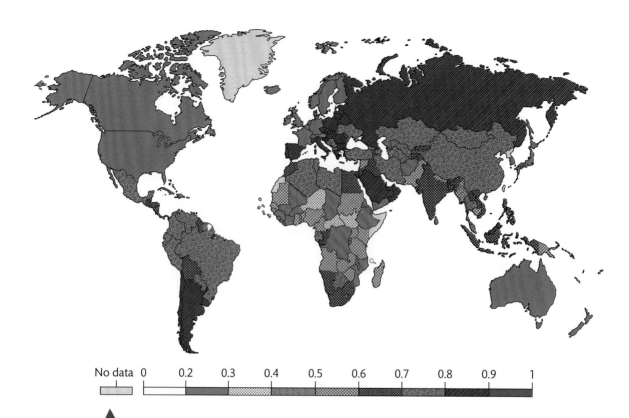

No data | 0 | 0.2 | 0.3 | 0.4 | 0.5 | 0.6 | 0.7 | 0.8 | 0.9 | 1

Figure 27.1 The Human Development Index 2017: a summary measure of key dimensions of human development

Why has the focus shifted from growth to development?

For the decades that followed the Great Depression of the 1930s, in the early years of macroeconomics, economists mostly focused on economic growth. Growing economies, it was logically reasoned, would improve the lives of most citizens. The emphasis was on investment in infrastructure, creating productive capacity, stimulating spending, and generally improving income level. In Chapter 13, we discussed the many measures economists have devised to assess those levels, from gross domestic product (GDP) to per capita GDP, to adjusting for purchasing power and the creation of purchasing-power-parity-adjusted per capita GDP. Eventually, the limits of GDP to assess the activity it claims to record have been acknowledged. Economists, it could be said, grew better and better at keeping score, but only in a particular way.

Beginning in the late 1940s and early 1950s there began an age of independence from colonial rule in many developing countries. From this, there emerged a concern that growth alone did not always provide a better quality of life. Sheer economic growth had a mixed record in terms of improving health, education and other basic living standards. Economists began seeking out new ways to look at economic well-being, especially for developing countries, which had either missed out on growth or found its promises unfulfilled.

Development, as noted earlier, takes into account factors beyond monetary income to include health, education, and other social indicators. Development economics is a branch of economic theory that has grown up around the idea that it is possible to understand what makes developing countries poor (and rich countries rich) and to make policy changes that can turn developing countries into richer ones.

A sign of the shift to a wider focus came in 1966, when the United Nations created the UN Development Programme (UNDP), and by 1971 had consolidated most of its development-related agencies together. Funded by voluntary contributions of UN members, the UNDP has contributed technical assistance, consultants' services, equipment, and fellowships for advanced study abroad. It has funded projects in resource planning, training institutes, the application of modern technology to development, and the building of the economic and social infrastructure.

In 1990, influenced by the work of Amartya Sen, the UNDP began to compile and publish the HDI, a more inclusive evaluation of economic well-being that has become the standard international benchmark measure for quality of life. This drive towards a development focus, rather than pure growth, has gathered momentum through the work of the UN as well as from a wide variety of academics in the last few decades. It accelerated in the UNDP's Millennium Development Goals (MDGs) Project, an ambitious effort to draw attention and resources to the struggles of developing countries. And it continues today in the Sustainable Development Goals (SDGs), discussed later in this chapter.

How are economic growth and economic development interrelated?

Economic growth is rather strictly defined as an increase in real GDP over the previous year. Economists strive to refine and clarify the idea by measuring it against population size and relative spending power. But it remains the defining characteristic of a country's economic success. Growth, because it usually means more money and activity and employment, generally suggests that something is going right with the economy. A recession, a lack of growth or a decrease in the economy's size, triggers attention and policy changes.

Development, in contrast, emphasises specific changes in aspects of people's lives in many different dimensions. A primary focus of development economics is the reduction of poverty, the raising of incomes among the world's poorest. Furthermore, development economics seeks the improvement of general living standards. Typically, living standards are measured by long life, general health, education achievement and opportunities, as well as measures of income. Development economics, like mainstream views of growth, also focuses on employment, in particular on the types of employment offered in developing countries, and how countries can adapt and respond to the challenges of their workforces.

TOK Economic development draws from a set of values set out by Denis Goulet in 1971 (life sustenance, self-esteem and freedom). Does this make the pursuit of economic development unscientific?

Case study – modern economists – Amartya Sen

What does it mean to be free? For Amartya Sen, the question has been personal, political and professional. Sen was born in West Bengal, then a colony of Great Britain. As a child, he witnessed the devastating Bengal famine of 1943, an event that lingered with him and shaped his research as an economist.

Sen achieved top marks at prestigious prep schools in Bengal and India, and eventually studied at Cambridge. His early years of graduate work were marked by intense debates between the advocates of Keynesian and new classical economics.

Eventually, though, Sen made his mark by pursuing a different perspective on national economic well-being. His study of famines and deprivation led him to conclude that most famine was unnecessary, a consequence of factors that had little to do with a lack of resources. More important, he argued, were the capabilities of the people to fend for themselves. Freedom, he argued, was more than the lack of government interference in one's life, but rather the ability to positively do something to help oneself. To Sen, it is on this basis that all governments should be evaluated. Famine, he later noted, was far less likely in functioning democracies because the government is compelled to respond to its people in times of critical shortage.

Sen also promoted a focus on gender inequality, writing famously that 'more than 100 million women are missing', in China and India because of preferential healthcare for men and sex-selective abortion of girls. Among the most influential economists, if not intellectuals, of the 20th century, Sen questioned the view that humans function mainly with a mindset of *homo economicus*, as purely self-motivated actors. He was awarded the 1998 Nobel Prize for his work on social choice theory and his interest in poverty and development. His work in the causes of famine and on social welfare, drove much of the thinking behind changes in UN development policy in recent decades, including the formulation of the HDI.

What are the sources of economic growth?

While economic growth occurs with any increase in GDP over the previous year, it is relevant to make a distinction between the growth of actual production and growth of potential production. Potential output is an increase or shift to the right of long-run aggregate supply (LRAS) or a country's production possibilities frontier (PPF), as explained in Chapter 17. Once the sources of economic growth are established, it is possible to examine the relationship with economic development.

The natural resource base

When it comes to natural resources, each country must make the best out of their 'gifts of nature'. Some countries are blessed with an abundance of water, arable land, timber, and other natural resources. The US attributes some part of its enormous wealth to a breadth and depth of natural bounty. Other countries, like Singapore and the Netherlands, resort to increasing resources like their actual land area by means of impressive technological achievement. Still other countries toil away in hopes of discovering a precious new resource, as happened in Afghanistan in 2009 when vast mineral deposits, some including lithium (which is used to power all kinds of modern batteries) were discovered. The estimated worth of Afghan deposits is nearly 3 trillion dollars. Such a windfall is extremely rare; the only practical alternative is to seek out ways to improve the resources already known.

Physical capital and technology

Growth can be achieved by increasing or improving the amount of physical capital. This includes buildings, machinery, vehicles, offices, and equipment. The resources to purchase these goods come from savings (and the income earned from savings); the intellectual power to improve them comes from a more highly educated workforce. Some technology can be imported from overseas capital products and by hiring foreign expertise.

- *Capital widening* refers to the extension of capital goods to a larger segment of workers (e.g. more farmers using simple tools).
- *Capital deepening* refers to increases in the ratio of capital per worker, so that workers have more capital to work with (all farmers using better farm tools).

Improved technology refers to acquiring more sophisticated capital goods as well as better methods for production, and is clearly a source for economic growth.

Human capital

A larger, healthier, and better-educated population would improve the human capital of the country.

The quantity of human capital can be increased by encouraging childbirth with better prenatal and maternal healthcare. It can also be accomplished by encouraging immigration to the country, adding to the labour force. However, many countries have too large a population and are seeking ways of reducing it. China's one-child policy and Singapore's incentive system for families are two prominent modern examples.

The *quality* of human capital can be improved through a variety of approaches to make the average person more productive. Improved healthcare keeps children healthy, and parents able to care for them. It also lowers the amount of time workers are absent or ill during working hours. Furthermore, education and worker training are all investments in human capital, and thus should contribute to the productive capacity (LRAS) of the country.

Institutional factors

Enduring economic growth can only occur when minimum levels of institutional factors are in place. A generally equitable and stable legal system is desirable. Political stability is a prerequisite. A stable banking system ensures the flow of capital. A minimum level of infrastructure is necessary, so that goods can be transported, and a minimum level of public health is required. An orderly legal system that affirms property rights encourages investment. A reasonably good education system, one that successfully trains students in numeracy and literacy, is also important.

Economic growth is indispensable to enduring economic development. While it is true that some basic and inexpensive changes to public policy in areas like healthcare can yield positive results, many of the requirements for development require the money that growth provides to pay for them. Better education requires more resources, as does capital formation, as does improved technology, and a growing economy can fund these efforts. At the same time, economic growth does not always yield positive or sustainable development results.

27.2 What is sustainable development?

Learning outcomes

At the end of this section you will be able to:

- define sustainable development
- outline and explain the United Nations' Sustainable Development Goals
- **HL** analyse the relationship between economic development and poverty.

One way to understand the concept of sustainable development is to place it within the context of macroeconomic perspectives of the last 100 years. The catastrophe of the Great Depression (1929–39) inspired the creation of macroeconomics, and the primary focus of this new field was to analyse and engineer economic growth. Whether one subscribed to the Keynesian school of government intervention or the non-interventionist classical school approach, growth was the goal.

Starting in the 1960s, during the peak of the post-Second World War boom period, a small number of thinkers and writers began to question the effects of industrialisation. In rich countries, worries about air pollution, oil spills, water quality, toxic waste and nuclear accidents led to the flowering of an environmentalist movement. In the 1970s and 1980s, environmentalism took political shape in the formation of green parties in many countries, who sought renewable energy resources, clean water, and clean air.

Among the first to identify sustainable development as a worldwide goal was a 1980 report by the International Union for the Conservation of Nature. Shortly after, it was expanded upon by the United Nations World Commission on Environment and Development in 1987, who defined the concept as follows:

> 'Sustainable development is development that meets the needs of the present without compromising the ability of future generations to meet their own needs. The idea encapsulates worries about the impact of human activity on the planet's ecosystem, and whether that ecosystem will survive the ravages of human use. This can run contrary to the notion of economic growth as it was once understood.'

In theory, economies getting richer led to unequivocally positive outcomes: more goods and services, perhaps access to transportation, more housing and energy use across the population. All of this led to a rise in the standard of living of many millions of people. It also puts an ever-greater strain on the planetary ecosystem as a whole.

In 2000, the United Nations launched the UN Millennium Development Goals (MDGs), a wide-ranging effort to specifically target, promote, and channel efforts towards development goals. The MDGs sought to eradicate extreme poverty, achieve universal primary education, promote gender equality, reduce child mortality, improve maternal health, combat disease, develop a global partnership for development and to ensure environmental sustainability.

Upon the target date of 2015, the United Nations reported impressive results on the MDGs. Extreme poverty in developing countries had been reduced from 47% to 17% since 1990. The number of extreme poor dropped by over 1 billion people. The number of children not in school dropped by 43 million. The period also saw large gains in school enrolment of girls, and lower mortality rates worldwide. The number of people with access to piped safe drinking water rose from 2 billion to 4 billion.

The SDGs, released in 2015, replaced the MDGs. They reflect a more ambitious effort by the UN to improve lives in a more comprehensive manner. The SDGs add to their goals by including inequality, age considerations, working life, gender equity, consumption patterns, sustainable industry, and direct action on climate change.

The theme of sustainability runs through many of the goals. The SDGs demonstrate an understanding that many human systems need to change rapidly in response to the climate crisis brought on by carbon emissions. Climate change is known to have the following effects:

- ice melting worldwide, especially at the north and south poles
- sea-levels are rising at 3.2 mm per year, and the rate is likely to increase
- species collapse as rising temperatures affect ecosystems
- increased rain and (paradoxically) more severe drought
- drinking water shortages
- risk of massive crop failures.

Climate change is expected to have further effects on the global environment:

- increased incidence of disease, such as mosquito borne malaria
- less available fresh water as melting glaciers store the majority of the world's remaining fresh water
- decades-long 'megadroughts'
- more frequent and more intense extreme weather events causing more natural disasters.

Climate change is a global crisis that requires global cooperation to solve. However, those most likely to be affected are the poor, living in coastal areas all around the world. And with their limited resources and structural vulnerability, they are least equipped to cope. The SDGs should be viewed as a drive for collective action in the face of extreme danger. At the same time, the SDGs suggest that progress in the quality of life for all is synonymous with action on climate change not a question of choosing one or the other.

The SDGs, shown in Figure 27.2, have a target date of 2030.

Each goal is broad on the surface but includes more specific *sub-goals* designed to achieve the larger goal. The targets for SDG #2, End hunger, are as follows.

By 2030, **end hunger** and ensure access by all people, in particular the poor and people in vulnerable situations, including infants, to safe, nutritious, and sufficient food all year round.

End poverty in all its forms everywhere

End hunger, achieve food security and improved nutrition and promote sustainable agriculture

Ensure healthy lives and promote well-being for all at all ages

Ensure inclusive and equitable quality education and promote lifelong learning opportunities for all

Achieve gender equality and empower all women and girls

Ensure availability and sustainable management of water and sanitation for all

Ensure access to affordable, reliable, sustainable and modern energy for all

Promote sustained, inclusive and sustainable economic growth, full and productive employment and decent work for all

Build resilient infrastructure, promote inclusive and sustainable industrialization, and foster innovation

Reduce income inequality within and among countries

Make cities and human settlements inclusive, safe, resilient, and sustainable

Ensure sustainable consumption and production patterns

Take urgent action to combat climate change and its impacts by regulating emissions and promoting developments in renewable energy

Conserve and sustainably use the oceans, seas and marine resources for sustainable development

Protect, restore and promote sustainable use of terrestrial ecosystems, sustainably manage forests, combat desertification, and halt and reverse land degradation and halt biodiversity loss

Promote peaceful and inclusive societies for sustainable development, provide access to justice for all and build effective, accountable and inclusive institutions at all levels

Strengthen the means of implementation and revitalize the global partnership for sustainable development

Figure 27.2 United Nations Sustainable Development Goals

SDG #2 To end hunger, achieve food security and improved nutrition and promote sustainable agriculture

- By 2030, **end all forms of malnutrition**, including achieving, by 2025, the internationally agreed targets on stunting and wasting in children under 5 years of age, and address the nutritional needs of adolescent girls, pregnant and lactating women and older persons.
- By 2030, **double the agricultural productivity** and incomes of small-scale food producers, in particular women, indigenous peoples, family farmers, pastoralists and fishers, including through secure and equal access to land, other productive resources and inputs, knowledge, financial services, markets and opportunities for value addition and non-farm employment.
- By 2030, **ensure sustainable food production systems** and implement resilient agricultural practices that increase productivity and production, that help maintain ecosystems, that strengthen capacity for adaptation to climate change, extreme weather, drought, flooding and other disasters and that progressively improve land and soil quality.
- By 2020, **maintain the genetic diversity of seeds**, cultivated plants and farmed and domesticated animals and their related wild species, including through soundly managed and diversified seed and plant banks at the national, regional and international levels, and promote access to and fair and equitable sharing of benefits arising from the utilisation of genetic resources and associated traditional knowledge, as internationally agreed.

TOK

Are the values on which development is based universal or do they depend on culture? Are there some goals among the SDGs that may not be acceptable to some cultures?

Research and inquiry

Is the UN hitting its SDGs?

As we approach 2030, it is a good idea to see what kind of progress is being made against the SDGs. Conduct an internet search for the 'Sustainable Goals Progress' or 'Sustainable Goals Tracker'. Use the information you find to conduct research and discussion with your class.

For discussion and debate:

1 Allocate the goals across the group.

2 Find information on each of the targets of your goal.

3 Identify areas where more attention or resources are needed.

4 Share a written or verbal summary with your group.

- **Increase investment, including through enhanced international cooperation, in rural infrastructure**, agricultural research and extension services, technology development and plant and livestock gene banks in order to enhance agricultural productive capacity in developing countries, in particular least developed countries.

- **Correct and prevent trade restrictions and distortions in world agricultural markets**, including through the parallel elimination of all forms of agricultural export subsidies and all export measures with equivalent effect, in accordance with the mandate of the Doha Development Round.

- **Adopt measures to ensure the proper functioning of food commodity markets** and their derivatives and facilitate timely access to market information, including on food reserves, in order to help limit extreme food price volatility.

HL What is the relationship between sustainability and poverty?

One theme we see in the study of environmental sustainability is the challenges of affluence. Richer people tend to consume more, in general, than poor people and so put more pressure on the planets' resources than the poor do, on a per capita basis. Their carbon footprint, and individual effect on climate change, is larger than those who consume fewer fossil fuels and those people tend to be poorer.

However, one cannot ignore how extreme poverty can lead to fairly high contributions to pollution and climate change among the poorest. About two-thirds of the world's poorest 900 million people work in agriculture, and several examples help demonstrate this connection between poverty and sustainability. Poor farmers rarely own their own land, letting out extraneous lots that are the least-good land available. This leads to inefficient crop production, so it takes more land to get the same amount of food. Because many poor farmers do not own their land, either because it is rented or because they cannot get property rights in their land, they do not invest in the long-term care of the soil. They will choose to neglect crop rotation practices to get the most of the much needed cash for the crop right away. This contributes to soil erosion. It is not uncommon for such farming to take place on commonly held land, demonstrating the overuse of common pool resources.

Deforestation is hastened for similar reasons. In need of cheap farmland, the poor will cut or burn down forests. The wood can be used for heat or cooking, and the land used for farming, even if it is of relatively poor quality.

It would be a mistake to blame those in this situation. Just the opposite, as the poorest are far more likely to be affected by climate change effects (droughts and famine, sea level rises and floods) than the rich. It is instead very important to understand that the desperation of the poor can put a greater strain than one might expect on the planet's resources, and that addressing inequality (SDG #10), which is an ethically important goal on its own, will also help take action on responsible consumption and production (SDG #12) climate action (SDG #13), and life on land (SDG #15).

27.3 What do developing countries have in common?

Learning outcome

At the end of this section you will be able to:

- discuss, using examples, the similarities between developing countries.

Less economically developed countries tend to share common characteristics, some of which are outlined below.

Low standard of living

Almost by definition, countries who score lowest on the HDI have low levels of educational attainment, low incomes, and poorer health, because these attributes are the chief standards for the HDI. And so, one would expect these countries to struggle in areas of infant mortality, life expectancy, fewer years of education, and general poverty.

High population growth and birth rates

Measured as the crude birth rate (CBR), global birth rates have dropped steadily over the last 100 years, but the rates for developing countries have dropped much more slowly. The global average CBR for 2018 is approximately 18.5 births per 1000 women of child-bearing age per year. In less developed countries (LDCs), this figure is far exceeded, with CBRs as high as 31 births per 1000 women of child-bearing age per year. In other words, birth rates in many LDCs can be about 1.5 times higher than the global average. On trend, this gap has narrowed in recent years and is expected to narrow even more in another decade.

High dependency ratios

The dependency ratio is the combined number of people not in the labour force compared to those who are in the productive population (labour force). In other words, how many working people are there compared to the number of old and young people who rely on them? High birth rates tend to lead to high dependency ratios, another common characteristic of LDCs. Countries with high birth rates and large populations of younger people fall easily into this category.

At the same time, richer countries with ageing populations are also seeing their dependency ratios climb. Countries with high dependency ratios are likely to struggle to meet the needs of their relatively large dependent population. The highest ratios, typically at or above 80%, imply that for every productive, working person there is another person to support. Table 27.1 shows several more developed countries (MDCs) with relatively high old age dependency ratios, with several of the lowest ranking LEDCs ranking high child dependency ratios.

High dependence on agriculture and primary production

The UN defines commodity dependence as having more than 60% of your total merchandise exports composed of commodities. Often this is a reliance on

Table 27.1 Old age and youth dependency ratios for selected countries

Country (HDI rank)	Dependency ratio, old age (%)
Japan (19)	47
Italy (29)	36
Finland (12)	36
Portugal (40)	35
Country (HDI rank)	**Dependency ratio, child (%)**
Niger (189)	105
Mali (184)	94
Chad (187)	92
Angola (149)	90

agriculture, but it can be mined goods as well. A larger percentage of labour is employed in agriculture in LEDCs. Generally speaking, developed countries tend to employ less than 10% of the population in agriculture, while the proportion in LEDCs may be 50–80%. These countries, along with a large portion of their employed population, remain vulnerable to weather changes and the typically volatile market for agricultural commodities.

Commodity dependent LEDCs who rely not on agriculture tend to be oil or mineral exporters. Table 27.2 shows the relative dependence of several LEDCs on commodities as a share of their exports.

Note the dominant share of exports for oil exporters, whose export income is entirely dependent on oil prices. Some countries are heavily dependent on agriculture, and others on ore and minerals. Cambodia, shown here as a textile exporter, is heavily reliant on manufacturers in one industry. We could also add some service dominant countries, typically island countries that rely on tourism. Some countries export several commodities, such as Côte d'Ivoire, which produces cocoa, nuts, rubber, gold, to have a diversified but still commodity-heavy portfolio of exports.

Large urban informal sector

The informal sector is defined as being unorganised, unregistered, and unsupported by the state and its institutions. It may include subsistence production, cottage industry,

Table 27.2 Commodity dependence, selected countries

Country (main exports)	Share of exports (%)
Chad (oil)	96.4
Angola (oil)	96.1
Guinea-Bissau (fresh fruit, nuts)	88.4
Zambia (copper)	75.7
Burkina Faso (gold)	60.8
Ethiopia (coffee)	22.9
Cambodia (textiles)	93

unreported merchant activity, and black market trade. Most LDCs have relatively high proportions of their economy operating informally. Because such activity goes untaxed, it does not generate tax revenues the state can use for merit goods.

Poorly functioning markets

Developing country markets face considerable obstacles to smooth operation. Transport infrastructure can be poor, making logistical efficiency hard to achieve. Businesses cannot get adequate credit because of an inadequate banking system. Legal institutions are poorly developed, and so property rights and fair treatment are often in doubt. All of these make the lives of entrepreneurs far more challenging than they would be in their developed world counterparts, and slow the growth of industry.

Unequal power relationships to major countries

The small and weak countries that orbit their larger and more powerful neighbours find themselves negotiating at a disadvantage in many areas: the terms of foreign investment, foreign aid, and the opening of rich-country markets. The continued stalling of the Doha Development Trade Round of the World Trade Organization (WTO), started in 2001 and still yet unfinished, largely over access to rich world agricultural markets, is one example of this unequal relationship.

27.4 How diverse are developing countries?

Learning outcome

At the end of this section you will be able to:

- discuss the differences between developing countries, using examples.

While many less economically developed countries share the imposing challenges discussed above, they can differ quite profoundly in other ways. These differences are important to bear in mind as the policies recommended to LEDCs cannot be applied without consideration for the differences. Some categories of difference are discussed below.

Different resource endowments

While it is understandable to think that a country is developing because it has little in the way of natural resources, this is not necessarily true. Angola, a country disrupted by decades of civil war, was once considered the breadbasket of its region and holds major oil reserves. Myanmar is known to possess large quantities of oil, natural gas, teak wood, and gems, yet it still languishes in poverty. Brazil, considered to be as resource rich as nearly any country in the world, has considerably underperformed in development terms given its resource endowment. At the same time, some countries have done rather well despite limited natural resources. Japan, with little arable land and no in-ground resources to speak of, has consistently been ranked among the top few developed countries in the world. Famously, Singapore has almost no resources to speak of but has expanded its land base by increasing its shoreline. Liechtenstein and Andorra, two tiny European principalities, enjoy very high development levels with perhaps their only natural resource being their geographical location in Europe.

Different historical experiences

Many developing countries were once colonies of developed countries. However, the effects of colonisation are varied, as well as being disputed. It has been argued that countries that experience long-standing occupation, like India and Hong Kong, benefited by the establishment of legal order and effective institutions. In contrast, countries that were used primarily for resource extraction, such as Myanmar and Vietnam, have fared less well. Other studies suggest that the duration of colonisation played a significant role, and that the terms of independence also made a difference.

Different political systems

Developing countries have a wide range of political systems. These include democracies, monarchies, single-party states, theocracies, and military rule. Several have disputed governments, where conflict has rendered government almost completely ineffective, and the problem of governance is discussed in detail in Chapter 29. With such variety it is necessary to create policies with consideration of the distinctive political structure in any given developing country.

Different degrees of political stability

Civil war or intra-state conflict certainly interferes with plans for prosperity and development. Many of the countries at the bottom of the HDI have suffered from one or the other of these dangers. However, many other countries have had relatively stable governments, with little conflict over changes in power. This, of course, does not confirm the relative efficacy of these governments – even the most stable can still be corrupt.

Different geographical or demographic makeup

Developing countries can be big, such as China, Russia, Brazil, and India, or quite small like Haiti, Vanuatu, and Kiribati. Some are landlocked countries, like Bolivia, Lesotho, Congo, Laos, and Burundi. Evidence suggests that being landlocked is a disadvantage in terms of access to trade. However, many developing countries have plenty of coastline, such as Mozambique, Somalia, and Indonesia. Some also have very large populations, with the obvious examples of China and India, and others like Kiribati who have populations in the hundreds of thousands.

Different composition of industry

The clichéd notion of a developing country is one that is primarily agricultural, and indeed two-thirds of people who are in extreme poverty work in agriculture, however, as countries many LEDCs specialise in non-agricultural industry like basic manufacturing of textiles and others may specialise in tourism service industries.

In summary, one can say that there are commonalities between developing countries but also significant differences. As students of developing countries, it is of little use to generalise broadly, especially when considering the needs and possible solutions for any particular country.

Ethics TOK

Economic development considers the question of 'Why is development uneven?' but also provokes the question of 'What is to be done?' Some ethicists have challenged the rich world to do more to help the poor generally, but developing countries in particular. Among those is Peter Singer, an Australian moral philosopher, who argues that helping the poor is an essential part of a good life.

"If it is in our power to prevent something bad from happening, without thereby sacrificing anything of comparable moral importance, we ought, morally, to do it."

– Peter Singer

To take this argument to its extreme, as long as a fellow human is in need, any money spent by others on frivolities is basically immoral. This is connected to the notion that the marginal utility of money actually diminishes the more one acquires of it. So, the marginal utility of one dollar to a billionaire is practically nothing, but the same dollar may mean life or death for a child on the verge of starvation.

For discussion:

1 Do you agree with Singer's premise, shown above?

2 If you agree with Singer's conclusion, what do you think should be done about it?

3 What kind of knowledge would persuade you that Singer is correct or incorrect?

4 On what basis might you accept the immorality of wealth accumulation, but still defend it?

Practice exam questions

Paper 1, part (a) questions – (HL & SL)

1. Distinguish between economic growth and economic development. (10 marks)
2. Define sustainable development and explain two of the Sustainable Development Goals. (10 marks)

HL Paper 1, part (a) questions –

1. Explain the relationship between poverty and sustainability. (10 marks)

Paper 1, part (b) question – (HL & SL)

1. Using real-world examples, evaluate the idea that economic growth ensures sustainable economic development. (15 marks)

Measuring development

28

As described in Chapter 27, economic development is multidimensional. The most commonly accepted standard, the UN HDI, includes measures of income, health and education. Broader measures can encompass other quality of life measures like safety and political freedom. This chapter will consider the many ways development can be measured.

How do economists objectively classify countries at various stages of development? Countries are usually first ranked by their per capita income levels. However, no single indicator on its own can render an accurate portrait of any country's overall development, and there are a variety of other indicators available. Indeed, because development involves so many facets of economic life, evaluations of a country's progress must involve many indicators taken together, and for this reason a number of composite indicators have been developed.

28.1 What are the single indicators that are used to measure economic development?

Learning outcomes

At the end of this section you will be able to:

- distinguish between GDP per capita figures and GNI per capita figures
- compare and contrast these figures for economically more developed countries and economically less developed countries
- distinguish between GDP per capita figures and GDP per capita figures at PPP exchange rates
- compare and contrast these figures for economically more developed countries and economically less developed countries
- explain and give examples of economic and social inequality indicators, energy indicators and environmental indicators.

Single indicators are specific individual statistics that are intended to demonstrate a level of economic development. These can come from the realms of health, education, income, or other measures. Economic indicators are specific points of data gathered systematically and continuously to better inform economists and policymakers. For each area, health for example, there may be dozens of different ways of assessing the level of development.

Much like the gathering of national income data, the compilation and study of measurement data is useful because:

- baseline indicator data can help set an agenda for progress, with specific goals
- indicator data measured from one year to the next can indicate the level of progress on that goal
- continued data gathering enables policymakers to reformulate and adjust policies to improve performance
- indicators across countries allow for cross-country comparisons of relative development.

It is important to bear in mind that conclusions based on statistics gathered from developing countries must be read with caution. Many countries cannot afford the resources needed for consistent and rigorous information gathering. For this reason, many countries provide only limited data. Still more challenging is the extraordinary variety of development indicators. The language and purposes of these can vary significantly. As a result, some scepticism with regard to the reliability of the data is warranted. However, where a long-term trend is evident, it is likely that the data have a certain level of reliability and validity.

Income-based development indicators

GDP and GNI

National income data are usually the starting point for understanding development levels. You will recall from Chapter 13 that real gross domestic product (real GDP) is the inflation-adjusted value of all the goods and services produced in the country in the past year. As such, it provides an indicator of the level of activity within a country's borders. GDP counts activity regardless of the flows of income in or out of the country. So, one could say the GDP still counts production that is foreign owned and so the profits flow out of the country. GDP will not count the production of domestically owned companies in other countries, even though that is clearly beneficial to the home country.

A different measure called gross national income (real GNI) takes the ownership of resources into account. Rather than tracking production geographically, it considers the flow of incomes across borders. Real GNI is the total money value of all final goods and services produced in an economy in one year, plus net property income from abroad (interest, rent, dividends and profit). In short, $GNI = GDP - net\ income\ flows$.

For example, take IKEA, a popular Swedish furniture retailer operating in China. Its sales in China count towards Chinese GDP, but would go to Sweden's GNI. For some countries, the different calculation can mean a higher GNI value than GDP or a lower one, depending on the amount of net flows of income. As the level of foreign direct investment activity (FDI) has increased in the last several decades, some countries with large international distribution of company ownership can have higher GNI than GDP.

Per capita GDP versus per capita GNI

To get a better understanding of the average level of production or income, per capita measures are used. These divide national totals by the population to get average income levels. Compared to national income totals, per capita income data provides a better sense of the average standard of living.

When viewed comparatively, a number of high-income countries have rather different per capita GDP and GNI results. Table 28.1 shows such a selection, where Ireland, with the highest per capita income in terms of GDP, has over $16,000 less income per capita in GNI terms. What does this mean? It suggests that there is far more economic activity happening within Ireland than is actually being paid to Irish-owned factors of production. This also appears to be true, to a lesser extent, for Singapore. Meanwhile, for Germany the opposite appears to be true. German-owned factors of production abroad (including repatriated corporate profits and salaries), contribute to Germany's income beyond what is generated solely within the borders of the country.

Table 28.1 GDP per capita versus GNI per capita for select countries

Country	GDP per capita (current US$) 2019	GNI per capita (Atlas method) (current US$) 2019	GNI – GDP (% of GDP)
Ireland	78,661	62,210	−20.9
Germany	46,258	48,520	4.8
Singapore	65,233	59,590	−8.6
Vietnam	2,715	2,540	−6.4
Botswana	7,961	7,660	−3.7
Kenya	1,855	1,750	−5.6

In the case of richer countries, GNI may be higher than GDP because firms in those countries have spread overseas and now generate significant profits that are sent back to their corporate homes. Germany is such an example.

Some countries, but more often developing ones, may also have a discrepancy between GDP and GNI numbers. The income generated by production within Vietnam slightly outpaces the income generated by Vietnamese-owned factors. The same is true for Singapore, Botswana, and Kenya.

For less developed countries, the differences between GDP and GNI may be for different reasons. For Kenya, with increasing amounts of FDI, we may see a significant amount of corporate profits sent out of the country. In the case of developing countries with higher GNI numbers, it is possible that many have citizens living abroad as guest workers who repatriate salaries home. These migrant salaries can be a significant source of income for developing countries. While relatively small in total size, these remittances can be very important to the local economy. For Tonga (40.7% of GDP), Haiti (38.5%), and Nepal (26.9%) such income flows are essential for economic stability. And in those countries GDP alone would likely undercount the income level because remittances would not be included.

GDP and GNI using purchasing power parity

Of course, when doing any national income accounting, statisticians first calculate output and incomes in the local currency. But comparisons between Norwegian krone and Thai baht, for example, would seem meaningless without being translated into a single currency, usually the US dollar.

While this translation makes comparisons more useful, the spending power of money in Norway may be very different from that in Thailand. Resources, goods and services may be more expensive in Norway than in Thailand, which means that more income is needed in Norway to enjoy the same standard of living as in Thailand.

To more accurately reflect the buying power of any amount of income, and so to better assess the standard of living in a country, economists use a comparison called purchasing power parity (PPP). Purchasing power parity is based on the law of one price, which states that an identical good in one country should cost the same in another country, and that the exchange rate should reflect that price. This has implications for the way we look at exchange rates (Chapter 25). For our purposes here, PPP is a tool to assess more accurately the standard of living available for a given amount of income in a country.

For example, the Norwegian equivalent of $100 (kr588) may buy a certain amount of food, perhaps three pizzas. The Thai baht equivalent of $100 (฿2,994) may buy six pizzas, because staple goods are cheaper in Thailand (kr is the symbol of the Norwegian krone, the currency of Norway. ฿ is the symbol of the Thai baht, the currency of Thailand). This means that every $100 of income earned in Norway will buy less in goods and services than the same amount in Thailand. Therefore, Norway's high GDP per capita may overrate the standard of living there. When the purchasing power is factored into national income measures, it produces a refined view of the GDP data.

When PPP-adjusted per capita GNI is greater than nominal GNI, it suggests that the potential standard of living is underestimated. For example, Burundi's GNI per capita is only $280, but adjusted by PPP measures is actually $782, which better reflects the standard of living relative to price levels there. The same is true for many developing countries. Ethiopia's income by GNI per capita is only $850 per year, while by PPP measures it rises to $2,311. It is with this in mind that economists pay attention to PPP-adjusted GNI levels to better understand the attainable quality of life, and to compare one country with another in this regard.

Health-based development indicators

Life expectancy at birth

Life expectancy at birth, which tells us how many years a person will live on average, is the primary measure of health used in the HDI, the UN's composite ranking of a country's overall development. According to the Organisation for Economic Co-operation and Development (OECD), life expectancy at birth is defined as 'how long, on average, a newborn can expect to live, if current death rates do not change'. What causes long life spans? Lack of conflict, good nutrition, better basic health practices, better sanitation and disease prevention have all contributed to longer life spans. The global life expectancy at birth in 2016 was 72 years. However, life expectancy varies by region and country, and within countries can vary by gender, economic level, and ethnic group.

Infant mortality

Infant mortality measures the number of deaths among children under one year of age for every 1000 live births. Globally, this rate is 39 deaths per 1000 live births, which is approximately 15,000 every day. In some countries this rate is as low as 2, while in others it can be nearly 100, or 10% of live births. Infant mortality is seen as an important signifier of overall health levels because prenatal and neonatal care can help reduce the risk of long-term health conditions early in life, as well as influencing the life expectancy at birth trends.

Maternal mortality ratio

The maternal mortality ratio (MMR), which measures maternal deaths per 100,000 live births, also tends to be highly correlated with overall development levels. This metric shows death rates for women caused by factors related to childbirth either before, during, or after pregnancy. When a country has an especially high MMR it is an indicator that women's health around pregnancy should be a priority, and this can support infant health levels as well.

Education-based development indicators

Expected years of schooling

Expected years of schooling refers to the number of years of schooling that a child of school entrance age can expect to receive if prevailing patterns of age-specific enrolment rates persist throughout the child's life. Countries that score lower in development terms average around 9 such years, while developed countries tend to have about 16.

Mean years of schooling

Mean years of schooling is the average number of years of education received by people aged 25 and older. This can range from five years in the least developed countries to about 12 in the highly developed ones.

Other development indicators

Inequality measures

Lorenz curves, Gini coefficients, and poverty indices are among the indicators of the degree of economic inequality within society. Social inequality can be measured as well by analysing different outcomes based on gender and ethnicity. Other measures that tend to reveal social inequalities are undernourishment rates, rates of child poverty, adolescent fertility rates, and child labour participation.

Energy indicators

Measures of how much energy is produced and consumed within a country can give an idea of the level of development. Some useful indicators are electric power consumption, access to electricity, and affordability.

Environmental indicators

Measurements of environmental sustainability are numerous, and the utility of such indicators depends on the area of the environment being examined. To study climate change, one might seek carbon emissions relative to GDP per capita. To measure water availability, one might measure the population having access to improved drinking water sources. And to study soil erosion, one may use desertification levels.

In summary, the use of single indicators provides useful but narrow information about a country's overall well-being and level of development. This is why composite measurements are increasingly used to give a broader view of the multidimensional aspects of development.

Researchers and policymakers have turned to composite indicators to get a better view of the many sided nature of development. These indicators combine two or more single indicators, weighting each according to the design of the measurement, and putting them together in an index.

The Human Development Index

The most influential and important composite indicator is the HDI. The HDI is a composite index that brings together three variables that reflect the three basic goals of development: a long and healthy life, a good education, and a decent standard of living. The variables measured are life expectancy at birth, mean years of schooling and expected years of schooling, and GNI per capita (PPP US$). It was created by the UN Development Programme (UNDP) in the late 1980s and put into use in 1990. It was created as a response to dissatisfaction with the emphasis on economic growth as the sole means to measure development.

The UNDP was attempting to shift the paradigm for development away from a purely growth-based model to a broader view, one that encompasses health and education levels. Amartya Sen, whose work is recognised as providing the intellectual framework of the HDI, put it this way:

> 'Human development, as an approach, is concerned with what I take to be the basic development idea: namely, advancing the richness of human life, rather than the richness of the economy in which human beings live, which is only a part of it.'

> – Amartya Sen

With this ideal in mind, the HDI evaluates the performance of a country in three areas:

- long life – measured by life expectancy
- education – measured by adult literacy and combined primary, secondary and tertiary enrolment ratio
- standard of living – measured by GDP per capita (PPP-adjusted).

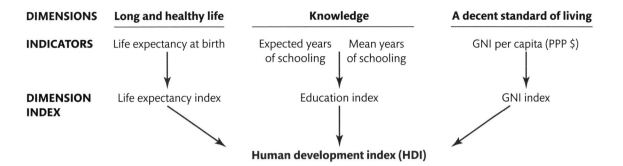

| DIMENSIONS | Long and healthy life | Knowledge | | A decent standard of living |
| DIMENSION INDEX | Life expectancy index | Education index | | GNI index |

INDICATORS Life expectancy at birth — Expected years of schooling — Mean years of schooling — GNI per capita (PPP $)

Human development index (HDI)

Figure 28.1 shows the flow of dimensions to indicators to the dimension index used to calculate the HDI.

These dimensions are weighted and aggregated into a composite index. Each country's performance in an area earns a score between 0 and 1; 0 is lowest, 1 the highest. These areas are then compiled for the composite HDI ranking. Table 28.2 shows the HDI value range and the scoring classifications.

Table 28.3 shows a selection of countries from each category. For some the HDI ranking in overall development is similar to the ranking on sheer income, here shown as GNI per capita. Some degree of correlation between development and income is to be expected, both because money is required to pay for essential healthcare and education but also because the HDI itself weights income as a third of its measurement. This makes discrepancies between these rankings more interesting. How does a country manage to 'overachieve' by ranking highly on development but lower on income? What is happening when a country scores highly on income but lower on development?

Where there is a difference between HDI and GNI performance, it is typically only a few spots. In many more, like El Salvador and Indonesia, they are very close. It would appear that, based on this list, some countries slightly overperform in development, relative to what their income rank would suggest (Norway, South Korea, Poland, Cameroon, and Pakistan), while Madagascar (+19) scores significantly better. Several others, the USA, Nigeria, Senegal among them, slightly underperform in development compared to their income level, and a few such as Brunei and Qatar, significantly fall short of what their income levels would suggest.

What are the overperforming countries doing right, and the underperforming countries doing wrong? Policymakers can use this information to assess their priorities and change their approach. Chapter 29 will explore the barriers to development, which may help explain why some countries misuse their wealth, and in Chapter 30 we will consider the strategies that countries can use to make development decisions.

Table 28.2   HDI country classification levels

Classification	HDI value
Very high human development	0.800 and above
High human development	0.700 to 0.799
Medium human development	0.555 to 0.699
Low human development	Less than 0.555

Table 28.3   HDI and GNI per capita information for selected countries

HDI Category	Country	HDI value	HDI rank	GNI per capita (PPP US$)	GNI per capita (PPP US$) rank	GNI per capita (PPP US$) minus HDI rank
Very high human development (62 countries)	Norway	0.954	1	76,684.5	7	+6
	USA	0.920	15	65,880	10	−5
	South Korea	0.906	22	43,430	29	+7
High human development (54 Countries)	Poland	0.872	40	32,710	45	+5
	Brunei Darussalam	0.845	43	80,393	9	−34
	Qatar	0.848	41	94,170	2	−39
Medium human development (36 countries)	Indonesia	0.707	111	11,930	109	−2
	El Salvador	0.667	124	8,700	124	0
	Cameroon	0.563	150	3,730	158	+8
	Pakistan	0.560	152	5,210	144	+8
Low human development (36 countries)	Nigeria	0.534	158	5,170	146	−12
	Senegal	0.514	166	1,450	159	−7
	Madagascar	0.521	162	1,660	183	+19
	Afghanistan	0.496	170	2,330	173	+3

The values and limitations of using the HDI

While the HDI is a major improvement over the crude use of simple GDP per capita to measure development *between* countries, it is likely to mask the vast differences *within* each country. Many countries have major differences in development between different regions, where major cities could rank in entirely different categories of the HDI than other parts of the country. Gender differences can be stark, with lower levels of health, income and education for women and girls. Attainment of all three of these key life measurements can also vary significantly between ethnic groups. With this in mind, economists and researchers are creating new indices that study other areas of the issue.

Exercise 28.1

With the data provided in Table 28.3 study the following groups of countries and make inferences about the difference between their GNI results and their HDI rankings. In other words, if the HDI consists of income, education and health, what can be said of countries that are overperforming (+) or underperforming (−) compared to their income?

1   What would you say about the differences between Poland and Brunei?
2   Nigeria and Madagascar score closely on the overall HDI, but have very different GNI levels. What do you think might be true of each country relative to the other?

Other composite indices used to study development

The Gender Inequality Index

In 2010, the UNDP created the first **Gender Inequality Index (GII)**, a composite indicator of the disparity in well-being between women and men in three areas: reproductive health, empowerment, and the labour market. The reproductive health dimension is measured by two indicators: MMR and the adolescent fertility rate. The empowerment dimension is measured by two indicators: the share of parliamentary seats held by each gender and their secondary and higher education attainment levels. The economic dimension is measured by women's participation in the workforce.

According to the UNDP, the GII 'is designed to reveal the extent to which national human development achievements are eroded by gender inequality, and to provide empirical foundations for policy analysis and advocacy efforts'.

Comparison of overall HDI rank to GII rank reveals that in some countries, gender inequality performance is holding back total development. Table 28.4 shows selected countries and their HDI as well as their GII ranks. The higher the GII rank, the greater equality between females and males.

The top countries in Table 28.4 have a GII rank well below their HDI rank. This suggests that the HDI scores for these countries would be even higher if there were to be some improvement in women's healthcare, women's comparative education levels, female employment, or political representation.

The bottom countries in Table 28.4 have scored extremely highly on the GII (more equality) compared to their overall HDI rank. As the HDI rankings attest, none of these are especially wealthy or highly developed. But gender equity scores are 'better than expected' when compared to their HDI rankings.

Inequality-adjusted Human Development Index

With the **Inequality-adjusted Human Development Index (IHDI)**, the UN has adjusted the HDI measures by how those achievements are distributed among the country's

Research and inquiry

What is the relationship between development and gender equality? Select from Table 28.4 one country with large negative disparities and one country with large positive disparities. What are the factors or policies that result in such high or low scores in each country? Use search terms like 'gender equality policies', or 'gender disparities/equality in _____ [your selected country]'.

Table 28.4   Countries with large disparities between HDI and GII ranks

Country	HDI rank (higher rank = more developed)	GII rank (higher rank = more equal)	HDI – GII disparity
Large negative disparities			
Saudi Arabia	36	49	−13
USA	15	42	−27
Iran	65	118	−53
Panama	67	108	−51
Large positive disparities			
Libya	110	41	+69
China	85	39	+46
Tajikistan	125	84	+41
Portugal	40	17	+23

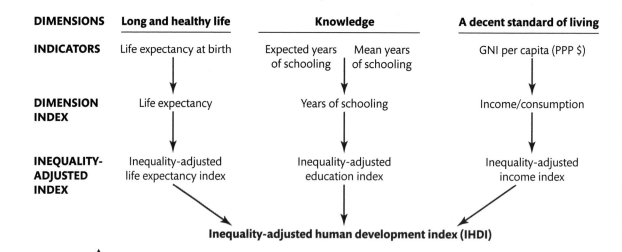

DIMENSIONS	Long and healthy life	Knowledge		A decent standard of living
INDICATORS	Life expectancy at birth	Expected years of schooling	Mean years of schooling	GNI per capita (PPP $)
DIMENSION INDEX	Life expectancy	Years of schooling		Income/consumption
INEQUALITY-ADJUSTED INDEX	Inequality-adjusted life expectancy index	Inequality-adjusted education index		Inequality-adjusted income index

Inequality-adjusted human development index (IHDI)

Figure 28.2 The Inequality-adjusted Human Development Index

population by 'discounting' each dimension's average value according to its level of inequality. This approach strives to account for the human costs of inequality.

Because all countries have some inequality in their distributions of income, education and health, all countries' IHDI decreased their overall HDI value. In other words, all of the IHDI values are lower than their HDI ones because all countries suffer development costs because of their inequality. However, those with the greatest inequality fall furthest in the rankings while some move up because of their smaller relative inequities.

The table below shows a selection of countries and their HDI score and rank as well as their IHDI score and rank, as well as the difference between the two. The final column therefore shows the rise or fall in rankings because of the IHDI adjustment.

Notice that Singapore dropped several places while Japan moved up. One way to explain this is to say that the high levels of development in Singapore are concentrated and not as widely distributed as they are in Japan. We could say the same thing about Brazil and Chile (both marked down by the IHDI), compared to Kyrgyzstan. By these measures, the UN is saying that the social costs of inequality will drag down overall development, and this is especially true for some countries.

Table 28.5 **Selected countries' HDI and Inequality adjusted HDI values and ranks**

Country	HDI value	HDI rank	IHDI value	IHDI rank	HDI rank – IHDI rank
Norway	0.945	1	0.0889	1	0
Singapore	0.935	9	0.810	23	−14
Japan	0.915	19	0.882	4	+15
USA	0.920	15	0.845	28	−13
Chile	0.847	42	0.696	56	−14
Brazil	0.769	79	0.574	102	−23
Kyrgyzstan	0.674	122	0.610	99	+23
Namibia	0.645	130	0.417	144	−14

As described in Chapter 18, inequality carries costs that show up in health levels and education attainment. Specifically, higher levels of many bad social outcomes such as obesity, mental illness, depression, and infant mortality are found in unequal societies.

Why keep track of these distinctions? As the UN says, 'The IHDI allows a direct link to inequalities in dimensions, it can inform policies towards inequality reduction, and leads to better understanding of inequalities across population and their contribution to the overall human development cost'. Advocates for more equitable policies in countries like the USA, Brazil, Singapore, Chile, and Namibia can point to these results as the inspiration for changing course.

Exercise 28.2

Using the information in Table 28.5, discuss the probable differences between the following countries who scores similarly on the HDI, but differently on the IHDI.

1   Japan and the USA.
2   Kyrgyzstan and Brazil.

The Happy Planet Index

We have already discussed the Happy Planet Index (HPI) in Chapter 13. The HPI measures well-being, life expectancy, and inequality and adjusts these for the ecological footprint per person. By doing so, the HPI tries to measure equitable well-being with sustainability factored in. The results for the HPI vary significantly from traditional HDI rankings.

The multidimensional poverty index (MPI)

The MPI was explained in more detail in Chapter 18. The MPI is a composite indicator that contributes to the understanding of the complexity of poverty, one that combines traditional measures of education and health with specific indicators on standard of living. The indicators are:

- health – nutrition, child mortality
- education – years of schooling, school attendance
- standard of living – cooking fuel, sanitation, electricity, housing, assets, drinking water.

The Inclusive Development Index

The Inclusive Development Index (IDI) is a project that comes from the World Economic Forum's System Initiative, one whose stated goal is 'to inform and enable sustained and inclusive economic progress through deepened public–private cooperation.' The IDI itself has three pillars: growth and development; inclusion; and intergenerational equity with sustainable stewardship of natural and financial resources.

The IDI tries to incorporate many factors into each of its dimensions, including measures of income and wealth equity, as well as the financial and environmental sustainability over time.

Table 28.6 shows sample scores for selected countries from the two groups, advanced and emerging economies. Among the advanced economies, Switzerland is near the top at number 4, and the UK, significantly lower at number 21. Switzerland ranks in the top 20% for seven of the elements, while the UK is in the bottom 40% for seven elements.

In the emerging economies group, Lithuania is at the top, ranking in the top 20% for five of the elements measured. China, while scoring highly in three elements, is in the bottom 20% for income and wealth inequality, as well as net savings.

The data offered by the IDI, as well as the numerous other composite indices being offered, is to energise debate around the ways to best achieve development aims.

What are the strengths and limitations of the different approaches to measuring development?

With all the measurements available, the study of development may seem intimidating. How does one compare and evaluate the different approaches? It may be evident that

Research and inquiry

Using the IDI, look up your home country, or your country of residence. Do the rankings make sense to you, or is there something surprising? Now seek out the results for one emerging and one advanced economy and share the results with your class.

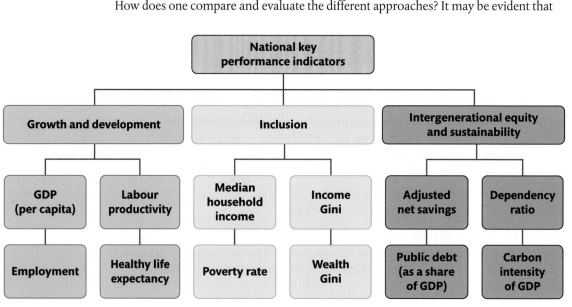

Figure 28.3 Inclusive Development Index dimensions and indicators

Table 28.6 The Inclusive development index, selected countries from advanced and emerging groups

	Growth & development				Rank	Inclusion				Intergenerational equity & sustainability			
	GDP per capita ($)	Labor productivity ($)	Healthy life expectancy (YRS)	Employment (%)		Net income Gini	Poverty rate (%)	Wealth Gini	Median income ($)	Adjusted net saving* (%)	Carbon intensity, KG per $ of GDP	Public debt (%)	Dependence ratio (%)
Advanced economies													
Switzerland	75,726	98,724	73.1	65.4	4	29.3	7.8	69.4	55.6	17.9	11.8	45.4	49.4
UK	41,603	80,371	71.4	59.6	21	32.8	10.9	73.5	39.4	4.4	21.8	89.2	56.2
Emerging economies													
Lithuania	15,873	60,195	66.1	53.9	1	34.2	2.7	51.6	18.2	18.8	63.7	40.0	50.5
China	6,894	25,369	68.5	67.5	26	51.0	12.1	78.9	7.7	23.3	201.1	46.2	38.5

Rank

Bottom 20%   Top 20%

single indicators are less useful than composite indicators at evaluating the many facets to human well-being in any given country. And all such data is only as good as the methods used to compile it.

One might compare this trend to the notion of an 'open source' environment where the standard no longer is measured through one statistic (GDP per capita) and distributed by one or two agencies, like the World Bank and the UN. Instead, the open approach has many different non-governmental organisations (NGOs), research groups, and intergovernmental agencies all trying out new perspectives and new models. Just as the HDI surpassed old measures of economic growth, so too may one of the alternative measures here evolve into the baseline standard for country well-being, ones that include the distribution of well-being, the sustainability of each country's way of life, and whether such well-being is broadly enjoyed.

TOK

What knowledge questions might be encountered in constructing a composite indicator to measure development?

Exercise 28.3

Using the information in the chapter and your own knowledge of economics, evaluate the strengths and limitations of any two of the composite indices discussed in this chapter.

Practice exam questions

Paper 1, part (a) questions (HL and SL)

1. Explain the difference between GDP per capita and GNI per capita as a measure of economic growth. (10 marks)
2. Discuss how three different indicators might be used to measure health. (10 marks)
3. Explain what the Human Development Index measures. (10 marks)
4. Compare two composite indicators, explain how economic development can be measured differently. (10 marks)

Paper 1, part (b) questions (HL and SL)

2. Using real-world examples, examine the distinction between economic growth and economic development. (15 marks)

HL and SL Paper 2, 2-mark and 4-mark questions

Country	HDI rank	HDI value	GNI per capita (PPP US$)	GDP growth rate (%)	Cause of death by communicable disease and nutrition conditions (% of total)
Ireland	3	0.942	55,660	5.5	5
China	85	0.752	16,127	6.1	4
Myanmar	145	0.584	5,764	6.5	24
Tanzania	159	0.528	2,805	6.3	56
South Sudan	186	0.413	1,716	11.3	63

2-mark questions (HL and SL)

1. Define the following terms:
   a. HDI   (2 marks)
   b. GDP growth rate.   (2 marks)

4-mark questions (HL and SL)

1. Explain why cause of death by communicable disease and nutrition conditions would correlate highly with levels of economic development.   (4 marks)
2. Explain two reasons why the GDP growth rate is not a useful indicator of overall economic development.   (4 marks)

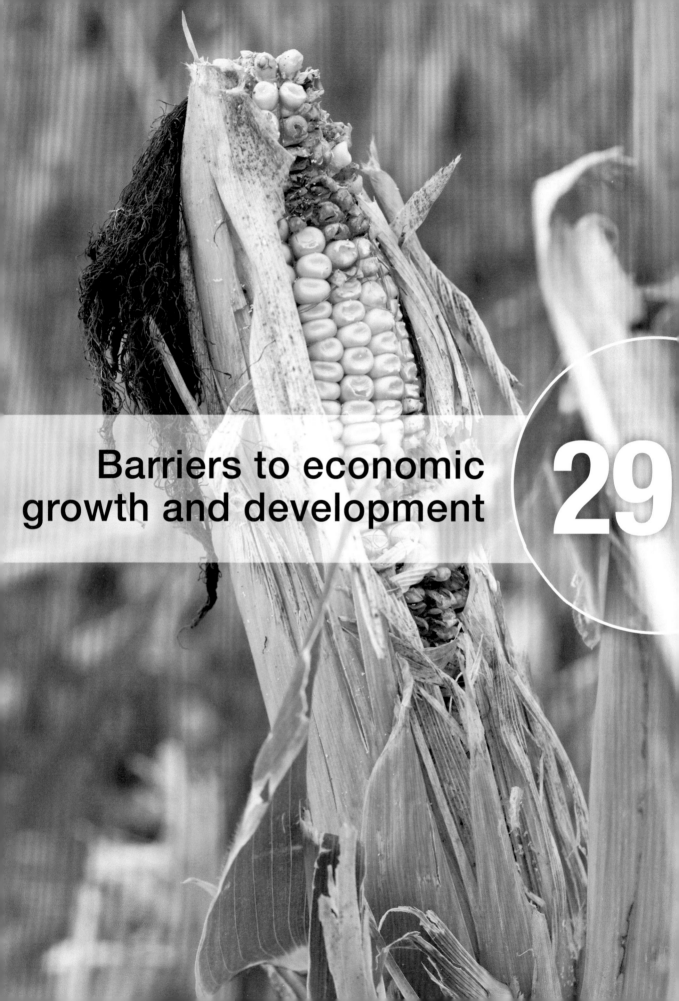

Barriers to economic growth and development

In our last two chapters we established a definition of economic development, with an acknowledgement that sustainable development requires a broad look at human well-being that incorporates economic, social, political, and environmental considerations. We have also examined the common characteristics of less economically developed countries and looked at the different measurements of economic development, both single indicators and composite indicators.

In this chapter we will ask the question, 'What are the barriers to economic development?' In order for countries to overcome poverty and raise living standards to a level at which a healthy, happy life can be enjoyed by all, an understanding of the obstacles their economies face is crucial.

29.1 What is a poverty trap?

Learning outcomes

At the end of this section you will be able to:

- explain, using a diagram, how certain factors can trap a country in a cycle that perpetuates poverty, including:
  - natural resource endowments
  - geography
  - education
  - poor governance
  - conflict.

A poverty trap is any self-reinforcing mechanism that contributes to the persistence of poverty in a nation. If a country finds itself in a poverty trap over a long period of time, it is unlikely to escape unless meaningful steps are taken either domestically or initiated by an outside force to allow the country to escape the trap.

Poverty traps usually have at their core a fundamental obstacle that perpetuates itself and thereby keeps the country poor. Some examples of poverty traps include the natural resource trap, the geography trap, the poor education/poor governance trap, and the conflict trap.

What is the natural resource trap?

A developing country with few natural resources may find itself in a poverty trap for two reasons. First, without mineral, energy, forest, or marine resources it cannot sustain its domestic need for such resources. Second, it cannot export resources to earn much needed foreign exchange. Without a developed secondary, manufacturing sector, many developing countries (such as the Democratic Republic of Congo and other mineral-rich countries in Africa) depend greatly on the export of raw materials to Europe and East Asia.

A country without a secondary sector and a poor supply of natural resources, however, could find itself in a particularly difficult situation in which the foreign capital required to invest in its secondary sector is inaccessible due to the lack of exchangeable commodities from within the country. Figure 29.1 provides an

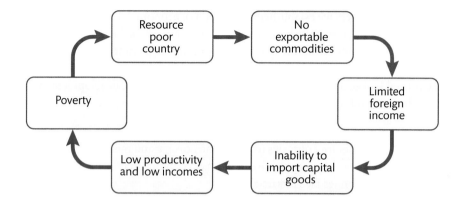

Figure 29.1 In the natural resource poverty cycle the lack of exportable commodities hampers economic development

illustration of a poverty trap in which a developing country is kept poor because of its lack of exportable natural resource commodities. The trap is illustrated in a circle, or a **poverty cycle**: a self-perpetuating cycle of poverty from which the country cannot escape.

Poverty persists because a poor resource base prevents the country from accessing foreign capital. Since the country has few valuable natural resources to exchange with the rest of the world, it has only limited access to the foreign exchange it would need to acquire the capital goods needed to develop a secondary sector. Without capital, worker productivity and incomes remain low, and the people remain impoverished.

Paul Collier, an economics professor at Oxford University, proposes another kind of natural resource trap, in which a developing country is kept poor because of its *abundance* of natural resources. His seemingly contradictory theory is explained by the fact that if all a developing country has to offer the global market is one valuable natural commodity (such as diamonds from Sierra Leone or Liberia), domestic conflict arises over the control of the one natural resource. Political and social upheaval may result from the struggle for control of the exportable commodity, creating conditions completely antithetical to those necessary for economic development.

What is the geography trap?

Collier also suggests that a major source of persistent poverty for some nations is their geographical location. If a nation is landlocked and surrounded by developing countries, that country is extremely likely to be developing itself. Being landlocked alone does not mean a country is developing. There are several landlocked countries in Europe that are among the richest in the world, such as Luxembourg, Switzerland, Austria, and Liechtenstein. But all these countries are fortunate to have rich neighbours with whom they have good economic relations.

A look at the map of Africa, Asia, or South America identifies many landlocked countries that are among the least developed in the world, including Bolivia, Paraguay, Niger, Zambia, Nepal, and Afghanistan.

Some of the least developed countries in South America, Africa, and Asia are landlocked and surrounded by other developing countries, a situation that makes it incredibly difficult for the landlocked country to begin a journey on the path of economic development. Figure 29.3 provides an example of the poverty cycle a landlocked country might find itself in.

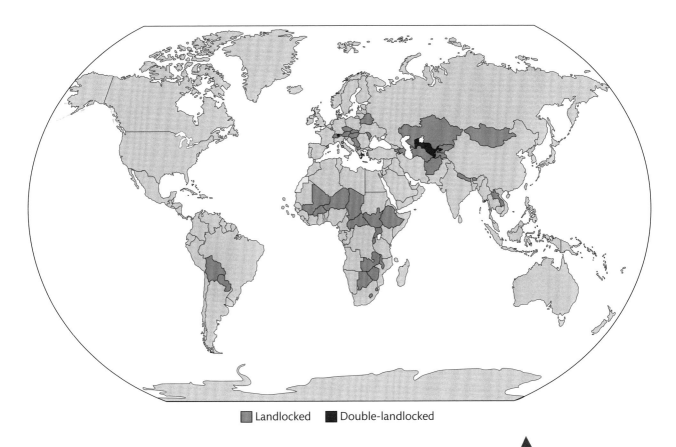

Landlocked ■ Double-landlocked

▲
Figure 29.2 The landlocked countries of the world

The key to the geography trap is the lack of access to sea ports even in neighbouring countries. Without access to sea ports, it does not matter how politically stable and economically attractive a country is to foreign producers and consumers. If there are no means to safely and reliably export their output to the rest of the world, such a country would not even be on the radar of international investors looking for places to produce goods for the global market. Without reliable demand from other countries, it would be nearly impossible for a developing country to increase its national income and the standards of living of its people.

What is the education and poor governance trap?

One of the most important functions of government is to collect taxes and provide public goods to the nation's people, including education, healthcare, and infrastructure.

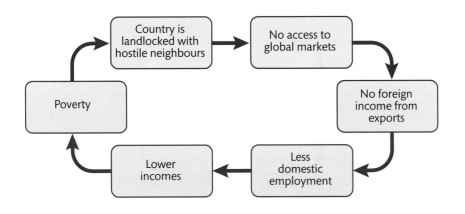

◀ **Figure 29.3** In the geography poverty cycle a lack of sea ports blocks access to global markets and stunts growth

591

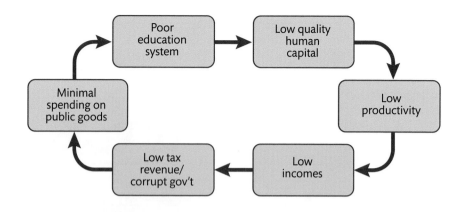

Figure 29.4 In the education poverty cycle under-provision of education perpetuates poverty and bad governance ▶

Developing countries are poor because their leaders keep them poor. To what extent is this statement true? Is a good leader all that is needed to achieve economic development in a developing country?

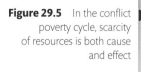

In a developing country with a corrupt government, an ineffective tax system and a poor education system, economic development is nearly impossible to achieve. And under-provision of education perpetuates the bad governance and poverty, as can be seen in Figure 29.4.

A poorly educated workforce makes a country less attractive for foreign direct investment, limiting the amount of capital available to workers. Low skill levels and limited capital make the nation's workforce unproductive, meaning lower incomes, less tax revenue, and less ability for the government to provide the very public goods needed to get the country on the road to economic development.

What is the conflict trap?

Perhaps the worst poverty trap for a country to find itself in is a conflict trap. Unfortunately, any of the three poverty traps described above can easily deteriorate into conflict, and if a country finds itself in all three situations (landlocked with poor natural resources, and a corrupt government) the likelihood of conflict arising is extremely high. Civil unrest perpetuates poverty for many reasons, but Figure 29.5 shows the basic problem with conflict in a developing nation.

Much of the conflict in developing countries is over the resources that are needed to generate income that could then be put to work improving people's lives. But the existence of conflict ultimately intensifies the scarcity of resources and creates an environment of political and economic uncertainty that makes the country unattractive to foreign investors who might otherwise invest in the nation's economy.

Figure 29.5 In the conflict poverty cycle, scarcity of resources is both cause and effect ▶

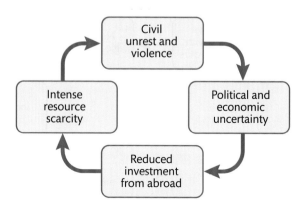

In this way, conflict born from scarcity actually intensifies scarcity and thereby fuels more conflict. A country in which many resources are going towards waging an internal war is most certainly going to remain developing until stability is achieved and an atmosphere deemed safe for international investors is restored.

29.2 What are the economic barriers to growth and development?

Learning outcomes

At the end of this section you will be able to:

- examine the role of barriers to economic development including:
  - inequality
  - lack of access to infrastructure and **appropriate technology**
  - low levels of human capital
  - lack of access to healthcare and education
  - dependence on primary sector production
  - lack of access to international markets
  - **informal economy**
  - capital flight
  - indebtedness
  - geography including landlocked countries.

What is the relationship between inequality and economic growth and development?

An unequal distribution of income, demonstrated by a nation's Gini coefficient, is common in developing countries. While the vast majority of the population remains poor, what little income is generated by the economy is often enjoyed by a tiny elite. Unequal income distribution may be a result of an ineffective tax system, without which an equitable distribution of income is impossible. Without a system of transfer payments, the ability of the poor to escape poverty by improving their human capital is limited, keeping the majority of the country's population in poverty.

Inequality can be considered both a cause and a consequence of underdevelopment. In a way, growth and development present a pathway towards greater equity and equality in society; after all, the larger the pie, the more there is to go around. However, a low level of economic development can also be caused by inequality, as without a level playing field and an equitable opportunity for all in society to pursue and maintain a higher standard of living, economic development can never get underway. Equity requires that all people are offered the same opportunities, including access to education and healthcare. While gaps between rich and poor might exist, they are not so great that they cannot be overcome through individual perseverance and hard work.

The picture painted here is idealistic; in reality the many other social, cultural, economic, and political barriers to economic development complicate the picture and make improved equity and a more equal distribution of income that much harder to achieve.

Why do a lack of access to infrastructure and appropriate technology slow development?

Infrastructure includes roads, highways, airports, rail track, ports, and communications technologies such as cellular towers, phone lines, and internet. It also includes a nation's stock of schools, hospitals, clinics, community centres, cultural centres, office buildings, and all other 'manufactured inputs' that contribute to economic growth and development.

A lack of access to infrastructure leaves a country in a permanent state of underdevelopment. Infrastructure is like the essential biological systems that support the life of a functioning economy. Roads are the arteries of commerce, telecommunications the neurons, school the brains, and hospitals the immune system. Without infrastructure, the organism that is the economy is sick and cannot function efficiently.

Where does infrastructure come from? Once again we return to a chicken and egg question. Without economic growth, a country cannot afford to invest in infrastructure, which itself is necessary for economic growth. In other words, some income is needed before infrastructure improvements can be made. For very under-developed countries, international aid or foreign investment could provide infrastructure, either through private investments from multinational corporations or via aid from international organisations like the World Bank (which will be explored more in Chapter 30).

What is human capital and why does it matter?

Human capital refers to the level of skill, knowledge, and education among a country's workforce. A low level of human capital occurs in countries in which access to education is inadequate, while good schooling improves human capital.

Why is it important? While growth and development can take place even in a country with low levels of human capital (an export-oriented growth strategy based on the employment of unskilled workers in agriculture, mining, or manufacturing industries, for example) there is ultimately a ceiling at which improvements in living standards will be capped without investing in human capital. The most developed countries in the world, in which households enjoy higher incomes, but also better health and a cleaner environment, are typically those in which human capital has been invested in through providing high quality education systems for decades. The jobs available to high-skilled workers are typically safer, pay higher incomes, offer more benefits like paid holidays, and take a smaller toll on the physical well-being of those who do them. Therefore, improving human capital is a sure means to promote economic growth and development.

An educated population is able to contribute more to the economic output of a developing country than if the population has less access to education. There is a strong correlation between education and income; as access to education increases, productivity of workers rises, allowing them to contribute to the nation's output and increase their own income in the process.

How does a dependence on primary sector production affect development?

In Section 29.1 we looked at the 'resource trap' that many developing countries that are overly dependent on the production of primary commodities have found themselves in.

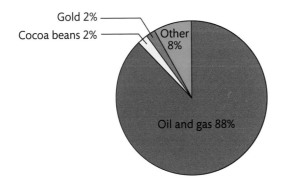

Figure 29.6 Most of Nigeria's exports are of oil and gas

Many less economically developed countries tend to over-specialise in a narrow range of products, oftentimes primary commodities such as energy resources, minerals, and agricultural goods. Consider Figure 29.6, which shows the composition of Nigeria's exports to the rest of the world.

Observe from the pie chart that 88% of Nigeria's exports are of energy resources (oil and gas). While specialisation in petroleum allows Nigeria to achieve a high level of efficiency in the production of this valuable resource, it also leaves the country highly vulnerable to fluctuations in global petroleum prices.

When oil prices are high, Nigeria can expect to enjoy booming export revenues, strong aggregate demand (AD), higher levels of employment and income, and a strong currency. However, when global oil prices fall, Nigeria's AD, employment, price level, aggregate output, and currency exchange rate will all decline. The current account balance will move towards a deficit and Nigeria's foreign income will fall, making it difficult to afford the imports of manufactured goods and technology that it depends on for economic development.

Consider Figure 29.7, which shows the world oil price between 2005 and 2017. As the price of its only major export fluctuated, Nigeria's economy would have experienced macroeconomic shocks as its export earnings rose and fell. When oil prices rise, Nigeria's currency appreciates as demand for its major exports increases. High export revenues and a strong currency allow Nigeria to buy imported technology and consumer goods relatively cheaply and promote improvements in economic development as the cost of welfare-improving products becomes more affordable.

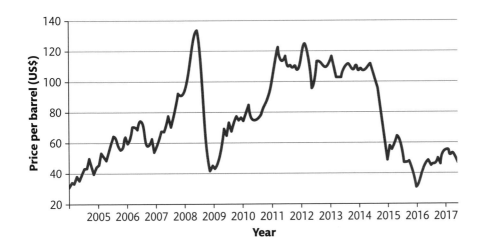

Figure 29.7 Global oil price fluctuations, 2005–17

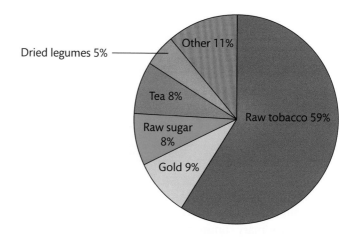

Figure 29.8 Malawi's exports are almost all agricultural goods

However, when oil prices fall, Nigeria's ability to buy those development-supporting imports decreases. The problem with primary commodities, as we learned in our microeconomic chapters, is that their prices tend to be highly volatile due to relatively inelastic demand and supply. For this reason, over-specialising in a single or a small number of primary commodities leads to instability and poses a barrier to economic development for developing countries.

Let us consider another country that is overly dependent on a narrow range of exports. Figure 29.8 shows the composition of Malawi's exports.

Malawi specialises almost entirely in agricultural goods (80% of exports), which like oil tend to have highly volatile prices on global markets due to their highly inelastic supply and demand. Consumers are not highly responsive to price changes, so changes in supply year to year tend to result in sharp spikes or dips in global price. In the short run, supply of agricultural goods is highly inelastic, resulting in price volatility as demand rises and falls.

For comparison, let us look at the composition of goods produced in a more economically developed country, the UK. Figure 29.9 shows the UK's exports by category.

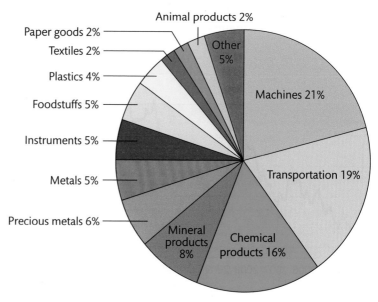

Figure 29.9 United Kingdom exports include a diverse range of goods

Obviously, the UK produces a much more diverse range of goods for export to the rest of the world, which shelters its economy from swings in the prices in any single category of goods. As a result, the UK's economy is much more resilient and able to survive the volatility that is common in the markets for primary commodities.

Does access to international markets matter?

In short, YES! Poet John Donne wrote, 'No man is an island.' In the same vein, no *country* is an island. I mean, yes, there are countries that are literally islands, but metaphorically speaking, no person (or country) is truly self-sufficient. The degree to which less developed countries are integrated with the rest of the global economy plays a huge role in their access both to markets for their exported commodities or manufactured goods and their ability to import the capital and consumer goods necessary for economic development.

Access to markets means more than just more places to sell exports to or buy imports from. Globalisation means financial integration as well, and at the higher levels free movement of labour and capital. Trade blocs in the developing world have increased regionalisation in less developed countries, while bilateral and multilateral trade agreements between more developed and less developed economies have broadened the markets for producers on both ends of these deals.

For all the reasons outlined in Chapter 22, Benefits of international trade, and Chapter 24, Economic integration, broadening access to global markets provides a path towards economic development. On the other hand, an inward oriented strategy through which a country attempts to achieve growth and development on its own, is bound to result in perpetual poverty and low living standards. 'Self-sufficiency is the road to poverty', argues American economist Russ Roberts. Increased economic integration, therefore, provides a pathway to prosperity.

What is the informal economy, and why might a large one affect development?

Large informal markets, or black markets, are common in less developed countries, again largely because of the lack of effective institutions such as a legal system, law enforcement, property rights, or a system of taxation. When an entrepreneur in a developing country sees a business opportunity, her natural instinct might be to take the steps necessary to meet the demand she sees, and do so at the lowest possible cost in order to maximise her own profits and well-being.

Black markets may bring to mind illicit or illegal activities, such as drugs or prostitution, but in fact, most informal markets in the developing world are just enterprising businesspeople meeting the needs in their communities, but doing so without going through the formal, official, process of starting a legal business, recording and reporting income to the government, paying taxes and licence and permit fees, and all the other 'red tape' that goes along with running a legitimate business.

In other words, black markets in themselves are not necessarily *barriers* to economic development; rather, the benefits an economy would experience from more of the informal economy becoming formalised. There are benefits to individuals who run their businesses informally, but there are costs to society as a whole, including reduced tax revenues and a diminished public sector that, were more of the economy taking

Research and inquiry

The diversity of a country's economic output is important for the level of resilience to economic shocks the economy might face. Overdependence on a small number of primary commodities, as we have shown, can present a barrier to economic development.

A great resource for visualising the composition of countries' output is available at the Observatory of Economic Complexity. Look it up in a web browser, or visit https://oec.world. Complete the following tasks, making observations along the way, then answer the questions that follow.

Tasks:

1 Choose one less economically developed country, perhaps from sub-Saharan Arica, South Asia, or Central Asia. In the search bar where it says 'Explore World Trade', type the name of the country you selected and the word 'exports'. Click enter.

2 Study the chart that is returned, which should show the composition of your selected country's exports.

3 In a separate tab in your browser, do the same thing for a more developed country, perhaps one from Western Europe, North America, or East Asia. Study the resulting chart.

With the two export charts on your screen, answer the questions that follow.

1 What percentage of total exports are made up by the three largest exports from the less developed country you selected? What about from the more developed country?

2 What are the largest exports from each of your countries?

3 Choose one of the primary commodities that make up a significant percentage of your less developed country's exports. Do a web search for the name of the commodity and 'price chart'; for example, 'copper price chart'.

  a Find a price chart showing the changes in the commodities price over several years.

  b How would you describe the changes in the commodities price over the years?

  c What might account for the fluctuations observed in the commodity's price over several years?

4 Why do the prices of manufactured goods tend to be more stable and therefore fluctuate less than the prices of primary commodities?

5 Why does a country's dependence on the export of a small number of primary commodities pose a barrier to economic development?

place formally, would be able to provide more of the public goods on which continued economic development depends.

What is capital flight?

Capital flight occurs when financial and physical assets are withdrawn from a country due to uncertainty over economic conditions or events that have made the country less attractive for foreign investment. Domestic capital flight occurs when domestic investors withdraw their assets and place them in safer, overseas accounts or invest in physical assets abroad rather than at home.

Capital outflows might occur due to political turmoil, such as a contested national election or a government takeover by a party hostile to foreign investment. Economic causes might include an increase in taxes on foreign investment or a decrease in interest rates that suddenly makes investments in the country less profitable to foreigners. Exchange rate fluctuations also might make foreign investors jittery and lead them to withdraw their investments.

When financial and physical capital are withdrawn from a developing country, the economy will find its capital stock decreased, slowing the rate of economic growth, or even causing a recession. Foreign investment provides a source of domestic tax revenue, so with less foreign capital in the country the domestic tax base, along with the government's ability to provide public goods like education and infrastructures, is diminished.

Capital flight can be prevented when a developing country tackles some of the other barriers to development that it faces, including political, banking and finance, property rights, and legal challenges. Stable institutions foster confidence among both international and domestic investors and create an environment more conducive to attracting and retaining international capital flows.

Is indebtedness a concern?

In the macroeconomics section of this course we learned how countries accrue debt: when a government's budget is in deficit, it must borrow money to finance that deficit, adding to the national debt. Every year a country experiences a budget deficit, its national debt grows.

Debt in and of itself is not always a bad thing. The ability to borrow funds to finance a budget deficit allows a country to fund the current and capital expenditures necessary to keep the government running, to invest in the nation's infrastructure, and to provide the public goods required for economic development.

The countries with the highest debt levels in the world are hardly on the brink of economic collapse. The USA, with a national debt of over $20 trillion (around 100% of gross domestic product (GDP)), enjoys macroeconomic stability and a strong currency. Japan has debt that equals nearly 250% of its national income, yet it is considered one of the safest economies in the world to do business in.

The problem arises when a country's debt is mostly owed to foreign investors, AND when the burden of that debt limits the country's ability to provide necessary public goods and to invest in infrastructure. External debt, or foreign debt, is the proportion of a country's debt that is owed to international lenders, including commercial banks, governments, and international financial institutions like the World Bank and the International Monetary Fund.

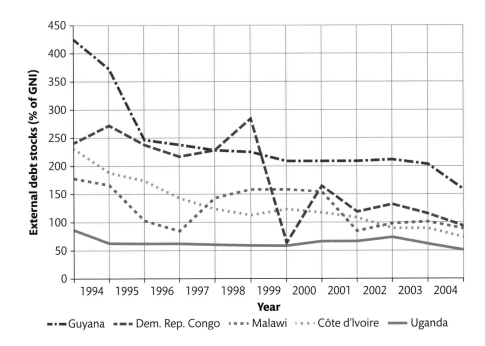

Figure 29.10 External debt stocks as a percentage of GNI for selected sub-Saharan African nations

When a less developed country accumulates a large amount of foreign debt, servicing that debt can crowd out essential spending on public goods and infrastructure, and thus limit the level of economic development in the developing country. Debt servicing refers to the money that a government must spend to pay the interest on past debts. The larger a country's foreign debt, the more of its limited tax revenues it must allocate to service that debt. If the country has to borrow money to service past debts, its total debt stock will increase.

Figure 29.10 shows the total debt stocks of several less developed countries as a percentage of their gross national incomes (GNIs) from 1994 to 2004.

Note that nearly all the countries averaged external debt stocks of well over 100% of their GNIs over the decade from 1994 to 2004.

To give an idea of the burden high levels of external debt can put on a country's economy, consider a country that must service external debt of 200% of GNI, such as Democratic Republic of Congo (DRC) in 1999.

- Assume DRC owed external creditors 10% interest on its debt.
- With debt equal to 200% of GNI, this means that as much as 20% of DRC's total income in 1999 was owed to foreign creditors in interest payments alone.
- DRC's government must then collect taxes on its citizens of at least 20% of their total income, which would be just enough to service its debt.
- That 20% of income would then be handed over to foreign lenders, leaving DRC with little or no money to spend on infrastructure, health, or education.

High levels of external debt can result in a poverty cycle or poverty trap in which foreign debt payments limit the ability of a country to achieve economic development, requiring the government to accrue more debt, leading to higher debt servicing costs. As Figure 29.10 shows, external debt levels as a percentage of GDP have declined across sub-Saharan Africa in the decades since 2000, largely the result of debt relief efforts, which will be explored further in Chapter 30.

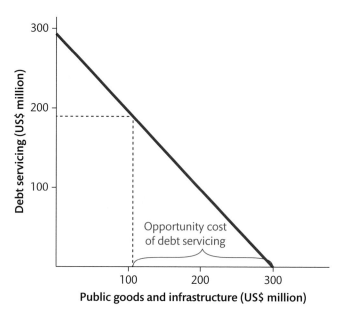

Figure 29.11   PPC showing the trade-off between debt servicing and the provision of public goods

The dilemma of foreign debt can be illustrated in a simple production possibility curve (PPC) model showing the trade-off between servicing debt and investing in public goods and infrastructure. Figure 29.11 illustrates the trade-off between debt servicing and public goods in a PPC model.

Assuming Guyana's GNI is $1 billion and that the government collects $300 million in taxes, it must spend $200 million on interest payments to foreigners to service its debt, leaving only $100 million to invest in public goods and infrastructure. Guyanese households lose 30% of their income to taxes, but get only 10% back in the form of public goods, while 20% 'leaks' from the economy, ending up in the pockets of foreign creditors.

Servicing international debt also creates balance of payments problems. Recall that the balance of payments consists of the current account (which measures the flow of money for the purchase of goods, income flows, and current transfers) and the financial account (which measures the flow for financial and real assets). Debt servicing leads to an outflow of funds in the financial account, moving it towards deficit.

To pay back foreign creditors, a country must have foreign currency, which it can earn from selling exports (measured as a credit in the current account). However, if a country does not have exports to sell or if the demand for or the value of its exports suddenly falls (not uncommon in less developed countries that largely specialise in primary commodities), then the ability to service its external debt is limited, and a country runs the risk of defaulting on its foreign debts. A default would result in a country being cut off from international credit markets and limit the government's ability to finance future budgets.

Do geography and climate matter for economic development?

Many observers note that some of the least developed countries in the world lie in the equatorial zones, leading them to posit that geography and climate might matter for economic development. While it is true that some of the least developed countries do lie at or near the equator, there may be more correlation at work than causation. It is also true that some of the richest countries in the world lie near the equator. The oil-rich emirates of the Middle East, Singapore, Panama, and some of the more prosperous cities in India all lie near the equator. Geography and climate, in other words, are not destiny.

A country's geographic location can, of course, be a huge boon to economic development. Singapore is a case in point. Practically straddling the equator, Singapore began its modern history as a former British colony that upon gaining its independence in 1965 was left with a system of institutions established by the British, automatically giving it an upper hand in its path towards development. However, unlike many other former British colonies, many of which remain underdeveloped in 2020, over 50 years since their independence in 1965, Singapore was left with a system of institutions that gave it an upper hand in its path towards development. However, unlike many other former British colonies (many of which remain underdeveloped, over 50 years since their independence), Singapore was also blessed with advantageous geography.

Despite its steamy, equatorial climate, Singapore's location along key international shipping routes between the economic powerhouses of East Asia (Japan, Taiwan, China) and the large consumer bases of South Asia, Africa, and Europe, made Singapore a natural hub from which international commercial operations could be established. Though economic development there has many causes, Singapore's geography served as a major advantage in its path towards economic development.

As we discussed in Section 29.1, geography can pose a trap. Only a couple of thousand kilometres northwest of Singapore lies Laos, the only landlocked country in Southeast Asia, and not surprisingly a country that is far behind Singapore, and even its more immediate neighbours of Vietnam and Thailand, on its path to economic development.

Climate can also pose both an obstacle to and provide opportunities for economic development. As the global climate changes, growing warmer in an era of increased greenhouse gas emissions, some countries are experiencing changes that could accelerate development, but more are seeing the adverse effects of a warming planet. More frequent and intense extreme weather events, from floods to typhoons to droughts and forest fires, are creating environmental and human catastrophes that can set countries back in their path towards development. In some cases, entire regions are becoming uninhabitable due to climate change, leading to mass migration and putting increasing pressure on the limited resources available in already over-populated areas, especially cities, of the developing world.

Sometimes a country's climate itself can pose obstacles to development, especially if the climate is harsh and conducive to endemic diseases like malaria. According to the World Health Organization:

> 'Globally, an estimated 3.4 billion people in 92 countries are at risk of being infected with malaria and developing disease and 1.1 billion are at high risk. According to the World Malaria Report 2018, there were 219 million cases of malaria globally in 2017 (uncertainty range 203–262 million) and 435,000 malaria deaths … The burden was heaviest in the WHO African Region, where an estimated 93% of all malaria deaths occurred, and in children aged under 5 years, who accounted for 61% of all deaths.'

The map in Figure 29.12, produced by the International Association for Medical Assistance for Travelers, shows the countries with high and limited risks of malaria infection.

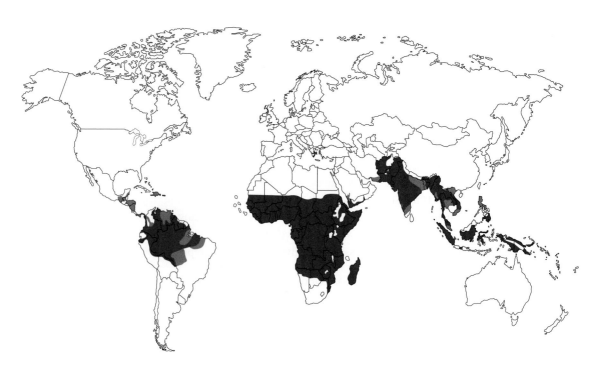

■ Areas with high rates of Malaria ■ Areas with limited risk of Malaria

Figure 29.12 Malaria infection risks impede economic development in many countries

A climate conducive to infectious disease means a country will have to allocate its limited resources towards protecting human life from illnesses that most countries in cooler climates would never have to worry about. The 435,000 deaths in 2017, mostly among children, represent lost lives that will not grow up to participate in the growth and development of their economies. The human, social, and economic impact of climate-related diseases poses an obstacle to development across the developing world, even in the 21st century.

29.3 What are the political and social barriers to economic growth and development?

Learning outcomes

At the end of this section you will be able to:

- outline how weak institutional frameworks create barriers to economic development, including the lack of effective:
  - legal systems
  - taxation structures
  - banking systems
  - recognition of property rights
- examine the role of gender inequality as a barrier to economic development.

How does a country's institutional framework affect its ability to develop?

Other domestic obstacles to economic development are rooted in the failure of institutions to lay the groundwork for meaningful improvements in people's lives.

Legal system

The legal system, a key institution needed to promote growth and development, is a public good that many take for granted in a country. A legal system includes the laws themselves, which are typically agreed upon and enacted by government officials, a constitution or some foundational document on which the laws are based, and the institutions and structures for interpreting and enforcing those laws.

A legal system is a public good, meaning that it is not provided by the free market because the benefits it conveys society are non-excludable and non-rivalrous. A well functioning government is therefore needed for a sound legal system to exist, and the existence of one will assure businesses, consumers, and investors (the drivers of economic activity) that it is safe and secure to participate in a country's economy.

Without a legal system, a country is essentially in a state of chaos and anarchy: hardly the characteristics investors, entrepreneurs, and multinational corporations are looking for when deciding where to do business.

Ineffective taxation structures

With an unclear or ineffective tax structure, a nation is unattractive to foreign investors who might otherwise invest in the country. Uncertainty about how taxes are collected deters investment and reduces the amount of foreign capital in the country. In addition, rich domestic households may choose to save their incomes and wealth abroad in a country whose tax structure is more stable and predictable. An ineffective tax structure may allow domestic firms and households to hide their income in overseas accounts, representing a form of capital flight that deprives the country of much needed funds for investment in public goods.

A tax structure should be neither too progressive nor totally regressive. A progressive tax structure is one that places a greater burden on high-income earners than on low-income earners. The degree of progressivity of a country's tax system determines to some extent the effectiveness of the system at incentivising and collecting tax revenues. Too progressive and the rich will hide their income or send it abroad, depriving the economy of tax revenues. Too regressive (or not progressive enough) and the poor will shoulder a larger burden, perpetuating inequality and preventing development from occurring.

Banking system

Many developing countries lack an effective banking system that is able to offer secure deposits to savers and access to credit to borrowers. Without a functioning domestic banking system, households with money to save will likely save it abroad, leading to capital flight. Without a supply of loanable funds domestically, it becomes nearly impossible for small businesses to access credit to finance productivity-enhancing investments. Consumers also find it difficult to borrow money to invest in real estate or to buy consumer goods, both of which make up significant proportions of more developed countries' economies' AD.

Microcredit is a much talked about and widely used development strategy that provides financial credit or technology loans to entrepreneurs in poor communities to create small businesses – ideally businesses with a socially beneficial purpose. Loans may be issued by community banks or by international micro-finance institutions. Community banks act like commercial banks in the developed world, collecting deposits from local savers and using them to make loans to local borrowers. International microcredit organisations match lenders in the developed world with borrowers in the developing world.

Such programmes differ from traditional commercial credit like that those in the rich world have access to. Entrepreneurs with access to financial capital, either through a community bank or a microcredit institution, are able to put their business skills to work employing others in providing goods and services that are in demand in their local communities. Often, the loans entrepreneurs receive are very small, as

Installation of microcredit financed solar home system, Bangladesh ▶

little as $100 or $200, which may be all that is needed to acquire some simple capital equipment such as a sewing machine or a vendor stand from which the entrepreneur can begin producing output demanded by their community. The more successful borrowers eventually gain access to larger amounts of credit, allowing them to expand their businesses, employ more workers, and add more value to the developing nation's output.

Community banking and microcredit promote the entrepreneurial talents of the people in less developed countries, and for that reason promise great potential for long-run economic development. Whereas many of the obstacles to development and strategies for overcoming them outlined in this chapter require a top-down approach, microcredit and community banking are grassroots in nature, empowering individuals within the poorest communities in the developing world to create their own opportunities while meeting the demands of their community and creating income and employment for others in the process.

Case study – microcredit in action in Kenya

Microcredit is not always in the form of financial capital. Some development projects aim to put physical capital directly into the hands of poor entrepreneurs. In Kenya, for instance, a non-governmental organisation (NGO) known as WISER aims to match young entrepreneurs with the tools they need to start their own businesses using donated technology such as copy machines, laptop computers with cellular internet connections, foot pumps for water, and digital LCD projectors.

The technology is sold on credit to entrepreneurs who are required to pay back the value of the capital through their business revenues. The capital, once in the hands of local entrepreneurs, is immediately put to use providing services to the community. Here are some examples.

- The copy machine was installed and powered by a generator. It was the first such machine ever installed in the community. Local businesses, students, job seekers and others could, for a few cents, photocopy their documents locally, avoiding the two-hour drive previously required for such a service.
- The laptops were installed in an internet café and made available to local students and businesses. Farmers and fishermen could check product prices in the cities hours away, increasing efficiency and bargaining positions when intermediaries came to town to buy their produce. Job openings in the city newspapers' classifieds could be printed and posted for the local community to see, improving information symmetry between the poor countryside and the cities where job opportunities existed. The cost of access to these services was cheap, yet the entrepreneurs who were granted the laptop loan were able to pay back the cost of the technology in no time at all, and the community as a whole benefited from their existence.
- The LCD projector was the first of its kind ever seen in the community. The entrepreneur who received the projector hooked it up to a satellite dish in order to capture and project English Premier League football matches onto the wall of a large room in a local building. The business was to sell tickets to local football fans who were more than happy to pay to watch English football matches in full

colour on a wall-sized screen. Before the projector arrived in the community, football fans had huddled around tiny black-and-white televisions with poor reception to watch football matches. The football-theatre business was the most successful of all, and paid back its loan fastest.

Property rights

If foreign investors cannot be sure that their property rights will be respected by the domestic government, they are unlikely to invest their capital into a developing country. The guaranteed protection of property rights makes a country more attractive to foreign investors and increases the amount of capital and thus the productivity and income of the nation's workforce. Domestically, a lack of property rights deters investors at even the lowest levels. Domestic entrepreneurs feel secure in their ability to reap the rewards of the business ventures when property rights are respected.

Without sound and secure protection of property rights, the entire market system is undermined, because confiscation of property, either by the government or by criminals, is a real possibility faced by prospective investors and entrepreneurs.

Does unequal access to political power and status limit development?

Inequality can extend beyond economic differences between rich and poor to gaps in political power and status. Often, economic inequality and political inequality are two sides of the same coin; political influence and status, to no one's surprise, can often be bought, giving those with the most income and wealth the ability to influence government policy in ways that entrench their own wealth and power, excluding those in society with the fewest economic resources from the political system through which the playing field could be levelled and greater equity achieved.

For evidence of the lack of access to political power and status among those on the lower rungs of the income ladder, we need only look at who the political players are in nearly every country, both more and less developed. From sub-Saharan Africa to the USA and Western Europe, national political leaders usually arrive at their posts after growing up among the elite rungs of society. It is relatively rare that someone born into poverty rises to the level of national political figure; surely if they did, more attention would be paid among the world's government to the challenges and barriers to economic development faced by the world's poor.

Does gender equality matter?

The extent to which women play a role in society is a crucial factor in determining whether a developing country is able to achieve meaningful improvements in the standards of living of its people. Female education in particular should be a goal of developing countries wishing to promote development. Better-educated women mean improved chances at development for many reasons, including the two discussed below.

When girls and young women have better access to education, society's fertility rate tends to decrease. Fewer children reduce the financial burden on families in developing countries, allowing limited resources to be better applied towards the continued education. Children raised in households in which both parents are educated have better opportunities. Better education means a more productive workforce; one in which both genders participate and in which the economy achieves a higher level of potential output than would be possible without women in the workforce. Greater national output means higher per capita incomes and an increased standard of living, thus economic development.

TOK Quite a lot of the subject matter in this chapter is about the many problems associated with developing countries. Is an understanding of the perspective of other knowers essential in the pursuit of knowledge?

Practice exam questions

1. Read the extract below and answer the questions that follow.

Karnataka tourism set to gain from admissions fever

Being admitted to professional courses in medical, dental, and engineering institutions in India is the biggest ambition of most of the academically brilliant students and their parents. Given the limited number of places available in the Indian Institutes of Technology (IITs), there is a huge demand for admission to professional colleges – as in the State of Karnataka where thousands apply every year, not only from within the state, but also from other parts of India and even from abroad.

Despite a fee of ₹3,000, there is **excess demand** for places. This year, a record number of 127,343 students have applied to Karnataka's colleges. Of these, as many as 59,299, or roughly 46.7%, are from outside the state. These candidates are competing with each other for the 26,000 places in the state's professional colleges – medical, dental, and engineering.

With such large numbers of non-Karnataka students, possibly accompanied by at least one parent or adult to guide them, it is natural that there will be enormous business opportunities for the hotels, lodgings, and travel operators. The state-owned Karnataka Tourism Development Corporation (KTDC) has taken the initiative to offer an elaborate and attractive package.

A spokesperson for the KTDC said, 'We believe there are many **social benefits** arising from the demand for places at IITs and it is our intention to take advantage of them.'

---

a. Define the following terms indicated in bold in the text:
  i. excess demand (2 marks)
  ii. social benefits. (2 marks)
b. With the aid of a diagram, explain how the social benefits resulting from the provision of education promote economic development in India. (4 marks)
c. Identify and explain two possible government responses to the shortage of spots at the IITs. (4 marks)
d. To what extent is education an essential requirement for reducing poverty in less economically developed countries like India? (15 marks)

2. Study the extract and data below and answer the questions that follow.

'Singapore is a high-income economy in South-East Asia. The country provides the world's most business-friendly regulatory environment for local entrepreneurs and is ranked among the world's most competitive economies. Presently, the strong manufacturing and services sectors have become the main drivers of the Singapore economy. There is a wide range of businesses, with a particular focus on high value added goods and services.'

'Timor-Leste (formerly known as East Timor) is a developing economy in South-East Asia. Timor-Leste gained independence from Indonesia in 2002. The country and families were torn apart by violence in the years before independence. Nearly 70% of all buildings, homes and schools were destroyed. An estimated 75% of the population were forced to move due to the violence.'

'After serious challenges, Timor-Leste has progressed, particularly due to its endowment of natural resources, especially oil. With the petroleum revenue boom, fiscal policy has been expansionary and the economy has grown rapidly as a result of government spending, focusing on major **infrastructure**, development of skills, and other institutional changes. A main goal was to generate increased and sustainable private sector investment as a means to increase job opportunities and to reduce **poverty**. These developments are starting to contribute to poverty reduction and improved social outcomes.'

Table 1   Selected economic data for Singapore and Timor-Leste – 2013

	Singapore	Timor-Leste
Human Development Index (HDI) data		
HDI rank	9	128
HDI value	0.901	0.62
Life expectancy at birth	82.32	67.54
Mean years of schooling	10.20	4.42
Expected years of schooling	15.40	11.70
Gross national income (GNI) per capita (2011 purchasing power parity (PPP) US$)	72371.23	9673.61
Other selected data		
Population (millions)	5.41	1.13
Gross domestic product (GDP) per capita (2011 PPP US$)	71474.89	11814.79
Urban percentage of population	100.00	29.11
Foreign direct investment (FDI), net inflows (% of GDP)	20.62	4.31

a. Define the following terms indicated in bold in the text.
   i.   infrastructure   (2 marks)
   ii. poverty.   (2 marks)
b. Using a poverty cycle diagram, explain how its history of violence
   has presented a barrier to economic development for Timor-Leste.   (4 marks)
c. Explain how its 'business-friendly regulatory environment' has
   contributed to economic growth and development in Singapore.   (4 marks)
d. Outline the advantages and disadvantages of Timor-Leste's
   dependence on the export of a single primary commodity, oil, for
   its economic growth and development.   (8 marks)
e. Referring to data in Table 1, discuss the importance of education
   and health as a determination of economic development.   (15 marks)

Economic growth and development strategies

30

At the end of this section you will be able to:

- outline the various strategies to promote economic growth and development, including: trade, diversification, **social enterprise**, market-based policies, interventionist policies, the provision of merit goods, FDI, aid, **multilateral development assistance**, and institutional change.

Is economic development a destination towards which countries are striving or is it a process that countries are always undergoing? This is an important question, because if it is a destination, then the implication is that at some point all countries could become 'developed', and therefore achieve some end beyond which there is no further need for improvement. While there is no one correct answer to this question, let us consider the second alternative, that economic development is not an *end* towards which countries strive, rather it is the ongoing process that even the richest, healthiest, best educated countries in the world are constantly undergoing.

When we think of economic development as an ongoing process that every country in the world is constantly undergoing, the very idea of 'developing' versus 'developed' countries becomes blurred. There is no such thing as a 'fully developed' country; rather, all nations have room to improve the lives of their people. There is no 'perfect', 'developed' country we can look at as a model for all other countries to emulate.

With this idea in mind, the last chapter in this unit will explore some of the economic development strategies that countries can pursue. Just as there is not one ideal of economic development countries can strive for, there are many paths they can follow to promote both economic development and economic growth, paths that might look very different from one another. While some countries have achieved growth and development following free market-oriented principles, others have harnessed government intervention as a guiding principle. While many countries have promoted exports to the rest of the world, others have focused on reducing imports so domestic firms face less competition as they serve their consumers. While some have turned to aid from outside organisations, others have promoted trade.

Strategies for growth and development can appear as varied as the languages, currencies, races, and religious views of the people in the countries implementing them. Throughout our final chapter, we will explore the various strategies for growth and development and wrap up our study of economics by reviewing some of the key themes of the course.

How can international trade help growth and development?

In Chapter 29 we argued that the idea that 'no man is an island' applies to countries as well. No country can grow its economy and improve the lives of its people without, to some extent, depending on trade with the rest of the world. Self-sufficiency is the road to poverty, so at some point countries must decide how they will harness the advantages of trade to grow and develop their own economies. There are two basic approaches to harnessing trade to the advantage of a less developed economy: the import substitution approach and the export promotion approach.

Import substitution

When a less developed country (LDC) has a large population among which there is a high level of demand for consumer goods, that demand could be met by foreign producers in more developed economies, whose advantages of scale and efficiency allow them to produce the consumer goods that the LDCs households demand at lower prices than domestic firms in the developing country could achieve. In such a case, the LDCs would benefit from trade by opening its economy to cheap imports, allowing low-income consumers to benefit from foreign-produced goods.

However, while low-cost foreign goods stand to benefit poor consumers in an LDC, the disadvantage is that producers in the developing country will struggle to compete with more efficient, lower cost, foreign firms. Because imports are cheaper, consumers in the developing country will choose to buy products from foreign firms over domestic firms.

A strategy for promoting domestic economic growth in LDCs, therefore, is to enact protectionist policies that raise the price of foreign goods to the extent that domestic consumers will substitute domestically produced goods for the now *more expensive* imports. Tariffs and quotas (Chapter 23) are the typical tools in an *import substitution* model for economic growth. A developing country government can tax imported goods to the point where it becomes cheaper for domestic households to buy from domestic firms.

Over time, domestic firms will grow in scale as they meet the demand from domestic consumers. As they achieve economies *of scale* that allow them to produce at a cost competitive with foreign firms, the government will ideally begin rolling back protectionist measures, at which point they are no longer needed.

In short, an import substitution model of economic growth is aimed at increasing domestic aggregate demand (AD), and therefore inducing domestic investment in capital and infrastructure, which in turn increases aggregate supply (AS) and promotes long-run economic growth. While this sounds like a sure means of achieving growth, there are many disadvantages, all of which were outlined in Chapter 23.2, What are the different types of protection. Protectionist tariffs and quotas create a deadweight loss in the developing country, as consumers, who already live on relatively low incomes, are forced to pay more in the short run for essential goods that could be bought for less under free trade.

Additionally, when an LDC imposes tariffs on the imports from its trading partners, those countries are more likely to retaliate by imposing tariffs on producers from the LDC. This may not be an issue if the developing country does not have a large export sector, but there will be losers as exports to other countries will likely be affected to some extent.

Clearly, if an LDC wishes to grow its export sector, and is willing to allow domestic consumers to depend more on imports, then an import substitution policy is not desirable; instead, an *export promotion* strategy might be more appropriate.

Export promotion

Export promotion policies are an alternative set of policies for promoting economic growth and development. The aim is to increase the overseas market for domestic producers by employing subsidies and exchange rate controls that give domestic producers an advantage in foreign markets. In contrast to import substitution, which aims to grow demand for domestically produced goods within the domestic market, export promotion aims to grow demand for domestic output among *foreign consumers*. To do so, domestic producers must be given a *competitive advantage* on foreign markets.

We use the term *competitive advantage* carefully and intentionally here. Recall from Chapter 22, Benefits of international trade, that a country has a *comparative advantage* in a good's production when it can produce it at a lower opportunity cost than other countries. In theory, when countries specialise their production in the goods for which they have a comparative advantage, and then import the goods that other countries can produce more efficiently, global resource allocation is most efficient and the highest possible overall production across countries can be realised. In turn, incomes will be higher due to greater productivity, and living standards should therefore improve.

When countries implement export promotion policies, they attempt to give domestic producers that lack a *comparative advantage* an artificial *competitive advantage* by offering them subsidies or by devaluing the currency on forex markets. Both of these actions make domestic output cheaper to foreigners and therefore should stimulate demand from abroad. The result is a less efficient allocation of global resources as countries that might not be able to compete in certain industries produce goods that could, under free trade, be produced more efficiently somewhere else.

Additionally, export promotion comes at an opportunity cost for consumers in the country that is enacting the policies. A devalued currency, while helping exporters, makes imports more expensive and reduces the real incomes of consumers. Subsidies, while helping producers, allocate scarce taxpayer money towards production and away from consumption, or require allocating funds away from public goods like infrastructure and healthcare and towards goods meant for export to other countries.

Clearly, export promotion, just like import substitution, has winners and losers. There are opportunity costs that go along with using government funds to help exporting firms and with interventions in the forex markets, and just as with import substitution, there is a deadweight loss as overall global resource allocation is made less efficient by government intervention in international trade.

Export promotion has been employed for decades by many LDCs, particularly those of East and Southeast Asia, with varying degrees of success. Malaysia, Thailand, and the Philippines have all aimed to grow their export sectors through currency devaluation and targeted subsidies for domestic industries. All three countries achieved strong economic growth and meaningful improvements in their peoples' living standards throughout the 1980s, 1990s, and early 2000s, but this growth came at a great cost to certain stakeholders within these economies.

Case study – Malaysia aims to boost exports to grow its economy

In the 1990s, Malaysia was experiencing rapid economic growth with the stated goal of achieving developed nation status in a very short period of time. Vision 2020 was an ambitious government plan to make Malaysia the economic powerhouse of Southeast Asia by the year 2020. In order to achieve this goal, the Malaysian government believed it needed a large export sector, able to compete with its more developed Asian rivals, Singapore, South Korea, Taiwan, and Japan.

The Malaysian government believed the nation needed a large exporting automobile sector in order to be a developed country. The government aimed to develop the country's automobile sector through an aggressive set of protectionist policies focusing on both import substitution and export promotion. Substantial tariffs were levied on imported automobiles, sometimes as high as 100%, while the state-owned automobile company, Proton, received billions of Malaysian ringgit over two decades.

Malaysian car manufacturer Proton has announced an ambitious new five-year plan to massively boost exports in a drive to halt falling profits due to declining domestic sales.

The government-backed company hopes new models such as the Suprema S will prove popular with foreign consumers as it earmarks half of total volume for overseas markets. Proton currently sells to over 20 countries but its sales lag at below 5%.

Proton's share of the Malaysian car market dipped below 25% in 2013 as sales stalled, while exports have also slumped in recent years, with only 6000 units sold in 2013 compared to over 16,000 in 2011.

The Malaysian government, however, remains committed to bucking this downward trend.

'Although running at a loss, Proton will continue to export its models to create future markets', International Trade and Industry Minister Datuk Seri Mustapa Mohamed said.

But has the government's policy of export promotion led to an overall improvement in the welfare of the Malaysian people and therefore promoted economic development? To answer this question, we must look at the overall cost to society of increased car exports and compare it to the benefit the policy added.

The cost to the Malaysian taxpayer to achieve the government's objective of greater car exports and thus a stronger industrial sector was substantial. A not insignificant chunk of the national income was reallocated from taxpaying Malaysian households to domestic car manufacturers, representing reduced real incomes of hard working Malaysians. Opportunity costs include the higher disposable incomes Malaysian taxpayers could have enjoyed and all the other investments the country could have made with the tax revenue, including education, healthcare, and infrastructure investment.

The benefit of the export promotion strategy includes the revenues from overseas sales of domestically produced cars and the lower prices enjoyed by domestic car consumers. But as with all forms of protectionism, or any other government interventions that target specific industries, welfare is not necessarily increased, rather it is transferred from one set of stakeholders to another.

Economic development requires improvements in human health, education, and access to life-improving goods and services; the cheaper cars resulting from the subsidy clearly fall short of these goals. Malaysian households might have benefited more in economic development terms if their tax money had gone towards improving the Malaysian education system, building more hospitals, training more doctors, or providing access to sanitation to the poorer parts of Malaysia. These are just a few examples of what government could have done to bring more economic development to Malaysia than its decision to promote the export of Protons to China and India.

Economic integration

Import substitution and export promotion strategies for growth and development both represent government intervention-oriented approaches; without tariffs, quotas, subsidies, and forex market interventions, these two strategies would not work. For countries choosing the free market-oriented approach to growth and development, increased economic integration, involving the removal of protectionist measures, offers an alternative approach.

The World Trade Organization (WTO) has tried to alleviate global poverty by addressing the constraints to global trade that put developing countries at a disadvantage in the global economic system. Some of the challenges the WTO has attempted to address and will continue to address in future rounds of trade negotiations include the following.

- Encouraging LDC to refocus their development agendas away from high tariff barriers and towards strategies relying on trade liberalisation and integration into the global trading system.
- Encouraging developed countries to take into account the needs of developing countries when considering their own trade policies.
- Promoting access to new markets for manufactured goods and primary commodities from developing countries.
- Working towards meaningful cuts in protectionist agricultural subsidies in developed countries.
- Making sure that future bilateral or multilateral trade agreements do not undermine the industrialisation prospects of developing countries.
- Providing duty-free and quota-free access to imports from LDCs in the developed world.
- Promoting increased movement of labour, both high skilled and low skilled, among LDCs and between LDCs and the developed economies. The WTO's role in poverty alleviation is to bring countries together to develop a fair trade framework that promotes meaningful development in developing countries.

In the absence of progress at the multilateral or WTO level, a better option for an LDC than removing all barriers to trade with other nations may be to start locally in trade liberalisation by joining regional trading blocs or entering into preferential trade agreements with neighbouring countries.

The East African Community (EAC) is a common market agreement that includes Burundi, Kenya, Rwanda, South Sudan, Tanzania, and Uganda. The aim of the EAC is to enable free movement of labour, services and capital to significantly boost trade and investments and make the region more productive and prosperous.

By embracing free trade first with its neighbours, and from there entering into additional preferential and free trade agreements with geographically more distant trading partners, developing countries may begin to enjoy the benefits of trade liberalisation without being subjected to the unfair disadvantages that would result from the failure of more developed countries to reciprocate the removal of protectionist policies such as agricultural subsidies and import tariffs.

How does diversifying economic output promote development?

Perhaps the best strategy for a developing country to overcome the external obstacles to economic growth and development is to diversify the composition of its output. A developing country that is overly dependent on one or a few primary commodities, or even low-skilled manufactured goods, faces great obstacles in growing its economy in a manner that ensures higher incomes, better health, and improved education among its people.

Investing in human capital may be the best way a government can achieve the diversification of its national output. Better-educated workers attract foreign investment from multinational corporations (MNCs) eager to tap the relatively low-wage, but well-educated workforce available. The inflow of foreign investment allows the LDC to acquire much needed foreign capital and productivity-enhancing technology that can be employed in the production of manufactured goods, thus providing the nation's households with higher incomes. Higher incomes increase the level of savings in the nation, providing loanable funds to entrepreneurs and businesses at home, and further contributing to the nation's growth and development.

The key for a developing nation's government is to identify the poverty trap in which it is ensnared, and then pursue policies that enable it to escape that trap and begin the journey towards growth and development. This may be harder than it sounds, but some of the strategies described here will help a nation improve the standard of living of its people.

What is 'social enterprise'?

A recent field of development economic studies is the examination of the role of *social enterprises*, which are 'organisations that address a basic unmet need or solve a social or environmental problem through a market-driven approach'.

In short, social enterprises meet the development needs of society through their pursuit of profits. The basic principle is that the solutions to development challenges do not always lie in the hands of governments, outside experts, foreign investors, aid organisations, or MNCs, but may exist within the stock of domestic entrepreneurial talent. Social enterprises can address problems at the hyper-local level, ones that may not draw the attention of government policymakers or international investors. The aim is to benefit a specific group of people by meeting development needs that are unmet by the existing resources in their communities.

An entrepreneur who sees that residents in a poor community lack internet access may open a computer lab or install a Wi-Fi hub, charging a small fee for locals to use the service. As a result, an entire community is given access to the internet at a relatively low cost. Where major infrastructure investments by national or global telecommunications firms might have been required under a traditional model of economic development, a social entrepreneur has made a relatively small investment in an enterprise that has met a development need at a much lower cost. Residents of the poor community are now able to access the internet to conduct business, enhance their education, or apply for jobs in the city. A promising business model, the rural Wi-Fi hub provides spillover benefits that go far beyond improved individual access to communication infrastructure, making it a social enterprise.

In Chapter 29, we learned about microcredit organisations, which offer small loans to individuals and businesses in LDCs who otherwise would lack access to credit. Microcredit organisations are another example of social enterprises; while the concept began as an experiment in aid assistance to poor individuals, microcredit organisations have emerged as successful enterprises that actually turn profits for the investors who finance them. Thus, an experiment in aid turned into a widespread model of economic development rooted in the social enterprise model.

Social enterprises offer the best example of how markets, as envisioned by the father of modern economics, Adam Smith, benefit all the actors that participate in them. 'Give me that which I want', wrote Smith, 'and you shall have this which you want.' While Smith's sentiment could be applied to markets for all sorts of goods from toys to cars to smartphones and luxury cruises, in the case of economic development, it applies rather nicely to social enterprises that emerge in the markets for welfare-enhancing goods that might otherwise not be provided through mainstream channels such as the government, aid organisations, and national or multinational corporations.

What can the free market offer?

So far in our examination of strategies for economic growth and development we have swung back and forth from market-driven approaches to interventionist-oriented models for development. We will continue exploring development and growth strategies rooted in the market-oriented approach in the following section.

Trade liberalisation

An alternative to using protectionism to promote growth and development is for a country to embrace trade liberalisation. The risks associated with a developing country opening its market to free trade are of course substantial. There is no guarantee that one country's opening itself to trade will be reciprocated by its trading partners.

For example, Kenya, an LDC in East Africa, may choose to remove tariffs on imported grain from Europe in the hope that European nations will remove protectionist duties on Kenya's exports, thereby liberalising trade between Europe and Kenya. However, when Kenya embraces free trade it risks exposing its own grain producers to the heavily subsidised European grains that would likely flood into the domestic market. Free trade is an elusive goal, as the removal of tariffs in one country does not guarantee that all its trading partners will likewise roll back protections like domestic tariffs and subsidies that give foreign producers an unfair competitive advantage over the LDC's producers.

While the intention of trade liberalisation was to make imports cheaper for Kenyans and to make Kenya's exports more attractive to foreign consumers, the result may be a reduction in the welfare of the primarily rural population of Kenya who find it increasingly difficult to compete with subsidised food from Europe.

Privatisation

Many of the developing countries in the world today are former colonies of European empires (primarily in Africa, South America, and South and Southeast Asia), or 'emerging market' economies of the former Soviet bloc (mostly in Eastern Europe and Central Asia). Their historical legacies left many developing countries in the world with state-run industries, originally established to serve either foreign colonial masters or the domestic market in a command and control economic system. State-controlled industries across the developing, emerging market economies of the world have struggled to compete with the more efficient, free market MNCs that have grown to dominate global commerce in the 21st century.

One of the surest ways to increase efficiency in developing countries, therefore, is to break up or sell off state-run enterprises, attracting domestic or foreign investors who have an eye for efficiency and productivity. Examples of previously state-run enterprises that have been privatised in developing countries include the sale of state-run mines and farms across sub-Saharan Africa, petroleum, infrastructure, heavy machinery, and steel companies in India and China, and state-run airlines around the world.

In each of these cases large swathes of the economies of developing countries that had previously been run at a loss by the governments (and therefore propped up with limited taxpayer funds that could have gone towards public goods) were sold to private investors. In many cases, the privatisation resulted in efficiency and productivity improvements that allowed the industries to be run at a lower cost, even becoming profitable businesses.

The disadvantage of privatisation, of course, is that once an industry is no longer under control of the government, its ability to provide its output to its consumers at competitive prices (be those airline passengers, car manufacturers, or petroleum refineries) is diminished, creating a cascading effect felt across the economy as key production operations are handed over to profit-seeking firms. However, as is the case with all forms of government intervention, the operation of state-run enterprises, particularly those that incur large losses at the expense of taxpayers, comes with opportunity costs to society that are relieved when the industry is sold to private investors.

Deregulation

Globalisation is sometimes referred to by its critics as a 'race to the bottom'. In their efforts to attract inflows of international investment, LDCs may find themselves deregulating their industries to make it cheaper, and more attractive, to operate a business in their country. In a purely free market economy, there would be no regulations governing workplace safety, product quality, the environment, labour rights, wage rates, or any other area of the economy. In such a hypothetical case all types of industries would likely thrive, as the cost of opening and operating a business would be low relative to that in economies with more government regulation. The trade-off, of course, would be high levels of *exploitation* of both human and natural resources.

High levels of onerous regulations imposed by LDC governments could deter foreign and domestic investment; in such a case some degree of deregulation could drive capital inflows and lead to a more dynamic, efficient, and globally competitive economy.

When is intervention needed?

Trade liberalisation, privatisation, and deregulation are three means by which a country can increase its economic efficiency in order to attract domestic and foreign investment that will stimulate growth, leading to higher incomes and improved standards of living. We must remember, however, that the free market, which is good at providing some things (factories, jobs, efficiency, income) fails in many ways. Economic development is multidimensional; it does not happen simply through income and job creation. The public and merit goods the free market fails to provide must be provided by the government; and this is where intervention is needed.

Redistribution policies

Recall from Chapter 18, Economics of inequality and poverty, that the free market tends to create an unequal playing field, on which those with access to the most resources, lucky enough to be born into higher income families, are most likely to end up rich, while those who are born poor are likely to stay poor. The free market does little to level the playing field, leaving it up to the government to enact equity-enhancing policies like progressive taxes, transfer payments, minimum wages, and social safety nets.

Progressive income taxes are those that increase in percentage as income rises, thereby placing a larger burden on higher income earners than lower income earners. Transfer payments are the means by which income is redistributed to those who have less in society, either through subsidies for food, education, or housing, or through direct payments to people with lower incomes or those who are unemployed, too old, disabled, or unable to work for other reasons. Together, these systems are sometimes referred to as a country's *social insurance*.

While markets for private insurance exist in most countries, the countries with the highest level of human development tend to have strong and stable systems of social insurance. A report prepared by the International Labour Organization found that 75% of the 150 million people unemployed around the world lack any unemployment insurance protection. The report showed that the countries providing the most generous support to unemployed workers were Austria, Belgium, Denmark, Finland, France, Germany, Iceland, Luxembourg, Netherlands, Norway, Portugal, Spain, Sweden, and Switzerland. These 14 countries provide unemployed workers with benefits averaging 60% of their last salary for more than one year following the loss of their job. This benefit allows workers and their families to maintain a suitable standard of living during their period of economic hardship while they have time to look for a new job.

Countries with medium-level systems included Australia, Canada, Ireland, Japan, New Zealand, the UK, and the US. In these countries, fewer of the unemployed workers receive benefits and the compensation provided is lower, averaging around 40% of salaries earned before being laid off.

In the countless countries not mentioned above, there are literally tens of millions of unemployed workers receiving no benefits whatsoever from the private or public sectors during their times of hardship. The total lack of any social insurance is an obstacle to economic development in a low-income country. The families of unemployed workers in a country without a social safety net suffer:

- children are more likely to go undernourished
- children are more likely to supplement the family income by working rather than going to school
- healthcare is out of reach for a family with no income.

The lack of social safety nets perpetuates poverty in developing countries and reduces the likelihood that human welfare will improve over time.

What merit goods promote growth and development?

A merit good, you will recall, is one that is *underprovided* by the free market. The benefits of merit goods are not *purely private*, but include external social benefits beyond those enjoyed by the individuals consuming them. For this reason, the private firms that might provide the goods to the free market will provide them only to the extent that the market demand (or the marginal private benefit) dictates, ignoring the spillover benefits they provide, resulting in an underprovision of the good.

Education

Education is good with countless external benefits of consumption. When a nation educates its children, the nation's human capital is improved and they are more likely to grow up to become productive members of the workforce, contributing to the production of goods and services that benefit fellow citizens, and paying taxes that can in turn be used to provide more education to future generations.

Without government intervention in the market for education, resources would be vastly under-allocated towards schooling for the nation's youth. Most more developed countries provide education as a benefit for all citizens to at least the secondary level. LDCs can learn from the model that has successfully contributed to the economic growth and high living standards of Western European, East Asian, and North American countries.

A private education system has many benefits for a nation, but without the support of the government, only the most privileged and richest members of society are able to improve their human capital to a level that leads to a higher standard of living. A publicly supported education system reduces inequalities in society and improves the well-being of all members of a nation.

Health

Healthcare, like education, is a *merit good*, or one that is underprovided by the free market. The benefits of consuming healthcare are clearly *private* (the person getting care is likely to be healthier and more productive) but they are also *social* (society as a whole is more productive and healthier when each individual has access to healthcare). Therefore, the amount of healthcare provided by the free market will be less than what is socially optimal.

Without some degree of government provision, healthcare will be underprovided, leaving a developing country's people with poorer health, and therefore a lower level of human development. Healthcare can be supported through government provision, or through aid from international development organisations like Médecins Sans Frontières. One thing is certain, however. There needs to be some effort to increase the level of access to healthcare beyond what the free market would achieve if a country is to achieve meaningful improvements in people's standards of living.

Case study – Ukraine's hybrid approach to healthcare

Since gaining its independence from the Soviet Union in 1991, the country has undergone a transition from government-provided healthcare (a guaranteed benefit under the Soviet Union) to a mixed government and free market model for healthcare. Today, Ukraine has a dual healthcare system: a publicly funded service available to all citizens, and a private health system available to those willing and able to afford private insurance premiums.

The state-run health programme is subject to price controls determined by government policies aimed at making healthcare affordable to all Ukrainian citizens. On the other hand, in the market for private healthcare, hospitals and clinics are allowed to charge consumers higher prices, and thus the providers are willing and able to supply a greater quantity of healthcare than the public system.

Under a government-run monopoly, Ukraine's healthcare system charged prices that made healthcare affordable to all, but resulted in shortages, as there was little incentive for individuals to go into medicine and no room for entrepreneurs to enter the market to meet the needs of society.

Privatisation of the healthcare system led to an inflow of investment from private entrepreneurs seeking to soak up the excess demand for care, attracted by the chance to earn profits by meeting citizens' healthcare needs. As a result, throughout the early 2000s hundreds of healthcare clinics opened across the country, with prices set not by the government, but by the willingness of consumers to pay for the service.

On the one hand, the privatisation of the healthcare industry led to an explosion in investment and a broadening of access to care to millions of Ukrainians. We might be tempted to assume, therefore, that healthcare is best left to the free market. On the other hand, without the baseline level of care provided by the government for free or for very low prices, the free market would exclude millions of Ukrainians (and billions of people across the developing world) from access to basic care.

Some of the most effective healthcare systems in the more developed countries combine a hybrid approach where individuals are automatically enrolled as residents of the country in the national healthcare system, but have the option to purchase supplemental insurance that provides a higher quality or more immediate care in cases where the public system falls short. The model could be applied to LDCs as well, where there are many who are willing and able to pay for high quality healthcare, but far more who simply could not afford to get care on the free market.

Infrastructure

A nation's infrastructure includes more than its roads and railways, although such capital goods are also necessary for a nation to achieve economic development. Infrastructure includes telecommunications, transportation, and utilities such as sewerage, running water, electricity, and gas.

When private firms are given control of a nation's infrastructure, the results can be detrimental to the nation's economic development and growth. Without government provision or subsidies to providers, such capital goods as electricity and water systems will be underprovided. Certain types of infrastructure such as roads and railways, it could be argued, are in fact public goods. Very few private firms would find it economically feasible to construct highways across a developing country, for instance. It would simply be too difficult to recover the costs of production through charging for the use of such a system of roads. Therefore, without government provision, such major capital investments would simply not take place.

On the other hand, certain types of infrastructure can be provided by the free market in a cost-effective, profitable manner. The market for cellular phone service, for instance, has been a hotly contested one in many developing countries.

For instance, in the Democratic Republic of the Congo (DRC), a nation with one of the lowest Human Development Index (HDI) rankings in the world, there were 22 million cellular service subscribers in 2016, ten times the number of a decade prior, representing 25% of the population. Of the four providers of cellular service in the DRC, only one (in fact the one with the fewest subscribers, Congo Chine Telecoms) was partially controlled by the DRC government. The three leading providers of this service, so vital to the nation's human development and economic vitality, were private MNCs.

Case study – cellphones and electricity in Africa

Cellphones have led to huge improvements in the well-being of the rural poor all over the developing world. According to the United Nations:

> 'Cellphones today are nearly ubiquitous in African society. Teenagers and young adults are obsessed by them, carrying them around everywhere.'

> 'The World Bank and African Development Bank report there are 650 million mobile users in Africa, surpassing the number in the United States or Europe. In some African countries more people have access to a mobile phone than to clean water, a bank account or electricity, the agencies add.'

> 'Youth are using mobile phones for everything: communicating, listening to the radio, transferring money, shopping, mingling on social media and more. Furthermore, the industry has transcended divides between urban and rural, rich and poor.'

The ability of remote, poor communities to engage in economic activities across vast distances quickly and efficiently with a cellphone increases the incomes of the poor and empowers them as contributors to the economic well-being of the country.

While mobile phones and the network infrastructure needed to operate them have been sufficiently provided by the private sector, a much more basic, related good needed to operate the phones has been grossly underprovided. Many of the remote, rural communities that benefit most from cellphones are so far off the grid that they do not even have access to the electricity needed to charge mobile phones. Ironically, the phones, provided efficiently by the free market, depend on electricity, which has historically been provided by the government, but is currently underprovided in much of Africa. This poses problems for the rural poor in Africa.

Africa's 46 sub-Saharan countries collectively have the same electricity generation capacity as Spain. But dilapidated infrastructure means as much as a quarter of even this capacity is unavailable, meaning power shortages and regular interruptions to supply. These outages are particularly acute away from the main urban centres.

The inefficiency of having to spend hours or even days just to charge a cellphone poses an obstacle to the extent to which this technology can improve the well-being of those with access to it. The cost to the government of a rural African country of providing the most remote communities with electricity on the national grid is prohibitive. But it turns out the free market has recently come up with a possible solution to a problem traditionally solved by government infrastructure spending. Entrepreneurs have begun to provide the rural poor in Africa and other parts of the world with low-priced solar electricity units.

Manufactured cheaply in China, a solar electricity unit can be purchased in Africa for as little as $80. One unit provides enough electricity for a household to power several electric lights, a few common appliances and to charge electronics such as cellphones. The benefits enjoyed by households that have acquired such systems quickly outweigh the costs. The renewable electricity provided by solar panels has reduced poor families' dependence on increasingly scarce heating and cooking fuel, improved health and provided children with the ability to study under electric lights after dark, thereby improving the quality of education received.

Solar electricity and other such sustainable, low-cost methods of providing the rural poor with access to those goods traditionally provided by big, government infrastructure projects are still emerging. Markets have popped up around the developing world, but there is no reliable supply of resources to meet the ever increasing demand of the hundreds of millions of poor households still living without electricity in the world.

What roles does foreign direct investment play in economic development?

As you now know, countries can become trapped in the poverty traps. In its simplest form, the poverty cycle shows how limited income makes it difficult to accumulate savings. Without savings, there is little available capital to grow the economy. To break free, many countries seek out foreign injections of money and capital goods. These injections may take the form of foreign direct investment (FDI).

As Figure 30.1 illustrates, inflows of FDI can break the poverty cycle and put an LDC on a path towards prosperity. FDI refers to the long-term investment by a company into the market of another country. Inward flows of FDI to a country are when foreign companies invest in the domestic market of that country. Outward flows of FDI are when domestic companies do the same in foreign markets.

Typically, FDI occurs when foreign companies purchase productive assets, such as factories, mines and land. These private companies are, by the act of FDI, MNCs that

Figure 30.1 FDI and/or foreign aid break the poverty cycle and put a country on the path towards prosperity

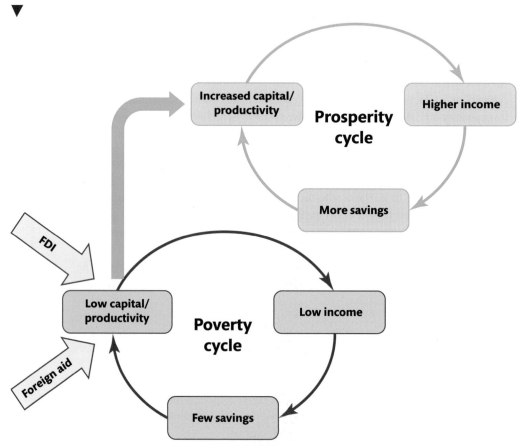

are seeking profits by moving or expanding operations to new countries. FDI can be classified as either greenfield investment (when companies construct new facilities from scratch) or brownfield investment (when investors purchase or lease existing facilities).

What attracts MNCs to LDCs?

Multinational firms looking to invest in a developing economy may be attracted to particular characteristics in economies receiving investment, characteristics that many LDCs happen to share.

Low-cost labour

Many MNCs choose to relocate production to countries where the per-unit labour costs are much lower. This lowers overall costs of production for labour intensive manufactured goods, even when transport costs are included. LDCs may, therefore, hold a comparative advantage in the production of labour intensive, lower tech manufactured goods, which could make them an attractive destination for foreign direct investment by multinational manufacturing firms.

Natural resources

Access to natural resources – be they mineral, metal, timber, or fossil fuel – can draw the interest of many foreign investors. Some countries in Africa and Southeast Asia have recently been recipients of attention from China, in the form of aid and foreign investment. Typically, these countries are resource rich, reflecting China's need to create new supply lines for its growing economy.

Domestic market

Part of the attraction of emerging markets is that the MNCs' products can be sold to the local population as well. Thus, for some MNCs, the attraction of foreign investment is to export to the rest of the world (and perhaps back to the home country) and to expand the market for the MNC's goods by having a direct presence in the country. This explains the natural advantage that China and India possess, having huge domestic markets and major growth potential as incomes rise.

Relaxed regulatory environment

Developing countries may have lax regulations that make it profitable for MNCs to invest, including in the following areas.

- **Profit repatriation.** When profits earned by foreign firms can easily be reported in the country where the firms are headquartered, it becomes more attractive for foreign firms to invest. However, the downside is the recipient country is deprived of much needed tax revenues, limiting the government's ability to invest in merit and public goods.
- **Environmental regulations.** Lax environmental rules are more common in LDCs than they are in more developed countries, making them more attractive for MNCs that participate in manufacturing or resource extraction activities that create negative externalities of production. Again, the trade-off for the developing country is a less sustainable path towards economic growth and development, as investment comes with increased environmental destruction.

- **Health, safety, and workplace standards.** Similar to environmental controls, LDCs often have more relaxed rules around worker health and safety and minimum workplace standards, meaning it is cheaper to operate a production facility than it would be in a higher income country. While lax standards make developing countries attractive to foreign firms, they also mean there is a limit on how much development can take place, with the trade-off being more economic growth.

Case study – FDI and government intervention in Ethiopia

Isabella Socks Manufacturing, PLC, is located in a large industrial park in the southern Ethiopian city of Hawassa. Considered Ethiopia's flagship industrial park, it was built by a state-owned Chinese firm and cost $250 million. It contains 55 industrial sheds, designed to house up to 20 MNCs.

In 2017, the author visited Isabella Socks and interviewed its Sri Lankan ownership. The firm, which sews and processes socks that are later sold in the EU, has been awarded the highest standard for the Business Social Compliance Initiative (BSCI), a supply chain management system that supports companies to drive social compliance and labour standards.

Isabella Socks has 70 employees, operates tax-free, and gets government rent subsidies on the space as a way of encouraging investment. The owner said that the programme was part of the Ethiopian government's drive to encourage FDI, to raise labour standards and wages, and to increase higher value exports from what has traditionally been an export sector reliant on agriculture and basic goods.

What role does foreign aid play?

Foreign aid is defined simply as, 'money, food, or other resources given or lent by one country to another'. Note that aid can be 'given' (meaning there is no expectation of repayment) or 'lent' (in which case, the recipient country is required to repay some of what is given to the donor country).

The vast majority of the over $150 billion in aid given annually is in the form of official development assistance (ODA) which is aid extended by one government (the donor) or from multilateral development institutions such as the World Bank and the International Monetary Fund (IMF) to another government (the recipient).

Aid is also extended, but at a much smaller level, by non-governmental organisations (NGOs). Some well-known examples of NGOs providing aid to economically LDCs, along with their primary focuses, include:

- The Bill and Melinda Gates Foundation – global health
- World Vision – food aid and emergency assistance
- Oxfam – poverty alleviation and debt relief
- Médecins Sans Frontières – healthcare services
- CARE International – poverty alleviation
- International Red Cross and Red Crescent Movement – humanitarian relief

While these well-known organisations target specific areas of economic development, aid in general falls into one of two categories, summarised in the table below.

Foreign aid	
Humanitarian aid	**Development aid**
Examples: food aid, medical aid, disaster relief aid	Examples: grants, concessional loans, project aid, programme aid

Most ODA (government to government) is in the form of development aid. Figure 30.2 shows the dollar value of ODA extended worldwide from 1990 to 2016.

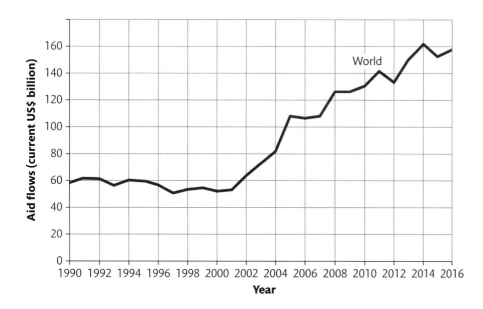

Figure 30.2 **Official development assistance** exceeded $150 billion in 2016.

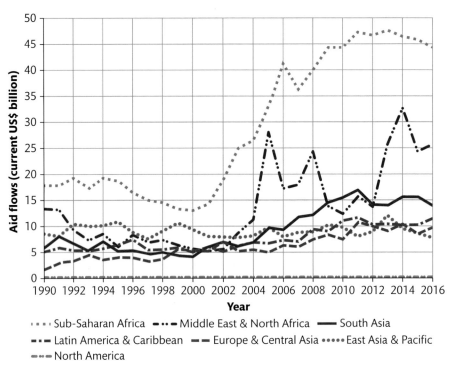

Figure 30.3 Most ODA flows to Africa and the Middle East

At last count over $150 billion per year was being extended in foreign aid, mostly from rich countries to developing countries. When we look at aid flows by region, as in Figure 30.3, we can see where most of the money given for development assistance is flowing to.

Note in Figure 30.3 that the region receiving by far the largest proportion of foreign aid is the 46 countries of sub-Saharan Africa, where around 1 billion people live and where average incomes are lower than in any other region of the world.

Development aid comes in many forms defined below.

- *Grants* are money gifted by a government to another government for the purpose of improving the country's infrastructure or other factor contributing to economic development. Grants are not required to be repaid by countries that receive them.
- *Concessional loans* are money lent by a government to another government, at least 25% of which does not have to be repaid. A loan is 'concessional' in nature when the interest rate is below what the recipient country could receive from a private lender, which classifies such loans as 'aid'.
- *Project aid* is money given for specific investments in healthcare, education, or other infrastructure (hospitals, schools, ports, railways, bridges, among others).
- *Programme aid* is money given to a country that is not designated for a specific project, including money to help balance a government's budget or to stabilise its currency's value on the forex markets.

Tied aid

According to the Organisation for Economic Cooperation and Development (OECD), tied aid describes 'official grants or loans that limit procurement to companies in the donor country or in a small group of countries'. In other words, a government makes a grant or a loan to another government, but requires the recipient to use the money to buy technology or hire services from companies in the donor country.

Tied aid is aid with 'strings attached'. It effectively limits the ability of the recipients to 'shop around' for the best value for the goods, services, or work it wishes to invest in with the granted or loaned funds. Tied aid acts as an indirect stimulus to the donor country's economy, masked as development assistance for a developing country. Since the money has to be spent in the donor country, it boosts domestic output and employment at the expense of the recipient having the freedom to choose where and how to spend the money in a way that maximises its impact on the country's development.

According to the OECD, the proportion of aid that is 'untied' (e.g. the recipient is able to spend it wherever it gets the most bang for the buck) has increased from 46% to 82%, vastly increasing its potential impact for good in the recipient countries.

Tied aid provides an obvious benefit for the donor country, but untied aid can stand to benefit both the recipients and the donors. What may appear as a 'selfless act' can in fact benefit both sides of the aid transaction. Donor countries (mostly rich, more economically developed countries) are better off when the rest of the world experiences rising incomes, longer lives, and greater levels of education and health.

Debt relief

Debt relief helps countries escape the debt poverty cycle, freeing up scarce government resources for investments in infrastructure, health, and education. Furthermore, the foreign revenues earned from exports can be used to buy much needed imported capital goods and technology, including medical equipment, drugs, communications and transportation technologies, and other goods that improve the living standards of the country's people, rather than on servicing external debt.

Debt relief reduces the chance of a sovereign default (i.e. government bankruptcy) and leads to greater exchange rate stability on the forex markets, as international investors are more confident in a developing country's ability to repay new debts if it has a smaller level of past debts.

In concert with domestic factors such as improvements in education and health, international factors such as diversification of exports and economic integration, FDI, and foreign aid, debt relief has played a crucial role in the economic development experienced by the world's developing countries over the last couple of decades, and will likely continue to do so in the decades ahead.

Official development assistance

When a donor country's government gives directly to another country it is called bilateral aid. Alternatively, donors can contribute to multilateral organisations like the UN, World Bank, IMF, or regional development banks like the Inter-American Development Bank. Subgroups with specific goals (e.g. United Nations International Children's Emergency Fund (UNICEF)) can also be the focus of specific giving. These organisations administer the flow of aid according to their aims and goals.

ODA flows are concessional in nature: they are required to consist of at least 25% grant money, and the rest in long-term loans with relatively easy terms. These loans can be in some combination of local currency and the currency of the donor. In reality, up to three-quarters of ODA funding is grant money, the rest is loans.

Non-governmental organisations

Aid provided by NGOs typically has a more specific purpose or operates on a smaller scale than ODA. Oxfam, which is dedicated to poverty relief and the advocacy of fair trade, is one of the more famous NGOs. Also well known is Médecins Sans Frontières, which sends medical relief to areas of emergency and long-term need.

NGOs focus on areas that official aid may not reach. Poverty relief, accomplished by working closely with desperate communities, is a major emphasis. Many NGOs focus specifically on women's issues, in particular prenatal care, abuse prevention, childcare, and women's healthcare.

What are the motivations for donor countries to give aid?

Improving development in developing countries creates more consumers for rich-country firms, a better-educated workforce willing and able to contribute to global production, and greater economic, political, and social stability, all of which contribute to favourable conditions for economic growth and increased revenues for firms and higher incomes for households in rich and developing countries alike.

Case study – foreign aid

Vietnam

In 2016 Vietnam received $2.37 billion in ODA, making it the world's third largest recipient nation after Afghanistan and India. Figure 30.4 breaks down the extent, nature, and sources of the ODA received by Vietnam in 2016.

Note that the largest donor country to Vietnam was Japan, followed by 'IDA', or the International Development Association, the part of the World Bank that helps the world's developing countries. According to the World Bank:

> 'The IDA aims to reduce poverty by providing loans (called 'credits') and grants for programmes that boost economic growth, reduce inequalities, and improve people's living conditions.'

> 'IDA is one of the largest sources of assistance for the world's 75 poorest countries, 39 of which are in Africa, and is the single largest source of donor funds for basic social services in these countries.'

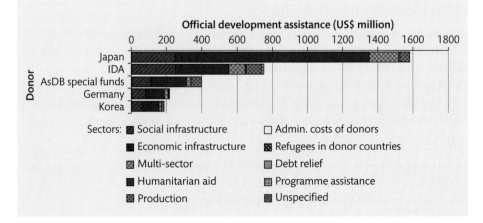

Figure 30.4 Vietnam's ODA by donor and sector, 2016

'IDA lends money on concessional terms. This means that IDA credits have a zero or very low interest charge and repayments are stretched over 25 to 40 years, including a 5- to 10-year grace period. IDA also provides grants to countries at risk of debt distress.'

The colours represent the sectors within Vietnam that received aid, including 'economic infrastructure' (the roads, bridges, transportation hubs, communication technologies, and other physical infrastructure that makes a country's economy function efficiently) and 'social infrastructure' (which includes schools, universities, hospitals, housing, and other goods that improve social welfare).

As we can see, humanitarian aid makes up only a tiny proportion of Vietnam's total aid, which is almost entirely in the form of development aid.

Ethiopia

In 2016, Ethiopia was the world's fifth largest recipient of ODA, receiving $1.98 billion. Figure 30.5 shows the extent, nature, and sources of aid received by Ethiopia.

Like Vietnam, the IDA wing of the World Bank is a major donor to Ethiopia, providing $1.2 billion of its almost $2 billion in total aid. Concessional World Bank loans are being used largely to provide social infrastructure to Ethiopia (schools, clinics, hospitals, etc), followed by economic infrastructure.

Following the IDA is the United States, which unilaterally provided Ethiopia with almost $900 million in aid, much of which was in the form of humanitarian aid.

Note also that compared to Vietnam, which received almost no humanitarian aid, over one-third of the aid received by Ethiopia ($700 million) was humanitarian. The difference can be explained by the fact that Vietnam is a relatively rich-country that is not as prone to humanitarian emergencies like drought, conflict, flooding, and outbreaks of disease as compared to Ethiopia.

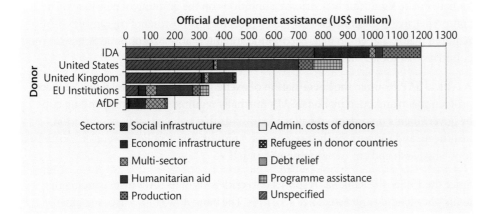

Figure 30.5 Ethiopia's ODA by donor and sector, 2016

What role does multilateral development assistance play?

Multilateral development assistance is not from individual countries, groups or countries, or non-governmental organisations, rather from *multilateral* organisations work to support global development goals. The two biggest multilateral development organisations are the World Bank and the IMF.

The World Bank

The World Bank is an international development assistance organisation that was created with the purpose of enhancing economic development and structural change. The bank was created at Bretton Woods, at the same conference as the system of international exchange rates, the IMF and the General Agreement on Tariffs and Trade (GATT), which later evolved into the WTO. These institutions were developed to establish a system of economic order that it was hoped would prevent further economic collapses like the Great Depression of the 1930s, which created the conditions for the Second World War.

The World Bank was initially made up of a handful of countries, with the former Allied countries forming its core. It has since grown to 187 members. Membership influence is directly related to the amount of donor money given to the bank. In 2010, the bank revised voting rules to allow a greater voice from developing countries. Currently the largest voting shares go to the USA (15.8%), Japan (6.84%), China (4.42%), Germany (4.00%), the UK (3.75%), and France (3.75%).

From the late 1940s through the 1960s, a sort of fiscal conservatism dominated the bank's thinking and lending. Making safe loans with an emphasis on projects that would repay the loans easily, the bank focused on infrastructure projects that would directly increase economic growth. This approach established the financial credibility of the bank but limited its impact on broader development issues.

By the 1970s, the bank was under new leadership, and its priorities changed to emphasise the meeting of basic needs in developing countries. Spending on social programmes increased significantly, including healthcare, education and poverty alleviation. Lending increased significantly, as did the debt levels of many LDCs, during this period.

In the 1980s, the bank revisited its fiscally conservative roots under the leadership of AW Clausen. During this period, the increasing debt loads of LDCs inspired the bank to create significantly restrictive conditions on the granting of new loans. The comprehensive economic reforms, called Structural Adjustment Programmes (SAPs), required major changes in macroeconomic and international economic policy for the countries that took loans at this time.

A typical SAP required the liberalisation of exchange rates and capital flows, reduced protectionism and open markets. SAPs normally required significant spending cuts by governments (in order to repay the loan), cuts that reduced levels of education, healthcare and support for the poor or unemployed. These policies were later criticised for being harsh and anti-development in practice.

Since the 1990s, the bank has responded to criticisms of its SAPs by expanding the focus of its lending and assistance activities. The bank now emphasises sustainable development methods as opposed to pure economic growth. It supports poverty alleviation and debt relief for developing countries as well. With these aims in mind, the bank has supported the work of the UNDP to reach the Millennium Goals of 2015.

So, has the World Bank made meaningful contributions to economic development in the developing world? The influence and role of the World Bank has received regular criticism, especially after the introduction of the SAPs in the 1980s. What follows is a discussion of some of the more common complaints about the bank.

Conditionality

World Bank loans come with conditions attached. Recipient countries must follow the often strict guidelines to receive the funding. The cutting of budget deficits, in particular, in order to pay back the loans, force large cuts in social welfare spending on unemployment relief, medical services, and education subsidies. These cuts hit the poorest and most vulnerable rather hard, critics say. These policies may be mixed with compulsory liberalisation of domestic industry and trade.

Privatisation may be causing increased unemployment, with fewer resources available (because of budget cuts) to help the jobless. Increased foreign competition may also cause domestic industries to fold, creating more unemployment and suffering. While this criticism of the World Bank has lessened in recent years, as the bank has adapted its conditions to more specific circumstances, it remains probably the chief complaint of borrowers and critics.

Loss of sovereignty

A related issue to World Bank conditionality, separate from the effectiveness of the conditional requirements, is that these loan terms may dramatically reduce a country's economic sovereignty. The scope of the change can be all-encompassing. When monetary, fiscal, and international trade policies are all apparently dictated by non-elected international officials, the borrowing country's people will question the legitimacy of the policies.

Dominance of rich countries

The voting procedures of the bank give heavy weight to donor countries, most of them highly developed countries, and chief among them the USA. Such countries, it is argued, know little of the challenges faced by developing countries, and thus World Bank policies are disconnected from the needs of developing countries. More worrisome is that policy prescriptions too often resemble the harsh medicine that is easier for a doctor to give than to take. During the 2008–10 global financial crisis, when the USA and European budget deficits began to soar, the World Bank was demanding fiscal austerity from its borrowers. Such disparities, if not completely validated by the evidence, do perhaps undermine the bank's legitimacy.

Mixed results

The free market emphasis of the World Bank's approach has, according to some economists, led to rising inequality in a number of recipient countries. Even further, the resulting cuts in social spending have potentially lowered some countries' performance on the HDI, in effect worsening the quality of life in those countries. More pointed criticism has come from a former chief economist of the bank, Joseph Stiglitz. While serving for three years in the late 1990s, Stiglitz reported dismay at the results of the ten-year studies of World Bank policy towards former communist countries. He left the bank, and has since advocated a much greater government role in creating economic growth and development.

To Stiglitz, the timidity of developing country businesses and individuals to spend or invest results in a lack of growth that can be compensated for only by governments. However, such a role is practically impossible when World Bank/IMF conditionality forces austere fiscal and monetary policy, as well as compulsory liberalisation. In part as a reaction to these lingering critiques from Stiglitz and many others, the bank has refocused its efforts on a broad array of specific development issues that are designed to more directly target development goals. These include sustainable development through carbon-trading funds, conservation efforts, and water-sanitation initiatives.

The bank has sought to fortify institutions by working against corruption, and for the promotion of legal reform and property rights. It spends on human development by funding childcare projects, malaria treatment, and HIV/AIDs projects worldwide. Thus, the World Bank appears to be changing strategy as the development consensus changes, even if these changes are occurring rather slowly.

International Monetary Fund

The IMF is an organisation of 187 countries, whose dues go towards funding IMF activities. Among the stated aims of the IMF are to be working towards fostering global monetary cooperation, securing financial stability, facilitating international trade, promoting high employment and sustainable economic growth, and reducing poverty around the world.

Created alongside the World Bank and GATT, the IMF's initial purpose was to act as the overseer of the Bretton Woods fixed exchange rate system. The IMF was to monitor the balance of payment situations of member countries and when necessary, act on behalf of those countries to solve current account problems. Typically, this involved the risk of some kind of rapid currency depreciation.

The IMF would then loan the country money (an inflow on the financial account) to finance the current account deficit that is a symptom of the depreciation. Without this financing, countries with current account deficits might need to devalue their currencies and upset the fixed rate system. The IMF, to some extent, still plays this role, as the international lender of last resort. In the 1980s, the IMF expanded its role beyond management of exchange rates to a form of debt relief. Many LDCs experienced crippling debt crises, and the IMF worked with these countries and the countries and banks that had lent to them. By acting as a final guarantor of privately loaned funds, the IMF provided a backstop for many debt crises. Furthermore, most countries avoided defaulting on IMF loans because this would eliminate their financial safety should any future crisis arise. However, complying with the IMF's loan rules proved challenging for many countries. The stabilisation policies associated with these rules could be far-reaching. This resulted in most of the criticism directed at the agency.

The agency may well be the world's 'financial fire department' but it does not work for free, nor is it considered a kind of public good. The policies, according to the IMF, are justified because they are aimed at paying back the IMF so that funds will continue to be available for countries in need and at enabling the IMF to impose unpopular policies that would have prevented the crisis in the first place.

The policies include a range of market-oriented reforms that, depending on the country in question, could have enormous impact.

Government budget austerity

In order to pay back loans, governments need to cut their spending. This nearly always results in significant cuts to social programmes, often in times of crisis, when the need is greater than usual.

Supply-side policies

The IMF may insist on the reduction of minimum wage laws, the privatisation of industries, and the cutting of state subsidies to firms.

Inflation control

To establish stability and to reduce the drag downwards of exchange rates, governments may be urged to control inflation with significantly higher interest rates. These high rates could reduce investment and consumption and usher in a period of recession, with all the unemployment and social dislocation that goes with it.

Currency floating

Since the ending of the Bretton Woods system, currencies are encouraged to float to avoid over- or under-valuations. For many, floating rates could lead to a painful depreciation of the currency.

Trade liberalisation

This includes reductions in protectionist tariffs, quotas and subsidies, as well as ending restrictions on FDI.

So how does the IMF score in its efforts to promote economic development in developing countries? Because countries in need of IMF help have such poor credit reputations, the IMF's willingness to lend offers a hard-won seal of approval, a kind of stamp of credit-worthiness. This makes countries ever more desperate to land IMF help when international consensus determines it is necessary for foreign credit and investment to return to the country. Nevertheless, many of the same criticisms levelled at the World Bank have been applied to the IMF, including the following.

- **Rich-country dominance:** Voting follows IMF rules, with the percentages of votes being, in line with those of the World Bank, heavily dominated by rich countries. Rather than 'one country – one vote', the rules dictate that monetary donations determine the percentage of voting power.
- **Moral hazard:** IMF lending, it is argued, frees countries from fiscal responsibility, and allows them to mismanage their monetary and fiscal policies. With the IMF around to help, the consequences of poor management are one step removed from short-run concerns.
- **Harsh policies:** IMF stabilisation policies have a reputation for hitting hardest when the population is most vulnerable. The decreased spending on merit goods, the cutting of already low wages, cuts on food and medical subsidies, and reduction in unemployment benefits at times of greater unemployment, all these have been cited as extraordinary and inhumane policies, especially when applied to developing countries where the reserves of savings and private help are low to begin with.

 Ethics

Do economically more developed nations have a moral obligation to assist economically less developed nations, such as through foreign aid or World Bank lending? What criteria should economists use to make such judgements?

What institutional changes will promote growth and development?

A country's *institutions* are like the operating system on a smart phone or laptop computer. Even a phone with the flashiest hardware (biggest, sharpest screen, thinnest body, high quality camera) will be ineffective if it does not have a well functioning operating system. Countries are the same way; an LDC can invest all it wants in human capital, infrastructure, and technology, but in order for it to achieve meaningful economic development it must have well-run institutions that assure secure, stable, equitable economic growth and development.

In Chapter 29 we outlined how the lack of strong institutions poses a barrier to economic development. By developing and protecting their institutions, therefore, LDCs can expect a more stable and equitable economy that is more attractive for investment and therefore likely to promote both economic growth and development.

Improved access to banking

A banking system provides the medium through which lenders and borrowers can be matched with one another. Disposable incomes among workers and businesses can be saved, creating funds that can be loaned to individuals and businesses in turn. Access to credit is a mandatory ingredient for economic growth and development to take place.

In Chapter 29 we learned about microcredit organisations, which have emerged to fill the void left by the lack of traditional commercial banks in the developing world. As developing countries see incomes rise, it becomes increasingly important for a banking sector to emerge to serve the needs of savers and borrowers, allocating capital to where it is needed most in the growing economy.

Increased women's empowerment

Women make up half the world's population, yet, in many parts of the world they still play a secondary role to men in the economic realm. Empowering women through extending equal rights, expanding access to education, and providing equal opportunities in the workplace vastly expands a country's production possibilities. Not only do women become productive members of the economy, increasing national income, but the act of extending rights to women itself directly improves human welfare, helping a country achieve its development goals.

Reducing corruption

In Chapter 29 we learned about Paul Collier's poverty traps. One of those was the poor governance trap, which arises when corrupt officials undermine society's advancement towards economic development by demanding bribes, siphoning off state resources for their personal gain, and engaging in other corrupt acts at the highest level. Corruption can occur in the private sector, as well, as workers or business owners put their own wealth and interest above those of the businesses they are meant to work for.

Ending corruption will make for a more efficient public and private sector, allowing resources to be allocated to where they are needed most, but also making a country a more attractive place to do business, which could attract FDI and help increase a developing country's capital stock and productivity levels.

Protecting property rights

A final institution needing protection for growth and development to occur is that of property rights. As explained in Chapter 29, the lack of property rights creates an environment of economic uncertainty and instability. Investors, both domestic and foreign, will only feel safe putting their capital in a country if they are sure that their assets will remain in their hands no matter what.

30.2 What are the strengths and limitations of strategies for promoting economic growth and economic development?

Learning outcomes

At the end of this section you will be able to:

- evaluate the strengths and limitations of trade strategies for growth and development
- evaluate the impact of FDI for economically less developed countries (LDCs)
- evaluate the effectiveness of foreign aid in contributing to economic development.

Trade strategies

When a country trades with other countries it is guaranteed to broaden the market for the country's output and increase the variety of goods available to the country's households. When a country specialises in the goods for which it has a comparative advantage and trades for other goods, it experiences an increase in its production possibilities, greater efficiency, and higher incomes. Trade, as it turns out, is a wonderful way for a country to promote economic growth.

Trade does have several limitations, however. It is not a development strategy, since free trade, despite all its benefits for the countries that participate in it, does little to protect human and environmental welfare. Trade increases productivity and therefore incomes, but cannot provide for improvements in living standards beyond more income. Trade creates externalities, from the increased fossil fuel consumption and resulting carbon emissions created by the ocean liners that transport commodities all over the world to the race to exploit the natural resources of countries with lax regulatory environments, often in a way that profits MNCs but does little to develop the economies of the countries the resources are extracted from.

In other words, international trade is a means to an end. Through trade an LDC can expect to increase its incomes, attract foreign investment, and grow its stock of infrastructure and capital. However, human capital requires more than what trade can offer. The merit goods of education and healthcare are rarely provided through trade; in order to achieve economic development, a mixed market and interventionist approach must be taken. Trade also creates many losers, so countries often adopt an import substitution or export promotion policy, as described earlier in this chapter.

However, no man is an island, and economic development is unlikely to take place without first a country opening itself to international trade.

Foreign direct investment

Because the expansion of FDI in the developing world is expected to continue, it is critical for LDCs to assess the value of FDI for their own development plans. Keeping in mind the variety of developing countries, as well as the differences between types of FDI, it is still possible to make some generalisations about the desirability of foreign investment.

Advantages of FDI

When a developing country receives incoming FDI, valuable financial and physical capital are injected into the recipient economy, creating several positive outcomes, including the following.

- Capital injections can help to break the poverty cycle by injecting much needed capital goods and finance.
- The foreign purchase of domestic assets brings money into the capital account of the balance of payments, enabling more imports of foreign consumer and capital goods.
- Foreign investment can induce LDC governments to invest in infrastructure to support the new firms. This may have spin-off benefits to the country at large if the works projects have other useful applications.
- Some forms of FDI provide opportunities for enhanced research and development, which may expand technical capital in the greater economy.
- FDI can stimulate domestic industry when the MNC buys locally produced capital goods and services.
- Technology transfer improves the country's capital stock. As foreign firms bring in new and more advanced technology, domestic rivals and suppliers are inspired to adapt technologically as well.

FDI also has positive impacts on income and employment in the recipient country, including the following.

- If foreign firms hire significantly from the domestic workforce, increased employment increases incomes and tax revenues.
- Often MNCs will invest in the skills of workers; here FDI can increase human capital through training.
- The increased income accruing to workers and to the MNC is subject to taxation, increasing tax revenues that might be used for development purposes such as improved healthcare and education.

Finally, FDI leads to increased market efficiency and choice, benefiting consumers in the recipient economy. Some of the benefits in this area include the following.

- MNCs may compete with complacent domestic industries. The added competition should lower prices and increase market efficiency domestically.
- If MNCs help a country realise its comparative advantages, world trade is enhanced and lower prices result.
- For domestic consumers, the arrival of foreign firms may initiate meaningful choice in the market for goods and services.

Disadvantages of FDI

In reality, FDI may not achieve the outcomes expected in developing countries that receive it. In the area of employment, for one, there are several possibilities that may render it an ineffective development strategy.

- Foreign firms may choose to bring large amounts of management personnel to launch and administer the company. In this case, the employment growth only comes to the low-skilled and low-wage labour force.
- Where foreign management stays in place, the expected training and skills transfer effect is limited.
- Some industries do not hire workers extensively as they are capital intensive. Thus, some FDI companies that earn large revenues have relatively few domestic workers.

The impact on domestic income may also be less than expected due to MNCs' tendency to repatriate profits earned through overseas investments, and their ability to use sophisticated accounting methods to avoid paying local taxes in the developing country.

Additionally, FDI may come with only limited capital injections. In some cases, the government of the country receiving FDI will require that foreign firms partner with a domestic company in a joint venture. In other instances, domestic companies are bought through transfers of share ownership in the new foreign parent company. In either case, the FDI may simply mean increased foreign ownership of already existing domestic assets, with little or no injections of foreign capital resulting.

There is no guarantee that the investment spending undertaken by foreign investors actually originates outside the domestic economy. In reality, many corporations borrow from local financial markets to finance their investments in developing countries, pushing up borrowing costs and crowding out investments that might have come from domestic firms seeking credit in the developing country.

Finally, one likely outcome of FDI in LDCs is a loss of economic sovereignty by the recipient country's government and businesses. MNCs hold great power and influence in the developing countries where they do business. This may include influence over the regulatory environment and the ability to bully elected officials into keeping tax rates low at the risk of losing billions of dollars in foreign capital flows. Likewise, attempts by the recipient country's government to make policies aimed at improving worker safety and health or raising the environmental standards to which producers are held could be undermined by lobbyists for the foreign firms doing business in the home country.

In other words, in their efforts to attract and retain FDI, governments in less economically developed countries may find their hands tied when it comes to implementing policies that could lead to meaningful improvements in the lives of their citizens and promote sustainable development. Once again we are reminded of the apparent trade-off between health and wealth, between growth and development, and, in this case, between the desire to attract foreign capital while also protecting the well-being of domestic stakeholders.

What are the strengths and limitations of foreign aid?

There has been much debate over the effectiveness of aid in contributing to economic development. On one side of the discussion are economists like Columbia University's

Jeffrey Sachs, who argued in a January 2014 column in Foreign Policy Journal that 'the recent evidence shows that development aid, when properly designed and delivered, works, saving the lives of the poor and helping to promote economic growth'. As evidence, Sachs points to the reduction in instances of malaria in sub-Saharan Africa since the turn of the 21st century:

'At the turn of the new century, malaria was front and centre of the global aid debate. Research by myself and others … showed that in addition to being a health catastrophe, malaria imposes a significant economic burden, particularly in sub-Saharan Africa. Luckily, though, the world was starting to take notice. In 2000, the UN Millennium Declaration, The African Summit on Malaria, and the G8 Declaration all addressed the burden of malaria and committed the world to action. The debate soon turned to the issue of policy: how could the malaria burden be reduced?'

'The combination of bed nets and effective medicines, supported by rapid diagnosis of infections, makes for a powerful one-two punch in saving lives and reducing malaria transmission.'

'Without financial support, poor people could not afford either the (bed nets) or the new medicines. Attempts to sell the nets at a discount, known as social marketing, had very little take up, since many poor families simply lacked any cash income at all. The prospect of achieving 'mass action' protection through social marketing was very small. Moreover, impoverished households would often scrape together the needed money only to buy the cheaper but ineffective nets, rather than the more expensive but more effective (ones).'

'Governments of low-income African countries needed donor support for the scale-up effort since their own domestic tax revenues, even when amply allocated to public health, could not cover the costs of a basic primary health system including scaled-up malaria control. The financial calculations, laid out by the Commission on Macroeconomics and Health, showed that an impoverished country with a GDP of around $500 per capita, typical for a poor country in Africa, may be able to muster around $15 per person per year out of domestic revenues for primary health, while the costs of a basic public health system would be around $50–$60 per person per year.'

' … The WHO (World Health Organization) swung its powerful weight behind the mass free distributions of bed nets throughout sub-Saharan Africa. Soon after, UN Secretary-General Ban Ki-moon established the mass free distribution of bed nets as policy for all UN agencies, and called on the world's governments and NGOs to support the scale-up effort. Ban's leadership tipped the global scales decisively. Close to 300 million bed nets were freely distributed from 2008–10, with the global fund to fight AIDS, tuberculosis and malaria and the US President's Malaria Initiative program paying for a substantial share of the scale-up.'

'The evidence is overwhelming that malaria declined precipitously as a result of these bold measures. WHO's latest report finds a stunning 51 percent drop in malaria deaths of African children under the age of five between the years 2000 and 2012. These results are historic. Roughly a half-million children, if not more, are being saved each year that otherwise would have succumbed to malaria.'

According to Sachs and other aid proponents, without the work of both NGOs and official development agencies, and the governments that support them, the poverty reduction and improvements in health and education experienced across the developing world in recent decades would have been significantly less pronounced.

On the other side of the debate are economists like New York University's William Easterly, who argues that due to factors like a lack of accountability and feedback, corruption, and the fact that recipient countries can become dependent upon and beholden to donor countries, rather than developing their own capacities as contributors to global trade, aid has failed to achieve meaningful improvements in the development of developing countries.

According to Easterly:

> 'Economic development happens, not through aid, but through the homegrown efforts of entrepreneurs and social and political reformers. While the West was agonising over a few tens of billion dollars in aid, the citizens of India and China raised their own incomes by $715 billion by their own efforts in free markets. Once aid agencies realise that aid CANNOT achieve general economic and political development, they could start concentrating on fixing the system that fails to get 12-cent medicines to malaria victims.'

> 'The two key elements necessary to make aid work, and the absence of which has been fatal to aid's effectiveness in the past, are FEEDBACK and ACCOUNTABILITY. The needs of the rich get met through feedback and accountability. Consumers tell the firm 'this product is worth the price' by buying the product, or decide the product is worthless and return it to the store. Voters tell their elected representatives that 'these public services are bad' and the politician tries to fix the problem.'

> 'Of course, feedback only works if somebody listens. Profit-seeking firms make a product they find to be in high demand, but they also take responsibility for the product – if the product poisons the customer, they are liable, or at least they go out of business. Elected representatives take responsibility for the quality of public services. If something goes wrong, they pay politically, perhaps by losing office. If it succeeds, they get the political rewards.'

> 'Aid agencies can be held accountable for specific tasks, rather than the weak incentives that follow from collective responsibility of all aid agencies and recipient governments for those broad goals that depend on many other things besides aid agency effort. Examples of the latter include such unaccountable goals as the very fashionable campaign to achieve the UN Millennium Development Goals, or the sweeping goals of economic growth, government reform, and democracy for poor countries mentioned above. If a bureaucracy shares responsibilities with other agencies to achieve many different general goals that depend on many other things, then it is not accountable to its intended beneficiaries – the poor. No one aid agent is individually responsible for successfully achieving any one task in the current aid system. Without accountability, then the incentive for finding out what works is weak. True accountability would mean having an aid agency take responsibility for a specific, monitorable task to help the poor, whose

outcome depends almost entirely on what the agency does. Then independent evaluation of how well the agency does the task will then create strong incentives for performance.'

At the very least, opponents argue, aid has played a secondary role, while the primary driver of economic development has instead been the opening up of global markets to less economically developed countries, trade liberalisation, FDI, and other market-oriented approaches to raising incomes and reducing poverty.

To summarise, aid is effective when:

- it is targeted at specific needs for specific communities in developing countries
- it meets a need that the free market and domestic government has been unable to meet
- it is temporary and has achievable, measurable goals.

Aid fails when:

- there is a lack of feedback and accountability, making it impossible for the aid givers to know whether the aid is working or not
- it is too broad or its objectives are not clearly defined
- the countries receiving the aid become dependent upon it, creating a moral hazard under which there is less incentive to promote development through their own means.

30.3 What are the strengths and limitations of government intervention versus market-oriented approaches?

Learning outcomes

At the end of this section you will be able to:

- discuss the strengths and limitations of market-oriented policies (such as liberalised trade and capital flows, privatisation and deregulation), including a more efficient allocation of resources and economic growth
- discuss the strengths and limitations of interventionist policies, including the provision of infrastructure, investment in human capital, the provision of a stable macroeconomic economy and the provision of a social safety net
- discuss the view that economic development may best be achieved through a complementary approach, involving a balance of market-oriented policies and government intervention.

Economics is sometimes called the dismal science. Originally this term referred to the fact that it dealt with the inevitable problem of scarcity faced by all human societies and the myriad conflicts that arise over the use and allocation of scarce resources. Throughout your course, you have explored situations both micro and macro, local, national and international, ranging from the efficiency of the elusive perfectly competitive market to the inefficiency of protectionism.

You have learned about the theories, models, graphs, and other tools economists employ to try and deal with scarcity efficiently and equitably, with the well-being of society as the ultimate goal. The competing objectives of efficiency and equity may not always coincide but the outcome achieved by Adam Smith's invisible hand of the market can be improved on. This can be brought about through the implementation of re-allocative policies such as taxes, subsidies, and price controls by an economically informed and well intentioned government.

In this regard, economics is hardly dismal at all. It offers a toolkit for making the world a better place. By quantifying the seemingly unquantifiable, such as the 'marginal social benefit of healthcare', economists are able to present realistic, achievable solutions to challenges affecting human welfare. The central problem of scarcity is dismal indeed but economics is ultimately a hopeful science offering market-based solutions to humankind's biggest problems.

Yet the dismal truth is that good economics is not always valued by those in power who have the greatest ability to affect the allocation of the scarce resources we depend on. In reality, good politics does not always equal good economics – a claim for which the poor decisions of politicians and leaders in countless countries, day after day, present ample evidence.

Whether it is a decision to cut taxes and increase government spending in a country on the brink of a debt crisis, or the decision to control the price of fuel in a city where long queues are already forming at petrol stations, or to privatise a water system in a region where poor people already find it difficult to maintain health, government decisions often reflect poor economic judgement.

And the free market itself rarely has all the answers to the problem of scarcity. The idea that markets promote efficiency and therefore achieve a socially desirable outcome places great faith in the assumption that competition exists to ensure that efficiency emerges. In reality, a market system driven by individuals pursuing self-interest does not always lead to the most desirable outcomes for society as a whole, despite Adam Smith's belief in the allocative power of the invisible hand.

Markets tend to experience cyclical fluctuations over time, evolving from periods of innovation and competition to periods of increasing concentration of market power among a few large firms, stagnation and inefficiency. The creative destruction of the free market and innovation in welfare-improving technologies sometimes requires the guiding hand and watchful oversight of a socially conscious government.

The markets for goods that are vitally important to a nation's economic development (healthcare, education, infrastructure, social insurance) and certain welfare-improving technologies must all be examined carefully with the tools and models of economics so as to decide the extent to which the free market is capable of promoting human welfare and development. The motives of the free market pursuit of profits lay the foundation for efficiency, while the interests of society must be attended to by watchful government regulators.

Development will not be achieved in any country left entirely to the free market; nor will total government control promote improvements in human welfare. The complementary approach of a market-oriented development strategy combined with careful government oversight is the most likely to promote economic development while creating an atmosphere for sustainable economic growth.

Is economics the dismal science or the hopeful science?

Despite all your reading, the conversations in class, the diagrams you have drawn in your notes, and the pages and pages of analysis and evaluation you have laboured over, the theories and tools of economics only get us so far in our understanding of how to make the world a better place. The welfare of human societies ultimately rests in the establishment and maintenance of economic systems that take into account the costs and benefits of human behaviour on society, on the environment including other species with which we share the planet, and on generations of humans both present and in the future.

Sustainability is defined as 'the ability to endure'. The ability of any economic system to endure depends on the extent to which it accounts for the future in its decisions as to how resources should be allocated in the present. Unfortunately, neither the free market nor government intervention has done a sufficiently good job of accounting for future generations in the economic interactions and policies of the 20th and 21st centuries.

In the 2003 documentary film *The Corporation*, the economic and environmental challenges the world has faced since the Industrial Revolution are compared to the challenges faced by the earliest pioneers of human flight. Those intrepid adventurers would push their crafts off high cliffs, flap their mechanical wings, and think they were flying because the ground was still so very far away. But eventually they would crash to the ground, as they were doomed from the moment they pushed off the cliff's edge. Without knowledge of flight mechanics and good design, their craft could never fly. Like the early flight pioneers, society has yet to develop an economic system that allows all human civilisation to soar.

Again, like those pursuing the dream of flight, Western civilisation pushed itself off a massive cliff into the unknown when it embarked on the path towards industrialisation that began in England over 300 years ago. Today, LDCs around the world are travelling the same path. The ground in this analogy is the point at which the world's resources are depleted to a degree beyond which they are unable to be replenished. It once seemed so far away that very few people ever considered the likelihood of civilisation crashing into it. But today it is growing ever closer.

The economic systems we have developed, some argue, are as unsuited to making our civilisation sustainable as mechanical wings were to flight. Eventually, if we do not realise that the ground is growing nearer, human civilisation will crash. The question is, at what point will our civilisation realise it is on a path towards total resource depletion and self-destruction? At what point will we begin implementing much needed reforms to the economic systems that govern our allocation of resources?

Can sustainability be achieved?

When will good economics – an economics that accounts for all stakeholders, those living now and those of future generations – prevail in our exchanges with one another on a local, national and international level? Only when an economic system prevails that accounts for the true costs and benefits of our behaviour to society, to the environment, and to future generations will human civilisation enter an era in which it can truly fly and thereby avoid the fate of the flight pioneers and their flapping mechanical wings.

Economics is only dismal insofar as it is ignored by policymakers and politicians. Economics offers a design for a civilisation that could truly fly, allowing humans to survive indefinitely in a world in which resources are allocated efficiently between the competing wants and needs of society in a sustainable manner.

The ability of humankind to endure, to sustain itself into the future, is increasingly questionable. A greater understanding of economic theories, and an implementation of the models and tools economics teaches us can help ensure that future generations will live in a world in which human societies everywhere can live happy, healthy lives, free of fear and conflict. In this regard, economics is the most hopeful science of all.

Practice exam questions

1. Read the extract below and answer the questions that follow.

EU's secret plans target markets in developing countries

The European Union (EU) has drawn up secret plans aimed at opening the service sector markets in the world's developing countries in return for reducing its farm subsidies.

The demands made by the EU would allow European firms to charge for providing water to some of the 1.2 billion people living on less than a dollar a day. Water has always been regarded as a free good, but this idea is changing. It would give large gains to European banks, telecommunication businesses and business service firms.

The EU is under intense pressure to remove export subsidies that depress global food prices and impoverish farmers in the developing world. Reform of Europe's agricultural policy is a top demand from developing countries.

Supporters for less developed countries argue that the EU proposals are not pro-development, nor do they encourage sustainable development. Many developing countries would be tied to unfair and irreversible commitments if they agree to European requests. If these economic decisions go wrong, developing countries would be affected for generations to come. A more effective approach would be to encourage **export-led growth**.

While the **privatisation** of water would result in a higher price for the consumer, the advantage is that the water will be clean and filtered, enabling the population to be healthier and live longer, acting as a positive externality. Against this is the cost of implementing the privatisation, possible social and economic upheaval, and institutional and political factors that would act as significant barriers to economic growth and development.

Among its demands, the EU wants Bolivia to let in more overseas water companies despite a recent case where a multinational company increased water prices by 200% in one city. The EU is also looking at Panama with similar plans where water privatisation plans were scrapped in 1998 after strikes and demonstrations.

---

a. Define the following terms indicated in bold in the text:
   i.   export-led growth   (2 marks)
   ii. privatisation.   (2 marks)
b. Using an appropriate diagram, explain how European agricultural subsidies help to 'impoverish farmers in the developing world'.   (4 marks)
c. Using an appropriate diagram, explain why consumers will buy nearly a constant quantity of water despite higher prices.   (4 marks)
d. Using information from the text and your knowledge of economics, evaluate the extent to which the privatisation of the water supply in a less developed country would benefit consumers in that country.   (15 marks)

2.   Read the extracts below and answer the questions that follow.

Fighting poverty in Africa

Item 1: There are those, not least in Africa, who fear this massive debt relief will produce the same circumstances that have followed smaller debt write-offs. Incompetent governments will run up large new debt, spend the money on unrealistic projects and place spare cash into Swiss bank accounts.

– *Arab News*, Editorial, Saudi Arabia, 12 June 2005

Item 2: Doubling official aid, even if it is **tied aid** and cancelling Africa's debt are theoretically very attractive proposals. They fail because they are based on a misguided faith that you can rely on human unselfishness to end human misery. Tony Blair and his partners would do the continent a lot of good if they promoted trade, removed agricultural subsidies and encouraged investment relationships, rather than offering kindness and generosity through more aid and debt relief.

– Andrew M. Mwenda, *Sunday Monitor*, Uganda, 12 June 2005

Item 3: If we are serious about addressing Africa's poverty, far more money and effort will be needed as well as freeing these countries from debt repayment, which then allows them to invest in economic development and improve the health and education of their citizens. Africa has 11% of the world's population, but accounts for only about 1% of the world's economic output. Export-led growth is needed. Without more help from the developed countries, the future looks bad.

– *Seattle Times*, Editorial, 12 June 2005

Item 4: Africa is not poor. As the Africa commission report has noted, while it lacks **infrastructure**, Africa is rich in human and natural resources. The problem is that Africans have been forced to live in countries that have not wanted to enrich the lives of people within them, but rather to transfer resources abroad. The struggle of Africa is to be part of the world economic order based on mutual respect, not exploitation.

– Ken Wiwa, *The Observer*, 12 June 2005

---

a. Define the following terms indicated in bold in the text:
    i.   tied aid   (2 marks)
    ii. infrastructure.   (2 marks)
b. Using an appropriate diagram, explain how
    domestic farmers would be affected by the
    removal of their subsidies.   (4 marks)
c. Using an AD/AS diagram, explain the effect of a
    successful export-led growth policy.   (4 marks)
d. Using information from the text and your knowledge
    of economics, evaluate the effectiveness of increased
    aid and debt forgiveness policies.   (15 marks)

External assessment

31

There are many ways to approach exam revision, and this chapter will address paper-specific approaches in the following sections. Before doing so, it may be helpful to discuss some general approaches that are useful across the external and internal assessments.

Fluency with economics terminology

Economics has its own vocabulary, and your mastery of that vocabulary is assessed throughout. There is a glossary of subject-specific terms provided in Chapter 33, and these terms have also been defined where they are used in the text. While the subject is grounded in logic and common sense, putting your explanations in your own words should only be a last resort. Command of economic terms is a prerequisite for a solid performance and can enhance your overall understanding.

Note that fluency is not the same thing as repeating the definitions for every term. You are only asked to specifically define terms in Paper 2, part a. For writing short answers or essay-type questions, only define the key terms and strive to demonstrate an understanding of the other terms in the context of the question.

Clear and well explained diagrams

As you well know by now, the majority of economics theory in this course is enhanced by a diagram at some stage. Your diagrams are a fulcrum around which your explanations will revolve. There are simple but important things you can do to make sure your diagrams are effective.

- *Large diagrams* are better than small ones. To fit the information needed and to make it clear, use nearly one-third of a page to draw your diagrams.
- *Fully label* your diagrams. Use arrows to indicate shifts, and dotted lines to connect graph coordinates to their respective X and Y axes.
- Use a *pencil and a small ruler*. To keep it neat, be prepared to erase as needed and use the ruler to draw clear lines.
- *Explain your diagram with specific references*. Diagrams that are unexplained do little for your paper. General references to a diagram score slightly better. Fully explained diagrams that refer to specific points, e.g. 'demand shifts from D to D_1, causing price to rise from P_E to P_1', will score well.

Real-world examples (RWEs)

Where questions elicit a real-world example, students should provide an actual specific instance that demonstrates the theory of a particular situation. These can be current or historical, provided they accurately reflect the principle you are describing. Some examples include the following.

- An example of supply inelasticity in the short run is surgical masks and other personal protective equipment (PPE) in 2020. After a huge and sudden spike in demand for PPE, prices were high and supply was short, but after several months, manufacturers massively increased output and prices dropped accordingly.

- An example of a company that is alleged to command monopoly power is Google, which has been the subject of regulatory scrutiny over internet search and search advertising market dominance in recent years.
- An example of a demand deficient recession is the Great Depression of the 1930s, where output fell by some measures up to 40% and unemployment was as high as 20%.
- Norway consistently scores among the highest countries in terms of human development, even when adjusted for inequality, gender equity, and sustainability.

It is recommended that you identify and clearly label your RWEs throughout your notes. For example, indicate each example with a bold 'RWE' for each appropriate topic. For revision purposes, comb through your notes to find all the RWEs and add more where the topic calls for it.

31.2 What is Paper 1 and how should you prepare for it?

Paper 1 is an essay paper that is drawn from all parts of the syllabus. For SL students, it is worth 30% of the final grade, and for HL students it accounts for 20% of the final grade. You are given three options and you are to choose one question and answer it within 1 hour and 15 minutes. Each question is generally tied to a single and different unit of the syllabus (i.e. introduction, microeconomics, macroeconomics, global economy). HL questions are likely to encompass the HL extension material, allowing or encouraging that material to be included in the response.

For each paper, you will be given *5 minutes of reading time*. Use this wisely to both read each question carefully and to organise your thoughts in response.

It is recommended to use part of this time to be sure you *understand the specific demands of the question*. By doing so you can write efficiently and clearly and access the top marks. Many students only catch a general idea of the question and unload all they can remember on the topic. This takes extra time away from answering other parts of the paper and does not help your score.

Use another part of this reading time to *map your answer*. For part (a), this may be a short list of terms and graphs you want to discuss. For part (b) the notes you write may be more complicated, but that is the point. It is extremely helpful to have these reference notes as you look up from writing out a portion of your answer. Instead of forgetting your brainstormed plan, you have it for reference. This makes following through on your thoughts, as well as making the synthesis and evaluation points, easier to make when you are well into your essay.

Paper 1 is typically divided up into two sub-questions or *parts* on a related topic.

How do you answer part (a)?

Part (a) usually requires you to demonstrate the skills in AO1, AO2, and AO4 (knowledge and understanding, application and analysis, and the use of appropriate skills and techniques). Part (a) is always worth 10 marks. Note: part (a) questions nearly always require the use of a diagram, even when it is not explicitly stated in the question.

A typical part (a) question might look like these. Some typical descriptors are used with sample questions.

1. a. *Explain* the concepts of price floors and price ceilings. (10 marks)

     Here *explain* asks you to tell the reader something in a way that makes it clear with relevant ideas and possible causes.

    b. *Analyse* the relationship between the application of a tax and allocative efficiency. (10 marks)

     To *analyse* something is to examine something and break it down into its different parts to make it better understood.

    c. *Suggest* three ways in which the government could address the problem of a negative output gap. (10 marks)

     To *suggest* is to offer possible answers without going into specific detail.

    d. *Distinguish* between expenditure switching policies and expenditure reducing policies used to correct a persistent current account deficit. (10 marks)

     Here to *distinguish* is to make the difference between the two clear to the reader.

To give you a sense of the requirements for full marks, and the distinction between the top levels, the descriptors for Level 4 and 5 are listed below.

How do you answer part (b)?

Part (b) is typically related to the part (a) question, and it often requires some combination of all four assessment objectives, with a heavy emphasis on synthesis and evaluation (AO3). It is always worth 15 marks. You will not need to repeat the definitions you wrote in part (a), but you may want to redraw diagrams if there is a new

Table 31.1 Paper 1 part (a) levels, marks, and descriptors

Marks 0–10	Level descriptor
7–8 (Level 4)	• The specific demands of the question are understood and addressed. • Relevant economic theory is explained. • Relevant economic terms are used mostly appropriately. • Where appropriate, relevant diagram(s) are included and explained.
9–10 (Level 5)	• The specific demands of the question are understood and addressed. • Relevant economic theory is fully explained. • Relevant economic terms are used appropriately throughout the response. • Where appropriate, relevant diagram(s) are included and fully explained.

application. For example, part (a) may ask you to discuss a price control, but part (b) asks about an efficient allocation of resources or may imply that you discuss another policy as well. This may require new diagrams or redrawn revisions to the previous ones you wrote in part (a).

A typical part (b) question might look like the following. *Evaluate* and *discuss* are the most common command terms. Example questions, related to the part (a) question above, are shown below.

b.   Using real-world examples, evaluate the effectiveness of price-control policies designed to improve producer and consumer welfare.   (15 marks)

   Here *evaluate* is used to prompt the student to make a judgement about the effects on different groups and the advantages and disadvantages of the policy.

b.   Using real-world examples, discuss the effectiveness of a minimum wage to improve welfare and income for low wage workers.   (15 marks)

   Here the term *discuss* asks the student to share the different perspectives on the issue, supported by evidence and theory.

One might less frequently see *compare and contrast*, as well as *to what extent* as command prompts.

Note the repetition of the call for RWEs. These are essential for you to score in the top range. With the awareness that you are going to be asked about RWEs in Paper 1, the collection of RWEs for each topic is very important.

Part (b) is different in that it asks that you *evaluate* – to make a critical judgement on the policies in question, based on evidence from the real world, and demonstrating your understanding of, in this case, the economic concept of price controls. Evaluation of price controls requires you to measure the effectiveness of price-control policies against their stated goals of helping either producers or consumers. You also need to apply relevant knowledge of price-control programmes, and explain the advantages and disadvantages of such schemes. Do your best to outline the issues, dilemmas, and key challenges of an issue, using your theory and your real-world example.

While evaluation will be discussed in some more detail later three tips are worth noting here. Part (b) is a mini-essay unto itself, and needs some basic structure to be done well.

1   You need an **introduction** that defines the scope of your answer and the outline of your thesis. The more specific you can make your thesis, the better.

2   Your main **arguments**, of course. But every argument has a **counterargument**, and these should be acknowledged and addressed in your answer.

3   A **summative conclusion** is important for part (b). Often, you 'write your way to a thesis' and land on the clearest version of your thoughts when you finish. Be sure to include that in your answer.

To give you a sense of the requirements for full marks, and the distinction between the top levels, the descriptors for Level 4 and 5 are listed below.

Table 31.2 Paper 1, part (b) levels, marks, and descriptors

Marks 0–15	Level descriptor
10–12 (Level 4)	• The specific demands of the question are understood and addressed. • Relevant economic theory is explained. • Relevant economic terms are used mostly appropriately. • Where appropriate, relevant diagram(s) are included and explained. • The response contains evidence of appropriate synthesis or evaluation that is mostly balanced. • A relevant real-world example(s) is identified and developed in the context of the question.
13–15 (Level 5)	• The specific demands of the question are understood and addressed. • Relevant economic theory is fully explained. • Relevant economic terms are used appropriately throughout the response. • Where appropriate, relevant diagram(s) are included and fully explained. • The response contains evidence of effective and balanced synthesis or evaluation. • A relevant real-world example(s) is identified and fully developed to support the argument.

31.3 What is Paper 2 and how should you prepare for it?

Paper 2 is a data response paper. There are two question options and you are to select and answer one of them. Within each question, the prompts will cover all four areas of the syllabus. Paper 2 is worth 40 marks, and the time allowance is 1 hour, 45 minutes. For HL students this paper is worth 30% of the final IB Economics grade, and for SL students it is worth 40%.

For each question the format is that you are asked to read a selection of information from a news story and/or study a selection of economic data; you then answer questions based on the readings. Your answers should also demonstrate your own knowledge of course topics. Data response questions are more specific and directed than the extended response questions of Paper 1.

Here you also have 5 minutes of reading time.

1   Use it to *skim the questions and question prompts to make a thoughtful selection.* Select the question with prompts that you know well, and feel confident to answer.

2   *Next, read the question carefully.* Part (g) is a synthesis and evaluation question worth 15 of 40 points. Answering it well requires an understanding of the whole set of information in the question, not just a few parts.

3   *Annotate the text* with notes or underlining. This makes it easy to go back and find RWEs or relevant text to answer a question part.

The 1 hour, 45 minute time frame may seem like a lot of time, but it is very important to manage your time wisely. The final question (g) is the most valuable, worth over a third of the points. A common mistake is to focus on doing a good job on easier questions and then run out of time on the last question.

What are the four parts of a Paper 2 question?

Part (a)

Part (a) always requires you to define two terms from the document or data supplied. No more than a definition is required to receive the full two marks for each definition. Only a clear definition, perhaps a sentence or two at most, is required. Part (a) totals 4 marks.

Part (b)

Part (b) will require two simple calculations, and will be worth a total of 5 marks.

Parts (c) to (f)

Parts (c) to (f) typically require you to use an appropriate diagram or to use data in the tables given to explain something relating to the document or data. Your diagrams, as always, should be clearly labelled and specifically explained. Pay attention to the demands of the question and the marks awarded. Your notions of an answer may appear larger than the question actually requires. Use examples from the text anywhere you can. Each of the parts (c) to (f) totals 4 marks.

Table 31.3   Paper 2, part (g) levels, marks, and descriptors

Marks 0–15	Level descriptor
10–12	• The specific demands of the question are understood and addressed. • Relevant economic theory is explained. • Relevant economic terms are used mostly appropriately. • Where appropriate, relevant diagram(s) are included and explained. • The response contains evidence of appropriate synthesis or evaluation that is mostly balanced. • The use of information from the text/data is generally appropriate, relevant, and applied correctly.
13–15	• The specific demands of the question are understood and addressed. • Relevant economic theory is fully explained. • Relevant economic terms are used appropriately throughout the response. • Where appropriate, relevant diagram(s) are included and fully explained. • The response contains evidence of effective and balanced synthesis or evaluation. • The use of information from the text/data is appropriate, relevant and is used to support the analysis/evaluation.

Part (g)

Part (g) typically begins with the words 'Using information from the text/data and your *knowledge of economics, evaluate* …'. Clearly, the assessment objective assessed here is synthesis and evaluation (AO3). To earn top marks, you must refer to evidence from the given text, and make an informed judgement regarding the issue addressed. Part (g) totals 15 marks.

In general, part (g) is also a mini-essay and should include the basic elements outlined above: *introduction, arguments* and *counterarguments*, and a *summative conclusion*.

To give you a sense of the requirements for full marks on part (g), and the distinction between the top levels, the descriptors for Level 4 and 5 are listed below. Notice that there is only one important difference between the descriptors for Paper 1, part (b) questions and the Paper 2, part (g) questions. Instead of an emphasis on RWEs in Paper 1, Paper 2 prompts you to *use the information from the article*. Moreover notice that the top marks come to an answer that *use the* information 'to support the analysis/evaluation'. In other words, the best part (g) answers will *take a position* on the question and support it with economic theory evidence from the article.

31.4 What is the Higher Level Paper 3 and how should you prepare for it?

Paper 3 is a policy paper and is written only by HL students. It is worth 30% of their IB final grade. Paper 3 consists of two questions and students must answer both of them. Each question is worth 30 marks and the paper lasts 1 hour and 45 minutes.

You are allowed a calculator for Paper 3, in order to do basic numerical analysis on the HL extension topics covered in the course. For example, you might be asked to calculate the amount of welfare loss from a tax, or the opportunity costs to determine the gains from trade, or the amount of tax paid from a set of data. You will also be given a policy-based question that requires your judgement.

What are the sub-questions in HL Paper 3?
Part (a)

Part (a) will consist of approximately eight questions. These will provide tables of data, diagrams, and short selections of text, and then ask you to make calculations, draw inferences based on your knowledge of the theory, write definitions, or make explanations. No synthesis or evaluation will be required for these questions.

Specific requirements and suggestions include the following.

- Your calculations should be figured up to *two decimal places*.
- Two-mark questions require the *workings to be shown* on your paper.
- It is recommended that you *work quickly* through the calculations questions to allow extra time to answer part (b).
- Early errors will not count against further results if the *reasoning is correct*. Finally, you should be aware that you will receive a separate answer booklet for your Paper 3 answers.
- Express answers with the *units provided* (litres, kilograms, GBP, USD, etc.).

Part (b)

Part (b) will ask you to 'Recommend a policy …' and by recommend the IB specifically says to 'Present an advisable course of action with appropriate supporting evidence/reason in relation to a given situation, problem or issue.' For example, a question that discusses the cocoa market and its effects on a particular country might conclude with the following part (b) question.

b. Using the data provided and your knowledge of economics, recommend a policy which could be introduced by the government of Country X in response to the expected fall in the world price of cocoa.
(10 marks)

Some advice on 'answer these policy' questions.

- Use appropriate economic theory to support your recommended policy.
- Make specific reference to the data in part (a) to support the analysis and your choice of policy.
- Diagrams may be useful, but may not be necessary.
- Your argument should be well-developed but not strident or overly firm. Qualifying language is useful here. Phrases like 'it is likely that', 'usually', and 'probably' are examples of this.
- A summative conclusion will connect your evidence back to your initial recommendation.

You will have 5 minutes of reading time for HL Paper 3. You can use that time effectively by:

- looking at the part (b) questions
- as you work through part (a) questions, think about how that information might be used to support your answer in the part (b) question (much like your final question of Paper 2, some useful information is likely to be found above in the provided tables, diagrams, and data).

The following is a suggested breakdown of how to allocate your time on HL Paper 3, for which you have a total of 1 hour and 45 minutes:

- Reading time: 5 minutes
- Q1 part (a): about 30 minutes in total
- Q1 part (b): about 20 minutes
- Q2 part (a): about 30 minutes in total
- Q2 part (b): about 20 minutes.

Again, to give you a sense of the requirements for full marks, and the distinction between the top levels, the descriptors for Level 4 and 5 are listed in Table 31.4.

Note the similarity between the descriptors for the Paper 3 policy question and the final questions from Papers 1 and 2. The use of data, in particular, is important again here, as is a balanced synthesis and evaluation. Like Paper 2, there is a significant amount of data that you can use to support your answer, and the data act as 'clues' to the correct interpretation of the issue. Also, like Paper 2, you use your own knowledge, in this case the recommended policy, to answer the question. Clearly, you want to have a solid command of the range of government policy options here.

Table 31.4   Paper 3, part (b) levels, marks, and descriptors

Marks 0–15	Level descriptor
7–8 (Level 4)	• The response identifies and fully explains an appropriate policy. • The response uses relevant economic theory to support the recommendation. • Relevant economic terms are used mostly appropriately. • The use of information from the text/data is generally appropriate, relevant and applied correctly to support the recommendation. • The response contains evidence of appropriate synthesis or evaluation that is mostly balanced.
9–10 (Level 5)	• The response identifies and fully explains an appropriate policy. • The response uses relevant economic theory effectively to support the recommendation. • Relevant economic terms are used appropriately throughout the response. • The use of information from the text/data is appropriate, relevant and supports the analysis/evaluation effectively. • The response contains evidence of effective and balanced synthesis or evaluation.

31.5 What is synthesis/evaluation?

Several components of the SL and HL assessments (both external and internal) require you to employ effective evaluation. In the examinations, it is required to reach the highest mark bands for part (b) of Paper 1 questions and part (d) of Paper 2 questions. In the internal assessment, 4 of the 14 marks available for each commentary are awarded for effective evaluation. Consequently, this discussion of evaluation is relevant to the IA component of your course as well as to the examinations.

Evaluation is perhaps the most challenging skill to master. Along with the related skill, synthesis, it requires that you go beyond the explanation, application and analysis of economic theory that is required for AO1 and AO2.

Effective evaluation requires you to make a judgement based on evidence. This sounds simple enough, but making a well-informed, intelligent judgement based on evidence from the real world is one of the most challenging tasks you face.

Here are some examples of examination questions that require the skill of evaluation.

• Using real-world examples, discuss the ways a functioning price system uses the signalling and incentive functions to ration resources in a free market economy.
• Using real-world examples, evaluate the effects of government intervention into the market for petrol.
• Using real-world examples, to what extent should governments attempt to influence markets where positive externalities exist?
• Using real-world examples, discuss the economic, social, and personal consequences of unemployment.

- Using real-world examples, evaluate the alternative ways in which a trade deficit might be reduced or eliminated.
- Using information from the text/data and your knowledge of economics, discuss methods that the Brazilian government might employ to achieve greater economic growth and/or economic development.
- Using information from the text/data and your knowledge of economics, discuss possible economic outcomes for economic growth and economic development that might arise from Vietnam's current international trade situation.

These questions are all in the style of Paper 1 part (b) questions or Paper 2 part (g) questions. The first thing to notice is that only a few of them actually use the word 'evaluate'. Some other prompts that require you to 'use economic concepts and examples to construct and present an argument' include: discuss, justify, examine, suggest, recommend, compare and contrast, and to what extent.

What approaches can be taken to answer an evaluation question?

There are several approaches you can take when answering a question that requires you to evaluate. The four most trusty and true methods are considered below. In each case, one of the above questions are given as an example.

Consider short run versus long run

The concepts of short run and long run in economics have different applications depending on whether the question relates to micro- or macroeconomics. Depending on the period of time following a particular policy or economic decision by an individual, a firm or a government, there may be very different outcomes.

Worked example 31.1

Evaluate the alternative ways in which a trade deficit might be reduced or eliminated.

In the short run, a government may choose to employ protectionist policies to reduce a current account deficit. Higher taxes on imported goods and services will make them less attractive to domestic consumers, reducing expenditures on imports and moving the current account towards surplus.

However, owing to the misallocation of resources resulting from protective tariffs, and the likelihood that trading partners will impose retaliatory tariffs on the deficit country, a longer-term solution to a current account deficit requires investments in human capital, infrastructure and technology.

Such investments will increase the productivity and international competitiveness of the deficit country. Reducing the country's dependence on cheap imports and making its own exports are more attractive to foreign consumers. Such a strategy will, in the long run, reduce the nation's current account deficit, increase net exports, and in the process grow the economy, creating more jobs and a more productive workforce.

Worked example 31.2

Discuss the economic and social consequences of globalisation.

It is helpful to first identify all the stakeholders who are affected by globalisation. These may include:

- domestic households
- domestic firms
- government
- foreign households and firms
- workers in the primary, secondary, and tertiary sector
- foreign workers
- the environment.

Globalisation is generally beneficial for those who experience it; however, not everyone is necessarily better off as the world's markets become increasingly interconnected.

In a globalising world, in which different countries have comparative advantages in different goods and services, the opening of domestic markets to international trade can lead to major social and economic disruptions for domestic households, firms, workers and the government. In Europe and North America, globalisation has led to the loss of millions of manufacturing jobs which, over the last two decades, have increasingly shifted to low-cost developing countries in which labour-intensive production is relatively cheap.

On the other hand, skilled workers in the developed world, particularly those with high levels of education, have benefited greatly from globalisation as the demand for services such as banking, law, finance and business has expanded dramatically in the global marketplace.

Examine the impact on different stakeholders

Throughout the economics course, various stakeholders are mentioned. Discussing the impacts of a particular economic decision, policy or action on the various stakeholders involved is an effective method for evaluation.

This evaluation could continue by examining the effects of globalisation on workers and firms in the developing world. It could even discuss the environmental effects that international trade has wrought, including increased greenhouse gas emissions and the unsustainable extraction of primary commodities in less developed countries.

Discuss advantages and disadvantages

This may be the easiest and most obvious way to evaluate. Throughout the IB course you have read about and discussed with your class the advantages and disadvantages of various economic policies. This approach is best suited to macroeconomics questions. In approaching a question such as the one below, you may choose two or three policy options, and weigh the advantages and disadvantages of each.

Worked example 31.3

Suggest and evaluate measures to deal with high unemployment.

Both fiscal and monetary policies can be used to reduce unemployment in an economy. Both policies have their advantages and disadvantages. Expansionary fiscal policy, for instance, has the advantage of directly stimulating aggregate demand through government spending and higher disposable incomes among households who enjoy lower taxes. With greater consumption and government spending, job creation is highly likely and unemployment should fall.

On the other hand, expansionary fiscal policy financed through increased government borrowing may have the effect of driving up interest rates in the private sector, as the government must offer lenders higher rates on its debt. The corresponding increase in demand for loanable funds may drive up interest rates and thereby crowd out private investment. In this way, the fall in unemployment that may have resulted from increased government spending might not occur if private sector investment decreases at the same time.

Such an approach as this to evaluation is highly effective, especially if the response were to evaluate the advantages and disadvantages of monetary policy and, based on the evaluation, draw a conclusion which argued for one type of policy response over the other.

Prioritise the arguments

This approach to effective evaluation involves prioritising the arguments for a particular position which you have taken in your response. For example, in answer to the question below, you may decide to identify and then rank according to importance the threats posed by a high rate of inflation.

Worked example 31.4

Examine the view that the control of inflation should always be the most important objective of governments.

The most important reason a government should keep inflation under control is that a rapidly rising price level drastically reduces the standard of living of a nation's people. A high rate of inflation erodes the purchasing power of households' nominal incomes; therefore, if incomes are rising at a rate slower than that of the price level, then the real incomes of the nation's households decline and the average citizen is actually getting worse off over time.

Second, inflation makes a country's exports less competitive in the global market, and, therefore, over time a high rate of inflation will lead to an increasing deficit in the nation's current account. The higher price of the nation's goods makes imports more attractive to domestic consumers, and exports less attractive to foreigners. The growing current account deficit will require the nation to sell increasing amounts of its assets to foreign investors, whose funds will flow back into the nation in the financial account.

The above evaluation could continue by identifying a third and perhaps even a fourth argument for why low inflation should be the most important objective of governments. On the other hand, you could have taken a very different approach to the question and argued that inflation should not be the most important objective, and then prioritised the arguments for why unemployment, economic growth, or income distribution should be of greater importance to governments.

31.6 What is the Extended Essay?

The Extended Essay (EE) is an exciting and rewarding component of the IB Diploma Programme. The EE is a detailed paper of 4000 words on a topic in a subject that interests you. You can choose a topic that fits into one of the subjects on the approved EE list, which can be obtained from your school's IB coordinator. The EE encourages you to think critically and research deeply on your topic, with the goal of gaining real-world knowledge that furthers your understanding in a meaningful way.

What follows is advice on the EE writing process. Before you start, it is important to put some of your greatest energy into identifying your topic and refining your research question. By making a solid start in this, you set yourself up for a clear, focused, and arguable essay that scores well. The longer you wait to clarify your topic and research question, the harder your research process and writing will be.

How do you decide on a topic and research question?

An excellent source for guidance is the *Extended Essay Guide*. Because the start of your essay is so important, this exercise from the Guide is reproduced here.

Practice exercise: Formulating well-focused research questions	
Developing a narrow, focused research question is an integral part of your extended essay process. A research question will provide a path to guide you through your research and writing.	
Step 1. Choose your subject area	*Which subject area is of most personal interest to you? Is there something you are especially curious about in one of your IB courses? Did your personal project (if you completed the Middle Years Programme) spark an idea that can be researched?*
Step 2. Choose a topic that interests you	*Describe your work in one sentence.* I want to learn about _____. ***Example:*** I want to learn about public funding for the arts.
Step 3. Suggest a question	*Try to describe your research by developing a question that specifies something about your topic.* I am studying _____ because I want to find out (who, what, when, where, whether, why or how) _____. ***Example:*** I am studying public funding for the arts because I want to find out how accessible the arts are to those people who are on low incomes.

	Direct question: To what extent are the arts accessible to people who belong to the class of the working poor?
	Include a command term from your subject area to help form the research question.
	Will you be able to argue a specific position? What are some possible issues or arguments?
Step 4. Evaluate your question	*Answer the questions:*
	Is there a range of perspectives on this topic?
	Does the research question allow for analysis, evaluation and the development of a reasoned argument?
	I am studying _____ because I want to find out _____ in order to understand (how, why or whether) _____.
	Example: I am studying public funding for the arts because I want to find out how accessible the arts are to the working poor so I can determine whether tax dollars support cultural enrichment for all citizens regardless of their socio-economic status.
Step 5. Restate your question using a different command term	*Asking the question in a different way might help you view your topic in a different way.*
	How does analysing …
	To what extent …
Step 6. Review with your supervisor	*Is your supervisor able to understand the nature of your research?*
	Is it clear to your supervisor how and why your topic is relevant in your subject area?
Step 7. Reflection	*If you can adequately respond to the 'so what?' question, you may be on your way to a clear and focused research question using your initial topic idea.*
	Do that here:
You must now start some preliminary reading around the issue or topic. Remember that you will most likely need to revise your research question once you start to undertake your research. In this sense your research question should always be considered provisional until you have enough research data to make a reasoned argument.	

Table 31.5 Evaluating research questions

Here are some suggestions on evaluating your question. Is your question …	
Clear?	Will the reader understand the nature of my research? Will it direct the research being undertaken?
Focused?	Will the research question be *specific* enough to allow for exploration within the scope of the task (that is, the number of words and time available)?
Arguable?	Does the research question allow for analysis, evaluation, and the development of a reasoned argument?

Table 31.6 Improving your research question

Unclear, unfocused, and unarguable research questions	Clear, focused, and arguable research questions
Why do African countries suffer so much in the way of poor health outcomes?	To what extent has the lack of antimalarial medicine in the Democratic Republic of Congo reduced life expectancies?
Do price controls and taxes on soda really work?	To what extent have specific taxes on sugary beverages in the UK reduced consumption?
What are the costs of palm oil production?	Faced with a European boycott of palm oil, to what extent can Malaysia profitably switch to sustainable alternatives?

In Table 31.6 are some examples of poor research questions that have been refined into quality research questions.

Once you have chosen your subject area, you must meet the following general requirements.

Observe the relevant regulations

You must have an EE supervisor, who ideally is a teacher of the subject you have chosen to write on and who works at your school. This teacher, or your school's IB coordinator, is responsible for providing you with the Extended Essay Guide, an official IB publication in which the regulations relating to the EE are laid out.

Meet deadlines

You and your supervisor should agree deadlines for intermediate and final drafts of your EE. It is likely that your school will have internal deadlines agreed by all IB teachers. Make sure you are aware of these deadlines, and plan accordingly to meet the requirements of each deadline so as to ensure your final essay is of the best quality possible.

Acknowledge sources in an approved academic manner

The easiest way to fail the IB Diploma Programme is to be caught plagiarising. In your research and writing of the EE, it is crucial that you acknowledge all sources of information and ideas in an approved manner, most likely through footnotes or a bibliography following either the APA or the MLA structure.

In addition to these requirements, you are strongly recommended to:

- start work *early*
- think very carefully about the *research question* for your essay
- consult your school *librarian or library web page* for EE research guidance
- plan a *schedule* for both researching and writing the essay, including extra time for delays and unforeseen problems

- *record sources* as your research progresses (rather than trying to reconstruct a list at the end)
- *outline* your essay before starting to write it
- check and *proofread* the final version carefully
- make sure that all basic requirements are met (e.g. word count, section headings).

How do I prepare for EE work?

Before starting work

Read the assessment criteria in the Extended Essay Guide, then read previous essays to identify strengths and possible pitfalls. Your supervisor should be able to provide you with past, marked essays to give you ideas of how to begin your own, or you can also find examples on the ibo.org website.

Spend time working out the research question. A strong research question is essential; without one, your essay will be weak at best.

Work out a structure for your essay. Before you begin writing in earnest, create a comprehensive outline of the essay.

During the research and writing

Start work early and stick to your deadlines. Maintain a good working relationship with your supervisor. Check in with your supervisor often, at least once every few weeks. Remember, it is your responsibility (not your supervisor's) to make sure you have regular meetings. Without initiative on your part, you will not benefit from your supervisor's guidance.

Construct an argument that relates to the research question. The research question is only the starting point for your essay. In attempting to answer it, you must construct a reasoned argument supported by evidence gathered in your research.

Use the library and online resources, and consult librarians for advice. Librarians today deal with more than just books. Most school libraries have access to online databases of scholarly journals, which could be great sources for research. Using search engines successfully requires sound search technique; be sure to consult a specialist in your school to get tips on how to go about conducting your online and library research.

Do not be afraid to change your topic and research question if there is a problem with your original one. If you start early enough, there should be plenty of time to change topics a few weeks or a month or two into the process if you decide you cannot successfully write an essay on your original topic.

Use the appropriate language for the subject. Keep the course syllabus, a textbook, and your class notes in front of you at all times while writing. The biggest threat to your success is writing 4000 words that repeatedly drift away from the topics covered in your chosen subject. Keep your essay grounded in the subject by continuously checking your progress against the course syllabus.

Let your interest and enthusiasm show. Hopefully you have chosen a topic that genuinely interests you. It is perfectly acceptable to express interest and emotion in your writing. Some of the best essays are those in which the writer's voice and personality are clearly visible.

Wrapping up the essay

Carefully proofread your essay. Try to have at least one or two of your classmates also proofread your essay for you (perhaps you can agree to proofread theirs for them). In addition, you should ask your supervisor to give your final draft one last look before you submit the true final copy. Check the Guide for the heading and formal requirements. Check the Guide and with your EE coordinator or librarian to find guidelines for citations.

What is some subject-specific advice on the Economics EE?

Make sure economics is the right subject for you

Economics is a very popular subject for the EE at many schools. Some students are under the impression that economics is an easier subject in which to write an essay in than, say, the physical sciences such as physics or chemistry.

You should know that this is a myth. There is no sound evidence to support the assumption that economics is any easier to write a strong EE for than the physical sciences. In fact, the best economics EEs tend to be those which take a highly scientific approach to the research and writing process.

Why is this? The higher levels of economics are extremely empirical in their analysis. Economics is a social science, yes, but in their study of human interaction in markets, economists seek to quantify human behaviours to as great an extent as possible. By collecting, organising, displaying, and then analysing data representing the interactions of individuals, firms or governments in a mathematical way, economists are able to observe the interactions between two or more variables and develop hypotheses about human behaviour.

In this regard, a top-notch economics essay may appear very scientific indeed; students hoping to avoid doing experiments and gathering data should perhaps avoid writing an economics essay.

What does an economics essay look like?

Core principles throughout

An EE in economics should employ the core principles of economics as a basis for researching a particular topic. Both primary and secondary research should be conducted to gather data and background information for the essay. Theories outlined in the course syllabus, as well as the tools, models, graphs, and skills learned during the IB Economics course should be applied to the topic.

Avoid narrative, descriptive writing

You should avoid writing an historical, narrative essay, even on an economic topic. In general, topics that are older than five years will be marked down.

Essays should be analytical rather than descriptive. The purpose is not so much to tell a story as to analyse events in the world around you through the lens of economics. To this end you can employ the tools and models of economics to develop a deeper understanding of human interactions and behaviour.

Answerable research question

It is important that you can answer your research question using economic concepts and theories. Often, students choose a topic they think is appropriate for economics, but which would be more suited to business and management. For instance, you may wish to analyse the costs and revenues of a particular firm in which you have a relative who is employed. Be aware that firms do not like to share this information, and it may not directly relate to the syllabus anyway.

Data, data, data!

Your researched data are very important. While it is not explicitly required, primary research tends to be a part of the best essays. For an essay in which you undertake an analysis of a particular product market, for example, you may include historic price and output data for the market, surveys of consumers in the market, interviews with sellers in the market, and so on.

Data should be presented in a visually appealing manner. Where possible, create charts and graphs rather than presenting large tables full of small numbers.

Do not waste too many words summarising your data. If presented well, it does not need it. Focus on analysing your data. Attempt to find and explain patterns within the data, and once identified, apply the tools of micro- or macroeconomics to explain those patterns.

Secondary research

Secondary research should include analyses of data that already exist from studies done by others on topics similar to yours. Successful secondary research can bolster your argument, offering evidence found through similar studies that either supports or refutes your own hypothesis.

For further guidance on choosing a topic and developing a research question, along with more information on treatment of the topic in an economics EE, check the IB Extended Essay Guide.

How do I interpret the EE criteria?

EEs are externally assessed on assessment criteria by examiners appointed by the IB. Essays are marked out of 34 points allocated between criteria A to E as shown in Table 31.7. The total score for your essay is used in conjunction with your theory of knowledge score to determine the number of points awarded jointly to these two components of your Diploma.

Notice that the largest section of points is C: Critical Thinking. This is where the quality of your research and your discussion of it is assessed. Obviously, valid and relevant information is essential, but also your ability to break it down (analyse it) shows your understanding as well. When it comes to discussing your research, it is here that you try to connect it to your research question, stating why it is of use to your essay.

Finally, when it comes to evaluating your findings, be aware that you should do so *continuously*, as you bring each piece of evidence forward into the essay. Do not wait until the last pages to do 'evaluation'. Each article, survey, or data set, should be

Table 31.7 Extended Essay criteria

Criterion	Descriptors	Marks
Criterion A: Focus and Method	Topic Research question Methodology	6
Criterion B: Knowledge and Understanding	Context Subject-specific terminology and concepts	6
Criterion C: Critical Thinking	Research Analysis Discussion and evaluation	12
Criterion D: Presentation	Structure Layout	4
Criterion E: Engagement	Process Research focus	6
Total Marks		34

evaluated 'in real time', as to its values and limitations. Some of your research will be just what you were looking for, but others may be supplementary, or only somewhat helpful to you.

Be honest about your evidence. Papers with great evidence that is poorly explained and not properly evaluated will score poorly on Criterion C. Papers with weaker evidence but whose writers are candid about how the information might be useful but also carefully point out its flaws will score reasonably well.

This advice, honesty in your reporting, applies to Criterion E: Engagement. Your grade here is based essentially on your own writing of the 'Reflections on Planning and Progress Form (RPPF)'. For these entries, written over the course of your essay process, try to capture your thinking at each stage. Generally, you will write one after forming your research question, another after an initial draft, and finally one for the viva voce when you have completed the paper. Describe your progress and your problems, and how you are trying to overcome them. Here the IB is rewarding your adherence to the EE research process, rather than looking exclusively at your finished product. This is a great place to score points, so see the IB resources for specimen paper examples of good reflections.

Internal assessment 32

The Internal Assessment (IA) is a very important part of the IB Economics course. It is required of all students, and many find the task enjoyable and challenging. You are encouraged to pursue personal interests within the boundaries of the course syllabus, and because each commentary is researched outside class time, more deliberation and planning are possible. This means that the IA process provides an opportunity to enrich your knowledge.

Building your IA portfolio requires you to engage with real news items and to apply the economic concepts you have learned. You will write economics commentaries on three news items.

To find appropriate articles, you will need to read a variety of news items from various sources, and judge their relevance to economics topics. For each of the three articles that you choose, you will identify in your commentary the concepts and aspects of economic theory that are at work in the article. The commentary will analyse the event, apply the concepts in detail, and explain how the theory works. This requires good evaluation skills and good command of diagrammatic skills.

Besides this review of the IA writing process, you are advised to read and review the IA section of the IB Economics Guide, which should be available from your teacher.

What are general requirements of the IA?

The IA portfolio is worth 20% of your final mark for HL students and 30% for SL students. The IA writing process should be integrated into your class and use 20 hours of class time; it is not an independent project. The IA process is summarised as follows.

Variety of sources

You will produce three commentaries from a variety of news sources. Each commentary will focus on a different part of the IB syllabus. Articles must come from print news media that include newspapers, magazines, and internet news sites. Television or radio broadcasts are not suitable. Blogs or other opinion or editorial articles are strongly discouraged.

Articles should be brief. Long articles are very much discouraged. If you do select a longer article, the commentary should focus on a short section indicated by highlighting in the portfolio.

Articles should be in the same language as the commentary. If different from the commentary language, a translation and the original article should be attached to the commentary.

Articles must be current, published within one year of the writing of the commentary.

Articles must be from a variety of news sources, a different one for each commentary. You may not choose two articles from, say, the *Financial Times*. You are encouraged to choose articles from a mixture of local, national and international news sources.

Table 32.1 IA criteria, descriptors, and marks

Criterion and section	Top level descriptors	Marks
A: Diagrams	Relevant, accurate and correctly labelled diagram(s) are included, with a full explanation.	3
B: Terminology	Economic terminology relevant to the article is used appropriately throughout the commentary.	2
C: Application and analysis	Relevant economic theory is applied to the article throughout the commentary with effective economic analysis.	3
D: Key concept	A key concept is identified and the link to the article is fully explained.	3
E: Evaluation	Judgements are made that are supported by effective and balanced reasoning.	3
Single IA Total		14

Other guidelines

Commentaries should be no longer than 750 words (the IB Guide has a list of items that are not included in the word count). Do not stuff the graph legend with extra explanations to stay under the word count. This will be marked down.

Commentaries should be your own work, not done in collaboration. Try not to use the same articles as anyone else. Your teacher may not assign articles for you to use.

What are the IA rubric requirements?

Your commentaries will be marked by your teacher against a set of rubric requirements defined by the International Baccalaureate (IB). Table 31.1 shows you the five criteria that apply to each of your three commentaries, the skill area each criterion tests, the marks available for each criterion, and the highest descriptor for each criterion.

In addition to the criteria in Table 31.1, criterion F (worth three marks) is applied to the entire portfolio. Criterion F assesses your complete portfolio on the following five points:

- each commentary is not more than 750 words
- each article relates to a different section of the syllabus
- each article comes from a different and appropriate source

Table 32.2 Total IA scores

Single IA scores	(14 points × 3)	42
Criterion F: Rubric Requirements	Each article is… • based on a different unit of the syllabus • taken from a different and appropriate source • published no earlier than one year before the writing of the commentary.	3
Portfolio total		45

- each article is no more than a year old
- the portfolio has a summary cover sheet, each commentary has a cover sheet, and each article is included in the portfolio.

So, each commentary is marked on criteria A–E and is given a score out of 14 marks. The entire portfolio is then given a score out of three marks for criterion F. Thus, the full portfolio is scored out of 45 marks (3 commentaries $\times$ 14 marks + 3 marks).

32.2 How do I write high-quality commentary?

How do I find a good article?

Finding a suitable article may seem like the easiest part of the process, but you will be surprised at just how difficult it can be.

Information balance

For IA purposes, a useful news article should say neither too little nor too much. The article should describe an issue sufficiently to allow room for analysis and discussion of an event's implication. But the article should not provide that analysis itself – that is your job. This is why general news articles from daily newspapers (or news agency services) can work out very well, while articles from more economics-focused publications (e.g. *The Economist*) or scholarly journals are often less suitable.

Conduct an effective search

The internet has made it possible to search far and wide with incredible speed, but the volume of information can be overwhelming and stall your progress at a very early stage. With this in mind, search for a good article with care.

Where to look

Search engines are well suited for finding articles on specific topics. So rather than going to the homepage of your favourite search engine, begin your search in the news section. For example, do not start at www.google.com, begin at http://news.google.com, which ensures that your search results will already be filtered from news websites. But beware – not all news sites are appropriate for an IB commentary. Be sure to avoid opinion and editorial pages, and try to use trusted news sources.

Use keywords

Often, a web search for a topic from the syllabus that is commonly referred to in the media (e.g. demand, taxes, trade) will turn up thousands of hits. Searching for an article by browsing the results of such a broad search will prove tedious and you are not likely to find more than a very few appropriate articles. However, terms such as 'income elasticity of demand' or 'aggregate supply' are not typically used by the news media, even though the concepts themselves are regularly the subject of reports in the business and economic news.

To find articles relating to such concepts, you must be critical and flexible in your browsing of search results; move on quickly if your first search attempts fail to yield any promising results. When this happens, try out associated terms that are linked with the overall concept. And ask your teacher if there is another way of phrasing your searches to get better results for the topic you are interested in.

Vet your article

So how can you tell if your article is a worthy candidate for a commentary? Do not take the first one, as a rule. Of the many articles you have read, you are likely to have decided early on that a few have the right balance of not-too-little/not-too-much information and analysis. Once you have narrowed down your options to two or three for each choice, vet the articles for final selection. You might take the following steps.

- **Brainstorm.** Pull out a copy of the current IB Guide and turn to the list of topics. Or you might want to use the vocabulary list for the relevant unit. As you read the article, check off the relevant terms.
- **Identify concepts.** As you read each article, make notes in the margin (or on the website if you are using a social bookmarking tool) of the concepts from the syllabus to which the article relates. This will help you decide if the article is appropriate for the section of the syllabus you wish to address.
- **Identify diagrams.** Typically, a high-quality commentary includes at least two (but perhaps more) diagrams. Diagrammed items should be part of the core topics of the commentary, not merely introductory material or of tangential interest. As you read the article, take note of potential diagrams you can include in your analysis. If you are not able to identify at least two relevant economics graphs to include in your commentary, the article may not be of use to you.
- **Outline.** Create a simple outline of each section of your commentary. List what each paragraph will do, including the types of explanation and areas of evaluation. Remember that diagrams must be clearly explained in the body of the text, and not merely attached to the commentary.

After completing these steps for each potential article, it should be clear which of your options is best suited to be the subject of an economics commentary that meets the requirements of the IA.

How do I write my first draft?

Now that you've outlined the key ideas for each paragraph, you can begin to link together the main ideas in complete prose for your draft commentary.

Satisfy the IA criteria

The IA criteria require that each commentary includes diagrams, definitions, application, analysis and evaluation of relevant economic theory. The discussions below will help you more clearly understand these requirements.

Diagrams

Diagrams must be highly relevant and fully explained in the text. Explanations must make specific reference to graph points (e.g. quantity increases from Q_1 to Q_2.) Graphs should be given priority in your analysis. Make them large and centre them on the page rather than writing text around them. They should be introduced and then clearly explained in the text.

Video suggestions:
You have read about it, now you can review what you've just learned by watching a few videos by the author!

 The IB Economics IA – getting started.

 The IB Economics IA – making an outline.

Define and explain

Definitions of relevant terms should be included in each commentary. Not all economics terms need to be defined – it would be easy to use up half of your 750 word count defining terms. Only define terms that are integral to the analysis and evaluation you plan to conduct in each commentary. Once a term has been defined, do not define it again in a later commentary in the same portfolio. Explanations require students to describe clearly, make intelligible and give reasons for an economic concept or idea. It is your job to bring clarification to the economic concepts relating to your article.

Analysis and application

Analysis requires you to closely examine the events laid out in your article through the tools and theories learned in your economics course. A clear analysis will identify the key ideas and your application will match these ideas to issues in the article. Economic diagrams should form the heart of your analysis; anything that can be explained graphically should be explained graphically. With only 750 words, you must be concise and selective in how you analyse the news on which your commentary is based.

Key concepts

Each entry should identify a key concept from the course list of concepts which include **scarcity**, **choice**, **efficiency**, **equity**, **economic well-being**, **sustainability**, **change**, **interdependence**, and **intervention**. Top marks in this category come from correctly identifying and fully explaining the link between the key concept and the issues in the article.

Evaluation

This is your opportunity to discuss the implications of an economic issue, and to assess the effects the issue (or policies to redress it) have on stakeholders. Evaluation is the skill many students find the most difficult. It requires you to make a judgement based on evidence. In your commentaries, you can evaluate throughout the text, or you may choose to conduct the evaluation at the end of each commentary. To make an evaluation, you can:

- weigh the advantages and disadvantages of certain economic policies
- discuss the effects on different stakeholders in society of a particular policy or event
- compare the short-run and long-run effects of an economic policy or a decision by a particular stakeholder in a market
- critically assess the validity of the economic theories you have applied to your commentary.

Critically assessing the validity of economic theories is the thing many students find the most difficult to do successfully. Evaluation requires that you call into question the economic theories themselves. For instance, economic theory would argue that a progressive tax system is inefficient due to its negative effect on the incentive to work and earn higher incomes. However, you may argue that in reality there is little evidence that progressive taxes reduce efficiency, and that the resulting reduction in income inequality more than justifies the use of such a system in a modern, developed economy. You have now called into question the economic view that taxes are inefficient.

There are more ideas on how to evaluate effectively in Chapter 31.

Avoid unnecessary summary

The article supplies the fundamental information for your commentary. The grader will read the article you have supplied, so it is not necessary for you to recap that information. To do so would waste precious words that count against your limit. You should reference the article by including direct quotes and references to data.

Reference the article

In each commentary, it is critical that you cite the article in several instances. Each commentary should include references to the specific circumstances as laid out in the article. Include at least one direct quote, and whenever there are numbers, such as prices, quantities or percentage changes mentioned in the article, attempt to incorporate them into the analysis in your commentary.

For example, if there is mention of airline ticket prices changing for a particular route, then in your graph of the airline market, include the original price and the new price on the Y-axis, rather than a generic P_1 and P_2. This demonstrates that you are a skilled economist able to apply economic theory to real examples. If you use direct quotes, they should be a brief phrase, or a word or two. Avoid long quotes that will count against your word limit.

How do I revise my commentary for the final draft?

When you have finished your draft, you submit it to your teacher. He or she will provide you with brief but useful advice about how to improve each commentary. Take this help seriously – it can significantly improve your marks. You should continue to seek advice, but remember your teacher can give only limited help from now on. Be sure to observe all the appropriate language conventions and you can ask a classmate to help copy-edit your work. Finally, use the following checklist of requirements before handing in your final draft.

- Do I have a cover sheet with all the appropriate information? What is my word count?
- Are all the relevant economic terms defined? Have I used economic terminology throughout my commentary, not just occasionally?
- Have I included at least two diagrams? Have I explained them carefully in the body of the text?
- Have I referenced the article to a degree that makes it clear my commentary is on the particular circumstances described in the article, not just a repetition of what I read in my textbook or took notes on in class?
- Is my analysis complete? Have I considered the major areas of theory that are related to this topic?
- Have I evaluated effectively? Have I considered the short run and the long run, the implications for various stakeholders, and the validity of the economic theory itself?

The IA portfolio is intended to be an enriching learning experience. Feel free to seek out articles in areas of your own interest. You are far more likely to bring insight to issues in which you are already interested. However, another equally important motivation is to encourage you to broaden your knowledge of economics and the world by reading widely.

After writing each entry, your teacher will mark it and likely give you feedback to help you write the next one. After completing the portfolio, your teacher will award the rubric requirement marks accordingly, and your work will be uploaded to the IBIS system. The marks for the entire class will be subject to moderation by IB examiners.

Glossary

This is not an exhaustive list of terms that may be assessed. Any technical term within the Guide can be assessed.

Abnormal profit
This arises when average revenue is greater than average cost (greater than the minimum return required by a firm to remain in a line of business).

Absolute advantage
A country has an absolute advantage in the production of a good if it can produce more of it with the same resources or, equivalently, if it can produce the same amount using fewer resources compared to another country.

Absolute poverty
People living below the minimum income necessary to satisfy basic physical needs (food, clothing, and shelter); as of October 2015, the World Bank international poverty line is set at US $1.90 PPP per day.

Administrative barriers
Trade barriers in the form of regulations that aim to limit imports into a country. These barriers may take the form of product safety standards, sanitary standards or pollution standards but may also include more stringent than necessary application of customs procedures.

Adverse selection
A type of market failure involving asymmetric information, where the party with the incomplete information is induced to withdraw from the market. The buyer, for example, of a used car, may hesitate to buy without knowing about the quality of the vehicle. The seller, for example of health insurance, may hesitate to sell a policy without knowing the health of the buyer.

Aggregate demand (AD)
Planned spending on domestic goods and services at different average price levels, per period of time. Consists of consumption, investment and government expenditures plus net exports.

Aggregate demand curve
A curve showing the planned level of spending on domestic output at different average price levels.

Aggregate supply (AS)
The planned level of output domestic firms are willing and able to offer at different average price levels.

Aggregate supply curve
A curve showing the planned level of output that domestic firms are willing and able to offer at different average price levels.

Allocative efficiency
Achieved when just the right amount of goods and services are produced from society's point of view so that scarce resources are allocated in the best possible way. It is achieved when, for the last unit produced, price (P) is equal to marginal cost (MC), or more generally, if marginal social benefit (MSB) is equal to marginal social cost (MSC).

Allocative inefficiency
When either more or less than the socially optimal amount is produced and consumed so that misallocation of resources results. MSB MSC.

Anchoring
Refers to situations when people rely on a piece of information that is not necessarily relevant as a reference point when making a decision.

Anti-dumping
Typically refers to tariffs that aim at raising the artificially low price of a dumped imported good to the level of the higher domestic price. A dumped good is one that is exported at a price below the cost of producing it.

Anti-monopoly regulation
Laws and regulations that are intended to restrict anti-competitive behaviour of firms that are abusing their market power.

Appreciation
When the price of a currency increases in a floating exchange rate system.

Appropriate technology
Technology that relies mostly on the relatively abundant factor an economy is endowed with.

Asymmetric information
A type of market failure where one party in an economic transaction has access to more or better information than the other party.

Automatic stabilisers
Institutionally built-in features (like unemployment benefits and progressive income taxation) that tend to decrease the short-term fluctuations of the business cycle without the need for governments to intervene.

Average costs
Total costs per unit of output produced.

Average revenue — Revenue earned per unit sold; average revenue is thus equal to the price of the good.

Average tax rate — The ratio of the tax paid by an individual over their income expressed as a percentage.

Balance of payments — A record of the value of all transactions of a country with the rest of the world over a period of time.

Balance of trade in goods — Part of the balance of payments, it is the value of exports of goods of a country minus the value of imports of goods over a given period of time.

Balance of trade in services — Part of the balance of payments, it is the value of exports of services of a country minus the value of imports of services over a given period of time.

Barriers to entry — Anything that deters entry of new firms into a market, for example, licenses or patents.

Behavioural economics — A subdiscipline of economics that relies on elements of cognitive psychology to better understand decision-making by economic agents. It challenges the assumption that economic agents (consumers or firms) will always make rational choices with the aim of maximizing with respect to some objective.

Biases — Systematic deviations from rational choice decision-making.

Bounded rationality — A term introduced by Herbert Simon that suggests consumers and businesses have neither the necessary information nor the cognitive abilities required to maximise with respect to some objectives (such as utility), and thus choose to satisfice. They therefore are rational only within limits.

Bounded self-control — The idea that individuals, even when they know what they want, may not be able to act in their interests. Findings of bounded self-control include evidence of procrastination (for example, among students, professionals and others) that may result in self-harm, and submitting to temptation (for example, dieters).

Budget deficit — When government expenditures exceed government (tax) revenues usually over a period of a year.

Business confidence — A measure of the degree of optimism that businesses have about the economic future.

Business cycle — The short-term fluctuations of real GDP around its long-term trend (or potential output).

Business tax — Tax levied on the income of a business or corporation.

Capital — Physical capital refers to means of production that include machines, tools, equipment and factories; the term may also refer to the infrastructure of a country. Human capital refers to the education, training, skills and experience embodied in the labour force of a country.

Capital account — A subaccount of the balance of payments that includes credit and debit entries for non-produced, non-financial assets as well as capital transfers between residents and non-residents.

Capital gains tax — A tax on the profits realised from the sale of financial assets such as stocks or bonds.

Capital transfers — Include financial or non-financial assets for items including debt forgiveness, investment, non-life insurance claims. They are part of the capital account of the balance of payments.

Carbon (emissions) taxes — Taxes levied on the carbon content of fuel. They are a type of Pigouvian tax.

Central bank — An institution charged with conducting monetary and exchange rate policy, regulating behaviour of commercial banks, and providing banking services to the government and commercial banks.

Ceteris paribus — A Latin expression meaning 'other things being equal'.

Choice architecture — The design of environments based on the idea that the layout, sequencing, and range of choices available affect the decisions made by consumers.

Circular flow model — A simplified illustration that shows the flows of income and expenditures in an economy.

Collusive oligopoly — A market where firms agree to fix price and/or to engage in other anticompetitive behaviour.

Common market — When a group of countries agree not only to free trade of goods and services but also to free movement of capital and labour.

Common pool resources — A diverse group of natural resources that are non-excludable, but their use is rivalrous, for example, fisheries.

Comparative advantage — When a country can produce a good at a lower opportunity cost compared to another country.

Competitive market — A market with many firms acting independently where no firm has the ability to control the price.

Competitive market equilibrium — Occurs if in a free competitive market, quantity demanded is equal to quantity supplied.

Complements — Goods that are jointly consumed, for example, coffee and sugar.

Composite indicator — An indicator that is comprised as an average of more than one economic variable, for example, the HDI.

Concentration ratios — The proportion of industry sales accounted for by the largest firms; the greater this proportion, the greater the degree of market power of the firms in the industry.

Consumer confidence — A measure of the degree of optimism that households have about their income and economic prospects.

Consumer nudges — Small design changes that include positive reinforcement and indirect suggestions that can influence the behaviour of consumers.

Consumer price index (CPI) — The average of the prices of the goods and services that the typical consumer buys expressed as an index number. The CPI is used as a measure of the cost of living in a country and to calculate inflation.

Consumer surplus — The difference between how much a consumer is at most willing to pay for a good and how much they actually pay.

Consumption (C) — Spending by households on durable and non-durable goods and on services over a period of time.

Contractionary fiscal policy — Refers to a decrease in government expenditures and/or an increase in taxes that aim at decreasing aggregate demand and thus reducing inflationary pressures.

Contractionary monetary policy — A policy employed by the central bank involving an increase in interest rates and aimed at decreasing aggregate demand and thus inflationary pressures. Referred to also as tight monetary policy.

Corporate indebtedness — The sum of what a corporation owes to banks or other holders of its debt.

Corporate social responsibility (CSR) — A corporate goal adopted by many firms that aims to create and maintain an ethical and environmentally responsible image.

Cost-push inflation — Inflation that is a result of increased production costs (typically because of rising money wages or rising commodity prices) and illustrated by a leftward shift of the SRAS curve.

Credit items — Refers to transactions within the balance of payments of a country that lead to an inflow of currency (for example, the export of goods); these transactions enter the account with a plus sign.

Credit rating — A grade assigned by certain agencies (such as Moody's or Standard and Poor's) on the borrowing risks a prospective issuer of debt (for example, of a bond) presents to lenders.

Crowding out — The idea that expansionary fiscal policy is not very effective in increasing aggregate demand because the increased borrowing needs of the government to finance the increased expenditures could lead to increased interest rates. Thus, reducing private sector investment, consumer spending, and other components of AD.

Current account — A subaccount of the balance of payments that records the value of net exports in goods and services, net income and net current transfers of a country over a period of time.

Current account deficit — Exists when the sum of net exports of goods and services plus net income plus net current transfers is negative (or simply when debits or outflows are greater than credits or inflows).

Current account surplus — Exists when the sum of net exports of goods and services plus net income plus net current transfers is positive (or simply when credits or inflows are greater than debits or inflows).

Current transfers An entry in the current account that records payments between residents and non-residents of a country without something of economic value being received in return and that affect directly the level of disposable income (for example, workers remittances, pensions, aid and grants, and so on).

Customs union An agreement between countries to phase out or eliminate tariffs and other trade barriers and establish a common external barrier toward non-members.

Cyclical (demand-deficient) unemployment Unemployment that is a result of a decrease in aggregate demand and thus of economic activity; it occurs in a recession.

Debit items Refers to transactions within the balance of payments of a country that lead to an outflow of currency (for example, the import of services); these transactions enter the account with a minus sign.

Debt relief A reduction of the debt burden of developing countries organised by the World Bank and the IMF.

Debt servicing Refers to the repayment of principal and interest on the debt of a person, a firm or a country.

Default choice When a choice is made by default, meaning that when given a choice it is the option that is selected when one does not do anything.

Deflation A sustained decrease in the average price level of a country.

Deflationary/ recessionary gap Arises when the equilibrium level of real output is less than potential output as a result of a decrease in AD.

Demand The relationship between possible prices of a good or service and the quantities that individuals are willing and able to buy over some time period, *ceteris paribus*.

Demand curve A curve illustrating the relationship between possible prices of a good or service and the quantities that individuals are willing and able to buy over some time period, *ceteris paribus*. It is normally downward sloping.

Demand management Policies that aim at manipulating aggregate demand through changes in interest rates (monetary policy) or changes in government expenditures and taxation in order to influence growth, employment, and inflation.

Demand-pull inflation Inflation that is caused by increases in aggregate demand.

Demand side policies Refers to economic policies that aim at affecting aggregate demand and thus macroeconomic variables such as growth, inflation and employment; demand side policies include fiscal policy and monetary policy.

Demerit goods Goods or services that not only harm the individuals who consume these but also society at large, and that tend to be overconsumed. Usually they are due to negative consumption externalities.

Depreciation A decrease in the value of a currency in terms of another currency in a floating or managed exchange rate system.

Deregulation Policies that reduce or eliminate regulations related to the operation of firms so that production costs decrease—resulting in increased competition and higher levels of output.

Devaluation A decrease in the value of a currency in a fixed exchange rate system.

Development aid Aid aimed at assisting developing countries in their development efforts. Includes project aid, programme aid and debt relief. It is concessional, meaning there are low interest rates and long repayment periods.

Direct taxes Taxes on income, profits or wealth paid directly to the government.

Discount rate The interest rate that a central bank charges commercial banks for short-term loans (also referred to as the refinancing rate).

Disinflation When the average price level continues to rise but at a slower rate so that the rate of inflation is positive but lower.

Dumping When a firm sells abroad at a price below average cost or below the domestic price.

Economic development A multidimensional concept involving a sustained increase in living standards that implies higher levels of income and thus greater access to goods and services, better education and health, a better environment to live in as well as individual empowerment.

Economic growth Refers to increases in real GDP over time.

Economic integration Economic interdependence between countries usually involving agreements between two or more countries to phase-out or eliminate trade and other barriers between them.

Economics Economics is the study of how to make the best possible use of scarce or limited resources to satisfy unlimited human needs and wants.

Economic well-being A multidimensional concept relating to the level of prosperity and quality of living standards in a country.

Economies of scale Falling average costs that a firm experiences when it increases its scale of operations.

Efficiency In general, involves making the best use of scarce resources. May refer to producing at the lowest possible cost or to allocative efficiency where marginal social costs are equal to marginal social benefits or where social surplus is maximum.

Elasticity A measure of the responsiveness of an economic variable (such as the quantity demanded of a product) to a change in another economic variable (such as its price or income).

Elasticity of demand for exports A measure of the responsiveness of the volume of exports to a change in their price.

Elasticity of demand for imports A measure of the responsiveness of the volume of imports to a change in their price.

Engel curve A curve showing the relationship between consumers' income and quantity demanded of a good. It indicates whether a good is normal or inferior.

Entrepreneurship Refers to the ability of certain individuals to organise the other factors of production (land, labour, capital) and their willingness to take risks.

Equilibrium A state of balance that is self-perpetuating in the absence of any outside disturbance.

Equity The concept or idea of fairness.

Excess demand Occurs when quantity demanded at some price is greater than quantity supplied.

Excess supply Occurs when quantity supplied at some price is greater than quantity demanded.

Exchange rate The value of one currency expressed in terms of another currency; for example, €1 = US$1.5.

Excludable A characteristic that most goods have that refers to the ability of producers to charge a price and thus exclude whoever is not willing or able to pay for it from enjoying it.

Expansionary fiscal policy Refers to an increase in government expenditures and/or a decrease in taxes that aim at increasing aggregate demand and thus real output and employment.

Expansionary monetary policy Monetary policy aiming at increasing aggregate demand through a decrease in interest rates; also referred to as easy monetary policy.

Expenditure approach One of three analytically equivalent approaches of measuring GDP that adds all the expenditures made on final domestic goods and services over a period of time by households, firms, the government and foreigners.

Expenditure reducing Contractionary demand side policies aiming at decreasing national income and thus expenditures on imports so that a current account deficit narrows.

Expenditure switching Policies aimed at switching expenditures away from imports towards domestically produced goods and services by making imports more expensive in order to narrow a current account deficit. It includes lowering the exchange rate as well as adopting trade protection.

Exports Goods and services produced in one country and purchased by consumers in another country.

Export promotion Growth policies aiming at expansion of export revenues as the vehicle of economic growth; often contrasted to import substitution.

Export revenue The revenues collected by exporting firms.

Export subsidy Payments made by the government to exporting firms on the basis of the number of units exported.

External balance A situation where the value of a country's exports is balanced by the value of its imports over a period of time, such that a current account surplus or deficit does not persist over long periods.

Externalities External costs or benefits to third parties when a good or service is produced or consumed. An externality arises when an economic activity imposes costs or creates benefits on third parties for which they are not compensated or do not pay for respectively.

Factors of production Resources used in the production of goods and services; include land (natural resources), labour, capital and entrepreneurship.

Financial account In the balance of payments this records inflows and outflows of portfolio and FDI funds over a period of time, official borrowing and changes in reserve assets.

Firm An entity such as a business that uses factors of production in order to produce and sell goods and services and earn profits. It is an important decision maker in a market economy.

Firms Productive units that transform inputs (factors of production) into output (goods and services), usually aiming at earning profits.

Fiscal policy A demand-side policy using changes in government spending and/or direct taxation to influence aggregate demand and thus growth, employment and prices.

Fixed exchange rate An exchange rate system where the exchange rate is fixed, or pegged, to the value of another currency (or to the average value of a selection of currencies) and maintained there with appropriate central bank intervention.

Floating exchange rate An exchange rate system where the exchange rate is determined solely by the market demand and market supply of the currency in the foreign exchange market without any central bank intervention.

Foreign aid Refers to flows of grants or loans from developed to developing countries that are non-commercial from the point of view of the donor and for which the terms are concessional (that is, the interest rate is lower than the market rate and the repayment period longer).

Foreign direct investment (FDI) When a firm establishes a productive facility in a foreign country or acquires controlling interest (at least 10% of the ordinary shares) in an existing foreign firm.

Foreign sector In an open economy the term refers to exports and imports.

Framing In behavioural economics, the term refers to the way choices are presented as a simple change of the 'frame', that may affect the choice made. For example, highlighting the positive or the negative aspects of the same choice may lead to different decisions.

Free goods Goods such as air or sea water that are not considered scarce and thus do not have an opportunity cost.

Free market economy An economy where the means of production are privately owned and where market forces determine the answers to the fundamental questions (what/how much, how and for whom) that all economies face.

Free rider problem Arises when individuals consume a good or service without paying for it because they cannot be excluded from enjoying it.

Free trade International trade that is not subject any kind of trade barriers, such as tariffs or quotas.

Free trade area/ agreement An agreement between two or more countries to phase-out or eliminate trade barriers between them, members of the agreement are free to maintain their own trade policy towards non-members.

Frictional unemployment Unemployment of individuals who are in-between jobs, as people quit to find a better job or to move to a different location.

Full employment A goal of macroeconomic policy that aims at fully utilizing the scarce factor of production labour. Full employment exists when the economy is producing at its potential level of real output and thus there is only natural unemployment (the AD–AS model considers the AD and AS curves together). In the production possibilities curve (PPC model), full employment exists when the economy is producing on the PPC.

Full employment level of output
The level of output that is produced by the economy when there is only natural unemployment.

Game theory
A branch of mathematics that studies the strategic interaction of decision-makers that may be individuals, firms, countries, and so on.

Gender inequality index (GII)
A composite indicator that measures gender inequalities in three dimensions of human development, namely reproductive health, empowerment and economic status.

Gini coefficient
A measure of the degree of income inequality of a country that ranges from zero (perfect income equality) to one (perfect inequality). Diagrammatically it is the ratio of the area between the Lorenz curve and the diagonal over the area of the half-square.

Government (national) debt
The sum of all past budget deficits minus any budget surpluses; the total amount the government owes to domestic and foreign creditors.

Government spending (G)
Refers to all spending by the government that is distinguished into current expenditures, capital expenditures and transfer payments.

Gross domestic product (GDP)
The value of all final goods and services produced within an economy over a period of time, usually a year or a quarter.

Gross national income (GNI)
The income earned by all national factors of production independently of where they are located over a period of time; it is equal to GDP plus factor income earned abroad minus factor income paid abroad.

Happiness Index
An index that is used to measure economic well-being of a population using several quality of life dimensions.

Happy Planet Index
An index that combines four elements to show how efficiently residents of different countries are using environmental resources to lead long, happy lives. The elements are well-being, life expectancy, inequality of outcomes, and ecological footprint.

Homogeneous product
Goods that are considered identical across firms in the eyes of consumers; examples include mostly primary sector goods like corn, wheat, or copper.

Household indebtedness
The money that households owe.

Households
Groups of individuals in the economy who share the same living accommodation, who pool their income and jointly decide the set of goods and services to consume.

Human capital
The education, training, skills, experience and good health embodied in the labour force of a country.

Human Development Index (HDI)
A composite index of development that reflects the three basic goals of development, which are a long and healthy life, improved education, and a decent standard of living. The variables measured are life expectancy at birth, mean years of schooling and expected years of schooling, and GNI per capita (PPP US$).

Humanitarian aid
Aid given to alleviate short-term suffering, consisting of food aid, medical aid, and emergency relief aid usually as a result of a natural catastrophe or war.

Imperfect competition
A market structure where firms have a degree of market power as they face a negatively sloped demand curve and can thus set price.

Imperfect information
When the information about a market or a transaction is incomplete.

Import expenditure
The value of imports of goods and services.

Imports
The value of goods and services purchased domestically that are produced abroad.

Import substitution
A growth strategy where domestic production is substituted for imports in an attempt to shift production away from the primary sector and industrialise. This strategy requires that the domestic industry is protected from import competition.

Incentive-related policies
Policies that aim at improving economic incentives of individuals and firms.

Income
A flow of earnings from using factors of production to produce goods and services. Wages and salaries are the factor reward to labour and interest is the flow of income for the ownership of capital.

Income approach
One of the three equivalent ways that GDP can be measured, by adding all the incomes generated in the production process (wages, profits, interest and rent) for a given time period.

Income effect — The law of demand is explained by the substitution and the income effect. The income effect states that if the price of a good increases then the real income of consumers decreases and, typically, they will tend to buy less of the good—thus working in the same direction as the substitution effect.

Income elasticity of demand (YED) — The responsiveness of demand for a good or service to a change in income.

Indirect taxes — Taxes on expenditure to buy goods and services.

Industrial policies — A type of interventionist supply-side policies whereby the government chooses to support specific industries through preferential tax cuts, subsidies, subsidised loans and other means as they are considered pivotal in the growth prospects of the economy.

Inequality adjusted Human Development Index (IHDI) — A composite indicator consisting of an average of a country's achievements in health, education, and income all adjusted for the degree of inequality characterising each.

Inferior goods — Lower quality goods for which higher quality substitutes exist; if incomes rise, demand for the lower quality goods decreases.

Inflation — A sustained increase in the average level of prices.

Inflationary gap — The case where equilibrium real output exceeds potential output as a result of an increase in AD.

Inflation rate — The percentage change between two periods of the average price level, usually measured through the CPI.

Informal economy — Refers to the part of an economy where activity is not officially recorded, regulated or taxed. The activities of the informal economy are not included in a country's national income figures.

Infrastructure — Physical capital typically financed by governments that is essential for economic activity to take place, including roads, power, telecommunications and sanitation, generating significant positive externalities.

Injections — Within the circular flow model these refer to spending on domestic output that does not originate from households and thus includes investment spending by firms, government expenditures, and exports.

Interest rate — The cost of borrowing money or the reward for saving money over a period of time expressed as a percentage.

International Monetary Fund (IMF) — An international financial institution of 189 countries whose objectives include to improve global monetary cooperation and secure financial stability by monitoring the economic and financial policies of its members and providing them with advice and with loans, if they face balance of payments difficulties.

International trade — Trade that involves the exports and imports of goods or services between countries.

Interventionist supply side policies — A set of policies that aim to increase an economy's productive capacity that relies on a greater role for the government; these include expenditures on infrastructure, education, health care, research and development, and all industrial policies.

Investment (I) — Spending by firms on capital goods such as machines, tools, equipment, and factories.

J-curve — Following devaluation or a sharp depreciation, a trade deficit will typically widen before it starts improving thus tracing the letter "J" if plotted against time, because the Marshall-Lerner condition is satisfied only after a period of several months following the decreased value of the currency.

Joint supply — Goods jointly produced, for example beef and cattle hides; producing one automatically leads to the production of the other.

Keynesian multiplier — The idea that an increase (or, more generally, a change) in any injection will lead to a greater increase (change) in real GDP or national income because an increase in spending generates additional income that leads to further spending, and thus more income. Its size depends on the size of the withdrawals from the circular flow, as these reflect income not spent on domestic output.

Labour — One of the four factors of production that refers to the physical and mental contribution of workers to the production process.

Labour market flexibility	The labour market is considered flexible if it can adjust fast and fully to changes in labour demand and labour supply conditions.
Labour union	An organisation of workers whose goals include improving working conditions and achieving higher compensation for members. Unions permit workers to negotiate more effectively with employers.
Laissez-faire	The view that if market forces are left alone unimpeded by government intervention the outcome will be efficient.
Land	One of the four factors of production that refers to the natural resources with which an economy is endowed; also referred to as 'gifts of nature'.
Law of demand	A law stating that as the price of a good falls, the quantity demanded will increase over a certain period of time, *ceteris paribus*.
Law of diminishing marginal returns	A short-run law of production stating that as more and more units of the variable factor (usually labour) are added to a fixed factor (usually capital) there is a point beyond which total product continues to rise but at a diminishing rate or, equivalently, marginal product starts to decrease.
Law of diminishing marginal utility	The idea that as an individual consumes additional units of a good, the additional satisfaction enjoyed decreases.
Law of supply	A law stating that as the price of a good rises, the quantity supplied will rise over a certain period of time, *ceteris paribus*.
Leakages	Income not spent on domestic goods and services. It includes savings, taxes, and import expenditure.
Less economically developed country (LEDC)	According to the UN these are low-income countries facing severe structural constraints to sustainable development, with low levels of human assets, highly vulnerable to economic and environmental shocks.
Long-run aggregate supply (LRAS)	Aggregate supply that is dependent upon the resources and technology in the economy, thus being independent of the price level. It is vertical at the level of potential output. It can only be increased by improvements in the quantity and/or quality of factors of production as well as improved technology.
Long-run Phillips curve (LRPC)	A curve showing the monetarist view that there is no trade-off between inflation and unemployment in the long run and that there exists a natural rate of unemployment at the level of potential output.
Long run in microeconomics	The period of time when all factors of production are variable.
Long run in macroeconomics	The period of time when the prices of all factors of production, especially wages, change to match changes in the price level.
Long-term growth	Growth over long periods of time. In the PPC model this is shown by outward shifts of the PPC. When shown in the AD–AS model (the AD–AS model considers the AD and AS curves together), it is shown by rightward shifts in the LRAS curve.
Long-term growth trend	Refers to average growth over long periods of time shown in the business cycle diagram as the line that runs through short-term fluctuations, indicating changes in potential output.
Lorenz curve	A curve showing what percentage of the population owns what percentage of the total income or wealth in the economy. It is calculated in cumulative terms. The further the curve is from the line of absolute equality (along the diagonal), the more unequal the distribution of income.
Loss (economic)	Occurs when total costs of a firm are greater than total revenues. It is equal to total cost minus total revenue.
Luxury goods	Goods that are not considered essential by consumers therefore they have a price elastic demand (PED > 1), or income elastic demand (YED > 1).
Macroeconomics	The study of aggregate economic activity. It investigates how the economy as a whole works.
Managed exchange rate	An exchange rate that floats in the foreign exchange markets but is subject to intervention from time to time by domestic monetary authorities, in order to prevent undesirable movements in the exchange rate.
Mandated choices	Choices made by consumers who are required to state whether or not they wish to take part in an action.

Manufactured products	Products or goods that have been produced by workers often working with capital goods.
Marginal benefit	The extra or additional benefit enjoyed by consumers that arises from consuming one more unit of output.
Marginal costs	The extra or additional costs of producing one more unit of output.
Marginal propensity to consume (MPC)	The proportion of extra or additional income that is spent by households on goods and services (consumption).
Marginal propensity to buy imports (MPM)	The proportion of extra or additional income that is spent by households on imported goods and services.
Marginal propensity to save (MPS)	The proportion of extra or additional income that is saved by households.
Marginal propensity to tax (MPT)	The proportion of extra or additional income that is paid in taxes, also referred to as the marginal tax rate.
Marginal revenue	The extra or additional revenue that arises for a firm when it sells one more unit of output.
Marginal social benefit (MSB)	The extra or additional benefit/utility to society of consuming an additional unit of output, including both the private benefit and the external benefit.
Marginal social cost (MSC)	The extra or additional cost to society of producing an additional unit of output, including both the private cost and the external costs.
Marginal tax rate	The proportion of a person's extra or additional income that is paid in tax, usually expressed as a percentage.
Marginal utility	The extra or additional utility derived from consuming one more unit of a good or service.
Market	Any arrangement where buyers and sellers interact to carry out an economic transaction.
Market-based supply side policies	A set of policies based on well-functioning competitive markets in order to promote long-term economic growth, shown by increases in long-run aggregate supply.
Market demand	The sum of the individual demand curves for a product of all the consumers in a market.
Market equilibrium	In a market this occurs at the price where the quantity of a product demanded is equal to the quantity supplied. This is the market clearing price since there is no excess demand or excess supply.
Market failure	The failure of markets to achieve allocative efficiency. Markets fail to produce the output at which marginal social benefits are equal to marginal social costs; social or community surplus (consumer surplus + producer surplus) is not maximised.
Market mechanism	The system in which the forces of demand and supply determine the prices of products. Also known as the price mechanism.
Market-oriented approaches	Approaches or policies that are based on the actions of private decision-makers operating in markets with a minimum amount of government intervention.
Market power	The ability of a firm (or group of firms) to raise and maintain price above the level that would prevail under perfect competition (or P > MC).
Market share	The percentage of total sales in a market accounted for by one firm.
Market supply	The horizontal sum of the individual supply curves for a product of all the producers in a market.
Marshall-Lerner condition	A condition stating that a depreciation or devaluation of a currency will lead to an improvement in the current account balance if the sum of the price elasticity of demand for exports plus the price elasticity of demand for imports is greater than one.
Maximum price	A price set by a government or other authority that is below the market equilibrium price of a good or service, also known as a price ceiling.
Merit goods	Goods or services considered to be beneficial for people that are under-provided by the market and so under-consumed, mainly due to positive consumption externalities.
Microeconomics	The study of the behaviour of individual consumers, firms, and markets and the determination of market prices and quantities of goods, services, and factors of production.
Minimum income standards (MIS)	A measure of poverty that is based on the beliefs of people regarding what is essential in order to achieve a minimum acceptable standard of living.
Minimum lending rate	The interest rate that is charged by a central bank when it lends to commercial banks. Also known as discount rate or refinancing rate.

Minimum price

A price set by a government or other authority above the market equilibrium price of a good or service, also known as a price floor.

Minimum reserve requirements

A requirement by the central bank that sets the minimum amount of reserves that commercial banks must maintain to back their loans.

Minimum wage

A type of price floor where the wage rate or the price of labour is set above the market equilibrium wage rate.

Mixed economy

An economy that has elements of a planned economy and elements of a free market economy. In reality, all economies are mixed. What is different is the degree of the mix from country to country.

Monetarist/new classical model

An economic school of thought arguing that the price mechanism along with well-functioning competitive markets are sufficient to lead the economy to full employment. In this school of thought, government intervention is not necessary to manage the level of aggregate demand.

Monetary policy

A demand-side policy using changes in the money supply or interest rates to achieve economic objectives relating to output, employment, and inflation.

Monetary union

Where two or more countries share the same currency and have a common central bank.

Money

Anything that is generally accepted as a means of payment for goods and services. It usually consists of currency and checking accounts.

Money creation

The process of creating new money by commercial banks, which occurs when they make loans.

Money supply

The total amount of money available at a particular time, consisting of currency plus checking accounts.

Monopolistic competition

A market structure where there are many sellers, producing differentiated products, with no barriers to entry.

Monopoly

A market structure where there is only one firm in the industry, so the firm is the industry. There are high barriers to entry.

Moral hazard

A type of market failure involving asymmetric information where a party takes risks but does not face their full costs by changing behaviour after a transaction has taken place. It is very common in insurance markets.

Multidimensional Poverty Index (MPI)

An international measure of poverty covering over 100 of the economically least developed countries. It complements traditional income-based poverty measures by capturing the deprivations that each person faces at the same time with respect to education, health, and living standards.

Multilateral development assistance

Assistance provided by multilateral organisations such as the World Bank when they lend to developing countries for the purpose of helping them in their development objectives.

Multilateral trade agreement

An agreement between many countries to lower tariffs or other protectionist measures, currently carried out within the framework of the WTO.

National income

The income earned by the factors of production of an economy, equal to wages plus interest, plus rents, plus profits.

National income accounting

The services provided by a statistical entity in every country that measure the economy's national income and output as well as other economic activity.

National income statistics

The statistical data used to measure a nation's income and output, and perform national income accounting.

Natural monopoly

A monopoly that can produce enough output to cover the entire needs of a market while still experiencing economies of scale. Its average costs will therefore be lower than those of two or more firms in the market.

Natural rate of unemployment (NRU)

The rate of unemployment that occurs when the economy is producing at its potential output or full employment level of output. It is equal to the sum of structural, frictional, and seasonal unemployment.

Necessity

The degree to which a good is necessary or essential.

If the increase in demand for a necessity good is less than proportional to the rise in income; then the necessity good is income elastic.

If the change in quantity demanded for a necessity good is less than proportional to a change in price; then the necessity good is price inelastic.

Negative externalities of consumption
Negative effects suffered by a third party whose interests are not considered when a good or service is consumed, so the third party is therefore not compensated.

Negative externalities of production
Negative effects suffered by a third party whose interests are not considered when a good or service is produced, so the third party is therefore not compensated.

Net exports (X − M)
Export revenues minus import expenditure.

Nominal gross domestic product (GDP)
The total money value of all final goods and services produced in an economy in a given time period, usually one year, at current values (not adjusted for inflation).

Nominal gross national income (GNI)
The total income earned by all the residents of a country (regardless of where their factors of production are located) in a given time period, usually a year, at current prices (not adjusted for inflation).

Nominal interest rates
Interest rates that have not been adjusted for inflation.

Non-collusive oligopoly
Firms in an oligopoly do not resort to agreements to fix prices or output. Competition tends to be non-price. Prices tend to be stable.

Non-excludable
A characteristic of a good, service or resource where it is impossible to prevent a person, or persons, from using it.

Non-governmental organisation (NGO)
Organisations that are not part of the government that promote economic development and/or humanitarian ideals and/or sustainable development.

Non-price competition
Competition between firms that is based on factors other than price, usually taking the form of product differentiation.

Non-produced, non-financial assets
A measure of the net international sales and purchases of non-produced assets (such as land) and intangible assets (such as patents and copyrights).

Non-rivalrous
A characteristic of some goods such that their consumption by one individual does not reduce the ability of others to consume them. It is a characteristic of public goods.

Normal goods
A good where the demand for it increases as income increases.

Normal profit
The minimum return that must be received by a firm in order to stay in business. A firm earns normal profit when total revenue is equal to total cost, or when average revenue or price is equal to average cost.

Normative economics
Deals with areas of the subject that are open to personal opinion and belief, thus not subject to refutation.

Nudge theory
Nudges (prompts, hints) are used to influence the choices made by consumers in order to improve the well-being of people and society.

(OECD) Better Life Index
An index to compare well-being across countries, based on several dimensions that the OECD has identified as essential, in the areas of material living conditions and quality of life.

Official Development Assistance (ODA)
Aid that is provided to a country by another government or multilateral agency. It is the most important part of foreign aid.

Oligopoly
A market structure where there are a few large firms that dominate the market, with high barriers to entry.

Open market operations
A tool of monetary policy involving the buying or selling of (short-term) government bonds by the central bank in order to increase or decrease the money supply, thus influencing the rate of interest.

Opportunity cost
The next best alternative foregone when an economic decision is made.

Output approach
One of the three equivalent ways that GDP can be measured, it adds up the value of final goods and services produced in a given time period.

Overvalued currency
A currency whose value or exchange rate is greater than its equilibrium exchange rate, usually achieved through central bank intervention; may occur in a pegged or managed exchange rate system.

Payoff matrix
A table showing all possible outcomes of decisions taken by decision-makers in game theory.

Per capita
Per person. Per capita values are found by dividing the variable by the size of the population.

Perfect competition	A market structure where there is a very large number of small firms, producing identical products, with no barriers to entry or exit, and perfect information. All the firms are thus price takers.
Perfect information	Where all stakeholders in an economic transaction have access to the same information.
Perfectly elastic demand	Occurs with a horizontal demand curve signifying that any amount can be bought at a particular price. (PED is infinite.)
Perfectly elastic supply	Occurs with a horizontal supply curve signifying that any amount can be offered at a particular price. (PES is infinite.)
Perfectly inelastic demand	Where a change in the price of a good or service leads to no change in the quantity demanded of the good or service. (PED is equal to zero.)
Perfectly inelastic supply	Where a change in the price of a good or service leads to no change in the quantity supplied of the good or service. (PES is equal to zero.)
Personal income taxes	Taxes paid by individuals or households on their incomes, regardless of the source of the income, such as wages, salaries, interest income, or dividends.
Phillips curve	A curve showing the relationship between the rate of unemployment and the rate of inflation.
Pigouvian taxes	An indirect tax that is imposed to eliminate the external costs of production or consumption.
Planned economy	An economy where the means of production (land and capital) are owned by the state. The state determines what/ how much to produce, how to produce, and for whom to produce.
Portfolio investment	The purchase of financial assets such as shares and bonds in order to gain a financial return in the form of interest or dividends. Appears in the financial account of the balance of payments.
Positive economics	Deals with areas of the subject that are capable of being falsified, or shown to be correct or not.
Positive externalities of consumption	The beneficial effects that are enjoyed by third parties whose interests are not accounted for when a good or service is consumed, therefore they do not pay for the benefits they receive.
Positive externalities of production	The beneficial effects that are enjoyed by third parties whose interests are not accounted for when a good or service is produced, therefore they do not pay for the benefits they receive.
Potential output	Output produced by an economy when it is at full employment equilibrium, or long-run equilibrium according to the monetarist/new classical model.
Poverty	Arises when the lack of material possessions or money prevent an individual or a family from achieving a minimum satisfactory standard of living.
Poverty line	A level of income determined by a government or international body (such as the World Bank) that is just enough to ensure a family can satisfy minimum needs in terms of food, clothing, and housing.
Poverty trap/cycle	Any circular chain of events starting and ending in poverty—for example, low income leads to low savings, leads to low investment, leads to low growth, leads to low income.
Preferential trade agreement	Where a country agrees to give preferential access (for example, reduced tariffs) for certain products to one or more trading partners.
Price ceiling (maximum price)	A price imposed by an authority and set below the equilibrium price. Prices cannot rise above this price.
Price competition	Competition between firms that is based on price; for example, a firm that wants to increase its sales at the expense of other firms will lower its price.
Price controls	Prices imposed by an authority, set above or below the equilibrium market price.
Price elasticity of demand (PED)	A measure of the responsiveness of the quantity demanded of a good or service to a change in its price.
Price elasticity of supply (PES)	A measure of the responsiveness of the quantity supplied of a good or service to a change in its price.
(Price) elastic supply	Where a change in the price of a good or service leads to a proportionately larger change in the quantity supplied of the good or service in the same direction. (PES is greater than one.)
Price expectations	The forecasts or views that consumers or firms hold about future price movements that play a role in determining demand.

Price floor (minimum price) A price imposed by an authority and set above the market price. Prices cannot fall below this price.

(Price) inelastic demand Where a change in the price of a good or service leads to a proportionately smaller change in the quantity demanded of the good or service in the opposite direction. (PED is less than one.)

(Price) inelastic supply Where a change in the price of a good or service leads to a proportionately smaller change in the quantity supplied of the good or service in the same direction. (PES is less than one.)

Price maker A firm that is able to influence the price at which it sells its product. Includes firms in all market structures except perfect competition.

Price taker A firm that is unable to influence the price at which it sells its product, being forced to accept the price determined in the market. It includes firms in perfect competition.

Price war Occurs when firms successively cut their prices in an effort to match the price cuts of other firms, resulting in lower profits, possibly losses.

Primary commodities Raw materials that are produced in the primary sector. Examples include agricultural products, metals, and minerals.

Primary sector Anything derived from the factor of production land. Includes agricultural products, metals, and minerals.

Privatisation The sale of public assets to the private sector. May be a type of supply-side policy.

Producer surplus The benefit enjoyed by producers by receiving a price that is higher than the price they were willing to receive.

Product differentiation The process by which firms try to make their products different from the products of other firms in an effort to increase their sales. Differences involve product quality, appearance, services offered, and many others.

Production possibilities curve (PPC) A curve showing the maximum combinations of goods or services that can be produced by an economy in a given time period, if all the resources in the economy are being used fully and efficiently, and the state of technology is fixed.

Productive capacity The greatest capability of an economy to produce, usually measured by maximum possible output of an economy.

Profit maximisation A possible objective of firms that involves producing the level of output where profits are greatest: where total revenue minus total cost is greatest or where marginal revenue equals marginal cost.

Progressive taxation Taxation where the fraction of tax paid increases as income increases. The average tax rate increases.

Property rights The exclusive, legal, authority to own property and determine how that property is used, whether it is owned by the government or by private individuals.

Proportional tax A system of taxation where tax is levied at a constant rate as income rises.

Public goods Goods or services that have the characteristics of non-rivalry and non-excludability; for example, flood barriers.

Purchasing power parity (PPP) A method used to make the buying power of different currencies equal to the buying power of US$1. PPP exchange rates are used to make comparisons of income or output variables across countries while eliminating the influence of price level differences.

Quantitative easing An expansionary monetary policy where a central bank buys (long term) government bonds or other financial assets, in order to stimulate the economy and increase the money supply.

Quantity demanded The quantity of a good or service demanded at a particular price over a given time period, *ceteris paribus*.

Quantity supplied The quantity of a good or service supplied at a particular price over a given time period, *ceteris paribus*.

Quota An import barrier that set limits on the quantity or value of imports that may be imported into a country.

Rational consumer choice Occurs when consumers make choices based on the following assumptions: they have consistent tastes and preferences, they have perfect information and they arrange their purchases so as to make their utility as great as possible (maximise it). It is assumed in standard microeconomic theory.

Rationing	A method used to divide or apportion goods and services or resources among the various interested parties.	**Revaluation**	An increase in the value of a currency in a fixed exchange rate system.
Real GDP	The total value of all final goods and services produced in an economy in a given time period, usually one year, adjusted for inflation.	**Revenues**	Payments received by firms when they sell their output.
		Rivalrous	Goods and services are considered to be rivalrous when the consumption by one person, or group of people, reduces the amount available for others.
Real GDP per person (per capita)	Real GDP divided by the population of the country.		
Real GNI per person (per capita)	Real GNI divided by the population of the country.	**Rules of thumb**	Rules of thumb are mental shortcuts (heuristics) for decision-making to help people make a quick, satisfactory, but often not perfect, decision to a complex choice.
Real interest rates	Interest rates that have been adjusted for inflation.		
Recession	Occurs when real GDP falls for at least two consecutive quarters.	**Satisficing**	A business or firm objective to achieve a satisfactory outcome with respect to one or several objectives, rather than to pursue any one objective at the possible expense of others by optimising (maximising); for example, profit, revenue, or growth. It is essentially a mix of the words 'satisfy' and 'suffice'.
Refutation	A method used in the natural sciences and social sciences where any proposition must be subjected to an empirical test in order to see if it can be disproven or refuted. If it is disproven or refuted, then the proposition must be rejected.		
Regional trade agreement	An agreement between a group of countries, usually within a geographical region, to lower or eliminate trade barriers.	**Say's Law**	A proposition stating that the supply of goods creates its own demand.
		Scarcity	The limited availability of economic resources relative to society's unlimited needs and wants of goods and services.
Regressive taxation	Taxation where the fraction of tax paid decreases as income increases. The average tax rate decreases. All indirect taxes are regressive.		
		Seasonal unemployment	Unemployment that arises when people are out of work because their usual job is out of season; for example, agricultural workers during winter months.
Relative poverty	A comparative measure of poverty according to which income levels do not allow people to reach a standard of living that is typical of the society in which they live. It is defined as a percentage of society's median income.		
		Shortage	Arises when the quantity demanded of a good or services is more than the quantity supplied at some particular price.
Remittances	The transfer of money by foreign workers to individuals, often family members, in their home country.		
		Short-run aggregate supply (SRAS)	The total quantity of real output (real GDP) offered at different possible price levels in the short run (when wages and other resource prices are constant).
Reserve assets	Foreign currencies and precious metals held by central banks as a result of international trade. Reserves may be used to maintain or influence the exchange rate for the country's currency. Reserves appear as an item in the financial account of the balance of payments.		
		Short run in macroeconomics	The period of time when the prices of factors of production, especially wages, are considered fixed.
Resource allocation	Apportioning available resources or factors of production to particular uses for production purposes.	**Short run in microeconomics**	The period of time when at least one factor of production is fixed.
Restricted choices	This is when the choice of a consumer is restricted by the government or other authority.	**Short-run Phillips curve (SRPC)**	A curve showing the inverse relationship between the rate of unemployment and the rate of inflation, which suggests a trade-off between inflation and unemployment.

Signalling
In asymmetric information, the participant with more information sending a signal revealing relevant information about a transaction to the participant with less information, to reduce adverse selection.

Social/community surplus
The sum combination of consumer surplus and producer surplus.

Social enterprise
A company whose main objective is to have a social impact rather than to make a profit for their owners or shareholders. It operates by providing goods and services for the market in an entrepreneurial and innovative fashion and uses its profits primarily to achieve social objectives.

Social sciences
Academic studies of human societies and how people in society interact with each other.

Specialisation
Refers to when a firm or country focuses on the production of one or a few goods or services. This forms the basis of theory of comparative advantage in international trade.

Speculation
Refers to a process where something is bought or sold with a view to making a short term profit; for example, currency speculation where currencies are bought or sold so that a profit can be made when the exchange rate changes.

Stakeholder
An individual or group of individuals who have an interest, or stake, in an economic activity or outcome.

Structural unemployment
A kind of long-term unemployment that arises from a number of factors including: technological change; changes in the patterns of demand for different labour skills; changes in the geographical location of industries; labour market rigidities.

Subsidies
An amount of money paid by the government to a firm, per unit of output, to encourage production and lower the price to consumers.

Subsidy (international)
An amount of money paid by the government to a firm, per unit of output, to encourage production and provide the firm an advantage over foreign competition.

Substitutes
Goods that can be used in place of each other, as they satisfy a similar need.

Substitution effect
When the price of a product falls relative to other product prices, consumers purchase more of the product as it is now relatively less expensive. This forms part of an explanation of the law of demand.

Supply
Quantities of a good that firms are willing and able to supply at different possible prices, over a given time period, *ceteris paribus*.

Supply curve
A curve showing the relationship between the price of a good or service and the quantity supplied, *ceteris paribus*. It is normally upward sloping.

Supply-side policies
Government policies designed to shift the long-run aggregate supply curve to the right, thus increasing potential output in the economy and achieving economic growth.

Surplus
An excess of something over something else. It occurs:

* when quantity supplied is greater than quantity demanded at a particular price
* when tax revenues are greater than government spending (budget surplus)
* on an account when credits are greater than debits in the balance of payments.

See also 'consumer surplus' and 'producer surplus'.

Sustainability
Refers to the preserving the environment so that it can continue to satisfy needs and wants into the future. Relates to the concept of 'sustainable development'.

Sustainable debt
Refers to a level of government debt such that the borrowing government can make its payments of interest and debt repayment while at the same being able to meet the economy's growth objectives.

Sustainable development
Refers to the degree to which the current generation is able to meet its needs today but still conserve resources for the sake of future generations.

Tariff
A tax that is placed on imports to protect domestic industries from foreign competition and to raise revenue for the government.

Total costs	All the costs of a firm incurred for the use of resources to produce something.
Total revenue	The amount of revenue received by a firm from the sale of a particular quantity of output (equal to price times quantity sold).
Tradable permits	Permits to pollute, issued by a governing body, that sets a maximum amount of pollution allowable. These permits may be traded (bought or sold) in a market for such permits.
Trade creation	In international trade it occurs when higher cost imports are replaced by lower cost imports due to the formation of a trading bloc or a trade agreement.
Trade diversion	In international trade it occurs when lower cost imports are replaced by higher cost imports due to the formation of a trading bloc or a trade agreement.
Trade liberalisation	The process of reducing barriers to international trade.
Trade protection	Government intervention aiming to limit imports and/or encourage exports by setting up trade barriers that protect from foreign competition.
Trading bloc	A group of countries that have agreed to reduce protectionist measures like tariffs and quotas between them.
Tragedy of the commons	A situation with common pool resources, where individual users acting independently, according to their own self-interest, go against the common good of all users by depleting or spoiling that resource through their collective action.
Transfer payments	Payments made by the government to vulnerable groups in a society, including older people, low income people, unemployed, and many more. The objective is to transfer money from taxpayers to those who cannot work, to prevent them from falling into poverty.
Undervalued currency	A currency whose value or exchange rate is lower than its equilibrium exchange rate, usually achieved through central bank intervention; may occur in a pegged or managed exchange rate system.

Unemployment	When a person (who is above a specified age and is available to work) is actively looking for work, but is without a job.
Unemployment benefits	Payments, usually made by the government, to people who are unemployed (and actively seeking employment).
Unemployment rate	The number of unemployed workers expressed as a percentage of the total workforce.
Unfair competition	In international trade this refers to practices of countries trying to gain an unfair advantage through such methods as undervalued exchange rates.
Unitary elastic demand	Occurs when a change in the price of a good or service leads to an equal and opposite proportional change in the quantity demanded of the good or service (PED = 1).
Unitary elastic supply	Occurs when a change in the price of a good or service leads to an equal proportional change in the quantity supplied of the good or service (PES = 1).
Universal basic income	A regular cash payment given to all persons in an economy that is independent of any other source of income they may have. It is intended to reduce poverty and income inequality.
United Nations Sustainable development goals (SDGs)	The UN set out 17 global goals including those that aim to end all forms of poverty, fight inequalities, and tackle climate change.
Utility	A measure of the satisfaction derived from consuming a good or service.
Wage	Payment received by the factor of production labour, which is a certain amount per unit of time.
Wealth	The total value of all assets owned by a person, firm, community, or country minus what is owed to banks or other financial institutions.
Weighted price index	A measure of average prices over a period of time that gives a weight to each item according to its relative importance in the consumers' budgets. It is used to measure changes in the price level.

Welfare loss   A loss of a part of social surplus (consumer plus producer surplus) that occurs when there is market failure so that marginal social benefits are not equal to marginal private benefits.

World Bank   An international organisation that provides loans and advice to economically less developed countries for the purpose of promoting economic development and reducing poverty.

World Trade Organization (WTO)   An international body that sets the rules for global trading and resolves disputes between its member countries. It also hosts negotiations concerning the reduction of trade barriers between its member nations.

Index

World Economic Forum: The Inequality-adjusted Human Development Index. World Economic Forum. 586; Data taken from World Forum Inclusive Development Index Tables, 2018 587; **Wikimedia Foundation, Inc.:** File:Landlocked Countries. svg. Wikimedia Commons 593; **The World Bank Group:** External Debt Stocks (% of GNI) - Guyana, Congo, Dem. Rep., Malawi, Cote D'Ivoire, Uganda." Data. The World Bank Group. 601; **World Health Organization:** Malaria, World Health Organization 603; **The Economic Times:** Adapted from The Economic Times, India, Sunday 6 May 2001 609; **The Economic Times:** Taken from ECONOMICS STANDARD LEVEL PAPER 2 Friday 7 November 2003 609; **United Nations Development Programme:** Adapted from UNDP Human Development Reports. 609; **The Economic Times:** Taken from Economics Standard level Paper 2 Tuesday 3 May 2016 610; **Social Enterprise Alliance:** What is Social Enterprise?.Social Enterprise Alliance 618; **W. Strahan and T. Cadell, London:** Adam Smith, The Wealth of Nations (Book 1), 1776, ch. 2 619; **United Nations Africa Renewal:** Jocelyne Sambira, "Africa's mobile youth drive change. Cell phones reshape youth cultures". United Nations Africa Renewal. 625; **The Slate Group: The List:** The World's Most Powerful Development NGOs." Foreign Policy, Foreign Policy, 9 May 2019 629; The World Bank Group : Data taken from World Bank via Google Public Data explorer 629, 630; **World Bank:** Macroeconomic Management Weakens While Social Inclusion Policies Improve Slightly in Africa's Poorest Countries." World Bank 632; **The Slate Group:** Sachs, Jeffrey. "The Case for Aid" Foreign Policy. The Slate Group 642; **The Economic Times:** Taken from ECONOMICS HIGHER LEVEL PAPER 3 Wednesday 14 May 2008. 648; **The Seattle Times:** Taken from Seattle Times, Editorial, US, 12 June 2005 648; **The Observer:** Taken from Ken Wiwa, The Observer, 12 June 2005 648.

Photos Acknowledgements:

123RF: Wichan Sumalee/123rf.com 3; Rafal Olkis/123rf.com 8; macor/123rf.com 9; tomas1111/123rf.com 12; ANDREY GUDKOV/123RF 87; Alessio Moiola/123RF 341; Norman Kin Hang Chan/123RF 497; **Alamy Stock Photo:** CPA Media Pte Ltd/Alamy Stock Photo 13; dpa picture alliance / Alamy Stock Photo 17; Valentino Visentini / Alamy Stock Photo 39; World History Archive / Alamy Stock Photo 42; agefotostock / Alamy Stock Photo 58; Foto 23 / Stockimo / Alamy Stock Photo 60; LJSphotography / Alamy Stock Photo 76; Lars Johansson / Alamy Stock Photo 82; Y.Levy / Alamy Stock Photo 91; Panther Media GmbH / Alamy Stock Photo 97; vm2002 / Alamy Stock Photo 105; JK21 / Alamy Stock Photo 111; robertharding / Alamy Stock Photo 137; Cristiano Fronteddu / Alamy Stock Photo 165; Arterra Picture Library / Alamy Stock Photo 174; REUTERS / Alamy Stock Photo 241; Cultura Creative RF / Alamy Stock Photo 261; Zoonar GmbH / Alamy Stock Photo 310; IanDagnall Computing/Alamy Stock Photo 318; JLBvdWOLF / Alamy Stock Photo 339; C.MALE / Alamy Stock Photo 350; DENIS BALIBOUSE/REUTERS/Alamy Stock Photo 375; XiXinXing / Alamy Stock Photo 399; LAMB / Alamy Stock Photo 408;

World History Archive / Alamy Stock Photo 443; Kathy deWitt / Alamy Stock Photo 464; REUTERS / Alamy Stock Photo 484; John Rees / Alamy Stock Photo 499; Jerónimo Alba / Alamy Stock Photo 551; Jeff Morgan 11 / Alamy Stock Photo 562; Dmytro Zinkevych / Alamy Stock Photo 567; uskarp / Alamy Stock Photo 585; Joerg Boethling / Alamy Stock Photo 606; Sally Weigand / Alamy Stock Photo 619; **Getty Images:** DenBoma/Gettyimages 158; Keystone/Hulton Archive/Getty Images 318; Hulton Deutsch/Corbis Historical/Getty Images 318; David Levenson/Getty Images Entertainment/Getty Images 459; Chapter openers: Zanariah Salam/EyeEm/Getty Images; **Shutterstock:** Michael Potter11/Shutterstock 2; Orientaly/Shutterstock 3; 527/Shutterstock 4; Yupa Watchanakit/Shutterstock 4; PopTika/Shutterstock 5; lowsun/ Shutterstock 6; Pormezz/Shutterstock 6; Romolo Tavani/Shutterstock 7; Fotoluminate LLC/Shutterstock 8; Parilov/Shutterstock 9; Dean Drobot/Shutterstock 10; Heartland Arts/Shutterstock 10; funnyangel/ Shutterstock 12; Radachynskyi Serhii/Shutterstock 25; faroukb16/ Shutterstock 27; Everett Historical/Shutterstock 29; Everett Collection/ Shutterstock 30; Rido/Shutterstock 31; hxdbzxy/Shutterstock 50; Dmitry Kalinovskiy/Shutterstock 71; Andrea Danti/Shutterstock 100; Tanathip Rattanatum/Shutterstock 120; Keith Homan/Shutterstock 124; Travelpixs/Shutterstock 131; GWImages/Shutterstock 134; CHEN HSI FU/Shutterstock 160; yelantsevv/Shutterstock 186; Kzenon/ Shutterstock 192; Dmitry Naumov/Shutterstock 206; alphaspirit. it/Shutterstock 217; Drazen Zigic/Shutterstock 225; M-Production/ Shutterstock 233; Creative Lab/Shutterstock 237; MAGNIFIER/ Shutterstock 254; ESB Professional. Shutterstock 288; Galushko Sergey/ Shutterstock 307; Humannet/Shutterstock 333; maigi/Shutterstock 379; 360b/Shutterstock 403; Gubin Yury/Shutterstock 426; Jerry Horbert/ Shutterstock 439; Shutterstock 457; AePatt Journey/Shutterstock 526; Nelson Marques/Shutterstock 527; arrowsmith2/Shutterstock 558; Tooykrub/Shutterstock 574; AZP Worldwide/Shutterstock 590; Stephen Mcsweeny/Shutterstock 612; wavebreakmedia/Shutterstock 675; **Fibonacci Blue:** Fibonacci Blue/Flickr 431; **Jules Selmes:** Jules Selmes/ Pearson Education Ltd 477; **Rachel Hulin:** Photo of Professor Emily Oster. © Rachel Hulin 24; **Naki Kouyioumtzis:** Naki Kouyioumtzis/ Pearson Education Ltd 36; **Sean Maley:** Exterior of Isabella Socks facility in Hawassa. © Sean Maley 628; **Christof Van Der Walt:** Christof Van Der Walt/Pearson Management Systems Limited 656.

All other images © Pearson Education